Effective Public Relations and Media Strategy

SECOND EDITION

C.V. Narasimha Reddi, Ph.D.

Editor, *Public Relations Voice*

Formerly
UGC, National Professor in Public Relations
Vice-Chancellor's Visiting Scholar, University of Canberra, Australia
National President, Public Relations Society of India
Director, Department of Information & Public Relations
Government of Andhra Pradesh

PHI Learning Private Limited

Delhi-110092

2014

₹425.00

EFFECTIVE PUBLIC RELATIONS AND MEDIA STRATEGY, Second Edition
C.V. Narasimha Reddi

ISBN-978-81-203-4871-4

The export rights of this book are vested solely with the publisher.

Third Printing (Second Edition) ... ... **January, 2014**

Published by Asoke K. Ghosh, PHI Learning Private Limited, Rimjhim House, 111, Patparganj Industrial Estate, Delhi-110092 and Printed by Baba Barkha Nath Printers, Bahadurgarh, Haryana-124507.

Contents

Foreword xxvii

Preface xxix

Preface to the First Edition xxxv

PART ONE
PRINCIPLES OF PUBLIC RELATIONS AND COMMUNICATION

Chapter 2: Communication

Chapter 3: Principles of Public Relations

Chapter 4: Evolution of Public Relations: Ancient India to Modern India (World's Biggest Democracy)   64–92

PART TWO

STRATEGY

Chapter 8: Public Relations Departments and PR Agencies   140–163

Chapter 9: Crisis Management: PR Centre Stage   164–176

PART THREE

PUBLIC RELATIONS PRACTICE

PART FOUR
MEDIA STRATEGY AND TACTICS

Chapter 27: Audio-Visual Media: Films 458–466

Chapter 28: Visual Media—Photographs and Exhibitions 467–476

PART FIVE
PROFESSIONAL EXCELLENCE IN PUBLIC RELATIONS

Chapter 32:   Effective Writing for Public Relations   515–524

Chapter 33:   How to Be a Good PR Manager   525–539

Chapter 34: **Public Relations into the Future**   **540–551**

PART SIX
ACTIONS SPEAK—PR CASE STUDIES

Chapter 35: **Actions Speak: PR Case Studies**   **555–588**

Foreword

Public relations is emerging as a key strategic and operational discipline to meet the global communication and marketing environment. In fact, it is ubiquitous profession being practiced by every organisation.

Dr. C.V. Narasimha Reddi who has been called the Father of public relations in India has strived hard to make public relations as an independent discipline and get it its rightful place in the corporate board rooms. Reddi and I worked together more than a half century ago on the subject, when I was the Director of the Information and Public Relations Department. We worked to confer respectability on what was generally known as publicity. Publicity is a one-way street, which has graduated into public relations as a highway communication with a built-in feedback loop. PR is a device of democracy. While I moved way, Reddi has kept working on the subject and refined its definition and scope. He became Director of the State Department of Information and Public Relations and UGC National Professor of the subject.

He started India's first and the only journal '*Public Relations Voice*', has lectured on the subject nationwide and abroad and written a number of books on public relations. He has thus exhibited a rare competence on both the practice and theory of PR which reflects in this volume. He is doubtless the high priest of the subject in India. His current book has already proved its popularity. Its second revised and enlarged edition will continue to provide valuable guidance to teachers, students and practitioners of the subject in India and abroad.

Narendra Luther
Formerly Director of Information and
Public Relations Department and
Chief Secretary, Government of Andhra Pradesh

Preface

The Hindu, India's national newspaper, while reviewing the first edition commented the book under review, "Effective Public Relations and Media Strategy" joins the few textbooks that seek to plug this gap in the lack of good textbooks written by Indian authors, in an Indian context and its currency is commendable. The author, Narasimha Reddi, verily qualifies for the appellation, 'Guru' of Public Relations Education in India (*The Hindu*, 1 March 2011).

This revised and updated second edition continues to successfully blend theory, principles and actual practice illuminated by much needed case studies to give a new look and to keep pace with the rapid changes taking place in the practice of public relations discipline.

State-of-the-Art

What is the State-of-the-Art Public Relations in India? It is a 'Mixed Bag' with a few professionals, a few in-house PR departments and public relations agencies which are second to none in the world on the one side and many non-professionals without any grounding in PR education and training on the other. The distinguishing trait of Indian public relations is the 'Quantity of Public Relations Personnel' rather than 'Quality of the Public Relations Profession'. What is needed today is professional excellence.

The revision of the text draws on my five decades of professional experience in government and public sector undertakings as the Head of Public Relations Departments and my academic career as University Grants Commission's National Professor in Public Relations and as Senior Academic Consultant, Dr. B.R. Ambedkar Open University, where I had introduced Mass Communication and Public Relations as one of the optional subjects at undergraduate level and Bachelor of Public Relations, besides being instrumental in launching MS Public Relations at Sri Venkateswara University, Tirupati and M.A. in Journalism and PR at Osmania University. M.A. in Mass Communication and Public Relations and M.A. in Mass Communication and Journalism are also in the offing.

New to the New Edition

As public relations is a multidisciplinary course, an attempt has been made to convert the new edition into a 'Four-in-One Combo Textbook' covering four major areas of academics such as public relations, corporate communications, advertising and media studies as a comprehensive text with international standards. A specialty of this textbook is the inclusion of seven new chapters, six new case studies, completely revised chapters with additional information, quotations from eminent personalities, new examples from well-known campaigns relevant to students, faculty and practitioners. The new chapters included in this new edition are: 1. History of Public Relations in USA, 2. Public Relations and the Law, 3. Standards and Ethics in PR, 4. Celebrity Public Relations, 5. Event Management—Open House, 6. Public Relations into the Future, and 7. Mahatma Gandhi: World's Greatest Communicator.

Structure of the Book—Six Parts

The book is divided into six key parts which are as follows:

Part One: Principles of Public Relations and Communication
Part Two: Strategy
Part Three: PR Practice
Part Four: Media Strategy and Tactics
Part Five: Professional Excellence in PR
Part Six: Actions Speak: PR Case Studies

Part One: Principles of Public Relations and Communication

In **part one, Chapter 1** starts with definitions of public relations, communication, propaganda, publicity, advertising, public affairs and lobbying, along with basic principles of public relations and communication on which the edifice of public relations profession stands. This is followed by an outline of communication models in **Chapter 2**, which expolers how and why people communicate. The basic difference between public relations and communication has been detailed. **Chapter 3** focuses on truth, public interest, social responsibility and two-way communication besides identification of publics and the court of public opinion. **Chapters 4 and 5** highlight the evolution of public relations in India and USA with historical case studies to indicate how public relations grew over a period. However, the history of public relations in India has been divided into five periods based on records and experience of the author. The five periods are: the State of Propaganda (1500 BC–1858 AD), the Era of Publicity (1858–1947), Gandhian Era of Public Communication (1919–1947), the Age of Public Relations (1947–1991) and Indian Public Relations with Global Perspective (1991–2012).

Since advertising and public relations are intertwined in organisational communication, corporate advertising has been elucidated in clear terms with a major difference between advertising and public relations. Once the students are through with the definitions, principles and historical perspective, it will be easy for them to proceed further into the areas of public relations practice.

Part Two: Strategy

Part two discusses important areas of strategic public relations, public relations process that includes four stages, PR Departments and PR Agencies, Crisis Management, the RPCE PR Model, which elaborates on the four-stage PR process (Research, Planning, Communication and Evaluation) explaining the practical case problems to give insight into the practice of public relations. Some of the PR managers landed in the defamation cases by issuing controversial press notes. A new **chapter** "Public Relations and the Law" enlightens the implications of various Acts such as Law of Defamation, Copyright Act, Official Secret Act, Right to Information Act, etc. to deal with corporate-related legal matters. 'Standards and Ethics in PR' is yet another new **chapter** included to gain credibility for PR practice with truthful information. Effective PR professional body is a *sine qua non* with the growth of public relations discipline. **Chapter 12** not only describes the functioning of the national and Global PR Associations but also gives a clear picture of Global Protocol on PR Ethics.

Part Three: PR Practice

The crux of the public relations discipline—corporate public relations versus corporate communications—is discussed in detail in **part three**. It enlightens the students on the differences and similarities between these two areas. Stakeholders relations, dimensions of public relations practice in government, public sector, municipal government, police, banks, tourism, political parties, NGOs, etc. are illustrated with case studies and practical examples. As Indian public relations is gaining global recognition, **Chapter 20**, while explaining the concept of globalisation as integration of trade, finance and information into a single market, emphasizes on implications of global public relations.

Celebrity Public Relations has emerged as a specialised form of communication to promote the image of celebrities on the one side and making use of celebrities to promote corporate reputation/brand, products and services on the other. This topic has been discussed in **Chapter 19** with a case study of a renowned actor Amitabh Bachchan, who as goodwill ambassador of UNICEF Pulse Polio Campaign made a significant contribution in creating awareness on polio disease which resulted in WHO declaring India as a polio free country.

Part Four: Media Strategy and Tactics

Part four analyses the linkage between media and public relations practice. As a conduit to stakeholders relationships, media gets top priority in the implementation of all public relations campaigns. **Chapter 26** has been thoroughly revised with new inputs to highlight the relevance of social media in public relations and its networking to convey messages on one-to-one basis for better impact. However, the classification of media in this part has been designed based on the ITMN Theory of Gandhian Public Communication, where **I** represents Interpersonal Media, **T** Traditional Folk Media, **M** Mass Media and **N** New Media (Modern). Management of events including media events has been an integral part of public relations profession. Therefore, a new chapter, **"Event Management: Open House"** has been added with a case study. Multimedia PR campaigns and Media Relations are the other two key areas that enable the students not only to learn the art of designing campaigns but also to evolve an appropriate media strategy to reach out to the target audiences.

Part Five: Professional Excellence in PR

Lack of professionalism is the key pitfall due to which public relations recognition as a strategic management function is not gaining importance on par with other disciplines such as HR or Marketing. **Part five** is completely revised and it explores the key characteristics of a successful public relations manager with Four 'As', which describe the roles as Analyst, Adviser, Advocate and Antenna, and four 'Ps', Personal Characteristics, Professional Qualification, Professional Skills and Psychologist Bent of Mind, which emphasize on the qualities and qualifications needed. Writing skill is the rock foundation of public relations to communicate messages effectively so as to influence the mind of audiences. It is in this context that **Chapter 32** introduces the 10 Golden Guidelines for Effective Writing.

The blend of theory and practice of public relations, corporate communications and media tactics ends with a thought provoking chapter **'Public Relations into the Future'**. It examines whither Indian public relations in the backdrop of its pitfalls and recommends five growth engines towards a bright future for Indian public relations. In fine, the new edition contributes to the much needed professional excellence of international standards towards effective corporate public relations for good governance, good business and better reputation for organisations.

Part Six: Actions Speak: PR Case Studies

"An ounce of action is worth more than tons of preaching", said Mahatma Gandhi. **Chapter 35** in **part six** throws light on practical application of theory into practice to accomplish corporate goals. Thirteen case studies have been discussed in this chapter to testify as to how public relations techniques applied in dealing with the organisational problems yielded good results. Subjects such as curbing stray dog bites menace, higher productivity, media relations in crisis situations, employees' motivation, rural communication, education of tribals, Bharat Nirman public information campaign, etc. have been covered in the case studies. "India: A Polio Free Country: A Case Study in Health Communication" is a model study which highlights the need for micro-level household communication to solve many problems confronting our nation.

World's Greatest Communicator

The uniqueness of this new edition, in contrast with other public relations books lies in its last **Chapter 36 "Mahatma Gandhi: World's Greatest Communicator"**, which focuses on public relations exercise in the freedom struggle. With his distinguishing communication techniques in tune with the Indian environment, Gandhi not only created public opinion against the British rule towards independence but also laid a solid concrete foundation for the future of public relations in India. The Public Relations Voice in its inaugural issue (1997) aptly described Mahatma Gandhi as the Father of Indian Public Relations. As such, the last chapter symbolizes the Indian public relations model.

"Reach out to Every Village, Every Household" with public relations message to inform, educate and enlighten the people of India as active partners in the world's largest vibrant democracy is the essence of this new edition.

Every chapter is self-contained by itself. However, certain teaching aids such as chapter opening contents, tables, figures, points to remember, review questions, suggested reading, glossary, index are included to help students understand and remember the various aspects of public relations to apply in real-life situations. Every effort has been made to update facts and figures. If any omissions, useful comments or suggestions are notified, we will undertake to rectify and improve the contents. Feel free to contact me anytime at drcvn@hotmail.com and Mobile No. +91 09246548901. We can share our experiences and compare our perspectives on the subject.

Naredra Luther, former Chief Secretary to Govt. of Andhra Pradesh, who as a Director, Information and Public Relations Department laid a strong foundation for the public relations network in the State, wrote the foreword which has added value to this edition. I express a deep debt of gratitude to him.

Finally, I would like to thank PHI Learning for their untiring efforts and support in bringing out this second edition.

C.V. Narasimha Reddi

Preface to the First Edition

Over a period of last 34 years, Public Relations (PR) in India had witnessed a sea change both in its quantity and in its quality. From being mere propaganda during medieval India, publicity in British India and public relations in the independent India, the Indian public relations has now graduated into global public relations. This is all due to the New Industrial Policy 1991 which envisaged economic liberalisation, privatisation and globalisation. What was the result of this policy? It led to the end of State Control of Licence *Raj* in the industry, and marked the beginning of a new *Raj* of reposing confidence among the management of corporate India and the stakeholders.

As a result, multinationals came to India, and Indian companies, by acquiring foreign enterprises, became multinationals. Thus, the need for public relations communication increased manifold to meet the global competitive marketing environment. In the recent times, there has been an upswing in public relations activities in the government, public sector, private industry and even NGOs. When multinationals came to India, they came along with their own public relations agencies. Indian public relations agencies also tied-up with foreign public relations firms as to serve the cause of global market. In the process, there emerged a holistic, integrated corporate public relations or corporate communications embracing total relationships of corporate India.

Though the profession is growing in India with its increasing number of in-house public relations and independent public relations firms, there is a dearth of trained and competent public relations professionals who can handle the ever-increasing corporate communication programmes. A key reason for this pitfall is lack of public relations education, training and standard textbooks. Public relations academicians, students, professionals and other communication specialists still refer to foreign textbooks, especially those from the USA and the UK. No doubt, the Western books are very useful in understanding the basic principles of public relations, but their usage in application to Indian conditions is minimal. Unlike Western public relations, Indian public relations has a distinct role to play in promoting the largest democracy with a pluralistic society in the world that is poised to become the world's third biggest economy next only to China and USA. It undoubtedly beckons a bright future for Indian public relations communication discipline.

The need of the hour is, therefore, standard textbooks on public relations with international standards in the Indian socio-economic environment. Against this backdrop, this book *Effective Public Relations and Media Strategy* emerges out of more than forty years of my experience as a public relations professional.

The book is divided into six key parts: Part One: Principles of Public Relations and Communication; Part Two: Public Relations Practice; Part Three: Media Strategy; Part Four: Effective Public Relations; Part Five: Historical–Indian Perspective of Public Relations; Part Six: Actions Speak—Case Studies.

In Part One, the book discusses the basic principles of public relations and communication on which the edifice of public relations profession stands.

Topics, such as definitions of public relations, communication, basic elements and principles, public relations as a strategic management function, structure of in-house public relations and public relations firms, history of public relations are explained in this part. Once the students are through with the basic principles, it will be easy for them to proceed with the practice of public relations.

In Part Two, the book takes the academicians and students in sequence through the four stages of public—relations process research, planning, communication and evaluation, and stakeholders' relations. Another significant area—Corporate Public Relations has been analysed in this part which explains the difference between public relations and corporate communications.

Media is the lifeblood of public relations. It is both a constituency and a conduit to all other organisational constituents—employees, investors, customers, etc. It is media that links the internal and external audiences besides promoting reputation of the company. Therefore, Part Three focuses on different public relations media and tactics used as opportunities there in the practice of public relations to reach and influence the target public. The classification of media has been designed on the ITM Theory of Gandhian Public Communication as: Interpersonal Media, Traditional Folk Media, Mass Media and Modern IT New Mass Media.

The success of public relations practice ultimately depends on the professionalism and efficiency of the public relations manager. Part Four of this book envisages the eight attributes that have to be acquired by a public relations professional not only to add professional excellence in public relations, but also to promote effective corporate public relations for better governance, for better business, for better image and for higher productivity of organisations.

Part Five deals with the origins and development of public relations in the world's largest democracy. Public relations in India is as old as the Indian civilisation itself. No formal research has been undertaken to analyse the origins and development of public relations in India.

However, an attempt has been made to divide the History of Public Relations into five periods based on records available and experience of the author. The five periods are: The State of Propaganda (1500 BC–1857 AD); The Era of Publicity (1858–1918); The Gandhian Era of Public Communication (1919–1947); The Age of Public Relations (1947–1990); and Indian Public Relations with Global Perspective (1991–2009).

"An ounce of practice is worth more than tons of preaching" said Mahatma Gandhi. Case histories are the best way of studying practical applications of public relations programme. Part Six includes some of the case studies reflecting employee relations, media relations, customer relations, reputation management, crisis management.

Every chapter is self-contained by itself. However, certain teaching aids have been included to help students understand and remember the various aspects of public relations and give them the practical areas of public relations to apply the principles to real-life situations.

Finally, I would like to thank PHI Learning for their untiring effort and support in bringing out this book.

Any useful comments or suggestions to improve the contents will be warmly appreciated.

C.V. Narasimha Reddi

P
A
R
T

O
N
E

Principles of Public Relations and Communication

✓ What is Public Relations?

✓ Communication

✓ Principles of Public Relations

✓ Evolution of Public Relations—
Ancient India to Modern India
(World's Biggest Democracy)

✓ History of Public Relations in USA
(World's Oldest Democracy)

What is Public Relations?   Chapter 1

> *We do not need to Proselytise either by our speech or by our writing.*
> *We can only do so really with our lives. Let our lives be open books for*
> *all to study.*
>   **—Mahatma Gandhi**

CONTENTS

DEFINING PR

'Definition' is a statement giving the exact meaning of a word, a phrase, a term, and the nature and scope of a subject: The heart and soul of any discipline, be it medicine, journalism, or public relations is reflected in its definition. Therefore, no public relations professional can practise the profession without knowing its meaning in the shape of a definition. Various authors, and professional bodies have defined public relations in different ways. In *Public Relations and Communication Handbook-2002*, Dr. C.V. Narasimha Reddi has quoted over 100 definitions. Probably one of the best is, "The management of a two-way communication process between an organisation and its publics".

The Stanford University Professor Emeritus (USA) Rex Harlow who identified 500 definitions of public relations in 1976 had come up with the following definition: "Public relations is a distinctive management function which helps establish and maintain mutual lines of communication, understanding, acceptance and cooperation between an organization and its publics; involves the management of problems or issues; helps management to keep informed on and responsive to public opinion; defines and emphasises the responsibility of management to serve the public interest; helps management keep abreast of and effectively utilise change, serving as an early warning system to help anticipate trends; and uses research and ethical communication techniques as its principal tools" (Wilcox 2009).

The Chartered Institute of Public Relations (CIPR) London, defines "Public relations is the planned and sustained effort to establish and maintain goodwill and mutual understanding between an organization and its publics...public relations is about reputation—the result of what you do, what you say and what others say about you" and "public relations practice is the discipline which looks after reputation with the aim of earning understanding and support and influencing opinion and behaviour".

According to the **Public Relations Society of America** "Public Relations helps an organization and its publics to adapt mutually to each other. Public relations is an organization's effort to win the cooperation of groups of people. Public relations helps organizations effectively interact and communicate with their key publics".

Public relations is the attempt by information, persuasion, and adjustment to engineer public support for an activity, cause, movement or institution.
Edward L. Bernays (1891–1995)

The management function which evaluates public attitudes, identifies the policies and procedures of an individual or an organization with public interest and executes a programme of action to earn understanding and acceptance.

Denny Griswold

The International Conference of Public Relations Institutions held in Mexico in 1978 came up with a definition of PR, popularly known as Mexican Statement, "Public relations practice is the art of social science of analysing trends, predicting their consequences, counselling organizations, leaders and implementing planned programmes of action, which will serve both the organization and the public interest".

The definition offered by the author Dr. C.V. Narasimha Reddi, who is also the Editor, *Public Relations Voice,* is: "Public relations is the management of a two-way communication process between an organisation and its publics to promote the corporate vision, mission, services, products, reputation and gain public understanding".

Public relations in any organization has to promote the corporate vision, mission, goods, products, services and reputation. These keywords have been added to this definition, making it distinct from other PR definitions.

An analysis of definitions reveals the following key elements which give us a working definition of public relations:

- Organization
- Corporate vision, mission, products/services/reputation
- Plan of action with public interest
- Publics—internal (employees), External (customers)
- Management Principles
- Two-Way Communication process
- Effect or impact of action plan and communication
- Mutual understanding

A combination of these elements summarises the basic functions of public relations in any organization to gain public understanding for its smooth functioning.

IS PR ALL ABOUT WINING AND DINING?

Public relations in India is a much misunderstood discipline. It is not about wining and dining as some people think. As public relations' intention is to create goodwill for the organisation, it is but natural to meet not only stakeholders, but also opinion leaders, media persons, etc. Organisations arrange such meetings over lunches or dinners, which are often misunderstood by people and they give a bad connotation to the public relations practice itself. Lunches are not exclusive only to public relations, every profession organises them. When foreign dignitaries visit India, the President of India hosts dinners to discuss matters of mutual interest. Entertainment is a part of corporate culture. Even Government and private sector have provisions for such entertainment.

Luncheon meetings are common when important persons are invited for discussion. There is an element of social contact in such meetings because it uses the time more effectively since we all have to eat. The image of public relations being limited to lunches in luxurious hotels and restaurants probably owes more to wishful thinking and satire rather than reality.

In fact, 'business lunch' or, for that matter, breakfast and dinner have contrasted dramatically in importance in the changing corporate world. One-to-one meetings have taken some beating for quality of communication, but these days public relations professionals tend to skip lunch in favour of hurried snacks, and use many more communication channels than were available to them a few years ago. Public relations is not just about 'wining and dining', although the perpetual urgency to achieve more output with the available time has not destroyed the observance of common courtesies in those countries where social etiquette remains a key component of doing business.

Journalists are always busy gathering news from sources. Often they meet people over breakfasts, lunches and dinners to save their time. Public relations professionals organise such one-to-one meetings between a CEO and a journalist over lunches or dinners to create an informal environment. Thus, public relations cannot be termed as a 'wining and dining' profession because it is not without a meaningful dialogue. Such meetings are result oriented in gaining media coverage.

Lok Sabha Speaker's Breakfast Meeting

The National Democratic Alliance withdrew its decision of boycotting the Parliament Committees at a breakfast meeting arranged by the Lok Sabha Speaker Somnath Chatterji, with the Leader of the Opposition L.K. Advani on 3 August, 2004. The breakfast as the first meal of the day not only provided a social contact between the Speaker and the Leader of the Opposition, but also enabled them to discuss the issues of boycotting Parliament Committees. As such wine and dine is a process of get-together and it should be taken in a positive sense.

WHY DO PEOPLE SEEM TO RESPOND TO PR?

Public relations has become both invasive and pervasive—thanks to economic liberalisation and globalisation. There has been an upswing in public relations activities in India and abroad. Trade wars on the one hand and media explosion on the other hand have made almost all organisations, both in the government and in the private sector realise the importance of communication with internal and external public. As a result, most of the organisations respond to the call of public relations these days which has fuelled its growth as a strategic management function.

In the last decade of economic liberalisation, the public relations profession has injected new words into the language, filled news items in the newspapers, inspired numerous television and radio programmes, transformed policies, and persuaded even the former Prime Minister Atal Bihari Vajpayee to launch a nationwide public communication campaign, *India shining*. These testify the need for such campaigns in government and private sector.

The constant media conferences, sponsorships, corporate social responsibility, exhibitions, printing of colourful information brochures, employee relations, customer relations, financial relations, crisis communication—all give the impression that public relations is at the very heart of Indian corporate culture. Corporations today vie with one another to attract efficient and energetic public relations professionals. Therefore, people depend on public relations practice for solving organisational problems. Unfortunately, the supply of professionals is not in tune with the demand.

Can PR be Self-taught?

Yes, but patience and application are needed for sustained success. There are many 'How To' books and courses on public relations. The techniques are easy to learn, at least in principle, and most people can turn their hands to them. Writing press releases, and producing brochures, house magazines etc. can be learnt on the job.

Even when there were no public relations educational facilities in the country, India produced self-taught and on-the-job trained professionals. In sum, public relations can be learnt from open universities and correspondence courses besides studying books and journals on the subject. However, internship in the public relations department is essential because on the job training helps to be more effective.

WHAT CAN PR DO?

Public relations is all pervasive, but it can never be held as a panacea for every problem. When working with public relations, the management of an organisation must have a clear understanding of its limitations. However, public relations is a sustained effort that can provide good results over time.

The functions of public relations practice which can help your organization include:

- Analysis/research of the internal and external organizational environment to study its problems and pulse of the public.
- Advising/counselling the management on the identified problems
- Promote the corporate vision, mission, products, services with dissemination of public information
- Promote internal communication within employees through house journals
- External communication with customers and, shareholders through customers meet, annual reports
- Better community relations with the neighbourhood community by undertaking welfare programmes and communicating with them through meetings
- Bringing out corporate publications, newsletters and corporate profiles, success stories for distribution among internal and external stakeholders

- Better media relations by providing newsworthy information to journalists through press releases
- Build trust and reputation with stakeholders that promote mutual understanding and goodwill for the organization. Convert ill will to goodwill
- The last but the most important function of public relations is to assess the reactions of stakeholders towards organizational policies and products/services and keep the management constantly informed with such feedback reports

WHAT IS PROPAGANDA?

Propaganda, one of the earliest forms of communication, is different from publicity, public relations, or advertising, because it attempts to achieve a response that furthers the desired intent of the propagandist. *Webster's New World Dictionary* defines propaganda as "the systematic, widespread promotion of a certain set of ideas, doctrines etc., to further one's own cause".

Reader's Digest Great Dictionary of the English Language describes propaganda as "information of a biased or misleading nature, used to promote a political cause or a point of view".

Joseph Goebbels, the Propaganda Minister of Hitler (1897–1945), defined propaganda as "an instrument of politics, a power of social control". The function of propaganda is not essentially to convert; rather its function is to attract followers and keep them in line. The task of propaganda, given suitable avenues, is to blanket every area of human activity so that the environment of the individual is changed to absorb the 'Nazi movement'. Propaganda is defined as a deliberate manipulation by means of symbols, words, gestures, images, flags, music—of other people's thoughts, behaviour, attitudes and beliefs. Communication intended to influence belief and action, whether true or false is called propaganda. In *white propaganda*, the information source is identified, while in *black propaganda,* information source is not divulged. The recipient of the propaganda is discouraged from asking about anything outside the content area.

Goebbels adopted 'You Can' theory based on 'Man believes anything, if you tell in a proper way' and followed his Guru's principle, Adolf Hitler: "*more lies, more people would believe*". Goebbels said that propaganda had no fundamental method, only the purpose—the conquest of the masses.

College of Propaganda

The word 'propaganda' is derived from the word of Latin "*Congregation de propaganda fide*", meaning the "Congregation for the Propagation of the Faith" of the Roman Catholic Church. The Vatican established a College of Propagate in Rome in 1662 AD for training missionary priests and also for spreading the faith of Christianity through foreign missions. Propaganda has been used from the late 18th century to refer to a scheme or organisation for promoting a particular doctrine. However, it seems to have acquired its modern meaning in the 1830s. From this, it came to be known as spreading a belief of any organisation or movement. This principle applies to all religions, be it Hinduism, Jainism, Buddhism, Sikhism or Islam. The Imperial Roman Empire used propaganda techniques between 50 BC and 50 AD to build up its image and develop a strong centralised government.

Propaganda is more or less a systematic effort to manipulate other people's beliefs, attitudes, or actions by means of symbols, words, gestures, banners, monuments, music, clothing, insignia, hairstyles, designs on coins and postage stamps, and so forth. Deliberateness and a relatively heavy emphasis on manipulation distinguishes propaganda from casual conversation, or the free and easy exchange of ideas. The propagandist has a specific goal or set of goals. To achieve these, one deliberately selects facts, arguments, and display of symbols and presents them in ways he or she thinks will be most effective. To maximise effect, the propagandist may omit pertinent facts or distort them, and he or she may try to divert the attention of the reactors (the people whom he or she is trying to sway) from everything but his or her own propaganda.

One Empire, One People, One Leader

The word 'propaganda' has negative connotation today because of its implications of bias, deception and misinformation. But such connotation was acquired only in the 20th century. In 1919, Adolf Hitler (1889–1945) co-founded the National Socialist German Worker's Party, which later became known as the Nazi party. While in Landsberg prison, he dictated his political testament *Mein Kampf* (My Struggle). This was his political manifesto which laid the foundation of his propaganda technique, *Ein Reich, Ein Volk, Ein Fibrer* which means "One Empire, One People, and One Leader".

He imposed this ideal on his country at the expense of millions of lives. Hitler, however, based his propaganda on the dictum: *The greater the lie, the more people would believe it.* In his attempt to succeed in his mission, Hitler appointed his most trusted colleague Paul Joseph Goebbels, the architect of propaganda, as the Propaganda Minister during the Second World War. In fact, Goebbels gave a derogatory connotation to the word propaganda. He made full use of propaganda techniques as an instrument to win the war, misused the concept and brought a wrong connotation to this discipline. In tune with the objectives set by Hitler, Goebbels developed a two-pronged propaganda strategy. One was "Sycophancy and Flattery" and the other was "Your Country Needs You, You Can".

ARCHITECTS OF PROPAGANDA

Both Adolf Hitler and his Propaganda Minister Joseph Goebbels remained as the architects of propaganda during the Second World War. They gave a distinct negative concept to the age–old propaganda technique by giving priority to lies, sycophancy and flattery rather than truth and reality. Their main aim was to win the war and establish their own empire.

What was the result of their efforts? What inference can we draw from their propagandism? Hitler shot himself dead on 30 April 1945, while Joseph Goebbels after poisoning his six children and wife Magada shot himself. Any publicity or public relations programme without performance will also meet the same fate.

Usage has rendered the word propaganda pejorative. To identify a message as a propaganda is to suggest that it is dishonest. Words frequently used as synonyms for propaganda are: lies, distortion, deceit, disinformation, manipulation, psychological warfare, brainwashing, double talk, omission of facts, prejudiced appeals, etc. Many of these synonyms are suggestive of techniques of propaganda message production, rather than the purpose or process.

PR Differs from Propaganda

A clear distinction needs to be drawn between *public relations* and *propaganda*. The elements of *deliberateness* and *manipulation* along with a *systematic plan* to accomplish a purpose which is advantageous to the propagandist distinguish propaganda from a free and open exchange of ideas brought about by honest public relations. If public relations is a two-way traffic, then propaganda is only one-way communication with no provision for feedback. They are two different approaches. Propaganda does not necessarily call for an ethical content, and the word is used nowadays mainly to describe those types of persuasion which are based only on self-interest and in which it may be necessary to distort the facts or even to falsify them (War Propaganda) in order to achieve the purpose.

Public relations, on the other hand, recognises truth as the basic principle and also a long-term effort, and seeks to persuade to achieve public acceptance for a cause, service or product. It can succeed only when the basic policy is ethical and the means used are truthful. In public relations, the ends can never justify the use of false, harmful or questionable means.

Public Interest

It is not possible to use public relations techniques to bolster a weak cause, or a defective product. In fact, a successful public relations campaign may only expose the weaknesses and offer suggestions for corrective course. Moreover, public relations cannot use the techniques of propaganda. In the practice of public relations, the policy should always be in the public interest and positive.

Public interest is the prime concern of public relations, while in propaganda the intentions of the propagandist are important. Social responsibility to serve the cause of the community is yet an important area of public relations. But, the propaganda has no value for social responsibility. It is against this background, no government, industry, corporation or not-for-profit organisation can operate successfully without public relations.

In fact, the basic difference between propaganda and public relations can be described by comparing with Kauravas led by Duryodhana as propaganda and Pandavas headed by Yudhisthira as public relations in the great epic of *Mahabharata.*

WHAT IS PUBLICITY?

Publicity has graduated from propaganda. It is only intended to draw the attention of the audiences and create awareness by any means that is both credible and relevant. Scott M. Cutlip and Allen H. Centre define publicity as "the dissemination of information, making matters public from the point of view of one who wishes to inform others". *It is also called a systematic distribution of public information about an institution, individual, a product, an idea or a service.* Placing information in a news medium to attract the attention of the public towards the products or services' is also publicity. Thus, it can be described as telling a story without payment.

Media persons are hungry for good sources of information for writing stories. The public relations manager as a source could be of great use to them by providing publicity material in the form of press releases, backgrounders, press kits, features, press photos, etc. Public relations is about striving to achieve and improve a two-way communication, whereas publicity is mainly a one-way communication not seeking either any dialogue or feedback. The disadvantage in publicity compared to advertising is that one has full control over the message in advertising and the posters and brochures. But, one does not have the control over publicity message. It is controlled and managed by the media depending on the news values, availability of space and time.

If publicity is the front cover of a news magazine which is published free of cost, advertising is the back cover which carries paid forms of communication in the shape of an advertisement either to sell a product or a service. The front cover is free, because it carries pictures and messages of news value and public interest, while the back cover is a paid one. Newspapers offer free space for new products of consumers' interest. This is called product publicity.

Publicity Boards

The attempt to draw attention for commercial advantage, publicity began in the United States of America in the 1860s. So it is long established form of communication (Anthony Davis, p. 89). The Government of India needed extensive propaganda to secure greater response and support for the First World War effort during 1914–1918. The Government had set up a number of provincial publicity boards throughout the country with a Central Publicity Board in New Delhi (Dr. C.V. Narasimha Reddi, *Public Relations and Communication Handbook, 2002*, p. 101). The main aim of the publicity boards was to create awareness among the people towards war effort through media and seek their support.

In 1930, the Great Indian Peninsular Railway established its publicity bureau in England to carry publicity campaign with the help of mass media to attract tourists to India. The publicity bureau also introduced a travelling cinema within India to promote tourism.

After India got its independence, a greater thrust was given to publicity with the launch of first Five Year Plan (1951–1956). A nationwide Plan Publicity Campaign was launched with the appointment of Plan Publicity Officers not only to inform about the objectives of various schemes of planning but also to enlist people's cooperation and participation in the successful implementation of Five Year Plans.

PR as Distinct from Publicity

Publicity should not be confused with PR. Publicity is part of public relations. Both are free as they provide news of public interest. Publicity is one of the main strands of public relations described as the term 'press agentry' which is public relations through newspaper.

Public relations and publicity are not two independent disciplines, but two sides of the same coin. Public relations is often used as a synonym for publicity. Publicity is strictly a communication function whereas public relations involves a management function also. But publicity is not public relations. It is a tool used by the public relations practitioners. While the boundaries of these two disciplines may well overlap, they differ in the technique of their approach. Public relations deals with the people individually in mass as distinct from general public in publicity. The former always adopts segmented audience approach to disseminating information, while publicity disseminates information to the general public. Therefore, publicity has been defined as 'the art of dealing with the people in masses'. Its chief function is to gain public attention for companies, clients, products or services. For example, when a scientist invents a new thing, the news about the invention hits the front page in newspapers and becomes the main story of electronic media. This, in brief, is publicity and utilises all media of communication such as press releases, leaflets and posters.

Publicity achieves its goal when it provides information to the target audiences. In publicity, news is published free of cost at the discretion of the media. The source of publicity is always known and the information disseminated is also credible.

Publicity material must be interesting to the people. Financial reports, scientific findings, news of corporate performance, annual general body meetings, press conferences, new product launches, sponsorships, community relations service, national calamities—all have obvious news value and get publicised in the media without any payment, provided the source is known and credible. Public relations makes use of publicity tactics to achieve its objectives. Publicity is a one-way communication, while public relations is a two-way traffic—a very important distinction.

Handling publicity demands professional skills. When handled well, it confers tremendous benefits; if handled badly, it can do more harm than good. In other words, it may become counterproductive.

WHAT IS ADVERTISING?

The word 'advertising' originates from the Latin word *advertise* which means 'to turn to'. It is turning one's attention to the message of either a product or a service. According to *Concise Oxford Dictionary*, the verb 'to advertise' means: "To make generally or publicly known; describe publicly with a view to involving sales". The *Webster Collegiate Dictionary* gives the meaning of advertising as "the action of calling something to attention of public by paid announcement". The *Encyclopaedia Britannica* says, "advertisement is a form of paid announcement intended to promote the sale of commodity or service to advance an idea or to bring about some other effect, desired by the advertiser". In this way, advertising began when someone had some product to sell and at the same time there was someone who wanted to buy that particular product. It became a process of 'selling' and 'buying' through public announcements.

The American Marketing Association defined Advertising as *"any paid form of non-personal presentation or promotion of ideas, goods or services by an identified sponsor"*. Advertising presents the most persuasive possible selling message to the right prospects for the product or service at the lowest possible cost. It is the means by which we make known what we have to sell or what we want to buy.

The process of buying sponsor identified media space or time in order to promote a product or an idea.

B.S. Rathor

Advertising is the life of trade.
John Calvin Coolidge, Jr. (1872–1933), 30th President of the USA

Advertising is communicating with and influencing someone to do something—usually to buy a product or service—and often to think something.

Sushil Bahl

Advertising is the paid dissemination of information for the purpose of selling or helping to sell commodities and services or of gaining acceptance of ideas that may cause people to think or act in a desired manner.

Subrata Banerjee

Advertising is a substitute for the human salesman.

Sydney Bernstein

Components of Advertisement

First, advertising is a paid form of communication intended to promote sales. **Second**, advertising is non-personal. **Third**, advertisement is identifiable with its sponsoring authority. Since advertising and public relations use the media either to create awareness or to influence markets, they share some common attributes but the terms are not interchangeable. Advertising is logically a part of public relations, since it affects relationships between an organisation and the public.

Corporate Advertising

Corporate advertising is designed to portray a desirable reputation of an organisation, as such it is advertising not to sell a product but sell the company's image. Corporate advertising is also called general promotion, or institutional, image, strategic issue or umbrella advertising.

Corporate advertising and public relations are often closely allied. Both deal with the image of a corporation as expressed through its paid public communications and attempt to shape public attitudes.

The main difference between corporate advertising and public relations is that the former unlike public relations can select the exact content of the message as well as the media in which it will appear. Many corporations have chosen to supplement their traditional public relations programmes with paid corporate advertising. In fact, corporate advertising is the prerogative of public relations.

If I say "I am good", it is advertising. "If I say I have heard that you are Good", it is public relations. Public relations sometimes is confused with advertising. But the fundamental ways in which both the disciplines work are very different. It is true that they are part of communication in reaching the audience with a message. It is also correct that both seek to influence the minds and attitudes of the people. But, from thereon, they take separate paths.

One author described the difference between public relations and advertising by comparing them to a car and a boat. Both are modes of transport to reach one's destination, but each takes a very different approach. However, when public relations and advertising are converged or coordinated (as a car and boat may be used at different stages in the same journey), powerful communication campaigns result. Convergence of public relations and advertising as an integrated approach is the current trend.

Although both public relations and advertising utilise mass media for dissemination of messages, the format and content are different. In public relations, information about an event or a product is published as a news item of public importance. Such news stories are prepared by public relations managers and sent to newspapers and electronic media for publication. However, editors (known as gatekeepers) determine the news value of such news items and use them if they are of interest to the readers or listeners/viewers.

Advertising, in contrast, is paid space and broadcast time. Organisations normally contract with an advertising agency which in turn is in touch with the advertising department of mass media outlet for a full page advertisement or a one-minute commercial. An organisation writes the copy, decides the type and graphics, and controls where and when the advertisement will be published. In other words, advertising is simply renting space in a mass medium. In it the message is controlled by the sponsor, while in public relations, the media decides what to be published.

How does public relations differ from advertising? (refer Table 1.1)

TABLE 1.1: Differences between Public Relations and Advertising

Public Relations	*Advertising*
I. Strategy	
PR aims to persuade people to buy or take some desired action–creates desire, motivates demand for product/service. PR is a top management function.	Advertisement seeks to create awareness and understanding of the public for products/services
II: Target Audience	
PR audiences are segmented as employees, customers, shareholders, media, etc.	Target audience is based on market demographic distribution, product/ service, social background, age and sex. Consumers in general.

Public Relations	*Advertising*

III: Purpose

Mutual understanding, goodwill, building reputation of the organisation among its public.	To increase sales and motivate people to purchase goods/services, marketing effort, announce new products, challenge the competition, build brand image.

IV. Message

PR message has credibility. No superlatives no self-praise. Trustworthy information, interest and value to the public. No decorative device. Message is given in simple language without elaborate window dressing. Media releases and stories are independent of advertising.	Advertising is to compete for attention and must use clever devices, street cries, circus drum. Messages are emotive such as stage makeup and voices and artiste makeup as decorative device. In radio, TV, magazines and newspapers messages are advertised.

V. Media Choice

PR messages to segmented groups. Unlimited and variety of multiple media from interpersonal media/electronic media to IT new media/traditional folk arts.	Advertisement messages to the largest buying groups. Limited depending on the product and audience. For example TV, Radio, Film, Press, Hoarding, Banner.

VI. Presentation

Subtle, simple to inform.	Competitive and creative copy to influence.

VII. Cost

PR stories are unpaid for. It has no rate card. PR editorial information not paid because of public interest. PR is time-cost.	Media cost of advertising is high as it is paid, based on time and space.

Publicity involves conveying information to a mass or targeted audience about a product, or programme in the form of a news story, feature story, by-lined article or other kinds of non-paid media coverage. Generating publicity in newspapers, radio and TV is one of the most effective ways of popularising the use of contraceptives to contain population and promote family planning. Factual and public interest are the two ingredients of publicity.

Publicity depends much on media. Media publicity has news value. Publicity material gives a lot of information to journalists who sort the wheat from the chaff according to their needs and feed the media. Publicity is carried in the media free of cost as against advertising which is a paid form. Because publicity cost is primarily the cost of producing background materials, media release and the cost of coverage in placing a story are relatively cheaper. It is considerably less expensive than advertising.

The other differences between PR and advertising are as follows:

1. Advertising functions mainly through mass media outlets, while public relations relies on a variety of communication media, including interpersonal, traditional media.
2. Advertising is always aimed at external publics (customers, shareholders). Public relations presents its message to both internal (employees) and external publics (all stakeholders).
3. Advertising is readily identified as a specialised communication, while public relations is broader in nature and scope, and wider in subject dealing with the policies and performance of the entire organisation from building the morale of employees to promoting customers' loyalty, besides gaining public understanding.
4. Advertising often is used as a communication tool in public relations (product publicity, corporate advertising), while public relations programme often supports advertising campaigns.
5. Advertising is 100 per cent controlled by the advertiser, while public relations is directed but not completely controlled by the organisation.
6. Advertising is to sell goods and services, while the public relations function is to create a conducive environment in which organisation can prosper and reach its goals. The job of public relations is also to promote reputation of an organisation.
7. Advertising is expensive, while public relations is more cost-effective and often more credible because the message of the product is published in a news context without any cost. The news release, interview, and press conference—the traditional workhorses of publicity—are examples of uncontrolled public relations messages. But the advertising department can control content, placement and timing.

Commercial Vs Social

The most astute distinction between advertising and public relations, as one General Manager of an advertising agency said, is that generally speaking, advertising is 'commercial' while public relations is 'social'. Public relations differs from advertising. The strategy of advertising is to create desire, motivate demand for a product. Public relations is the strategy of confidence which alone gives credibility to a message. A public relations manager who has no expertise in advertising will engage the services of a professional advertising agency.

Public relations creates awareness among the public about a product or service while advertising promotes sales—a prerequisite for marketing and advertising. Both, public relations and advertising are the two forms of communication which brings these two disciplines closer and sometimes they function in unison. However, the messages are complementary rather than exclusive.

Advertising and public relations are integral parts in the integrated marketing communication. Similarly, the integrated public relations communication embraces advertising as one of the components. Most of the in-house public relations departments have advertising as one of its key functions. Also advertising agencies deal with public relations. Accordingly, some advertising agencies have opened public relations divisions in their firms.

Advertising agencies deal with public relations of a client either directly or through a public relations division within the agency or an independent PR agency. Since they have distinct functions, advertising and public relations agencies function independently all over the world. There is likely to be a swing towards integrated approach in future wherein these two functions will be converged.

New Dimensions in Advertising

In their book *The Fall of Advertising and the Rise of PR*, Al Ries and Laura Ries (2002) provide valuable ideas for marketers, all the while demonstrating the **why** of PR:

- Advertising lacks credibility, the crucial ingredient in brand building, and how only PR can supply that credibility.
- The big-bang approach advocated by advertising people should be abandoned in favour of a slow build-up by PR.
- Advertising should be used only to maintain brands once they have been established through publicity and public relations.
- While narrating that the public relations 'era cometh', the authors say, "We see a dramatic shift from advertising-oriented marketing to public relations-oriented marketing".
- PR creates brand while advertising will maintain the brand.
- Advertising is one-sided message, while PR is supported by third party endorsement.

PUBLIC AFFAIRS

Public affairs is a term born in the USA and mostly practised in the US, UK and in a few countries like Australia as a specialised area of public relations that involves government relations, legislative and community relations. In fact, public affairs focuses on relationships that have a bearing on the development of public policy and issue management of public concern which if acted upon by significant groups will have an impact on business activities.

How Do You Define Public Affairs?

According to Newsom, Turk, and Kurucerberg (2000), "Public Affairs is actually a highly specialised kind of public relations that involves community relations and government relations—that is dealing with officials within the community". Public affairs is the professional maintenance of legislative, government and community relations. Public affairs is the planned management of public and political issues which may have an impact on the reputation, performance or licence to operate any business or organization. It also includes management of internal and external communications. It is a critical part of public relations practice, but it is not the whole public relations programme. For example, before Dallas Airport was inaugurated, two PR firms were engaged, one to handle public affairs (government and municipal relations) and the other to handle media relations. Relations with the Government, statutory bodies, government departments and various semi-official organisations that wield power in the Government come under the purview of public affairs.

The Public Relations Society of America (PRSA) also identifies public affairs as a specialist area of practice within public relations. Many public relations personnel use the term public affairs to connote their functions. The legislative, government relations on the one hand and welfare activities as part of social responsibility on the other hand are but one important area in the broader term of public affairs which is used by non-government organisations as a synonym for government relations.

It will be interesting to know how the term public affairs came into existence in the USA. Although the US government is the largest employer of public relations professionals in the world, the term 'public relations' is not used in government departments. Instead, it is public affairs or public information that is used in the US government. However, almost all other fields in private sector, corporations and business organisations use public relations or corporate communications.

Prohibitive Words

Why is it so? The October 1913 Inter-State Commerce Commission Act of the USA precluded governmental use of public relations talent (Doug Newsom). The prohibitive words were attached to the last paragraph of the Inter-State Commerce Commission Statute "Appropriated funds may not be used to pay a publicity expert unless specifically appropriated for that purpose".

The amendment to the Bill was introduced by the Representative Fredrick H. Gillet, and, thus, is referred to in public relations studies as the Gillet Amendment. Most of the public relations work in the 1930s was publicity, and the intent of the amendment was to identify and control government publicity. Legislators then were concerned that the Government would become involved in propaganda directed at the US citizens. This amendment was not repealed because the government currently carries public relations functions under the mask of public affairs or public information.

Therefore, each Ministry in the US such as Ministry of State, Ministry of Agriculture, Ministry of Education, etc. has 'Public Affairs Division' manned by Public Affairs Officers to handle public information and public relations. They use public affairs to designate a broader responsibility than public information which involves merely dissemination of public information or publicity. Thus, the Public Information Officer is a publicist, whereas the Public Affairs Officer in the government has a bigger policy-making responsibility. For example, the Defence Public Affairs Officer often has the responsibility for all the facets of internal and external communication. It is against this backdrop that the term 'public affairs' for anyone in the employment of the United States Government is accepted as that of public relations. Public relations practitioners in the USA operate under a variety of job titles including press secretary, public information officer and public affairs officer.

PR Vs Public Affairs

How does public affairs differ from public relations? There are two schools of thought on this. One is that public affairs is equivalent to government relations; the other which is much broader than public affairs and covers a variety of activities such as government relations, community relations, media relations, employee relations, corporate advertising. The argument about public relations versus public affairs may be summed up as while public relations is concerned with the management of overall relationships such as media relations, financial relations, employees relations, institutional advertising; public affairs focuses on relationships which evolve public policy such as monitoring policy, representation to ministers, civil servants, legislative bodies. Maintaining public wise relationships—employees, shareholders, customers, media suppliers, dealers—is the job of public relations, and dealing with government relations and community relations as a specialised area is the task of public affairs.

Distinctions between public relations and public affairs are often blurry, but certain differences are clear. The public affairs function usually operates through either the political (government) process or the social service process (community relations). In contrast, public relations usually operates through the communications process with practitioners oriented towards media.

Services

Like public relations, the public affairs officer also offers services to influence the employer's customers. If it is government relations, the public affairs division's communication tasks include preparation of materials, reports; testimony for government hearings; producing brochures, videos for political affairs committees, and parliamentary committees. Public affairs specialists often serve as representatives of their organisations on task forces and commissions. The purpose is to develop a dialogue between the company and the community. Public affairs officials, while presenting the company's viewpoint, also listen and monitor emerging issues based on the feedback information. Thus, they can keep the management informed about any public or governmental concerns that directly or indirectly affect the company.

Public Affairs in India

Public affairs as a distinct discipline is not in practice in India. However, we have pressure groups, professional bodies which take care of government relations and also legislative relations. However, US embassy, and US Consulates in India have public affairs officers. It may, however, develop even in India under the impact of globalisation and information revolution.

LOBBYING

Among the many dictionary meanings of the word 'lobby', the one we are dealing here is "a group of people who try to influence politicians on a particular issue". There are special interest groups in the US that openly attempt to influence government and legislative actions especially Federal and State Legislative processes. In India, for example, the Andhra Pradesh Retired Employees Association is one of the most effective lobby groups which advances the interests of the retired persons.

What is Lobbying?

Lobbying is described as a process of corporate advocacy to influence decision-making by the legislators, regulatory bodies and government officials. It is in this context corporations use the technique of lobbying to present their case with facts and figures, whenever any proposed legislation is likely to affect their operations. The origin of lobby is from the Latin word *Lobia* which means "covered walk"—first used in the sense of monastic cloister. From the Latin word, there emerged lobbying as one of the techniques of management to influence legislative process. "Lobbying is a process in which individuals or groups seek to influence those in power" (James Watson and Anne Hill, *A Dictionary of Communication and Media Studies*). Lobbying is aimed at directing attention to influence legislative and regulatory affairs in government at a local, state and national level. It is also directed towards non-governmental public whose voices are heard by Members of Parliament/ Members of Legislative Assembly and/or officials in the government. It is a long process of forging an interactive relationship between a particular industrial lobby and politicians who are beneficial to an organisation. For example, the anti-nuclear lobby is becoming stronger all over the world and the sugar industry lobby in Maharashtra is very powerful as it has influences over the state government also.

Functions

Lobbying is, therefore, a specialised subset of public affairs, but it is not the whole story in terms of the public affairs function and cannot and should not be used as a synonym for public affairs. Lobbying involves direct attempts to influence legislative and regulatory decisions in the government. It is closely aligned with government relations, and the distinction between the two areas often blurs.

However, certain functions insofar as legislature is concerned overlap between public affairs and lobbying. Public affairs is a specialised area of public relations designed to build and maintain government, legislative and community relations, while lobbying centres around only legislative relations as a specialist function. Lobbying can be either defensive, designed to get abolished or amended an existing law, or offensive, aimed at influencing the authorities and legislators to enact a new law. What are the basic functions of lobbying? It has three functions: (i) to 'inform' and to pass persuasive information to officials and legislators, (ii) to 'persuade' for an action and (iii) to monitor the implementation of decisions and the laws affecting the company.

Who is a Lobbyist?

The term that first appeared was lobby agent in the early 19th century, meaning someone who visits the lobbies of government administrative buildings to speak to officials or legislators.

A lobbyist is someone who, acting on behalf of a special interest group, tries to influence various forms of government regulations. He or she is also a specialist whose prime activity is directed towards ministers, politicians, legislators and the media persons for getting things done. A lobbyist generally passes persuasive information to the government officials.

Webster's New World Dictionary defines a lobbyist as "a person acting for a special interest group, who tries to influence the voting on legislation or the decision of government administrators". In other words, a lobbyist directs his or her energies to the defeat, passage or amendment of a proposal on legislation and regulatory agency policies. The term 'lobbyist' has several meanings. In its broadest sense, it is often used interchanging with the term 'pressure group' to mean any organisation or person that carries on activities as their ultimate objective to influence the decisions of Parliament. In a narrower sense, a lobbyist means any person, acting for a specialist interest group usually for pay, who tries to influence legislation or the decisions of government administration.

Lobbies and lobbyists are regulated in the USA by the Lobbying Disclosure Act which mandates that people who are paid to lobby the Congress or the executive branch of the Federal Government must register with the government, and paid lobbyists must specify who they represent and how much they are being paid. The law requires that lobbyists publicly identify themselves through registration. They must also file quarterly reports on their expenditures so that legislatures, regulators, the media and the public can see who is spending, how much and on what. Lobbyists by law are barred from giving gifts either to legislators or to civil servants.

What do Lobbyists do?

Lobbyists perform the functions envisaged under lobbying mainly to inform, persuade, plant and monitor ideas with legislators on the one side and keep the managements of the organisations that they represent informed of their efforts on the other side. In fact, a lobbyist acts as a bridge between a company, and legislators and government. However, the specific functions performed by individual lobbyists vary with the nature of the company or the group represented. Their activities and functions include the following:

1. *Background information:* Before undertaking lobbying, the first task of a lobbyist is to collect background information on the issue which is to be handled through lobbying. The government has enormous information, statistics, reports on the proposed legislation which is to be collected and collated to evolve a strategy and proper interpretation.

2. *Interpretation:* A key function of a lobbyist is to interpret the background information on the issue, as related to the client organisation with potential implications on the company. Implications are based on lobbying.
3. *Company's views:* It is the function of a lobbyist to interpret the company's viewpoint on the issue to government officials and legislators. Such briefings further the objectives of lobbying.
4. *Advocate:* The lobbyist finally assumes the role of an advocate to present the issues of the clients in the court of government servants and legislators. Lobbyist's advocacy plays a major role in shaping the new legislation concerning the client's company.

In essence, lobbyists closely monitor public policy developments, identify the policy-makers and decision-makers in order to approach a matter that is of concern to their organisation or client, and secure access and/or make representations, with supporting information. They also keep rapport with those people that they have lobbied with and apply whatever pressure they could create to secure the outcome they sought. One of the methods through which lobbyists could involve MPs is to persuade them to ask questions in Parliament on behalf of a particular organisation to support the company's cause.

Successful Lobbyist and Lobbying

As lobbying is skill-oriented discipline, research carried out amongst MPs in the UK has found that certain factors are required for being a successful lobbyist. The key attributes and knowledge are as follows:

1. Access to decision-makers and lawmakers with better image of lobbying company.
2. Research on the issue.
3. Knowledge of government structure and hierarchy of officials.
4. Knowledge of government rules and regulations.
5. The public interest on the issue, but not clients' interest only.
6. Support of public leaders and opinion leaders.
7. Communication skills and presentation techniques.
8. Effective targeting of officials and legislators.
9. Good timing.
10. Favourable media coverage.

Is Lobbying Part of PR?

Lobbying is communication and persuasion to influence parliamentarians in legislation. While negotiating, lobbyists also aim at media coverage for their efforts so as to bring the subject to the notice of relevant legislators and civil servants. As such lobbying is present in media relations and government and legislative bodies and their members. While lobbying or negotiating, a careful balance of public relations skills is required, especially when trying to develop coalitions of shared interests that create congenial environment towards sought-after decisions. While retaining the basic principles of lobbying, it is now integrated into a broader range of corporate public relations programmes. Lobbyists make representations to politicians, civil servants and legislators in order to influence the subject and timing of legislation and regulations from which they, or those on whose behalf they act, will benefit. Lobbyists are employed by the interests they represent or act as consultants on a specific matter. Many lobbyists are not public relations specialists. But many public relations practitioners get involved in lobbying activities through their jobs with companies or a particular industry. They work closely with the officials of Federal or State Governments and Senators, who depend on them to explain the implications of a proposed legislation.

It is a specialist branch of public relations and there are dedicated lobbying firms, commercial organisations, trade associations, charities and pressure groups. Investment companies dealing with mutual funds make heavy use of lobbying.

Difference

The Public Relations Voice, the only journal of Indian PR professionals, made an attempt to distinguish between PR and Lobbying as two distinct disciplines from the angle of practice and academics. These two areas adopt different approaches in strategy, objectives, target audience, media choice, message formulation, cost-effectiveness and presentation. Lobbying aims at reaching out to limited audience such as Legislators and government officers, while public relations has diversified audiences, internal and external. Strategy of lobbying is to get either the existing law amended or a new law passed, while PR strategy aims at creating mutual understanding between an organization and its public, including the government. However, the subject of government relations brings public relations and lobbying together.

Lobbying Scenario in India

In India, lobbying is yet to grow as a discipline. But there are some pressure groups present in our country. Professional organisations which influence the Members of Parliament are: Confederation of Indian Industry and Federation of Indian Chamber of Commerce and Industry, to name a few. They exercise considerable influence on decision-making of government, particularly in the areas of tax, licensing, imports, exports, etc. These groups are also associated with various committees constituted by the government to advise on policy-making. In the wake of globalisation, lobbying as a specialised area of public relations may also develop in India.

Case Study

The corporate lobbyist Niira Radia was the owner of three companies: Vaishnavi Corporate Communications Pvt Ltd, which dealt with public relations and lobbying of Tata Group of Companies; Neucom Consultancy, which handled public relations of Reliance Industry, and the Noesis Consultants, which was set up with former bureaucrats, including Pradip Baijal, former Chairman, Telecom Regulatory Authority of India as a Policy Advocacy Agency to look after Government Relations. Niira Radia was grilled by both CBI and the Enforcement Directorate in 2010 for her alleged lobbying in 2G Spectrum and Licence Allocation Scam, particularly about her role as a lobbyist with her clients in telecommunications as well as in bringing foreign investment into telecom firms in India.

One of the major alleged allegations was about her taped telephonic conversations with Tatas, politicians, bureaucrats, media in getting license to a telecom company and other favours to her clients. The Chairman, Tata Group asserted that his group had never used Niira Radia to make payments or to seek favours from Government. However, Ratan Tata stated: "we have advocated changes in policy through Niira Radia or directly. But never once have we done something to exploit a political or policy issue".

The Chairman, Tata Group, Ratan Tata filed a writ petition in the Supreme Court seeking action against those involved in the leakage of his conversation with Niira Radia as infringement of his fundamental right to privacy. The Centre for Public Litigation in its writ petition had prayed that all conversations of Niira Radia on tapes be made public except the ones which were purely personal. The Supreme Court had directed the Director General of Income Tax to furnish the transcripts of the 5800 conversational tapes of Niira Radia for the perusal of the court (2012).

An analysis of Niira Radia's three companies, according to a few experts, reveals that she played 'Three in one Role' by mixing corporate communications/public relations/lobbying and public affairs consultancy. Her taped telephonic conversations with CEOs, bureaucrats, politicians and media as a lobbyist to gain undesirable favours for her clients landed her and her companies in trouble. It is alleged that she not only misused the concepts of lobbying as practised in the West, but also generated much radiation in the public relations profession by creating confusion between lobbying and public relations.

What was the result of Niira Radia's operations as a lobbyist? In a surprise move, Niira Radia announced the closure of her company. She said, "To give precedence to my personal priorities of family and health, I have decided to exit the business of communication consulting". But many in the industry were not convinced with her decision. "If you build a business from scratch to such a level, then you would never want to shut it down and that too because your health is not allowing. There is something also to say", said the founder of a leading PR firm (The Week). Tatas also had appointed Rediffsion as their new PR agency in place of Vaishnavi Corporate Communications even before Niira Radia decided to quit her business.

Niira Radia, it is alleged, became the self-imposed lobbyist as no rules and regulations were formulated by the Government or industry and she acted as such with her own modus operandi to influence public authorities for her clients. As a result, she had to close her flourishing business operations. The need of the hour is to enact a law as in the case of USA to regulate lobbying in India.

WHAT IS MARKETING PR?

Philip Kotler, the Marketing Guru, has defined marketing as "a social and managerial process by which individuals and groups obtain what they need and want through creating, offering and exchanging products of value with others". "Marketing is the management process responsible for identifying, anticipating and satisfying consumer requirements profitably". Such processes include: product or service development, pricing, packaging, advertising, merchandising, distribution and public relations promotion. Kotler also said that "public relations is the fifth 'P" of marketing strategy, which includes four other Ps: (a) **P**roduct, (b) **P**rice, (c) **P**lace and (d) **P**romotion. Sales promotion is different from public relations. Sales promotion is devoted towards increasing sales in a particular period by offering premium, reduced price, free offers, vouchers and coupon distribution, charity linked promotions, sales and trade inclusive.

When public relations is applied to marketing, it becomes marketing public relations or marketing communications. Public relations supports marketing function as a marketing public relations in all seven 'Ps'. This describes that public relations, when it is part of (i) promotion within the marketing mix, is aimed at fulfilling marketing objectives, as against public relations as fifth P. However, (ii) public relations also has a keen interest in and may be involved with other aspects of the marketing mix as well, particularly in (vi) corporate identity, as well as customers and employees. Marketing public relations may be defined as the use of public relations techniques to promote the marketing of goods and services with customers satisfaction.

Social Marketing

Many public relations professionals employed in public sector and not-for-profit organisations, such as colleges, schools, hospitals, government agencies and local authorities, are engaged in *social marketing* designed to foster or change social behaviours. For example, marketing campaigns are mounted to encourage parenting, school attendance, personal hygiene and safe food preparation or to discourage cigarette smoking, alcohol abuse, drug abuse and unsafe sex. The professionals engaged in social marketing are expected to have some additional formal marketing expertise and/or qualification. Social marketing is also marketing PR. It will benefit society or promote socially desirable actions.

In other words, public relations is concerned with building relationships and creating goodwill for the organisations. Marketing is concerned with markets, customers, and selling products and services. However, functions of both disciplines—marketing and public relations—are to promote customers' relations.

PUBLIC INFORMATION

Freedom from information poverty (ignorance) is as important as freedom from hunger.

Jawaharlal Nehru

Good Governance

What is a good government? According to the Chinese philosopher Confucius a good government is one which can feed the people, provide adequate weapons for the defence of the State and which has the trust of the people. While emphasising on 'trust' as a prerequisite for the success of a government, he said: "A people that has lost faith in the government is a people without a future". *Upanishads* also say "*Bahujana Hitaya, Bahujana Sukhaya*", meaning greatest happiness of the greatest number, the cardinal principle of good governance. Kautilya in his *Arthashastra*, while discussing the role of the king, says: "In the happiness of his subjects lies his happiness, their welfare, is his welfare; whatever pleases his subjects, he shall consider as good; but whatever pleases himself, he shall not consider as good".

How do we ensure good governance? It is through a two-pronged strategy:

1. Effective implementation of people-centred socio-economic development programmes and efficient delivery of public services.
2. Effective two-way flow of information from the government to the people and from the people to the government on public policies and welfare measures.

It is in this background that both the first Prime Minister of India, Jawaharlal Nehru, and the fourth President of USA James Madison in their statements highlighted the importance of public information and that any investment in public information is an index for both individual and nation's development and prosperity. India's commitment to democracy, development, and secularism can be successful only when there is a free flow of information from the government to the public and vice versa.

Information

What is information? It is a fact conveyed and reception of knowledge or intelligence. Information is wealth. It is also power and a form of energy which act as an input for change and development. People have a surprising range of ideas and pronouncements on what information is. The *Oxford English Dictionary* defines information as "which is appraised or told, intelligence, news, facts, data, knowledge, or anything conveyed". *Roget's Thesaurus* equates information with knowledge, enlightenment and acquaintance. *The Reader's Digest Great Dictionary of the English Language* defines information as "facts or knowledge provided or learnt". What is conveyed or represented by a particular sequence of symbols, impulses, etc. is information.

Knowledge acquired in any manner and ideas and facts that have been communicated in any format is information. An information agency is an organization such as a government department whose primary function is to provide news and other information to the public. The Press Information Bureau of the Ministry of Information and Broadcasting is a good example of public information agency.

The importance of information was felt even in the cave age when the primitive tribal people had to exchange information for their survival. Wilbur Schramm (1907–1987), an American communication expert, explained the three key roles of information as seen in the early society:

The watchman role (to scan the horizon and report back); **the policy role** (to decide policy based on the information to lead and to legislate); and **the teacher** role (to socialise the new members with the skill and beliefs valued in the society).

Explaining the role of information in a developing country, Y.V.L. Rao, an expert in communication, says, the amount of information available and the wideness of its distribution is thus a key factor in the speed and smoothness of development. He further elaborates that if sufficient information is available, it contributes to a special developmental activity. It helps farmers improve methods and produce more. As such, 'information' and 'development' are described as the two eyes and ears of a developing country.

Dr. P.C. Joshi said, "if economic poverty is bad for a nation, information poverty is worse". In a democratic polity, information is the people's fundamental democratic right and also it is the fundamental duty of the government to provide full information to the people. The study of 'information' and 'public information', therefore, assumes great importance in the context of a democratic and developing country like India.

What Then is Public Information?

The process of communication to provide information of public interest by public authorities including government departments to various groups of public either directly or through media is called public information. Each public authority in India under the Right to Information Act has a public information officer to provide information to the public.

Information of public interest is termed as **public information**. Here public interest represents the citizenry, whose informed opinion is of vital importance to a democratic society. Such information normally emanates from public authorities and the government. Well-informed citizenry is an asset to the nation, while ill-informed citizenry a liability.

Public information in the Indian context is what the Central Government, State Governments, public authorities, local bodies and the public sector undertakings disseminate that is advantageous to both the government and the public. The message "Light up your child's life. Take your child up to five years of age to the nearest booth for polio drops" is a good example of public information publicised by the Ministry of Health and Family Welfare, Government of India, under the Pulse Polio Immunisation Campaign. Similarly various ministries, and departments also disseminate information about their respective policies, programmes and achievements to inform, educate and motivate them for participation. That is the philosophy of public information.

A public information officer is one who is given the responsibility to disseminate information and handle media relations on behalf of the government.

Public Information Campaigns (PIC)

The Press Information Bureau, Ministry of Information and Broadcasting organizes Bharat Nirman Public Information Campaigns across the country to disseminate information on Government's Flagship programmes directly to the target beneficiaries at the grassroot level. These are multimedia campaigns organized by PIB in association with other sister media units of the Ministry of Information and Broadcasting. The strategy of a PIC is to combine information dissemination with the delivery of public services at the doorsteps for the beneficiaries, particularly in rural areas.

HISTORICAL PERSPECTIVE

India is one of the oldest civilisations in the world with great diversity and rich cultural heritage. With over 5,000 years long known history, India occupies a strategic position in Asia. Communication, as a discipline of sharing knowledge, has been a binding force in preserving the cultural heritage and integrity of the nation. In fact, communication as a process and information as input are the lifeblood of a society. Public communication in India as part of its civilisation has grown over centuries. Communication system which is a *sine-qua-non* of Indian civilisation had passed through different periods to reach its present stage. Indian history can be divided into four broad periods: the Indian mythology; the ancient India, the medieval India and the modern India. Each period had its own role in the growth of communication and dissemination of public information, as a system it had existed in each period but with a difference. Here are a few examples of dissemination of public information.

Rock edicts

Emperor Ashoka (273–236 BC), the Father of Indian public communication system, disseminated public information through rock edicts, inscriptions on stone pillars, folk arts and pictures drawn on temple walls. He was, perhaps, the first king in ancient India to think of public information as a two-way traffic not only to inform the public but also to keep the king informed of the ground realities of the kingdom. Each king adopted his own system for public communication.

Jharoka Darshan

Among the Great Mughals, Akbar the Great (1556–1605 AD) is known for effective means of communication called '*Jharoka Darshan*' (window audience). *Jharoka darshan* means the appearance of the Emperor at the *jharoka* (window) to the people freely and receiving their grievances. It was like an open communication court (*darbar*) resulting in a two-way communication process. Badauni, a contemporary of Akbar, wrote that the *jharoka darshan* worked effectively under Akbar who spent about four and half hours in such person-to-person meetings to redress people's grievances. '*Jharoka Darshan*' was a means of giving and receiving information.

Bell of justice

If Akbar introduced *Jharoka darshan*, his son Jahangir (1569–1627) paved the way for 'Bell of Justice' which was tied in front of the palace enabling the people to ring the bell if anyone had grievance and the king used to come out to listen to the grievance. The bell of justice was intended to receive information—an instrument of people's feedback.

Beating of drum

Beating the drum, a medium introduced in ancient India as a method of conveying information, is popular even today. It is recorded that in 1569, the news of the birth of his son Salim was conveyed to King Akbar in Allahabad from Agra, a distance of about 500 km, in about two hours and twenty minutes by beating drums, with drummers positioned one mile from each other. Different types of drum beatings were developed for different purposes—births, deaths, marriages, etc.

POINTS TO REMEMBER

1. Public relations is the management of a two-way communication process between an organisation and its publics to promote the corporate mission, services, products, reputation and to gain public understanding.

2. Organisation, corporate vision, mission, publics, management of two-way communications, public understanding are the key components of public relations definition.

3. Globalisation, on the one hand, and media explosion (Information Revolution), on the other hand, made all organisations realise the importance of public relations. As a result, such organisations respond to the call of public relations for solving their communication problems.

4. Public relations can help organisations in promoting mutual understanding, providing feedback information, disseminating information on policies and programmes.

5. Propaganda is described as information of a biased or misleading nature, used to promote a political cause or a point of view. It is also an instrument of politics and a power of social control. Propaganda is intended to manipulate people's beliefs, and their actions.

6. Adolf Hitler and Joseph Goebbels are regarded as architects of Second World War Propaganda. Their dictums were "The greater the lie, the more people would believe it", "One empire, One people and One leader".

7. Public relations is different from propaganda. If public interest is the key in public relations, the intention of propagandist is of prime concern in propaganda. **Duryodhana** is recognised as a propagandist while **Yudhisthira** is considered as a true public relations personality.

8. Publicity is the systematic distribution of public information about an institution, an individual, a product, a service or an idea. Placing information in news media to attract the attention of the public towards products or services is also called publicity. It is telling a story in the media without payment.

9. Advertising is a paid form of non-personal presentation or promotion of ideas, goods or services by an identified sponsor. Corporate advertising portrays reputation of an organisation.

10. Public Relations differs from Advertising. It is not paid form of communication. Media releases of public relations which are of public interest are published free of cost. If advertising is commercial, public relations is social.

11. Public affairs more popular in the USA is a kind of public relations that involves community relations and government relations. The US government uses the term public affairs for public relations as a part of government public relations.

12. Lobbying is a process in which lobbyists seek to influence those in power, legislators, bureaucrats. It is a specialised branch of public relations.

13. When public relations supports marketing, it amounts to marketing public relations. Fifth 'P' in marketing mix concerns public relations. It helps marketing in customers relations and reputation management.

14. Information of public interest that emanates from public authorities is called public information. Well-informed citizenry is an asset to the Government, while ill-informed citizenry a liability.

15. Public information had passed through the stages of public be fooled, public be damned, public be informed. Ivy Ledbetter Lee is the Father of public information concept. Emperor Asoka is regarded as the Father of Indian Public Information System.

REVIEW QUESTIONS

1. What is the definition of public relations?
2. Does public relations mean only wining and dining?
3. Why do people seem to respond to public relations?
4. Can public relations be self-taught?
5. What can public relations do for the organizations?
6. Distinguish between propaganda and public relations as tools of communication.

7. What is publicity? How does it differ from public relations?

8. What is advertising? Distinguish between public relations and advertising.

9. What is public affairs? How do you differentiate between public affairs and public relations?

10. What is lobbying? Is it a part of public relations?

11. What is marketing public relations? How does public relations support marketing?

12. What is meant by public information? Explain its genesis and growth as a tool of public communication and education.

Communication

> *Positive communication builds relationship. Negative communication severs relationship.*

CONTENTS

WHAT IS COMMUNICATION?

The cry of a new born baby is nothing but an act of communication. The child cries because he is hungry. The word 'Communication' is derived from the Latin word *communis*, which means 'common'. In its application, communication creates a common ground of understanding. It is a process of exchange of facts, ideas, opinions. Moreover, it is a means through which individuals or organisations share meaning and understanding with one another. In other words, it is the transmission and interactions of facts, ideas, opinions, feelings or attitudes. Communication is an interdisciplinary concept because theoretically, it is approached from various disciplines such as mathematics, accounting, psychology, ecology, linguistics, systems, analysis, journalism, public relations, advertising, etc. If communication is the means, public relations is the end.

Definitions

Communication is an exchange of facts, ideas, opinions, or emotions by two or more persons. It is also defined as intercourse by words, letters, symbols, or messages and as a way that one organisation member shares meaning and understanding with another.

Communication is the process of passing information and understanding from one person to another. It is the process of imparting ideas and making oneself understood by others.

Theo Haiemann

Communication is defined as sharing of information, knowledge, abilities and efforts towards achieving a happy life, happy organisation, happy country and establishing a more happy relations with other people around the organisation/world.

Wilbur Schramm

What is Corporate Communication? Corporate communication is defined as the integrated approach to all communications produced by an organization and directed at all relevant target groups.

Blaw

Communication is the sum of all the things one person does when he/she wants to create understanding in the mind of another. It involves a systematic and continuous process of telling, listening and understanding.

Allen Louis A

A conversation or a message that creates mutual understanding between the sender and the receiver on a given topic is communication.

Dr. C. V. Narasimha Reddi

Facets of Communication

People generally believe that communication means talking to someone. Communication has four facets—reading, writing, speaking and listening. In fact 80 per cent of our waking time is spent in communication either talking or listening or writing and reading. If we spend 25 per cent of time in reading and writing, one survey says, we spend 75% time in talking and listening. A successful communicator is one who has adequate skills in all the facets.

FIVE KINDS OF COMMUNICATION

Human beings are engaged in a variety of communications which are broadly divided into five types. These are: (i) Intrapersonal communication, (ii) Interpersonal communication, (iii) Group communication, (iv) Mass communication and (v) Non-verbal communication. Although each type appears to have distinctive features, they are all alike in the sense that one enters into a meaningful relationship with one or more persons by means of words, signs and symbols.

1. Intrapersonal communication: It refers to communication that transpires inside a person; and this happens all the time. It is like talking, listening and relating to oneself. What goes on inside our mind is conditioned and controlled by our self-view that has emerged from a vast complex of past and present influences. Intrapersonal communication, therefore, is important for contemplating, conceptualising and formulating our thoughts or ideas before we actually indulge in interpersonal communication. Just think about your daily activities and involvement with others in the form of a dialogue, etc. Every time you do something or speak, you rehearse it first within yourself. Is it not? Meditation comes under this type of communication. However, interpersonal communication is a prerequisite to interprasonal communication. Lord Buddha attained enlightment through meditation and intrapersonal communication—Intrapersonal communication either creates bridges of understanding or battlements.

2. Interpersonal communication: This is the universal form of communication that takes place between two individuals. Since it is person-to-person contact, which includes everyday exchanges that can take place anywhere by means of words, sounds, facial expression, gestures and postures. In interpersonal communication, there is face-to-face interaction between two persons, that is, both are sending and receiving messages. This is an ideal and effective communication situation because you can get immediate feedback. You can clarify and emphasise many points through your expressions, gestures and voice. It is possible in this type of communication to influence the other person and persuade him or her to accept your point of view. Since there is proximity between the sender and the receiver, interpersonal communication has emotional appeal too; it can motivate, encourage, and coordinate work more effectively than any other form of communication. Also in a crisis, through interpersonal channel, the flow of information has tremendous impact, e.g. news of violence, famine or disaster. In the process of interpersonal communication, two people exchange the roles of speaker and listener.

3. Group communication: It is an extension of interpersonal communication where more than two individuals are involved in the exchange of ideas, skills and interest. Groups provide an opportunity for the people to come together to discuss and exchange views of common interest. There could be many different groups for as many different reasons. For instance, casually formed groups with friends over a coffee break, or a religious both have different purposes when compared to groups attending a meeting or seminar to help fight AIDS. Good employee relations can be promoted through group meetings of workforce in an organisation.

Communication in a group, small or big, serves many goals including collective decision-making, self-expression, increasing one's effect, elevating one's status and relaxation. Group communication is considered effective as it provides an opportunity for direct interaction among the members of the group, it helps in bringing about changes in attitudes and beliefs. Group communication has limitations too as group interaction is time consuming and often inefficient, especially in an emergency.

4. Mass Communication: Outside the realm of interpersonal communication there exists another form of communication which involves communication with mass audiences and, hence, the term 'mass communication'. And the channels through which this kind of communication takes place are referred to as mass media. Both mass communication and mass media are generally considered synonymous for the sake of convenience. Mass communication is unique and different form of interpersonal communication as is evident from the following definition.

"Any mechanical device that multiplies messages and takes it to a large number of people simultaneously is called mass communication". The media through which messages are transmitted include radio, TV, newspapers, films, etc. and require large organisations and electronic devices to put across the messages. Media organisation arranges mass communication. The President of India speaking to the nation on the occasion of our Republic Day through Doordarshan is a fine example of mass communication.

5. Non-Verbal Communication: The transmission of a message or meaning from one person to another using non-word symbols or body language is called non-verbal communication. In non-verbal communication, people send messages to each other without talking. They communicate with five major channels of non-verbal communications, such as body angle, face, arms, hands and legs. The face, which is an autobiography of a man, is a major source of non-verbal communication. For example, smiling face indicates the positive attitude of a person, while a sudden flush in the face sends out a vivid warning that something is wrong with the person or one is angry.

MODELS OF COMMUNICATION

A model is a perspective of communication that tells as to how it could be applied in an organisation. In fact, a model is an abstracted representation of a reality developed, based on one's experience. For example, a model of one's proposed house gives a fair idea how it will be when constructed. Similarly, communication model as developed by scholars will explain how it could yield results when implemented in organisations.

Communication is based on a simple model as shown in Figure 2.1.

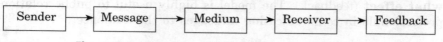

Figure 2.1 Simple model based on communication.

Shannon and Weaver Model

C.E. Shannon and W. Weaver (1949) developed the 'Mathematical Theory of Communication' which can be applied in a wide variety of information transfer situations, whether by humans, machines or other systems. In the Shannon and Weaver model, no provision has been made for feedback nor is there any acknowledgement of the importance of context—social, political, cultural—in influencing all stages of the communication process. Nevertheless, Shannon's publication of *Mathematical Theory of Communication* was recognised as a turning point in technological history.

The Shannon and Weaver model of communication is given in Figure 2.2.

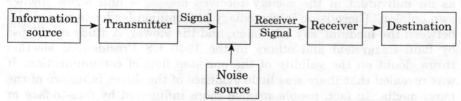

Figure 2.2 Shannon and Weaver model of communication.

This is a one-way communication model, but included in it are the concepts of noise source which amounts to feedback. In the above, the sender communicates well with the receiver, but there is a problem between senders and receivers. Breaks are seen in the transmission of the messages.

Lasswell's Model of Communication

The process of communication has been summed up in Harold Lasswell's (1948) model:

Who
Says what
In which channel
To whom
With what effect?

To amplify the model into different components, **who** refers to the source (communicator or sender), **says what** indicates the message;

in **which Channel** (medium) **to whom** (the receiver) and **with what effect** (feedback). The model is highly useful to public relations professionals in communicating messages to the audience.

Hypodermic Needle Model of Communication

The model describes the effects of the mass media. The hypodermic needle model highlights the power of media over audiences. The basic assumption is that mass media have a direct, immediate and influential effect on audiences by 'injecting' information into the minds of the masses.

STEPWISE FLOW OF COMMUNICATION

One-step Flow of Communication

In the one-step flow of communication model, mass media communicate directly to mass audience who have access to the media. The receiver as an individual in the society receives messages and forms his/her own opinion. There is no intermediary like opinion leader in this model between the medium, say television, and the viewer. A study conducted by Paul Lazarsfeld and others in the 1940 US Presidential election threw doubt on the validity of the one-step flow of communication. It was revealed that there was little evidence of the direct influence of the mass media. In fact, people seemed more influenced by face-to-face or interpersonal communication which is often directed through an opinion leader who plays a vital role in both spreading and interpreting the message.

Two-step Flow of Communication

Another theory developed which was called the two-step flow of communication model. In this model, message from the media flows to the opinion leader who has access to the mass media and, in turn, he/she conveys the message to others who have no access to the media. It presents the mass audience as being composed of interacting and responsive individuals of the society rather than isolated passive atoms of earlier mass society theories. This model is more useful in communicating public relations messages through opinion leaders with access to mass media.

Multi-step Flow of Communication

The multi-step model is a development of the other two models of communication, allowing for the sequential relaying of message. It is not specific about the number of steps there will be in the relaying process nor does it specify that messages must originate from a source and then pass straight through the media organisations. The model suggests a variable number of relays in the communication process and that receivers may receive the message at various stages along the relay networks.

The exact number of steps in the process depends on the following: (a) the intention of the source, (b) the availability of the mass media, (c) the extent of the audience exposure to media of communication, (d) the nature of the message, and (e) the importance of the message to the audience.

All these communication models, if applied properly, will be useful to organisations in improving relationships with stakeholders.

McLuhan's Theory of Communication

Marshal McLuhan (1911–1980), in his classic volume *Understanding Media—The Extension of Man* (1964) had advocated a theory of communication as "Medium is the Message". He regarded medium as an extension of human senses, the sensory organs of human senses. The sensory organs such as eyes and ears act as both media and message. For example, music is a medium as well as a message for the audience.

However, McLuhan, to substantiate his theory, has taken the instance of electric light. It is a medium without message unless it is used to spell out some action. If the electric light is used for brain surgery, McLuhan says, it acts as the content or the message of the electric light. As such he underlined the point that the medium is also the message because it shapes and controls the form of human action. This fact is the characteristic of all media because the content of any medium is always another medium. He believed that the particular attributes of a medium help to determine the meaning of the communication.

McLuhan, as part of his communication theory, made a controversial classification of media as hot media and cool media. A hot medium (like radio, movie, print) is the one that extends one single sense in high definition with well-filled data. A photograph, he said, is visually, 'high definition'. Hot media are low in audience participation.

A cool medium (such as—television and telephone) is of 'low definition' because the ear is given a meagre amount of information. As such hot media are low in participation and cool media are high in participation or completion by the audience. TV as a cool medium is visually low on data with a lot of high audience participation (McLuhan 1964).

Flow of Communication

One author of business management, while discussing the purpose of communication, said, "Doing business without communication is like winking at a pretty young girl in the dark. "You know what you are doing, but nobody else does".

Communication in any organization mainly flows in three directions:

1. The Downward Communication—information from top management flows to the grassroots level or field staff.
2. The Upward Communication—flow of information from grassroots level to the top management through different hierarchical structures.
3. The Horizontal or Sideway Communication—communication between two managers of equal rank in hierarchy.

Five Principal Objectives

The communication as a process has the following five purposes in any organization:

1. **Communication for sharing the vision, mission of an organization:** Communication ensures that the vision, mission or organization reaches to all employees and people concerned for better understanding.
2. **Communication for integrating the roles of different wings and their efforts:** Communication brings about coordination between different departments such as Finance, HRD, Production, Marketing and Public Relations to accomplish organizational goals.
3. **Communication for sustaining healthy and loyal stakeholders:** It is the organizational communication that reaches all the stakeholders such as shareholders, employees, customers and dealers with corporate messages and promotes better understanding between the management and stakeholders.
4. **Communication for making intelligent decisions:** Policy decisions are made based on the information collected from different sources. Efficiently collecting, structuring and transmitting information from different levels to the top management ensures intelligent decision-making.
5. **Communication for feedback information to gauge pulse of the public:** Communication facilitates feedback information to the decision-makers to know the reactions of the people towards its policies and programmes, which in turn helps management to make changes in policies or design a new one.

With the above five objectives, communication can play a pivotal role in informing, educating, motivating and entertaining people of India as partners in our democratic and development process. If India has been declared as a polio free country, we must admit that communication stood as a strong pillar behind its success.

DIFFERENCE BETWEEN COMMUNICATION AND PR

Communication gave birth to different disciplines such as propaganda, publicity, advertising, public affairs, public information, corporate communication, marketing communication, lobbying and public relations. Each form has its own principles, purpose and methods. However, public relations is a distinct art and science as compared to other forms of communication. It is used as an umbrella term on a worldwide basis to create mutual understanding between an organisation and its stakeholders. A public relations student and a practitioner must understand the difference between communication and public relations.

Means Vs End

If communication is sharing of information and public relations is the management of a two-way communication process between an organization and its public to create mutual understanding, a question arises as to how do they differ. Human understanding is the key to success of every institution or individual, and centres around public relations. Various communication methods are used to reach the goals of public relations. Both are supplementary. Communication is the lifeblood of public relations. If communication is the means, public relations is the end product of mutual understanding.

PUBLIC COMMUNICATION

Public communication is the conscious attempt of public relations professionals to change or modify the beliefs, attitudes, values, and behaviours of an audience in the public arena through symbolic manipulation of the senses. In fact, communication that emanates from the government and all other public authorities is intended for the benefit of the community, is called public communication.

The media units of the Ministry of Information and Broadcasting, Government of India such as the Press Information Bureau, Directorate of Advertising and Visual Publicity, Films Division, Publications Division, Directorate of Field Publicity are known as public information disseminating divisions which basically deal with public communication.

PR COMMUNICATION

What is then public relations communications? When communication is applied as a means to public relations end, we call it as public relations communication. Telecommunication is yet another form of communication, a science that deals with communication at a distance. Therefore, telecommunications and public relations communications are distinct and different. The term 'public relations communications' spells out more clearly what they actually do in reaching the stakeholders. Communication between an organisation as a whole and its internal and external publics practised in public relations comes under the purview of public relations communication. Employee relations, media relations are the examples of PR communications.

SEVEN 'Cs' OF COMMUNICATION

1. **Credibility:** Communication starts with the climate of belief. This climate is built by performance on the part of the practitioner. The performance reflects an earnest desire to serve the receiver who must have confidence in the sender. The receiver must have a high regard for the source's competence on the subject.

2. **Context:** A communication programme must square with the realities of its environment. Mechanical media are only supplementary to the word and need that take place in daily living. The context must provide for participation with feedback: the context must confirm and not contradict the message.

3. **Content:** The message must have meaning for the receiver, and it must be compatible with his value system. It must have relevance for him. In general, people select those items of information which promise them the greatest rewards. The content determines the audience.

4. **Clarity:** The message must have meaning put in simple terms. Words must mean the same thing to the receiver as they do to the sender. Complex issues must be compressed into themes, slogans or stereotypes that have simplicity and clarity.

5. **Continuity and Consistency:** Communication is an unending process. It requires reception and achieve penetration. Repetition with variation contributes to both factual and attitude learning. The story must be consistent.

6. **Channels:** Those established channels of communication should be used that the receiver uses and respects. Creating new ones is difficult. Different channels have different effects and serve effectively in different stages.

7. **Courtesy:** Courtesy keeps everybody happy. Courteous messages strengthen friendships, build goodwill and gain new friends.

Courtesy involves consideration in the tone of communication. Use tact instead of bluntness and avoid expressions that irritate, hurt the receiver.

Public relations is basically a communication function. If these seven Cs' are used effectively in public relations communication, the key objectives of public relations can be realised—building relationships, goodwill, better understanding for organisations. It also enhances the credibility of public relations in the eyes of the public.

POINTS TO REMEMBER

1. Communication is an exchange of facts, ideas, opinions by two or more persons. It is defined as sharing of information, knowledge, abilities and efforts towards achieving a happy life, happy organisation and establishing more happy relations with other people around the organisation.

2. Communication has four facets: Reading, Writing, Speaking, and Listening.

3. Communication is classified as intrapersonal communication, interpersonal communication, group communication and mass communication.

4. If intrapersonal communication refers to communication within oneself, interpersonal communication takes place between two individuals. The latter is also called person-to-person communication.

5. When messages are communicated to mass audiences through mass media—newspapers, radio, television—it is termed as mass communication.

6. Model is a perspective evolved by experience and research which tells as to how it could be applied to a practical situation. Communication model also is a theory that is applied to practical communication in an organisation.

7. Shannon & Weaver Model, Lasswell's Model and Hypodermic Needle Model of Communication are popular models in the communication process.

8. In the one-step flow of communication, the audience receives messages direct by getting exposed to the mass media. The receivers are called opinion leaders. If the opinion leaders who receive messages from the mass media in the first step tend to communicate or share their knowledge with others through interpersonal communication, then it is known as two-step flow of communication.

9. Multi-step flow of communication enables information to flow from different media at different stages. The audiences receive messages from different sources. Medium is the message is a communication theory evolved by McLuhan.

10. If communication is sharing of information and knowledge, public relations is to create and maintain mutual understanding. Communication is the means while public relations is the end, i.e. public understanding.

11. When the principles of communication are applied in the practice of public relations, we call it public relations communication. It is public relations communication that carries messages to the target audiences.

12. Seven 'Cs' of effective communications include: credibility, context, content, clarity, continuity, channel and courtesy. These seven 'Cs', if adopted, will enhance credibility of public relations.

REVIEW QUESTIONS

1. Define communication. Explain different kinds of communications.

2. What is a model? Describe communication models.

3. How do you distinguish between one-step flow of communication and multi-step flow of communication?

4. 'Medium is the Message'. Discuss

5. What is the difference between communication and public relations?

6. Why do we call public relations communication? How does it help in reaching out to the target audiences.

7. What are the seven 'Cs' of communication. Elucidate their role in public relations practice.

Principles of Public Relations | Chapter 3

Politics without principles is a sin.

—Mahatma Gandhi

CONTENTS

- Basic Principles of PR
- Identification of Publics
- Major PR Publics
- Court of Public Opinion
- Public Opinion Polls

BASIC PRINCIPLES OF PR

Every discipline be it economics, journalism or marketing is based on certain principles which act as guidelines for the practice. Objectivity is the basic principle of journalism, and journalists are always guided by an adage of C.P. Scott the great editor of *The Manchester Guardian* *"Facts are sacred, but comment is free"*. Accordingly, public relations also as a body of knowledge has its own principles. 'Public interest' and 'two-way communication' are the two cardinal principles of public relations practice. Here are the following 10 basic principles of public relations.

1. **Audience analysis:** The word 'audience' has long been familiar as the collective term for 'receivers' in the simple sequential model of mass communication process. Receivers of messages are the target audiences in the public relations practice. Like *Nose for News* in journalism, *Audience Analysis* is the first principle in public relations. As the insects and creatures feel the external environment through their sensory organs, similarly public relations department also must analyse the pulse of the audience, and the external environment of an organisation and its policies and programmes through audience analysis. This principle applies even to the press as it tries to glean information on the feelings of the audience and makes it public. Thus, audience analysis is the foundation of public relations process.

2. **Relationship management:** As a strategic management function, public relations has to manage the relationships between an organisation and its publics. The management of relationship is a key factor in the public relations process to reach organisational goals.

3. **Public interest:** Any policy or public relations programme of a corporation must be designed in the interest of the public. Public interest is the highest priority. Abraham Lincoln defined democracy as *a government of the people, by the people, and for the people.* According to public relations social philosophy, the management has to place the interest of the people first in all matters pertaining to the conduct of business and public service. People and their interests are of prime importance for any individual or institution. Public interest and public opinion go hand in hand. It is in this context, Mahatma Gandhi had said "public opinion alone can keep a society pure and healthy". This also applies 100 per cent to any organisation.

4. **Truth:** It is the touchstone of public relations. Public relations is not based on fiction but always on facts. For example, one cannot lie to a bride. If one tries to hide facts and project falsehood to the bride, the truth will eventually come out in due course. If the bridegroom tells a lie to the bride that he was a gold medallist in his bachelor's degree, the truth will surface out as marriage is a lifelong process. So the same applies to public relations practice also.

5. **Good cause and good deeds:** Good cause and good deeds are the prerequisites to successful public relations. The Chinese have a proverb: "You cannot carve a rotten wood". What has this got to do with public relations? Just as this, effective public relations must have a good cause, a qualitative product or a good policy. Public relations is not a substitute for a bad policy. It can promote effectively a good policy, a good programme, a good product or a good service. Bad policies, bad products that are not in tune with public interest must be changed. Therefore, it is the job of public relations to change the negative attitude into a positive mindset.

Mere good policy will not yield results. Policies must be grounded in the shape of good deeds. "An ounce of practice is worth than tons of big talk" said Swami Vivekananda. Actions speak louder than words. *"Facta non verba"*, the ancient Romans had said. This means: "Give us deeds, not words alone". The most striking principle is that public relations must be action oriented and give deeds to the public in concrete terms and not mere verbal promises. The most attractive poster, the most exciting film, the most glittering words in public relations messages or media release will achieve little, if there is no substance of good deeds in support that serves the public concerned.

6. **Two-way communication:** Public relations communication is not just telling people about an organisation, policies and programmes, but also listening to them to know their reactions and problems. Therefore, public relations is both speaking and listening, a two-way traffic. It is an art of both feedforward and feedback information process. They must go hand in hand to know the reactions of the public to the policies and programmes of an organisation. Thus, it is a two-way communication process.

7. **Multi-functional discipline:** Public relations is a multi-functional discipline that supports various management functions with a communications strategy. It supports human resource development, finance, marketing, production, crisis management by adopting an integrated public relations communication approach. Based on the performance of all departments, PR projects the total image of the organization.

8. **Social responsibility:** Since public relations is based on public interest, its practitioners work beyond organisational goals to serve the community cause. They are expected to play a constructive role in the society. So organisations owe a social responsibility to the community in fulfilling their needs. Public relations must identify the community needs and evolve suitable community relations programmes. Thus, public relations acts as a 'bridge' between the organisation and the community in implementing welfare programmes. In tune with the policy of public interest, public relations has the social responsibility to undertake the cause of the community, besides its professional responsibility.

9. **Sustained process:** Public relations is a planned, sustained and continuous process. As long as there is an organisation, there is a mission and there is an audience, public relations must continue to practise building bridges between the organisation and its publics. It is, therefore, said public relations is a sustained effort with long-range objectives. If public relations process is stopped, there would be a communication gap between an organisation and its stakeholders. This lowers the image of the institution/organisation.

10. **Change agent:** Public relations is a catalyst for change. As a change agent, it not only changes the attitudes of publics but also creates goodwill, trust and reputation based on the performance of the organisation. Table 3.1 gives a public relations change agent model.

TABLE 3.1 Public Relations Change Agent Model

From	To
Ignorance	Awareness
Ill-informed	Well-informed
Apathy	Interest
Negative	Positive
Ill-will	Goodwill
Reactive	Proactive

The change process is intended to bring about a transformation in the behavioural attitude of the people through public relations techniques.

IDENTIFICATION OF PUBLICS

The two key words, 'public' and 'relations', constitute the entire philosophy of public relations practice which is now an omnibus profession from grassroots to international understanding. However, 'publics' is literally the first word in public relations profession. If there is no public, the question of developing relationships does not arise. Similarly, if the concept of relationships does not exist in the society, the scope for public relations is redundant. Therefore, the word public is the lifeblood of public relations profession.

Public means people as a whole. When public relations professionals use the word 'public', they talk in general terms without thinking that too many people would mean the faceless mass. But this should not be the case in public relations. In fact, there is no general public in public relations. It is because, if one takes the general public as one's target public, it will result in missing not only opportunities but also the position to promote one's company's image among certain target constituent groups. Public relations professionals require to identify the public in specific terms as to reach them with specific messages and persuade them towards organisational goals.

The Director, public relations of State Bank of India might prepare a press release about the increase in rate of interest to be targeted towards customers; a chairman of an organisation might issue a letter on wage revision to the employees; an annual report to the stockholders, an e-mail to the regulator—Reserve Bank of India; a direct mail with a message on social responsibility to the community in the bank's neighbourhood, a folder giving the details of its products to the district magistrate, a backgrounder to the media representatives. Such publicity materials are intended for different sections of the public.

Different sections of the public react differently to the same message. And the message should also be designed in different ways to suit different public interests. The impact of the message is in the eyes and ears of the receiver. For example, the State Bank of India targets seven types of public with different methods. These seven different kinds of public have their own specific sets of concerns that need to be addressed, different socio-economic background and they respond to different messages with their own specific mental self-perception.

The challenge for a public relations professional is to identify the target public in specific terms and answer the following questions:

1. Who are the public that can influence and promote organisational goals?
2. What is the demographic profile of the public?
3. What is the psychographic profile of the public?
4. What is the public opinion about the organisation?
5. Who are the opinion leaders and decision-makers that can help the organisation?
6. How do we reach the public with the public relations messages?

Who are the Public?

'Public' may be defined as a group of people sharing a common interest or common values in a particular situation. In public relations, *public* (active audience) encompasses any group of people who are tied together, however, loosely by some common bond of interest or concern and who have consequences for an organisation (Newsom, 1999).

Longman Dictionary of Mass Media and Communication defines public as "people, who all have the same relationship to same person or group, constantly changing and not necessarily organised, the individual of a public may or may not know and communicate with each other". Public is also described in public relations as a group of persons, especially one that is interested in or affected by an action or an idea of an organisation. *Reader's Digest Great Dictionary of the English Language* gives the meaning of the public as "people in general, the community". A group of people having common interests or characteristics is public.

Publics are those who have a stake in the organization, are affected by the organization or can affect what the organization does?

Thus, the people interested in the publishing of newspapers and magazines are considered as one type of public, while those who are interested in distribution and selling them form another type of public of the press. The readers who are the actual consumers of newspapers constitute the third kind of public. Publishers, distributors and readers are the three types of public for a newspaper. Each category of the public has its own characteristics and interests.

How are public formed? All public relations communications begin with an individual. And these communications are received by individuals. In fact, individual is the kingpin of public relations practice.

The best way to understand the public is to think of individuals. People with similar interests make groups which constitute the public. Such groups having common traditions form the society. The main objective of public relations is to reach the individual in a group. As an individual, one belongs to a group of customers either for a television company or an automobile manufacturer.

Stakeholders

In the modern corporate world, stakeholders is the term used for public. The idea or concept of stakeholders has come from the term 'stockholders' which means people who have bought shares from publicly held company and, thus, developed vested interest in that company. In a way stockholders are the owners of the company with specific interest in the shares and profits of the company. Similarly, there are many others with similar vested interests in an organisation, such as employees, customers who may or may not actually own the company's stock. But they have interest in the company as customers, suppliers or opinion leaders, and are collectively called stakeholders. Thus, stakeholders cover a broader spectrum of public. Sometimes, public also stands for the audience in public relations who receive messages through media.

One Message—Different Public

If the Director (Public Relations), Andhra Pradesh State Road Transport Corporation, prepares a media release on bus fare hike, the release is intended for diverse passengers, such as government employees, business community, farmers, students, transport regulatory bodies. And even if the message is essentially the same for everyone, it is being directed to different publics, where each of them have their own set of concerns on the increase of passenger fare that need to be addressed.

Since generalising the public is not useful when delivering public relations messages, it is most appropriate that the audience be identified in specific term such as employees, shareholders, customers, dealers, media. This identification of the public is fundamental in the practice of public relations.

Segmentation of Public

An individual may belong to a social organisation like the Lions International or a professional body like Public Relations Society of India. The same individual may belong to a religious or cultural organisation. As a result, such an individual is not only a member of the general public but also a member of a specific social club. Therefore, general public does not exist in public relations. Instead, as an individual one is a member of many definable, describable groups. It is the job of public relations practitioners to identify these groups. Segmentation of the public will undoubtedly facilitate in putting across the public relations manager's message more effectively. As an individual, you may be a driver, a conductor, a stockholder, an employee, a farmer, a music lover, a consumer or a pilgrim. But at the same time, you belong to a group of customers. The motive should be to reach the individual in the group. For example, the bank and its publics may explain the role of the individual as a potential customer. The individuals may belong to different groups. The bank can reach the group made up of individuals.

Understanding the public helps a public relations manager to determine the feasibility of reaching these individuals economically with a tight budget. Such individuals become the target audience for public relations. Different kinds of public react differently to the same message and news. How individuals in different regions, situations and demographic segments react to a particular piece of news and whether or not those reactions will have to be considered is a matter for public relations. As such general public in public relations is a myth.

MAJOR PR PUBLICS

Every organisation has public. But care is needed to be taken as not to slip into the popular misconceptions of thinking of public in terms of the general public, which has no place in the practice of public relations or in its terms. Public in public relations management, by and large, are divided into two broad categories as **internal public** (employees) and **external public** (customers). A third type of public also emerged as **international public** in the wake of globalisation and information revolution. Such division is highly essential to identify organisational public to reach them with need based messages. Individuals and institutions constitute organisational public as individual public and institutional public. Both are equally important for public relations.

Categories of Public

The public in public relations may be as impossible to count as the stars, but like the stars they can be grouped into different categories. Public of the Indian Oil Corporation may be grouped as follows:

1. Employees—(internal publics)
2. Financial publics—shareholders, financial analysts, stockbrokers
3. Suppliers
4. Distributors
5. Customers
6. Government—Central, Local State Government Departments, Regulatory bodies, Bureaucrats, Ministry of Petroleum

7. Opinion leaders—Community and Caste Leaders, M.Ps, M.L.As.
8. Media public—Newspapers, Radio, T.V. Films, Internet
9. General Community—Neighbourhood Community
10. Special public—Women, farmers, tribals, minorities, youth, Community Relations
11. International public

Employees

Employees are the first in any organisation. The functioning of any organisation—be it a commercial or government department—is linked with the employees working in the organisation. However, employees are the first among the public relations publics, for the organisation cannot function without employees in providing services either to the investors or to the customers. In fact, the company cannot exist and start operations without employees. Over one lakh employees of various categories work in Andhra Pradesh State Road Transport Corporation (APSRTC) to transport over one crore passengers every day.

Even among employees, we have sub-divisions such as management executives, general managers, section officers, ministerial staff, factory workers, sales force, attenders, office boys. The mix of employees creates considerable communication problems in motivating them towards organisation's goals. Each type of employees has to be tackled differently depending on the nature of the work and needs.

Financial Publics

The growth of any organisation depends much on the financial resources. Without initial investment, one cannot start any company. How do we raise money? Is it through the proprietor's own resource or shares, loans or investments. Therefore, investors who purchase shares or invest money constitute financial public for an organisation. In fact, they are the owners of the company. Investors rely on growth in share price over time and any sudden or consistent fall may generate a merger or takeover of the company. The financial market is closely linked to investors and bankers. The financial public can be divided into three broad categories: (a) shareholders; (b) investment analysts, stockbrokers, institutional buyers of large blocks of shares such as insurance companies, unit trusts, pension funds; (c) financial media of both print and electronic. Financial public have to be tackled in a different way compared to employee public.

Suppliers

The suppliers of materials and services are of great importance to any manufacturing company. Without raw material, no products can be manufactured. Tyres, tubes, chassis, auto spare parts are the materials that are supplied to APSRTC in running about 20,000 buses. Similarly, a chemical company handling dangerous chemicals would be wise to keep doctors, hospitals, ambulance and fire services. The company will keep the police aware of special hazards so that it can seek their help in the case of emergency. The maintenance of good relations with suppliers and services will help in smooth running of the organisation.

Distributors

We have a very broad groups of distributors who play a key role in marketing of products and services. One of the 'Ps' in marketing represents 'Place' where the product is sold through distributors. For manufacturers and service providers, distributors mean wholesalers, departmental stores, supermarket chains, malls and appointed dealers or agents, franchises, hotels, Internet retailers, exporters and overseas importers, etc. The Indian Oil Corporation has a nation-wide distribution/dealer network in thousands. Distributor relations is an aspect of public relations and marketing support which no manufacturer or service provider can afford to neglect. Distributors are unlikely to sell a new product in which they have no confidence.

Customers

"Customer is the master" and "the Customer is always right" are the adages that are followed by all organisations. A business will not be successful unless people like its products. APSRTC has over one crore passengers as its valued customers. The Indian Railways also carries over one crore passengers every day. These customers are vested with rights under the Consumer Protection Act 1986. One of the rights is the right to be informed, about the quality, quantity, purity, standard and price of goods or services. Good customer relations are the essence of the success of any company. And the good customer relations are the roots of public relations. The target of public relations communication is not only the current customer but also the potential customer of the future. The customers are to be carefully identified for communication purpose and treated as very important persons. "Customers Meet" is an important tool of customers' public relations.

Government

In government, bureaucracy is the key role player. All organisations need the support of the government, consisting of several departments and regulatory authorities. The government affects business through taxes and monetary policies and provides water, power, sanitation, municipal services. Government Departments (Police, Industries, Labour, Electricity, Municipality), ministers, secretaries, heads of departments who run the public administration constitute the key government public for most of the organisations both in the government and in the private sector.

In government relations, business organisations primarily are concerned with weighing impending legislation for its impact on the company. Therefore, it is necessary to identify government as a public and make contacts to improve communications with government officials and departments. At the grassroots level, village panchayat president and its secretary are the key government public.

Media Public

A good media relationship is always useful for any successful public relations programme. Ours is a mass media society, where learning and knowledge come from the media—print as well as broadcast. The mass media greatly influences the public opinion. It is, therefore, imperative to identify the media and separate the public of any organisation to launch public communication programmes. Even in the case of media, we cannot treat all the representatives of media as media public. It is advisable to identify them in specific terms such as editors, news editors, sub-editors, chiefs of bureau, special correspondents, reporters and stringers. Andhra Pradesh, for example, is one state in India where about 13,000 stringers and reporters work in rural areas. It is a must for every organisation to be in touch with the media, be it print or electronic, which, in turn, enables the public relations professionals to get a fair coverage of corporate activities.

General Community

In broad terms, the general community consists of those who may not be directly related with the business of an organisation. But their moral support is required for the success of the business. For example, the neighbourhood community who lives very close to the company influences the organisation. Another example of this is an airport, where a number of communities will suffer from noise pollution. The general community may also contain present and future customers, future employees and their families. Community relations programme is undertaken for the welfare of local community.

Special Public

As we have specialised periodicals in journalism to cater to the needs of specialised category of readers, there are special public in public relations as well. In fact, magazines are classified based on their contents and the relevant readers. For example, *Women's Era* is a journal meant exclusively for women. Similarly, *All India Reporter*, an English monthly journal, covers legal issues. So also special public is a distinct category in public relations based on its characteristics and needs. For example, women in India who number about 49 per cent (59 crores) of country's population constitute an important segment of public relations public. Similarly, other specialised publics include: farmers, industrial workers, scheduled castes, scheduled tribes, minorities (Muslims, Christians), etc.

International Public

With liberalisation and globalisation concepts, international public relations is growing as part of doing business abroad. A basic problem facing Indian public relations practitioners either representing multi-nationals within India or national companies with export business, is that the various aspects of public relations are handled quite differently abroad. Local culture and language have to be taken into consideration while practising international public relations. International public include host country clients, customers, public officials, political leaders, media, Regulatory bodies, etc. In international public relations, one has to follow the principle of "Think and act globally and locally".

International public are those who reside out of the country but have interest in your business. Microsoft, a worldwide organisation, has its domestic clients in the USA and international clients and customers in other countries like India. It is in this context, public relations professionals are dealing with both national public and international public.

Communication with Stakeholders

As an organisation's operations affect its stakeholders, it is an ethical duty of the former to communicate about its dealings to the latter. For example, in 2006 a well-known soft drink manufacturer's products were found to have pesticides in it. It did not matter what was the percentage of pesticide contained in the drink but every stakeholder and the general public who constitute the prospective customers came to know via media that the soft drinks were contaminated with pesticides. This information needed to be communicated. There are times when an organisation knows 'in its heart' that it should be advising, telling, forewarning about some of the activities it is engaging in relation to its products and services. In fact, there should be a two-way communication process between an organisation and its stakeholders with segmented approaches. Public relations, in order to reach different categories of public and stakeholders, takes different dimensions such as employees' public relations, investors relations, customer relations, media relations, etc. Such a segmented approach is not only effective, but can also change the attitudes of the target audience. All relationships are handled by public relations/ corporate communications.

COURT OF PUBLIC OPINION

Public opinion alone can keep a society pure and healthy.

—Mahatma Gandhi

With public opinion on our side everything succeeds, without public opinion on our side nothing succeeds.

—Abraham Lincoln

Success of an organisation is closely linked to public opinion. In terms of public opinion, public relations is defined as the science of creating opinions and building relationships with the public to secure their understanding and goodwill. Public relations always aims at developing a favourable public opinion for social, economic or political institution. In fact, public opinion is the lifeblood of public relations practice.

Opinion Leaders

If public relations is to create a favourable public opinion, it is well-nigh impossible for a public relations manager alone to impinge or influence the belief of the whole gamut of organisational publics. It is here that a public relations manager must identify and work with the opinion leaders who are likely to have more impact on public thinking. Who is an opinion leader? Opinion leader is an important person in a particular group of people who, as a 'public thought leader' will have impact on public thinking. They are knowledgeable and articulate in specific issues and subjects, and are also well respected in the society. Sociologists describe 'opinion leaders' as intellectuals in their subject, well informed on the issue than an average person, avid consumers of mass media, early adopters of new ideas and good organisers who can get other people to take action. Public opinion on an issue may have its roots in self-interest in events, but the primary catalyst is 'public open discussion' when public opinion begins to crystallise which could be measured by a public relations manager. Public opinion leaders can be any people who, whether well or ill informed, may express opinions and influence people because of their apparent authority. They could be knowledgeable, well disposed or at least tolerant.

Types of opinion leaders

Opinion leaders may be categorised into two broad types: (i) formal opinion leaders and (ii) informal opinion leaders.

1. **Formal opinion leaders:** They are those who hold official positions either by appointment of the Government or by elections; for example, the Chairman, Zilla Parishad or Member of Parliament, who hold position by election. A District Collector holds the district administration by virtue of his appointment by the Government. Very often media persons interview such formal leaders in official positions for their opinions or comments on issues. Leaders in formal positions are also called power leaders. They are vested with powers by law as long as they hold such positions and influence the public opinion with their views.

2. **Informal opinion leaders:** In the second category, we have informal opinion leaders who have power with a peer group because of special characteristic. They may be role models who are admired and emulated because they can exert peer pressure on others to adopt on the issue. A knowledgeable and well-informed village barber can be a good informal leader to influence the minds of his community, and the customers. Former Chief Minister N T Rama Rao, it is said used to consult barbers on public issues. Newspaper readers could be informal leaders. In general, informal opinion leaders exert considerable influence on their respective peer groups by being highly informed, articulate and credible on certain issues.

Opinion leaders of a corporation may also be grouped as:

1. Government officials; central, state, local government, politicians; trade union leaders; social activists; NGOs and all professionals
2. Teachers; academicians; doctors and lawyers
3. Media persons—editors, reporters (print, radio, TV), authors and writers
4. Businessmen; bankers; professional associations; religious leaders; village heads; service clubs, rotary, lions clubs and postmasters.
5. Religious leaders—priests, clergy, mullahs

In this list an attempt has been made to group together certain kinds of opinion leaders. However, for some organisations they may be regarded as relevant opinion leaders. Who have direct interest in the organisation. In fact, people who have access to mass media can be termed as opinion leaders in comparison with those who do not have access to it.

It is the job of public relations to act as a catalyst, create public opinion and change the attitudes of the public towards organisational goals. Negative attitudes have to be changed into positive ones. Ill-will has to be transformed into goodwill. Such a change is possible only through opinion leaders. In this context, public relations professionals must deploy strategies that will assist corporations to forge strong relationships with the opinion leaders and through them the target audience.

Opinion Leader and Two-step Flow of Communication

In a two-step flow of communication model, the opinion leader plays a predominant role in changing the behaviour of the general people. Research has proved that the flow of communication to individuals is often directed through opinion leaders who play a vital role in both spreading and interpreting the information. It is for this reason, the two-step model of communication flow was introduced. In the *first* step, the information is conveyed to the mass audience through mass media—newspaper, radio, television or film. In the process, those who have access to mass media and who are exposed to it become opinion leaders as they have knowledge on the subject. In the *second* step, these opinion leaders, in turn, exchange information through interpersonal communication with those who have no access to the mass media and also educate them. Therefore, a message through opinion leaders will have greater impact on the audience. For example, Green Revolution was possible in India because messages on the subject, on improved variety of seed and the use of chemical fertilisers were first heard by rich farmers through All India Radio, and they, in turn, in the second step transmitted this information to those farmers who did not have access to All India Radio.

Four Components

An understanding of the process of opinion formation and behavioural change is fundamental to the study of public relations. To understand the relationship between public relations and public opinion, we need to divide the four key terms of public relations into four components, namely, 'public', 'relations', 'public interest' and 'public opinion'. This facilitates in deriving the meaning of public opinion.

Nature of public

A public is a group of people with similar interest and common opinion on an issue. The issue may be a controversial subject, for example, whether prohibition of liquor be introduced or not.

Methods of relations

The second step in public relations is to build good relations with the public through various tools of services and communication media. All messages intended for the public must be loaded with public interest and should be result-oriented programmes.

Public interest

The first basic principle of public relations is public interest in all matters of organisational operation. An institution functions only to serve the cause of the public. In reaching the organisational goals, a corporation has to serve the interest of its varied public. Good relations can be maintained only when such relations are accompanied by actions that serve the interests of the public. A business organisation that succeeds in satisfying the needs of its customers, enjoys the understanding and goodwill of the general public. It is the primary objective of public relations to communicate the good deeds of the organisation to the stakeholders.

Public opinion

When the elements of public interest, action oriented relations and the 'public' are combined in operation, it results in favourable public opinion—the impression of the people either about an organisation or a product or a service. What is an opinion? According to *Reader's Digest Great Dictionary of the English Language*, "opinion is a view or judgment, based on fact or knowledge, formed in the mind about a particular issue".

What is then public opinion? It is also the collective views of a significant part of any public. Public opinion is an expression of a belief held in common by members of a group or public on a controversial issue of public importance. German political scientist, Elisabeth Noelle-Neumann defines public opinion as that "which can be voiced in public without fear of sanctions and upon which action in public can be based". Public opinion is what most people think about a particular issue, e.g. it could be a collective perception of what voters think about a particular political party during elections. It is the complex of preferences expressed by a significant number of persons on an issue of general importance like introduction of prohibition of liquor.

Research

Public opinion and public attitudes go hand in hand. It is in this context public relations undertakes research to gauge public opinion and take actions to maintain favourable public opinion. Public relations professionals, therefore, function in a climate of public opinion that often conditions their own perceptions and responses. When appropriate relations are created with the public in public interest, public relations creates a favourable public opinion based on good actions and good services. Therefore, public relations communication plays a vital role in creating public opinion.

PUBLIC OPINION POLLS

'*Vox populi, Vox dei*', meaning "The voice of the people is the voice of God" is an old proverb. Public opinion is the ultimate determinator of success and failure of organisations, government and political parties alike. It is in this background that public opinion polls are conducted on the eve of General Elections in different countries. Major newspapers and news channels conduct such surveys to read the pulse of the public before and after the elections as pre-poll and exit-poll survey.

Public opinion research has been in use for many decades now. Political parties, media and social scientists generally use public opinion research to gauge the opinion of the people on various issues. Public opinion research, however, is increasingly used to gauge the mood of the electorate before an election. It started with Gallup Polls in the USA in the last century. In the Indian context, the terminologies such as psephology, pre-poll and exit-poll were alien to an average Indian a few decades back. The last two decades have seen a great spurt in public opinion polls giving Indian elections a flavour it had never known.

Do polls really reflect opinions of the people? What is the impact of opinion polls on the outcome of the polls? Opinion on whether the opinion polls play a decisive role in elections and their power in politics differs among experts. The issue is two pronged, viz. the alleged manipulative nature of opinion polls on the psyche of the electorate, and the genuineness and scientific base of various polls. Many opinion polls have gone wrong in the past. The 2004 Parliamentary Elections in India proved almost a nemesis for various pollsters, as most of the surveys could not gauge the mood of the electorate. Why did they go wrong? Among various reasons we can say selection of the representative sample, research instrument and the quality of surveyors were the important cause for the failure.

POINTS TO REMEMBER

1. Every discipline be it journalism or marketing is based on certain principles which act as guidelines for the practice.

2. Public relations also has basic principles on which it operates. They are: public interest, audience analysis, truthfulness, good cause and good deeds, two-way communication, sustained process, public opinion.

3. Public may be defined as people who all have the same relationship to same person or group. Public is also described as a group of persons that is interested in an organisation or affected by an action of an organisation. A group of people having common interests or common characteristics is also termed as public.

4. Public in public relations is broadly categorised as internal public (employees) and external public (customers).

5. There is no general public in public relations. Public relations messages are targeted to specific public or segmented public.

6. The major types of public include: employees, shareholders, customers, suppliers and dealers, media, opinion leaders.

7. Stakeholder is a person with an interest or concern in an organisation. All the public who matter to the organisation are treated as stakeholders.

8. Communication with stakeholders is an integral part of corporate strategy to inform, educate and motivate them towards organisational goals, products and services.

9. Public opinion is the collective view of a significant part of any public. Public opinion is what most people in a particular public think about a particular political party in elections or on a particular controversial issue.

10. Opinion leader is an important person in a particular group of people who as a public thought leader will have impact on public thinking. A member of Parliament is regarded as an opinion leader. Teachers, trade union leaders, social activists are considered as opinion leaders.

11. Opinion leaders, under the two-step flow of communication, create public opinion by exposing themselves to the mass media.

12. Public opinion polls read the pulse of the public towards various political parties before the elections.

REVIEW QUESTIONS

1. Describe the basic principles that govern the practice of public relations.

2. How do you classify the public relations public? Identify the major types of publics in corporate public relations.

3. Why do we need to communicate with stakeholders? Discuss.

4. What is public opinion? Explain the role of opinion leaders in creating public opinion.

5. How does the public opinion poll reflect the mood of the electorate?

Evolution of Public Relations:
Ancient India to Modern India
(World's Biggest Democracy)

"India is the cradle of the human race, the birthplace of human speech, the mother of history, the grandmother of legend and the great grandmother of tradition. Our most valuable and most instructive materials in the history of man are treasured up in India only".

—**Mark Twain**

C O N T E N T S

MYTHOLOGICAL AND CELESTIAL PR

India is one of the oldest civilisations in the world with a kaleidoscopic variety and rich cultural heritage. The American writer Mark Twain described India as not only the cradle of the human race but also the mother of history, the grandmother of legend and the great grandmother of tradition. Indian mythology with a number of legends connected with Gods and Goddesses over the years have not only influenced music, dance and other art forms but also developed a good communication system for disseminating public information. In fact, Indian mythology is the source of many inventions and innovations. So also the mythological and celestial public relations communication system was the forerunner of modern public relations.

The Epics

The two great epics—*Ramayana* and *Mahabharata*—tell us the system of exchange of news and information adopted by the renowned characters of the epics to harmonise relationships between the Gods, Goddesses and various rulers and the ruled. The '*Rayabaras*' (negotiations) in *Mahabharata* like the *Krishna Rayabara* or *Sanjaya Rayabara* are the shining examples of negotiations and communication between *Kauravas* and *Pandavas* towards peace.

Lord Krishna was a great communicator of pre-historic period when he delivered his sermon to Arjuna in *Mahabharata* to fight for the cause of righteousness. The Bhagavad Gita, the essence of Krishna's sermon, is the perfect guide to those who aspire to build a perfect personality with all characteristics of a good public relations personality. Lord Krishna as a public relations personality and man in the middle harmonised relations between the two groups whenever there was a conflict. Gita is an eternal beacon for PR professionals in their relations with stakeholders.

Vidura

Vidura, a close friend and advisor of the blind king Dhritarashtra, was also a good communicator. The advice of Vidura is a treatise on virtue known as *Vidura Neethi* (code of conduct) embedded in the epic *Mahabharata*. The media journal of the Press Institute of India is named after him as '*Vidura*'. Sage Narada, for example, the first mythological public relations personality, who figured in both *the Ramayana* and *the Mahabharata*, would disseminate information between Gods and Goddesses and the rulers and the ruled with the motive of establishing '*Lok Kalyan*'—universal peace and prosperity. Indian public relations, therefore, cannot ignore the mythological period as the basis for the origin of public relations techniques which serve as beacon lights to the present-day public relations practitioners.

Five PR Models

Based on the Western PR models, the evolution of public relations in India can be divided into five broad models:

1. *The state of propaganda (propaganda model):* From 1500 BC to the end of the East India company rule in 1858
2. *The era of publicity (publicity and public information model):* The British India rule from 1858 to 1947
3. Gandhian Era of Public communications, 1919–1947
4. *The age of public relations (two-way asymmetric public relations model):* Independent India (1947–1991)
5. Indian public relations with global perspective-global PR (1991)

FIRST PERIOD: THE STATE OF PROPAGANDA (1500 BC–1858 AD)

Ancient India

It is very difficult to determine the origins of public relations in India. History of public relations can be traced based on two factors: (i) media of communication and (ii) maintaining relations with the public. The existence of public relations dates back to Indus Valley civilisation when people lived a good civilised life and some sort of a government existed there. Moreover, it can be said that human communication is the origin of public relations. India is considered as the birth place of human speech.

Indus Valley Civilisation (3000–1500 BC)

It is generally agreed that Indus valley civilisation flourished between 3000 and 1500 BC. Such an earliest Indian civilization existed in the beautiful twin cities of Mohenjo-daro and Harappa. A unique contribution of the Indus Valley civilisation to the Indian communication system was the introduction of seals made of terracotta and stone. Some of the seals were engraved with figures, while others with pictographic script. The seals depicted religious beliefs, trade marks, and some seals even showed 'Yogi', a rearing 'cobra', animals, Gods and other inscriptions. Such seals were the means of effective communication. The decline of Indus Valley civilization was attributed to the invasion of Aryans.

Vedic Age (1500–600 BC)

The Vedic Age (1500–600 BC) began in India with the arrival of Aryan invaders from the North-West. Unlike Harappan urban culture, the Aryans settled in small villages or 'Gramas' (tribals) and became semi-agriculturists. Each Grama was headed by a Gramani (the chief officer of the village administration). Group of villages formed into small cities with a leader called Rajan or King. There were also two popular assemblies— the Samithi—first, a gathering of a large group of people for the discharge of tribal business which was presided over by the King, while the second one 'Sabha' was a body of a few selected people to advise the King in administration. The three key officials, the Purohita (the chief Priest), the Senani (the commander of the Army), and the Gramani (the village Head), assisted the King in administration.

Foreign trade was established with West Asia and Egypt. The barter system in local market was also introduced. Coins, called Nishka sere, was introduced. Common rituals like 'Yagas' and 'Yagnas' were observed to worship the nature.

Rural Society

As the society was confined to villages, the technique of communications centred around oral tradition and word of mouth. The four Vedas were preserved mostly in oral tradition and the knowledge of all Vedas was passed on from one generation to another only through oral communication. In fact, the oral communication as a medium of public relations was not only invented but also systematised with Sanskrit as a language.

What were the media of public relations communication? The key officials such as Gramani, the Chief Priest, the Senani, the travelling traders, farmers, vedic carpenters, heads of different castes on the one side and institutions such as Grama, the Samithi, the Sabha, the village market, rituals on the other became the fora of public communication so as to create a happy and prosperous community. Other media included the symbols, pictorials, folk arts and coins.

An interesting feature of the Aryan Age was the Sanskrit language (Illustrated History of India, Wilco, 2010). As a result, four Vedas—the Rig Veda, the Sama Veda, the Yajur Veda, and the Atharva Veda—were composed with the collection hymns, prayers, invocations offered to Gods of fire, rain, etc.

The Vedic Age with village administration and the King as a Head witnessed far-reaching developments in various spheres such as social, economic, political, cultural and religious. These changes demanded an effective public relations communication system to promote better relations between the King and the people on the one side and relationships between various institutions/key officials and their subjects on the other. The village priest and Gramani became the public communicators of the vedic period.

Propaganda

In the propaganda model of PR communication, the purpose is to promote an ideology/rule among the public with motives. Great religious leaders like Mahavira, the apostle of Jainism (599–527 BC), Gautama Buddha (566–486 BC), the founder of Buddhism and the Hindu philosopher Aadi Sankara (788–820 AD) belong to this category. They influenced the Indian mind to absorb and assimilate their respective faiths. The audiences, in this case, had to reinforce or modify their attitudes to the messages of their leaders. It was a sort of propaganda of their faiths.

As there were rigid caste distinctions and high rituals were the order of the society in the Vedic period, there came two reformers Mahavira and Gautama Buddha who changed the society towards their religions through appropriate communication methods.

Jainism: Mahavira

The central theme of Jainism as enunciated by Mahavira is that religion as a science of ethical practice, one should practice harmony between the self and one's environment. *Ahimsa* (non-violence) is the cardinal principle of Jainism. How did Mahavira propagate his religion? A distinguishing feature of Mahavira's preaching was that he travelled the whole country barefoot and bareheaded. That was his unpretentious style as compared with other religious leaders. After he attained enlightenment at the age of 42, Mahavira spent the next 30 years spreading message in his ascetic lifestyle. He spoke in simple language—the language of the masses and converted people of all walks of life. His teachings held no regard for social class—all people are equal in Jainism.

'Samgha' Centre of Propaganda

Mahavira, for the purpose of spreading Jainism, organized a fourfold holy Samgha (religious order) with monk (sadhu), nun (sadhvi), layman (shravak) and laywoman (shravika). Their job was to move into the field and propagate Jainism in tune with the aspirations of the local people. Eleven religious heads called 'Ganaharas' or chief disciples were appointed to oversee the propaganda of Samghas.

Buddhism

In his famous first sermon near Benaras, Lord Buddha had set forth four noble truths: (i) life is full of Dhukka (pain), (ii) pain is caused by a constant craving for sensual pleasures and material gains, (iii) agony will cease when a person is freed from desires and (iv) eight-fold path for the cessation of pain. The eight-fold paths included:

1. Right faith
2. Right endeavour
3. Right speech
4. Right conduct
5. Right livelihood
6. Right action
7. Right thinking
8. Right meditation

A unique teaching method of the Buddha was through parables. Buddha always taught the truth. But people sometimes had difficulty in understanding the philosophy of truth. To make people understand his philosophy, the Buddha told them stories to explain the glory of *Dharma*. If common people could not understand the truth in the abstract arguments, he would illustrate them with parables.

Household Approach

Buddha as Mahavira constituted 'Sangha' as a primary form of Buddhist community with Bhikshus (disciples) for propagating Buddhism and introduced the household approach. Each Bhikshu on a day-to-day basis had to contact the individual householder to exhort him on Buddhism and to restrain him from doing evil deeds, clear his doubts and constantly direct his attention to the right path that he should follow to attain salvation. Household approach propaganda was indeed a unique communication technique that had spread Buddhism in the entire Asia. Therefore, the Buddha is regarded as the Light of Asia and the World Teacher.

Aadi Sankara: Communicator Par Excellence

Aadi Sankara, founder of Advaita Vedanta, was a communicator par excellence. He travelled all over the country on foot three times in the 8th century AD, when there were no means of communication and transport facilities. To promote his philosophy of *Advaita Vendanta*, Aadi Sankara established four *'Mutts'* in four corners of India. They are:

1. *Jyotir Mutt* at Badrinath in the north
2. *Goverdhan Mutt* at Puri in the east
3. *Kalika Mutt* at Dwarka in the west
4. *Sharada Mutt* at Sringeri on the banks of Tungabadra river in the South

Each head of the mutt like the king was omnipotent in religious matters whose decision was final. *Mutts* were the source of information and religious communication and propaganda.

Sadharanikaran

Indian communication centres on the word *'Sadharanikaran'*. It is derived from the Sanskrit word *'Sadaran'* meaning simple, common or ordinary. This word is equivalent to the Latin word *'communis'* that is communication, meaning commonness of experience. Through sharing of information, communication creates commonness between the sender and the receiver on any given subject.

Sadharanikaran has been vividly described in Bharata's *Natyasastra* discovered in the 10th century. This book is said to have been authored in a period of as early as 500 BC. How does *Sadharanikaran* take place? Bharata (the Father of Indian Dance) describes *Sadharanikaran* as that point in the climax of a drama when the audience becomes one with the actor who shares an experience and leaves lasting impression through his acting on the stage and starts simultaneously revealing the same experience. In this process, the individual in the audience identifies himself with the actor on the stage and becomes emotional in that character. *Sadharanikaran* creates commonness of experience in full form between the communicator on the stage and the receiver in the audience. As a result, if the actor on the stage weeps or laughs, the audience also responds by repeating such gestures. Here, the receiver participates in communication. In essence, this type of communication achieves 'commonness' or 'oneness' among the people through communication.

Another format of *Sadharanikaran* is manifested in folk songs. The leader of the folk song troupe sings while all other participants join in group singing. This is otherwise known as 'participative communication'. Therefore, *Sadharanikaran* as enunciated by Bharata forms the foundation of the Indian communication system which is not only effective but also leads to participative communication process. Such a communication process was evolved by Bharata over 2000 years ago, much before the Westerners coined the word communication.

Kings in Propaganda Age

Like religious leaders, the kings of ancient India (Mauryan empire Chandragupta Maurya, 324–300 BC), Medieval India (Mughals, 1526–1707 AD) including the Governor Generals of East India Company (1757–1857) attempted with informaztion to instil a massive wave of faith in the people to support and preserve the government rule and build the image of the ruler. The religious leaders and the kings of yesteryears adopted propaganda techniques to preserve their rule by hook or crook. It remained a one-way communication, the message being the intent of the religious leader or the ruler.

Chanakya's Arthasastra

One of the celebrated ministers of Chandragupta Maurya (321 BC) was Kautilya, also known as Chanakya, who through his work *Arthasastra* gave an exposition on dissemination of information and collection of people's reactions through intelligence network especially suited for big monarchical kingdoms. In fact Chanakya laid the foundation in the Mauryan Empire. Kautilya launched mass propaganda through his intelligence network to guard against enemy's intrigues and reduce the enemy's subjects. His network was based on news carriers, spies in disguise, sanyasis, musicians, palmists, astrologers, dancers, etc. It was a marvellous system of communication or propaganda to preserve the rule of the king.

Emperor Ashoka (273–326 BC)

Emperor Ashoka's empire was so large that it was not possible for him to keep in touch with his subjects himself. Hence, he devised a novel method for reaching his subjects through rock edicts, stone pillars, copper plate inscriptions, stupas, paintings, pictures, music, and dance. Emperor Ashoka's edicts known as '*Dharma Lipis*', '*Dharma Sravanas*' and pillars of morality were erected where people gathered in large numbers, such as pilgrim centres, crossroads, etc. While emperor Ashoka used stone pillars, the Guptas introduced 'iron pillars' as media of communication. Even today we have one such iron pillar near Qutub Minar in Delhi.

Dharma Yatra

One of the stone edicts says that Ashoka gave up Vihara Yatras (pleasure tours) and undertook Dharma Yatras to preach Dharma and Buddhism. His greatness lies in his declaration: "All the people are my children and just as I desire for my children that they enjoy every kind of prosperity and happiness, so also do I desire the same for all my countrymen".

Golden Age of Guptas : Iron Pillars

After the decline of Mauryas, India had witnessed the Golden Age of Guptas (320–500 AD). Chandragupta I started a line of Kings who were great scholars and good administrators. It was under their patronage that magnificent architecture, sculpture, painting, literature, music developed. There was economic prosperity and peace in the country with a strong central Government. The cluster of 48 Ajanta caves carved out of a rock, filled with stories from Buddhism, at Aurangabad in Maharashtra, one of the greatest poets of all times Kalidas and the inventor of theory of astronomy Aryabhatta, who lived in Guptas period, represent the pinnacle of Indian Golden Age.

PR Communication

Alongside economic prosperity and the development of literature, public relations communication also developed as means for flow of information between the Government and the people within and outside India. Buddhism had opened its communication with foreign countries due to which Chinese travellers (HuienTsang) and missionaries came to India to study Buddhism and pay respects at the sacred places. Gupta literature, which had fables and folk role written in Sanskrit, had spread to countries such as Persia, Egypt and Greece which developed mutual relations between the people of India and those countries. Thus began Global public communication in the Golden Age of Guptas.

The greatest contribution of Guptas to the Indian communication system was introduction of iron pillars and beautiful Buddha copper statues as a media of communication. The iron pillar with the message of that Age at Qutub minar near Delhi is a shining example of public relations communication and propaganda of the Golden Age. The fifty feet Ashoka stone pillar at Sarnath Buddhist Vihara is the most popular, at the top of which are carved four majestic lions. Other media include: paintings, music, literature, poetry and word of mouth.

Mughal Rule (1526–1707): Medieval India

Six famous emperors known as the Great Mughals ruled India for about 200 years. They were Babar, Humayun, Akbar, Jahangir, Shajahan and Aurangzeb. It was in this period (1526–1707) that public communication system was developed. The Mughals appointed three categories of news writers or informers known as *Vaquia Navis, Khufia Navis* and *Harkara* for the purpose of regular bilateral communication of information between the Central Government and provinces. The *vaquia navis* (public news writer) was intended for the purpose of informing the administration of the day-to-day happenings in their respective regions. They were posted in capital cities of the provinces. The *Khufia Navis* (secret informer) was appointed for intelligence purpose and to provide information of secret nature. The *Harkara (Mokbar)* was the oral informer who gave his reports orally to the authorities.

Nicola Manuicci, a Venetian traveller, who lived in the court of Aurangzeb, recorded as follows:

> *It is fixed rule of the Mughals that the 'Vaquia Navis' (public news writer) and the 'Khufia Navis' (secret news writer) of the Empire, must once a week enter what is passing in a 'Vaquia' that is to say, a sort of gazette containing an account of events of great importance. These newsletters are commonly read in the King's presence by the women of the Mahal (palace) at about nine O'clock in the evening, so that by this means the king knows what is going on in his kingdom.*

The method of conveying information improved considerably during the Mughal period. Besides trained carrier pigeons, horse-riders, tunnel runners and drummers were used in fort-to-fort and post-to-post communication for transmitting distress or emergency messages. It is recorded that in 1569 the news of the birth of Salim, the son of Emperor Akbar, was conveyed to the King from Agra to Allahabad, a distance of about 500 km, in about two hours and twenty minutes by drum-beats, with drummers being positioned one mile from each other. Different types of drum-beating were developed for different types of messages. The style of drum-beating conveyed whether a child was born or someone had died. Similarly, marriage drum-beating had its own style. For making official announcements in villages drum-beating was used. This practice continues even today.

Jharokha darshan (Widow Audience)

Another important and very effective means of communication introduced by the medieval kings was face-to-face audience by the King. It was called *Jharokha Darshan* (window audience), introduced by Emperor Akbar. It became an established practice during the reign of his successors. *Jharokha Darshan* meant the appearance of the Emperor at the *Jharokha* (window) with the intention of freely meeting the people and receiving their petitions and grievances. It was like an open information court (*darbar*) resulting in a two-way communication process. All kinds of people, high and low, men and women, were permitted to meet the Emperor and present their petitions. Badauni, a contemporary of Akbar, said that "the *Jharokha Darhsan* worked effectively under Akbar who spent about four and a half hours regularly in such *Darshan*". The information system evolved by Mughals is relevant even today insofar as collection of feedback information on the policies and programmes of the government is concerned.

Bell of Justice

If the Emperor Akbar had Jharoka Darshan, his son Jahangir introduced Justice Bell to redress public grievances on the one side and get feedback on the policies and programmes on the other. A big bell was hung outside the King's Palace in Agra. Anyone with a grievance could pull the bell and he would be allowed to meet the Emperor to interact on his grievance. It was indeed a golden public relations communication exercise.

The East India Company rule (1757–1857)

The East India Company formed at the end of 1600 AD for the purpose of trading with East Indies, India and South East Asia obtained permission from Mughal Emperor Jahangir in 1617 to build a factory in Surat. The company expanded its trade and bought Indian commodities.

When the Mughal empire had become very weak, and native kings were fighting among each other, Robert Clive, the leader of East India Company in India, defeated Siraj-ud-Daula, the Nawab of Bengal, at the battle of Plassey and established the British East India Company rule in India in 1757. The East India Company ruled for one hundred years from 1757 to 1857. Though newspapers emerged as a means of public communication, the British East India Company did not encourage the press and rather it was suppressed.

First Newspaper—Bengal Gazette

An European, James Augustus Hicky, considered the Father of Indian Journalism started the first weekly newspaper, *The Bengal Gazette* or *Calcutta General Advertiser* on 29 January 1780. He described the objective of his paper as "a weekly political and commercial paper, open to all but influenced by none". Hicky wrote against the administration of East India Company, exposed their faults and also reflected public opinion by publishing letters to the editor. Hicky can also be regarded as the pioneer of public communication through his newspaper. But he was forced to close the newspaper within two years. The British East India Company neither made use of newspapers for dissemination of public information nor attempted to inform the people by any means of communication. They kept the people in dark.

Christian missionaries

Though the then Government (East India Company) suppressed the press, Christian Missionaries were allowed to carry out their religious propaganda. As a result, Christian missionaries at Serampore in Bengal started three newspapers: (i) *Dig Darshan*, a Bengali monthly (1818); (ii) *Friend of India*, an English monthly (1818); (iii) *Samachar Darpan*, a Bengali weekly (1819). These journals served as both a propaganda vehicles for promoting Christianity and British Empire in India and a source of information to the public for their enlightenment.

Commercial information

If Christian missionaries were involved in religious propaganda, there emerged a second front to promote business and commercial information. James Silk Buckingham, an European, with the support of a well-known salt merchant John Palmer started a weekly *The Calcutta Journal* in 1818. Buckingham made the journal more broad based to not only serve the cause of business but also support the cause of social communication launched by Raja Rammohan Roy. The objective of *Calcutta Journal*, according to Buckingham, was 'it would be a chronicle of political, commercial and literary news and views'. By printing the weekly, it was also intended that the Governor be admonished of their duties, warn them furiously of their fault and to keep public informed with the disagreeable truths. James Silk Buckingham paid for his boldness and was deported to England in 1823 for his anti-British and pro-Indian writings.

Father of social communication: Raja Rammohan Roy

Raja Rammohan Roy, the Father of Indian Language Journalism, started newspapers to create an awareness on the social evils of the Hindu Society and to counter the Christian missionaries propaganda against Hinduism. He started three newspapers: (i) *Sambad Kaumudi*, a Bengali weekly in 1821; (ii) *Mirat-Ul-Akbar*, a Persian weekly in 1821; (iii) *Brahmin Sevadhi*, an English and Bengali bilingual magazine in 1821. Through his journals, Raja Rammohun Roy mobilised public opinion against the practice of *Sati* (burning of Hindu widow with her dead husband) and got it abolished by the Government in 1829. His journals undoubtedly enlightened the people on social evils and became Father of social communication in India.

The first war of Indian independence—1857

The year 1857 was a momentous landmark in the history of India, when the first war of Indian independence or the Indian Sepoy Mutiny broke out. The first shot was fired by Mangal Pandey, an Indian soldier from Bengal Infantry, on 29 March, 1857 against the British. Mangal Pandey was hanged at Barrackpore in Bengal on 8 April 1857. There was also revolt by Indian soldiers at Meerut on 10 May 1857, where Britishers were killed. The mutiny against British rule spread to other places including Delhi. One of the reasons for the revolt was that the Hindu and Muslim soldiers had to bite the cartridges before the rifles were loaded and the grease of the cartridges was the fat of either cows or pigs. This was against the religious sentiments of the soldiers. Apart from this the other causes such as political, religious, economic, social and cultural were also at the root of the war for independence. The Hindus and Muslims resented Christian Missionaries' attacks on them. The kings developed hatred against the British as they lost power. Rani of Jhansi Laxmi Bai, Tantia Tope, Nana Sahib, Begum Hazrat Mahal were some of the heroes of the uprising.

Underground press

Information and communication played a significant role in the first war of independence. When the government suppressed the Indian owned press, underground press emerged that created awareness about the misrule of the East India Company and made people revolt against the British. The *Bombay Samachar* and *Jam-e-Jamshed* strongly supported the *Sepoy* mutiny. The Gujarati and Bengali press played an effective role in mobilising public opinion against the British. To a great extent the vernacular papers were responsible for the outbreak of the mutiny.

Bahadur Shah Zafar, the last Mughal Emperor of Delhi, was dubbed as the leader of the revolt. The British soldiers captured Delhi. Bahadur Shah was arrested and deported to Rangoon, Burma, where he died in 1862. His two sons were shot dead. Thus the Sepoy Mutiny got suppressed by the British. But the first war of Indian Independence witnessed the end of the British East India Company Rule in India. The first period of Indian public relations which is considered as the State of Propaganda paved the way for the Era of Publicity or Public Information with the end of the East India Company Rule in 1858. In other words, public relations was born out of propaganda.

SECOND PERIOD: THE ERA OF PUBLICITY (1858–1947)

Publicity is defined as "the dissemination of information, making matters public from the point of view of one who wishes to inform others". Placing information in a medium to attract the attention of the public towards products, services or events is also called publicity.

The era of publicity or public information—the second period in the evolution of Indian public relations—began in 1858 with the end of East India Company rule. In response to the mutiny, the British Government abolished the rule of the East India Company. In 1858, Queen Victoria took reins of the Indian Governance, after the sepoy mutiny. The British Government then ruled India through Viceroys till 1947.

Lord Canning in 1858 was appointed as the first Viceroy of India. The negative feelings of Indians against the East India Company's rule got suppressed were highlighted during first war of Indian independence. The East India Company had kept the Indians in the dark as they refrained from giving any information. There was a change in this attitude of the British Government and they gave impetus to public information with the aim of converting the ill feelings of the people. As the British government understood that they could no longer think only trade and making money and to stay in India they would have to take the local people into confidence, the new Viceroy, Lord Canning (1856–1862), evolved a method of keeping the newspapers informed with official information to woo and win the journalists.

Editor's Room

In order to better the relations between the Government and the press and through the press to the people, Lord Canning founded 'The Editors Room' in 1858, where journalists could come and peruse government papers of public interest. Some official papers were printed and pasted on the notice-boards and while others were included in the official gazette for public information. Such steps not only were the beginning of the government's publicity structure but also promoted good relations between governance and newspapers. When Sir John Lawrence became the Viceroy in 1864, he revived the idea of having a government newspaper for publicity purpose. The proposal was dropped as it was found financially unwise and some Indian newspapers severely criticised him.

First Press Commissioner

In 1876 Viceroy Lord Lytton wanted to better the relations with the press. Robert Knight, the founder editor of *Times of India* and *The Statesman*, was appointed as Consultant to Government on press relations. While lamenting the attitude of the government towards public information, Robert Knight demanded that the inherent utility of the press as a public welfare institution should be duly recognised. He then suggested the establishment of a Press Bureau with a Director for developing rapport with the newspapers. His suggestion in 1876 was a landmark in government information system and became the basis for press relations through the government information machinery. In the process, the Government appointed the First Press Commissioner in 1880, exactly hundred years after the inception of India's first newspaper in 1780. This marked the beginning of the Government's publicity which became a tool of public relations in the independent India.

Philanthropic Age and Community Relations (1911–1912)

J.N. Tata founded the House of TATAs with the aim to endow higher education for Indian graduates of merit abroad and also to construct a model industrial township for industrial workers of Steel Company at Jameshedpur, Bihar. The policy found its most striking expression with the establishment of the TATA Iron and Steel Company which went into production in 1912. This marked the beginning of community relations, an important element of public relations and as a measure to maintain better employee relations.

FIRST WORLD WAR—PUBLICITY BOARDS (1914–1918)

The Government of India, initially reluctant to have a regular official information set-up to deal with the public, realised its importance during the First World War (1914–1918). Extensive propaganda and war publicity were required to secure greater response and support for the war efforts both from the newspapers and from the general public. The Government, therefore, set up a number of Provincial Publicity Boards throughout the country with a Central Publicity Board in Shimla. This may perhaps be called as the first organised public information disseminating agency established in 1914 as part of the First World War Propaganda. With this the publicity of the government gained importance. Publicity Boards developed cordial relations with journalists who were till then looked on as anti-government. Tours were organised and Indian journalists were taken to the battlefronts. Sir Stanley Reed, Editor of *Times of India*, was appointed as Officer-in-Charge of the Central Publicity Board at Shimla in 1918. Following his recommendations, Government of India set up the Central Bureau of Information in 1919, now called the Press Information Bureau. Professor Rush Brook Williams, an academician of Allahabad University, was appointed as its first Director. The duty of the bureau then was to extract the most critical statements which appeared in newspapers and bring them to the notice of the departments concerned for comments and issue of rejoinders.

SECOND WORLD WAR (1939–1945)

In 1939 the Second World War broke out in which India was also involved. For war propaganda, Government of India improved the structure of government publicity machinery, which was fully utilised after Indian independence. The Bureau of Public Information and All India Radio were placed under a new organisation called the Directorate of Information and Broadcasting for better coordination and effective war publicity. Sir Frederick Puckle was appointed its first Director-General to control and coordinate the war publicity.

In 1941, subject broadcasting was transferred from the Department of Communications to Department of Information and Broadcasting. A separate Directorate of Inter-Services Public Relations was set up with Ivor Jehu, Assistant Editor of *Times of India*, as the Chief of the New Directorate. In the history of Indian Information system, in 1941 the Government used the word 'Public Relations' for the first time. The name of the Bureau of Public Information was changed to Press Information Bureau, which continues even today.

The war with Japan came to an end on 14 August 1945 but the official publicity machinery developed for war propaganda continued even after the war ended. The war publicity structure had changed its stand from war information to public welfare information for the welfare of the people.

THIRD PERIOD: GANDHIAN ERA OF PUBLIC COMMUNICATION (1919–1947)

Public relations or public communication played an active role in Indian independence. There was a close linkage between the Indian war of independence and the public communication system. From the birth of the Indian National Congress in 1885 to the dawn of Independence in 1947, almost all freedom fighters who turned journalists used the newspapers as 'vehicles of public communication' to carry the message of the freedom movement and mobilise public opinion against the British Government. They also adopted other tools of public relations such as word of mouth, folk media, printed word, etc.

Gandhian Era

Mahatma Gandhi returned to India from South Africa on 9 January 1915 to intensify the freedom movement from the grassroots. His ascendancy in Indian politics and his assumption of the leadership of the Indian independence gave fillip not only to journalism but also to public communication system.

Bharat Yatra

When Gandhiji met Gopala Krishna Gokhale in Poona after his arrival from South Africa, Gokhale took a promise from Gandhiji that he should travel in India for gaining experience and that he should not express any opinion on public questions. The idea behind the tour was Gandhiji must understand the land and the people.

As per his promise, Gandhiji criss-crossed the country, mingling with common man with a view to first understand his publics and also learn from the people what India needed then before embarking on preaching for any action against the British Raj. His eyes and ears were open during the Yatra but his mouth was shut not to express and opinion. At the end of his year-long wandering, Gandhiji settled at Sabarmati Ashram on the banks of river Sabarmati near Ahmadabad. Gandhiji's one year Bharat Yatra was like today's fact-finding/situation analysis stage in the practice of public relations.

In the period between 1919 and 1947, Mahatma Gandhi launched four major mass agitations of national character against the British Government. Mahatma Gandhi gave the first nation-wide call for satyagraha on 14 April 1919 against the British by observing *Satyagraha*, a movement against the Rowlatt Act and the massacre of 1200 unarmed people by the British General Michael Dyer at Jallianwala Bagh in Amritsar. In 1921 Gandhiji gave a nation-wide call to practice non-cooperation with the British (teaching Hindi, lawyers to suspend practice, boycotting foreign cloth, etc.).

Civil Disobedience Movement

In 1930, Mahatma Gandhi as part of the Civil Disobedience movement drew up a pledge for *'Purna Swaraj'* (complete independence) and organised the 241 mile long Dandi March on 12 March 1930 to break the Salt Law. Gandhiji collected a group of 78 Ashram people residing at Sabarmati ashram, Ahmadabad and reached Dandi on the shores of Arabian Sea on 5 April 1930. He broke the Salt Law by collecting contraband salt and manufacturing salt by boiling the sea water. He urged people to promote *'Swadeshi'* goods and boycott the foreign ones. Gandhi and his gallant band of *Satyagrahis* united the entire nation of about 350 million against the British Empire through the Civil Disobedience Movement.

An interesting feature of the Dandi March was musicians, who followed the March and recited *bhajans, kirthans, Ram Dhun* and other songs to attract the attention of the people. He also addressed people through roadside public meetings that we now call road shows.

Quit India

On 8 August 1942, Mahatma Gandhi gave a final call "Do or Die" for the 'Quit India' as part of India's freedom struggle and asked the British to leave the country. He adopted a multimedia approach to reach out the people in both the urban and the rural India. Before Gandhi came to India in 1915, the freedom movement was confined to the elite and in a few major cities. He wanted that the movement must spread to all villages as India lives in her villages. In an effort to create awareness of the freedom struggle, the flag of nationalism was planted in every village and a dozen or more peasants' households were actively drawn into the orbit of freedom struggle. In the process, the 'National flag' and a few opinion leaders from each village became media of independence message.

Newspapers

Mahatma Gandhi launched his own newspapers and the nationalist press also marched shoulder to shoulder. His newspapers included: (1) *Young India* (1919); (2) *Navajivan*, a Gujarati Weekly (1919); (3) *The Harijan Weekly* (1933). With the support of his own newspapers and the support of nationalist newspapers, Gandhi could enlighten the educated section of the society against the British. The true function of Journalism is to educate the public mind.

During the freedom struggle, what was the role of publicity machinery of the government? The British Indian Information Service was wholly used to promote the Second World War effort on the one hand and to contain India's freedom movement on the other hand. The then Prime Minister of Great Britain even called Mahatma Gandhi as *'half-naked fakir'*. But the Nobel Laurate Rabindranath Tagore called him "the Great Soul in Beggar's Garb". But the very same half-naked fakir not only communicated his message of freedom struggle to millions of people but also mobilised their public opinion against the British which forced them give India full freedom. How could Gandhi create such a massive public opinion? It was his two-way communication process based on principles of public relations. According to one estimate, Gandhi could literally mobilise ten per cent of the nation's population which came to about 400 million people in action against the imperial power. Gandhiji believed in the dictum "An ounce of practice is worth more than tons of preaching". Against this background he practised what he preached. That was his secret of success.

Father of Indian PR

Mahatma Gandhi is regarded as the Father of the Nation, Man of the 20th Century and the Great Mass Communicator of the World. What was the reason for his greatness? His philosophy of non-violence and the style of communication strategy in tune with Indian environment. In fact, Gandhi by practicing two-way public communication policy laid the strong foundation for the modern Indian public relations. *Public Relations Voice*, an Indian PR professionals journal, in its first inaugural issue (1997) named Mahatma Gandhi as the Father of Indian

Public Relations, which was lauded by the then President of India K.R. Narayanan.

At a time when the modern means of mass communication were not available, and All India Radio was controlled by the British Government, a question arises as to how Gandhi was successful in communicating with millions of diversified and illiterate masses. His communication strategy was based on what we call ITM Theory of Gandhian Techniques of Public Communication which was in a way a two-way traffic in the sense that he informed the people about freedom message and the people responded to his messages on the freedom struggle giving full support and active participation. There cannot be a better example of a two-way communication process in public relations. Such a communication strategy enabled us to attain freedom from the British.

In the ITM theory **I** stands for interpersonal media (prayer meetings, public meetings, padayatras, roadside interactions); **T** represents traditional folk media (*bhajans*, *keertans*, devotional songs, music); **M** represents of Mass Media (nationalist press). Gandhi made use of combination of these three types of media for urban and rural, rich and poor, literate and illiterate. After independence, the Government followed Gandhian techniques of communication, which is still relevant even today.

FOURTH PERIOD: THE AGE OF PUBLIC RELATIONS (1947–1991)

"Perhaps more than any other person in India at present, I have come in contact with vast masses. And because I am receptive to them, I can make them somewhat 'receptive to what I say. If I went about like a schoolmaster or a boss ordering them about, their receptiveness would close up. I go as a colleague and a comrade and I credit them with intelligence to understand the most intricate problems" (Pandit Jawaharlal Nehru).

India won its freedom on 15 August 1947. The first Prime Minister of independent India, Pandit Jawaharlal Nehru, was a devout believer in the free flow of public information and mass contacts for enriching people with intelligence. It was his view that if economic poverty is to be removed, we should first eradicate information poverty. It is against this backdrop several measures were taken to strengthen the public communication system, to inform, to educate, to persuade, to motivate and to entertain people as social partners of the world's largest democracy.

Communal Harmony

When partition took place between India and Pakistan, there arose the need for maintaining communal harmony between Hindus and Muslims. In the process, publicity machinery was stepped up to reach the people with the message of peace and maintaining religious harmony.

A Separate I&B Ministry

A major landmark in independent India was the creation of a separate Ministry of Information and Broadcasting in 1947 itself. Sardar Vallabhbhai Patel as the Union Home Minister held the charge of Ministry of Information and Broadcasting. As independent India's first Minister of Information and Broadcasting, Sardar Patel laid a strong foundation for the public relations communication in India which also dawned the new age of public relations.

However, publicity, a by-product of British India, graduated to public relations in independent India. The legacy of Gandhian techniques of communication in the freedom struggle had a great impact on the Nehru Government in informing and educating the public on democratic values. In fact, it was Mahatma Gandhi who had sown the seeds of public relations philosophy as part of the freedom struggle.

Plan Publicity

The Industrial Policy 1948 and the First Five Year Plan (1951–1956) gave much impetus to the growth of public relations in India as a measure to involve people in the socio-economic development of the country. Plan publicity machinery was developed all over the country as an integral part of public relations practice in all Government departments to publicise both industrial and agricultural development. Private industrial concerns major oil companies and steel companies also started developing communication divisions.

PR Growth Factors

The growth of public relations structure in India can be attributed primarily to the following factors:

- The Industrial Policies 1948 and 1956
- Launching of the Five Year Plans (1951)
- General elections and emergence of democratic institutions (1952)
- Establishment of Public Relations Society of India (PRSI) (1958)
- Growth of public sector (1960s)
- Mixed economy—the role of public and private sectors

- Nationalisation of the scheduled banks (1969)
- New industrial policy and the economic liberalisation (1991)
- Proliferation of the media and revolution of information and communication technology.
- Coalition Governments—NDA 1999, UPA I 2004 and UPA II 2009—stepped up publicity campaign.

All these efforts are but an indication of the emerging trends on the role and scope of public relations in India. As a result of various socio-economic development programmes, the information and public relations service was strengthened in the government, public sector, the private industry and non-profit organisations.

General Elections (1951–2009)

The General Elections to the Lok Sabha and to the Legislative Assembly of every State held on the basis of adult franchise was another reason to the intensification of public relations activity. If the first General Elections were held from 25 October 1951 to 21 February 1952, the fourteenth General Elections were held in April–May 2004. As many as 70 crore voters were eligible to vote. Educating the voters how to cast their vote was the major responsibility of both the Government and the political parties. As a result, public relations set-up in Central Government and State Governments was strengthened. Similarly political parties developed political communication to woo voters towards their ideologies. Multimedia communication was the strategy of both government and political parties to reach out to the urban, rural and tribal voters.

Coalition Governments NDA and UPA: Publicity Campaigns

In 1999, 13th General Elections, the Bharatiya Janatha Party (BJP) led by Prime Minister Atal Bihari Vajpayee in association with 14 other political parties formed coalition Government called National Democratic Alliance (NDA). In 2004 General Elections, the Indian National Congress (INC) led by Dr. Manmohan Singh in association with other political parties formed the coalition Government known as United Progressive Alliance (UPA) and UPA II in 2009 General Elections.

With the concept of coalition politics, both NDA and UPA Central Governments stepped up information and public relations activities to project the performances of their respective Governments besides building image. If NDA launched a major multimedia public relations campaign "India Shining" in 2004, the UPA Government launched nationwide "Bharat Nirman", public information campaign in 2006, which is being continued even in 2013. This campaign was aimed at creating awareness among the common people about the policies and programmes of the Government. As such, coalition Governments for their survival not only stepped up publicity activities but also strengthened public relations machinery in India. This forms an important segment in the evolution of Indian public relations.

Public Sector PR

The Industrial policy 1956 gave strategic role to public sector. As a result, there emerged public sector public relations to project the image of public sector undertakings. It was mixed economy where public and private sector co-existed. In 1956 General Insurance companies were nationalised and banks were nationalised in 1969. Almost all Central and State Public Sector Undertakings like BHEL, NTPC, Air India, ITDC, SAIL, APSRTC, Banks, insurance companies established public relations divisions to maintain good relations with stakeholders and motivate the workforce to achieve organisational goals. In the private sector, mention may be made of Tatas and Birlas, which developed public relations set-up.

National Emergency—Misuse of Media (1975–1977)

When Indira Gandhi was the Prime Minister, a proclamation of National Emergency was issued on 25 June 1975 on the ground of 'internal disturbance'. Emergency was in force for one year and nine months, during which period the Government misused not only the media units such as All India Radio, Doordarshan and Press Information Bureau, but also the private media such as newspapers, films which were otherwise outside the control of the government. The private media were made to dance to the tune called by the rulers by a ruthless exercise of censorship powers, enactment of a set of draconian laws which reduced press freedom to naught and an unabashed abuse of authority in the matter of releasing government advertisements, allocation of newsprint and release of raw stock for films.

All media units of the Ministry of Information and Broadcasting were made instruments of Government propaganda with a single point national agenda—projection of the image of Indira Gandhi and her 10-year rule—"Decade of Achievements" (1966–1976). This was the darkest period in government public relations after independence.

Das Committee Report

Emergency was revoked on 21 March 1977. In the 1977 elections, the Congress (I) under the leadership of Indira Gandhi was routed.

Mrs. Gandhi even lost her Lok Sabha seat. The Janata Party with Morarji Desai as Prime Minister came to power on 26 March 1977, ending 30 years of continuous Congress rule. A one-member Enquiry Committee was set up in the Ministry of Information and Broadcasting under the chairmanship of K.K. Das, ICS (Retd), a former Secretary of the Ministry of Information and Broadcasting, to enquire and collect facts for the preparation of a White Paper by the Government on the misuse of mass media during the Emergency. The Das Committee's report based predominantly on government records was submitted on 22 June 1977. The Government of India then prepared a White Paper on 'Misuse of Mass Media during the Internal Emergency'. This paper gives a vivid picture of the misuse of the government media units for projecting the personality of Indira Gandhi and her 10-year rule.

Government Advertising Agency

Private advertising agencies, when they release advertisements to newspapers, get 15 per cent commission. In 1985, the Chief Minister N.T. Rama Rao hit upon the idea of creating a Government advertising agency so as to get 15 per cent commission from newspapers and earn about ₹10 crores on the ads released by Government departments, public sector undertakings, local bodies, etc. The author Dr. C.V. Narasimha Reddi, who was then the Director, Department of Information and Public relations, was asked by the Chief Minister to launch the advertising agency. The Director in turn made enquiries with the Indian Newspapers Society (INS), an association of newspaper owners which gives accreditation to advertising agencies for getting commission from newspapers. The INS and major newspapers informed that the Government advertising agency will not be given 15 per cent commission as it would mix advertising and press information to influence the fourth estate.

When the negative response of INS was brought to the notice of Chief Minister, he was annoyed at the Director as if the Director was at fault. Later the Chief Minister posted the Additional Postmaster General, Andhra Pradesh V.V. Saidulu on deputation as Commissioner, Information and Public Relations over the Director in March 1986. In April 1986, Telugu Samacharam, an autonomous publicity agency, came into being for building the image of the state government including release of advertisements. The INS did not give accreditation to the new agency and the newspapers also did not allow any commission. In the process, the Director who became the victim of the agency got himself transferred out of the department. Later the agency was closed.

Indira Gandhi and N.T. Rama Rao

Just as Indira Gandhi misused the official public information disseminating agencies like All India Radio, Doordarshan for projecting her image and her 10-year rule during the internal emergency in 1975–1977, N.T. Rama Rao (NTR), Chief Minister of Andhra Pradesh, also misused the State Official Information machinery through an autonomous agency called *Telugu Samacharam* to glorify his personal image during 1986–1989. Incidentally, N.T. Rama Rao also held the Information and Public Relations portfolio from 16 September 1984 to 2 February 1989. Since NTR hailed from the film industry, he knew the value of the publicity given to film heroes and encouraged full-page advertisements about himself at public expense.

The autonomous publicity agency besides releasing ads also brought out a fortnightly *Telugu Samacharam* in 1987, which focused only on Chief Minister and his personal image. All the lead stories and editorials glorified the Chief Minister irrespective of readers-oriented columns. About 6–9 photos of Chief Minister were published on the edit page. *Telugu Samacharam*, an autonomous propaganda agency, was considered as a black spot in the history of Indian public relations communication.

The Andhra Pradesh High Court in a writ petition (2884/87) directed the Commissioner (Information and PR) to desist from publishing advertisements of the Chief Minister, as it might promote the Telugu Desam party's chances in the then *Zilla Parishad* elections (1987). The Court felt that prima facie the wall posters and the full-page newspaper advertisements failed to indicate that they constituted the material printed by the Government, as the Government monogram was insignificantly tucked away in a corner, thereby making it appear perilously close to Telugu Desam Party material (*Indian Express*, 14 May 1987). Public relations in any democratic government should be neutral to party politics. But this was not followed in Andhra Pradesh during 1986–1989 and the government public relations was misused.

The misuse of government authority under the National Emergency by the Central Government in 1975–1977 and in the guise of autonomy by the *Telugu Samacharam* (1986–1989) in State Government of Andhra Pradesh is unparalleled in the history of independent India's public communication and is, therefore, regarded as a 'pockmark' on the credible public information system.

PRSI Professional Approach (1958–2013)

Public relations in India took a new turn in 1958 when a national professional body Public Relations Society of India (PRSI) was formed to promote the recognition of public relations as a strategic management function. A decade later, on 21 April 1968 public relations professionals for the first time met at the first All India Public Relations Conference held in New Delhi. The conference, which had the theme 'Professional Approach', also adopted a *Code of Ethics* formulated by the International PR Association. In fact, this conference marked the beginning of professional public relations in India.

As many as 35 All India PR Conferences including the World PR Congress in 1982 at Bombay and World PR Festival in 2005 in New Delhi were organised till the end of 2013. These conferences undoubtedly enriched the knowledge of public relations professionals on the one hand and created greater awakening on the role of public relations among management on the other hand. From 1958 the birth of Public Relations Society of India to 2013 when the 35th All India PR Conference was held in New Delhi, a period of over 55 years, was a momentous era in which Indian Public Relations not only developed rapport with international public relations associations but also public relations set-up was strengthened in government, public sector, private industry and NGOs. In 2009, PRSI celebrated its Golden Jubilee to commemorate the completion of 50 years. As such, the practice of public relations became firmly established as an integral part of Indian economic, political and social development, thanks to the professional development programmes of PRSI. Three more professional bodies in India promote public relations. They are: (i) The Association of Business Communicators of India (ABCI), Mumbai, established in 1957, is an organization of PR professionals. ABCI conducts Comfest every year and presents awards. (ii) The Public Relations Council of India (Bangalore) came into being in 2004 which conducts Global Conference every year when senior PR professionals are inducted into Hall of Fame. (iii) The Global Forum for Public Relations, an initiative of Prajapita Brahmakumaris (World Spiritual University) which was launched in 2006, promotes the Golden Triangle—Professionalism, Ethics and Spirituality in public relations.

Public Relations Voice (1997–2013)

Professional Journal reflects the growth of the profession. Unfortunately, there was no professional journal for public relations profession in India. To fill this void, Dr. C.V. Narasimha Reddi, launched Public Relations Voice, the only journal for Indian PR professionals in October 1997 as a quarterly. The first issue devoted to Mahatma Gandhi as the Father of Indian Public Relations was released by the former Union Minister for Information and Broadcasting S. Jaipal and Reddy. The journal entered 17th year of its service to the PR profession in October 2013, with 52 issues to its credit.

The journal has not only helped the PR professionals in updating their knowledge and skills but also contributed to narrate the growth of public relations from ancient India to modern India. In has covered almost all major areas of public relations practice besides 16 great communicators of India from Lord Buddha, Emperor Ashoka, Saint Singer Kabir, Mahatma Gandhi, Pandit Jawaharlal Nehru to Ramana Maharishi. Dennis L. Wilcox professor, Emeritus of Public Relations, School of Journalism and Mass Communication, San Jose State University, USA said, "Public Relations Voice is making a great contribution to the compilation of public relations literature in India which will assist both students and professionals".

FIFTH PERIOD: INDIAN PR WITH GLOBAL PERSPECTIVE (1991–2013)

What is Globalisation? According to Thomas L. Friedman of New York Times, "Globalisation means the integration of trade finance and information that is creating a single market and culture". The United Nations Development Programme (UNDP) defines "Globalisation as the growing interdependence of the World's people through shrinking space, shrinking time and killing the distance". In the process, the World has become a Global Village.

With the spread of globalisation in the field of economy and marketing, there developed global public relations to handle international publics and global business. Global public relations is defined as the planned and organized communication effort of a government/company to establish mutually beneficial relations with the publics situated in other countries and to promote the products or services. Global public relations is an inter-governmental and multinational PR programme that has certain coordination between corporate office public relations department and various countries where offices and/or publics are located and that has potential consequences or results in more than one country. For example, the Pepsi Cola's corporate office is located in USA and the corporate communication department of Pepsi handles public relations activities in other countries from USA.

With the introduction of New Industrial Policy in 1991, which envisages economic liberalisation, privatisation and globalisation, the Indian public relations practice earlier confined only to national companies had developed global perspective to meet the growing competitive marketing environment between Indian companies and multinationals, on the one hand and among national and multinational corporations on the other hand. In fact, it paved the way for global public relations in India. Today there are a few international PR firms in India either through acquiring an Indian firm or on their own. These include Genesis Burson – Marsteller, iPAN Hill & Knowlton, etc. Multinational PR firms needed the expertise of Indian PR agencies to deal with the global competitive marketing environment.

An interesting feature of globalisation has been that many multi-national companies with foreign capital came to India and at the same time some of the Indian companies became multinationals by acquiring foreign concerns. Multinationals such as Ford Motors, Coco-Cola, Pepsi, Microsoft, etc. established their subsidiaries in India with local market. The Indian company Mittal Steel became the World's biggest steel producer with the acquisition of France based Arcelor Company as Arcelor-Mittal Steel Company.

Mergers and Acquisitions

If the UK-based Vodafone, the world's largest mobile company, acquired the India's fourth largest cellular operator, Hutchison-Essar, the Indian-based Mittal Steel acquired France-based Arcelor Steel and the Arcelor Mittal Steel has now become the world's biggest steel producer. Tata Motors took over truck operations of Daewoo to access markets in Korea and China. India Inc is now witnessing 'trade wars' in the shape of car war, cell phone war, media war, insurance war, banks war, etc. Earlier, there was only one State-owned Life Insurance Corporation of India, but today, we have over 30 insurance companies vying each other with aggressive communication messages to woo the customers. As a result, PR communication gained momentum.

Information Revolution

Alongside the trade wars, the information revolution and its globe girdling communication media BBC and CNN, have far-reaching impact on public relations practice. When foreign brands came to India, multinational public relations firms also came to boost their clients products. Indian public relations agencies tied up with foreign public relations firms to meet the global market needs. Major industries such as Reliance, Tata, Birla, IT companies and public sector undertakings strengthened their corporate communications. As a result, the number of public relations firms and in-house public relations departments increased in India with a global perspective. This resulted in the upswing of public relations activities in corporate India and public relations entered into new phase—global public relations with better professionalism. Global public relations practice in India adopted a strategy to implement distinctive programme in multiple national markets with each programme tailored to meet the acute distinctions, cultures and audiences of the individual geographic area. Professional excellence has become the hallmark of Indian public relations with a global perspective.

FDI in Retail

In 2012, India witnessed another economic reform, when Government of India allowed Foreign Direct Investment into multi-brand retail.

As a result, more foreign companies like Wallmart enter India with a big business proposition. Indian retail companies also will collaborate with foreign ones. This has given a further boost to both marketing and public relations communication activities. As such, Indian public relations is now passing through the phase of global public relations.

POINTS TO REMEMBER

1. Public relations in India is a 20th Century discipline. However, mythological communication was the forerunner of modem public relations. Lord Krishna was a great communicator of Indian mythology—*Mahabharata*. Sage Narada was yet another pioneer of public relations in India.

2. Period from 1500 BC to 1858 AD is regarded as the first period of public relations known as the *State-of-Propaganda*, when the religious leaders and the then kings practiced propaganda techniques. Jainism, Buddhism. Hinduism and Christianity were popularized through these methods.

3. Information and communication played a significant role in awakening the Indians towards the first war of Indian Independence called the Sepoy Mutiny in 1857.

4. With the end of the East India Company rule, the British Government in 1858 took reins of the Indian Governance after the first war of independence was suppressed. And the second period of public relations began with the Era of Publicity in 1858 which continued till 1947. In order to better relations with the press and the people, the British India founded 'Editors Room' in 1858. The First Press Commissioner was appointed in 1880 and Publicity Boards were set up in 1914 as part of the First World War Publicity. Sir Stanley Reed, Editor of *The Times of India*, was appointed as Officer-in-Charge of the Central Publicity Board at Shimla in 1818.

5. The Third Period of public relations 1919–1947, known as Gandhian Era of Public Communication in the evolution of public relations, played a significant role in the Indian Freedom Struggle with Mahatma Gandhi as a supreme leader.

6. Non-Cooperation Movement 1921, Civil Disobedience Movement 1930 and Quit India Movement 1942 were the three major mass freedom movements launched by Mahatma Gandhi to mobilize public opinion. Interpersonal media, folk art media and mass media were used to reach the public which came to be known as Gandhian techniques of communication and became part of Indian public relations.

7. The Second World War, 1939–1945, gave much impetus to Government publicity machinery in India when the Bureau of Public Information and All India Radio were placed under a new organization called Directorate of Information and Broadcasting to boost war publicity.

8. With the dawn of Indian Independence in 1947, there emerged the Age of Public Relations with the intensification of public information system to inform, educate, persuade, motivate and entertain people as social partners of the world's largest democracy.

9. Five Year Plan Publicity (1951–1956), General Elections (1951–2009), Public Sector Public Relations, Nationalization of Banks in 1969, birth of professional body 'Public Relations Society of India' in 1958 were the certain landmark events that strengthened the roots of public relations in post-independence era.

10. In the Fifth period 1991–2012, Indian public relations developed global perspective with the economic liberalisation, globalisation and privatisation. An interesting feature of globalisation has been that many multinationals came to India and Indian companies became multinational with business operations in foreign countries. In the process, India witnessed trade wars in the shape of Cars War, Cell Phones War, Insurance War, Banks War, Media War, vying each other with aggressive communication messages to woo customers. This has resulted in the upswing of public relations activities in corporate India and public relations entered into new phase—global public relations with better professionalism. The number of in-house public relations departments and public relations firms increased to meet the growing demand of corporate communications.

REVIEW QUESTIONS

1. The origin of Indian public relations extend deep into the Indian mythology. Describe the mythological public relations communication system from the great epics of Ramayana and Mahabharata.

2. What were the media and methods used by great religious leaders and the kings in the first period of public relations, which is otherwise called the State-of-Propaganda?

3. What do you mean by *Sadharanikaran*. Explain its relevance to modern communication system?

4. The era of publicity—the second period in the evolution of Indian public relations—began in 1858 with the end of East India Company Rule. What were the landmarks of the Era of Publicity?

5. Enumerate the major developments in the Gandhian Era of public communication that created public opinion against the British to win Independence. Describe briefly the types of media Mahatma Gandhi used to reach the people?

6. Mahatma Gandhi is regarded as Father of Indian public relations. Discuss.

7. Independent India in 1947 witnessed the age of public relations. Describe the various factors that strengthened public relations machinery during the period 1947–1991.

8. With economic liberalisation, privatisation and globalisation as part of the New Industrial Policy 1991, public relations in India entered into a new phase called global public relations with better professionalism. Describe important features of global public relations.

History of Public Relations in USA | Chapter 5

(World's Oldest Democracy)

C O N T E N T S

- American Independence
- Ivy Ledbetter Lee: Publicity Bureau
- Father of Modern PR
- Second Half of the 20th Century
- Four US PR Models
- Edwards L. Bernays: The Father of Modern Public Relations

The United States was first settled by immigrants from Europe, primarily from Britain, and various land companies with a license from the British Crown, actively promoting colonization to generate revenues from what the colonists were able to manufacture or grow. The Virginia Company (refers collectively to a pair of English joint stock companies chartered by James) was carried in 1606 with the purpose of establishing settlements on the coast of North America. In 1620, for example, the Virginia company distributed leaflets and booklets throughout Europe offering 50 acres of free land to anyone willing to migrate to the USA in an attempt to attract people to the country and this effort was one of the earliest exercises in public relations. After the American colonies were well established, publicity techniques were used to promote various institutions like colleges and to raise funds for running such institutions. In 1641, Harvard College published a fund-raising brochure.

AMERICAN INDEPENDENCE

Public relations also played an active role in the American independence. The colonists threw crates of tea leaves from British trade ship into Boston harbour to protest excessive British taxation. As such, public relations techniques were used in the American independence struggle to free the country from British rule. In the 19th century, American railroads used extensive publicity for promotion of trains and to attract people to travel by rail.

Politics and Publicity

The early 19th century also saw the development of publicity tactics on the political arena. Amos Kendall, a former Kentucky newspaper editor, became the first Press Secretary to President Andrew Jackson. Kendall assessed public opinion on various issues and skilfully interpreted the President's policies and issued news releases.

Corporate PR

As the country went ahead with industrialisation after the Civil War, the Westinghouse Corporation in 1889 established the first in-house publicity department. In 1897, the term 'public relations' was first used by the Association of American Railroads Company. Groups advocating the right of women to vote used a variety of public relations tactics to press for their cause. Street demonstration was one of the tactics.

IVY LEDBETTER LEE: PUBLICITY BUREAU

Professional public relations was born out of adamant attitudes of managements towards employees on the one hand and labour unrest and public criticism of management policies on the other hand. Most of the corporations had the notion that they were not accountable to the customers and the people and were reluctant to share information with the media. It is in this background the first publicity agency known as the Publicity Bureau was opened in Boston in 1900 by Ivy Ledbetter Lee (1877–1934), the pioneer of public relations and the father of American public relations. Lee and George F. Parker established the Publicity Bureau in New York City in 1904. It marked the beginning of the 20th century public relations effort in the USA. George Parker remained in publicity field. However, Lee became a counsellor and advisor to individuals and institutions, mostly corporations. This firm and Ivy L. Lee's declaration principles changed the adamant attitudes of companies from "Public be damned" to "Public be informed" and thus was born a new model of public relations called Public Information. AT&T Corporation was one of the important companies that had promoted public relations through its press relations and customer relations programmes in the beginning of the 20th century. Henry Ford, the owner of the Ford automobile company, promoted media relations to gain wide coverage for the company and had said "everyone should own a car and that it should be affordable to people". It was a good effort in promoting car consciousness. President Teddy Roosevelt was another key person who promoted public relations efforts and was involved in numerous press conferences and interviews to draw support for his projects.

Declaration of Principles

Based on the open society policy, Ivy Lee issued what he called the 'Declaration of Principles' for the guidance of both the management and the newspapers. Here is an extract:

This is not a secret Press Bureau. All our work is done in the open. We aim to supply news. This is not an advertising agency. Our matter is accurate. Further, details on any subject needed will be supplied promptly and any editor will be assisted most carefully in verifying directly any statement of fact.

This paved the way for the growth of public relations in the USA.

George Creel and World War I

One great public relations professional who emerged after Ivy Lee was George Creel (1876–1953), the head of the United States Committee on Public Information, a propaganda organisation created by President Woodrow Wilson during First World War. President Woodrow Wilson asked Creel to organize a massive public relations campaign to unite the nation and influence world opinion during the War. Creel developed good media relations by involving talented journalists to mobilise public opinion towards the war effort. He also involved scholars and artistes as the symbols of public opinion to unite the nation during the war period. The committee publicised the war aims and ideals of Woodrow Wilson, which was to make the world safe for democracy and to make the First World War, the war to end the wars. As such, the First World War gave much fillip to the practice of public relations techniques.

FATHER OF MODERN PR

On the basis of the strong foundations laid by George Creel during the First World War, others also took lead in organizing publicity efforts in the footsteps of Creel. One such person was Edward L. Bernays who by emphasising on the feedback information gave a new turn to the public relations practice. He became the Father of modern public relations by the time of his death in 1995 at the age of 103.

Two-way Asymmetric Model

According to Dennis L. Wilcox (2005), "Bernays conceptualized a third model of public relations (after press agentry and public information models) two-way asymmetric model that applied social science research and behavioral psychology to formulate campaigns and messages that could change people's perceptions and encourage certain behaviours".

Unlike Lee's public information model that emphasised the accurate distribution of news and information, Bernay's model was essentially one of advocacy and scientific persuasion. It also included the art of listening to the public with the aim of collecting feedback information to design a better persuasive message. James Grunig at the University of Maryland, a major theorist in public relations, has described this as the "two-way asymmetric model".

PR Counsel

In 1923, Bernays published the book *Crystallizing Public Opinion* which paved the way for the new concept of public relations. The book not only had set down the broad principles of the new profession of public relations counsel but also outlined the scope, function, methods, techniques and social responsibilities of a public relations counsel—a term that became the core of public relations practice.

Edward L. Bernays became famous in the field of public relations through his three main campaigns—(i) **Propaganda Campaign of First World War** as an arm of the US Defence Department, (ii) **Parade of Cigarette smoking debutantes** to promote the American Tobacco Company and to symbolise an act of liberation for women (iii) and the **Campaign sponsoring soap culture contests** for school-aged children to promote 'Ivory soap'. Proctor and Gamble sold its ivory soap by millions after Bernay's soap culture contests for school children were introduced.

Some of the other eminent personalities in relation to public relations are discussed in the following paragraphs.

Arthur W. Page

Arthur W. Page, who became Vice President of the American Telephone and Telegraph Company in 1927, is credited for establishing a new trend which is public relations is a top management function which must have an active voice in the overall management. Page also indicated that it is not press relations but it is the performance of the company that comprises its basis for public approval. In fact, he laid the foundation for the field of corporate public relations involving the management in the process of public relations.

Rex Harlow (1892–1993)

Rex Harlow, a professor at Stanford University's School of Education, taught public relations courses and conducted workshops around the nation. He is regarded as the 'Father of Public Relations Research'. Harlow also founded the American Council on Public Relations, which later became the Public Relations Society of America.

Elmer Davis (1890–1958)

President Franklin D. Roosevelt appointed Elmer Davis as the Head of the Office of War Information during the Second World War. Davis mounted a larger public relations campaign to promote the sale of war bonds, gain press support for war time rationing and spur higher productivity among American workers to win the war. The Voice of America was established during this period to carry news of the war to all parts of the world. The film industry made a number of feature films in support of the war.

SECOND HALF OF THE 20TH CENTURY

However, public relations in the USA witnessed an upswing in its growth only during the second half of the 20th century and it became part of America's economic, political and social development. Wilcox et al. (2005) identified five reasons of public relations growth:

1. Major increases in urban and suburban populations
2. The growth of a more impersonalised society represented by big business, big labour and big government
3. Scientific and technological advances including automation and computerisation
4. The communications revolution in terms of mass media
5. Bottom-line financial considerations often replacing the more personalised decision-making of a previous more genteel society.

Dialogic Model

In 2000, the public relations academicians and practitioners began to evolve a new philosophy of public relations practice as 'Relationship Management', the bottom-line being that public relations practitioners are in the field of fostering relationships with an organisation's various stakeholders. This involves active, interactive and equal participants of an ongoing communication process of an organisation—balancing the views of the management and the various publics. The relationships management has resulted in the **Dialogic Model of Public Relations**. The World Wide Web became an important tool of dialogic public relations. The web is used to communicate directly with public by offering real-time discussions, feedback loops, places to post comments, sources for organizational information and postings of organisational member biographies and contact information.

American business and industry turned to public relations counsel for audience analysis, strategic planning, issues of management and even the creation of conducive environment for selling of products and services. Mass media also became more complex and sophisticated.

Specialists in media relations who understood how the media worked were also in demand. Since 1960, the number of public relations practitioners has increased dramatically to about 200,000 nation-wide. The latest estimate from the US Department of labour predicts that public relations will be one of the fastest growing fields and that there will be a demand for public relations experts and managers.

Six Stages of PR in USA

In conclusion, public relations in the USA emerged from propaganda and passed through the stages of

1. Press agentry
2. Dissemination of public information
3. Persuasive communication (two-way asymmetric model)
4. Involving the public in corporate policy and to generate public goodwill—two-way symmetrical public relations model
5. Public relations as a strategic management function. To support all management functions through strategic identification of all types of publics and issues of management leading to relationship management and reputation management based on social responsibility
6. The last but not the least, the public relations practice entered dialogic model with the World Wide Web in the centre stage

However, the present-day public relations practice in the US represents different models. But all models of linear progression must result in future in an effective integrated public relations communication model with equal representation to the management of an organization and the publics of the organization, where these two segments must be equal partners in the progress of a company/organisation.

FOUR US PR MODELS

James Grunig of the University of Maryland and Todd Hunt of Rutgers State University in their book *Managing Public Relations* presented a **four-model typology of public relations practice in the USA**. These four models indicate the different stages through which public relations practice developed.

1. **Press agentry/publicity model:** The purpose of this model is to disseminate information through newspapers that may be exaggerated distantly or even incomplete to hype policies, a cause, product or service. In a way, it is a type of propaganda and the communication is also one way from the sender to the receiver to help the organization, without any scope for feedback and research. Theatre, music, film companies practice this model.

2. **Public information model:** From press agentry, there developed public information model in the second stage of the growth of public relations in the early 20th century. The purpose of this model was to disseminate public information, but it was to be truthful, and accurate without any content of propaganda material. This is also one way communication from the sender to the receiver. There is a scope for fact finding in content but little audience research regarding attitudes and dispositions. This was developed by Ivy Lee from 1910 to the 1920s. Government, not-for-profit organisations and other public institutions are practicing this model even today.

3. **Two-way asymmetric model:** This model propounded by Edward L. Bernays in the 1920s is a two-way communication system from the sender to the receiver, but the power is rested with the sender whose intention is to persuade the receiver to accept and support the senders' organisation, products or services. It is in a way a scientific approach in communication, based on behavioural science and two-way communication with imbalanced effects more tilted towards the organisation. This model has a feedback information loop, but the primary purpose of the model is to help the sender of the message to understand the audience and how to persuade them. The feedback is used for manipulate purposes, i.e. to determine what public attitudes are towards the organisation and how they have to be changed.

    Research based on the principles of social science research is used in this model to design public relations programme with clear objectives and also to know whether the objective has been accomplished or not. Marketing and advertising agencies in competitive business and public relations departments are still practicing this model which is better than the earlier public information model, which was only one way.

4. **Two-way symmetric public relations model:** In the 1960s, the USA was confronted with certain basic issues such as Vietnam War Protests, the Civil Rights Movement and the Environmental Movement. In addition, corporations and industry wanted that the corporate policies must be developed in tune with the pulse and needs of the customers. The issue management, on the one hand, and the development of corporate policy to suit the needs of public, on the other hand, forced a new approach in public relations management where it had to generate public understanding and public goodwill for issues and corporate policies. It was during this period that the managements of various business organisations and even the government departments developed a new concept. The concept was that it would be more useful to have rapport and interactions with each segment of public to assess their viewpoints and evolve corporate and public policies acceptable to them. James

Grunig again categorised this approach as a two-way symmetric model where both parties are capable of being persuaded to adjust and modify their attitudes and behaviours according to the needs as a result of public relations effort/programme. The element of dialogue is more in this model. Another development over earlier models is that formative research is used in this model mainly to understand how the public perceives the organisation and to determine what consequences organisational policies/actions might have on the public. Edward L. Bernays promoted this model, which has been used by many professionals since 1980s.

Though these four models are practiced today in varying degrees, the ideal one is the two-way symmetric model.

Table 5.1 shows the five distinct stages of the development of public relation in the USA.

TABLE 5.1 History of PR in the USA

1.	Preliminary period—an era of development of the channels of communication and exercise of PR tactics (publicity, promotion and press agentry)	1660–1779 Initial Colonization American Revolution
2.	Communicating/initiating—a time primarily of publicists, press agents, promoters and propagandists	1800–1899 Civil War, Western Expansion Industrial Revolution
3.	Reacting/responding—a period of writers hired to be spokespeople for special interests	1900–1939 Progressive Era Muckrakers—the action of publicising scandal about famous people. The word was coined by President Theodre Roosevelt in a speech (1906) alluding to the man with the Muckrake, a character in *Bunyan's Pilgrim's Progress* (muck—dirty or indecent). World War I, Roaring Twenties, Depression
4.	Planning/preventing—a maturing of PR as it began to be incorporated into the management function	1940–1979 World War II Cold War of the 1950s Consumer Movement
5.	Professionalism—an effort by PR practitioners to control PR's development, use and practice on an international level	1980—Present Global Communication

Source: Adapted from Newson et al. (2000). *This is PR: The Realities of Public Relations, Wadsworth.*

EDWARD L. BERNAYS: THE FATHER OF MODERN PUBLIC RELATIONS

Great Son

Born in 1891, Edward L. Bernays, another great son of the US, became the Father of Modern Public Relations. His name is synonymous with professional public relations practice on the one side and PR academics on the other, for he enjoyed a unique niche in the galaxy of PR professionals of the new world. A combination of practice, academics and his art of writing made him popular in the USA.

PR Counsel

Edward L. Bernays, a young man of 30, was the first to call himself a public relations counsel in 1921. Two years later, he wrote the first book on the subject "Crystallizing Public Opinion" and coined a term to describe the function that became the hard core of public relations. Not only did he write the first book, but he also taught the first college course of public relations in 1923 in New York City and laid a strong foundation for public relations academic in the United States, which spread throughout the world later.

Public Relations Term

In fact, he began his public relations practice during the First World War (1914–1918). He joined the War Department's Committee on Public Information, the propaganda arm of the US defence. However, he began his regular career in the 1920s as one of the first and most successful practitioners of public relations in America. Thus, it was around the 20th century that public relations came into being as a term as well as an occupation and an academic discipline. His vision in defining public relations as a vocation and developing its techniques exercised enormous impact.

So the entire credit for this development goes to Edward Bernays who had made all this possible.

Engineering Consent

In 1955, Bernays further defined his approach in another book titled the *Engineering of Consent* in which he gave a new description of public relations. To many, the word 'Engineering' implied manipulations through propaganda and other devices. Bernays defined his terminology and concept in the following words: "The term 'Engineering' was used advisedly. In our society, with its myriad of group interests, interest groups and media, only an engineering approach to the problems of adjustment, information and persuasion could bring effective results... "Public relations practiced as a profession is an art applied to a science in which the public interest and not pecuniary motivation is the primary consideration. The engineering of consent in this sense assumes a constructive social role." If engineering is the activity of applying scientific knowledge to the building, public relations also as a science helps build good relations between an organisation and its publics.

Who is a PR Professional?

Against this wider background, Bernays defined public relations as "the attempt by information, persuasion and adjustment to engineer public support for an activity, cause, movement or institution". He described Public Relations Manager as "a professional equipped by education, training and experience to give consent to a client or employer on relations with the public".

He had over 400 clients in his 40 years of full-time practice. They included General Electric and General Motors. Proctor & Gamble was one of Bernay's biggest clients. Its primary product was Ivory Soap.

PR Counsellor

Before World War I, he was content to call himself a press agent. When he opened his first office in 1919, he based his work on 'publicity direction'. But a year later he called himself as 'public relations counsellor'.

A unique way of Bernays was to generate events, the events generated news and the news generated a demand for whatever he happened to be selling.

Torches of Freedom

Edward L. Bernays through brilliant public relations campaigns became known as the 'Father of Modern Public Relations' in the USA. He is remembered for his unique 'Torches of Freedom' campaign for the American Tobacco Company in 1929, climaxed by a parade of cigarette smoking debutantes, young upper class women, down fifth avenue, New York City on Easter Sunday that recast smoking as an act of liberation for women and helped convince a generation of women to light up in public.

Lucky Strikes

American Tobacco Company's fastest growing brand was 'Lucky Strikes'. George Washington Hill, the head of the American Tobacco Company, became obsessed with the prospect of winning over the large potential female market for Luckies. "It will be like opening a new Gold Mine right in our front yard," he said. So he hired Edward L. Bernays for promoting 'Lucky Strikes' among women.

In 1929, George Hill summoned Bernays and said, "How can we get women to smoke on the streets. They are smoking indoors, but damn it if they spend half the time outdoors and we can get them to smoke outdoors, we will damn double our female market. Do something and act."

Edward L. Bernays developed a theory which was very simple. Slimness was coming into vogue and cigarettes could be sold to the public especially to women, as a fat-free way to satisfy their hunger. He coined a slogan 'Reach For a Lucky Strike Instead of a Sweet'. Hill loved the way Bernays used the anti-sweets campaign to promote Luckies but that only whetted his appetite to crack the female market. "The benefits of tobacco are: (1) it is a pleasure; (2) a good laxative after breakfast; (3) checks obesity by lessening the appetite; (4) aids nutrition by stimulating the secretory functions of stomach; (5) it aids contemplation. Nicotine is, of course, poison. So is coffee or tea."

Cigarettes which are equated with men became torches of freedom; an idea developed why not organise a parade of prominent women lighting cigarettes as their torches of freedom. And do it on Easter Sunday, a holiday, symbolizing freedom of spirit on Fifth Avenue, America's most prestigious promenade.

So Edward Bernays gathered a list of 30 debutantes from a friend at vogue and then sent each of them a telegram signed by his secretary Bertha Hunt. "In the interest of equality of the sexes and to fight another sex taboo, I and other young women will light another torch of freedom by smoking cigarettes while strolling on Fifth Avenue Easter Sunday" the dispatch explained. "We are doing this to combat the silly prejudice that the cigarette is suitable for the home, the restaurant, the taxicab, the theatre lobby, but never, no, never for the sidewalk. Women smokers and their escorts will stroll from Forty-Eighth Street to Fifty-Fourth Street on Fifth Avenue between Eleven-Thirty and one O' clock".

A similar appeal was made through an advertisement in New York newspapers signed by Ruith Hale, a leading feminist and the wife of New York World Columnist Heywood Brown. The object of the event it explained would be to generate stories that for the first time women had smoked openly on the street.

March of Women

The actual march went off more smoothly than even its scrip writing had imagined. Bernays persuaded the New York debutantes to conceal cigarettes while taking part in the early Easter Day parade. At a given moment, then all lit up. Newspapers and photographers had been alerted and event received exclusive press coverage.

Ten young women turned out, marching down Fifth Avenue with their lighted 'torches of freedom' and the newspapers leveled it. Two column pictures showed elegant ladies with floppy hats and fur-trimmed coats, cigarettes held self consciously by their sides, as they paraded down the wide boulevard. Despatches ran next day generally on page in papers all over the country.

Impact

During the following days, women were reported to be taking to the streets, lighted cigarettes in hand, in Boston and Detroit, and San Francisco. Women clubs, meanwhile, were enraged by the spectacle, and for weeks afterward, editorial writers churned out withering prose, *pro* and *con*.

The uproar he had touched off proved enlightening to Bernays. "Age-old customs, I learned, could be broken down by a dramatic appeal, disseminated by the network of media", he wrote in his memories. As a result of this campaign, Edward Bernays became known around the world as the Father of Public Relations.

The Torches of Freedom campaign remains a classic in the world of public relations, one still cited in classrooms and boardrooms as an example of ballyhoo at its most brilliant and more important of creative analysis of social symbols and how they can be manipulated.

Ethics

To be fair, there is an disagreement in the public relations community even today on what level of masking a client's identity is permissible as contemporary controversies over cigarette promotions make clear and there was far less consensus when Bernays was working for American Tobacco.

Edward Bernays Torches of Freedom stunt in 1929 was one of the most celebrated public relations events of the 20th century. It was designed to make cigarette smoking acceptable to women and features in many books and TV histories of PR. In most accounts Bernay's work is accepted uncritically as a brilliant PR stunt and a triumph of the public relations effort.

However, people see Bernays as a 'Master Manipulator' that they seldom pause for thought.

Although he retired from full-time consultancy, Bernays continued to write and give interviews and lecture about his favorite theme as a profession and an applied social science. He was widely acknowledged in his lifetime as the Father of Modern Public Relations. One historian even described him as 'the first and doubtlessly the leading ideologist of public relations'. The "LIFE" magazine cited Bernays as one of the 100 most important Americans of the twentieth century, a benchmark tribute. He counselled actors, Presidents, large corporations and government.

Edward L. Bernays, a legendary figure with a career spanning three quarters of a century, died in 1995 at the age of 103. His image endures and the discipline he fashioned for succeeding generations prevails. Three cheers to Bernays.

POINTS TO REMEMBER

1. Public relations in America began in 17th century when publicity war was carried out through booklets and leaflets offering free land to people who were willing to migrate to America. Public relations also played a key role in the American independence from British.

2. Ivy Ledbetter Lee, a pioneer of public relations, opened the first publicity Bureau in 1900 with a declaration of principles as "public be informed" which marked the beginning of a new model in public relations.

3. President Woodrow Wilson established United States Committee on public information, a propaganda Agency with George Creel as its head to organize public relations campaign and unite the nation and to influence the world opinion during the First World War (1918).

4. Edward L. Bernays, regarded as the Father of modern American public relations, authored a book *Crystallising Public Opinion* in 1923 that paved the way for the new concept of public relations —Two-Way Asymmetric PR model.

5. Arthur W. Page in 1927 established a new trend, i.e Corporate public relations involving the management.

6. James Grunig and Todd Hunt in their book *Managing Public Relations* presented four models of public relations:
   1. Press Agentry/Publicity model
   2. Public Information model

3. Two-way Asymmetric model
4. Two-way Symmetric model

7. Edward L. Bernays (1891–1995) is an icon of American public relations whose "Parade of Cigarette Smoking Debutantes" to promote American Tobacco Company to symbolise as an act of Liberation for women became historical.

REVIEW QUESTIONS

1. Describe the genesis of public relations in USA. What was the contribution of Ivy Lee, George Creel and Arthur W. Page?
2. Discuss Edward L. Bernays as the Father of American Modern Public Relations?

Strategy

Strategy

✓ Strategic Public Relations

✓ Public Relations Process: Four Stages

✓ PR Departments and PR Agencies

✓ Crisis Management: PR Centre Stage

✓ Public Relations and the Law

✓ Standards and Ethics in Public Relations

✓ PR Professional Organisations

Strategic Public Relations

CONTENTS

- PR as a Strategic Management Function
- Difference between Strategy and Tactics
- Boundary Spanning and Systems Theory in PR
- Is PR a Staff Function? Distinction between Line and Staff Functions

PR AS A STRATEGIC MANAGEMENT FUNCTION

Management is the process of getting things done with and through others; a manager is one who accomplishes the group objective by directing the efforts of others. It has also been defined as a process of decision-making, designing, strategic plans, controlling and co-ordinating activities to achieve organisational goals. Management scholar Henri Fayol described 'management is to forecast and plan, to organize, to command and to control' (1949).

Management Dimensions

Every organisation is run by the principles of management. The Chief Executive officer and the Directors of the Board constitute the top management who not only design plans for the company but also oversee its implementation. Management by nature of its functions in any institution takes different dimensions to accomplish the mission of the organisation or to reach its goal. Various types of management are as follows:

- Human Resource Management
- Financial Management
- Materials Management
- Production Management
- Marketing Management
- Business Management
- Office Management
- Industrial Relations Management

- Operations Management
- Communications Management
- Media Relations Management
- Crisis Management
- Public Relations Management

What is Strategy?

J.L. Thompson (1995) defined strategy as "a means to an end". Here the ends represent the vision, mission and goals of an organization. It is the strategy, a plan of a corporate body that accomplishes the objectives of an organization. Benett (1996) described strategy as "the direction that the organization chooses to follow in order to fulfil its mission".

In view of the global competitive marketing, Mintzberg et al. (1998) gave five uses of the word strategy:

1. A plan as a consciously intended course of action
2. A ploy as a specific manoeuvre intended to outwit an opponent or a competitor
3. A pattern representing a stream of actions
4. A position as a means of locating an organization in an environment
5. A perspective as an integrated way of perceiving the world

As there are different dimensions of management, the functional strategies contribute to the success of different management disciplines in decision-making.

Denny Griswold defines "Public relations is the management function, which evaluates public attitudes, identifies the policies and procedures of an organization with the public interest, and executes a programme of action to earn understanding and acceptance". The concept of strategy also applies to public relations management. Strategic public relations is concerned with managing relationships between an organization and a variety of stakeholders.

Public relations management as a process of developing harmonious relationships between an organisation and internal and external publics supports all management functions in achieving corporate goals. Therefore, public relations is called a strategic management function. In fact, an organisation seeks to manage its relationships with its stakeholders as well as the environment through identifying problems, responding to them and making necessary adaptations. Public relations here contributes as the corporate 'eyes and ears' for managing environmental interactions. Public relations helps the management with its fourfold functions—analyst, advisor, advocate and antenna. It anticipates the issues as they develop and also prepares solutions to solve them.

Relationships Management

Public relations as a two-way conduit provides the key linkages between the organisation and its subordinate strategic development and holds the organisation together and links the strategies at the corporate level. In the process, public relations embraces all relationships within and outside the organisation by undertaking the following:

- Employee relations
- Investor relations
- Customer relations
- Media relations
- Relations in crisis situations

As such public relations as a strategic management function will serve the strategies covering corporate goals, communication plans, corporate responsibility and all other relationships with both internal and external publics. These harmonious relationships undoubtedly not only create mutual understanding but also accomplish corporate goals. As a management discipline, public relations is to be found in all types of organizations. All these PR actions are undertaken under a strategy evolved by the management. As a measure to guide PR practitioners in strategy, the Public Relations Society of America launched a quarterly journal The Public Relations Strategist.

Areas where other departments consult PR manager

Public relations is a strategic management function. Like other functions of top management, public relations deals with the management as a two-way communication process to build good relationships with the public. In this process, the managers of other departments, say, HRD or Marketing, will have to consult the public relations professionals.

There are **five areas** in which a manager has to talk with the public relations manager. These are as follows:

1. To obtain advice from an expert about a communication problem
2. For help in communicating externally, say, with a supplier, investor or customer
3. To facilitate or mediate internal communication between units and employees
4. To bring news and views from outside through feedback mechanism
5. To undertake marketing communication

Tactics

What is a tactic? It is a method, a skilful device, a tool of influence and persuade and an important communication activity to achieve a particular corporate objective. The art of moving soldiers and military equipment during war in order to win the battle comes under the category of tactics. Press release is a good example of tactic. Tactics are also known as techniques and actions for achieving PR objectives. Tactics include: Written, Spoken, Visual and Audio-Visual. In fact, tactics emerge out of the strategy evolved by the management. In the cycle of planning, tactics come after strategy. Public Relations Society of America in 1994 started a monthly' Relations Tactics' for the benefit of practitioners.

Here are a few PR tactics, which are arranged media-wise. Each medium has its own tactics.

1. **Newspapers or the press**
   - Press release
   - Feature article
   - Press conference
   - Press tour
   - Press briefing—one-to-one briefing
   - Press interview
   - Backgrounder—success story

2. **New media**
   - Internet—Intranet
   - e-mail
   - e-press release
   - e-journal
   - website
   - blog, twitter, facebook

3. **Corporate publications**
   - House journal, Newsletter
   - Annual report
   - Posters, calendars
   - Brochures, flyers, leaflets
   - Direct mail

4. **Broadcast media**
   - Talks
   - Panel discussions
   - Features
   - News

5. **Films**
   - Documentary films
   - News magazines
   - Quickies
   - Animation film

DIFFERENCE BETWEEN STRATEGY AND TACTICS

Strategy and Tactics are the two sides of a coin. If the strategy is a plan designed to achieve a particular long-term objective, (eradication of pulse polio disease), the tactics are methods used as short-term measures not only to put the strategy on the ground, but also to accomplish the objective. The most important tactic used in pulse polio immunisation campaign was the appointment of the movie icon Amitabh Bachchan as Goodwill Ambassador for polio campaign. Twenty-four lakh vaccinators visited over 20 crore households. In the process the World Health Organisation declared India as a pulse polio free country. Strategy and tactics are intertwined and that no PR activity can be implemented without a strategy.

The public Relations Society of America, therefore, brings out two separate magazines—one for PR Strategy, the Public Relations Strategist and the second one for PR Tactics as The Public Relations Tactics.

PR as Top Management Function

If public relations is a strategic management function to evolve communication strategy for the corporation, PR professionals must have a place on the Board of Directors on par with finance, marketing or HRD. But a majority of PR practitioners in India are performing the technicians' role at a tactical level, implementing the communication tasks defined by CEO or other Heads of Departments of Finance, Marketing or HRD. They operate only as operation partners but not strategic partners.

PR in Designing Strategy

With PR as part of the top management team, the CEOs' job becomes easier, if PR head performs threefold roles as a strategic partner.

1. The PR team headed by Director can develop strategic communication plan and make it work through internal and external public relations process and media relations of internal and external publics.
2. The Head of PR will bring feedback information as collected from third parties to the CEO and the Board Room.
3. The Director PR has to create PR consciousness in every employee from top to bottom (Chairman to Watchman) that they have a responsibility to commit themselves to meet the organisational goals on the one side and to promote company's reputation on the other.

However, the CEO will be the visible symbol of the corporation with public face. He/she is an exemplary leader, visionary and embodiment of the organization, who, among other things, also guides PR function.

The success of communication strategy depends on how well we communicate with the key stakeholders, employees, shareholders, the financial community, government, industrial houses, suppliers, dealers, customers, media and the general community. As a result, many corporations are now investing in corporate communication efforts which ensure that their good deeds are communicated to the right audiences and when negative things get highlighted and middle course actions are taken to adjust the policies. Therefore, CEOs in the future are likely to play a more active role in setting communication goals for their corporations, as well as insisting on measurable programmes to achieve these goals. More and more of them will set aggressive benchmarks on which they will build their corporate reputation goals.

If public relations is given a place on the Board Room, public relations in India will not only have a right to be part of the organisation's decision-making process but also be indispensable to the CEO of a company. Public relations will then enter into a new era of professional excellence.

BOUNDARY SPANNING AND SYSTEMS THEORY IN PR

The concepts of boundary spanning and the systems theory have a close linkage with public relations management in promoting relationships and mutual understanding between an organization and its stakeholders. Four important words constitute this question—boundary, spanning, public relations and systems. If you study the literary meaning of each of the following words, one will understand the concept of boundary spanning in the context of public relations.

- **Boundary** means border or limits of an area or an organisation.
- **Spanning** is measuring the distance or the environment of an organisation.
- **Public relations** is a bridge of communication between an organisation and its publics.
- **System** is an interconnecting network within an organisation.

Boundary Spanning

What is boundary spanning? If you combine the above four words as applied to an organisation, one will come to know that boundary spanning means—measuring the within and outside organisational environment so that the system could work well in tune with the mindset of the public. Who does boundary spanning? Public relations as a two-way communication process does the boundary spanning to keep the management informed of the prevailing environment.

Boundary spanning as a process of an organisation's environment analysis emerges from systems theory. As such there is a close linkage between systems theory, public relations and boundary spanning. In fact, the concept of public relations as a boundary spanning function started only from the systems theory, which has been used by organisational theorists to explain the structure and working of organisations as well as their interactions with their social environment.

Systems Theory and Public Relations

What is a system? A system is defined as sets of interacting parts or subsystems which affect one another as well as all the functioning of the organisation as a whole. Scott M. Cullip defined a system as a "set of interacting units which endures through time within an established boundary of responding and adjusting to change pressure from the environment in order to achieve and maintain goal states".

Denny Griswold defined public relations as "the management function which evaluates public attitudes, identifies the policies and procedures of an individual or an organisation with the public interest, and executes a programme of action to earn understanding and acceptance".

The systems theory describes an organization as a set of parts (or subsystems) that interact within a boundary and which together respond and adjust to the organization's environment that is outside the boundary. Systems theory also underlines the role of public relations because it stipulates that an organization's progress is dependent on establishing and maintaining relationships both within the boundary and with its environment outside the boundary. As such the systems theory articulates the contribution of public relations as part of strategic management approach.

If a system is an interacting unit which enables the organisation to sustain, by adjusting to external environment process, public relations also promotes mutually dependent relationships between an organisation and its publics environment and behaviour. From this systems theory, public relations managers are usually considered as performing a boundary spanning function. White and Dozier define boundary spanners as "individuals within the organisation who frequently interact with organisation's internal and external environment and who not only gather and select but also relay information from the environment to the management (decision-makers in the organisation)". Boundary spanners are also described as 'exchange agents' between an organisation and its environment.

Since public relations acts as a bridge between an organisation and its public, it ensures that public relations professionals help support the other subsystems of the organisation to communicate across the boundaries of the organisation with both external public and other subsystems within the organisation.

Grunig and Hunt (1984), suggest that typically an organisational system might consist of five major subsystems: (i) the production subsystem; (ii) the disposal subsystem (marketing and distribution function); (iii) the maintenance subsystem (coordinating) the work of employees—personnel and training function; (iv) the adaptive subsystem (helping organisation adapt to change—R&D function); and (v) the management subsystem (control and integration of the systems).

In this systems model, public relations is seen as a part of the management subsystem of an organisation, no doubt it may support other subsystems such as the production subsystem or distribution subsystem. This theoretical organisational systems model is illustrated in Figure 6.1.

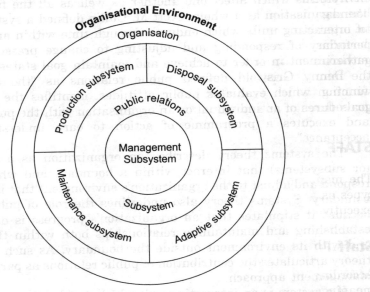

FIGURE 6.1 A generic view of organisational subsystems and of the location of the public relations subsystem Source: Adapted from Grunig and Hunt (1984). Source: Adapted from Gruning and Hunt (1984)]

The basic principle of dividing an organisation, according to this model, into a number of interacting subsystems can be applied to virtually any organisation irrespective of its size and complexity. This will develop important linkage between organisational departments and functions as well as the organisation as a whole and the key external groups.

Environmental Scanning

Public relations practice in its boundary spanning role helps keep an organisation aware of the changes taking place in its environment and, thus, helps it to adapt or adjust to the changing conditions it may confront. Public relations managers as boundary spanners can play a pivotal role in facilitating the transmission of information from across organisational boundaries to decision-makers in the management. This is popularly known as **environmental scanning** and is described as "the varied information gathering, analysis and dissemination activities that organisations pursue in order to keep up to date with changes in the organisational environment".

In the process, in their role as boundary spanners, the public relations practitioners act as exchange agents, between an organisation and its environment, and perform three functions: **information gathering, information processing** and **information feeding** of external environment. They act as collectors, filters and disseminators. As such boundary spanning by public relations is an important function useful to organisational decision-making. In this capacity, public relations performs a strategic role, both acting as an intelligence capacity—gathering feedback information from the environment—and counselling the management to explain their policies to external publics, thus winning the acceptance and support for the organisational mission and goals through sub-systems.

STAFF FUNCTIONS AND LINE FUNCTIONS

The management in any organisation divides its staff into two broad types as **staff executives** and **line executives** who perform different executives functions.

Staff Functions

According to Oxford Advanced Learner's Dictionary, staff has two meanings—one is workers employed in an organization, and the other meaning is a long stick used as a support in walking or climbing as a weapon. The Webster's Collegiate Dictionary describes the staff as the officers chiefly responsible for the internal operations of an institution or business, a group of officers appointed to assist a civil executive, or the personnel who assist a Director in carrying out an assigned task. Staff function also has been defined as "an organizational function that carries no direct executive power over the primary operational process, but that fulfils an advisory role to other functions within the organization." Staff function is pursuit of management objectives through suggestions, advice and recommendations of staff executives. Public relations is a staff function as it helps management in designing public relations communication strategy. In sum, staff executives function in the corporate office to assist CEO in designing strategy.

Line Functions

What is line function? Line executives are those who function on production line or field operational line. For example, a Lineman in power distribution company is the lowest employee who maintains or repairs the power lines at the grassroots. In army the combatant forces as distinguished from the staff corps and supply services fight in the front. Line function is pursuit of management objectives through a supervision, delegation of authority and work assignment to the field staff who are on the production or operational line. A General Manager of a textile company with powers vested in him or her can delegate authority, set production targets, appoint employees and directly supervise the work of all those involved in production line to attain the set target. The staff who actually produce are line executives. In contrast, staff executives have a little or no direct authority on line executives but they indirectly influence the work of line executives through suggestions and advices.

Military Origin

The line and staff principle of management which had originated in the military has been extended to most organisations in both public and private sectors. Military forces have long recognised the importance of maintaining unity and direct line of command. Staff officers in armed forces are attached at various levels to assist the Army Commander in the exercise of his position as commander and win the war. Here staff executives command no one but assist the commander in evolving a strategy and commanding every one. Thus, the staff-line function began in the military organisation.

In like manner, the staff executives assist the Chief Executive in corporations who is the line officer and actually sets policy and has the authority to see that the task of the organisation is accomplished. In an industry, for example, manufacturing product and profit making functions, such as engineering, production and distribution, are line functions.

Staff functions are those that advise and assist the line executives from CEO to General Manager—staff executives represent finance, legal, human resources, marketing and public relations. These functions became more and more necessary as organisations increased in size and complexity. Line executives have authority and responsibility to see that the work gets done, but they need assistance in the form of plans, advice and suggestions from staff executives. The job of staff officer is to advise top management and to support and assist the line officers.

Is PR a Staff or Line Function?

Public relations is a staff function, one of several that serve to advise the top management in evolving public relations communication strategy to maintain mutual understanding between an organisation and its publics. As such public relations professionals must understand the staff role to act as an advisor to the company.

Public relations practitioners are experts in communication, while line managers including Chief Executive Officer rely on the staff executives to use their skills in preparing and processing data, making recommendations and executing public relations communication programmes to achieve organisation goals.

Open House

If public relations research finds that the people have no understanding of what the company manufactures, the public relations department as staff function can recommend to the management to organise an Open House Programme at which product demonstrations, tours and entertainment could be featured. In organising the open house, the public relations department has no direct authority to implement the scheme suggested. But, top management, as line managers, have the authority to direct all departments to cooperate in the organisation of an open house. Such open house would undoubtedly bring the company and the public closer for a better understanding. Organising an open house at the ground level is a line function.

Access to Management

Though public relations is a staff function of advising the top management, its influence is of high order because of its close access to top management. That is why public relations, as well as other staff functions like human resources, marketing, are located high in the organisational chart and are called upon by top management to make recommendations on problems affecting the company.

Public Relations Role

Staff public relations practitioners who are employees of commercial or non-profit organisations or of departments of government such as Local, State or Central services perform specialised tasks of communications in their organisations. Public relations personnel have the role of being always in the middle—pivoted between their employers and the publics. This role in the middle is a specialty of public relations profession to act as eyes and ears of both the employer and the public concerned.

POINTS TO REMEMBER

1. Management is the process of getting things done through people. It has been defined as a process of decision-making, designing strategic plans, controlling and coordinating activities to achieve goals.

2. Management has different dimensions such as human resource management, financial management, marketing management, business management, materials management, production management, etc. Similarly, public relations management which promotes relationships between an organisation and its publics is another facet of management.

3. Like other management functions, public relations is also a strategic management function to develop and promote harmonious relationships between an organisation and its internal and external publics and also to support all other management functions with communication strategy in achieving corporate goals. Therefore, public relations is termed as a strategic management function.

4. There is a difference between strategy and tactics. Strategy is described as a plan designed to achieve a particular goal. The Indian Defence Force had evolved a strategy to win the Kargil war against Pakistan.

5. What is then a tactic? It is a skilful device or a method used to implement the strategy and accomplish the desired goal. Press release is a good example of public relations tactic to inform, educate and motivate the audience through newspapers. Tactics include: written, spoken, and visual tactics. Therefore, there is a direct link between strategy and tactics.

6. Public relations is a top management function like finance or human resource management. Director (PR) or Vice-President, like Director (Finance), must report to the CEO. In fact, CEO is in overall charge of organisational communication strategy whose direct involvement and commitment will yield good results in relationships management.

7. The future of public relations in India is based on a two-pronged strategy—making public relations indispensible to CEO and elevating the position of Chief of public relations to the top management level.

8. As the head of an organisation, the CEO is an exemplar, leader, visionary and embodiment of corporate culture, who among others guides public relations function. In fact, CEO is the first public relations officer of the organisation to build its reputation.

9. Boundary spanning means measuring the within and outside organisational environment so that public relations plan can be designed in tune with the mindset of the public.

10. A system is a set of interacting parts or subsystems which affect one another as well as all the functioning of the organisation as a whole. Boundary spanning, public relations and systems are interrelated in any organisation.

11. Communication is essential to all phases of the managerial process not only to integrate all the managerial functions but also to link the organisation with its internal and external environment. Therefore, other management functions such as finance, human resource, marketing consult public relations on communication problems and maintaining good relations with their respective publics.

12. The staff executives in the corporate office assist the CEO who is the line officer and actually sets policy and has the authority to see that the task of the organisation is achieved. Staff functions are those that advise and assist the line executives from CEO to General Managers. Staff executives represent Finance, HR, Marketing directors and Public relations.

13. Public relations is a staff function, one of several that serve to advise the top management in evolving public relations communication strategy. Public relations staff in the corporate office act as advisors to the company.

14. The line executives, with powers vested in them, set production targets and directly supervise the work of all those involved in production to reach the set target. However, there is a close link between the staff and line function in the operation of any organisation.

REVIEW QUESTIONS

1. Why do we call public relations as a strategic management function?

2. What is the difference between strategy and tactics?

3. Public relations is a top management function. Explain the role of a Public Relations Manager and CEO in the management of corporate public relations.

4. What do you mean by boundary spanning in public relations? Explain with examples.

5. What are the major areas where other departments would consult a public relations manager?

6. Is public relations a staff function? Distinguish between line and staff functions in relation to public relations profession.

Public Relations Process: Four Stages

CONTENTS

Public relations is the management of a two-way communication process. The word 'management' clearly indicates that public relations is not an 'ad-hoc' activity. All principles of management are equally applicable to public relations practice. What is management? It is a process of decision-making, formulating strategic plans, controlling and coordinating activities to achieve organisational goals.

PR PRACTICE

Public relations as a management function deals with activities such as:

- Two-way communication process
- Promotion of corporate mission, services, products and reputation
- Creating mutual understanding between an organisation and its publics

In other words, public relations involves a whole lot of communication process where a corporation speaks to its public and the public seeks to listen to the corporation as beneficiaries of organisational services or products. It is this communication process that makes each other understand better. Inherent in all this is that public relations professionals must know how these activities are planned and managed effectively in a structured way to the advantage of both the organisation and the public concerned.

PR POLICY

There are two prerequisites for successful public relations practice. One is *public relations structure* within the organisation and the other is *public relations policy*. The key requirement for a public relations practice is organisational public relations policy which has to be spelt out in clear-cut terms. This policy should define the areas of public relations programmes. The idea of policy is not to control or restrict but to give guidelines on areas of operation and responsibilities for the public relations department.

Public relations policy covers broad areas such as planning, strategy, media relations, media releases, government relations, comment on decision-making, identification of opportunities for favourable publicity, actions with prior clearance from the CEO.

Grounding a public relations programme can be an overwhelming task. It is not a press button operation. A systematic and scientific approach is needed. But as with any project, the secret of success lies in advanced planning and effective implementation. Planning and managing a public relations campaign encourage practitioners to consider carefully how programmes should begin and continue in a scientific way to benefit both the organisation and the public relations practice itself.

How do we create mutual understanding and mutual trust, or how do we practice public relations to create and sustain mutual understanding? It is a long drawn process, and must be researched, planned and provided for through an exchange of information and opinions. Such type of job is handled by a professional public relations manager who assumes the role of an analyst, advisor, advocate (communicator) and antenna (evaluator). One has to follow the four-stage PR process to perform the four roles.

RPCE MODEL: FOUR STAGES OF PR PROCESS

The four-stage public relations process is also called **RPCE model** as detailed here:

1. **R for 'research' or fact-finding:** In the first stage of public relations process, the internal and external environment of an organisation is analysed to elicit public opinion, public reactions, public attitudes towards policies and actions of an organisation. This stage answers two things: what is happening? and what is the problem confronting the organisation? In this process, the role of a public relations professional is that of an 'analyst'.

2. **P for 'planning':** Based on the environmental analysis and identified problems, necessary action plans, programmes have

to be designed and planned for solution to the issues. Here the public relations practitioner assumes the role of an 'advisor', to tell the management what should be done and how can it be done. Action plans must be designed.

3. **C for 'communication (implementation):** How should the action plan be implemented? All the programmes, services formulated have to be grounded with appropriate messages to reach the target audience. Communication and action plans have to move hand-in-hand for better impact. This stage answers: what is the communication strategy? What should be the media mix? The role of public relations practitioner in this process is that of an 'advocate' (communicator) to plead and communicate the messages in the court of target public.

4. **E for 'evaluation'.** The last but very important step in public relations practice is 'evaluation' or measurement of results of the programme implemented. Without evaluation process, the entire public relations programme will be a futile exercise. We do not know the results. Therefore, the evaluation answers: How did we do? What is the impact of public relations programmes?

Each of these steps is important in the public relations practice. However, the integration, overlapping and coordination of all the four steps must be kept in mind as part of the whole public relations programme for academic and practical discussion. While implementing a public relations programme or a campaign, each step can be divided into sub-steps for more clarity and better impact.

Table 7.1 gives the four-stages public relations process with four roles of public relations practitioner.

Table 7.1 Four-stages Public Relations Process with Four Roles of a Public Relations Practitioner.

1. PR Activity			
Research or Fact-finding	Planning Programme	Communication or Implementation	Evaluation/ Measurement
2. Role of public relations manager			
Analyst	Advisor	Advocate	Antenna

RESEARCH—THE FIRST STEP

The first step in the public relations process is research or fact-finding to elicit public opinion and their reactions towards policies and programmes of the organisation and also to identify the problems confronting the organisation. This step in other words is also known as 'situation analysis' or fact-finding.

As eyes and ears of an organisation, the public relations department not only tells the people, but also listens to them to gain insights of their feelings for guidance and action. Research findings can be used to generate goodwill and influence public.

According to a few experts in communication, the Soviet Union and its Communist Party collapsed because they only used the principle "Tell the People". They never observed the concept to 'Listen' to the people's problems. Therefore, research as a first step in public relations describes what is happening and what is the problem.

How does one undertake research? There are many research weapons to discover facts. Such techniques and tools include: primary research, (original survey, observation) and secondary research (books, online data basis, Internet). Personal contacts, content analysis, interviews, advisory committees, the call-in telephone line, mail analysis, media monitoring, cross-sections surveys, mail questionnaires, personal observations, informal interactions, institutional feedback mechanism are the other tools of research.

PEST Analysis

Here, **P** represents Political; **E**–Economic, **S**–Social and **T**–Technological. A commonly used and immensely valuable technique of research is the PEST analysis. PEST divides the overall environment of an organisation into four broad areas such as **political, economic, social** and **technological**.

The PEST analysis provides the environmental factors, affecting an organisation, to tackle such problems through public relations techniques. Some organisations are affected by one of the four PEST areas than others.

For example, political factors affected the US-based Enron's Power Project in Maharashtra. Political context is of vital importance to multinational corporations. By carrying out a thorough PEST analysis, it is possible to identify the significant issues likely to affect an organisation from political, economic, social and technological angles.

SWOT Analysis

Here, S represents–Strength; W–Weakness, O–Opportunities and T–Threats. Another way that helps fact-finding is **SWOT** analysis. The first two factors—**Strengths** and **Weaknesses** can be seen as internal factors and are concerned with the organisation. The other two—**Opportunities** and **Threats** are usually external and will have to be largely identified through the PEST analysis. It is sometimes essential to list the positive and negative elements confronting the organisation. SWOT analysis provides opportunities for public relations to design programmes. The four elements can be seen as mirror segments in a quadrant. A brief example is given here.

The Public Relations Department of the Municipal Corporation of Hyderabad made a SWOT analysis of various problems. People commented on the unclean areas, stray dogs menace, beggars nuisance (particularly leper patients), encroachment on footpaths by petty traders. They opined that the Corporation must take the responsibility to attend to such problems on priority basis.

In the research conducted by the Municipal Corporation of Hyderabad, among many other civic problems, the most important one that came to light was about stray dogs menace. As many as 200 persons used to be the victims of dog bites every day and about 25 people died of rabies every year. There were over 10,000 stray dogs in the twin cities of Hyderabad and Secunderabad in 1975. Such an important problem was identified by research and fact-finding mission. The role of individual public relations practitioner in this process is described as an 'analyst'.

PLANNING—THE SECOND STEP

The second step in the public relations process, after research, is planning a programme for its implementation. A good public relations programme is a prerequisite for the accomplishment of organisational goals. Careful planning prevents haphazard and ineffective communication. This stage primarily answers the question 'what should we do and why?' It involves a comprehensive public relations plan to solve the identified problem in the research stage, with objectives, target audience, programmes, resources, media strategy and selection of ways and means for putting the whole plan into action.

From the threads of fact-finding and identification of problems, the public relations manager must evolve a comprehensive plan to solve the problems through the following sub-steps in the backdrop of organisation's goals. Such a plan is also very useful in launching any PR campaign.

Setting Objectives

Management by setting objectives is the popular approach in reacting to the organisational goals. Setting realistic objectives is absolutely necessary if public relations programme is to achieve tangible results. The kinds of objectives public relations campaigns can have are: to inform, to educate and to motivate the people; to understand problems and participate in the programme/campaign.

Seven Golden Rules

Anne Gregory in her book *The Art and Science of Public Relations,* Volume 2, 2000 says that there are seven imperatives that must be borne in mind while setting objectives. They are discussed in the ensuing paragraphs:

PR objectives

There is a tendency among public relations professionals to set objectives that public relations cannot deliver. It is not reasonable to say that public relations should increase sales by 20 per cent. That depends on the sales force, but not public relations. However, it is reasonable to say that presentation of the new product should be made to 50 per cent of the key retailers, to tell them about the product and to encourage them to try it. It may well be that as a result, sales may increase by 20 per cent—but it is outside the scope of public relations to promise this.

Ally to organisational objectives

Public relations programmes and campaigns must support corporate objectives. If a corporate objective is major re-positioning of the company in the market, then the public relations effort must be directed to supporting this stance.

Be precise and specific

Objectives need to be clear. To create awareness is not good enough. Creating awareness of what, to whom, when, and how needs to be clearly spelt out. No element of ambiguity should be present.

Do what is achievable

It is better to set modest objectives and achieve them, than hitch one's wagon to the stars. Wherever possible, evaluate the likely benefits of idea and test the pilot schemes. If a major part of the programme is to contact all investors to inform them of a particular development, you must be sure you do it within the framework of the stock market rules.

Quantify as much as possible

Not all objectives are precisely quantifiable, but most of them are. If you aim to contact particular audience groups, say how many. Quantifying objectives make evaluation much easier.

Work within the budget

This goes without saying that one should work with the allotted budget. It is no good claiming to be creative, and not make money. A good planner and manager knows exactly how much the things will cost, and will run budget tracking programmes.

Work to a priority list

Public relations professionals always have too much to do and they can extend their list of activities without an end. They should know what their priorities are and stick to them irrevocably. If a professional has to work on non-prioritised work, then he should make sure to let the superiors know the consequence of their demands. Prioritising objectives enables one to seek where the major effort is to be focused. Examples of workable objectives are as follows:

1. Inform 50 targeted investors of reasons for management buy-out.
2. Ensure 100 top dealers attend annual dealers conference.
3. Increase levered editorial coverage of service by 20 per cent.

Public relations campaign can be effective and produce tangible results only if objectives are developed in relation to identified problems. The Municipal Corporation of Hyderabad had set the objective to reduce the number of dog bite victims. But it never promised that a particular percentage of dog bites would be brought down.

Target Audience

Audience are the lifeblood of a PR campaign/programme. There are groupings of audiences that are fairly common to most organisations. Public relations public could be divided into two broad segments as **internal** (employees) and **external** (customers). In fact, the general public in public relations is a myth. We have only specific target-oriented public such as employees, shareholders, customers, media, etc. The typical target public of any organisation includes: management public, employees, trade unions, shareholders and financial public, customers, community public, opinion leaders, government, suppliers and dealers, competitors, media public. The Hyderabad city population is over 60 lakhs. Though Hyderabad city is one, the people of the city can be divided into two broad segments on the basis of their socio-economic background as urban and rural (slum dwellers), educated and illiterate. Different linguistic and religious groups live in the city which also constitute a distinct category for communication purpose.

Services and Action Plans

If the public relations programme is intended to solve problems, the management must design services and action plans for the benefit of the target audiences. Programmes that aim at producing radical shifts in behaviour and attitude will be more useful. If there are no services or qualitative products, there is no programme for the public. In fact, they are the two prerequisites for a successful public relations campaign.

In a Pulse Polio Immunisation Programme, opening of centres with adequate provision for pulse polio drops acts as a service plan. Such centres were opened at all hospitals, health clinics, bus stations, railway stations, community centres enabling the people to get their children administered polio drops on a single day. Seventeen crore children were benefited on a single day by the pulse polio immunisation campaign in 2007.

PR Programme

The next sub-step in planning after services and action plans relates to public relations programme. Organisations very often forget the communication component in many of the campaigns and development projects. In fact, eradication of information poverty is a prerequisite for the eradication of economic information poverty. Unfortunately, the removal of ignorance or information poverty is not given due importance. Therefore, public relations communication content assumes great importance in any public relations programme and services plan.

Facta non-verba is a Roman dictum, meaning 'give us deeds not words'. Action projects/services of the organisation, on the one hand, and messages of the public relations department, on the other hand, act as two eyes of corporate planning and programming.

As a strategic management function and multi-disciplinary field, public relations is applied to various sub-areas of corporate management. For instance, human resource management, financial management, operation management, marketing management, media management and crisis management. In addition, public relations department has its own major responsibility of building harmonious relationships between an organisation and its various publics, otherwise known as corporate public relations. The public relations programme, based on the action plans, must sensitise the people concerned and it takes different dimensions depending on the type of audiences. Dimensions of public relations include: employee public relations, shareholders and financial public relations, customers public relations, government relations, community relations, media relations, relations in crisis situations and, finally, reputation management.

Tactics

Mere planning will not give results. The designed programme must be accompanied by tactics to ground the plan. This is the 'nuts and bolts' part of the plan that explains in sequence the specific activities that put the strategies into operation or implementation. Tactics are the tools of communication to reach the target audiences with key messages.

What is a tactic? It is a skillful device or method used to implement the planned programme. Media provides a variety of public relations opportunities which are otherwise known as *tactics or methods*. Some of the media tactics include press conference, news release and house journal. There is a direct link between the planning and programming, and the tactics. Programme is evolved based on corporate mission such as a long-term planning, while tactics or methods are used more often as short-term measure not only to implement the plan, but also to accomplish the objectives of the plan. Mere strategic planning will not get the message across to the target audience. We need to motivate the audience towards corporate planning. The messages are communicated through various media tactics.

Dr Dough Newsom (USA) compared the public relations campaign to a 'building'. The 'floor' is the organisation's mission statement and acts as the 'foundation' to support the entire campaign and that the 'roof' is the 'budget'. 'Supporting pillars' are the methods of research that give an insight into the correct approaches to the campaign. The roof of the building is equal to the budgeting of the campaign. Without a roof, a house is not habitable. So also a public relations campaign minus budget is equal to zero. That should be kept in mind while planning a public relations programme.

The Municipal Corporation of Hyderabad while managing the campaign on 'Keep the City Clean' allocated funds for hoardings, printing, production of films, advertising, song and drama, purchase of audio-visual equipment, evaluation, staff training, media relations, etc. That was the budget allocation for the campaign.

Calendar of Operations

Four things are peculiar to a public relations practitioner's life in preparing the calendar of operation. *First*, there will never be enough time to do everything that needs to be done because the tasks and possibilities for action are always far greater than the time available. So one must decide the timing of the programme as to when it should be conducted. *Second*, since public relations tasks often involve other people and the coordination of several departments always takes longer time than one thinks initially, a proper sequence of activities must be determined. *Third*, deadlines must be fixed so that the tasks associated with a campaign can be completed on time according to calendar, to produce results. *Fourth*, the right financial resources need to be allocated so that the tasks on hand can be completed satisfactorily. Thus, the calendar of operations must contain the timing, sequence of activities, deadlines and budget allocation.

There should be a well-thought out calendar of operations that has to be worked depending on the nature of an event. Topicality may be kept in view. Any campaign on agriculture must be organised in the monsoon season so that the farmers can be fully involved. Calendars and timelines take different forms. Year-wise, month-wise, week-wise, day-wise calendars can be prepared for undertaking both media programmes (printing of posters) and service-oriented programmes (action projects).

If a public relations professional is organising a media conference, he must see that his event does not clash with other major events. So timing the event is an important ingredient in campaign planning. Therefore, media conference is a part of the calendar of operations.

COMMUNICATION—THE THIRD STEP

The third stage in public relations process relates to communication and implementation of action-oriented programmes. If public relations has to succeed, the actions must speak louder than words. Therefore, actions and communication always must move hand-in-hand for better impact. Once a problem has been identified and a programme is designed to solve the problem, it is time to step into action-oriented services with appropriate messages. Such actions and services need supportive communication to reach the target audience.

Next to planning, communication gets priority. It is because no matter how well planned a programme is, it will fail if one does not *'see it', 'hear it' or 'read it' and 'understand it'*. Therefore, to assure the reach and impact, the first order of operation is to communicate the plan through various media of communication. A media list will be helpful in preparing the media plan which contains information, a client or PR executive needs such as the circulation and audience size, demographic profiles of each entry in the plan, where it ranks as part of the overall plan and its objectives. A media plan helps make certain that the information is not just about reaching an audience, but that it is to help reach the correct audience.

In the stage of communication and services, public relations has to be managed effectively and efficiently for getting good results. How do we manage communication? It is only through an appropriate media strategy and tactics that the public is kept informed of both services and action plans designed as part of the campaign besides grounding all plans.

MEDIA STRATEGY

Devising the media strategy for a communication plan or a campaign is the most difficult part of managing public relations process. If the media strategy is right, everything rolls on the back of it. What is media strategy? It is the overall approach to the media that is designed for a programme or a campaign to reach the target audience. It is the coordinating theme or the guiding principle, the big idea, the rationale behind the tactical programme. Media strategy is dictated by problems, programmes designed and the types of public to be reached.

Communication programme of any campaign is meant to change the attitudes of both internal and external audience. Such a programme is based on persuasive messages which is an important component of a communication plan. TATA Motor's slogan for Indica car was "more car per car" or that of VSNL "we carry the voice of India to the four corners of the world", Dogs are man's Best Friends: Let us Protect them Against Rabies" are good examples of public relations messages. Another example can be taken from the India Post that has its main message on commitment to the community "India Post delivers 4.3 crore pieces of services every day linking every nook and corner of the country. No other media can match the sheer expanse of India Post in terms of volume and direct personal reach".

PR Input

Public relations programme based on the action projects encompasses all the communication activities which an organisation undertakes as part of the campaign planning. The broad elements of a public relations programme include corporate identity; corporate advertising; issues management; crisis management; public-wise public relations programme such as employee communications, customer relations, community relations; sponsorship, media-wise programme and media relations, monitoring and reviewing. All these areas of public relations as applicable to a campaign must be grounded in the communication stage.

A very clear example of media strategy and tactics can be derived from the multimedia approach adopted by Ministry of Health, Government of India in the case of Pulse Polio Immunisation Programme. (Immunisation of pulse polio for all children under the age of 0–5 and get polio free certificate.) The World Health Organisation declared India a Polio free country in 2012, thanks to the multimedia communication campaign.

Multimedia Approach

Multimedia such as inter-personal media, traditional folk media, mass media and IT new media were used to reach both urban and rural target groups. The media strategy has been designed as part of information, education and communication programme of Ministry of Health and Family Welfare.

Household Microcommunication Approach: Case Study

Among others, the success of Pulse Polio immunisation programme was very much dependent on Household Microcommunication Approach. Under the scheme, the Ministry of Health and Family Welfare has positioned over eight lakh Asha Sevaks in six lakh villages of the country to be in touch with each household and create awareness about Pulse Polio immunisation programme. If a small village has one ASHA, big villages depending on the population had more than one ASHA. They were not only given orientation in household publicity approaches but also provided with drugs for supply to families. Each Asha visited households regularly and motivated the parents to get their children administered with Pulse Polio drops. They even took the parents and children personally to the Pulse Polio centres. ASHA mixed with household as one of their family members. So also households treated ASHA as one of the members of the household. Such a good camaraderie played the role of a big motivator for the success of Pulse Polio immunisation programme in India. WHO declared India as a pulse polio free country.

Media tactics

What were media tactics? Conferences, advertising, public meetings, radio, television talks, songs, street plays, press conferences, press tours, exhibitions, processions, rallies, publications, leaflets, etc. were used as part of media strategy to influence the target audience towards pulse polio immunisation programme.

ITMN Theory of Gandhian Public Communication

The media strategy in the Indian context must be based on ITMN theory of public communication.

    I : Inter-personal media such as symposia, public meeting
    T : Traditional folk media such as music, dance, drama, street plays, songs
    M : Mass media (conventional), press, radio, TV, film
    N : New mass media which include computer, Internet, e-mail

Such a combination of four types of media is an ideal communication model to suit the communication needs of the Indian public who belong to different religious, linguistic, rural and urban background. The media mix must be elaborate and extensive as the message has to reach every part of the area and every type of target audience. Internet was not there in Gandhian Communication.

Advocate

The public relations professional becomes an advocate in the third stage like a lawyer pleading the case in the court of law. The public relations programme is implemented to keep the public informed through an effective multimedia strategy and an effective communication process.

In the process, a public relations manager acts as an 'advocate' on behalf of the organisation to convey messages to the target public group.

EVALUATION—THE FOURTH STEP

The IBDO (1994) report observed that "evaluating the effectiveness of public relations programme remains a hotly debated issued and that the public relations industry may never be fully respected unless it can provide measurement of its value". Evaluation is the rocky but sunlit pathway for public relations practitioners to 'climb', once and for all out of the 'quacks' and 'where our work is judged by instinct, gut feeling and intuition. It has also a warning that there is a 'pain' factor in submitting work to the acid test of evaluation and it is the one that both clients and consultancies are frequently inclined to dodge" (Public Relations Voice, issue 43, Jan–March 2010).

Evaluation is indeed an ongoing process of review in order to determine the effectiveness/results of the public relations programme/plan. This is normally done against the objectives designed in the public relations plan. Public relations managers can evaluate media relations programme every month based on the media coverage the organisation gets. However, PR manager can undertake the evaluation of every PR campaign to show the results/impact to the management.

If first step in the public relations process is research, the fourth or last step is evaluation. Both research and evaluation are cornerstones of a good public relations practice. The principle of research 'Before', 'During' and 'After' the campaign is the key to gauge the effectiveness of public relations programmes. Unfortunately, public relations research, though very important, is neglected. The Central Government, State Governments and Public Sector Undertakings spend crores of rupees on their various public relations programmes, including advertising. The Government of India had spent over ₹500 crore on 'India Shining' public communication campaign before the 14th Lok Sabha Election in 2004. What was the result? The common voter in India failed to identify with the campaign as villages were burning for want of drinking water, power supply and employment opportunities instead of shining. Evaluation is not taken seriously in any government sector organisation. Consequently, the impact of public relations programmes on the target audience is not known.

PR Audit

It has been the author's experience that the authorities blame public relations when things go wrong in the government. But the same authorities do not attach any importance to public relations in normal times. Public relations department also does not report to the Government the results achieved by it through public relations evaluation and reporting. Like financial audit, there should be a public relations audit at the end of every year to know how public relations budget has been spent and what are the results. One of the pitfalls confronting the public relations profession in India is the lack of public relations research and evaluation.

Public relations should be subjected to rigorous evaluation as any other activity, but its distinct characteristics have to be taken into full account when deciding how best to measure and assess the results against communication objectives. The evaluation at this stage will answer how did we do, what are the results of the public relations programme, what did we learn for the future. Evaluation logically takes us back to the first step—fact-finding or research. But evaluation focuses on the measurement of PR programme.

Role of evaluation

Evaluation also acts as a key to identify likely dangers/threats before they occur and helps public relations practitioner to advise the management for corrective measures. In sum, the evaluation focuses on PR effort, demonstrates effectiveness, ensures cost efficiency, encourages good management of PR campaign and facilitates accountability of PR discipline. It tells in brief the outcome of the PR plan and the efficiency of the PR practitioner.

Evaluation is intended to do the following:

1. Demonstrate effectiveness of the public relations programme.
2. Ensure cost-effectiveness in terms of results.
3. Facilitate accountability.
4. Measure outcomes against objectives.
5. Measure exposure of audience to media and messages.
6. Measure the impact of services and action plans.
7. Measure the image of the organisation in terms of the services and draw inferences to guide future campaign.
8. Encourage good planning.
9. Encourage good management.
10. Evolve an effective communication strategy.

Dr. G.C. Banik, former Chief General Manager, Corporate Communications, Videsh Sanchar Nigam Ltd. at a Round Table organized by the Public Relations Voice said, "Lack of standard procedure for measurement of public relations is the weak link in the practice of public relations". He opined that specific criteria for evaluating public relations programme and its effect should be clearly stated in the objectives itself that will guide programme preparation as well as implementation.

Evaluation Methods

The research is undertaken to measure the effectiveness of public relations through different methods. They are summarised as follows:

1. Formal research
2. Informal research
3. Questionnaire
4. Interview
5. Observation
6. Website

Formal research

A formal research may be divided into two categories as qualitative and quantitative. The two complement each other. This is the reason why most public relations professionals employ both qualitative and quantitative research methods.

Informal research

An informal research is undertaken without generally agreed upon rules and procedures that would enable someone else to replicate the same study. An analysis of a public relations programme may be done through informal research method. It also makes use of opinion and its communication audits to evaluate various public responses to an organisation's communication programme.

Questionnaire

The most familiar survey data—a gathering devise is the questionnaire. A questionnaire is often used in face-to-face personal interviews with the interviewer asking the questions and noting the interviewees response on a form. E-mail is also being used to obtain information or responses to the questions.

interview

The interview is yet another method of collecting data. This can be done either through administering questionnaire or by personal contact.

PR analysis

A public relations analysis is another method often used as a tool of informal research. Clippings from print media and transcripts from broadcast media can be analysed to determine the quantity and quality of media coverage. The space given and the position of the item in the newspaper often give an idea of the coverage.

Website

The World Wide Web has given us a new research tool. The web is better than a traditional library because you get information at your finger tips. The web acts as an important source of information. As such, the web as a research tool is quick and easy but not always all that accurate.

Evaluation is always undertaken against objectives. For example, over 17 crore children between the age of 0–5 were administered pulse polio drops on a single day in the year 2000—thanks to the pulse polio immunisation campaign. However, there seems to be no proper evaluation of this nationwide campaign. Notwithstanding the advantages, the Indian public relations industry, in majority cases, does not get the programmes evaluated. Many organisations even do not allocate budget for evaluation. This is a major pitfall of the public relations profession in India. Unless evaluation is undertaken, the profession will not get management recognition.

POINTS TO REMEMBER

1. The successful public relations practice depends on public relations structure and policy. Public relations policy defines the areas of public relations programme, while structure with its personnel operates the programme.

2. RPCE Model represents **R** for research, **P** for planning, **C** for communication and **E** for evaluation. Public relations process is based on these four components.

3. Four **A**'s roles of public relations practitioner include analyst, advisor, advocate and antenna (evaluator).

4. PEST analysis divides organisational environment into four major areas as **P**olitical, **E**conomic, **S**ocial and **T**echnological environment. Such analysis will be useful in designing and implementing public relations plans.

5. Research is the first step in public relations process to elicit the public opinion and their reactions towards organisational goals and programmes. Research is also called the listening phase of public relations.

6. Research methods which discover facts include primary research (original survey, personal interviews), secondary research (books, online data).

7. Research tools include: personal contacts, interviews, advisory committees, the call-in telephone line, media monitoring, mail

questionnaires, informal interactions, feedback information mechanism.

8. Planning for a public relations process involves setting objectives, identification of target audience, formulation of action plans and public relations messages, creating calendar of operations and developing the budget.

9. Public relations process, from the stages of fact-finding, planning moves to the next step—action and communication. These two always must go hand-in-hand for effective impact and credibility.

10. Devising a media strategy for evolving a communication plan is an important step in the public relations process.

11. Formulation of public relations messages is a prerequisite for the implementation of communication plan. "We carry the Voice of India to the four corners of the world" is the message of VSNL, Mumbai.

12. Household microcommunication approach is a unique communication strategy wherein eight lakh Asha Sevaks positioned in six lakh villages in the country to visit every household regularly for motivating parents to get their children administered with Pulse Polio drops.

13. Media strategy in the public relations process must cover four types of media such as interpersonal media, traditional folk media, conventional mass media and IT new media.

14. If the research is the first step to know the problems, the evaluation is the fourth and the last step in the public relations process to study "How did we solve the problem" or the impact of public relations process.

15. Evaluation is intended to demonstrate the effectiveness of public relations programme, facilitate accountability, ensure cost-effectiveness in terms of results, measure the outcomes of public relations against set objectives.

16. Evaluation methods include formal research, informal research, questionnaire, personal interviews, observation, and websites.

REVIEW QUESTIONS

1. What are the four stages of public relations process? How are they related to public relations as a management function?

2. What is research (fact-finding)? Why is research important as a first step in the public relations process?

3. Why is planning (decision-making) so important as a second step of public relations process?

4. How does communication (action) as third stage help in the implementation of public relations programme?

5. What is the role of evaluation (measurement) as a fourth step in measuring public relations process?

6. You are a CPRO of a Municipal Corporation. About 500 persons in the city become victims of dog bites everyday. Design a multimedia public relations campaign indicating the four-step of public relations process to solve the dog menace problem in the city.

Public Relations Departments and PR Agencies

CONTENTS

KEY FUNCTIONS OF PR

Before we define the functions of public relations, it is most appropriate to recapitulate one of the definitions of public relations. Public relations is the management of a two-way communication between an organisation and its public to promote the corporate vision, mission, products, services and gain public understanding.

"PR, or Public relations to give it its full name, is the art of presenting a company (or person) to the public, usually via media, ideally in a positive manner that improves the reputation of that company (or person) and subsequently impacts positively on that company's sales/ uptake of that company's services/ the company or individual's overall reputation" (Cathey Bussey, 2011).

Public relations is all pervasive, but it can never hold as a panacea for every problem. When working with public relations, the management must have a clear understanding what public relations can do and what it cannot do; however, public relations is a sustained effort which can provide good results over a period of time.

Four 'As'

As a strategic management function, public relations encompasses four functions—Analyst, Advisor, Advocate and Antenna. The entire public relations process is based on these four **As**.

1. **Analyst:** In the role of an analyst, public relations undertakes the functions of analysing, anticipating, predicting and interpreting public attitudes and issues that might create positive or negative

impact on the operations of an organisation. Public relations begins with analysis.

2. **Advisor:** Based on situation analysis and organisational environment, public relations performs the role of an advisor in counselling the organisation to take policy decisions, courses of action and communication approach. Such an advice is intended not only to solve the problems identified in the first stage of the analysis, but also to improve the relations of the organisation with the people through effective communication and action-oriented programmes. Counselling helps the management in taking appropriate decisions with public interest.

3. **Advocate:** The third function of public relations envisages the role of an advocate. As an advocate, a public relations professional understands the policy decisions of an organisation and represents the organisation on the one hand and the people on the other hand in communicating policies and also ascertaining the feedback in the court of public opinion. As an advocate, it becomes a communicator and disseminates information to the public in a two-way traffic. It is in this role that public relations makes use of multimedia in reaching the target audience.

4. **Antenna:** In the fourth and final function, public relations becomes a TV antenna by researching and evaluating programmes of action and communications on a continuous basis and to achieve informed public understanding necessary to the success of organisational goals.

This may cover marketing, financial, employee, customer, shareholder, community or government relations and other programmes. Such an evaluation will be the basis of future programmes. As an antenna, public relations gives feedback information.

With its four-fold functions, public relations can help organisations in the following ways:

- Analyse the internal and external environment of the organisation to know its problems and pulse of the public and to advise managements.
- Dissemination of public information through various media of communication on organisational policies and programmes.
- Promote mutual understanding between an organisation and its internal and external stakeholders. Good communication based on the organisational performance can help develop stronger relationship at every level.
- Build trust and confidence with opinion-leaders that in turn promotes reputation which is a prerequisite to the success of a business.

- Stimulate discussion and encourage changes in attitudes, behaviour and public perceptions.
- Mobilise public opinion and overcome apathy, and convert ill—will to goodwill.
- Create awareness by dissemination of public information on a given product or service through multimedia approach.
- Provide feedback information to organisational policies and programmes through research and evaluation process.

PR Case

The four-fold functions of public relations can be explained from a campaign "Dogs Are Man's Best Friends. Let's Protect Them Against Rabies" launched by Municipal Corporation of Hyderabad in the 1980s. In the first stage of the analysis, the public relations department identified stray dog menace in the twin cities of Hyderabad and Secunderabad. There were about 10,000 stray dogs in the city and about 200 people were becoming victims of dog bites every-day. As many as 25 people died of rabies every year. Every dog owner is expected to take a license and get the dog vaccinated against rabies, but only 200 people had taken dog licenses. In the second stage of counselling, the public relations department based on the analysis advised the Corporation to evolve a plan of action to contain stray dogs and reduce the number of dog bites besides increasing the dog licenses.

In the third stage, the Corporation designed a plan of action based on the campaign theme. As part of communication and in its role of an advocate, not only the campaign theme was carried out but also action plans were implemented efficiently by opening public assistance cells, increasing the number of dog catching squads, supplying adequate vaccines for anti-rabies, opening more dog clinics to treat dog bite victims and communicating such plans effectively to the people.

What was the result of the campaign? In the fourth function of public relations—antenna, the public relations department got the programme evaluated through an independent organisation, Department of Communication and Journalism, Osmania University. The analysis revealed that the number of dog licenses increased from 200 to 6000 in two years and the cases of dog bites showed a steady decline from 200 a day to 63. In the process as many as 21,000 dogs were eliminated. An interesting feature of this evaluation was that about 71 per cent of Hyderabad's population had been educated on protecting dogs from rabies and taking dog licenses.

PR MANAGEMENT IN THREE SYSTEMS

Public relations, a two-way communication process is practiced all over the world as an industry of communication specialists, and their jobs are to build bridges of relationships with stakeholders; bridges of mutual understanding and bridges of corporate reputation. It is operationalised in three ways both in the government and in the private sector organisations. Some organisations have exclusive in-house public relations departments, while others entirely depend on public relations firms for the internal and external communication programmes. The third category of public relations operation is the combination of both in-house public relations department and use of expert services of public relations firms/agencies/consultancies. The three-fold system of public relations practice is not only an ideal system but also provides excellence in building relationships with corporate publics. Each system has its own advantages and disadvantages.

BASIC STRUCTURE OF PR DEPARTMENT: FIRST–SYSTEM

In fact, public relations is a relatively new management function. How do public relations professionals manage this function in an organisation? A prerequisite for effective implementation of public relations programme is the basic structure of a public relations department. The management style of the department will be influenced substantially by the nature, structure, and culture of the organisation within which the public relations department operates. Public relations within a business environment will require a different approach and balance of skills from that which might be required in the public sector or within a government department. It is a fact that no two organisations are the same.

Many industrial houses, government departments and public sector undertakings have set up in-house public relations departments within their own organisations. Similar to marketing, finance, human resources, organisations should also have internal public relations departments to deal with the subject of both internal and external communications. In-house public relations department may be described as a self-contained public relations setup with qualified public relations team and infrastructure to handle relationships with the organisation's employees and customers. Such public relations departments are headed by information officers/public relations officers, public relations managers, public relations directors/or Vice-President (Public Relations). The internal public relations department of Videsh Sanchar Nigam Limited, Mumbai is headed by Chief General Manager (Public Relations), while the Department of Information and Public Relations, Government of Andhra Pradesh is headed by a Director/ Commissioner, The head of public relations department in South Central Railway, Secunderabad is designated as Chief Public Relations Officer, while the head in the Railway Board in New Delhi is called Director (Public Relations).

The administrative set-up of public relations departments differs from organisation to organisation, depending on the nature of organisation, functions and the area of operation. The organisational set-up of public relations departments in government is different in scope and content from those under private management. In a private industry, the role of public relations is that of product promotion, with a keen eye on building up the image of the company. In this case, the interests of the shareholders also have to be safeguarded.

A public relations department is the unit within an organisation responsible for its internal and external PR functions.

Nomenclature

Public relations is the most common name and is used by many organisations as the title of the department. Other names include: corporate communication, information, publicity, etc. The Government which is the biggest employer of public communication officials in India uses the title 'information' and in some cases 'public relations' and 'publicity'.

In the case of State Governments, the public relations organisational set-up extends throughout the state concerned. The public relations organisational set-up in Government of India is spread throughout the country. National campaigns such as family planning, national savings and pulse polio immunisation programmes are carried out by Central Government media units at the national level, while State Governments carry out such programmes at the regional level.

Central Government

The Ministry of Information and Broadcasting, Government of India has various media units for dissemination of public information. The nomenclature of media units is totally based on the type of medium it uses. For example, the media unit intended to reach newspapers is designated as 'Press Information Bureau' while the Directorate of Advertising and Visual Publicity makes use of advertisements and films, and posters for communication purpose. The Government of India also uses the title of public relations in the case of Director, Public Relations, Ministry of Defence and Director, Public Relations, Ministry of Railways. The designation of the Head of Press Information Bureau (PIB) which used to be as Principal Information Officer is now designated as Principal Director General (Media and Communication). The PIB has offices at the state level also. The designation of state level PIB Head which was Director (Public Relations) has been changed as Additional Director General (Media and Communication). These changes are in tune with the changing scenario of media and public communication. All these designations are a legacy of the British Government. No major changes have been made after independence in tune with Indian heritage.

State Governments

In the case of State Governments, the departments are named as Information and Public Relations. While states such as Goa, Karnataka use the term Department of Information and Publicity, the Kerala Government designates its Head as 'Director of Public Relations'. There is no uniformity of titles with regard to public relations departments in the government sector. It is advisable to have a uniformity in the title of departments as Public Relations both in Centre and in State Governments. The Organisational Chart of the information and public relations department of Government of Andhra Pradesh is given in Figure 8.1.

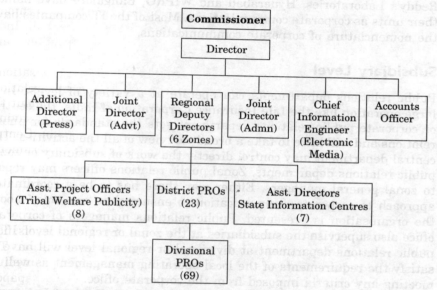

FIGURE 8.1 Organisational Chart of the Directorate of Information and Public Relations Department.

Public Sector

The public relations organisation in public sector undertakings is guided by the larger interests of social good. The interests of the society as a whole has to be safeguarded, while at the same time keeping the concern smooth-sailing, both with the internal and with the external public. It is the endeavour of the public relations department in a public sector undertaking to build up the image of the public sector as a whole in the larger interests of the country. Promoting sales of the products of the company is also one of the objectives of public sector public relations units. Most of the public sector public relations units are titled as public relations departments. But a few adopted the title corporate communications.

Heads of PR departments in various major public sector undertakings are designated as Director, Executive Director, Chief General Manager, General Manager, etc. If the Head of Public Relations in Air India is Director, the designation of marketing Division of Indian Oil Corporation is Executive Director, Corporate Communications.

Private Sector

When we come to private organisations, some have the title of public relations while others have corporate communications. For example, Dr. Reddy's Laboratories, Hyderabad and WIPRO, Bangalore have named their units as corporate communications. Most of the IT companies have the nomenclature of corporate communications.

Subsidiary Level

Public relations departments can operate at a variety of levels. In a large operation like the Life Insurance Corporation of India, the central or corporate public relations department sets the standards for public relations and will have to take a broad overview of all the activities. The central department may control directly the work of subsidiary or zonal public relations departments. Zonal public relations officers may report to zonal general managers. Either way there has to be a coordinated approach to corporate communication to ensure that 'one voice' about the organisation is presented. Public relations managers of corporate office also supervise the subsidiaries at the zonal or regional levels. The public relations department at divisional or regional level will have to satisfy the requirements of the local operating management as well as meeting any criteria imposed from the corporate office.

The General Manager (Public Relations), State Bank of India who is the head of public relations department reports to the Chairman and Managing Director at the Corporate Office in Mumbai. The General Manager is assisted by AGM (Public Relations) with four major sections, each headed by one officer. These sections are as follows:

1. Corporate image, advertisements and crisis management.
2. Media relations—press releases, press conferences, liaison with media.
3. Publications—house magazine (*Colleague*).
4. Community relations.

Local Head Office

The State Bank of India has 13 local head offices in the country. Each local head office is headed by a Chief General Manager. The Assistant

General Manager (Public Relations) who is incharge of public relations and community services at the local head office reports to the Chief General Manager, Local Head Office. The AGM (Public Relations) is assisted by four officers: (a) Officer, Community Services and Banking; (b) Officer House Magazine, Hyderabad Circle News; (c) Officer, Liaison with press; (d) Officer press releases and press conferences.

Zonal Office

Each local head office is divided into various zones. For example, the Hyderabad local head office has four zonal offices located at Hyderabad, Vijayawada, Visakhapatnam and Tirupathi. The zonal office is headed by one Deputy General Manager who is the head of zonal office. He is assisted by Deputy Manager (Public Relations) who reports to Deputy General Manager of zonal office. Public relations organisational chart of SBI is given in Figure 8.2.

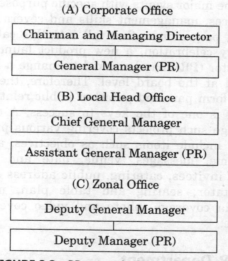

(A) Corporate Office

Chairman and Managing Director

General Manager (PR)

(B) Local Head Office

Chief General Manager

Assistant General Manager (PR)

(C) Zonal Office

Deputy General Manager

Deputy Manager (PR)

FIGURE 8.2   PR set-up in State Bank of India.

Areas of PR Department

The overall process of public relations can be conveniently divided into a number of areas. The terminology and divisions of these broad areas of public relations are not universally agreed and consistent, but most public relations managers look at the discipline in several main sectors comprising the following:

* Employees' public relations
* Financial and shareholders public relations

- Customers' relations management
- Marketing public relations
- Distributor and dealers' public relations
- Suppliers' relations
- Community relations and social responsibility
- Government relations
- Crisis management
- Corporate advertising
- Reputation management and media relations management

Each area of public relations department has its own specialised audiences, programme content, media and media tactics, working partnerships within the department and organisation.

Major Events

In addition to major areas of activities, the public relations department has to manage some major events with specific purposes, which demand substantial resources, management skills and several other elements. The major events, programmes that fall into this category include: a company centenary celebration, a new product launch or a company merger. The Director (PR) may be asked to mange a major event that has been initiated at the board level. Therefore, the management of major events will form part and parcel of public relations department. Advance planning is one of the keys to success. A checklist may be prepared to arrange such projects covering various programmes to be organised. It may include items such as objectives, audience, budget, detailed programme, messages, venue, date and time, invitation format and list of invitees, catering, public address system, lighting, flowers, commentator, seating and table plan, minute-to-minute programme, media coverage, photo and video coverage, rehearsals of the programme.

Functions of PR Department

From major areas and events, the head of public relations can move to the functions of the department. One of the pitfalls in Indian public relations is the lack of a defined job profile for a public relations manager. Even the functions of public relations units have not been enumerated clearly by the management. The functions of public relations department are determined by the number, size and importance of the public involved, the attitudes of the public towards the organisation, the size and financial resources of the organisation and the economic, social and political climate in which the corporation operates. Public relations is an information function. As such functions of public relations department relate to the dissemination of public information for bringing organisation and its public together.

The key functions are to:

- Interpret public opinion to the management by gathering feedback information about public attitudes towards the organisation.
- Keep the management informed of political, social and economic trends that have a bearing on the organisation and to advise the management for handling such trends and problems.
- Conduct opinion research, evaluate the impact of the programmes and policies of the organisation and advise the management on public relations techniques to be adopted.
- Carry out corporate public relations programme covering the major areas of public relations to inform and educate both internal and external public.
- Inform the public about the corporate objectives and programmes of corporation including the services taken up for the benefit of customers.
- Identify the adverse criticism on operation of corporation, behaviour of the employees as appeared in the newspapers and as obtained from other sources like written or oral complaints from opinion leaders.
- Issue clarifications on criticism appearing in the press without any basis.
- Arrange for the editing, printing and distribution of the house journal.
- Arrange for training in public relations and the code of etiquette for the employees of corporation.
- Launch employee communication programmes through various in-house communication methods as to create belongingness among the employees towards the corporation and increase their efficiency for better output.
- Organise 'open house' programmes and to bring the public closer to the corporation.

Feedback

Public relations is a two-way communication process. It is the duty of public relations professionals not only to disseminate information and ideas to the public outside but also to make correct assessment of public opinion and reactions towards policies and programmes of the organisation and bring them to the notice of the management. Public reactions and response are very important for an organisation, and also for the management to react suitably. Feedback findings are of great help and always provide information to some prevailing situations and problems, and the management can learn and benefit from the past experiences.

PR Budget

A public relations budget is a forecast of expenses that are incurred in the management of a public relations department and execution of its programme. The two basic considerations that go in to the preparation of a public relations budget are: public relations activities planned for the year, and the costs involved in executing the programmes. Administrative expenses are also added to the annual budget.

The Department of Information and Public Relations, which is the main agency for dissemination of public information of Government of Andhra Pradesh has about ₹100 crore as the annual budget. Details of this budget among others include: administration (salaries), films, research and training, advertising and visual publicity, press information services, song and drama, photo services, publications, community, radio and television programme, field publicity, etc. Similarly, each public relations department must have an annual budget.

PR Department Plan

Planning is a prerequisite for the implementation of any programme or activity. If public relations is to be cost-effective and valuable to the management, it must take its rightful place within the overall strategic development plan. A plan can be prepared based on budget allocation.

There could be a long-term and short-term plan in order to achieve corporate public relations goals. The long-term strategy should address the basic task of total reputation management as a long drawn policy. However, short-term plan envisages immediate results, for example, press relations campaign for covering an event or product launch. The plan must be approved by the CEO and the Board. Whatever the public relations plan may be, it must be communicated throughout the organisation. The plan must include emergency steps to deal with unexpected crisis situation.

Typical contents list for corporate public relations departmental plan are as follows:

- Executive summary
- Review of progress against previous year's plan
- Budget performance
- Budget proposals
- Implementation of corporate public relations
- Media-wise programmes
- Departmental structure
- Objectives and public relations policy

Creating PR Team

Who will implement the public relations plan? It is the public relations team created by the Director, Public Relations. Various factors go into the making of the team, such as size, scope of tasks, specialisation and experience, internal/external resource balance. All these factors will be influenced by the nature of the organisation, and driven by the responsibilities and goals of the department. The public relations department headed by Director, Public Relations has to handle all the specialist public relations programmes such as financial public relations, community relations. Each person in the department must specialise in one area of operation.

Recruitment

One must be careful about the methods of recruitment to select a well-qualified public relations personnel. After selection, the staff must be given induction training on company's strategies, philosophy, structure and public relations techniques.

PR Manual

The last but not the least, there should be a manual for public relations department. A manual is a must for every professional department, be it marketing or public relations. This will enable the personnel to work effectively without any confusion. The production of the public relations operating manual for any organisation is one of the most efficient ways of increasing the quality and consistency of public relations communication. Almost all organisations have financial manuals which are treated with a degree of reverence by the managers. On the same analogy, there should be a public relations manual for every organisation. The public relations manual must contain an introduction by Chief Executive on purpose and use and should do the following:

- Describe public relations policies and structures
- Explain the functional chart of public relations manager and team
- Provide guidance in implementing the public relations programmes
- Indicate financial and administrative powers of public relations personnel
- Give contact details for public relations team for accessing help
- Highlight the control mechanism where public relations activity needs to be cleared by the higher authority
- Contain Programme-wise contents
- Define internal communication
- Describe external communication

- Explain marketing communication
- Media relations
- Appointment of outside consultant
- Communication support materials

Merits of In-house Department

There are several advantages of having an exclusive internal or in-house public relations department in any type of an organisation. The merits are summarised as follows:

1. In-house public relations department is an integral part of the organisation, known to all other internal departments and organisational public. It enables to establish better communication with internal and external public including all internal departments such as finance, human resource department, production, etc. for collection of information.

2. Employees of public relations department enjoy permanency in the organisation who continue till their retirement while public relations firms' account executives are less permanent. This helps public relations team of the organisation to understand the company more closely.

3. The internal department can manage effectively the printed material/corporate publications effectively as it is easy to collect background material within the organisation. House journals, annual reports, corporate profiles, documentary films can be produced by collecting required material rather than a public relations firm coordinating such activities.

4. Internal public relations team will be on the spot as and when a crisis situation arises or whenever the organisation is in the news having immediate access to latest authentic information.

5. Above all, the internal public relations department can give a full-time service (24 × 7) which is not subject to any additional expenditure for the organisation. The time of Director/Manager, Public Relations will have to be devoted entirely only to the organisation and also to its public.

6. The internal public relations department will be more economical for it can dovetail various jobs such as the material used for house journal, including success stories, achievements, articles, photos can also be used for other media—press, exhibitions, posters, pamphlets within the organisations.

Limitations of In-house PR Department

Besides the advantages, in-house public relations department suffers from certain inherent limitations or disadvantages. Some of them are as follows:

1. The head of the public relations department who is an employee of the organisation tends to be uncritical and biased because of the influence of the management. The public relations firm can assume the role of oracle based on its professionalism and independent nature.
2. The in-house public relations department cannot have a varied experience of handling various areas of public relations management that a public relations firm enjoys.
3. The head of public relations department or his/her team members are liable for transfer. As a result the continuity suffers. The public relations staff in major national banks are drawn from officials of the regular banking cadre and transferred to their departments or branches after some period having worked in the public relations department. Therefore, continuity is lost.
4. In some cases, the heads of public relations departments are drawn without any training and education in public relations. They tend to be non-professionals causing great damage to the communication capital of the organisation.

PUBLIC RELATIONS FIRM/AGENCY—THE SECOND SYSTEM

A few small business organisations or institutions where there are no in-house PR departments engage the services of outside public relations firm/agency to handle public relations. This is the second system of PR practice which has its own merits and demerits.

What is a PR Agency?

Public relations firm/consultancy/agency is an independent specialised business organisation involved in the practice of public relations to counsel the client's organisation on communication and relationships management besides executing public relations programmes. It has creative and communication professionals to handle the client's public relations activities.

Public relations agency or firm may be defined as "a company hired by another organisation to provide certain communication services. Such public relations services range from strategic and management like planning and implementing major campaigns and providing high-level counselling to the more tactical operations such as generating news releases or printed promotional material".

Public relations firm is not an agency like advertising agency. Advertising agency is an agency of the media from whom it gains its income in the form of commission on the space and air time that the agency buys. The advertising agency procures business for the media.

The accredited advertising agencies to the Indian Newspapers Society not only get credit facilities for payment, but also get 15 per cent commission from the media. Therefore, the advertising agency is a commission agent for the media.

A public relations firm is an organised and specialised professional body in the art and science of public relations to render advice on public relations matters, besides undertaking the implementation of public relations programme on behalf of the client. The public relations firms derive income not through commission from the client but from professional fee charged based on man-hours and expertise.

The proliferation of media, challenges of globalisation and upswing in corporate communication activities demand the appointment of an outside public relations firm or consultancy which has vast experience and specialisation in public relations to counsel the in-house public relations of an organisation.

Agency

There are two types of public relations firms. The first category is of those that are independently owned and managed by a single individual, a group of individuals or a partnership. While the second type is of those that are a division or a subsidiary of national firm holding company. These companies are called firms or agencies. However, Public Relations Society of America preferred the nomenclature of public relations firm. The basic function of a PR firm is to serve its clients to the best of its ability and in their best interests at all times. Professionalism is the hallmark of a PR agency.

Important public relations agencies in India which handle Indian and multinational clients include: Genesis Public Relations, New Delhi (BBC World, National Geographic—Clients); Good Relations, corporate office in Mumbai with branches in New Delhi, Bengaluru, Kolkata, Chennai (Ten Sports Client); Corporate Voice Shandwick Public Relations, Mumbai (CNBC India Client); Burson-Marsteller Roger Pereira, Mumbai; Ogilvy Public Relations, Mumbai; R.K. Swamy BBDO, Chennai; Hill & Knowlton Strategies, Kolkata; and Perfect Relations, New Delhi.

PR Services

Public relations firms, by and large, provide a variety of services which include the following:

- *Marketing communications.* This involves promotion of products and services through such tools as news releases, feature stories, special events, brochures, and media tours.

- *Executives training.* Top executives are trained on government relations, media relations.
- *Research and evaluation.* Scientific surveys are conducted to measure public attitudes and perceptions.
- *Crisis communication.* Management is counselled on what to say and do in a crisis situation such as oil spill, recall of an unsafe product, fire accidents, natural disasters.
- *Media analysis.* Appropriate media are examined for targeting specific messages to key audiences.
- *Community relations.* The management is counselled on ways to achieve official and public support for such projects as building or expanding a factory or launching of a new product or service.
- *Corporate communications.* Promotes the corporate vision, to the internal employees and the external public, and reflects the corporate culture in all its positive dimensions.
- *Reputation management.* Projects the performance through the media to promote corporate image.
- *Events management.* Arranges news conferences, anniversary celebrations, rallies, symposiums, and national conferences on behalf of the client.
- *Government relations.* Materials and testimony are prepared for government hearings and regulatory bodies, and background briefings are prepared.
- *Branding.* Advice is given on programmes that establish a company brand and its reputation for quality.
- *Financial relations.* The management is counselled on ways to communicate effectively with stockholders, security analysts, and institutional investors, promotion of public issues.
- *Support for product launches.* Provides professional advice on launching of new products.

MelCole Public Relations

Established in 1985 as a proprietary consultancy, MelCole Public Relations New Delhi entered into an executive affiliation with Ketchum Public Relations, New York, a top global public relations firm, in 1990s to serve both Indian and foreign companies. MelCole has its full-fledged branches in Mumbai, and Chennai. MelCole offers a variety of services to clients, such as:

- Corporate communications
- Brand positioning
- Internal communication and External communication
- Investor Relations
- Media Relations
- Product and concept launches

- Event management
- Crisis management
- Training, Public Affairs
- Reputation management
- Feedback information and Research

Tactics

As part of its professional services, the public relations firm makes use of various tactics to reach the target audiences. Strategic counselling tactics include: message formulations, media relations through press releases, contributed articles, video news release, development and production of media kits, public relations writing for corporate publications/ posters, institutional advertisements, event management, organising exhibitions, open houses, road shows, customer meet, communication through Internet, intranet and extranet, managing bulletin boards and websites, speech writing, international relations through satellite media tours.

PR Counsel

Dealing with the basic role of public relations counsel, John W. Hill, the founder of Hill and Knowlton Inc. USA (a public relation firm), in his autobiographical book *The Making of a Public Relations Man* explains that a public relations firm must give counsel to the clients on the problems confronting them or on the issues asked by them. He cited the following examples on which his firm gave counsel to the clients.

- The company wanted to change its name
- The company's products are attacked on health grounds
- The industry is denounced by the government
- Two companies want to merge to gain efficiency
- The company plans to go public issue
- The company wants to adopt new technology
- The company wants to sponsor research programme that benefits its customers
- The company has important news announcement
- The company confronts violent strikes
- The company wants to celebrate its one hundredth anniversary

Public relations counsellors are not lawyers, who can cite statutes, judicial precedents and established legal procedures in arriving at their advice and counsel to clients. Public relations professionals must rest their counsel on experience plus opinions and judgement that are binding on everyone. Public relations in counselling must serve as 'a listening post for management' to appraise others reactions and viewpoints. In a way, a public relations firm or public relations professional must act as 'eyes and ears' of both the client and the public.

Justification for a PR Agency

Two key factors favour the appointment of an outside public relations firm.

- It provides independent and unbiased advice which is often listened to much more attentively than equally good advice from an organisation's own staff. Objective perspective given by the external public relations firm to a challenge or an issue confronting the organisation is useful.
- It provides a broad range of need-based specialised professional services and contacts that are more cost-effective and based on experience having worked with a number of clients of different nature.

Structure

Structure is a basic requirement for any organisational operation. The structure of a public relations firm/consultancy varies depending on the nature of the agency. For example, MelCole Public Relations Pvt Ltd, New Delhi, India's first professional public relations agency which has entered into an exclusive affiliation with Ketchum Public Relations (USA), functions with its headquarters in New Delhi.

The MelCole public relations is headed by its Managing Director. He is assisted by Director (Client Services), Director (Media), Executive Director and General Manager (Technology process). A number of Account Executives depending on the number of clients assist the Directors. MelCole public relations covers the entire country with its branches in Mumbai, Bangalore, Chennai, Kolkata, Ahmedabad and Hyderabad.

Advantages

1. **Independent service.** While an advertising agency may always project positive side of the organisation with glorification, a public relations firm is paid to be objective and criticise in its analysis of the organisation. The advice of a public relations firm can be positive and negative based on objective assessment.
2. **Long and varied experience.** A public relations firm handles many clients of various industries. As such it gains a lot of experience of various organisations. Experience is gained in areas such as print, production, film or audio-visual production, exhibition, institutional advertising, media relations, financial/

shareholder relations, market research, planning, budgeting and executing, evaluation of public relations programmes.

3. **Unsatisfactory service.** If the performance of a public relations firm is not satisfactory, it is easy for the organisation to terminate the contract by giving due notice.

Disadvantages

Certain practical disadvantages weigh against engaging a public relations firm. An outside public relations firm may have little practical knowledge of the client's organisation policies, programmes and its background.

Good Brief

A detailed briefing on the organisation and its problems has to be given by the in-house public relations manager to the public relations firm. The success of public relations firm in handling clients communication is entirely dependent on a good brief. A brief is a document which should be developed in consideration of the organisation's overall communication strategy. It should identify the public relations programme's objectives, tasks, target audience, budget, contract arrangements, timetable, and provide relevant background information. The brief is the foundation on which the public relations firm plans and costs its strategy. As such, the quality of the public relations manager's brief is the key to receiving high quality, tightly focused proposals from the public relations firm. If the brief is not comprehensive, it is a disservice to the organisation.

- Public relations firm has to act only through public relations managers. In case it needs any further information or information from other heads of departments, say Director, Marketing or Director, Finance, there will be a delay.
- Any query from the media, which is of complex nature, will be referred to the public relations manager of the organisation and this facilitates the speedy service to the media.

In general, the effectiveness of public relations programme depends on the ability and experience of those doing professional work, and not whether they are operating from within or outside the organisation. In-house or outside consultancy has to be professional, efficient and effective.

Appointment of a PR Agency

There are several ways through which one could select a good public relations firm to handle public relations work of an organisation. One procedure is recommendation from a reliable source be it another expert or media. However, a list of reputed public relations firms based on their profiles, experience, credentials, nature of specialisation, size may be compiled in the first instance for selecting a suitable agency. Out of the total list, a few may be asked to make competitive presentations paying for any creative work involved. The agency which makes best presentation may perhaps be selected on a contract basis for a specified period. Alternatively, a good public relations firm with vast experience and reputation may also be selected on nomination basis as we choose a specialist doctor for a particular disease. The Association of Public Relations Firms on consultancies may also be consulted for a list of public relations firms before selection is made. There should be a transparency in appointing a public relations firm based on merit.

Tata Group of Companies appointed Vaishnavi Corporate Communication Pvt Ltd, headed by Niira Radia, as their PR firm. However, Tatas did not renew the consultancy of Vaishnavi Corporate Communication, as Niira Radia was alleged to have been involved in 2G Spectrum scam. Tatas, therefore, appointed Rediffusion as their new PR consultancy in 2012.

PR Agencies Fee

A public relations firm charges for its professional services on man-hours and its expertise. The time given by each employee from the President to the Account Executive is taken into consideration in determining the fee to be charged to a client. An additional amount is also charged for professional services such as production charges, designing, creative work. Of course, separate charges are levied for media training, broadcasting, market research, press tours, etc.

Besides the method of basic hourly fee, some firms get retainer fee on monthly or any specified period under retained contracts of one, two or three years duration. A fixed project fee for a specific project is also levied and payed for placement charges, for placement of articles in media. However, the common methods of charging fee include—the basic hourly fee, retainer fee, fixed project fee and production charges. The public relations firm survives only on the fees charged to the clients.

PR Agency—Client Relations

The cordial relationship that an organisation has with its public relations firm is one of the most important factors in the overall success of the public relations programme. If the relationship is not functioning well, then no matter how much money and effort are put in one will ultimately fall short of achieving all that is possible from public relations.

The client–agency relationship is the state of interaction between an organisation and the public relations firm it engages to undertake public relations functions. Their mutual understanding is the most important factor in the success of the organisation's public relations programme and the firms effectiveness to serve the client well. However, best relationships can be maintained between the two on two basic factors: (i) skillful briefing of the organisation on its communication problems; and (ii) professionalism of public relations firm in providing excellent professional service. It is in this context, the client must repose confidence in the public relations firm and provide full information. The firm must also understand the problem of the client in clear perspective and act as a problem solver besides giving valuable counselling. Of course, the ability to counsel comes with experience and expertise.

Conflict

Sometimes, conflict might arise between the client and the public relations firm that may result in the termination of the contract. Such a situation comes only when the client is not satisfied with the work done by the public relations firm. Better communication between the agency and the client might prevent such an outcome. In some cases, a firm might withdraw its services from the client because it did not get proper treatment from the client. PR firms should be prepared to resign a good business offer rather than submitting their integrity, credibility and reputation. Agency should never compromise in communicating untruthful information or mis/disinformation.

In short, the client appreciates the expertise of the firm and looks to the agency to provide direction and considers the value of the agency's work well worth the cost. Similarly, a successful firm is able to produce excellent results to maintain a nourishing workplace and meet its own business goals while nurturing its client relationships to the betterment of both the client and the agency.

Six Responsibilities

A.C. Croft (1996), President of A.C. Croft & Associates Inc., a PR management consultant, identified six basic responsibilities of a successful PR firm. They are:

1. Listen to the voices and tides impeding on clients of PR firm (Media and Stakeholders' reactions)
2. Report and interpret to the client what you hear
3. Recommend policies and programmes that relate to corporate and public interests (to solve problems)
4. Communicate honestly and fully in anticipation of and in response to the voices and tides

5. Prove that your effort moved mountains. (demonstrate that your campaign influenced public behaviour, fostered product acceptance)
6. Get your Bills on time

THIRD SYSTEM: MIX OF IN-HOUSE AND PR AGENCY

There are advantages and disadvantages in the independent in-house public relations departments and independent public relations agencies. It is, therefore, difficult to compare the relative merits of establishing an internal public relations department or of using outside public relations consultancy. In the process, a third system emerged as an ideal way of handling the present-day competitive marketing economy. In this system, public relations is practiced with combination of both in-house public relations department and the outside help of public relations consultancy. This third method is most appropriate in the Indian context, particularly in the case of large industrial houses, public sector undertakings and Central and State Government public relations departments. Though Tatas have their own public relations/Corporate Communications Department, they appointed Rediffusion as their PR consultancy in 2012.

Benefits of Mixed System

The advantages of this mixed approach to public relations are obvious because not only does it give the company the required professional satisfaction that there is an in-house public relations manager just down the office who can be totally involved and immersed in the organisational communication but it has also the added advantage of a pool of outside public relations expertise to call upon to formulate and carry out professional public relations programmes. Despite certain pitfalls, however, a combination of in-house and consultancy PR does make a good job and can be a very powerful tool if set-up is appropriate. Combination approach can be successful only when we have the efficient internal set-up to feed the outside consultancy with good quality briefing material to enable it to use its professionalism for better impact.

Conclusion

The problem, however, is not which system is best—an in-house public relations department or a public relations firm. They are two different organisations and they serve different purposes. Rather than competing, they should complement each other in the promotion of professionalism in public relations and company's success. Professionalism is the hallmark for their success.

POINTS TO REMEMBER

1. As a management function, public relations and its public relations department encompasses four basic functions of analyst, adviser, advocate and antenna.
2. As an analyst, public relations manager undertakes the functions of analysing, anticipating and predicting organisation's problems and attitudes of people.
3. As an advisor, public relations counsels the organisation to design policies, programmes, action plans to solve the identified problems. Communication strategy will be suggested to reach the target audience.
4. As an advocate, public relations communicates the action plans of the organisation to the target audience for implementation. Action plans and communication go hand in hand.
5. As an antenna, public relations evaluates the programmes implemented to study the impact on the audience. It also tells the understanding of the public towards organisational goals.
6. With its four-fold functions—analyst, advisor, advocate and antenna, public relations department can help organisations in several ways to accomplish their corporate goals. The public relations department helps design communication programmes, disseminate the organisation mission and strategy, and collect feedback to organisation policies.
7. Public relations is practised in three ways. Some corporations have exclusive in-house public relations departments, while a few organisations entirely depend on external public relations firms. In the third category, public relations is practised with the help of both in-house public relations and external public relations agency.
8. The nomenclature of public relations department is used by different names such as Public Relations, Corporate Communications, Publicity or Information department.
9. The head of public relations department is designated as Director, Vice-President, Chief General Manager, Chief PRO, etc. who report to the CEO.
10. The advantages of having an exclusive in-house public relations department are: public relations department is an integral part of the organisation, employees of in-house public relations enjoy permanency in the organisation, easy for in-house public relations to collect background material within the organisation. The internal public relations team will be available round the clock during crisis situations. The internal public relations department is more economical for it can dovetail various jobs.

11. The disadvantages of in-house public relations include: in-house public relations head being a subordinate to the CEO tends to be uncritical and biased to the management, in-house public relations cannot have varied experience of an external public relations agency, in-house public relations personnel are liable for transfer leaving a gap in the operations.

12. Public relations firm is an independent specialised public relations business organisation equipped with skills in communication to counsel the clients on relationships management with public besides executing public relations programmes.

13. The public relations firm provides a variety of professional services to its clients such as: strategic public relations, marketing communication, research and evaluation, media analysis community relations, reputation management, financial relations, branding, product launchers, government relations, etc.

14. Companies seek the help of public relations firm—when a company wants to change its name, the products of the company are attacked on health grounds, the industry is denounced by government, two companies are merged, the company goes public, etc.

15. Advantages of engaging a public relations firm are: it offers independent service, and has a varied experience.

16. Responsibilities of a PR firm for its success include: Listen to voices and tides impacting on clients; report and interpret to the client what you hear; recommended policies and programmes of corporate and public interest; communicate honestly.

REVIEW QUESTIONS

1. What are the basic functions of public relations?
2. What is the structure of in-house public relations department? Explain its advantages and limitations.
3. Describe broad areas and functions of a public relations department. What principles do you follow in managing the department?
4. Why do we appoint a public relations firm/consultancy when we have our own in-house public relations department? Explain the advantages and disadvantages of a public relations firm.
5. Is there an established system to appoint a public relations firm? Discuss.
6. How public relations firms charge the fee for their professional services?
7. How do you sustain good client–public relations firm relations?
8. Describe the benefits of a third system of Public Relations practice.

Crisis Management: PR Centre Stage

The truth you resist is the battle you fight.

C O N T E N T S

- What is a Crisis
- Crisis Management: Meaning and Various Stages
- Crisis Team
- Crisis PR Strategy
- Ten-point of Crisis PR

Crisis such as Bombay High Oil Rig Blowout (1982), Bhopal Union Carbide Gas Leak (1984), Tsunami Disaster (2004) or even critical employees strike threats in any organisation clearly pose special problems in terms of public relations communication for companies and governments. Crisis can occur at any time, in any form. Crisis management, therefore, has become an essential aspect of public relations, which is termed as crisis public relations.

WHAT IS A CRISIS?

A crisis is an event which has possibly serious detrimental effects for an organisation. Regester and Larkin (2005) define a crisis as: "an event which causes the company to become the subject of widespread, potentially unfavourable, attention from the international and national media and other groups such as customers, shareholders, employees and their families, politicians, trade unionists and environmental pressure groups who, for one reason or another, have a vested interest in the activities of the organisation".

A crisis can be defined as "an unpredictable major threat that can have a negative effect on the organisation, industry or stakeholders". It has three broad features: (i) a crisis cannot be predicted, but it can be expected (one cannot say when it will occur); (ii) a major threat has the potential to disrupt organisational operations in some way (closure of production); (iii) the crisis can threaten the organisation, the industry or the stakeholders.

It is a major event that has potentially negative results. The event and its aftermath may significantly damage an organisation and its employees, products, services, financial condition and reputation. Some authors have also defined crisis as "a time of intense difficulty or danger, a moment of dissonance". Crisis means victims and explosive visibility. A crisis can be a dramatic change usually for the worse. It may be a disaster—an event which involves loss of life or extensive damage to property, or it may be a situation where an organisation finds itself under unwelcome scrutiny because of its behaviour or that of its employees. Crisis may also occur as a result of an accident and because of the negligence or criminal behaviour of an individual or organisation. It may happen to a company as a result of product tampering or other sabotage. Researchers have written that a crisis is a disruption that physically affects a system as a whole and threatens its basic assumptions, its subjective sense of self, its existential care.

The crisis runs the risk of the following:

- Escalating in intensity.
- Falling under close media or government scrutiny.
- Interfering with the normal operations of business.
- Jeopardising the positive image enjoyed by a company and its officers.
- Damaging a company's bottom line.

A crisis is also described from the following three dimensions:

1. That threatens high priority values of the organisation.
2. That presents a restricted amount of time in which a response cannot be made.
3. That is unexpected or unanticipated by the organisation.

The 'Blow Out' in Bombay High Oil Well which occurred on the night of 30 July 1982 is a good example of a crisis. It was a challenge to the Oil and Natural Gas Commission. Bhopal Gas leak in 1984, the most tragic industrial disaster that occurred in India, was yet another major crisis that the world witnessed.

Types of Crisis

In organisations, as in life, crises come in many varieties. One of the dimensions useful in classifying crisis is whether it is unexpected or unanticipated by the organisation. One has to identify the processes through which the organisation becomes aware of the crisis problem, and then the processes through which it responds and adapts to the need of the change. As such there can be crises that are totally unanticipated from those crises which are predictable and proactively managed.

Broad categories of corporate crises include the following:

1. **Technological crisis:** When modern technology is the key to success of any organisation, any failure in the technological process will have catastrophic consequences. Example of this type of crisis is Bhopal industrial accident when gas leakage from a Union Carbide Plant caused the death of thousands of people.
2. **Management failure crisis:** They are caused when management groups within the organisation fail to carry out their responsibilities. If the computer system is not checked properly, certain areas of bank services may not function to serve the customer.
3. **Malevolence crisis:** Such crises are caused by the malevolent actions of individuals or groups such as militants, terrorists and extremists by placing bombs and causing maximum disruption to business (sabotage—kidnaps).
4. **Natural calamities:** Crises caused by natural calamities such as cyclones, tidal waves, tsunami, earthquakes and droughts are known as natural calamitous crises.
5. **Man-made disasters:** They include plane crashes, derailments, mining accidents, chemical explosions.
6. **Governmental crises:** New legislation, investigations, regulatory actions can cause crisis situations.
7. **Product-related crises:** Defects in products. For example, the content of pesticides in Coca-Cola and Pepsi soft drinks which led to the recall of defective products.
8. **Takeover and merger crises:** When unexpected takeover or merger bids take place, crises are caused. Merger of two banks results in a crisis.
9. **Environmental pollution**
10. **Fire Accidents**

Crisis can also be classified as:

- The **starting crisis**—comes in the first or two years of starting the company with teething troubles.
- The **cash crisis**—excessive investment to enlarge sales.
- The **delegation crisis**—lack of control over day-to-day operations after delegating powers.
- The **leadership crisis**—because of not developing management team as next to take charge of top management.
- The **prosperity crisis**—over confidence of profits and complacency, and failing to read the emerging competition.
- The **financial crisis**—excessive dependence on loans, frauds.
- The **management-succession crisis**—no one groomed to takeover all management responsibilities.

CRISIS MANAGEMENT: MEANING AND VARIOUS STAGES

One of the findings of research is that when facing a crisis situation, management tends to react in very restrictive ways. Unfortunately, such behaviour may not prove to be in the best interest of the organisation. The critical balance, which is so difficult to achieve, is to ensure a full appreciation of the realities of the crisis situation and its potential seriousness, and to respond in a calm and rational way, and not to panic. Therefore, crisis has to be managed very carefully in the interest of both the organisation and the stakeholders.

Meaning

Crisis management by definition is the "planning, application and communication of strategies and tactics that can prevent or lessen the impact of the crisis on the company but also maintain its reputation". It is a way of thinking, designing and acting, when a crisis hits the organisation.

It is also a set of factors designed to combat crises and lessen the actual damage inflicted by a crisis.

Stages of Crisis Management

How do you manage a crisis? The three key stages of crisis management are: before the crisis, during the crisis and after the crisis. In all these stages, the crisis team should always keep in mind the stakeholders and organisation's goals.

1. Before the crisis: Every organisation must think, the unthinkable or 'expect the unexpected', and prepare an emergency plan for implementation as and when a crisis occurs. One should not wait for the public to bring problems to the attention of the management or media to highlight organisational problems. Organisations must be proactive and identify issues and problems so that they could not become crisis situations at a later stage.

One should invite comments at all times, welcome enquiries and pay attention to what people say. Such comments might reveal the first hint of a problem taking shape. Create a reservoir of goodwill with stakeholders that can be tapped if or when times get tough or crisis occurs.

2. During the crisis: When the crisis occurs, implement the crisis plan by telling the people what happened, how it happened what is the damage, what is the relief, what are rehabilitation measures. Relief measures and communication get priority in this stage.

3. After the crisis: When the worst of the crisis has passed, take a stock of all the steps implemented and prepare guidelines for the future. By maintaining a profile, being visible, accessible, involved in industry and community matters and not being known only for having experienced a crisis, the company has the best chance of regaining any ground lost during the crisis and winning respect from the industry and community. This could be a good case study for future.

Crisis management problems and strategies include: decision-making, dilemmas and moral challenges managers face, managing crisis victims, reducing litigations, recovering reputation, healing corporate wounds, dealing with organised opposition, selectively engaging the media and influencing employee community. Public attitude solutions to these problems lie in effective relief and public relations communication strategies.

Planning for a Crisis

The basic principle of crisis management is 'Expect the Unexpected'. The following is a road map:

- Catalogue the areas of crisis and evolve a policy to manage the crisis.
- Appoint a crisis committee which will act to both prevent and manage crisis.
- Put the plan in writing or bring out a crisis manual for the organisation.
- Define the role of communication.
- Test the plan, test and test again.

CRISIS TEAM

Who will implement the crisis plan? Someone has to be in total charge when the crisis takes place. In most cases it will take the time of all key persons. One person is designated as the head of the crisis team from the top management. The Commissioner and Ex-Officio Secretary to Government of Andhra Pradesh for Disaster Management acts as top management for all natural calamities in the state. However, the crisis team which handles the crisis is located at the place of crisis or corporate office, which consists of key representatives of the organisation from human resources, operation, safety, security, public relations, legal, finance, etc. If the CEO heads the team, it will be more advantageous. It is the crisis team that can offer focused, pragmatic, useful advice to deal with difficult situations strategically and immediately while limiting collateral damage.

Crisis PR Planning

Public relations as an anticipatory profession, which attempts to foresee events, trends and issues that disrupt operations of the company, has a critical role to play even in crisis situations. Public relations as a two-way communication process provides an interpretation of crisis situation to which everyone, both inside and outside the organisation, will react. In fact, crisis public relations is used in a variety of ways in the management of before, during and after the crisis. The crisis management team of which public relations is a part must move hand-in-hand for better impact. However, they must work under a crisis public relations communication policy. As a crisis management plan is designed, there should be a crisis public relations strategy also for pressing into action in such situations. Instead of facing tensions, rather becoming victims of stress, public relations must prepare crisis public relations communication plan.

What is crisis public relations communication? It may be defined as a corporate communication strategy of collecting and disseminating information, when a corporation is involved in a crisis situation affecting both the internal and the external public. In simple words, crisis public relations is the collection and dissemination of information on crisis situation. It is an important ingredient in crisis management when public relations practitioners use the information gathered during risk assessment to develop communication strategies for keeping the key publics informed of the crisis. The role of public relations in crisis is both fire preventive, fire brigade and fire fighting. One function precedes a conflict while the other comes when the conflict is on.

CRISIS PR STRATEGY

According to Coombs (2005), there are two general uses of the term 'crisis communication': (i) crisis communication as information, (ii) crisis communication as strategy.

(i) Crisis communication as information: It refers to the need to collect and disseminate information during a crisis. The information is collected to fill the information void of a crisis and thereby allows the crisis management team to understand what is happening and what actions and decisions they need to take in a crisis.

(ii) Crisis communication as strategy: It refers to the use of communication messages to repair relationships with stakeholders. What an organisation says and does after a crisis, the crisis response strategies, affects its relationships with stakeholders. Thus, the crisis communication is a factor throughout the four stages of a crisis: prevention, preparation, response and learning.

In the *before the crisis* stage, public relations can identify possible crisis risks. Collecting crisis risk information is the job of crisis public relations and a plan has to be designed for meeting the situation. In the *during the crisis* stage which is the most visible and widely studied aspect of crisis public relations, the organisation must provide full information and adjusting information. A crisis manager uses words and actions to shape stakeholders perceptions of the crisis or the organisation.

In the final *after the crisis* stage, the public relations team must collect information to complete a thorough post-mortem of the crisis management effort. Moreover, lessons from the postmortem are used to improve prevention, preparation and response to the crisis situation. These lessons must be communicated to the proper authorities in the organisation who can effect desired changes. The learning stage returns to crisis communication as information. Crisis public relations communication is the lifeblood of the entire crisis management effort. It plays a vital role in all the stages of crisis management.

TEN-POINT OF CRISIS PR

Based on an in-depth analysis, one must prepare crisis public relations communication plan covering all aspects of information dissemination to cover internal and external stakeholders. Once a crisis public relations plan has been formulated, the best way to test it is to rehearse. You are now ready to implement the plan as and when a crisis occurs. Expect the unexpected should be the principle for preparing a crisis plan. By the time you hear the thunder, it is too late to build the ark.

Advance Background Information

Every crisis is different but every response, media and methods of dissemination of information are not. A public relations manager must prepare background information in advance. However, the material will differ with each situation. A public relations manager in the Indian Airlines Corporation can get ready with the basic format of information to feed the media as and when an accident takes place by giving the details of the incident. The Trade Union strikes and product failures are other examples on which advance background material can be prepared.

When a crisis occurs, everything happens at once and very fast. The readymade background material with modifications based on the crisis must be provided to both internal public and media, including the external public. The background material must always contain information about good things done by the company, its products, services, safety record and style of management. Public relations must tell the story of the company. If public relations does not tell about the organisation, then nobody would tell about the company's past and present. A backgrounder will be of great value in such crisis situations. Which should help in fill-in-the blanks for the media.

Manage Inside and Outside Two-way Information Flow

In a crisis situation, it is the primary job of public relations to act truly and manage the two-way flow of information efficiently and effectively. It must interpret the crisis to which both inside and outside the organisation will react. A public relations manager while managing the flow of internal and external information must know—what to react, when to react, whom to react and when not to react. One must be aware of the information void and rumour mill. The false rumours spread like wild fire. The vacuum caused by a failure to communicate will be filled with rumours, misinformation. Avoid information void by providing full information with one voice. Public relations has to communicate, positively the organisation's credentials for not deserving a crisis.

Three Rs

The first response in managing the flow of information must be based on the '3 Rs'. They are: regret, resolution and reform.

Regret is a ticklish issue. Experts on the subject of crisis management may disagree on regretting. But there is a view that expressing regret is a difficult matter from making an apology. In the first act of communication, the management must say 'we are sorry' and convey regret on what happened. This is how the management must react with first 'R', responding to the crisis.

By **resolution** one communicates what action will be taken to resolve the crisis. Resolution of the organisation on the crisis creates confidence among the stakeholders. Public relations must communicate such resolution effectively.

Reform conveys the message that things will be **reformed** and such crises will not happen again.

Establish a Crisis Information Centre

Establishment of a crisis information centre with well-informed staff is a prerequisite for the successful implementation of a crisis public relations communication plan. Such a centre must be equipped with information technology such as computers, telephone, faxes, conference hall for media briefings, etc. The centre must act as a nucleus for all the information on the crisis including pictorial presentations.

Effective Media Relations Management

Napoleon Bonaparte, the French Emperor, had said, "Four hostile newspapers are more feared that a thousand bayonets". As such the media cannot ever be ignored in crisis situations and one spokesperson should always be designated for the media. Make sure a spokesperson is always available. It is desirable that the top management should become the spokesperson during the crisis. Regular media briefings should be held every evening during the crisis period or as and when the need arises. Press releases need to be issued regularly giving full facts and figures. Media should be taken into confidence and be taken to the site of crisis as quickly as possible for on the spot assessment. Reporters' questions should be responded immediately. They expect a return call or an onsite interview. Never go 'off the record'. In a crisis there is already much confusion. Do not add to it. Tell reporters only what you want to tell.

Monitoring of media reports is an important task of public relations, besides issuing rejoinders and clarifications on the reports published not based on facts. Keep a log of all press releases and key stories as the crisis develops and use it to uphold new reporters of the media as they enter the story. This will improve the accuracy of the coverage. Public relations officials must keep the management informed about the reactions of media on the crisis. Have media kits already prepared and keep in the crisis information centre ready for distribution.

Official Version

As soon as the crisis occurs, the first job of a public relations manager is to issue an official version media release of the incident giving all details based on the factual first information report. Such a report must have tacit approval of the chief executive. The official version of the press release, if it is an accident, must cover names of persons dead, injured, condolences, sympathies expressed, safety record, relief and rehabilitation measures being taken, etc. Such an official version will avoid speculation by the media. In the absence of an official version, the media develops stories from different angles from their own perception. Providing good media service in crises will earn goodwill and permanent friends in the media.

Relief and Rehabilitation Measures

As and when a crisis occurs, it is but natural that the media and others affected always point out negative aspects of the crisis. Accepting the ground realities, it is the task of public relations to project the positive work being done by the management to repair the damage caused by the crisis. That will create confidence among the stakeholders and also the media.

In November 1977, about 10,000 people died as a result of cyclone and tidal wave in Krishna District of Andhra Pradesh. The public relations cell attached to the then Chief Minister went on highlighting relief and rehabilitation measures of those affected areas. A segmented approach was adopted in providing information to the media everyday, at about 1.00 p.m. in the Secretariat Media Room. In this approach, separate media releases were prepared, say one day agriculture, another day fisheries, handloom, health, education, energy, industry, transport and so on covering the steps taken to restore and rehabilitate the people affected. Such positive projection will help maintain the reputation of the organisation. The organisation must face the crisis and take a proactive stance against the criticism and reaffirm its commitment to meet the crisis. Supplement everything you do with third party support. Make use of experts for third party opinion on relief measures.

In his memoirs, Dateline Andhra and an overview of political Movements in Andhra, R.J. Rajendra Prasad, the Deputy Editor of The Hindu, Hyderabad Edition, stated that the Chief Minister J. Vengal Rao noticed that it was necessary to present the nation a true picture of the devastation, because death tolls published varied from one lakh to 10,000 and an issue was made of dead bodies lying in the villages. A friendly and competent officer from the Information Department C.V. Narasimha Reddi (This Author) was brought to CM's office to deal with the press, and he took the press into confidence by daily issuing statements about the actual state of the relief operations.

Crisis No Longer Local, Always Global

We are now in the era of globalisation of economy and information media. With instant global access to information, news of crisis spans the world in seconds. Thus, quick responses from international humanitarian organisations and nations are received as happened in the case of tsunami in 2004. Its effect could be felt from Indonesia to India. But the spotlight also falls on the management of these crises. Sometimes nations are criticised for their bungling of the crisis itself as well as attempts of others to render aid. Therefore, no longer any crisis is local, they are always global. Crisis public relations must acquire global capabilities to handle crisis.

Accuracy

The public relations officials should provide accurate information to create credibility of the organisation. Be truthful and highlight both the bad and the good aspects of the crisis. Never concoct stories. Any inaccurate and false information will damage in the long run the reputation of the company. If a company at the centre of a crisis is seen to be unresponsive, uncaring, inconsistent, confused, inept, reluctant or unable to provide reliable information, the damage inflicted on its reputation will be everlasting and measurable against the financial bottom line.

Media Guidelines

Public relations professionals must follow certain media guidelines in crisis situations in regard to media conferences and the release of press notes. Here are a few:

- General guidelines of media relations should always be followed.
- A policy must be evolved by the management to allow media/photographers/TV crew inside the plant to see the scene of accident/crisis.
- Since spokesperson may be a technical person, necessary tips may be listed as to how he/she should answer questions from media.
- Media releases may be got cleared both by the competent authority (CEO) and Legal cell to avoid complications.
- Tell the Truth, even if it hurts. Credibility cannot be regained, once lost.
- Keep messages clear and consistent. Do not speculate. Be accurate in giving information on relief and rehabilitation.
- Avoid euphemism and jargon in your writings.
- Do not make off the record comment.
- Put the date and time at the top of media release.
- Include the details of the contact person who should be accessible 24 hours a day.
- Provide updates from time to time as new information becomes available.
- Review your organisation's website and remove any information which might be inappropriate during the crisis.
- Never say "No Comment"; it might fuel rumour or speculation.
- The last but most important, 'keep a Log' of what information is released, when, and to whom.

Learn from Case Study

Each crisis is a good experience and also a case study to learn for future. By keeping a log of what happened in the crisis during and after, and by proper interactions with the crisis team and affected people, conclusions can be drawn and lessons learnt which will be of great value in the future. Such reports must be prepared in a case study method. When the crisis is revisited, those case studies will be invaluable in managing crisis situations.

By maintaining a public profile, being visible, accessible, involved in industry and community matters, and not being known only for having experienced a crisis, the company or organisation has the best chance of regaining any ground lost during the crisis and winning respect from its industry and community.

What can go wrong during a crisis?

Notwithstanding careful planning, certain things can go wrong during crisis management. Public relations manager must be aware of such situations and know how to handle them. A number of issues that can arise on the spot include:

- Mass panic, making nonsense of the best-laid crisis plans.
- Multiple voices going out from different spokespersons on the crisis.
- Wanting to avoid media enquiries.
- Getting angry with the intrusiveness of the media.
- Suppressing the truth.
- Not being prepared to ask for help.
- Allowing the lawyers to dictate how to deal with the crisis.
- Not taking public relations into confidence.
- CEO meeting media without the public relations manager.
- Blaming the public relations for adverse reporting.

Case Study

For a case study on crisis public relations, please read "ONGC Gas Leak in Bombay offshore, 1999" under the chapter case studies "Action Speak".

POINTS TO REMEMBER

1. A crisis may be defined as "an unpredictable major threat that has a negative effect on the organisation or stakeholders". A crisis is also a disruption that physically affects a system as a whole and threatens its basic assumptions and objectives.
2. Any crisis has three broad features: (i) crisis cannot be predicted, but it can be expected, (ii) crisis disrupts organisational operation, and (iii) the crisis can threaten the industry.
3. Crisis can be categorized into eight types. They are: technological crisis, management failure crisis, malevolence crisis, natural calamities, man-made disasters, government-related crisis, defective product crisis, takeovers and mergers-related crisis. There may be other categories such as financial crisis, leadership crisis, etc.

4. Crisis management may be described as "the planning, application and communication of strategies and tactics that cannot only prevent or lessen the impact of the crisis on the company, but also maintain its reputation".

5. Crisis management has three stages: (i) before the crisis, (ii) during the crisis and (iii) after the crisis.

6. The basic principle of crisis management is 'expect the unexpected'. The road map of a crisis includes: evolving a policy to manage the crisis, appointing a crisis team to manage the crisis, preparing a crisis manual, defining the role of communications and pre-testing the crisis plan.

7. The role of the CEO who is the head of crisis team is especially important. It is the crisis team that offers pragmatic and useful advice to deal with difficult situations.

8. Public relations is an anticipatory profession which must foresee problems confronting the organisation. Public relations has a critical role to play even in crisis management. Public relations, therefore, prepares crisis public relations plan to keep the media and stakeholders informed about the crisis.

9. The crisis public relations communication is based on a 10-point formula. They are: (i) preparing a crisis public relations plan, (ii) compiling background information on the crisis, (iii) managing inside and outside two-way information flow, (iv) establishing a crisis information centre, (v) media relations management, (vi) giving official version of information, (vii) projecting relief and rehabilitation measures, (viii) crisis is no longer local always global, (ix) maintaining accurate information and (x) learn a lesson from the case study.

10. Media guidelines should be followed while issuing media releases.

11. Notwithstanding careful planning, certain things can go wrong in crisis management. They include: mass panic, running away from media enquiries, suppressing the truth, not taking public relations into confidence, blaming public relations for adverse media reporting.

REVIEW QUESTIONS

1. What is a crisis? Describe the three stages of crisis management.
2. Public relations is an anticipatory discipline. What is the role of public relations in crisis management?
3. Identify media guidelines to be followed while issuing media releases.
4. What can go wrong in crisis management? Explain with examples.

Public Relations and the Law

10

Ignorance of Law is no Excuse

CONTENTS

- Army Press Release—Defamation
- Two types of Legal Problems: PR
- Right to Freedom of Speech and Expression
- Intellectual Property Rights (IPR)
- The Patent Act, 1970
- The Copyright Act, 1957
- The Press and Registration of Books Act, 1867
- The Press Council Act, 1978
- The Emblems and Names (Prevention of Improper Use) Act, 1950
- The Official Secrets Act, 1923
- Law of Defamation
- The Consumer Protection Act, 1986
- The Right to Information Act, 2005

ARMY PRESS RELEASE: DEFAMATION

Public Relations Officers and their superiors should know that they cannot issue a press release with defamatory content. In one case, the Chief of Army authorized a press note which became the subject matter of writ petition before Delhi High Court and also litigation for defamation. This is an example to show how important it is for officers to know the basics of law. The details of the incident are as follows:

The Army's Additional Director General (Public Information), who is of the rank of Major General, issued a press release on 5 March 2012 authorized by the Army Chief V.K. Singh accusing Lt. Gen. (Retd) Tejjinder Singh of offering ₹14 crores bribe to clear a transaction of 600 sub-standard vehicles for the Army.

Lt. Gen. (Retd) Tejjinder Singh moved to the Delhi High Court seeking withdrawal of the press release that levelled serious allegations against him. The petitioner sought from the court the initiation of disciplinary action against the Army Chief. "The press release contained ex-facie defamatory statement and false accusations against the petitioner.

The press release is unauthorized and illegal. The army officers abused and misused their official power and authority for their ulterior personal gains by defamation and bringing dishonour to the petitioner", the petition said. The Delhi High Court in its verdict observed that the Army Chief V.K. Singh exceeded his jurisdiction by issuing a defamatory press release against retired Lt. Gen. Tejjinder Singh for offering him a bribe. The Defence Ministry also asked the Army to explain the functioning of its Public Information setup, including the authorization for the 5 March press release that contained allegations against Lt. Gen. (Retd) Tejjinder Singh.

Gandhi Pen: Legal Implications

There is a strong need for a PR wing of corporate to know the law and sentiments of the people before using great names for their business. Mahatma Gandhi is the Father of the Nation and he is not a poster boy for a pen making company. This is yet another controversy which gives the lesson on how business campaign should not be run. The details are as follows:

The global pen company Mont Blanc manufactured a luxury Mahatma Gandhi Pen at a price of ₹12 lakhs and depicted the picture of Mahatma Gandhi on the nibs of the luxury pen. The corporate communications wing of Mont Blanc launched a multimedia publicity campaign in promoting the new Gandhi pen. Mahatma Gandhi's picture, along with portrait of pen, was displayed on hoardings, in advertisements and other media. It is believed that Tushar Gandhi, the great grandson of Mahatma Gandhi, on behalf of Mahatma Gandhi Foundation had lent the name to the foreign pen maker by accepting about ₹70 lakhs. "Can Mahatma Gandhi be the poster boy for driving home the message that a super expensive Mont Blanc Gandhi pen is mightier than sword?" was questioned in the Supreme Court through a public litigation petition in December 2009. The Supreme Court issued notices to both the manufacturer Mont Blanc and the Government of India for their response. The Minister of State for Consumer Affairs K.V. Thomas informed the Lok Sabha that Mont Blanc violated the Emblems and Names (Prevention of Improper Use) Act, 1950.

These two cases, Army Press Release and Mont Blanc Gandhi Pen, clearly indicate the violation of law by both management and corporate communications personnel which might have resulted from either ignorance of law or negligence of knowing law before communicating.

TWO TYPES OF LEGAL PROBLEMS

In today's litigious society, particularly in the backdrop of global competitive marketing environment and consequent litigations between family concerns and other corporations, it is not just enough for a public relations practitioner to know only how to communicate effectively. Public relations professionals in their personal interest and in the interest of their employers and the stakeholders must acquire legal knowledge as they will encounter two types of legal problems:

1. The first type of exposure is corporate-related legal matters in relation to employees, stocks, consumers, etc.
2. The second type is that sometimes managements use public relations for misinformation campaigns to keep the stockholders in the dark.

A study conducted by 'Public Relations Voice' reveals that many public relations managers do not have a proper understanding of the laws and regulations governing both the corporates and the public relations profession. Of course, there is no separate law for public relations. However, the companies are required by law to inform shareholders about the company's financial health and other issues that could affect the value of the shareholders' investments. The SEBI regulations for an annual report include audited financial statements, profit and loss account, company's financial performance and a brief description of company's business products or services.

It is highly essential for public relations professionals to have a rule for stock/public issue related news releases so that no one is confused about investments. Press releases and advertisements on mutual funds scheme must carry a sterner message to read the 'Offer Document' carefully before deciding to invest money in the offer. Under the rules, messages should be worded in such a way that the warning should clearly spell out the risks involved in mutual fund investments. The causes of the risk and its consequences have to be underlined in such a message. The basic principle is that you must release the story only after clearance by the appropriate authority.

As every aspect of corporate life has to be within a framework of our Constitution and laws, public relations as a strategic management function also has to fall in the ambit of the Constitution of India and other related laws. As such, all the provisions of law dealing with corporations and communication aspects are compiled separately under the head Public Relations Law.

Though the Government does not license public relations professionals, several Acts and Laws of both Central and State Governments do have an impact on the practice of public relations. There are several regulatory authorities such as Securities and Exchange Board of India and the Companies Act, 1956 which regulate the corporates to protect the public interests.

Therefore, public relations managers require an intimate knowledge of the laws and regulations governing what they may or must say or do in a variety of corporate activities in relations to internal and external public communication.

RIGHT TO FREEDOM OF SPEECH AND EXPRESSION

Article 19(i) guarantees six freedoms to all citizens. They are as follows:
  (a) The right to freedom of speech and expression
  (b) The right to assemble peaceably, and without arms
  (c) The right to form associations or unions
  (d) The right to move freely throughout the territory of India
  (e) The right to reside and settle in any part of the territory of India
  (f) The right to practice any profession or to carry on any occupation, trade or business

Freedom of speech and expression means the right to express one's own convictions and opinions freely by words of mouth, writing, printing, pictures or any other mode. Thus, it includes the expression of one's ideas through any communicable medium or visible representation, such as gesture, signs and the like.

Though the Constitution does not contain in express terms the freedom of press, it was held by the Supreme Court in several cases to be an integral part of freedom of speech and expression under Article 19(1)(a).

Restrictions

Article 19(2) allows the legislature to impose reasonable restrictions in the public interest on the right of freedom of speech and expression on the grounds of security of the State, friendly relations with foreign states, public order, decency or morality, contempt of court, defamation, incitement to an offence and sovereignty and integrity of India. The term 'public order' is of broad relevance and synonymous with public peace, safety and tranquility.

Emergencies

Articles 352–360 of the Constitution allows the imposition of restrictions on all fundamental rights including suspension of the rights conferred by Article 19 whenever a State of Emergency is proclaimed on grounds of war, external aggression or armed rebellion.

INTELLECTUAL PROPERTY RIGHTS (IPR)

The expression 'Intellectual Property' is of recent origin. This term communicates the rights regarding five basic intellectual properties, namely, trade secret, patent, copyright, trade mark and mask work dealing with the design for element of semi-conductor chip. IPR law was basically a municipal law (Law of the Country). Later it became a significant subject of international law, which is now comprehended by several multi-lateral international conventions. Intellectual property is entirely different from 'real property'. The difference is because of the certainty of the value of IPR and the method and manner of the economic exploitation of the IPR. This property is of many forms— patents, industrial designs, copyrights, trade marks, know-how and confidential information. These can be stolen, pirated or misappropriated in a serious way than the ordinary movable or immovable property. Intellectual property is intangible or incorporeal. It is a product of human intellect. Copying it is an international problem with wider ramifications and faster spread all over the globe.

THE PATENT ACT, 1970

The Designs Act, 1911, the Copyright Act, 1957, the Trade and Merchandise Act, 1958 and the Patents Act, 1970 provided civil remedies for economic and commercial exploitation of the intellectual property rights, the enforcement of these rights and remedies available against infringement.

In case of patents for new inventions, the patentee gets the exclusive right to manufacture the product patented or to use the process patented for a maximum period of 14 years. But in case of drugs and food, the exclusive right accrues for a much shorter period of 7 years. After the expiry of the term of patent, the invention becomes public property and any person can freely use it. For an industrial design registered in the Designs Act, the registered owner of the design gets the exclusive right to apply the design to the article covered by registration for a maximum period of 15 years (5 years at a time).

THE COPYRIGHT ACT, 1957

The author of a copyright in literary, dramatic, musical or artistic work gets exclusive right to commercially exploit the work during his lifetime and thereafter for another period of 50 years. In regard to works such as cinematography films and music records, the copyright protection is limited to 60 years from the year of publication. Literary work is defined to include computer programmes, tables and compilations, including computer database. In 1994 and 2012, more amendments were carried out in the Copyright Act, 1957 to fulfil the criteria set out in TRIPS. Song writers, artistes and performers can now claim royalty as owners of the copyright which cannot be assigned to the producers as was the practice earlier. The international community is now asking for protection to computer programmes also under the copyright regime.

How to Complain?

A complaint for the offense of infringement of the copyright may be made by the owner of the copyright. Infringement of a copyright is not only a civil wrong for which a suit lies but also a statutory offense which is punishable under Section 63. Section 62 specifically deals with the jurisdiction for a civil proceedings vested exclusively in the district court. For a criminal complaint, provisions of Code of Criminal procedure will apply. Under Section 64, the Police has power to seize infringing copies. The owner of the copyright can file the suit for a civil remedy, which is an injunction to restrain the infringement before the mischief is done by publication or circulation, or for damages.

THE PRESS AND REGISTRATION OF BOOKS ACT, 1867

Generally, every person has a right to publish his own journal or newspaper. He need not take any license for such a publication. However, there is a need to declare the title of the newspaper and register it. By registering the title, the publisher will be preventing others from taking out any newspaper with the same name. Thus, he is required to register the title with which no newspaper was registered earlier in the same language or any other language. The declaration of publisher has to be authenticated by the Magistrate before the commencement of publication. Before that the title has to be cleared by the office of Registrar of Newspapers for India (RNI), which is constituted under the Press and Registration of Books Act, 1867.

House Journal

Even if it is a house journal, the clearance from and registration by RNI is required. Under this Act, every publisher must send the copy of published product to the RNI and to the office of magistrate, unless an exemption is granted by the RNI. Additional Executive Magistrate, Revenue Divisional Officer or PA to Collector in Districts and Deputy Commissioner of Police in corporations are authorized to receive and authenticate the declarations.

Penalties

Fine of ₹2000 or six months simple imprisonment is the prescribed punishment for hot exceeding printing books or papers contrary to rules under Section 8. Punishment for false statement without conforming to rules is also the same as above. Penalty for failure to supply copies of newspaper gratis to government is fine not exceeding ₹200 for every default. Penalty for failing to supply copy of newspaper to Registrar of the Newspapers is ₹50 for each default.

THE PRESS COUNCIL ACT, 1978

The Press Council Act, 1978 was enacted for the purpose of preserving the freedom of the press and maintaining and improving the standards of newspapers and news agencies in India. Under the chairmanship of a renowned former judge of the Supreme Court, the Press Council will consist of 28 members, who generally are prominent journalists and representatives of different walks of life. One of its main objects is to build a code of conduct for newspapers, news agencies and journalists in accordance with high professional standards. It is a forum to receive complaints by and against the press. There are two useful purposes of the Council:

1. Any threat against the independence of press and abuse of press freedom should not pass without anybody noticing it or raising a finger of protest.
2. The press should not in its own interest indulge in scurrilous or other objectionable writings which would lead to the very loss of much prized freedom of the press.

Section 13 explains the objectives of the Council, one of which is to help newspapers and news agencies maintain their independence. Under this provision, any newspaper or agency can file a complaint against any authority or individual for threatening the independence. A newspaper or a journalist or any institution or individual can complain against Central or State Governments or any organisation or person for interference with free functioning of the press or encroachment on the freedom of the press.

Section 14 says that when a complaint is made to Press Council that a newspaper or agency has offended against the standards of journalistic ethics or public taste or the journalist has committed any professional misconduct, the Council may after giving the newspaper or the editor an opportunity of being heard, hold an inquiry. PR professionals can lodge complaints with the press council if any adverse coverage is given in a newspaper without any basis. After recording the reasons, the Council can warn, admonish or censure the newspaper or agency or journalist. It may disapprove the conduct of the journalist.

Case Study 1

The Economic Times carried an article 'Bold Statement' on 30th June 2003 as part of the eight-page supplement "Futuristic", an Eastern Business Report. The article was on the natural wealth of Jharkhand State which can be harnessed only when the necessary infrastructure was provided as this being a new state. The crux of the problem was that along with this good article, an obscene photograph of a woman with a male partner handling her hips was shown, which was an indecent act. This author filed a complaint with the Press Council of India against the indecent representation of woman in July 2003. When the Press Council of India issued a notice to the newspaper, The Economic Times replied that it was not a picture of a real woman, rather a wax model of Jennifer Lopez at Madame Tussaud's museum. The person on the left is a staff member of Madame Tussaud who is seen to position the wax model at its inauguration in London in May 2003.

The Inquiry Committee of the Press Council after looking into all the aspects of the case expressed its displeasure over the selection and publication of the photograph in question and felt that it was an error of judgment and recommended to the council accordingly. "The Press Council of India, on consideration of the records of the case and report of the Inquiry Committee accepts the reason, findings and the recommendation of the committee and decides accordingly" on 20th October 2006. It took over three years for the Press Council to take a decision and informed the Complainant and the newspaper.

THE EMBLEMS AND NAMES (PREVENTION OF IMPROPER USE) ACT, 1950

This Act prohibits improper use of national emblems and names for promotion of products or for commercial advertisements. The names such as Shivaji, Mahatma Gandhi, and Tricolour National Flag, and Buildings such as Rashtrapati Bhavan or Raj Bhavan cannot be used as part of the design of the advertisement in an improper way. The Act imposes a penalty up to ₹500 for such an improper use.

THE OFFICIAL SECRETS ACT, 1923

This Act punishes two offenses—Spying and Wrongful communication of secret information. Section 3 of the Act makes it an offense if any person for any purpose prejudicial to the safety or interests of the State does spying. Under Section 5, it is an offense if any person willfully communicates any secret official code or password or any other information to any other person without authorization. Receiving any such secret information is also an offense under this section. This section covers only secrets of a Ministry or department of the government. A person guilty of an offence under this section shall be punishable with imprisonment for a term which may extend to 3 years or with fine or both.

THE LAW OF DEFAMATION

Defamation is an injury to a person's reputation. It is both a Crime and a Tort, i.e., a civil wrong. The Law of Civil Defamation is not codified. The Law of Criminal Defamation is codified in the Indian Penal Code, 1860. Section 499 states that when an act of imputation amounts to defamation, Sections 500, 501, 502 punish the defamation.

The wrong of defamation consists in the publication of a false and defamatory statement against another person without lawful justification or excuse. Truth or justification, fair comment, and privilege, absolute or qualified are the defenses available in an action for defamation. Remedy mainly is the damages. The amount of the damages depends on the rank and social position of the parties, nature of the imputation, mode of publication, mitigating circumstances and aggravating factors, apology and its acceptance. According to Section 499, IPC making any imputation in words, signs or visible representations, with the intention or knowledge of harming the reputation of the person concerning whom it is made, is crime of defamation. Imputation means accusation.

Rumours

The Criminal Law Amendment Act, 2010 provides for the offense of making, publication or circulation, in any notified area, of any statement, rumour or report which is or is likely to be prejudicial to the maintenance of the public order or essential supplies or services in that area or is prejudicial to the interests of the safety or security of India.

THE CONSUMER PROTECTION ACT, 1986

Public Relations depends on the credibility and credibility lives on the quality. A public relations professional cannot endorse a poor quality product and introduce it into the consumer market. Consumers have now gained greater consciousness and awareness. The society and law making body have properly responded in generating a movement and law to protect the interests of the consumer. It is the duty of any organisation and any PR professional to safeguard those interests. While propagating the product and campaigning for its purchase, the quality has to be assured and the norms prescribed by the Consumer Protection Act have to be strictly followed. This Act provides for better protection of the interests of consumer and for that purpose has made provision for the establishment of Consumer Councils and other authorities for the settlement of consumer disputes and for matters connected therewith.

Rights

The Act seeks to protect the following rights to of the consumer: (i) the right to be protected against marketing of goods which are hazardous to life and property; (ii) the right to be informed about the quality, quantity, potency, purity, standard and price of goods and Services to protect the consumer against unfair trade practices; (iii) the rights to assured of access to a variety of goods and services at competitive prices; (iv) the right to be heard and to be assured that consumers' interests will receive the consideration at appropriate forums; (v) the right to seek redressal against unfair trade practice or unscrupulous exploitation of consumers; and (vi) the right to consumer education.

The Act lays down substantive principles of law and also some principles of procedure. It defines defect, deficiency, restrictive trade practices and unfair trade practice and entitles a complainant to make a complaint on the ground of adoption of unfair or restrictive trade practice by a trader. Consumers can also complain against the defect in goods purchased or agreed to be purchased or the deficiency in the services availed or agreed to be availed and the act, on proof of the same, empowers the redressal agency to award one or more of the reliefs enumerated in Section 14(1) of the Act. The Act creates a right in favour of a purchaser of goods and a hirer or availer of services and a corresponding obligation on the manufacturer and trader of goods and provider of services.

A three-tier machinery has been created for redressal of grievances:

1. Consumer Disputes Redressal forum, in each district
2. Consumer Disputes Redressal Commission known as the State Commission in each State
3. National Consumer Disputes Redressal Commission known as the National Commission at the Centre

These Commissions are also referred to as Consumer Courts. An appeal can be permitted by the National Commission to the Supreme Court.

How to Make a Complaint?

A complaint can be filed by (i) a consumer, (ii) registered consumer association, if the consumer is the member of that association, (iii) one or more consumers, if there are more consumers, on half of a group of consumers, according to Section 12.

Reliefs to Consumers

A Forum/Commission may provide to the consumer one or more of the following types of relief.

1. Removal of defects from goods/services
2. Replacement of goods
3. Refund of the price paid
4. Compensation for any loss or injury suffered due to negligence of the opposite party
5. Award for adequate costs
6. Instructions to the opposite party to discontinue the unfair trade practice
7. Instructions to the opposite party not to offer hazardous goods for sale

Penalty for Non-compliance

Any non-compliance of the order of a Forum/Commission is punishable with imprisonment of 1 month to 3 years or with a fine of ₹2000–10,000 or both.

THE RIGHT TO INFORMATION ACT, 2005

The Right to Information Act provides the practical mechanism of right to information (right to know) for citizens to secure access to information under the control of public authorities. It has twofold objectives: to promote transparency and accountability in the working of every public authority. It is also intended to contain corruption and to hold government accountable to the governed. A legal sanctity has been given to the right to know under the Act by demarcating duties of public authorities and appointment of public information officers in every administrative unit.

What is Information?

Section 2(b) 'information' means any material in any form, including records, documents, memos, e-mails, opinions, advices, press releases, circulars, orders, logbooks, contacts, reports, papers, samples models, data material, held in any electronic form and information relating to any private body which can be accessed by a public authority under any other law for the time being in force.

What is Public Authority?

Public authority under the Act means any authority or body or institution of self-government established or constituted:

(a) by or under the Constitution;
(b) by any other law made by Parliament;
(c) by any other law made by State Legislature;
(d) by notification issued or order made by the appropriate Government and includes:
  (i) body owned, controlled or substantially financed; and
  (ii) non-government organisation substantially financed directly or indirectly by funds provided by the appropriate government.

What is Right to Information?

Section (2)(j), right to information, means the right to information accessible under this act, which is held by or under the control of any public authority and includes the right to (i) inspection of work documents, records; (ii) taking notes, extracts or certified copies of documents or records; (iii) taking certified samples of material; (iv) obtaining information in the form of diskettes, floppies, tapes, video cassettes, or in any other electronic mode or through printouts where such information is stored in a computer or in any other device.

Obligation of Public Authorities

Section 4(i) envisages that every public authority, having relevance to public relations, should disseminate public information in three ways:

  (i) Publish in the form of a guide the particulars of its organisation, functions and duties, the rules, regulations, manuals held by it, a statement of the boards councils, committees constituted, the budget allocated to each agency, the manner of execution of subsidy programmes, the information available or held by it, the particulars of public information officers.
  (ii) It shall be a constant endeavour of every public authority to provide as much information suo motu to the public at regular intervals through various means of communications including internal so that the public have minimum resort to the use of this Act to obtain information.
  (iii) Every information shall be disseminated widely and in such form and manner that is easily accessible to the public. Information may be disseminated to the public through notice boards, newspapers, public announcements, media broadcasts, the internet or any other means.

Public Information Officer

Every public authority shall designate as many officers as the Central Public Information Officers or State Public Information Officers as the case may be in all administrative units under it as may be necessary to provide information to persons requesting for the information under this Act.

Disposal of Requests for Information

Every public information officer shall dispose within 30 days of the receipt of the request. Request for information shall be deemed to have been refused by the PIO if decision on the request for information is not given within the period specified as above. In cases where a request has been rejected, the PIO shall communicate to the person making the request—(i) the reasons for such rejection, (ii) the period within which an appeal against such rejection may be preferred and (iii) the particulars of the appellate authority.

Information Commissions

If the Government of India constitutes the Central Information Commission with the Chief Information Commissioner and Central Information Commissioners, the State Governments appoint State Information Commissions with the State Chief Information Commissioner and State Information Commissioners to function as autonomous bodies to operate the Right to Information Act.

First Appeal

Section 19(1), (2) and (6)

1. Any person who does not receive a decision on request for information within the stipulated time or is aggrieved by a decision of the public information officer may within 30 days from the receipt of such a decision prefer an appeal to the designated Appellate Officer, senior in rank to the Public Information Officer, provided that such officer may admit the appeal after the expiry of the period of 30 days if he or she is satisfied that the appellant was prevented by sufficient cause from filing the appeal in time.
2. Where an appeal is preferred against an order made by a Public Information Officer to disclose third party information, the appeal by the concerned third party shall be made within 30 days from the date of the order.
3. An appeal under sub-section (1) or sub-section (2) shall be disposed of within 30 days of the receipt of the appeal or within

such extended period not exceeding a total of 45 days from the date of filing thereof, as the case may be, for reasons to be recorded in writing.

Second Appeal

Section 19(3), (4)

1. A second appeal against the decision of the appellate officer under sub-section (1) shall lie within 90 days from the date on which the decision should have been made or was actually received, with the Information Commission may admit the appeal after the expiry of the period of 90 days if it is satisfied that the appellate was prevented by sufficient cause from filing the appeal in time.
2. If the decision of the Public information Officer against which an appeal is preferred relates to Information of a third party, the Information Commission shall give a reasonable opportunity of being heard to that third party.

Decision of Information Commission

Section 19(7) and (8)

7. The decision of the Central or State Information Commission on appeal in accordance with the prescribed procedure.
8. In its decision, the information Commission has the power to—
   (a) require the public authority to take any such steps as may be necessary to secure compliance with the provisions of the Act, including:
   (b) by providing access to information, if so requested, in a particular form;
   (c) require the public authority to compensate the complainant for any loss or other detriment suffered;
   (d) impose any of the penalties provided under the Act;
   (e) reject the application.
9. The Information Commission shall give notice of its decision, including any right to appeal, to the complainant and the public authority.

Penalties

Section 20(1)

1. where the Information Commission, at the time of deciding any complaint or appeal is of the opinion that the Public Information Officer has, without any reasonable cause, refused to receive an application for information or has not furnished information

within the time specified or malafidely denied the request for information or has knowingly given incorrect, incomplete or misleading information or destroyed information which was the subject of the request or obstructed in any manner in furnishing the information, it shall impose a penalty of ₹250 each day till application is received or information is furnished subject to the total amount of such penalty not exceeding ₹25,000;

2. the Public Information Officer shall be given a reasonable opportunity of being heard by the Commission before any penalty is imposed on him or her;

3. the burden of providing that a Public Information Officer acted reasonably and diligently shall be on himself or herself. The Commission shall recommend for disciplinary action against the Information Officer under the service rules applicable to him or her.

Case Study 2   Motorcycle with Caste: Action for Defamation

This is a story of an advertising campaign that led for action against defamation. The Hero Motocorp Ltd, the largest motorcycle manufacturer in India released an advertisement in which it called its popular Splendor brand bike "Iyer" in Tamil Nadu. An organisation in Coimbatore lodged a complaint with the Commissioner of Police of that city seeking action against Hero Motocorp, Ad agency JWT which devised the campaign, and the newspapers that published the advertisement.

The complaint was that "Iyer" was part of the Brahmin caste and the advertisement had "denigrated" the community by using it as a surname for a motorcycle. As such the Brahmin Youth Federation of India sought action for defamation. According to Hero Motocorp, "the advertising communication of Splendor in various national and regional dailies showcases the bike as an integral part of the Indian family. We have depicted multiple societal groups in the campaign with the objective of connecting with the people by using local favours, e.g. Local language and local family names. In Mumbai and Karnataka, the bike was called Patil, while in Gujarat, it was Patel and in Delhi, Chauhan."

POINTS TO REMEMBER

1. Ignorance of Law is no excuse.

2. PR professionals encounter three types of legal problems. They are:

   (a) Personally as a citizen of the country, PR manager is subject to the law of the land

(b) PR professionals confront with corporate-related legal matters in relation to employees, stocks, consumers

(c) Misinformation campaigns by the corporates to keep stakeholders in the dark

3. A study reveals that many PR professionals do not have a proper understanding of the laws and regulations governing the corporate.

4. PR managers must have a rule that public issue related press releases, advertisements must carry the message of the risks and their consequences in investments of stocks.

5. The basic principle is that PR manager must release a press note on public issue only after it is cleared by an appropriate authority.

6. PR managers require an intimate knowledge of the laws and regulations governing the corporations.

7. The Indian Constitution gives a citizen certain fundamental rights which protect him/her against arbitrary and unfair actions of the State and create conditions of dignified wing.

8. The right to Freedom of Speech and Expression that includes freedom of the press enables a citizen to express one's own convictions and opinions. However, restrictions can be imposed on such freedom in the public interest on the grounds of security of the State, friendly relations with foreign States, public order, etc.

9. The Intellectual Property Rights relate to five basic intellectual properties namely: (i) Trade secret, (ii) Patent, (iii) Copyright, (iv) Trade mark, and (v) Mask designs.

10. The Patent Act, 1970 provides for civil remedies for economic and commercial exploitations of the intellectual property right.

11. The Copyright Act, 1957 provides the author the copyright in literary, dramatic, musical or artistic work, an exclusive right to commercially exploit the work during his lifetime. The owner of the copyright can file the suit for a civil remedy, which is either an injection to restrain the infringement before the mischief is done by publication or circulation or for damage.

12. The Press and Registration Books Act requires that one has to register newspaper with Registrar of Newspapers for India with a declaration before Magistrate. There is a fine of ₹2000 or six months imprisonment for printing books or newspapers contrary to this Act.

13. The Press Council Act, 1978 was enacted to preserve the freedom of the press as well as maintaining and improving the standards of newspapers in India.

14. Complaints can be made to the Press Council if aggrieved by the wrong reporting. Newspaper can also make a complaint if its freedom is threatened. The council can warn, admonish or censure the newspaper, news agency or journalist.

15. The Official Secret Act, 1923 punishes two offences—spying and wrongful communication of secret information. Punishment for the guilty includes imprisonment for a term which may extend to three years or with fine or both.

16. The Law Criminal Defamation is codified in the Indian Penal Code which states that an act of imputation amounts to defamation. Remedy is the damages.

17. The Consumer Protection Act, 1986 gives six rights to the consumers:
    (a) The right against marketing of goods which are hazardous to life and property
    (b) The right to be informed about the quality, quantity, purity and price of goods
    (c) The right to access to a variety of goods and services at competitive prices
    (d) The right to be heard and to be assured that consumers interests will receive the consideration at appropriate forums
    (e) The right to seek redressal against unfair trade practice or unscrupulous exploitation of consumers
    (f) Right to consumer education

18. A three-tier machinery has been created for redressal of grievances: (i) Consumer Disputes Redressal Forum in each District, (ii) State Consumer Dispute Redressal Commission and (iii) National Consumer Disputes Redressal Commission. Complaints can be made to the respective forums for redressal of grievances of consumers.

19. Forum or commission will provide relief to consumers in various types, such as removal of defects from goods/services, refund of price paid, compensation for loss or injury suffered, etc.

20. The Right to Information Act, 2005 provides the practical mechanism of right to information (right to know) to citizens to secure access to information under the control of public authorities.

21. The Act has twofold objectives: to promote transparency and accountability in the working of every public authority.

22. Every public authority under the Act must appoint Central Public Information Officer or State Public Information Officers as the case may be.

23. In all administrative units, information should be provided to persons requesting for the information.

24. Every Public Information Officer shall dispose within 30 days of the receipt of the request.

25. If the Government of India constitutes the Central Information Commission, the State Governments appoint State Information Commissions as autonomous bodies to operate the Act.

26. If the first appeal against the decision of PIO lies with the designated appellate officers, senior in rank to PIO, the second appeal lies with the Central or State Information Commission. The first appeal should be disposed of within 30 days of the receipt of all appeals while second appeal should be made within 90 days after the rejection.

27. The Central or State Information Commission shall impose a penalty of ₹250 each day till the application is received or information is furnished subject to the total amount of such penalty not exceeding ₹25,000. The Commission also shall recommend for disciplinary action against PIO under the service rules.

REVIEW QUESTIONS

1. What is public relations law?
2. What are the legal problems that confront the public relations professionals?
3. Explain the impact of law on the practice of public relations.
4. Describe the restrictions to be imposed on the right to freedom of speech and expression.
5. What do you mean by Intellectual Property Rights? Explain the remedies available under the Act?
6. How do you get your newspaper registered? Discuss.
7. Briefly discuss the Consumer Protection Act, 1986.
8. How does the Right to Information Act provide the citizens access to information under the control of public authority? Describe with examples.

Standards and Ethics in Public Relations

> *A lie gets halfway around the world before the truth has a chance to get its pants on.*
>
> **—Sir Winston Churchill**

CONTENTS

WHAT IS ETHICS?

The Oxford English Dictionary Thesaurus and Word Power Guide defines ethics as 'the moral principles governing or influencing conduct'. The rules of conduct recognized in a particular profession or an area of human life are also described as ethics. Ethics tells us the way in which we should live with an understanding about what is right and wrong, what is good or bad and what is responsible or irresponsible. The concept of ethics is derived from the Greek word 'Ethos', meaning an individual's character, belief and a community's culture (moral values). The Institute of Global Ethics defined ethics as 'the obedience to the unenforceable'.

TRUTH IN INDIAN CULTURE

India with over 5000 years of history not only has been a birthplace of unique culture but also has one of the oldest and greatest civilization of the world. Mark Twain, a renowned writer of America, described India as "the mother of history, the grandmother of legend and the great grandmother of tradition". Such a great tradition of India is evidenced in the philosophies of great sons of our country, from Gautama Buddha, Emperor Ashoka to Mahatma Gandhi, which are based on 'Satya' (the truth). Truth has been an integral part of Indian culture.

Lord Buddha (566–486 BC), the founder of Buddhism who is regarded as the Light of Asia, in his first sermon at Sarnath near Banaras exhorted the people about noble truths for cessation of pain and towards better life. One of his noble truths was based on the principle of Right Thinking, Right Speech, Right Action and Right Livelihood.

Emperor Ashoka (302–232 BC), who propagated the Law of Piety (Dharma) through rock edicts and stone pillars, was based on the tenet of 'Satya' (truth). In modern India, Mahatma Gandhi, who got independence for Indians through his ideology of truth and non-violence, has amplified his philosophy that "there should be truth in thought, truth in speech, and truth in action".

It is against this background of Indian culture, the words 'Satyameva Jayate', meaning 'Truth alone Triumphs' are inscribed below the abacus of Indian State Emblem. The State Emblem is an adaptation from the Lion Capital of Ashoka at Sarnath.

Truth and righteousness which are the strong pillars of ethics as derived from the Indian philosophers and Indian culture concern to all individuals and organisations—both government non-government—in their dealings with their publics on principles of public relations. If the key purpose of public relations is to earn the goodwill of the public for an organisation, it is incumbent upon public relations professionals to make decisions on dissemination of public information based on five considerations: truth, public interest (stakeholders' interest), the professional standards, personal behaviour (ethical and moral values) and corporate culture. In practice, these values enable the professionals to take the right ethical decisions in building better relations.

GOLDEN TRIANGLE PR ETHICS MODEL

Thus the need arises for Ethics in public relations which should be based on the principle of Trinity or Golden Triangle Public Relations Ethics Model—(1) Professionalism with standards of service and technical skills, (2) Ethics in public relations and (3) Corporate Ethics. If these three elements go hand in hand or in unison, the credibility and importance of public relations as a profession of relationships management and mutual understanding will gain due recognition on a par with other management disciplines such as marketing or human resource development.

PROFESSIONALISM

What is professionalism? The Oxford Advanced Learner's Dictionary defines professionalism as "the high standards that you expect from a person who is well trained in a particular job". The knowledge and hard skills and ability of a professional constitute professionalism. Professionalism is the competence of a professional based on professional skills. It also means the conduct or qualities that characterize or mark a profession or distinguish an occupation that serves the society with its own body of knowledge.

J.E. Grunig and Todd T. Hunt (1984), in their book *Managing Public Relations* listed five characteristics of a professional: (1) a set of professional values, (2) membership in a strong professional organisation, (3) adherence to professional norms, (4) an intellectual tradition or established body of knowledge and (5) technical skills acquired through professional training.

In the 1950s, Edward L. Bernays (USA), who suggested licensing (accreditation) as a means of ensuring professionalism, had identified six personal characteristics for a PR practitioner—(1) character and integrity, (2) truthfulness and discretion, (3) objectivity, (4) a broad *cultural background*, (5) intellectual curiosity and (6) effective powers of analysis and synthesis (Public Relations Voice 2012).

C.V. Narasimha Reddi wrote in Public Relations Voice, the journal of Indian PR professionals, "A round table has been organised to elicit views on what should be the attributes of PR professional." The consensus was that a PR professional should have five characteristics to exhibit one's professionalism. They are:

1. Professional qualifications—Degree or Diploma in Public Relations
2. Professional technical skills—communication skills in reading, writing, speaking and listening
3. Managerial skills—skills to advice the management in policy decisions
4. Personal characteristics—integrity, honesty, positive mindset
5. Psychologist's mindset—capacity to read and change the mindset of the public from negative to positive

Quantity Rather than Quality

A million dollar question arises as to what is the state-of-the-art of public relations. Public relations in India is now a 'Mixed Bag', containing a few highly qualified public relations professionals—second to none in the world—on one side and on the other we have many non-professionals without any grounding and education in the discipline. According to a survey, a large per cent of the Indian public relations practitioners are not involved in strategic management. Most of the practitioners are primarily performing the technician's role mainly involving, mediated communications, especially media relations or producing brochures, house journals, etc. The need of the hour is professional excellence.

Individual and Institutional Models

Such professionalism can be accomplished in two ways—the institutional model and the individual model. Under the institutional model, both educational institutions and public relations professional bodies must endeavour to promote all basic characteristics required for public relations profession, such as formal public relations education, training skills, research, accreditation and standard textbooks, code of professional standards and ethics. These are the institutional inputs for the growth of professionalism in public relations.

According to the individual professional model, every public relations practitioner must endeavour to acquire skills required to serve the society through the profession with public interest. *A high loyalty to the professional standards and professional values must be adhered to by every practitioner to gain credibility for the profession.*

PR CRITICS

It is ironic that the public relations profession which is devoted to promotion of corporate reputation, and building mutual understanding between an organisation and its publics, is viewed negatively by many. Study after study confirms that the journalists who have come to rely on public relations departments for much of their information still have a negative view of public relations professionals, such as 'manipulators', 'legitimisers', 'spin doctors' and 'flacks', because they project only management-oriented positive news, suppressing negative news. The bottom-line is that a lack of trust in the relationship between the public relations profession and the media is fundamental on ethical countdown.

Public relations, as a two-way communication process, is the primary source of corporate information to both internal and external public. If this source is not credible, the credibility of corporation and its mouthpiece public relations is lost. If credibility is lost, everything of the company is lost.

BIG LIE

Tactics that especially catch the eye of and 'against today's critic include what the PR industry detractors call 'the big lie', 'green washing', 'lobbying' against the public interest' (Public Relations: Good Spin; Bad Spin). The big lie is the process of disseminating information something that they know to be 'untrue'. Keeping the stakeholders informed about financial information that is not true, when the corporation wants to boost brand value and share value by manipulating audit reports. The fraudulent practices discovered of giant Satyam Computers a few years ago is a good example of manipulating financial information. Public relations professionals become part of the Big Lie or manipulation of information under the management pressure.

Advertorials

Critics believe that blurring the distinction between news and advertising through PR tactics like advertorials can impress media's function of providing consumers with accurate, unbiased information about the product or service. When some news reports are really advertisements in disguise, it casts doubt on everything presented as news. Advertorials mislead the reader with news as if from journalists.

While on one side some critics believe that the profession is basically untrustworthy, on the other side are practitioners who believe that public relations is criticized unfairly, while the good the industry does is ignored. Whichever side you happen to be on, there is no doubt that critics look for ethical dimension in the practice of public relations.

The need of the hour is professional excellence with ethical values to be followed by every public relations professional. Therefore, the second element of Golden Triangle Public Relations Ethics Model is public relations ethics.

PUBLIC RELATIONS ETHICS

Ethics is fundamental to the professionalism and credibility of the field. Professionalism and ethics are two sides of a coin. Good character of a professional is more to be respected than outstanding talent or skills of that professional. Most talents are to some extent a gift. Good character, by contrast, is not given to us as a gift. We have to build it piece by piece, by thought, choice, courage and determination. Good character always guides a person to function in an ethical way. Ethics in public relations is a prerequisite to its success.

Public relations ethics may be defined as 'the code of professional standards and practices evolved by public relations professional body as a useful guide for its members on their ethical and moral responsibilities in disseminating public information to both internal and external public.' Patricia J. Parsons in her book *Ethics in Public Relations—A Guide to Best Practice* states that public relations ethics is the application of knowledge, understanding and reasoning to questions of right or wrong behaviour in the practice of public relations.

The code of professional ethics embraces five basic areas of public relations discipline:

- Adhering to legal, regulatory, professional and company's code of ethics
- Practicing ethical values/integrity, truth, accuracy, fairness in promoting corporate vision, mission, services, brand products and reputation
- Truthfulness in the two-way communication process between the organisation and its publics
- Ethical dealings in media relations
- Counselling the management in ethical decision-making on policy matters without fear or favour
- Ethics in individual behaviour

Five things PR should not do:

- Deal in untruths, falsehoods or manipulation
- Operate in a vacuum and ignore valid criticism
- Be unreliable or inconsistent
- Make promises that it can't deliver
- Encourage unrealistic expectations

Public be Informed

In fact, ethics is the essence of public relations practice. When Ivy Ledbetter Lee, the Father of American Public Relations, started his Publicity Bureau in 1904, he declared that his policy was only to disseminate accurate and truthful information to the media and public. He changed the earlier concept of corporate world from 'Public Be Damned" to Public Be Informed'.

GLOBAL PROTOCOL ON PR ETHICS

The Global Alliance for Public Relations and Communications Management, a cooperative body of established national public relations associations, was founded in 2000 with its Secretariat in South Africa. It has 62 national PR associations representing 1,60,000 professionals around the world. It has evolved a Global Protocol on Ethics in Public Relations for adoption by all national associations.

The Public Relations Society of India, a constituent of the Global Alliance for Public Relations and Communication Management, has adopted the Global Protocol on Ethics in Public Relations at its 27th All India Public Relations Conference and the International Public Relations festival held in New Delhi on 2nd December 2005, and the theme of the conference was 'Quest for Leadership: Role of Public

Relations'. This new code of professional ethics replaces the earlier 'Code of Athens', adopted by PRSI on 21 April 1968 at its first All India Public Relations Conference held in New Delhi.

Declaration of Principles

A profession is distinguished by certain characteristics of attributes, including:

- Mastery of particular intellectual skills through education and training,
- Acceptance of a duty to a broader society than merely to one's clients/employees;
- Objectivity, and
- High standards of conduct and performance.

We base our professional principles, therefore, on the fundamental value and dignity of the individual. We believe in and support the free exercise of human rights, especially freedom of speech, freedom of assembly, and the freedom of the media, which are essential to the practice of good public relations.

In serving the interest of clients and employers, we dedicate ourselves to the goals of better communication, understanding, and cooperation among diverse individuals, groups and institutions of society. We also subscribe to and support equal opportunity of employment in the public relations profession and in lifelong professional development.

We Pledge

- To conduct ourselves professionally, with integrity, truth, accuracy, fairness and responsibility to our clients, our client publics, and to an informed society;
- To improve our individual competence and advance the knowledge and proficiency of the profession through continuing education and research and, where available, through the pursuit of professional standards for the practice of public relations.

Code of Professional Standards

We are committed to ethical practices, preservation of public trust, and the pursuit of communication excellence, professionalism, and ethical conduct.

Advocacy

We will serve our client and employer interests by acting as responsible advocates and by providing a voice in the marketplace of ideas, facts, and viewpoints to aid informed public debate.

Honesty

We adhere to the highest standards of accuracy and truth in advancing the interests of clients and employers.

Integrity

We will conduct our business with integrity and observe the principle and spirit of the Code in such a way that our own personal reputation and that of our employer, and public relations profession in general, is protected.

Expertise

We will encourage members to acquire and responsibly use specialized knowledge and experience to build understanding and client/employer credibility. Furthermore, we will actively promote and advance the profession through continued professional development, research and education.

Loyalty

We will insist that members are faithful to those they represent, while honouring their obligation to serve the interests of society and support the right of free expression.

Code of Practice

We believe it is the duty of every association and every member within that association that is part to the Code of Professional Standards to:

- Acknowledge that there is an obligation to protect and enhance the profession
- Keep informed and educated about practices in the profession that ensure ethical conduct
- Actively pursue personal professional development
- Accurately define what public relations activities can and cannot accomplish
- Counsel its individual members in proper ethical decision-making generally and on a case specific basis
- Require that individual members observe the ethical recommendation and behavioural requirements of the Code.

Corporate Governance

India's corporate sector is one of the major driving forces of its economic growth from major multinational corporations to small and medium enterprises. The Government of India has set up the Indian Institute of Corporate Affairs to provide much needed support in corporate governance and corporate social responsibility. The Government and the corporate sector are committed to good governance in their dealings with the public.

What is good governance? According to Chinese Philosopher Confucius, a good governance in one which has the trust of the people. Among others, the United Nations Development Programme prescribed five basic principles for good governance. They are (1) people's participation in decision-making, (2) transparency, (3) responsiveness, (4) accountability and (5) right to Information. If these five principles are followed, we would achieve good governance in every sector. Is the corporate sector following these principles?

CORPORATE SCAMS

A series of scams within and outside India beginning from Enron Power Corporation scam (USA), in which the Chairman of the company was imprisoned for manipulating the shareholders' money, Bofors Guns scam (1986), Bank Securities Scam (1992), 2G Spectrum (Telecommunication) Scam (2010) to Commonwealth Games Corruption (2010), not only defamed India in the world market but also generated a significant decline in people's trust both in government and in business organisations. The 2G Spectrum scam involving a battery of top politicians, including the Telecom Minister and bureaucrats, has been regarded as the biggest scam in India's history. The underpricing of the 2G Spectrum by the Department of Telecommunications allegedly resulted in heavy loss to the exchequer, to an extent of ₹1.76 lakh crores.

Kickbacks

New Industrial Policy 1991 bid goodbye to controlled economy, license Raj, inspection Raj and opened its economic doors to the world. As a result, many foreign companies with foreign capital came to India and, in turn, a number of Indian companies such as Tatas, Birlas, Ambanis, Mittals became multinationals and started doing business in a number of foreign countries such as USA, UK, China, and Africa.

What has been its consequence? The economy is now based on public–private–partnership which has brought greater complexity to the business environment, leading to kickbacks and corruption. "We have made a lot of progress economically in India, but there is a great shadow over progress—and that is corruption. Unfortunately with the economic growth of India, corruption has grown even faster", said Indian born industrialist Lord Paul of Maryleobone (UK). The need of the hour is ethics in corporate governance.

Business Ethics

Oscar Arias, former President of Costa Rica and Winner of the 1987 Nobel Peace Prize, once said, "In the twenty-first century, survival will be a more complicated and precarious question than ever before, and the ethics required of us must be correspondingly sophisticated" (Business Ethics-2008). A good business should be both completely successful and a force for good.

Brand Value

A more positive incentive behind the new focus on ethics is the growing evidence of boost to the brand value of the company and its product/service that can be gained if the brand is associated with ethical behaviour and moral values. Evidence also proved that employees are happier, loyal and prefer to work in such companies which are known for ethical principles.

CORPORATE ETHICS

Mahatma Gandhi said: "Business without morals is a sin". What is corporate ethics? A corporate code of ethics may be defined as "a statement of conduct or a set of ethical values, standards, integrity, accountability or guidelines for appropriate behaviour of members in relation to activities of a corporation". It is adopted by an organisation as part of its ethical behaviour.

A code of ethics underpins the values of any business and without it a corporation will have no moral compass. Corporate ethics spells out a company's obligations to six constituencies: (1) shareholders and other investors, (2) employees, (3) vendors and dealers, (4) customers, (5) the general community, (6) government and regulatory bodies, and (7) the media.

Bank's Ethics

Andhra Bank, a nationalized bank, in its corporate governance philosophy stated, "the principles of corporate governance require the commitment of the bank to attain high standards of transparency, accountability, responsibility and financial stability with the ultimate objective of building up values to the stakeholders. Values include: upholding the shareholders' interest within the principles of ethics, to ensure transparency and integrity in communication and make available full, accurate and clear information to all concerned".

Values

Values are just behaviour-specific nitty-gritty and they leave little to the imagination. People must be able to use them as 'Marching Orders' because they are the how of the mission the means to the end—winning nitty-gritty details.

One bank says: "we treat customers the way we would want to be treated" and that bank had literally identified 10 values of behaviour that created value to life. Here are some of them.

- Never let profit centre, conflicts get in the way of doing what is right for the customers.
- Give customers a good, fair deal.
- Great customer relationships take time. Do not try to maximize short-term profits at the expense of building those enduring relationships.
- Communicate daily with your customers. If they are talking to you, they can't be talking to competitors.
- Operations should be fast and simple.

Some companies in the West have appointed both ethical committees and ethical officers responsible for promoting the corporate ethics and enforcing its business standards.

Difference

What is the difference between corporate ethics and public relations ethics? Corporate ethics deals with good business. Ethical business is better than unethical business. Good ethics is good business. Public relations ethics in tune with corporate ethics focuses on ethical implications of public relations strategies and media tactics for providing accurate and truthful information to the stakeholders in public interest. Public relations is not a substitute for a policy. It cannot promote a bad policy.

If corporate ethics deals with overall business practices, based on morals, public relations ethics focuses on ethical and moral values in dissemination of public information through various media of communication. Public relations ethics provides credibility to the profession as well as to the corporates in the eyes of the society. PR practitioner is the 'eyes and ears' of both a corporation and public. Therefore, corporate ethics and public relations ethics must always go hand-in-hand in reaching organisational goals and earning reputation for both.

POINTS TO REMEMBER

1. Ethics is defined as moral principles governing or influencing the conduct of person, institution or profession. Ethics tells us what is right or wrong, what is good or bad and what is responsible or irresponsible.

2. Truth and righteousness are the strong pillars of ethics derived from our philosophers such as Gautama Buddha and Indian culture.

3. Mahatma Gandhi won independence for India through his ideology—truth and non-violence. He urged that there should be truth in thought, truth in speech and truth in action. "Truth is God", Gandhiji said.

4. Golden Triangle PR Ethics model is based on Trinity: Professionalism, PR Ethics and Corporate Ethics.

5. Professionalism is defined as the high standards with job, hard skills and knowledge.

6. PR professional should have five characteristics to qualify as a professional. They are (1) professional qualification, (2) technical job skills, (3) managerial skills, (4) personal characteristics such as honesty, positive mindset and (5) psychologist's mindset.

7. Public relations critics describe PR professionals as spin doctors, manipulators, legitimisers because they project only management-oriented positive news, suppressing negative news.

8. Public relations ethics is described as the code of professional standards, values and ethics evolved by public relations professional body as a useful guide for its members on their ethical and moral responsibilities in disseminating public information. It encompasses truth, accuracy and fairness in promoting corporate services, products and reputation.

9. The Global Alliance for Public Relations and Communication Management, a cooperative body of national public relations associations, evolved a Global Protocol on Ethics in Public Relations for adoption by all national associations. It envisages that PR practitioners are committed to ethical practices, preservation of public trust and the pursuit of communication excellence along with powerful standards of performance, professionalism and ethical conduct.

10. PRSI has adopted Global Protocol on Ethics, as its code of ethics in 2005.

11. Corporate ethics is defined as a statement of conduct or a set of ethical values, standards, integrity, accountability for appropriate behaviour of members of the company in relation to activities of the corporation.

12. If corporate ethics deals with overall business practices based on morals, public relations ethics focuses on ethical and moral values in dissemination of public information and media relations.

REVIEW QUESTIONS

1. What is ethics? Explain its key ingredients.

2. Truth and righteousness which are the strong pillars of ethics have been part of Indian culture. Discuss.

3. Define professionalism. Describe the characteristics that make a good professional.

4. How do you describe public relations ethics? What role do professional organisations play in evolving code of professional ethics for public relations professional?

5. Explain the key features of Global Protocol on Public Relations Ethics.

6. What are the contents of PRSI Code of Ethics?

7. Distinguish between corporate ethics and public relations ethics? Cite examples.

PR Professional Organisations | Chapter 12

CONTENTS

- Characteristics of Profession
- National PR Associations
- Global Alliance for PR
- PR Society of India
- PR Society of America
- Professional Code of Conduct

CHARACTERISTICS OF A PROFESSION

Any profession is distinguished by five key characteristics such as:

1. Mastery of a particular intellectual skill through professional education and training.
2. Professional literature, particularly textbooks and case studies.
3. Measurement and research methods in the field to assess the results.
4. Professional Association to promote the recognition of public relations as a distinct discipline.
5. Code of Ethics and high standards of conduct and performance.

If we judge the Indian public relations by the aforementioned attributes, we can infer that public relations in India as a profession is far behind other professions, such as advertising, journalism, marketing, human resource development or business management. How do we induct these characteristics in the profession? It is not possible for individual practitioners to promote professional traits. Therefore, the need is for a professional association to organise and infuse professionalism in the discipline.

NATIONAL PR ASSOCIATIONS

Public relations professional associations came into being as the profession grew in different countries. Public Relations Society of

America, Chartered Institute of Public Relations, U.K., to name a few, have done much to promote the profession as a strategic management function on the one side and to develop professional standards and code of ethics on the other to help the society in understanding the role of public relations.

It is against this background of characteristics of a profession that public relations professional bodies emerged as the fourth characteristic in different countries. If the Public Relations Society of America was established in 1947, the Institute of Public Relations, London, now known as Chartered Institute of Public Relations, London, came into being in 1948. Inspired by the Western models, the Australian public relations practitioners founded the Public Relations Institute of Australia in 1949. Similarly, professional associations were formed in different countries such as France, Germany, South Africa, Canada, Italy, Singapore, etc. After the national public relations associations were formed in different countries, the need was felt for an international public relations organisation. The International Public Relations Association was born (only individual members and not institutions are eligible for membership) in 1955 as a worldwide professional and fraternal organisation to serve as a catalyst in the development of the highest possible standards of public relations ethics, practice and performance.

GLOBAL ALLIANCE FOR PR

The Global Alliance for Public Relations and Communication Management came into being in 2000, located in South Africa. As an international PR association representing 62 national PR associations and 1.6 lakh professionals around the world, it evolved a Global Protocol on Public Relations Ethics in 2002. It envisages that every association and member within that association is a party to the Global Protocol on Ethics in public relations to commit to ethical practices and gain public trust with high professional standards. National public relations associations are members of this alliance. It organises World Public Relations Festival once in two years. The latest one was organised in Melbourne, Australia in November 2012.

PR SOCIETY OF INDIA

In 1958, India formed its first public relations society Public Relations Society of India (PRSI) with Mumbai as its headquarter. The Public Relations Society of India, the national association of public relations practitioners, is intended to promote the recognition of public relations as a profession, and to formulate and interpret to the public the objectives and potentialities of public relations as a strategic management function. Another objective of the society is to promote, seek, and maintain high professional standards among public relations practitioners. The Society functioned as an informal body till 1966, when it was registered under the Indian Societies Act. The headquarter is now in New Delhi.

Membership

The membership of the Society is open to a person who devotes the whole or a major portion of his/her time to the practice of public relations, and who is either employed in the public relations department of an organisation or practices as public relations consultant for any organisation. This category shall also include those engaged in teaching public relations. A member should have been engaged in public relations practice for a period of at least one year. Corporations which are engaged in the practice of public relations will become corporate members. A person who believes in the practice and promotion of sound and ethical public relations, but not qualified for regular membership, shall be designated as an Associate Member without voting right.

National Council

The Management of PRSI is vested in the National Council consisting of Honorary Officers of the Society and members nominated by the regional chapters. Honorary officers include: President, four Regional Vice-Presidents (one each for South, North, East and Western regions of the country), the Secretary-General and Secretary-Treasurer. The National Council is the supreme body in organising the programmes at the national level with the active support of regional chapters (30) located in various parts of the country. Most of the state capitals are covered by the regional chapters.

Code of Athens

The PRSI has adopted 'Code of Athens', an internationally accepted Public Relations code of Ethics for Indian public relations professionals. It was presented by Dr. Albert Oecki, the then President, IPRA, on 21 April 1968 at its first All India PR Conference held in New Delhi. (It was in Athens that IPRA had adopted Code of Ethics for public relations.) The PRSI, a constituent of the Global Alliance for Public Relations and Communication Management, adopted the new Global Protocol on Ethics in Public Relations of the Global Alliance in 2005 at its 27th All India Public Relations conference held in New Delhi. The theme of the conference was "Quest for Leadership: Role of PR". It replaced the earlier code of Athens adopted by PRSI in 1968.

All India PR Conferences

An interesting feature of PRSI has been its annual All India PR Conferences. The first All India PR Conference was held on 21 April 1968 in New Delhi with the theme 'Professional Approach', whereas 35th All India PR Conference was held in New Delhi, on 28–30 December 2013. The theme of the conference was inclusive growth through corporate social responsibility: Role of PR. Thirty-five All India PR conferences held in the country testify that public relations has come of age in India.

Regional chapters organise regular professional development programmes to enrich the knowledge of their members in the field of public relations and communication.

National PR Day

National Public Relations Day is observed every year by PRSI on April 21 as a mark of the beginning of professional public relations in India. Four World Public Relations conferences were held in India, first in 1982 in Mumbai second in 2003 in Bengaluru and third in 2005 in New Delhi and the fourth one hosted by PRSI was held in Mauritius in 2008.

The National Public Relations Day has been celebrated since 1986, based on the call given by this author, who was then National President of PRSI.

Other PR Bodies

Alongside PRSI, India has other professional bodies which are devoted to the promotion of public relations and corporate communications in the country. They include: The Association of Business Communicators of India (ABCI), Mumbai (established 1956); The Public Relations Council of India (PRCI), Bengaluru (established 2004); and The Global Forum for Public Relations (Association for values & Ethics in PR), a body promoted by the Prajapita Brahma Kumaris World Spiritual University, Mt Abu, Rajasthan (established in 2006). Its main purpose is to promote Golden Triangle Professionalism, Ethics and Spirituality in PR.

The future of Indian public relations is very much dependent on the effective functioning of these professional bodies. It is the onerous duty of every public relations practitioner in India to strengthen this national public relations body to promote all the attributes of public relations profession.

The growth and professionalism of public relations reflects in the public relations bodies. This has been proved by professional associations in the USA and the UK.

PR SOCIETY OF AMERICA

Established in 1947, the Public Relations Society of America (PRSA), headquartered in New York, is the largest national public relations association in the world. It has nearly 25,000 members organised in 116 regional chapters and 19 practice specific professional interest sections along with Affinity Groups representing business, industry and technology, counselling firms, sole practitioners, military, government associations, hospitals, schools, professional services firms and non-profit organisations (2013).

The Society's mission is to advance the package of public relations by the following:

- Uniting those engaged in the profession of public relations.
- Encouraging continuing education of practitioners.
- Interpreting the functions of public relations.
- Encouraging high standards of conduct in public relations.

Membership

There are two types of membership, member and associate member, to be eligible for admission. As a member, an individual must devote a substantial portion of time (at least 50 per cent) to the paid professional practice of public relations or the teaching or administration of public relations courses in an accredited college or university. Students who are members of the Public Relations Student Society of America are admitted as Associate Members. No individual member may remain as an associate member for more than two years, with the exception of fulltime graduate students pursuing degrees for the purpose of teaching or practicing public relations.

Member Benefits

As a member of the world's largest public relations organisation, one is entitled to the following benefits:

- *Public Relations Strategist*, the quarterly executive level magazine.
- *Public Relations Tactics*, the wide ranging monthly tabloid.
- *Professional Development Resources Guide*, the complete educational programming listing of their cost-effective professional development programmes (on site seminars, international and professional interest conferences, tele-seminars and e-learning).

Board of Directors

The business and affairs of PRSA are managed and controlled by a Board of Directors of 17 members who are accredited, consisting of four officers and 12 Directors. All of them are elected by the Assembly (General Body of delegates) at its annual meeting, and the immediate former President of the Society as ex-officio director.

Term of Office

The President-elect, Treasurer and Secretary are elected annually by the Assembly at its annual meeting and hold office for a term of one year beginning 1 January, next ensuing and until their successors are elected. The President-elect automatically becomes the President after serving a one-year term as President-elect. No person is eligible to hold more than one office.

The PRSA headquarters in New York is well established with a permanent office in a permanent building (22,000 sq ft.) on a 13-year lease with paid officials headed by Executive Director and Chief Operating Officer. The elected president of PRSA performs the duties with the assistance of an Executive Director and Chief Operating Officer, a paid official. The Executive Director and Chief Operating Officer are assisted by a Senior Counsel and four Vice-Presidents, each for one important division of PRSA, such as Membership, Sales and Publications, Marketing and Professional Development, Public Relations and Finance. An Executive Committee consisting of President, former-President, Treasurer, Secretary and Executive Director runs the day-to-day affairs of PRSA by making decisions.

PRSA Awards

A unique contribution of PRSA to promote professionalism among public relations practitioners is the institution of three categories of awards to recognise the excellence in public relations programmes. The awards are of three categories: (1) *The Silver Anvil Award*, which recognises complete public relations programmes incorporating measurable and sound research, planning, execution and evaluation; (2) *The Bronze Anvil Award,* which has been established to recognise outstanding public relations tactics such as a media kit, annual report, newsletter, video programme, speech or website as part of any public relations programme; and (3) *The Annual Individual Gold Anvil Award*, which is the society's highest individual award presented to a public relations practitioner and PRSA member whose accomplishments have made a major contribution to the public relations profession.

PROFESSIONAL CODE OF CONDUCT

The PRSA Assembly adopted the Member Code of Ethics in 2000. It replaced the code of professional standards that was last revised in

1988. In fact, the first code was written in 1950. Enforcement provisions were evolved in 1959 with a Grievance Board. The Code of Ethics has been designed to be a useful guide for PRSA members as they carry out their ethical responsibilities. The value of member reputation depends on the ethical conduct of everyone affiliated with the PRSA.

Accreditation

Accreditation in public relations (APR) is the mark of distinction for public relations professionals who demonstrate their commitment to the profession and its ethical practice. These professionals are selected based on broad knowledge, strategic perspective and sound professional judgement through the examination for accreditation in public relations. The examination is overseen by the Universal Accreditation Board, made up of representatives from PRSA and eight other organisations. Professionals with at least five years of full time public relations experience may sit for the examination. An accredited member has better prospects in employment.

The other key professional associations at the Global level include: The International Association of Business Communicators (headquarters in San Francisco, USA); the International Public Relations Association (IPRA, London); and China International Public Relations Association (Beijing; its mission is to "let the world know China to let China orient itself to the world).

<hr>

POINTS TO REMEMBER

1. The growth of any profession is closely linked to five key characteristics. They are: professional education and training; professional literature; professional research; measurement of results of the professional programmes, and a strong professional association.

2. Public Relations Society of America, the Chartered Institute of Public Relations, London, Public Relations Institute of Australia, Public Relations Society of India are some of the national public relations associations that work in their respective countries. However, the International Public Relations Association and Global Alliance for Public Relations and Communication Management function as worldwide professional organisations to serve the cause of high standards in public relations.

3. National Public Relations Day is observed every year in India on April 21 to rededicate to the cause of professional public relations. 21 April 1968 is a red letter day in the history of Indian public relations because it was on that day not only the first All

India Public Relations Conference was held in New Delhi, but also a code of ethics was adopted besides discussing the theme professional approach in public relations.

4. Accreditation in public relations is the mark of distinction for public relations professionals. These professionals are selected based on broad knowledge and sound professional judgement through an examination conducted by the national professional organisation. Professionals with at least five years of full-time public relations experience are entitled to sit for examination in the USA.

REVIEW QUESTIONS

1. What are the characteristics of a profession?
2. Discuss the role and functions of Public Relations Society of India.
3. How does a professional organisation promote the professional standards of public relations? Cite examples from PRSI or PRSA.
4. What is the role of international public relations bodies in promoting global public relations? Lite examples.

Public Relations Practice

- ✓ Corporate PR Vs Corporate Communications

- ✓ Stakeholders' Public Relations

- ✓ Public Relations in Government

- ✓ Public Sector PR, PR in Public Transport and Municipal Government

- ✓ Public Relations in Police, Banks, and Tourism

- ✓ Public Relations for NGOs and Political Parties

- ✓ Celebrity Public Relations

- ✓ Global Public Relations

Voice of the people is the voice of god

C O N T E N T S

- Concept of Corporate PR
- What is Corporate Public Relations?
- What is Corporate Communications?
- Corporate Identity
- Corporate Image
- Corporate Reputation
- Corporate Social Responsibility (CSR)

CONCEPT OF CORPORATE PR

The term 'corporate public relations' embraces all relationships that affect the corporation as a whole in reaching both the internal and the external publics. But the term 'corporate communications' also is used as a substitute for corporate public relations. The debate about the difference between corporate communication and corporate public relations is still on. In fact, there cannot be a substitute for corporate public relations. However, the identity crisis of public relations profession has created this difference. Public relations has to operate only under corporate public relations. Such misunderstanding will be cleared when we know the difference between communication and public relations.

The public relations profession is often described as being that of communications on the ground that it deals with communication activity between an organisation and its public. Not everyone agrees. According to Harold Burson, the doyen of public relations business, "the term communications has become synonymous with public relations but this does a disservice to our profession by making it tactical.... The best term for what we do is public relations". Long after he sold control of his public relations consultancy, Burson opted for perception management as a replacement for describing its service (Davis 2004). A debate is also going on about whether the term 'communication' or 'communications' is preferable. A few authors have pointed out that communications, belong to electronic equipment. Therefore, many professionals adopted the term 'communication' without the 's' as being more appropriate for public relations leaving communications with the 's' to the telecommunications professionals. It is a small point but a major step for it not only clears the confusion but also brings clarity. However, public relations practice comprises more than communication. Communication is means while public relations is the end to mutual understanding. There is a discrete area of public relations which deals with the corporate face of organisations and that is corporate public relations practice.

Corporation

What is a corporation? The dictionary meaning of corporation is "a large company or group of companies authorised to act as a single entity and recognised as such in law". It is also a group of people elected to govern a city or town. For example, the Municipal Corporation of Hyderabad and the Oil and Natural Gas Corporation. The term 'corporation' means a large company or group of companies authorised to act as a single entity and recognised as such in law. All corporations, such as industrial, commercial, financial, public service, transportation, telecommunication use public relations techniques in creating mutual understanding and goodwill of their corporate publics.

Corporate Public

The key public of a corporation are shareholders, employees, customers, distributors, suppliers, community neighbours, media and the government. Each of these is interested in a corporation as a source of benefits. Shareholders want dividend and profits, employees want better wages and welfare, customers demand quality of product and good service, media expect full information. The diverse interests of each of them call for a specific or specialised public relations communication programme to meet their demands and communication needs. The employees whose loyalty results in increased productivity; customers who provide running capital which pays the salaries and create profits, and stockholders, dealers, media, and the Government, all are essential in a complete corporate public relations plan. Thus, the need for an integrated corporate public relations strategy for every corporate body to maintain relationships with every segment of the public.

Corporate Face

The areas of corporate face include: corporate vision, corporate mission, corporate strategy, corporate identity, corporate image and reputation, corporate products and services, corporate conscience, corporate social responsibility, corporate governance, corporate brand, corporate philanthropy, corporate sponsorship. They constitute the total entity of a corporation. In all these spheres, public relations as a two-way communication process becomes an integral part of corporate planning.

While all strategic decisions of a corporation are the responsibility of the CEO and the Board of Directors, these decisions, of course, are taken based on the advice of the functional heads—the heads of finance, human resources, marketing and public relations or corporate communication. Thus, the corporate public relations process starts with the CEO and the Chief of public relations to evolve corporate communication strategy required to fulfil the corporate strategic goals enumerated above. For example, the Municipal Corporation of Hyderabad wants to eradicate mosquito menace with all action projects to eliminate the breeding of mosquitoes. If this is the corporate objective, it is for corporate public relations to put the plan into action with a communication strategy to educate the people to help the corporation in eliminating the mosquitoes. However, the corporate public relations has to adopt its own strategy/campaign techniques to reach different segments of the corporate public.

In implementing the public relations programme, corporate public relations has to follow the four steps of public relations process—fact-finding, planning, communication, and evaluation. As general public is a myth, public relations always identifies the public in specific terms, say investors, employees, customers, opinion leaders, competitors, suppliers, government, legislators. Public relations programmes are designed accordingly for each section of the public. The task of corporate public relations is not only to maintain relationships with each public but also to promote corporate reputation as a whole.

WHAT IS CORPORATE PUBLIC RELATIONS?

The *International Public Relations Encyclopedia* defines corporate public relations as "public relations for a company as a whole rather than for any of its primary functions; protecting the goodwill a company has already achieved and gaining additional goodwill in the process".

Heath 2001 defines public relations as "a relationship-building professional activity that adds value to organisations because it increases the willingness of markets audiences and publics to support them rather than to oppose their efforts". In their book *Strategic Communication Management: Making Public Relations Work*, Jon White and Laura Mazur (1999) states that "public relations in its true sense is a fundamental part of managing almost any organisation". The problem is its scope. Public relations is an umbrella term which can cover a wide range of areas including:

- Corporate communication
- Product publicity
- Issues management

- Investor relations
- Financial communications
- Lobbying
- Public affairs
- Media relations
- Community affairs
- Crisis management
- Event management
- Sponsorship
- Arrange of services which feed into all these

Principles of public relations as applied to a corporation in reaching its goals and maintaining good relations with the publics are termed as **corporate public relations** and cover developing relations through a communication process. This involves two different and contradictory postures—defensive in the face of a complaint, and attacking and aggressiveness in the effort to draw further goodwill for the company. Corporate public relations has also been described as a process of communication between an organisation and its various stakeholders. The underlying motive is to gain understanding and acceptance for the organisational goals, policies, programmes, products and services. It is also intended to promote corporate identity and image. Good corporate public relations begins at the top with the CEO. Effective management will set the agenda on all public relations efforts.

Areas of Corporate PR

The broad areas of a corporate public relations programme will vary depending on the fact-finding of the organisational issues and identified problems. Some of the areas of corporate public relations are: corporate identity, corporate advertising, issues management, crisis management, investor relations, employee relations, community relations, dealers and supplier relations, government relations, corporate sponsorship, corporate reputation, media relations, media monitoring and feedback mechanism. Each of these areas is discussed separately.

WHAT IS CORPORATE COMMUNICATION?

Corporate communication means any communication emanating from a company or occurring within it. The word 'corporate', however, refers to the whole body or corpus, and applies to any kind of organisation, regardless of whether it is in the private, public or not-for-profit sector.

All companies including non-commercial bodies are interested in corporate communications for building their images and reputations, besides maintaining relationships with the stakeholders.

Of late, many corporations in the USA and even in India are using the nomenclature corporate communication for public relations discipline. One student from Sri Padmavathi Mahila Vishwavidyalayam, Tirupati, selected the topic 'Public Relations in IT Industry' for her Ph.D. and went to various IT companies both in Bangalore and in Hyderabad for research. She was informed that there were no public relations departments in the companies. Based on the advice given by the author, she again went to these companies for information on corporate communication in the IT industry. They readily gave information.

Corporate communication has been defined by different authors in different ways. Here are some definitions in relation to public relations:

1. "Corporate Communication is about 'harmonising' all communication within an organisation to ensure consistency with corporate mission and objectives".

2. "The process of 'establishing' trust, social capital and legitimacy" (Weber 1968).

3. Corporate communication is the communication activities that an organisation undertakes as a corporate entity and includes 'public relations', the company website, the annual report, corporate identity programmes, the company logo, and any form of corporate advertising that the company carries out (Keith Butteric 2011).

4. Corporate communications focuses on responsibilities, for narrowing the gap between the organisation's desired image and its actual image; establishing a consistent organisational profile; and the organisation of communication by developing and implementing guidelines for coordinating all internal and external communications and controlling communications. Public relations complements marketing communication in achieving the aims of the organisation among external publics—it translates an identity into an image (Varey, 2007).

5. Corporate communication is primarily a mechanism for developing and managing a set of relationships with publics or stakeholders who could effect the overall performance of an organisation. These relationships must be viewed in a long-term strategic fashion (Kitchen and Schutz 2007).

6. Paul A. Argenti and Janis Forman in *The Power of Corporate Communication* (2003) describe: "By corporate communication we mean the corporation's voice and the images it projects of itself on a world stage populated by its various audiences or what we refer to as its constituencies. Included in this field are areas such corporate reputation, corporate advertising and advocacy, employee communications, investor relations, government relations, media management and crisis communications."

7. Corporate communication is an instrument of management by means of which all consciously used forms of internal and external

communication are harmonised as effectively and efficiently as possible, so as to create a favourable basis for relationships with groups upon which the company is dependent (Van Rie 2005).

8. Corporate communication is the integrated approach to all communications produced by an organisation, directed to all relevant target groups (Blauw 1989).

9. Jackson (1987) defines corporate communications as "the total communication activity generated by a company to achieve its planned objectives".

Corporate communication can be divided into **four** broad components:

1. Communication by a corporation to influence stakeholders and publics for establishing better relations

2. Marketing communication which is directed at achieving sales and support of other management disciplines such as finance, human resource development and production.

3. Organisational communication which engages those publics where there is 'interdependence' by implication with the major groups such as investors, employees and suppliers.

4. Reputation management based on organisational performance.

The popularity of corporate communication is also based on the idea that the term is broader than public relations, which is often incorrectly perceived as only media relations. Corporate communication encompasses all communications of the company, including advertising, marketing, government relations, community relations and employee communication.

The Difference

Is there any difference between corporate public relations and corporate communications? Many a student asks me about this confusion. If you make a critical analysis of definitions, functions, role and scope of both corporate public relations and corporate communications, the author in an unequivocal term answers the question 'No'. We find many commonalities in these two terms such as two-way communication process, relationships management, stakeholders, reputation management, internal and external communication, and media relations. One scholar in a lighter vein commented that public relations is an old wife and corporate communication is a bride. Public relations the oldest term born in the beginning of 20th century which has been hijacked by globalisation and information revolution as corporate communication in the last decade of 20th century. Jon White and Laura Mazur (1999) argue that corporate communication, the 'corporation's voice and images' it projects, is born under an umbrella term of public relations which covers a wide range of communication activities. Harold Burson of Burson-Marsteller public relations firm in USA described corporate communication as one of the many sub-sects of public relations which has been borrowed from the umbrella term of public relations with a variety of functions such as employee relations, customer relations, marketing communication, etc.

The greatest tragedy of public relations today is its identity crisis, which has taken different nomenclatures from public relations to corporate communication, from corporate communication to corporate affairs and public affairs, from public information to public communication and publicity. However, there is not much difference between corporate communications and corporate public relations. Both are applied to communication to corporations for management of stakeholders' relationships.

Information Revolution and Globalisation

The information revolution and media explosion on the one side and globalisation, including the concept of global village, on the other have created an unprecedented challenges to the corporate world to meet the global competitive marketing environment and also to keep the stakeholders satisfied. In the process there has been an upswing in communication activities of various organisations. Public relations which was confined to only media relations could not come up to the emerging expectations of the management.

When public relations became spin-doctor, when public relations was considered as mere media relations, a slick press agent, a hidden persuader or a devious manipulator of dummy fonts, a legitimiser, when public relations became non-professional; it failed to deliver results as expected by management, not only it lost its credibility but it also earned a bad name. As a result, the corporate sector in the US in response to the emerging global needs coined a new term corporate communications for public relations.

In many cases, corporations use both public relations and corporate communications. The Central Government in India uses the term 'information' as Ministry of Information and Broadcasting (British Legacy), while almost all the 28 State Governments use the nomenclature of Information and Public Relations. If most of the public sector undertakings use the term public relations, the IT sector in India uses the term corporate communications. This, in part, is a reaction to the misuse of the original term *public relations* by the public and the media. However, the future lies in corporate public relations as an umbrella term which will cover all communications aimed at stakeholders in the key agenda of 21st Century.

Areas of Operation

Notwithstanding the above exposition of difference, one university changed the title of the paper of corporate public relations overnight to corporate communication without changing a word in the original syllabus of public relations. Therefore, corporate public relations has been discussed in this chapter for corporate communication.

The broad areas of operation of corporate communication will vary depending on the nature, issues and mission of the organisation. Here are the dimensions of operation of corporate public relations to meet the needs of stakeholders:

- Promotion of corporate mission
- Corporate identity
- Strategic management function—PR strategy
- Employees relations
- Shareholders' and Investor relations (financial PR)
- Customer relations
- Suppliers and dealers relations.
- Government relations
- Community relations
- Relations in crisis situations
- Marketing communication support
- Media relations and Media Monitoring—New Media, Digital Media
- Corporate Sponsorship
- Issues Management
- Event Management
- Environmental Scanning
- Corporate Publications
- Research and Evaluation
- Feedback Information Mechanism
- Public Relations Reporting

Corporate public relations as top management function with its multiple operational areas adopts an integrated public relations communication approach not only to serve all internal management disciplines (finance, marketing) but also to reach out all internal and external stakeholders to create and sustain mutual understanding and promote reputation of the organisation.

Proactive and Reactive PR

Public relations depending on the nature of the public relations manager can be proactive and reactive. However, an effective public relations demands proactiveness in relation to the stakeholders. What is proactive? It is acting in anticipation of a problem rather than simply responding to a situation only when the public make a complaint. In contrast, reactive means showing a response to a stimulus, event or acting in response to a situation rather than creating a favourable atmosphere or controlling the probable problem.

It is in this context, public relations can be proactive public relations or reactive public relations based on the actions of the public relations department. The public relations department in one university was always reactive to the critical writings of a hostile newspaper. The newspaper once wrote that the University presents the look of a deserted graveyard. In such situations, public relations has to react and issue rejoinders to correct the wrong version published in the newspapers. But a successful public relations manager is one who is always proactive and takes action in anticipation of organisational problems.

Six areas of proactive PR

Environmental analysis is one of the functions of public relations. There has to be a value judgement based on the analysis and specific circumstances relating to objectives, the range and number of stakeholders, the number and types of competitors for share of voice, the availability of resources, and the number and range of proposed activities. Here are six areas to gain a general overview of how proactive a public relations professional may need to be:

1. Are we obtaining our fair share of feedback? If not, be honest: does it matter that much? Or is it a real problem that needs to be addressed? Find out the problem.
2. How confident are we about the quantity and quality of feedback information that is being collected from the internal as well as external environment? There is always scope for more, to be sure of the information. The bigger question may be: how much of this can we turn into usable intelligence for being proactive.
3. Do our image and our reputation satisfy our corporate needs? If not, can we be doing more to address this? If the current situation appears to be fine, as it is understood, ask then: What plans do we have to sustain our image and our reputation?
4. How are we doing at meeting our customers' communication expectations? Should we get real about this, with more measures and deeper analysis? Or are we confident that the current levels of service quality are appropriate and mutually satisfactory?
5. Can we fairly claim to be creative in what we are doing? Are we making best use of desperate, seemingly unconnected information and of our available resources, both knowledge and skills? Could we be coming up with fresh ways of looking at old communication to meet new challenges?
6. Are we identifying customers' grievances and problems unasked?

In short, it appears that everyone is doing it to analyse and anticipate problems and that this is an unstoppable trend in being proactive.

Right to Information

The Right to Information Act, 2005 not only accords the right for the citizens to secure access to information under the control of public authorities but also demands the public authorities to be proactive in dissemination of public information. The act envisages that every public authority must undertake proactive publication of information on the organisation; dissemination of information through all media; providing *suo motu* information at regular intervals so that the public have minimum resort to use the Act and also the publication of 'User Guide' with all details of the manner in which information can be obtained. All these efforts are shining examples of organisations being proactive in enlightening the people on the functioning of democratic government. This Act makes the government public relations to be more proactive. A proactive public relations creates better understanding between an organisation and its public and between a citizen and his or her public authority. While reactive public relations speaks volumes about the ineffectiveness of the organisation, proactive public relations as a means of a two-way communication results in effective relations with stakeholders.

CORPORATE IDENTITY

The importance of both the corporate identity and the corporate image has increased in the wake of globalisation, when all corporations are involved in global trade wars. In such a competitive marketing environment, the corporations which have better image will alone survive, while others will perish. Though these two terms 'identity' and 'image' are different, they are complementary to each other. In fact, corporate identity as the forerunner of public relations activity supports the corporate image. If the identity is the physical insignia of a corporation, image is the mental perception of a person about an organisation—one looks at identity while another thinks about the image of an organisation.

Corporate identity and corporate image are the two strong pillars of public relations edifice through which the goal of public relations, understanding of the public can be achieved.

What is Corporate Identity?

The dictionary meaning of identity is "the distinguishing characteristic or personality of an individual". The fact of being who or what a person or thing is. Such a meaning is applied to both individuals and corporations as a corporate citizen. *Corporate identity may be described as the distinctive insignia or logo of a corporation, easily recognised and remembered by the public.* It encompasses an organisation's core values, standards and its goals.

Corporate identity is also described as "visual identification of an organisation by the livery of its vehicles; logo, typography and colour schemes; dress uniform, badge; house style of print; fascia boards; and name displays and other special items such as ties, tableware, flags.

From a public relations angle, corporate identity can be defined as the strategic development of a distinct and coherent image of an organisation that is consistently communicated to stakeholders through symbolism, planned communications and behaviour. (ComLisson and Elving 2003). The authors in this definition have qualified that corporate identity is a corporate strategic effort to project the company to the stakeholders through symbolism. Such a pictorial presentation about the identity of an organisation like TATAs or Air India's Maharaja is easily understood by both literate and illiterates in the Indian context.

Symbols of Corporate Identity

Corporate identity has a historical background. In the early period, kings would lead their armies and identify themselves by means of an emblem or a flag. They later became the corporate identities of modern organisation. See Figure 13.1, the Indian national emblem, which is an adaptation from the Sarnath Lion Capital of Emperor Ashoka as the identifying symbol of the Government of India has four lions (the fourth being hidden from view). The wheel of the law (*Dharma Chakra*) appears in the centre of the abacus with a bull on right and a horse on left and the outlines of other wheels on extreme right and left. The words 'Satyameva Jayate' from *Mundaka Upanishad*, meaning 'truth alone triumphs' are inscribed below the abacus in *Devanagiri* script. This is the national emblem of our country and our nation is identified by this emblem all over the world which is also used in all the correspondence of Government of India from official diary to official Gazette. When you see this emblem, you think of India as a nation.

सत्यमेव जयते

Figure 13.1 The Indian National Emblem.

This principle also applies to the corporate India. People sometimes remember, a particular organisation by its corporate identity. For example, when we see *'Maharaja'* we think of Air India. Similarly, the inverted 'Vermillion Red Triangle', see Figure 13.2, has become an identifying symbol of Family Welfare.

Figure 13.2 Symbol of Family Planning.

The Life Insurance Corporation of India has a 'burning lamp protected by two hands' as its corporate identity. Its theme is *Yogakshema Vahamyaham* which means the date on which you insure, you are secure in the safe hands of the Life Insurance Corporation of India. This insignia has become very popular with the public as a physical symbol of LIC. Such symbols should always be very simple, easy to understand and capable of being imprinted in one's mind. See Figure 13.3.

Figure 13.3 Corporate Identity of LIC.

Togetherness is the theme of the logo of Andhra Bank where the world of banking services meets the realm of ever-changing customer needs, and establishes a link that is like a chain, inseparable. Derived from '∞' the symbol of infinity, the logo also denotes a bank that is prepared to do anything, to go to any lengths, for the customer. The keyhole indicates safety and security. The colours red and blue represent a fusion of dynamism and solidity. See Figure 13.4.

Figure 13.4 Logo of Andhra Bank.

Corporate identity is explicit in many visible forms of an organisation. It is conveyed through corporate products, services, stationery, uniforms, exhibition stands, corporate publications, house journals, annual reports, transport vehicles, advertisements, diaries and calendars so that the public could understand and form an impression of the organisation.

CORPORATE IMAGE

The *Reader's Digest Great English Dictionary* defines image as "a representation of the external form of a person or thing in art". It is derived from the Latin word *'imago'* which means to imitate. The image is the impression, the feeling, the conception which the public has of a person or a corporation. It is also regarded as a picture in the mind and has become a favourable term of public relations practitioners in implementing public relations activities. Some experts say public relations is an image building exercise. Maruti cars, Tata products, Microsoft software have their own image in the market.

What is corporate image? It is defined as "the impression of an organisation in the minds of the people". Corporate image is an image or impression of a company, based on knowledge of its activities and experience of its behaviour. Different people may attach importance to different factors of a corporate image, e.g., dynamic, cooperative, businesslike, successful (Aaron Spector). Such an impression of the public is based on their knowledge about the organisation and their experience with its products and services.

PR and Corporate Image

An individual knows all about his/her business and organisation, but an outsider knows very little about that particular organisation and its business. Unless the individual takes the initiative to tell the outsider about his/her business, the latter does not take initiative to know about the company. It is in this context that public relations as an information and communication function enters into the field. It is the primary task of public relations not only to tell about the organisation and its products and services but also to create a favourable image in the minds of various organisations' public based on its performance. It is because a corporation's identity and image reflects in its dealings with the employees on the one hand and customers on the other hand.

In fact, corporate image is the total public impression of an organisation as expressed by the internal and the external public. Of course, such an image depends on the organisation's mission, vision, policies, qualitative products and services, better financial performance and, in particular, its courteous behaviour with both the employees and the community. The better the service, the greater will be the image.

A good image of an organisation indicates its effective functioning and better performance.

The corporate image is not earned overnight. It is a long drawn process based on several factors, from good policy in the interest of public to better customer service. Good image is always built over a period, while bad image is created with one bad action. If the image is bad, it is the job of public relations to analyse the situation and keep the management informed of such bad images so that appropriate steps could be taken to rectify the defects and improve the corporate image of the organisation. Public relations with its persuasive techniques and messages must endeavour to reach all the public—the employees, customers, opinion leaders, regulatory bodies, government and the media who have the most accurate possible corporate image.

Corporate Identity Vs Corporate Image

The terms 'corporate identity' and 'corporate image' are sometimes confused with each other and often considered one and the same. The corporate identity of ITC Limited is printed on the cover page of a publication *Transforming Lives and Landscapes. ITC's Rural Development Philosophy of Work*. Here the organisation is communicating its identity as part of its rural development service. People look to ITC with its corporate identity whereas the corporate image is how ITC's target rural public actually view it after experiencing its rural development schemes, such as social and farm forestry, integrated watershed development, economic empowerment of women, web empowerment of farmer through *e-choupal* to transform them into powerful agents of social change. Today, ITC has a better image in the market. As such corporate identity is an identifiable visual symbol of the organisation whereas corporate image is the perception of the person that exists in one's mind. Both must run hand in hand and complement each other. See Figure 13.5

Figure 13.5 ITC Limited's Logo.

Public relations as an art of relationships management must promote both the corporate identity and the corporate image of an organisation.

CORPORATE REPUTATION

I don't know who you are.
I don't know your company.
I don't know your company's product.
I don't know what your company stands for.
I don't know your company's customers.
I don't know your company's record.
I don't know your company's reputation
Now what was it you wanted to sell me?

This is one of the most famous advertisements in which McGraw-Hill expresses the belief that a company's reputation is a prerequisite for effective selling of products. In fact, sales of products must start before the salesman calls on the potential customer. That is possible only when there is an excellent reputation for the organisation in the market. A good corporate reputation enhances the value of everything, an organisation does and says. A bad reputation devalues products and services, and it acts as a magnet for further deterioration.

What is reputation? The dictionary meaning of reputation is "the overall quality or character as seen or judged by people in general (good name), the beliefs or opinions that are generally held about someone or something". Reputation is the sum total of the corporation's daily actions, and it will determine whether recruits will join, consumers will buy, and journalists and legislators will give the benefit of doubt.

Edelman Public Relations (a public relations agency) defines the management of corporate reputation as "the orchestration of discrete public relations initiatives designed to promote or protect the most important brand you own—your corporate reputation". This reputation will be good or bad, strong or weak depending on the quality of strategic planning and service. Corporate reputation is defined as "the collective representation of an organisation's past performance that describes the firm's ability to deliver valued outcomes to multiple stakeholders. Expressed in plain terms reputation is the track record of an organisation in the public's mind" (Wilcox, Len and Cameron 2005).

The introduction of corporate reputation is a new dimension in corporate image. It causes further confusion between image and reputation. It may be difficult to distinguish between corporate image and corporate reputation.

It is opined that image is an immediate feeling or mental impression, whereas reputation is an assessment or judgement developed over a long period that relates to organisation's historical and future performance. If the image reflects the more recent beliefs about the organisation, the reputation is the perception of an organisation built over time (Balmer 1998). Reputation results from a reflection upon historical accumulated impacts of previously observed identity cues and transactional experiences (Melewar 2003). In other words, it is evaluative and is image endowed with judgement (Simoes and Dibb 2002).

Reputation unlike corporate image is owned by the public. It is not formed by slogans. A good reputation is created and destroyed by everything an organisation does, from the way it treats employees to the way it handles conflicts with outside constituents.

The management's commitment to achieving its stated goals, and the skill and energy with which all component programmes are implemented and communicated contribute to the creation of reputation. Corporate reputation is based on how the company conducts or is perceived as conducting its business. The attributed values (such as authenticity, honesty, responsibility and integrity) evoked from the person's corporate image constitute corporate reputation. Reputation like image is based on all impressions gained by the public, but there is difference. Unlike image, reputation is formed from personal experience. Image is based on beliefs developed from a distance without the benefit of contact. Reputation of a corporation, according to a few scholars, is based on three key factors: (i) economic performance of an organisation; (ii) social responsibility; (iii) the ability to deliver valuable outcomes to stakeholders.

Values of Reputation

A poor reputation will affect the company adversely, while good reputation will pay in both operational and financial ways. A survey reveals that the better the corporate reputation, the higher the stock price. There is a strong correlation between higher corporate reputation and higher price earnings. Some values are given as follows:

- It adds extra psychological value to your products and services (trust).
- It helps customers choose between products (TV set) and services (education) that they perceive as functionally similar.
- It increases employee job satisfaction.
- It enhances advertising and sales-force effectiveness.
- It supports new product introduction.
- It acts as a powerful signal to your competitors.
- It helps raise capital in the equity market.
- Tata group of companies have good reputation.

Some of the effects of poor reputation are as follows:

- The share market analysts do not like the company and undervalue its share price.
- Journalists pay particular attention to companies with poor reputation, and even when these companies do something good,

the journalists may remind their audience that this company has a bad history.

- Customers seem more concerned and price sensitive about products and services from less well-respected companies.
- Poor reputations tend to feed poor employees' morale.
- Satyam computers earned bad reputation.

Stakeholders' Reputation

A company has different types of stakeholders and the perception of the company differs from one group to another. This diversity presents a daunting task only if you try to manage all these separate perceptions. What is needed is a way of clustering people into groups which are likely to hold similar evaluations of the organisation. Here the task is to split these stakeholders into a manageable number of groups. These groups are linked to an organisation in different ways. The stakeholders include shareholders, employees, customers, government and regulatory agencies, financial analysts, media, dealers and suppliers. The better the reputation among these public, the better is the success of the company.

To create corporate reputation, it is necessary that programmes are designed to suit the different audiences. Such programmes must be developed based on the corporate strategy of the organisation. It is in the time of crisis that a good reputation acts as a 'shield' to save the company.

Role of PR

Public relations can play a pivotal role to build the reputation of a company based on its vision, mission, goals and performance. The Chartered Institute of Public Relations, London defines "Public Relations is about reputation, the result of what you do, what you say and what others say about you". Public relations practice is the discipline concerned with the reputation of an organisation (or products, services or individuals) with the aim of earning understanding and support.

Integrated public relations communication combines the work of all departmental communication of an organisation in relation to reaching their respective public on the one hand and also promote public relations culture, within and outside the organisation to persuade and influence the segmented public towards organisational goals on the other hand.

Corporate public relations programme either for internal publics or for external publics must be based on a strategic planning to reach all segments of public with good deeds. As part of integrated public relations communication, various media and tactics have to be used to achieve the following five communication objectives:

1. Awareness of the company
2. Customer needs and services
3. Corporate image and reputation
4. Stakeholders support
5. Company's performance and feedback

Reality

Public relations has a major role in publicising the various corporate activities that promote reputation. The schemes undertaken under the corporate social responsibility which add to corporate reputation are taken by public relations to target the audience.

Public relations must remember that good policies, quality of product and service, above all the reality and corporate reputation are inextricably linked. But, however, skilled a public relations professional may be, he or she cannot create and sustain a good reputation for a bad corporation. If asked to do, a professional public relations manager should not hesitate to tell the management about the 'reality' and that the top management must change the reality with new positive policies.

Case Study

In her book, *FACE UP Tenets, Techniques and Trends of Public Relations for the 21st Century*, Rita Bhimani says "that when the product is good, and the past reputation sound, the goodwill generated far outstrips any formal public relations efforts". In other words, it is the quality of the product and service that creates an image for the organisation. While presenting the case study of the Bengal Ambuja Housing Development Ltd., Kolkata, she pointed out that the reputation is garnered but not sought. The Ambuja Housing Development Ltd. is the joint venture project where the State Government and the private sector have collaborated to augment the provision of housing, particularly in the urban areas and have added to the governments' efforts to provide affordable houses to the masses. It was conceived by Harshavardhan Neotia with the simple vision: 'Housing for All'. The business model was simple as well: "Make Quality Homes charge reasonable prices and provide the customer with a product that is value for money". This was straight-from-the-heart philosophy of Neotia. An interesting feature of the Housing Project was that about 65 per cent of the area was left open sky to create the feeling of space and the perfect ambience for living in harmony with the nature.

The new concept was well received. Bengal Ambuja was hailed as a model housing project. Among others, the President of India visited the project site and commended. Neotia was also conferred with *Padmashree* by the Government of India. The project was so popular that there was never a week when the media did not contact the company to get a story. That is how reputation is built which has to be managed very carefully by public relations.

CORPORATE SOCIAL RESPONSIBILITY (CSR)

A company which abuses its workforce, or a company which employs forced labour, is not only in breach of the Universal Declaration of Human Rights, but is flying in the face of civilised thinking all over the world. Such a company is acting irresponsibly in an area over which it has direct influence. And in a world of increasing transparency and global communications such a company is also foolish if it thinks such behaviour will not attract attention, said one Chairman, Centre for Corporate Citizenship.

Jamshedji Tata, the pioneer of social responsibility in India, said, "Wealth that comes from the people as far as possible must go back to the people". It is against the background of this philosophy, the concept of corporate social responsibility began in India at Jamshedpur, Bihar where the Tatas built a township for the workers of the Tata Iron and Steel Company.

The importance of corporate social responsibility (CSR) has further increased because of changing corporate world. Everything from family life to ways of working in a corporation are changing. In consequence, every organisation has to confront with a global economy; a technological revolution, an information revolution and proliferation of sources of information; emergence of large companies with international business; mergers and acquisitions, and signs of increasing environmental damages. The changes have had an impact on ways of doing business. For instance, competition gets intensified when cheap goods produced by low-wage workers are imported into parts of the world where labour charges are high. Reputations are either strengthened or damaged as the information is flowing with lightening speed. As a result, the concept of corporate citizenship and corporate social responsibility is growing in the modern world.

Corporate Citizenship

What is a corporate citizen? Corporation is a legal entity registered under the law which assumes certain rights and duties like a citizen of the country. Involvement of a corporation in matters concerning to society as a whole is called corporate citizenship.

Corporate citizenship is an idea, which has both practical and ethical dimensions. It suggests a two-way relationship between corporations and society which are oriented towards meeting community needs. In fact, business organisations and the community have a symbiotic relationship with one thriving on the other. It is in this context, corporate citizen has the responsibility to serve the cause of the society like a citizen of a Nation. Interest in corporate citizenship and social responsibility is growing as the role of corporate and its business in society increases. As in the case of an individual citizen, corporate citizen which has emerged from a corporation has similar legal and moral responsibilities towards the needs of the society.

Definition

Corporate social responsibility is defined as "the process by which a corporation participates in the welfare of both internal and external community, enhancing its environment and well-being to the advantages of the organisation and the community concerned". It also aims at building relationships with all types of public and increasing the reputation of the company. Actions and community services that do not have purely financial implications and those are demanded or expected of an organisation by society at large, often concerning community welfare and ecological and social issues, come under the corporate social responsibility.

CSR and Business Organisation

Why should companies consider corporate social responsibility? This is not about dropping coins in a kitty. Corporations which are active in this area say that corporate social responsibility makes a sense to them in the enhanced quality of relationships with their publics. They treat this as part of their corporate strategy. Business companies which make a public commitment to improve the welfare of the society claim that they have substantial company benefits covering competition, performance and recruitment as well as creation of enduring healthy communities. In other words, corporate social responsibility can bring benefits in the four following areas:

1. Enhanced features of the corporate brand
2. Greater customer goodwill and loyalty
3. Improved workforce commitment and morale
4. Better image and reputation in the society

How does CSR help organisation: "CSR helps to greenwash the company's image, to cover up negative impacts by saturating the media with positive images of the company's CSR credentials." CSR enables business to claim progress despite the lack of evidence of verifiable change. Since much of the business case for CSR depends on corporation being seen to be socially responsible, CSR will continue to be little more than PR for as long as it is easier and cheaper to spin than to change (Fauset 2006). Cutlip (2000) believes that CSR can be good for PR, stating that "much good can be credited to ethical public relations practice, and opportunities for serving the public interest abound.

What are the programmes covered under corporate social responsibility? The programmes include wide range activities, often far removed from the corporation's economic function. Examples of such activities include sponsorship of sport event or the arts, donations to charity and contribution in either cash or kind such as office facilities, equipment, professional advice, training, technology, gifts normally given towards public or voluntary-sector activities in the community in which the organisation operates. They also include: education, population control, removal of poverty, illiteracy and ignorance; combating corruption, ensuring free and fair elections; providing employment; pushing through reforms, eradicating communicable diseases and finding answers to problems pertaining to gender discrimination, child labour, mother and child health, HIV AIDS, energy conservation, etc. The canvas is so large that there is need for coordinated action from the government, local and corporate bodies, NGOs and individuals. The staff of the corporation also participates in CSR.

Case Study: *Tata Council for Community Initiatives*

The Tata Group Companies have constituted the Tata Council for Community Initiatives (TCCI) mainly for the purpose of undertaking community welfare programmes. The mission statement of the Council reads:

> We will evolve a common direction for community development programmes from diverse activities of all Tata business units through sharing and participatory networking. We will strive together constantly to strengthen our professional and organisational abilities to fulfil our commitments towards society at large.

After the death of Jamshedji Tata, in tune with his deep commitment, the Tata group established many major institutions including Tata Memorial Centre for Cancer Research and National Centre for the Performing Arts. These corporate bodies are run out of profits earned by Tata companies as part of their social responsibility.

Since India lives in its villages, Tatas also have taken up their social responsibility in rural areas. Rural India's socio-economic development needs include—education, healthcare, agricultural inputs, transport, water supply and so on. It is in this context the Tata Steel Rural Development Society was established in 1979 and it had pioneered a rural development programme in 32 villages around Jamshedpur. Later its activities were spread to 500 villages in Bihar, Orissa and Madhya Pradesh.

PR and social responsibility

One of the objectives of corporate social responsibility is that having done good to the community, the corporation intends to improve its reputation as a responsible corporate citizen. The corporate contributions, undoubtedly, create good relations with employees, shareholders, consumers, community neighbours, media public, dealers, distributors, educators, the government, etc.

As ethical standards towards society change and the commitments to corporate social responsibility grow, public relations which is based on the principle of public interest and social purpose gains added importance to help the corporate world. "Do the Right Thing". It is here the role of public relations that *doing good* or *Performing well* by the organisation is reported to the community. Therefore, public relations means 'P' for performing good and 'R' for reporting which will build goodwill of key publics. Many corporations operate their corporate social responsibility programmes through their public relations/corporate communications departments. State Bank of India has kept CSR programme under its corporate communications department.

Two Themes

Public relations literature in the West highlights two main themes with regard to corporate social responsibility and public relations. The **first theme** points out the relationship between the public relations function and society which clearly says that public relations in itself has the social responsibility to serve the cause of the community and has a role to promote the public welfare and public good. The **second theme** argues that public relations performs the role of conscience keeper of the organisation and it has a moral obligation to promote the social responsibility programmes of the corporation.

Public relations, in social responsibility, plays dual role. It communicates to the target audience about the programmes of social responsibility on the one hand and also identifies the community needs such as educational facilities, drinking water, medical facilities, etc. and brings such needs to the notice of management on the other hand. The second role enables the management to undertake corporate social responsibility programmes.

Thus, there is a close link between corporate social responsibility and public relations function. The ideal role of public relations is often described as that of "a person in the middle", between the corporation and the society without any scope of the possible conflict that might result in this role. In fact, the objective of public relations in a society is to harmonise an organisation with the social environment by communicating honestly, consistently and continuously to gain in return credibility, public goodwill, mutual understanding and mutual respect.

POINTS TO REMEMBER

1. The corporation is a large company or a group of companies authorised to act as a single entity and recognised as such in law. Corporation means a business organisation formed into an association by law with the rights and liabilities of an individual or relating to a corporation. It is also a group of people joined together under the law to accomplish the corporate goals.

2. Corporate communication is the integrated approach to all communications generated by an organisation directed to all relevant target groups. It is also described as the total communication activity of a company to achieve its planned objectives.

3. Corporate public relations is a process of a two-way communication between an organisation and its various stakeholders to promote goodwill, and organisational products and services.

4. There is not much difference between corporate communication and corporate public relations. Both areas applied communication to corporations or companies for management of stakeholders relationships. When public relations became non-professional and failed to deliver goods and carried bad name like spin doctor or mere media relations, the corporate sector in the USA coined a new word for public relations as corporate communication. In fact, both are the same in reaching the goals of organisations but only titles are different. Both nomenclatures—Public Relations and Corporate Communication are popular all over the world.

5. Proactive public relations is a process of acting in anticipation of a problem rather than simply responding to a situation when the public lodges a complaint. Proactive public relations redresses a complaint or a problem unasked based on the assessment of public relations practitioner. The Right to Information Act envisages that public authorities should endeavour for proactive disclosure of information so that the public have minimum resort to the use of the Act to obtain information.

6. Reactive public relations means showing a response to a stimulus, or acting in response to a situation or a complaint rather than creating a favourable situation or showing the probable problem. Public relations, therefore, has two faces as proactive and reactive.

7. Corporate identity is the distinctive insignia or logo of a corporation easily recognised and remembered by the public. 'Maharaja' is the corporate identity of AIR India.

8. Corporate image is defined as the impression of an organisation in the minds of the people. Image describes the perception of an

organisation or individual. It is the collective perception of an organisation by all of its public, based on what it says and does which constitute the image. The better the service, the greater the image.

9. Corporate reputation is the sum total of the corporation's daily actions that determine the image to attract recruits, consumers, etc. Reputation unlike image is formed from personal experience and a long range process.

10. Public relations is about reputation, the result of what you do, what you say and what others say about you. Public relations is concerned with reputation management as a measure to gain public understanding. Therefore, public relations promotes corporate reputation by taking the messages to all its stakeholders about the good products and good services of the organisation.

11. Jamshedji Tata once said "wealth that comes from the people as far as possible must go back to the people". It is in this context that the concept of corporate social responsibility began in India at Jamshedpur in Bihar where the Tatas built a township for the workers of the Tata Iron and Steel Company.

12. Corporate social responsibility is defined as the process by which a corporation participates in the welfare of both internal and external community, enhancing its environment and wellbeing to the advantages of the organisation and the community concerned.

13. Corporate social responsibility brings benefits to a company in four ways: enhancement of the value of corporate brand, greater customer goodwill, loyalty and improved commitment of workforce and corporate reputation.

14. Corporate social responsibility programmes intended for the benefit of community include: sponsorship of sports event, donations to charity, supply of technical equipment, training, public education, award of scholarships, measures for population control, eradicating communicable diseases, HIV AIDS, energy conservation, etc.

15. One of the objectives of corporate social responsibility is to improve corporate reputation by doing good to the community. As such public relations has to report to the community about the community welfare undertaken by a corporation. When public relations is based on public interest, it has the responsibility to promote corporate social responsibility. Public relations also identifies the community needs and brings to the notice of corporation for undertaking community welfare programmes. Therefore, there is a close linkage between corporate social responsibility and public relations practice.

REVIEW QUESTIONS

1. What is corporate public relations? Explain the broad areas of corporate public relations.

2. What exactly is corporate communication? Is it different from corporate public relations? Describe the role of corporate communication in building relationships between an organisation and its stakeholders.

3. How proactive do we need to be for being effective in public relations practice?

4. What is the difference between corporate identity and corporate image?

5. What is corporate reputation? How does public relations help in reputation management?

6. What is corporate social responsibility? How does public relations promote social responsibility?

Stakeholders' Public Relations | Chapter 14

> *If you want to plan for a year, plant a corn. If you want to plan for 30 years, plant a tree. But, if you want to plan for 100 years, plant people.*
> **—Chinese Proverb**

CONTENTS

WHO IS A STAKEHOLDER?

The terms stakeholder and shareholder confuse the students as to who is the actual stakeholder who is a shareholder. The stakeholder is 'a person with an interest or concern in an organisation. Stake means money invested in a company, or an interest of a person in a company. Oxford Advanced Learner's Dictionary defines stakeholder as a person or a company that is involved in a particular organisation, project, system, etc. because he/she has invested money in it. The idea of stakeholder comes from the stockholders, people who have bought shares into a publicity held company and thus have a vested interest. A shareholder is a stakeholder, but all stakeholders who do not have shares cannot be shareholders. Therefore, shareholder is distinct from general stakeholders such as customers and media who do not have shares.

The definition of a stakeholder provided by Freeman is "a stakeholder is any group or individual who can affect or is affected by the achievement of the organisation's purpose and objectives". An organisation's stakeholders are those publics who have an interest in the organisation. They are also 'publics' of public relations practice who they have to motivate towards organisational goals, products and services.

TYPES OF STAKEHOLDERS

Stakeholders publics are classified into different categories based on their nature and interest of the people.

1. One classification is based on stakes:
   * Equity stakes—shareholders, owners
   * Economic stakes or market stakes—customers
   * Influencer stakes—consumer advocates, opinion leaders
2. The second classification is as internal stakeholders (employees) and external stakeholders (customers, suppliers, dealers)
3. The third category is of two types as: (i) contractual stakeholders, who have some contract with the organisation by way of an agreement such as employees, suppliers, dealers, shareholders; (ii) community stakeholders, who can influence and affect the organisation such as consumer advocates, regulators, government, media, pressure groups, lobbyists.

Stakeholders or public relations publics are categorised as follows:

(i) **Management publics**
   * Members of Top Management
   * Directors of the Board, CEO
   * Heads of Departments
   * Senior Level Managers
   * General Managers and Other Managers

(ii) **Financial publics**
   * Shareholders, investors
   * Security analysts
   * Financial media: Economic Times, NDTV Profit
   * Business Magazines
   * Securities and Exchange Board
   * Stock Exchanges
   * Banks: Reserve Bank of India and Commercial Banks

(iii) **Employee publics**
   * Clerical personnel
   * Workers, secretariat personnel
   * Security personnel, drivers
   * Trade unions
   * Telephone operators

- Receptionists
- Potential employees

(iv) **Consumer publics and users**
- Customers
- Consumers Activist Groups
- Consumer Publications

(v) **Supplier publics**

Who supply raw material and other logistics

(vi) **Trade Distributors and dealers**
- Retailer
- Dealers

(vii) **Government publics (executive)**
- Central Government—Department, Bureaucrats
- State Government—Department, Bureaucrats
- Local Government—Department, Mayor, Bureaucrats
- Panchayati Raj Institutions
- Zilla Parishad, Blocks, Mandals, Village Panchayats
- Regulatory Bodies—Electricity Commissions

(viii) **Legislative branch publics**
- Members of Parliament—Speaker and Chairman
- Members of Legislative Assembly—Speaker and Chairman
- Members of Legislative Council—Chairman
- Members of Local Bodies

(ix) **Community publics**
- Community leaders
- Religious leaders
- Professionals—Professional Associations
- Community Organisations—civic, social service, cultural, political, opinion leaders

(x) **Third party publics**
- Not-for-Profit organisations
- Non-governmental organisations
- Voluntary organisations
- Leaders of NGOs

(xi) **Specialised publics**
- Women
- Youth
- Farmers
- Tribals
- Scheduled Castes and Scheduled Tribes
- Senior citizens
- Minorities
- People below the Poverty Line

- Illiterates
- Sports fans
- Artistes

(xii) **International/global publics**
- Global Media: BBC, CNN
- Host country government, regulatory bodies, bureaucrats, political parties and leaders

(xiii) **Media publics**
- Print Media, Broadcast Media
- New and Social Media
- Folk Arts
- Media Representatives
- Specialised Media—Finance, Business

The key job of public relations is to create and maintain cordial relations with all types of stakeholders/publics who are concerned with the organisation. Thus there is the need for stakeholders' relationship management. Stakeholders relations is described as building of bridges with each type of stakeholder groups/individuals that effect the corporate mission of the organisation. Therefore, the success of every organisation is inseparably linked with the relations of stakeholders and their goodwill for the organisation.

Case Study: Manesar Maruti Plant

"Not a single mishap of such nature has happened in Suzuki Motor Corporation's global operations spread across the world", said Maruti Suzuki Managing Director Shizo Nakanishi. The General Manager (Human Resource Development) of Maruti Plant at Manesar in Haryana was killed and 91 people were injured in a violent confrontation between workers and the management in July 2012. Office property was damaged, burnt beyond repair along with heavy damages of the main gate, security office and fire safety section. Manesar Plant has an annual capacity of about 5.5 lakh cars and accounts for about a third of Maruti's total production in India. The relation between workers and management had been under strain. As a result, it took violent form. This incident is not only a conflict between workers and management but also a serious industrial relations problem.

Why did it happen? The Hindu in its editorial on 23 July 2012 commented: "while condemning the violence unleashed by the workers, it is important to find out why they reacted in such an extreme way. Maruti's Manesar Plant workers and management have been in an uneasy relationship for over a year now. The Plant witnessed labour protests for more than four months last year, culminating in a 33-day lockout following a dispute over *employment of contract labour wages,* the creation of a new union and speed-ups. The truce since then was an uneasy one as borne by the unfortunate events last week".

The Economic Times in editorial on 23 July 2012 stated: "The immediate provocation at Maruti is reported to be an altercation between a supervisor and a worker that resulted in the worker's suspension *which the newly recognised union failed to reverse*. The union had also failed to secure wage settlement or end the system of Maruti deploying temporary contract workers who outnumber the permanent workers by far and are paid a fraction of what the permanent workers are paid."

If that was the story narrated by media about the Manesar incident, here are the comments of shareholders and investors as reported in the media. "Shareholders of Maruti Suzuki criticised the management for intelligence failure and poor handling of labour issues, where festering worker discontent led to rioting and loss of production last month. The Industrial Relations Department needs to be strengthened. It should not let evils crop up." (31st AGM). "Investors also voiced concern over poor intelligence gathering, Maruti needs to revamp its internal intelligence. Better information gathering would have helped it know about what was happening within the company". The lockout had cost Maruti a production loss of over 30,000 cars or over ₹1500 crores in revenue. The plant was reopened on August 21, 2012.

Responding to shareholders concerns, Maruti Chairman R.C. Bhargava said, "The violence at the Manesar plant was unprecedented in the history of Maruti and Indian Industry. There was no ostensible cause for this violence; there were no outstanding demands of the workers pending with the company. We are introspecting on the reason for this incident and will address them" (as reported in the Economic Times).

Whatever may be the reason for this crisis at Manesar, the fact remains that the relations between the Maruti Management and its workforce were strained over a period on the demands of workers. Therefore, the need for employee communication arises on account of high profile crisis situations such as trade union agitations against managements on employees' demands, strikes, factory closings, lockouts, layoffs, etc. Such crisis demands the need for constant employee relations process to promote better relations and mutual understanding between management and workforce. Such relations can be better handled by public relations personnel. A corporation's long-term practice of two-way communication, transparency and fair consistent treatment of employees becomes its most imaginative tool in employee relations. Thus, there is the need for employees public relations.

EMPLOYEES' PR—EMPLOYEES ARE THE FIRST

The people who affect or are affected by an organisation's programmes, policies, services or products are mainly the stakeholders. An organisation's stakeholders include—customers, shareholders, financial suppliers, employees, suppliers, distributors, neighbourhood community, media, etc. Communication with all these segments of population is an important area in public relations of an organisation.

The business of every organisation is inseparably linked with the interests of its employees (E), shareholders (S), and customers (C). These three groups constitute a tripod—'ESC' on which a corporation strongly rests. It is the job of the management to see that each of these segments receives a fair and considerably good treatment so that the corporation could engineer a firm public support.

Employees First

According to some authors, employees are the first priority among the publics of a corporation. Granted a corporation cannot exist without customers who buy its products, granted shareholders are so basic that they cannot be relegated to a minor position. Despite these facts, one social scientist Edger Queen thoughtfully and intentionally listed employees 'first' knowing that without them there would be no company either for the customers to patronise or for the shareholders to invest.

Internal Customers

Of late, a new term 'internal customers' has been coined for employees giving them equal importance on par with customers or external customers. Unfortunately, most of the organisations' managements tend to ignore public relations in relation to employees'. Internal communication regrettably is the cinderella of organisations.

New Trend in Recruitment

The concept of globalisation, information revolution, concept of global village, the international competitive marketing environment and the global trade wars, more than ever, warrant the corporations to have, well informed, empowered, loyal and fully committed workforce to compete the trade wars in the global economy effectively.

Beyond Employees

The concept of employee relations sometimes goes beyond internal audiences. It is because the confidence of customers, shareholders and investors can be strained when there is unrest between employees and management, may be on workers' demands or on the quality of service and product. Even other stakeholders such as suppliers, dealers, community leaders and regulators may form adverse opinion about the company.

An appointment advertisement in a daily newspaper read, "Here is a company that rewards you to work, to somebody else's satisfaction". Another company Wintech Software Solutions carried the headline in its advertisement campaign in all major newspapers "These are not our employees. They are yours" (Customers). These appointment advertisements highlight the key role of employees to attain the targets of a company and to serve the customers.

What is then employees' public relations? 'It is the systematic and symmetrical process of public relations communication through which organisations listen to employees, share information, build their support and commitment, and manage change to achieve organisational goals'. It is systematic because in that all tools and techniques are used to disseminate information in order to be highly effective and motivate the employees. Moreover, it is symmetrical in the sense that those who communicate also seek an interactive relationship. We speak and listen. We write and we read. It is quite simply a loop. Thus, employees' public relations is a two-way communication process, which not only gives job information but also ascertains employees' reactions and their needs. Finally, it is aimed at creating loyalty towards the company and commitment to its policies and programmes.

Principles of Employees' Relations

The communication between the management and the employees is based on the following basic principles:

1. Develop a comprehensive internal communication strategy as approved by management with media and tactics to cover all employees based on their needs and aspirations.
2. Produce the relevant printed, audio-visual material in advance that are tailored to the audience (backgrounders, handbooks).
3. **Share information:** Management must be genuinely willing to share information with the employees. Take the message directly to the employees.
4. **Truthfulness, avoid distortion of information:** Written messages should be used to avoid the distortion of meaning that may occur in oral communication.
5. **Media:** The media of communication should be carefully selected and messages be prepared by experienced public relations practitioners. House journal is a good medium.
6. **Timely:** Information should be timely and messages transmitted quickly to avoid misunderstanding.
7. **Loyalty:** Communication with employees must be aimed at gaining their loyalty and increase productivity.

8. **Feedback information:** As a two-way communication process, provision should be made to collect employees' feedback information.

Areas of Employees' PR

The following are the areas of employees' public relations:

1. Organisational information (promotion of corporate mission—product information)
2. Job information (skills, job profile)
3. Collective bargaining issues (trade union—agreements)
4. General education (health, social responsibility)

Tactical Objectives

A predetermined list of tactical objectives may be evolved for employee communication. They are to promote:

1. Achievement of targets in production to meet delivery promises on schedule.
2. Achievement of quality standards and reduction of defects to meet customer demands.
3. Achievement of cost-reduction goals.
4. Achievement of productivity, improvements from new equipment and procedures, changes in facilities, machines and methods.
5. Introduction of new practices/new technology, changes in work standards, restructuring of jobs, changes in classifications and pay rates.
6. Resolution of employee dissatisfaction, strike, threats through sound understanding of the issues.

The entire employees' public relations programme is dependent on the dictum "Well-informed employee is an asset, while ill-informed employee is a liability". It should be the endeavour of internal public relations to create a well-informed employee with loyalty, dedication and commitment towards organisational goals. How can we create such a commitment? It is through a well-formulated communication programme and employees' welfare measures.

Employees' Media and Methods

A key factor in employees' public relations and their motivation is communication. The organisation needs a blueprint on a well-planned and implemented public relations communication programme using a variety of media to meet employees' basic information needs and to facilitate the upward flow of information. The media of communication in any organisation is organised under the following heading: print media; visual media; electronic media; oral media; IT new media; upward communication (subordinate to superior); downward communication (superior to subordinate); and communication in crisis situation. The role of public relations manager in all these areas is that of a kingpin. Here are the following various methods of communication used under each medium.

1. **Print media:** Employee newspapers, house journals, newsletters, corporate publications, letters to employees, handbooks, manuals, brochures, folders, annual reports, posters, stickers, etc.
2. **Audio and oral media:** Radio – industrial workers programme, meetings, quality circles, open house, floor walking, voice-to-voice communication, grapevine, seminars, group discussions, workshops, individual and group briefings, conferences.
3. **Visual media:** Bulletin boards, displays, exhibitions, photographs, posters, demonstrations, etc.
4. **Audio-visual media:** Television, video, slides, cable TV, electronic bulletin boards, electronic house journals, electronic newspapers, closed circuit TV, film strips, documentary films, etc.
5. **IT new mass media:** Personal computers and computer networks, Internet, CD-ROM, e-mail, voice-mail, fax, blogs, twitter, facebook.

Employees' Feedback

Most of the Indian companies do communicate with their employees, but they do not give much importance to the feedback they receive from their own employees. In fact, it should be an in-built mechanism in the employee's public relations programme. The incident at Manesar in Haryana in which GM (HRD) was killed would not have happened had there been a good feedback information mechanism in place with the corporate communications department of Maruti Udyog Ltd.

Some of the methods of feedback mechanism include: employees workshops; seminars; open house; individual meetings; staff review meetings; suggestions scheme; active listening; orientation programme; visits of senior officers to field offices, etc. Employees may be encouraged to write their views in house journal.

Orientation Programme: A Case Study

The Andhra Pradesh State Planning Department organised an eight-day orientation training programme in July 2000 for about 1100 Nodal Officers of *Janmabhoomi Programme* (Rural Development) at the Administrative Staff College of India (ASCI), Hyderabad. The officers were divided into different groups for discussing the problems on the implementation of the Janmabhoomi Programme. Each group was supervised by a senior faculty member of the ASCI, who not only facilitated the group discussions but also collected the officer's reactions. The senior faculty member of each group briefed the Chief Minister at a Plenary Session of the Orientation Training Programme about the reactions of officers. This is a good example of collecting feedback information from employees in a seminar or a workshop.

Senior Managers' Meeting

On May 1, 1999, May Day (the Workers' Day), over 1200 senior managers of Tata Iron and Steel Company (TISCO) held a half-day session in Jamshedpur to thrash out key company issues such as investment, disinvestments strategies, future plans for social responsibility, marketing strategy, cost-competitiveness, human resources policy, and translate TISCO's new vision into action. This brain storming meet was intended to equip the company workers for the challenges they face in the future. Better service, customisation of products, quality norms, TATA code of conduct, all were discussed.

Dr. J.J. Irani, Senior Vice-President of the company, headed the strategy-cum-communication exercise session. After the session, the senior executives were made responsible to disseminate company's strategy and the new vision at the shop-floor levels. This is yet another method of employee communication.

Common Failings in Employee Communications

First, communication is weighed towards management views, priorities, perceptions and interests, with insufficient attention given to the views of non-management people—say employees, trade unions. In other words, the weight of the flow is downwards and not upwards, and there is insufficient attempt made to create a two-way dialogue.

Second, communication is not something public relations does in isolation. It has to be a combined effort with contributions from different units, coordinated but flexible enough to handle a variety of requirements. Sometimes communication requirements call for input from human resource department, because it alone has the relevant expertise. Employees' communication will succeed when it is converted into colleague communication involving human resource department. All employees should be treated as colleagues in a team.

What employees do not like

While handling employees' communication, public relations must bear in mind as to what employees do not like. Such dislikes include adding more hierarchical levels to treat employees like cheap labour when employee labour is anything but cheap; excluding employees from the decision-making process (empowered employees are happy employees); red tape; inefficient bosses; uncooperative management, an injudicious reward/punishment system. Building employee morale is just as hard as it is easy to break it. Thus, it should be handled with care. Appointment of temporary contract labour at cheaper wages ignoring permanent workforce is yet another cause for employees dissatisfaction.

Case Study

The employees of the Andhra Pradesh State Corporation gave a strike notice for wage revision in 1980. Negotiations were held with the recognised trade union and other unions of employees on the demands. Conciliation meetings with labour department officials were held. While negotiations were on, the public relations department brought out a 'Mini Poster' of 20" × 15" size explaining the Corporation's stand on the employees demands. The title of the poster was "Employees are lifeblood of the Corporation". The contents of the poster were: that the wage revision was done earlier involving an additional burden of ₹16.5 crores, that the corporation is ready to appoint a committee for revising the pay scales.

Detailing the welfare measures, the poster mentioned about temporary relief, additional dearness allowance, payment of ex gratia, incentive bonus, housing loans, medical aid, new dispensaries, child welfare centres, concessional bus passes to the children of employees and loans through cooperative credit society. The poster also presented the other side of the financial burden on the Corporation due to increase in the cost of inputs such as fuel, spare parts and tyres. "In view of the positive approach of the Corporation to demands of the employees, the strike is not advisable," the poster said. They were advised to keep the financial crisis of the Corporation in view and await the decision of the Pay Revision Committee.

This poster was displayed in all the depots, bus stations and at all workplaces where the employees of the Corporation meet. It was the practice earlier that the management negotiations should be confined only to the trade union leaders and that there was no direct communication with individual employees. This Mini Poster exposed all the employees to the positive attitude of the management to their demands and created great impact on the minds of the employees that they could wait till a decision is given by the Pay Revision Committee. Passengers were also exposed to this poster. Sensing the favourable mood of the employees, the Trade Unions also realised the difficulty of the corporation and called off the strike. This was the miracle of the mini poster, which helped in maintaining direct contact with individual employees.

HOUSE JOURNALS

The British Association of Industrial Editors, a professional body of business communicators, defined a house journal as "a publication issued periodically by industrial undertaking, a business house or a public service organisation, which is not primarily devised for profit but for the benefit of employees". House journal is also described as an in-house magazine issued regularly for either its internal public (employees) or its external public (customers) or both—internal and external for the purpose of information, education, motivation and entertainment.

Therefore, it contains news, views, events, humour and written by employees for the employees. The business of house journal forms part and parcel of corporate public relations/corporate communications.

History of house journal takes us back to 1840 when the first ever house journal 'Lowell Offering' was published by the Lowell Cotton Mills in America. However, the concept spread to all countries including India as a tool of employees' communication.

Why did they name the magazine of a company a house journal? The concept of house journal is derived from the house or home where the workforce employees live for more than eight hours and which is considered as the second house for them. It is a journal of the family of an organisation which regarded as house for them. House journal is also intended to bring about a sense of family environment among the employees of the company.

Types of House Journal

House journals are classified into three broad categories:

1. Internal house journal called employees' publication is exclusively meant for the workforce. For example, ITC News published by ITC Ltd, Kolkata.
2. External house journal published for the benefit of external public—customers, dealers, etc. The 'Swagat' is an example of external house journal brought out by the Air India as an in-flight magazine for the benefit of its passengers.
3. The third type of journal called mixed one, internal and external house, is intended both for internal and external stakeholders. The journal aims to meet the communication needs of an extended family of a company consisting of employees, customers, suppliers and general community. 'Sandesh' is an example of this type of journal brought out by the Shipping Corporation of India.

Objectives

A house journal must serve three basic objectives. It must act as a means of communication for employees with the management. The second objective is that the journal acts as a bridge of communication between the management and employees. The third purpose of a house journal is to act means by which the employees communicate with each other as members of the family within the organisation. These three purposes relate to the basic principles of corporate communications as downward, upward and horizontal communication.

Bertrand Canfield, a leading PR author, described objectives of a house journal as: "to inform employees about the policies and practices of a company; to stimulate increased production by publishing individual good performance and the need for increased output or productivity by workers; and to develop and promote loyalty towards organisation's goal."

Contents of an Internal House Journal

Contents of a typical house journal include: message from Chief executive, editorial, an article on any facet of the corporation needing the employees cooperation, a regular feature entitled our landmarks' spotlighting the achievements of the company; 'The Weal and Welfare' on the welfare of employees, the Humour Page containing light reading material such as cartoons and jokes; the cultural arena on the social and cultural activities of the employees including sports events, retirees' articles from retired employees, poems, short stories from employees, photos and illustrations, letters to the editor.

Safe Driving Poster

The Andhra Pradesh State Road Transport Corporation, which transports over one crore passengers every day, in its house journal 'Prasthanam' published a photograph of a poster that spelled out the benefits of careful driving and it informed the driver that if he would drive carefully, the passengers, the pedestrians and he too would reach home safely to a warm and affectionate welcome of the wife and children. The poster depicted the smiling face of a driver's wife with her two children, including a pet dog. This poster published in the house journal had great impact on the mindset of drivers towards safe driving, besides creating confidence among passengers on the efforts of APSRTC.

Staff Suggestions

'Without Reserve', the house journal of the Reserve Bank of India, once had brought its employees nearer to the management by introducing the "Staff Suggestions Scheme". It provided a channel of direct communication between the employee readers of the house journal and the top management of the Reserve Bank of India in tune with the philosophy of participative management. Out of over 3000 suggestions received from the employees, the management accepted 285 staff suggestions. As a result of accepted suggestions, the bank's savings came to an estimated amount of ₹2 lakhs. In terms of cash prizes, the journal distributed ₹12,500 to various winners of suggestions besides merit certificates.

R.K. Nair, former Executive Director, Corporate Communications, National Thermal Power Corporation, while dealing with the critical role of internal communication said: "Unfortunately the house magazines today do not effectively play the role assigned to them. The content, periodicity and distribution,—the three vital areas—are neglected in most organisations."

House journals by and large are management oriented because more coverage is given for management views. In fact, it should be a mix of management and employee orientation. Employees should feel that it is their journal. House journals do not reflect the views of recognized trade unions which represent the employees and their problems. Recognized trade unions should be given due place in the house journal. Unless a house journal is valued and appreciated by employee reader, its very purpose gets defeated. Employees' participation is a prerequisite for its success. Employees should be involved in contributing articles for the journal.

Though the printed house journal in India is still one of the most important media of internal communication, other formats of electronic journals are also in vogue.

Electronic newspaper/e-zine

Electronic newspaper or e-zine is another format of internal communications in which pages can be displayed in a computer for viewing at several workplaces on TV or on PC. The advantage of this type of house journal is that news can be flashed instantaneously

Video magazine

The news magazine type of house journal can be played back on a VCR at the workplace or at home.

FINANCIAL PUBLIC RELATIONS

Three 'Ms'

The growth of any organisation, according to one estimate, depends on '**Three Ms**'—**Men**, **Money** and **Material**. How do we raise money and financial resources? It is through shares, loans, investments, etc. Therefore, financial public relations in any company assumes great importance in acquisitions or mergers, public issue, resource mobilisation from the market. It is the function of public relations professionals to create an environment in which a company could mobilise funds.

Definition

Financial public relations is defined as "the management of two-way communication process between a public limited company and its financial stakeholders to promote its shares and investments". The shares of a company are traded on the stock exchange. The planning and implementation of financial calendar of a company through public relations communication in order to raise financial capital is also called financial public relations. It is a specialized area of public relations. The key task of financial public relations is to help build an awareness and understanding of the financial performance of the company among opinion leaders such as media, stockbrokers and financial analysts who influence potential investors. It is to ensure that the share price of a company adequately reflects its value in the market to help liquidity in shares.

The Public Relations Society of America defines financial public relations as "that area of public relations which affects the understanding of stockholders and investors generally concerning the financial position and prospects of a company and includes among its objectives the improvement of relations between corporations and their stockholders". Incidentally, financial public relations and investor relations are often referred to as being one and the same.

To interpret facts on financial matters to shareholders and influence investment decisions is a specialised area of public relations. A sound financial public relations programme wins and keeps the support of stockholders and financial community. It also contributes to corporate profitability.

Historical Background

Public companies as a measure to raise their finances have always communicated with their investors in one way or the other. Banks in India as institutional investors started their lending with the money on "Lender's Table" doing money lending on a small table, which was purely a private affair and individual oriented business. Later banking industry developed significantly to invest in companies.

Investors met in 'Coffee Shops' around the Bank of England in the 17th century to buy and sell shares (Keith Butterick 2011). The Lenders' Tables in India and Coffee Shops in the West now transformed into big financial institutions to invest in public companies which led to the emergence of financial public relations as 'a person in the middle' between companies and financial institutions.

With the introduction of New Industrial Policy 1991, that envisages economic liberalisation, privatisation and globalisation, the importance of financial public relations has gained further momentum. Public sector undertakings which were in a predominant sector have been privatised, such NTPC, ONGC and Indian Oil. In the process, privatisation became a shorthand term for selling of assets. Selling shares to public who were unfamiliar with the culture of share market necessitated in huge communication programme on television and newspapers. As a result, financial public relations acquired a specialised activity. This then led to a large increase in initial public offerings business in both private and public sectors. Entry of public sector into share market has given a fillip to financial public relations.

Financial Public

The financial publics of a company may be divided into three broad categories:

1. **Shareholders:** current shareholders, past shareholders, potential shareholders
2. **Institutional investors:** banks, mutual funds, pension funds, insurance companies, trusts, investment analysts and advisers, stockbrokers
3. **Financial media:** the financial and business media: Financial Express, Economic Times, Business Line, TV, Radio, Internet news services—Financial Journalists

Identification of financial public in specific terms is a prerequisite to the success of financial public relations. Each type of public needs a distinct media and a distinct method. However, annual report as a medium is common to all.

There are many listed companies in India, although the levels of trading in individual stocks vary greatly. When the Bombay Stock Exchange main market is operating, normally much of the dealing is concentrated in the stock of relatively few Indian companies such as ONGC, Reliance—that are in the news owing to corporate activity. Financial public relations has, therefore, become a very important part of a listed company's activities.

Good media coverage reflects financial public relations. There are many companies that have to fight for attention and find their shares undervalued simply because they are not obtaining their share of attention in the media. The companies will benefit substantially if they make use of public relations for media coverage.

To make a decision on which stock or bond to buy, investors need information. Many do some research before investing, and most require latest news and information. That is where the financial public relations function steps in. A financial public relations professional is one who breaks information between the investing community and the public trading company.

The financial calendar

Financial calendar which is a requirement of stock exchange is the lifeblood of a public company. For the public relations department, a financial calendar provides an opportunity to understand in detail how the public company operates and, therefore, in times of crisis such as take-over bids or defences, the public relations team hits the ground running.

The financial calendar comprises publication of preliminary results of a company, half-yearly figures, the annual report popularly known as once in a year communication and the Annual General Meeting. This constitutes food for financial public relations and a guide to shareholders. Shareholders need high dividend and better price for share.

Financial public relations programme

Although the financial calendar provides an ideal opportunity for a public company to develop its relationship with its public relations advisers and investors, there are yet three main areas of ongoing work which should be thoroughly undertaken throughout the year. They are: (i) a plan for communicating with stock brokers and financial institutions; (ii) a planned communication programme with the media; (iii) effective communication plan with its internal public—the employees.

Tactics

Once the financial public relations has developed a plan with specific strategy, it needs multiple tactics: annual report, quarterly reports, presentation before financial audiences, factbooks or factsheets, press releases, newsletters, telecommunication devices—ranging from the Internet to the old-fashioned telephone.

Finance can be public relations quagmire, but if it is neglected the company could go out of business and one could be out of job. The principles and methods discussed provide merely a basis for setting up and carrying out a successful public relations programme for stockholders. In applying them to a specific situation, the practitioner should always have in mind that the situation of no two companies is alike and, therefore, methods should be adopted to the specific situation. In another words, the approach should be flexible rather than rigid.

CUSTOMERS' PR

Customer is the master. Customer is always right.

Peter Drucker, the well-known management consultant, has said: "The primary purpose of a company is to create a customer. The primary business of every business is to stay in business and to do that, you have to get and keep customers".

Customer is the master and is always right. An organisation and its employees are totally accountable to the master customer. If the organisation has certain privileges in running the business, the customer also has certain inherent rights—the right to information, the right to know about the product or service, right to safety, right to choose. With these rights, the customer places an onerous responsibility on the management, the duty to inform or communicate to the customer. This philosophy brings us to the fact that every organisation has to devote itself to the subject of customer relations.

Describing the importance of a customer, Mahatma Gandhi once said:

> A customer is the most important visitor on our premises. He is not dependent on us. We are dependent on him. He is not an interruption in our work. He is the purpose of it. He is not an outsider in our business. He is a part of it. We are not doing him a favour by serving him. He is doing us a favour by giving us an opportunity to do so.

Another quotation from Mahatma Gandhi on the duty of a railway passenger is as follows: "If I were at the Head of the Railway Administration, I would advise the railway management to tell the public that unless they purchased tickets, trains would be stopped and they would resume journey only if the passengers willingly paid the fares due".

These two quotations bring two factors into light: in the first instance, the importance of a customer as a person who is doing us a favour by giving business is indicated, and in the second, the duty of the customer towards the organisation is highlighted as passengers should purchase the correct ticket for the smooth running of railways.

One Crore Passengers

On an average, Andhra Pradesh State Road Transport Corporation (APSRTC) with its fleet of 22,000 buses transports over 1.35 crore passengers every day covering about 85 lakh kilometres. Maintaining cordial relations with over one crore passengers poses the biggest challenge to the management and its over one lakh employees and to every transport manager in the Corporation. Good passenger relations and the public relations efforts by managers assume great importance in such corporations as the very success of the corporation lies in harmonious relations and better understanding with the passengers.

The passenger relations programme implemented by public relations department in APSRTC was basically based on the Corporation's services. However, the various media of communication were utilised in reaching the passengers not only to inform what the management is doing for them but also to educate them on their responsibilities as Mahatma Gandhi pointed out.

In conclusion, one needs to remember the words of Melody 'O' Shea and also spread it within the company. "A satisfied customer tells nine persons. A dissatisfied customer tells sixteen persons".

How do we make customers (passengers) to like our organisation? It is not just by our personal relations. But through our business, quality products and service. As such, a good product or good service is the key to successful customer relations. Good customer relations are based on good services and such relations lead to the satisfaction of the customer. This is the beginning of customer relations. Public relations in customer relations is regarded as marketing communications. Therefore, fifth 'P' public relations has been added to marketing strategy.

Cutlip, Center and Broom (1985) have identified seven forms of assistance to the marketing function which public relations can perform:

1. Publishing news and events related to the launching of new products or services
2. Promoting established products or services to the extent they are newsworthy
3. Creating a favourable image of the company behind the product
4. Arranging for public appearances of marketing spokespersons
5. Probing public opinion in market areas
6. Focusing news media attention on sales conferences and another marketing events
7. Assisting in programmes concerning promotion of consumerism

The above list underscores the key role of public relations in marketing which will ultimately promote customer relations.

A Chief Executive of a major public sector transport undertaking once posed a question to this author, "Why do I need public relations when my service is good?" The author replied:

There I beg to differ with you. Unless the information about good service is communicated to the customers, unless customers' satisfaction is sustained, there would be a communication gap between the service and the customer. Public relations is, therefore, required to sustain customer relations and their satisfaction. Customers' satisfaction certainly creates good reputation for the organisation, but public relations encase this reputation through its techniques by nurturing, maintaining and sustaining their satisfaction. This calls for a public relations-oriented management. Customer relations through public relations techniques is also required to find out what customers want. What problems do the product or the service have to solve in order to create customers' satisfaction?

Customer Service

The survival, growth and profitability of an organisation in a competitive environment are dependent on good customer service it offers. Good customer relations enhances the image of an organisation. The employees at all levels feel proud to work for an organisation which has an excellent image and this increases their efficiency and, thereby, the productivity and profitability of the organisation. It also has a great impact and influence on external public for getting their support to achieve the organisational goals.

Customer Satisfaction Index

How can we know whether our customers are satisfied? The answer is by simply asking them. By continuously carrying out customer surveys in which randomly selected number of customers reply to a number of questions. By this we obtain a large volume of data for processing and analysis. The results of this analysis will provide us with in-depth insight into what our customers think about us and what we can do to retain them, attract new customers, or win back any customers we may have lost. In addition they may also point out as to how we may best deploy our financial, technological and personnel resources to achieve better profitability. This, in other words, provides us what may be called our Customer Satisfaction Index (CSI), which can be effectively used to benchmark our customer satisfaction activities within our given objectives in marketing as well as public relations.

Educative Slogans

Education of customers assumes importance in an external public relations programme to seek their active cooperation in the smooth running of buses. Of course, the education depended much on the services provided by the Corporation.

The media utilised for external public relations in the Transport Corporation includes the following:

- Bus and bus stations
- Hoardings
- Newspapers
- Electronic display
- Radio
- Commuters' meets
- Doordarshan/ T.V. Channels
- Audio-visual aids
- Printed literature
- Face-to-face communication with passengers

The theme of the passenger relations programme was based on *Prayaneekule Mana Yajamanulu*, meaning 'passengers are our masters'. In tune with this theme, the Corporation has coined six slogans for educating the passengers through various media. They are as follows:

1. Follow the 'Q' while boarding. Avoid inconvenience to fellow passengers.
2. Ticketless travel is an offense. Fine up to ₹500.
3. Pay correct change for the fare. Cooperate with the Conductor.
4. Respecting women is our tradition. Allow women to sit in the seats allotted for them.
5. Footboard travel is dangerous.
6. Smoking is prohibited.

Customer relations for any company is a constant consideration, every time a customer encounters the company. If neglected, even a single incident can have serious consequences. One must adopt customer relations strategy depending on the nature of the organisation and the type of customers. The strategy adopted in APSRTC may not be useful in manufacturing industry, where consumers use products.

Consumer Awareness: A Case Study

JAGO GRAHAK JAGO

"An enlightened consumer is an empowered consumer". An aware consumer protects efficiency, transparency and accountability in the entire manufacturing and services sector. The most important milestone in consumer movement in India has been the enactment of the Consumer Protection Act, 1986, which applies of all goods and services, unless specially exempted by the Central Government in all sectors whether private, public or cooperative.

The Consumer Protection Act among others provides a right to be informed about the quality, quantity, potency, purity, standard and price of goods and services, right to seek redressal against an unfair or restrictive trade practice or unscrupulous exploitation and the right to consumer education. Consumer education, therefore, is an inherent right of every consumer/customer.

'JAGO GRAHAK JAGO' is the theme of consumer awareness publicity campaign under which the Ministry of Consumer Affairs makes use of multimedia to educate consumers. Publicity is done through AIR, FM stations, newspaper advertisements, telecast of video spots through electronic media, meghdoot postcards, display of posters in 1.55 lakh rural post offices and more than 25,000 urban post offices, advertisements on the website of the Ministry, www.fcamin.nic.in, publicity through outdoor media, traditional media such as "Nukkad Nataks", etc.

Complaint against Banks

The Ministry of Consumer Affairs, Food and Public Distribution and the Reserve Bank of India jointly issued an advertisement under the scheme 'JAGO GRAHAK JAGO', "Do You have a Complaint about Your Bank's Services". The Banking Ombudsman (BO) appointed by the Reserve Bank of India will help you in resolving your complaint. (for details visit: www.bankingombudsman.rbi.org.in).

ICICI Bank Education Series

The ICICI Bank, apart from its 'Customers Meet' programme, has launched 'customer education' advertising campaign, with a catch line "Be an Informed Consumer". Watch this Space Every Wednesday.

Three key objectives were behind this campaign:

1. Educating the customers on bank's products and services including their benefits
2. Creating awareness among stakeholders on 'How To Avoid Online Frauds'
3. Issuing clarifications on baseless reporting in media

While explaining the various products of the bank, the Education Series highlighted on subjects like "Discover the Benefits of Online Banking"; Menu-Based Mobile Banking; Bank Online—Save Your Time and Money; How to Derive Maximum Value from your Home; Home Loan Repayment, etc. Beware of Online Frauds; E-mail Frauds were some of the advertisements that enlightened the customers on online frauds. We get e-mails that we won one crore prize in a lottery. The ad educated that we must not be carried away by such messages.

SPONSORSHIPS

Sponsor was originally a Latin word derived from 'Spondere', meaning 'promise solemnly'. In English the first sense was 'Godparent', a person who promises to look after and guide a child. From there it came to mean a person who takes responsibility for the actions of another. The word 'sponsorship' is derived from 'sponsor', a person or an organisation that pays for or contributes to the costs of sporting or artistic event or radio or television programme in return for publicity and advertising. *Sponsorship may be described as an act of an organisation or individual as a sponsor to promote the company by underwriting the cost of an event.* Sponsorship is a specialised form of sales promotion where a company will help fund an event or support a business venture in return for publicity and reputation. It can be a form of advertising or a part of marketing strategy but it can also be a public relations tactic. In some cases the objective may embrace all the three.

Sponsored radio/TV programme is a distinct broadcasting when a controlled message of the sponsor is broadcast by advertisers or companies as different from commercial spots which are produced by contracting companies; similarly, a book is sponsored by a company or other sponsor with a vested interest such as a book to the company's history or products. For example, the Rashtriya Ispat Nigam Ltd, Vishakapatnam Steel Plant, sponsored a publication "Andhra Pradesh: A Great Synthesis"—a Pictorial Presentation by Vishakhapatnam Steel Plant. The book highlights the glory of Andhra Pradesh, but it also contains a message from CMD. This book is given as a gift from Vishakhapatnam Steel Plant as a "Coffee Table Book" as well as a humble tribute to the people of Andhra Pradesh. This book is presented to dignitaries in India and abroad to our Embassies, Missions to spread the charm of Andhra Pradesh. As a result such sponsorship gets good mileage for the company.

Objective

The primary objective of sponsorship is generally a strategic marketing effort to promote the brand/product or service. It is the responsibility of public relations profession to make use of the format of sponsorship to build image/reputation of an organisation. As such it is a tool of both marketing and public relations as in the case of organising an exhibition. There are two basic elements to sponsorship:

1. The organisations and persons concerned with events seeking funds
2. The advertisers/companies wishing to engage in sponsorship for their benefit

The main problem with these two elements is that one should match sponsor and sponsee appropriately in order to derive a win-win situation for both parties. In fact, sponsorship is 'a business relationship between a provider of funds, resources or services and an individual, event or organisation which offers in return some rights and association that may be used for commercial advantage in return for sponsorship advantage.

Sponsorship is used very often to promote a name or brand or to position or reposition a brand. It can also provide a variety of other benefits to the sponsor. These include the following:

1. Corporate image/reputation with stakeholders
2. Goodwill by association
3. Media coverage and publicity and audience awareness
4. Market penetration and sales campaigns: Employee–customer relations

5. Alternative advertising
6. Hospitality platforms
7. Employee benefits
8. Strengthened identity
9. Give product brands high visibility among purchasing publics
10. Corporate identity promotion

Most sports events get large sponsorships because these events receive extensive TV coverage, resulting in repeated naming of the sponsor by all the media. Sometimes, the name of the event includes the name of the sponsor, and so a vast volume of publicity results from the sponsorship.

Olympics is the pinnacle of corporate sponsorship, but companies also sponsor other events on a local, regional or national level. **Olympic Games Athens 2008,** held in Beijing, **Commonwealth** Games 2010 in Delhi and **Olympic** Game 2012 in London offered ample opportunities for companies to sponsor the events.

The sponsorships are given for various events. Some of them are as follows:

1. The performing arts—dance, drama, music, entertainment
2. Museums, art galleries, exhibitions and the arts
3. Various types of shows and outdoor public events
4. Expeditions and other exceptional athletic undertakings and sports events
5. Festivals and similar events and activities
6. Publications—books
7. Professional awards
8. Educational—scholarships, sponsoring chairs
9. Charity, rural development and social causes

COMMUNITY RELATIONS

What is community relations? Andrew Mann defines community relations as "a series of mutually beneficial business partnerships with one or more stakeholders which enhance the company's reputation as a good corporate citizen". Partnership can be either on local, regional, national or international basis, but the majority of community relations programmes are usually focused on either where the company's headquarters is located or around one or more of its operational areas.

Community relations has been also defined as "an institution's planned, active and continuing participation with and within a community to maintain and enhance its environment to the benefit of both the institution and the community". The community relations is also regarded as the social responsibility of a corporation undertaken to the mutual advantage of both the organisation and the community.

Fittest and Fastest

It has gained importance in the wake of globalisation and also due to cut-throat competitive marketing environment. Community relations has reached a stage wherein the fittest and the fastest to change will alone survive. It is in this context that any organisation has to maintain good community relations by undertaking community development scheme for the needy community so that the reputation of the organisation can become better.

In fact, any organisation, be it business or manufacturing concern, has symbiotic relationship with the community. What are the things that a company provides to the community? Take, for example, ITC Ltd., Kolkata. It provides its community goods and services of various nature ranging from food products to tobacco products. The company helps the community by providing employment to members of the society besides paying taxes for community development.

Corporate Citizen

What does a company get from the community? The community provides the employees to run the company and land, water, power, fire protection and police services among other things. A company, therefore, must accept its responsibility towards the community in which it operates not only by providing goods, services and paying taxes but also by being a good corporate citizen taking active part in community life, supporting education, community health, and providing facilities for recreation. It must encourage its employees to volunteer social services to the needy community. In the process, the company is recognised by the community as a good corporate citizen that cares for the community welfare. In return, the company gets name and fame from the community. Such corporate reputation will undoubtedly promote products and services of that company. This type of community services is also called **corporate social responsibility**.

Benefits

Why should companies consider community relations? Community relations is not about dropping coins in a collecting kitty for the benefit of someone. The CEOs of various corporations involved in social responsibility say that community relations makes a sense of relationship with their stakeholders. They treat it as a part of their corporate strategy to improve the welfare of the society on the one hand and build relationships with stakeholders on the other hand. Community relations programmes can bring benefits in the four broad areas: (i) enhanced features of the corporate brand and reputation,

(ii) greater customer goodwill and loyalty of stakeholders, (iii) improved workforce commitment and morale towards higher productivity and (iv) understanding the behaviour and needs of the community to evolve corporate strategy.

Employees' Role

The success of the community relations programme depends on the involvement of the employees, for they are the providers of services to the customers. In fact, it is essentially the responsibility of every employee in contact with the members of the community, neighbours, fellow club members and other stakeholders to improve the image of one's organisation. Employees are the ambassadors of the corporation and should speak for the corporation's community relations programme. Their words and actions have an important impact on the external publics about effective relations of the company. Employees' participation in the community welfare programmes is an important index of the effectiveness of community welfare activities.

Telstra Community Service: A Case Study

A good case study can be derived from the Telstra Corporation Limited, Australia, a telecommunication company, about its policy involving its employees in community relations programme. To meet the competitive environment, Telstra developed an internal marketing programme to inspire the staff and gain their help in keeping the stakeholders well served. It is called 'Telstra Friends'—a voluntary group, mostly after work hours programme, that provides staff members, their families and their friends with meaningful community service activities as part of the Telstra marketing objectives.

Telstra Friends network is made up of enthusiastic and energetic staff who are committed to maintaining and enhancing Telstra's image in the community. The activities of Telstra are linked to an equitable reward system structured so as not to undermine existing work-based performance and motivation programme.

What are the activities that the Telstra's Friends undertake? They include: cleanup Australia Day; national blood bank challenge, community open day programme; support for children's hospitals; Christmas collections, etc. Telstra Friends go to the localities and tell the customers that the Telstra is the best choice for them by highlighting the benefits of the company in both professional and social meetings. Employees in 1999 contributed 5000 hours of voluntary staff participation in out-of-hours work. Behind Telstra Friends, public relations and new media department stood like a rock and motivated them for community welfare work.

Staff Make a Social Impact

As part of the annual voluntary community service branded as 'Impact Day', the employees of Deloitte & Touche India, Hyderabad organised programmes in June 2006 on heritage conservation and an AIDS awareness camp. They cleaned the premises of Gandhi Hospital and those of protected monuments such as Mushaq Mahal and Fortification Baradari at Malkajgiri. Medical camps were organised for film workers and road safety awareness for motorists at Panjagutta and Khairtabad. In all 100 places were covered and 3500 volunteer employees participated.

Citizen First

ITC Limited, a major company in India which deals with multi-products such as foods, paperboards, agri-business, information technology, hotels, cigarettes, etc. believes in its social responsibility towards the needs of rural India—a home to 72 per cent of the poor. As part of its social responsibility, ITC has partnered with the Indian farmer for development. It is now engaged in elevating this partnership to a new paradigm by leveraging information technology through its trailblazing 'e-choupal' initiative.

ITC's unique e-choupal movement which commenced in 2000 is elevating farmers to a new order of empowerment. Using Internet stations installed by the company right in their villages, farmers are logging on to ITC created Indian language websites. From these websites, the farmers get access to local weather forecast, expert knowledge on best farming practices, agri-inputs and local national and international agri-commodity prices online. The e-choupal intervention is thus a significant step towards enhancing global competitiveness for over 2.4 million farmers across India in six states. Over the next decade, ITC aims to empower 10 million farmers in one lakh villages.

Additionally, ITC is significantly widening its farmer partnerships to embrace a host of valuating activities; creating livelihoods by helping poor tribals make their wastelands productive; investing in rain water harvesting to bring much needed irrigation to parched dry lands; empowering rural women by helping them evolve into entrepreneurs; providing infrastructural support to make schools exciting for village children and unique forestry programme to rejuvenate waste lands and generate income.

Through these rural partnerships, ITC touches the lives of every three million villagers across India. For ITC, these are expressions of social commitment beyond the market of a conviction that 'the country must come before corporation'. A true pride in being 'the Citizen First' and through empowering farmers. This story is a good example of community relations in rural India.

Auditorium

As a responsible corporate citizen, the National Thermal Power Corporation has adopted multifaceted social activity for community development in rural areas. The Corporation has set up resettlement colonies with facilities such as drinking water, roads, drainage system, schools dispensaries and electricity for street lighting. The Mangalore Electricity Distribution Company in Karnataka constructed Community Auditorium at Shimoga for the benefit of local community.

PR Perspective

According to the Chartered Institute of Public Relations, London, public relations is about reputation, the effect of what you do, what you say and what others say about you. Public relations is the discipline that looks after reputation with the aim of earning understanding and support, and influencing public opinion and behaviour. Community relations is largely a public relations responsibility focusing on the management of potential and existing communication interactive networks of organisations with publics for the benefit of both the groups. This assumes that public relations utilises its communication functions to interact with intent and commitment to create dialogue between a company and its internal and external public. Community relations, therefore, is a vital part of public relations programme as the local community can contribute to the reputation of the organisation.

Public relations also has been described as **P** for performance and **R** for reporting. If doing good and performing well is the responsibility of the organisation, then the primary task of its public relations department is to report to the community about the company's good work through various media of communication.

The essence of modern public relations practice is based on the principle that "First Deserve and then Desire". First deserve a good reputation based on good community service and then by planned communication enjoy the reputation that the company deserves. As such public relations is more applicable to community relations. Public relations manager must base his/her programme on the dictum *Deserve* and *Desire*. When you implement a community welfare scheme, you deserve and then desire for publicity through media.

Good Relations

One of the objectives of community relations is that having done good to the community, the corporation intends to improve its reputation as a responsible corporate citizen. The corporate contributions, undoubtedly, create good relations with employees, shareholders, consumers, community neighbours, media public, dealers, distributors, educators, the government, etc. In consequence, public relations which is based on the principle of public interest and social purpose gains added importance to help the corporate world by highlighting its welfare activities.

It is obvious that community relations, as described earlier, is action oriented. Such good work done must be communicated by the public relations department through all the available media to inform and educate both the internal and the external public.

Media

The principal media of communication in communicating the messages of community relations are newspapers, radio, television, corporate advertising, company publications, house journals and annual report, open houses, meetings with opinion leaders, cinema, exhibitions, visits to community organisations and new media—Internet, e-mail. All these must be utilised to highlight community relations activity. Employees who provide service also act as tools of PR.

GOVERNMENT RELATIONS

The functioning of the government today has become so complex that now it is a necessity for the business community or any organisation to establish and maintain good contacts with it. Governments—local, state and central, their attached offices and civil servants who run the administration constitute an important segment of the public for both the profit and the not-for-profit organisations.

Why are bureaucrats, legislators and the various public authorities important public for corporations? Richard E. Crable and Steven L. Vibbert (1985) said that organisations/corporations do not have authority in public policy. Rather, organisations have the ability to influence public policy. That is, organisations, whether profit seeking or not-for-profit, need to participate in the multiple state and central government's areas where public policy is being decided. If business is to have its voice heard and its views considered by government, then it must know what the latter is planning and the pressure points in the decision-making process, before legislation is tabled in the Parliament. Once legislation reaches the Parliament, the chances of major changes involving policy shifts are little. Therefore, government is an important organisational external public. Its importance has further increased in India from 1991 when the New Industrial Policy was introduced. It envisages economic liberalisation, privatisation and globalisation. India as a developing country is rapidly moving from mixed economy to privatisation, as the impetus for economic development shifts from government to private sector corporations. India has already witnessed privatisation in the fields of finance, telecommunications, transport, insurance, automobiles, media, etc.

Economic Reforms

During this time of transition, government offices are emerging as powerful public to the corporations that want to participate in and benefit from the economic reforms. Therefore, public relations professionals must build, maintain relationships with key government officials. But it is not an easy proposition to maintain relations with Indian bureaucrats who are part of the age-old colonial British steel frame administration. It is in this context a special area called government relations developed as part of the corporate public relations to improve contacts with the government officials who wield power.

What is government relations? It may be defined as "the art of working with myriad public authorities, legislative and regulatory bodies that can influence achievement of organisational and business objectives". It takes place at local, state and central government level. And if the organisation does any kind of business abroad or has clientele, overseas government relations occurs at the international level as well. Government relations is also described as "the maintenance of mutually beneficial relations between an organisation and the local, state and central government agencies".

The communication task of government relations include producing corporate literature such as brochures, folders, pamphlets, reports, videos and other publicity material giving the organisation's viewpoint on issues and also corporate profiles for presentation to government authorities and legislative bodies. Other duties of government relations cover testifying before government fact-finding commissions, monitoring government policy-making activities at all levels and preparing reports for the use of management. Federation of Andhra Pradesh Chamber of Commerce and Industry does government relations in relation to the problems of its members.

Regular Relations

Many corporations in the US maintain monitoring activities at State capitals in an effort to have early knowledge of activities that may help or hurt the corporation. Such research generally consists of maintaining regular personal contacts and reading government publications and press releases. Large and small organisations and their professional associations endeavour to build relationships with the government officials that are summarised hereunder.

1. Corporate leaders must be aware of the proposed legislation and public policies in the different areas of government that may affect their organisations. A backgrounder may be prepared with full information covering all the areas of public policy and the position of the organisation on the policy. Such background information is only one part of relationship building process with government officials.
2. Leaders of industry and professional associations will need to establish an interpersonal connection with bureaucrats and elected officials. Instead of individual organisations, industrial associations can influence the government effectively. For example, the Federation of Indian Industry of Chamber of Commerce and Industry can influence government policies.
3. To advance awareness and understanding among lawmakers of the activities and functioning of constituent organisations.
4. To win support for favourable legislation.
5. To keep the management informed of legislative development.
6. To develop public support for legislative goals.
7. Professional organisations connected with industry invite bureaucrats, ministers for dialogue at seminars, workshops.

Consultant

It is important to understand the stages that a legislation goes through before it reaches Parliament so that action can be taken in the early stages if necessary as part of government relations. In the Western countries, many organisations interested in government relations usually employ professional and registered lobbyists who inform and persuade the government to consider the viewpoints of the industry. In some cases the government relations consultant also works largely not only with the civil servants and government agencies but also with politicians and political parties. Lobbyists inform and persuade the government. They study the policy-making environment of the government and interpret the same to the organisations as to how it affects. At the same time, the lobbyists also interpret actions of the companies through their contacts including the attitude of the organisation towards governmental actions. Finally, lobbyists advocate positions on behalf of the clients both pros and cons.

Government relations in India is yet to develop as an art. It is being carried out through professional associations, individual organisations, liaison officers designated for the purpose. However, government relations as an activity of public relations will undoubtedly grow in the near future.

Benefits

Organisations, both public sector and private sector undertakings, will benefit from the government relations process in getting not only their views approved in policy-making, but also adjusted the organisational goals according to the government policies. Every organisation must establish government relations branch for creating and maintaining cordial relations with the government departments and the various regulatory bodies governing the industry. This is a sustained activity. Government relations include relations with municipal corporations, water works departments, electricity boards, State Government and Central Government departments, State Legislatures and Parliament.

POINTS TO REMEMBER

1. Employees stand first among the public of an organisation. It is because without them there would be no company either to serve the customer or to patronise the shareholders for investment.

2. Employees' public relations may be described as the systematic and symmetrical process of public relations through which organisations listen to employees to understand their problems, share good and bad information, build their support and commitment, and manage change to achieve organisational goals.

3. Employees media cover house journals, newsletters, manuals, annual reports, posters, quality circles, bulletin boards, close circuit TV, films, Internet, intranet, e-mail, seminars, group meetings.

4. Financial public relations is described as the area of public relations which affects the understanding of stockholders and investors concerning the financial position and prospects of a company and includes among its objectives, the improvement of relations between corporation and their stockholders. Financial public relations is also known as investor relations.

5. Financial calendar comprises publication of preliminary results of a company, half yearly figures, the annual report and the annual general body meeting. These components of financial calendar constitute food for financial public relations.

6. Financial public relations programme include: communication with the stockholders and financial institutions, planned media-wise programme to reach the financial public including the internal public.

7. Customer is the master and the customer is always right. This adage is the basis for customer relations.

8. The quality of the product, efficient customer service on the one hand and the public relations message on the other hand must go hand-in-hand to gain the understanding of the customer.

9. Sponsorships may be described as an act of an organisation or individual as a sponsor to promote the company by underwriting the cost of an event. Olympic games offer ample opportunities for a company to sponsor the event.

10. Sponsorship will benefit the organisation in several ways such as goodwill of the public, coverage in the media, market penetrations, promotion of corporate identity, etc. Examples of sponsorship cover sports, performing arts, publication of books, scholarships, awards, charity, etc.

11. Two basic elements are involved in sponsorship:

    1. The organisations/events seeking funds

    2. The companies which want to engage in sponsorship. One should match both the sponsor and beneficiary to their mutual advantage.

12. Community relations may be described as the institution's planned, active and continuing participation with and within a community to maintain and enhance its environment to the benefit of both the institution and the community. Community relations is also regarded as the social responsibility of a corporation undertaken to the mutual advantage of both the organisation and the community.

13. Benefits of community relations reflect in the four broad areas such as reputation of corporate brand, greater customer goodwill and loyalty of stakeholders, improved workforce commitment for higher productivity and understanding the community needs to evolve corporate strategy.

14. Public relations is the discipline that looks after the reputation of an organisation and gaining understanding and support of the public. As such public relations has a vital role to play to promote community relations to inform and educate both internal and external public. Good work such as provision of drinking water, organising medical camps, empowering rural women, provision of irrigation facilities undertaken under community relations, if reported properly will improve the image of the organisation.

15. Government is one of the publics for an organisation. Government relations is defined as the art of working with myriad public authorities, legislative and regulatory bodies that can influence achieving of organisational and business objectives. Government relations takes place at Local Bodies, State and Central Government levels. Organisation will benefit from the government relations

process not only in getting their views heard and approved in policy-making but also getting adjusted organisational goals in tune with the government policies. Government relations include relations with Municipal Corporations, Water Works, Electricity Board, State and Central Government departments and Legislatures.

16. Eradication of information poverty is a prerequisite to the eradication of economic poverty.

REVIEW QUESTIONS

1. What is employees' public relations? Explain the media and methods used in reaching out to the employees.

2. Evaluate the role of public relations department in promoting employees' relations and to create camaraderie among the workforce of an organisation towards higher productivity?

3. What are common failings in employee communications?

4. What is financial public relations? How does financial calendar help in building relations with investors?

5. What are the tactics of customer's public relations?

6. Why do organisations go for sponsorship? What has public relations got to do with sponsorship?

7. What is community relations? How can public relations promote community relations programme?

8. What do you understand by government relations? Explain its utility to an organisation.

Public Relations in Government

A popular Government without popular information or the means of obtaining it, is but a prologue to a farce or tragedy or perhaps both.
—**James Madison,** 4th US President (1809–1817)

CONTENTS

PR IN PUBLIC AUTHORITIES

What is government? A type of ruling or a system of governing by which a State or community is governed. Democracy, which is based on public opinion, is one of the types of government. India, a Union of States, is a Sovereign, Socialist, Secular, Democratic Republic with a Parliamentary system of government. In India, we have the central government, 28 states and 7 union territories. The Government of India consists of a number of ministries, departments; in 1947 the Central Government comprised 18 ministries; at present it has increased to 51 ministries for governing the country as a welfare State, besides six independent departments such as planning commission, cabinet secretariat, etc.

Characteristics

Democracy is a form of government in which the people have a voice in the exercise of power, typically through elected public representatives. It is in this context Abraham Lincoln described democracy as a "government of the people, by the people and for the people". Ancient Romans coined the words *'Vox Populi—Vox Dei'*, which means the Voice of the people is voice of God.

However, any democratic form of government is based on certain key factors which are as follows:

- Public opinion as supreme power.
- People are both sovereign and subjects.
- Bureaucrats are public servants.
- Welfare of the people is the welfare of the State.
- Government is accountable and answerable to the people.
- People's feedback a prerequisite for the success of democracy.

In fine, democratic government is not only open government but also people's participatory government. Kautilya, the author of the 4th century BC classic *Arthashastra*, a treatise on administration, said: "A king who observes his duty of protecting his people justly, according to law, goes to heaven, unlike the one who does not protect his people or inflicts unjust punishments". He further amplified the statement by his own words: "in the happiness of his subjects lies his happiness; their welfare is his welfare; whatever pleases his subjects, he shall consider as good; but whatever pleases himself, he shall not consider good".

State

The functions of the government may be divided into two broad categories:

- Obligatory or primary functions
- Optional or secondary functions

Functions which are essential to the preservation of the 'State', such as the right to life and the pursuit of happiness, come under obligatory or primary functions. Moreover, there are functions which contribute to better system of government and better living conditions in the society, like promotion of welfare, come under the optional or secondary functions. The secondary function takes us to the concept of Welfare State. The Directive Principles of State Policy mentioned in our Constitution are a good example of optional functions of the government. The Directive Principles shall not be enforceable by any court but the principles lay down fundamentals in the governance of the country, and it shall be the duty of the State to apply these principles while making laws. These functions are to be carried out to the satisfaction of the public.

Government's Public

Who are the 'publics' of a government? There is a difference between the public of a private enterprise and the government's 'public'. The stakeholders in the government are a vast and diverse group of internal and external public. They include: employees—All India Services;

employees in Executive, Legislative or Judicial branches; employees' unions and their leaders; political parties, their leaders, private industry and business people; professional interest groups—lawyers, doctors, architects; public in media, general community, specialised public such as women, children, farmers, industrial workers, agricultural labour, tribals, scheduled castes, scheduled tribes, minorities, etc. An interesting feature of the government's public is that the citizen is both the master and the subject. Some of the groups with vested interest closely monitor the government's programmes and form public opinion that influences the government's actions and policies. If there are about 50 lakh employees in Central Government, the number of employees in a State Government like Andhra Pradesh is about 12 lakhs. They constitute the backbone of Government public management.

Government–Citizen Interaction

The interaction, in a democratic society, between the government and the public called the *sequence of action* covers policy decision, communication of dissemination of public information, action by the public, and reaction. Such a cycle is much more direct and immediate in the government than in other types of social organisations. The government official must be intuitive by being public relations savvy because of the nature of public office he holds. The official must cultivate an acute sensitivity towards the needs and attitudes of the people, and be able to identify actions and communication with public interest based on the sequence of communication and reactions of the people.

It is in this context there arises government–citizen and citizen–government relationship to make the democratic polity a more participatory in nature. How do we make participatory government? How do we invite the people in the functioning of the government? It is public information that binds the government and the public, and brings them nearer for better understanding. In fact, government information and public relations service charged with the responsibility of providing information act as a *bridge* between the government and the people.

Information Poor and Information Rich

What is *information*? Anything that is meaningful and useful to the person receiving it can be called information. It follows that if something is not meaningful and useful, then it is not information. In other words, information needs to inform the receiver of something which will enable him to perform his duties. Information is a must, both for the sender organisation and for the receiver public. *Information is the means or the input, and public relations is the end product—better understanding between the government and the people.*

According to Dervin (1981), "information as thing" is the notion, an understanding of something that can be dumped into the heads of the individuals and corresponds directly to 'reality', independent of the observers. In fact, information is the product of social relations, and it is produced by and large by institutions to suit their own purposes. T.S. Elliot had said on the importance of information: *"Where is the life—We have lost in living; Where is the wisdom, We have lost in knowledge; Where is the knowledge, We have lost in information"*.

In other words, an 'information-poor citizen' is one who is ignorant or ill-informed cannot make a good living. An information-rich citizen is one who is well informed can make a good living and also participate in the functioning of the government with the help of his rights. As a result, we come across two types of citizens—*information poor* and *information rich*. A well-informed citizen is an asset to the government while an ill-informed citizen a liability. Information is, therefore, the lifeblood of democracy.

There is a close linkage between information and public relations. By providing full information public relations creates understanding and public opinion. Information is a source of knowledge for public relations. Following are the functions of public relations:

- Public relations practice is the management of a two-way communication process between an organisation and its publics to promote corporate mission, services, products and reputation to gain public understanding.
- Public relations is the attempt by information, persuasion, and adjustment to engineer public support for an activity, cause, movement or institution.
- Public relations is communication with internal and external publics of an organisation.
- The management of communications between an organisation and its publics, is pubic relations.

WHAT IS GOVERNMENT PR?

What is government public relations? It is the management of a two-way communication between the government organisations and their employees and the general public to create a well-informed citizenry and make them partners in democratic and development process. As a two-way communication process, public relations supports the government's efforts in promoting its goals, policies, programmes, services and achievements. A democratic government's information and public relations machinery is intended mainly to keep the people constantly well informed The machinery should be capable of making prompt and correct assessment of current public opinion and reaction to the programmes of the government, and be able to keep the government informed about the mood of the citizens. It also educates the public on legislation, regulations, health and all matters that affect lives daily. In this way alone can we ensure the maximum cooperative effort of those in authority and the people in general towards the promotion of national interests.

Justifications for Government PR

The practice of public relations in government within a democratic society is justified by the following:

1. A democratic government is best served by a free two-way flow of ideas and accurate information between the government and the people. This will help the citizens and the government make well-informed decisions and implement the same for the welfare of the nation.
2. A democratic government which is based on the will of the electorate is not only accountable to the public but also must report what it has done for them. It is because public opinion is the backbone of a democratic polity.
3. Citizens as masters have a right to know what the government is doing. This gives them the right to information with some exceptions. And the government also has the duty to provide full information to its citizens. A democracy, therefore, works best when the people have all the information that the security of a nation permits. Of course, today in India we have the RTI (Right to Information) Act which empowers the citizens to query the government and its many organisations on their functioning.
4. Media is the lifeblood of a society. The government depends on the mass media, both private and government, for keeping the people informed of the various policies and programmes.

The volume of public information that emanates from public authorities either in New Delhi or from State capitals is so great that it is almost well-nigh impossible for newspapers or electronic media to cover without the assistance of public relations professionals. The media persons who want to cover either the Central Government Secretariat news or the State Government Secretariat news have to depend on Press Information Bureau in the case of Central Government or the State Information and Public Relations Department for State Government news.

Media Relations

Media are the principal vehicles of disseminating public information and forming public opinion besides educating the citizens. Who has to maintain relations with the media? A specialist department must manage media relations based on their requirements and professional standard. The government in its dealings with the media is represented by the government public relations agency which acts as the chief window of public information between the government and the media in reaching the public with public relations messages.

Four Basic Goals

There are four rather basic strategic approaches to all government public relations practice. In all these four approaches, the existence of a two-way communication process assumes great importance—that is, a free flow of information back and forth between the government and the citizens it serves. These approaches are focused on the goals of providing (a) public policy communication, (b) information services (c) promoting positive institutional images, and (d) generating public feedback.

Public policy communication: gain public support

The goal in the public policy communication is to persuade and win domestic or international acceptance for a Government's existing, new or proposed budget, policy, law or regulation. In pursuing this goal, bureaucrats, leaders usually promote the policies and programmes to various constituencies. In simple words, this is a "battle to win public opinion and gain public support". Government public relations provides all information through publicity material, elected and appointed government officials so that they could keep the electorate informed of what the Government is doing.

Information services

Government public relations offers various information services; the goal is to inform various public about the types of government information and services available so that the citizens can access them. This is the day-to-day government's customer service role disseminating information or answering questions from citizens or the media concerning such areas as education, citizens entitlements, public health, public safety, public transportation, agriculture, government reports, development information and so forth. One of the best government public health communication examples was the case of Pulse Polio Immunisation Programme, under which 17 crore children were administered polio drops on a single day in 2002. The information services that are offered either by the Central Government or by the State Government public relations include: press information services, films, information centres, song and drama services, interpersonal field publicity services, photo services, printed word publication services, institutional advertising service, community radio and community television services, media monitoring service, etc.

Developing and protecting positive institutional image

The goal in developing and protecting positive institutional image is to inform and influence short- or long-term public support for a government branch, department, agency or unit. This goal often is pursued within a complex matrix of contention, criticism, and problems. Uneasy feelings and controversies can be expected when government officials try to sell such a positive image. Unique problems often arise when internal government critics (in Assembly, Parliament) or external media critics (news media) claim that the type of activity is a form of self-serving propaganda and a waste of tax payers' money in the form of government public information. In defence, the government units spokespersons usually reply that the public has a right to know what the government is doing and its public relations efforts are objectively and legitimately designed to inform the public about its mission, operations and people. It is for the government, based on its performance, to protect its image with constant ongoing engagement with the people through information services.

Generating public feedback

Public relations managers seek to see a flow of information from the public to the decision-makers in government in evolving policy decisions in the interest of the public. This is the most misunderstood strategic task of government public relations staff. In a large government bureaucracy, leaders can become isolated from those people who may be most affected by their policy decisions. In contrast to this, the government public relations officers, because of daily contact with a wide range of people (e.g. other government employees, news media representatives, community civic leaders, special interest groups, and the general public) hold a unique insight into how the segments of the society feel or might react to an order on a particular government policy.

Reality Check

Bringing feedback to the decision table is not enough. Leaders must have enough trust and confidence in the public relations officers to ensure such information is within policy decision. This means 'providing reality check' feedback at all stages of discussions, not just after decisions have already been made. This helps keep the government officials informed of what is happening in the nation and the world so that they can make informed decisions. One of the methods of keeping the government informed of public feedback is through media monitoring and field-based feedback information reports. The Directorate of Field Publicity (DFP), for example, acts as a two-way information dissemination and feedback bridge between the people and the Government. On an average, the DFP collects and submits about 3000 public reaction reports for redressing public grievances and also adjusting policy decisions.

Non-political

Public relations is essentially non-political in government, a position that is expected of civil servants. It promotes only the government, but not the party in power. Such neutrality alone will give credibility to the government public relations department and can expect cooperation from all parties.

Management of Public Information

Managing dissemination of public information is an art. One requires skills in handling information to have a better impact on the receivers. It has two aspects. The first is *providing information* and the second, *creating public relations*. While public relations is an effort of the organisation to engineer public support either for policies, programmes or products and services, information that flows from the authorities and the government departments called 'Public Information' acts as an input and knowledge on governmental policies and to understand the government. Who handles public information? Who manages public information? Like any other essential department of the government, public information/public relations is managed or administered professionally by a separate service called the **Information Service**. It is of two types in our country: Central Government's Indian Information Service and State Information and Public Relations Service of various state governments.

Types

For the purpose of public relations in Government, we can divide government in three types – Central Government, State Government and Local/Municipal Government. Functions of government public relations by and large are the same in the three types of government. But the structure, the nomenclature of PR departments and designations of PR officials differ in each type of government. In this chapter, we discuss the information and public relations structure in the Government of India.

Indian Information Service

Public information in Government of India is handled by both Indian Broadcasting Service, i.e. AIR and Doordarshan, while the information of all the departments including the News Services Division of All India Radio and the News Units of Doordarshan are managed by the Indian Information Service. The recruitment of officials under Indian Information Service (Group A) (Senior Cadre) is made through the Civil Services Main Examination, while that of Indian Information Service (Group B) (Junior Grade) posts through direct recruitment by UPSC. Professional qualification like Diploma in Journalism is essential for Group B officials.

In the case of the Central Government, it is the Indian Information Service that manages dissemination of public information through the various Central Government media organisations of the Ministry of Information and Broadcasting, like Directorate of Advertising and Visual Publicity, Press Information Bureau, Publications Division, etc. For each medium, there is a separate department at the national level. These are media units which act as public relations departments of the Government of India.

State Information Service

In the case of the state governments, there is a separate state service called the **State Information Service** which handles public information through State Information and Public Relations Department. Andhra Pradesh State has two cadres, namely, Andhra Pradesh Information Service (gazetted) and Andhra Pradesh Information Subordinate Service (non-gazetted). The employees for these two cadres are recruited through State Public Service Commission, who manage dissemination of public information and maintain public relations.

The Difference

Two areas distinguish the Indian Information Service from the State Information Services. The Central media units such as the Press Information Bureau, and DAVP provide 'one-to-one specialist service', while the State information and public relations departments offer all-in-one service under one roof. If a public sector bank wants to utilise the services of the Central Government media units or its information programmes, it has to approach 10 media organisations at the rate of one department for the medium, viz. Press Information Bureau for newspapers, the Films Division for films and so on. In State Government, all information services are provided under one umbrella—Director of Information and Public Relations.

Public Information: Achievements

Public information management in government is the dissemination of information at national, state, district, sub-division, block and village levels as well as creating and establishing goodwill and mutual understanding between the government and the publics. The information and public relations departments work in this direction.

The public information network of both the Government of India and the state governments must be proud of their role in taking India to the tenth largest economy in the world. At present, India is heading towards becoming the third new economic power of the world. Education of 75 crore voters on how to vote, administration of pulse polio drops on 17 crore children on a single day, the increase in the average life expectancy of an Indian from 32 years to 64 years for males and 67 for females, increase in the literacy rate from 18 per cent to 74 per cent, the Green Revolution, the White Revolution, and the Blue Revolution are only a few to quote to demonstrate the role played by the public information disseminating agencies in changing the socio-economic face of India. Both All India Radio and Doordarshan have played and continue to play pivotal role in the socio-economic development of the country.

Limitations

Notwithstanding the achievements of Indian Information Service, it has its own limitations which, among others, include lack of national policy on public information system; Official Secrets Act 1923, which prohibits officials to disclose even public information; lack of professionalism; and lack of evaluation of government information programmes. The Second Press Commission (1982) observed that the Press Information Bureau and the State Information Departments tend to function as trumpeters and drum beaters for the government, and even for the individual ministers whereas the objective of official information agencies is to provide full information to the public through the press.

Future

A bright future beckons the Indian public information system. It is because India is not only a democratic country but also a developing nation, where free two-way flow of information is a prerequisite for its success. In addition, the Government of India has enacted the Right to Information (RTI) Act and now people have easy access to public information with certain restrictions imposed for the security of the nation.

This casts heavy duty on the government to inform the people. India will emerge as the World's largest English speaking nation when foreign media turn to India for collaboration with Indian media Mughuls.

MEDIA UNITS OF MINISTRY OF INFORMATION AND BROADCASTING

Freedom from ignorance is as important as freedom from hunger.

Pandit Jawaharlal Nehru
Prime Minister of India (1947–1964)

Publicity which was the by-product of the British Government had graduated to public relations in Independent India. It was the Government of India that took the lead in the expansion of countrywide public information network to inform, educate, motivate and entertain the people as active partners in our democratic and developing society.

Ministry of Information and Broadcasting

In view of the importance assigned to public information in a democratic polity, a major landmark in independent India was the creation of a separate Ministry of Information and Broadcasting in 1947 with the objective to educate the public with full information and create better understanding between the government and the governed. If British India had a Department of Information and Broadcasting with a skeleton staff, independent India witnessed a separate ministry for public information, a far-reaching step in the evolution of information administration. The 'Iron Man' Sardar Vallabhbhai Patel as the Union Home Minister also held the charge of the portfolio of the Ministry of Information and Broadcasting.

The Ministry has four key departments which implement the mandate. They are:

1. The Information Wing which handles policy matters of the Print and Press media and publicity requirements of the Government.
2. The Broadcasting wing that handles matters relating to the electronic media. It formulates policies and frame rules and regulations for this sector, which include public service broadcasting, operation of cable television, private television channels, FM and community radio, etc.
3. The Film wing deals with the matters relating to the Film sector, including film festivals.
4. The Integrated Finance wing which looks after financial aspects, including plan coordination, etc.

The Ministry of Information and Broadcasting, as per the allocation of business rules, has a wide mandate in respect of information, education and entertainment to be executed with functions relating to print, and electronic media, and films.

The mandate is as follows:

1. News Services through All India Radio (AIR) and Doordarshan (DD) for the people including Indians overseas.
2. Development of broadcasting and television.
3. Import and export of films.
4. Development and promotion of film industry.
5. Organisation of film festivals, and cultural exchanges.
6. Advertising and visual publicity on behalf of the Government of India.
7. Handling of press relations to project the policies of the Government of India and to secure a feedback on public opinion.
8. Administration of the Press and Registration of Books Act, 1867, in respect of newspapers.
9. Dissemination of information about India within and outside the country through publications on matters of national importance.
10. Research, reference and training to assist the media units of the ministry.

Ministry

The Ministry of Information and Broadcasting consists of a main Secretariat, which is headed by a Union Minister, 21 media units attached and autonomous statutory organisations such as the National Film Development Corporation, the Press Council of India.

Media units

The Secretariat has 10 subordinate offices known as media units, directorates of executive departments which are the line agencies and are concerned with the execution and implementation of the Ministry's policies and public information campaigns.

The media units of the Ministry are as follows:

1. **Registrar of Newspapers for India, West Block No. 8, Wing No. 2, R.K. Puram, New Delhi 110 066**
   The Office of the Registrar of Newspapers for India (RNI) came into being in July, 1956 on the recommendation of the First Press Commission in 1954 as the registering authority for newspapers in India. The Registrar, commonly known as Press Registrar, is required, interalia, to submit an Annual Report to the Government of India of the status of newspapers by 31st December every year. This gives details of newspapers registered during the year, total number of newspapers, their circulation, etc. There were 82,222 newspapers and periodicals in 2010.

2. **Press Information Bureau, Shastri Bhavan, New Delhi 110 001**

   The Press Information Bureau (PIB), started as the Central Bureau of Information (1919) renamed as Bureau of Public Information in 1936, is now the nodal agency of the Central Government to disseminate information to the print and electronic media on government policies, programme initiatives, and achievements. It functions as an interface between the Government and media and also serves to provide feedback to the Government on people's reactions as reflected in the media. The Bureau has a total of 43 regional and branch offices and information centres. Public information is disseminated through press releases, press notes, feature articles, backgrounders, press briefings, photographs, press conferences, interviews, databases available on PIB's website, press tours, etc. The PIB's home page www.pib.nic.in makes available publicity material in English.

3. **Research, Reference and Training Division, Room No. 116, 'A' Wing, Shastri Bhavan, New Delhi 110 001**

   Set up in 1950, the Research, Reference and Training Division is an information serving agency for the Ministry of Information Broadcasting, its various media units. It serves as an information bank and information feeder service to the media units to help their programming and publicity campaigns. The agency also studies trends in mass communication media and maintains a reference and documentation service on mass communication. The Division provides background reference and research material besides bringing out *Diary of Events* every fortnight and compiles two annual reference works—*India: A Reference Annual* and *Mass Media in India*.

4. **Photo Division—Soochana Bhavan, CGO Complex, Lodhi Road, New Delhi 110 003**

   Established in the year 1959, merging the Photo studio of the Publications Division and the Photo Unit of the PIB, the Photo Division is responsible for visual support for the varied activities of the Government of India. It is the biggest production unit of its kind in the country in the field of photography. Photo Division organises the national photo contest every year on different themes. It provides photos to the media through PIB.

5. **Publications Division, Patiala House, New Delhi 110 001**

   Established in 1941 as a branch of the Bureau of Public Information, the Publication Division brings out a wide variety of books on subjects ranging from national policies and programmes to art, culture, history, the flora and fauna, the land and the people, speeches and writings, biographies and children's literature. This division uses the printed word as a medium of publicity.

Journals: Apart from books, the Division publishes 21 periodicals in English, Hindi and regional languages—Yojana (Planning) in 13 languages; Kurukshetra (rural development) in English and Hindi, Aajkal (Literacy) in Hindi and Urdu; Bal Bharati (Children) in Hindi; Employment News in English, Hindi and Urdu.

6. **Films Division, 24, Peddar Road, Mumbai 400 026**

The story of the Films Division begins with the formation of the Film Advisory Board in 1943 to use short films as a propaganda medium for the Second World War effort. Its successors, Information Films of India and the Indian News Parade, produced and distributed newsreels and documentaries mainly with a view to supporting the Second World War effort. They were wound up after the War creating a vacuum in this medium. The Information Films of India was revived as Film Producing and Distribution Unit after independence in December 1947. It was renamed as the Films Division in April 1948. With its headquarters in Mumbai, the Films Division is charged to record, propagate and preserve the achievements of resurgent independent India on the celluloid. It has been a vital link between the people and the government apart from its pioneering role in spreading the documentary film movement in India and the world. Moreover, it is the largest national agency devoted to the production and distribution of news magazines, documentaries and animation films. The Films Division produces story based short films and other educational and children's films distributed to about 8500 cinema houses in India through its 10 distribution branch offices located across the length and breadth of the country at Mumbai, Kolkata, Hyderabad, Lucknow, Chennai, Bengaluru, Madurai, Nagpur, Thiruvananthapuram and Vijayawada. It has a National Film Archive of India with more than 8000 films on the subjects touching almost all aspects of human life.

7. **Directorate of Advertising and Visual Publicity, PTI Building, Sansad Marg, Parliament Street, New Delhi 110 001**

The Directorate of Advertising and Visual Publicity (DAVP) is the multimedia advertising agency of the Government of India. It has been designated a single window agency for publicising government policies and programmes through various media such as newspaper advertisements, print publicity (posters, brochures, booklets), outdoor publicity (hoardings, kiosks, wall paintings), jingles, sponsored programmes and exhibitions on themes of national importance.

Started as an advertising branch in Shimla, DAVP was shifted to New Delhi in 1954. In 1955, the exhibition wing was made part of DAVP. It has two regional offices at Bengaluru and Guwahati, with 35 Field Exhibition units spread all over the country.

The functional units of DAVP include press advertisements, audio-visual publicity, print publicity, exhibitions, outdoor publicity, mass mailing, etc. The mass mailing wing of DAVP has over four lakh addresses in 138 categories to reach out to a wide spectrum of people across the country with information material. About two crore copies of publicity materials are distributed free of cost every year.

8. **Directorate of Field Publicity (DFP) East Block IV, Floor III, R.K. Puram, New Delhi 110066**
Established in 1953 under the name of Five Year Plan Publicity, renamed as The Directorate of Field Publicity in 1959, it is the largest rural-oriented interpersonal communication medium in the country which acts as a two-way information dissemination and feedback bridge between the people and the Government. Its areas of operation are: (i) to educate the people about the policies and programmes of government and the principles of secularism and democracy; (ii) to generate public opinion for the implementation of developmental programmes; (iii) to keep the government informed of the peoples' reactions to its programmes and policies. The DFP resorts very largely to interpersonal communication, such as group discussions, public meetings, seminars, symposia, etc. to convey its message to the people.

9. **Song and Drama Division, Soochana Bhavan, CGO Complex, Lodhi Road, New Delhi 110 003**
Set up in 1954 as a unit of All India Radio, the Song and Drama Division was given the independent media unit status in 1960 as a subordinate office of the Ministry of Information and Broadcasting. It was established for tapping the resourceful live media, particularly traditional and folk art forms for planned publicity. The division has the advantage of instant rapport with the audience and flexibility in its forms to incorporate new ideas effectively. The Division utilises a wide range of stage forms such as drama, folk and traditional plays, dance drama, folk recitals and puppet shows, besides the sound and light medium to focus the attention of the audience on important aspects of the country's life and development.

The Division has 12 regional centres at Bengaluru, Bhopal, Chandigarh, Chennai, Dehradun, Delhi, Guwahati, Kolkata, Lucknow, Raipur, Ranchi and Pune. Seven Border centres offices are working at Imphal, Jammu, Shimla, Nainital, Darbhanga, Jodhpur and Guwahati, while six Drama Troupes are located at Bhubaneswar, Delhi, Hyderabad, Patna, Pune and Srinagar.

Nine troupes of Armed forces Entertainment wing at Delhi, and Chennai, two sound and light units at Bengaluru and Delhi and a Tribal project at Ranchi.

10. **Directorate of Film Festival, New Delhi**
The Directorate of Film Festivals was set up in 1973 with the prime objective of promoting good cinema. Since then the Directorate has provided a platform for the best Indian cinema by holding the National Film Festival every year. It has also proved to be a vehicle for promoting cultural understanding and friendship at the international level. Within the country, it has made the newest trends in world cinema accessible to the general public. The Directorate organises the International Film Festival under the Culture Exchange Programme.

ALL INDIA RADIO AND DOORDARSHAN

The Prasar Bharati (Broadcasting Corporation of India)
Prasar Bharati, (Broadcasting Corporation of India), an autonomous body, is the public service broadcaster in the country with All India Radio and Doordarshan as its two constituents. The Prasar Bharati Act (Broadcasting Corporation of India), came into existence on 23 November 1997 with a mandate to organise and conduct public broadcasting services to inform, educate and entertain people, and to ensure balanced development of broadcasting on radio and television. Earlier, both All India Radio and Doordarshan were departments of the Government of India. With this Act, they attained autonomous status like BBC.

All India Radio, Broadcasting House, Sansad Marg, Parliament Street, New Delhi 110 001
The first broadcast programme in India was launched by the Radio Club of Bombay in 1923. However, the first regular radio station was started in Bombay by the Broadcasting Service in 1927 with a privately owned transmitter. The Government took over the transmitters in 1930 under the name of Indian Broadcasting service. It was changed to All India Radio (AIR) in 1936 and it also came to be known as *Akashvani* from 1957.

At the time of independence in 1947, All India Radio inherited only six radio stations which has now increased to 277 Radio stations with 91.85 per cent area and 99.18 per cent population coverage (2012). The News Services Division of All India Radio disseminates news and views to listeners in India and abroad through 647 news bulletins daily from Delhi and its 45 regional news units, 90 languages/dialects. 314 News headlines are broadcast on hourly basis.

***Doordarshan, Mandi House, Copernicus Marg, New Delhi* 110 001**
Television service as part of All India Radio was introduced as a pilot project at New Delhi on 15 September 1959. The regular service with a news bulletin was started in 1965. It was named **Doordarshan**. Television was delinked from All India Radio in April 1976 and a separate Directorate General was created to develop television as an independent medium. Doordarshan became autonomous in 1997.

Doordarshan operates 35 satellite channels (2012). It has a three-tier programme service—National (Delhi), Regional (States), and Local (Metro). Doordarshan has 11 regional language satellite channels which broadcast programmes in regional languages. Commercial advertisements were introduced on Doordarshan from 1 January 1976. Doordarshan commands the biggest reach among television channels in the country, boasting around 45 crore viewers, covering about 92 per cent of population.

Both All India Radio and Doordarshan as catalysts for socio-economic development act as the primary media channels of government for keeping the people over the entire length and breadth of our country well informed of government policies and programmes.

INDIAN INSTITUTE OF MASS COMMUNICATION

Indian Institute of Mass Communication, Aruna Asaf Ali Road, JNU New Campus, New Delhi 110 067
Established on 17 August 1965 in New Delhi, the Indian Institute of Mass Communication (IIMC) is an autonomous centre for advanced studies in mass communication, research and training. IIMC is fully funded by the Government of India through the Ministry of Information and Broadcasting. It has branches at Dhenkanal (Odisha), Dimapur (Nagaland), Kottayam (Kerala) and Jhabua (Madhya Pradesh).

Indian Institute of Mass Communication conducts major courses for:

1. Indian Information Service (Group A)
2. Post Graduate Diploma Journalism course in English and in Hindi
3. Post Graduate Diploma course in Advertising and Public Relations
4. Post Graduate Diploma course in Radio and TV Journalism
5. Diploma course in Development Journalism

In addition, the Institute runs short-term courses for middle-level and senior officers of the Indian Information Service and public relations personnel of different media units of Government of India. IIMC also conducts evaluation and research studies on a wide range of topics, such as audience reactions, communicators' views, impact studies of communication process. It organises seminars, symposia and conferences on communication.

A three-tier faculty system operates for teaching, and training, which includes the core faculty, practitioners from the industry and senior professionals, who are invited from time to time to share their experiences and enlighten the trainees/students about the industry.

POINTS TO REMEMBER

1. Democracy is a form of government in which people have a voice in the exercise of power. Abraham Lincoln described democracy as "government of the people, by the people and for the people". Ancient Romans believed that the "Voice of the People is the Voice of God".

2. Public information that brings government and the people together is the means, while public relations is the end product creating and maintaining mutual understanding between the government and the citizens.

3. We have two types of people—information poor and information rich. Information poor is a liability to the government, information rich an asset.

4. What is government public relations? It may be described as the management of a two-way communication between the government organisations and its employees and general public as a measure to create and maintain better understanding and also make the citizens as partners in the democratic and development process. It acts as a *bridge* between the government and the public in disseminating information.

5. The practice of public relations in government is justified by four major considerations:
   (a) A democratic government is best served by a free flow of information between government and citizens, which creates a well-informed citizenry.
   (b) A democratic government which is accountable to the people must also report to them what it has done. Such reporting by government public relations is the basis for public opinion.
   (c) In a democratic polity, the people have the basic right to know and the right to information. And the government has the duty to inform.
   (d) Government public relations is the chief window to the media in providing all information of public importance. Interface between government and media.

6. What are the basic goals of government public relations? There are four basic strategic goals to government public relations:

(i) Public policy communication to gain public support. (ii) To offer various information services both to the media and general public. Information services include: press information services such as press relations, media conferences, films, audio-visual aids, publications, institutional advertising, field publicity programmes, etc. (iii) Projecting positive image of the government based on its performance. (iv) Generating feedback towards policies and programmes of the government.

7. Who manages public relations and public information in the Government? Like any other government department, public relations is managed and administered by a separate service or department called information service. It is of two types. Indian Information Service is intended for Government of India, while the State Information and Public Relations Service is for State Governments.

8. The Ministry of Information and Broadcasting handles public information agencies in Government of India, while the State Information and Public Relations Department manages public relations in State Governments.

9. The public relations agencies, both in Central Government and in State Governments, played a pivotal role in changing the socio-economic face of India. For example, as many as 17 crore children were administered pulse polio drops on a single day in 2006, which speaks volumes about the role of public relations in Government.

10. A bright future beckons the Government public relations in India because free flow of information between the government and citizens is a prerequisite for the success of Indian democracy. WHO declared India as a pulse polio free country.

REVIEW QUESTIONS

1. What do you understand by government public relations? Explain the basic goals of government public relations.

2. What are the various media units of the Ministry of Information and Broadcasting, Government of India? Describe their role in disseminating public information.

3. Discuss the functioning of All India Radio and Doordarshan as public service broadcasters.

4. How does the Indian Institute of Mass Communication help public relations discipline? Enumerate its role in research and training of information and public relations personnel.

Public Sector Public Relations, PR in Public Transport and Municipal Government

Chapter
16

CONTENTS

FEATURES OF PUBLIC SECTOR

India started her quest for industrial development only after independence in 1947. In fact, the Industrial Policy Resolution of 1948 marked the beginning of the evolution of Indian industrial development. This Resolution had outlined the role of the State in industrial development both as an entrepreneur and as a controller. Successive industrial policies reiterated the basic tilt in favour of public sector. As a result, basic industries such as steel, coal, fertilisers, power were kept under the control of Government. The Industrial Policy Resolution of 1956 gave further impetus to the public sector in the Indian economy which envisaged mixed economy where both public and private sectors could progress hand in hand. Nationalisation of General Insurance Companies in 1956, and of banks in 1969, and the mixed economy policy led to the growth of public sector in Central and State Governments.

What is a public sector undertaking? It may be defined as a "legal entity created by the Government but exterior to Government organisation, functionally and financially independent for carrying on specific activities prescribed in the law creating it".

Earnest Davies described a public sector as "a corporate body created by public authority, with defined powers and functions and financially independent. It is administered by a board appointed by the public authority to which it is answerable. Its capital structure and financial operation are similar to those of public company, but stock holders retain no quality of interest and are deprived of voting rights and power of appointment of the board". However, this concept has changed when disinvestments was introduced in public sector.

The Corporations are constituted either under Central or State Legislature as the case may be. The objectives of public sector undertakings are threefold: (i) to gain control of the commanding heights of the economy; (ii) to promote critical development in terms of social gain or strategic value rather than on the consideration of profit; and (iii) to provide commercial surpluses with which to finance further economic development.

Features

Public sector undertakings compared to government departments and private companies have certain peculiar characteristics which are of vital importance to public relations practitioners. They are as follows:

1. Public sector enterprises are owned by Government and accountable to the people through Parliament or State Legislatures.
2. They enjoyed, prior to 1991, certain monopoly in their respective field. For example, there is no competition for Indian Railways.
3. They are subject to scrutiny by Government regulatory agencies. For example, the Insurance Regulatory and Development Authority regulates the functioning of the Life Insurance Corporation of India and other private insurance companies.
4. With liberalised economy since 1991 the disinvestment of Government equity in public sector was made through public offer. Earlier, public enterprises were entirely financed by the Government.

The public sector undertakings are broadly divided into two categories: Central Public Sector Enterprises (240) and State Level Public Enterprises (1100). These enterprises could be further divided into manufacturing units, such as steel, minerals, metals, and those rendering services in trading, marketing, transportations, construction sectors.

They have the basic responsibility to the growth of Indian Industrial Development.

The important Central Public Sector undertakings include: Oil and Natural Gas Commission; National Thermal Power Corporation Ltd.; Indian Oil Corporation; Bharat Heavy Electricals; Steel Authority of India; Gas Authority of India; Life Insurance Corporation of India. Some of the public sectors like Videsh Sanchar Nigam Ltd., Bharat Aluminium have been privatised.

CHALLENGES OF PUBLIC ENTERPRISES

1. **Competition with multinationals:** The liberalisation and enhanced foreign investment and participation have increased competition with multinationals. Now the Indian industries need to be geared to face this challenge of competition with multinationals as well as national companies in the process one has to develop global perspective.

2. **Globalisation of market:** Instead of limiting the market to the domestic needs, the liberalised market will be internationalised to meet the needs of the global market.

3. **Technological upgradation:** To generate more export, the emphasis needs to be given for technological upgradation to ensure better quality and productivity.

4. **Efficiency and high productivity:** To boost production, productivity and reduce the cost of operations and also to compete with the multinationals, the efficiency level in the PSUs needs to be pushed up. The productivity of the average Chinese worker is about 12 times more than that of his Indian counterpart, and a Japanese worker's productivity is 33 times that of an Indian worker.

5. **Improvement of communication:** Communications is considered as the lifeline of any economic system. The foreign investors like the multinationals, or NRIs expect efficient communication systems which they are used to. The communication system in our country must be made more efficient and upgraded to the expectation of the NRIs and multinationals. It should also meet the global competitive marketing environment.

6. Reduction in cost of production and distribution to meet the global market.

7. Quality of products and services with reliability and international standards.

8. Employees commitment to Economic Reforms.

9. Customer care and customers' satisfaction.

10. A paradigm shift in corporate strategy with global perspective and local culture.

Competitive Marketing

The public sector no longer enjoys monopoly. In the era of economic liberalisation (1991), public sector undertakings had to face new challenges such as competition with multinationals, globalisation of market, technological upgradation, high productivity with reduction in cost of production, improvement in communication with stakeholders, customers' satisfaction. As a result, there has been an upswing in communication activities of public sector to meet the growing competitive marketing environment. The concept of public sector public relations, envisaged in the 1960s, changed in the 1990s.

WHAT IS PUBLIC SECTOR PR?

What is public relations? Public relations is a relationship building professional activity that adds value to the organisations because it increases the willingness of markets audiences and publics to support them rather than to oppose their efforts (Health 2001). If the function of public relations is to increase the willingness of markets' audiences, and to provide the mechanics for explaining an organisation and its policies to its various publics, it has a vital role to play in public sector undertakings to meet the global corporate challenges. Similar to government public relations and financial public relations, there emerged public sector public relations to project the role of public sector in Indian economy, on the one hand, and to motivate employees and stakeholders towards higher productivity and also meet the growing competitive marketing environment on the other hand. It is against this backdrop, public relations in public sector kept the two-way channel of communication open between the public enterprises and their internal and external public.

Functions

The major functions of public sector public relations may be summarised as follows: (i) employees' relations; (ii) shareholders' relations; (iii) customers' relations; (iv) community relations; (v) media relations; (vi) communication about environmental protection; (vii) promotion of reputation of public sector; (viii) corporate advertising; (ix) management of crisis communication; (x) media monitoring and feedback information management and (xi) to advise management on policy and its effect on public relations. All these activities of relationship building are based on communication capital of the corporation. In fact, public relations in public sector is more professional and well organised in India than in government.

PR Structure

Bharat Heavy Electricals Limited (BHEL) has an exclusive corporate communication department headed by an Additional General Manager with the required managerial staff at its corporate office in New Delhi. There is a communication and public relations division at unit level in Bhopal, Haridwar, Hyderabad, Tirichy, Bangalore offices. Public relations division is headed by an Assistant General Manager, Deputy General Manager or Senior Deputy General Manager as the case may be.

Corporate communications department is responsible for policy formulation, budgeting, programme coordination and managing corporate communications activity for BHEL nationally and globally. Unit level communications and public relations divisions take care of this activity in their respective region with a close link with corporate office in New Delhi. This set-up is also a pace setter for others in public and even private sector organisations.

The Singareni Collieries Co Ltd., Hyderabad, the coal mining public sector organisation with a workforce of about one lakh employees, has an exclusive corporate communication department headed by Executive Director (Marketing and Public Relations), who reports to the Chairman and Managing Director. The Executive Director (Public Relations) is assisted by one Chief Public Relations Officer and a PRO, and also a Junior Communication Officer under the General Manager Personnel at the Corporate level. In the field, each Area General Manager (12 in numbers) is assisted by Communication and Coordinating Officer and also Coordinators. The Area General Manger reports to Executive Director (Marketing and PR) insofar as communication task is concerned. With this public relations structure, the Singareni Collieries Ltd. manages both macro level and micro level communication with the employees and customers, media and government.

FUTURE OF PUBLIC SECTOR PR

The policy of the Government of India on public sector as laid out by the United Progressive Alliance Government in the National Common Minimum Programme is as follows (2004). The Government is committed to a strong and effective public sector whose social objectives are met by its commercial functioning. But for this, there is a need for selectivity and strategic focus. It is pledged to evolve full managerial and commercial authority to successful, profit making companies operating in a competitive environment. Generally, profit making companies will not be privatised. The Government will not support any monopoly because that restricts competition.

Public relations must facilitate the change to meet a fierce competition from a wide spectrum of foreign companies. Employees have to be motivated towards change. Shareholders have to be satisfied with the share market. Image of the company has to be built up. All these challenges cast heavy responsibility, on the public sector public relations and it has to work with a new strategy as a specialist dealing with both internal and external communication.

PR IN PUBLIC ROAD TRANSPORT CORPORATION

Transport is the life-line of a nation.

Transport is not only a key industry but also one that holds the keys of all other industries. It is the single and powerful factor on which the social, economic, political and cultural fabrics of a nation wholly depend. A transport network which is basically concerned with the movement of men and materials, assumes great importance in any country, more so in a developing country like India.

Transport system takes different forms depending on its nature and the type of traffic it handles. However, all transport systems have to work in a coordinated manner in providing an efficient and convenient service to the public. The modes of transport comprise primarily the four systems: (i) the roadways, (ii) the waterways, (iii) the railways, and (iv) the airways. Each system has its own role to play in the transport map of the country.

Road Transport

India has one of the largest road networks in the world, aggregating to about 41 lakh kilometres. Road transport has a very important role in the growth of the national economy of a country. It stimulates the development and growth of trade and industry, culture and civilisation. It is the obvious choice of the majority of consumers because of its flexibility in operation and freedom to choose routes. It is vital to the development of the rural areas because of the inability of the railways to serve the interior villages. Road transport has brought about social changes in the countryside and has proved indispensable to the overall growth of the social, cultural and industrial development of the country. Travelling by bus alone represents about 80 per cent of the road-based passenger travel. That is why, India is basically a 'bus country', while the USA is a 'car country'.

Transport Management

The various modes of transport like the roadways, the waterways, the railways and the airways which carry both passengers and goods constitute the biggest human organisations. Management of such transport systems not only poses the biggest challenge to the discipline of modern management but also requires distinct technique and skills in handling such huge traffic.

The primary objective of transport management is to provide a safe, comfortable, regular and convenient service to the masses. Management of transport system is, therefore, of great significance as a distinct discipline. Any mismanagement in the transport system will result in a crisis affecting human beings. As such, the transport management should endeavour in providing safe and courteous service and not to cause any inconvenience to the people. It calls for greater coordination with other agencies included in the transport setup of the country.

ANDHRA PRADESH STATE ROAD TRANSPORT CORPORATION

Andhra Pradesh State Road Transport Corporation (APSRTC) which made its beginning in 1932 with 27 buses has now grown to its present day status as the country's second biggest state transport undertaking next to Maharashtra with a fleet strength of 20,000 buses and 113,728 employees. Everyday about one crore passengers are transported to different destinations by covering about 41 lakh km (2006).

The corporate objectives of APSRTC are summarised as:

1. To provide an efficient, adequate, economical and properly co-ordinated system of transport service in the State.
2. To provide for its employees, suitable conditions of service including fair wages and other amenities.

TRANSPORT PR

According to Howard Stephenson, Editor, *Handbook of Public Relations*, the credit for having originated the term 'public relations' goes to the American railroad industry. Samuel Spencer, the then President of the Southern Railway (USA), first used in 1906 the term in an address, "The relationship of the Railroads to the people".

> *Public relations means what it says—relations with the public. It is practically a self-defining term, it aims to create and maintain confidence. It is a system of communications to create goodwill and earns credit for achievements.*
>
> **Frank Jefkins**

Public relations plays a vital role in the public transport corporations by creating the right environment and understanding between the management and its public, particularly, the passengers. The need for public relations in a public sector transport undertaking like APSRTC or any other passenger transport undertaking including the railways, airways is all the more essential as these organisations are not only owned by the public, but also deal with millions of passengers. The main function of transport public relations arises on the ground that a public sector transport undertaking should assume the responsibility as a matter of highest importance to furnish the passengers with full and correct information. It is the primary role of public relations in the transport sector to tell passengers what it is doing. There are several other factors which justify the need for public relations in the transport sector. They include: transportation of lakhs of people from one destination to another every day: emergencies due to accidents, industrial disputes, natural calamities; the need for continuous communication with employees and passengers, building up of image of the undertaking based on its performance, etc.

PR DEPARTMENT IN TRANSPORT CORPORATION

Public relations is a top management function. If this function is entrusted either to personnel or marketing department, it tends to promote the specific interests of only those departments. In fact, public relations is intended to promote the overall corporate image and such image can be built up only when this department is directly placed under the Chief Executive who is in overall charge of the entire organisation. Against this background, Andhra Pradesh State Road Transport Corporation created a separate public relations department with Director (Public Relations) as the Head in 1987 who was made responsible directly to the Managing Director. The public relations department was treated as any other department in the Corporation, such as human resource, traffic, engineering, finance.

Regular Managers

The corporation entrusted the public relations responsibility to the regular managers at region, division and depot levels. It was the main objective of the corporation to manage a passenger relations programme by making use of the available resources. However, care was taken to impart public relations training to all the managers entrusted with the customer relations programme.

The public relations set-up introduced by APSRTC in 1987–1989 was a rare phenomenon in the public sector in the sense that a professional headed the public relations department at the corporate level, while public relations cells at the regional, divisional and depot level were headed by regular managers who were given the ex-officio designation in public relations. The Director (Public Relations) being the head of the public relations department at the corporate level was made responsible for providing professional guidance to all public relations cells at other levels besides supplying the publicity material and other inputs required for carrying out professional public relations work.

Corporate Office

The Director (Public Relations) who is the head of the public relations department reports to the Vice-chairman and Managing Director. The Chief Public Relations Officer, Deputy Chief Traffic Manager (Liaison), Editor (House magazine) and Asst. PROs were made responsible to the Director (Public Relations).

Field Officers

At the regional level, the Deputy Chief Traffic Manager of every region was designated as Ex-officio PRO, who reports to the Regional Manager. The Divisional Manager at the divisional level was designated as Ex-officio Divisional PRO while the Depot Manager at the depot level was nominated as Depot Public Relations Officer, who is assisted by the Chief Traffic Inspector. All these officials were given ministerial assistance to look after the additional work of public relations.

Airlines

Departments of Corporate communications function in AIR India, Indian Railways, even in private airlines like Jet Airways, etc. which are responsible for building good relations with both internal and external public. All airlines in India bring out in-flight journals for the benefit of air passengers. Mergers and acquisitions in airlines have increased the role of corporate communication. With Air India, Indian Airlines merger, Jet and Sahara, Kingfisher and Air Deccan these are a few examples that created challenges to corporate communications.

FUNCTIONS

One of the pitfalls in Indian public relations is the lack of a defined job profile for a public relations manager. Even the functions of public relations units have not been enumerated clearly by the managements. While reorganising the public relations department, APSRTC has clearly indicated the functions of the public relations department in an official communication signed by the Vice Chairman and the Managing Director.

They were as under the following:

- To inform the public through all available media about the corporate objectives and programmes of corporation including the passenger amenities taken up for the benefit of commuters.
- To highlight the problems of the corporation such as attacks on the crew, damage to buses during agitations, etc. so as to seek people's cooperation in the successful operation of its fleet.
- To instil better traffic consciousness among commuters such as maintaining queues, avoiding footboard travel, purchasing correct tickets, keeping change for ticket so that the corporation could provide comfortable transport.
- To identify the adverse criticism on operation of buses, behaviour of the bus crew as appeared in the newspapers and as obtained from other sources like written or oral complaints from opinion leaders/passengers.
- To issue clarifications on criticism appeared in the press without any basis.
- To arrange for the editing, printing and distribution of the house journal '*Prasthanam*'.
- To arrange for training in public relations and code of etiquette for the bus crew and other employees.
- To launch employee communication programmes through various in-house communication methods so as to create belongingness among the employees towards the corporation and increase their efficiency for better output.
- To evaluate the impact of the corporation's policies on the public and advise the corporation on policy matters by gauging the public reactions towards such policies through feedback information process.

PR CAMPAIGN: A CASE STUDY

The APSRTC adopted a multimedia approach and launched a public relations campaign for educating both internal and external public. The theme of public relations programme was based on "passenger is the master and every employee is accountable to the master passenger". A poster with five golden service rules was brought out for motivating employees. They included: safety, courtesy, punctuality, reliability and cleanliness. Driver's poster with illustrations was also brought out which inspired the drivers that "safe driving will not only enable the drivers to reach home safely but also passengers and pedestrians". A 10-point code folder for conductor was printed and distributed among about 40,000 conductors. The code said: (i) know your job, (ii) be neat in uniform, (iii) be courteous, (iv) aim at passengers satisfaction, (v) be helpful, (vi) passenger is always right, (vii) develop patient listening,

(viii) show interest in passengers problems, (ix) deposit found articles in the lost property room, (x) develop team spirit with colleagues and lead happy life.

Educative Slogans

In tune with the theme, the Corporation has launched a campaign to educate passengers with six slogans such as: (i) follow the 'Q', (ii) ticketless travel is an offense; fine up to ₹500, (iii) pay correct change for the fare and cooperate with the conductor, (iv) respecting women is our tradition: allow women to sit in the seats allotted to them, (v) footboard travel is dangerous and (vi) smoking is prohibited.

National Awards

As a result of sustained public relations campaign, which has motivated both the employees and the passengers, APSRTC bagged two national awards—one for having achieved the highest km per litre at 4.94 in 1989–90, the second award was given by the Transport Development Council, New Delhi in 1989–90 for recording the lowest accident rate in the country at 0.15 per one lakh kilometre. There was also complete industrial peace in that period—thanks to multimedia public relations campaign.

PR IN MUNICIPAL GOVERNMENT

The city is citizens, the city is the public character.

Different forms of governments exist all over the world—unitary, federal, state and local. In the unitary form of government, the supreme political authority is vested in the Centre, while in the federal form, the powers are shared between the Central and the State governments, within the sphere as enshrined in its Constitution. Local bodies exist both in unitary and in federal types of governments.

Municipal bodies have a long history in India. The first such municipal corporation was set up in the former Presidency Town of Madras in 1688 and was followed by similar corporations in the then Bombay and Calcutta in 1726. However, to provide a common framework for urban local bodies and help to strengthen the functioning of the bodies as effective democratic units of local self government, Indian Parliament enacted the Constitution (74th Amendment) Act 1992 relating to Municipalities. The Act came into force in June 1993. It provides the constitution of three types of municipalities, i.e. Nagar Panchayats for areas in transition from a rural area to urban areas, municipal councils for smaller urban areas and municipal corporations for large urban areas.

The need for local government arises from certain historical development. With all their multifarious functions, it is not possible for either the Central or the State governments to effectively administer the local units.

The scope of central administration covers the whole nation, that of the entire state. Local problems and needs stand on a different footing and require different kinds of treatment. Local governments have, therefore, been constituted within the state governments to perform administration and public activities of a purely local nature. In short, it is a government in a limited sense, within a government or it may be termed as a 'mini-government'.

Thus, the units of local government serve twin objectives:

1. Function as the agents of State government insofar as tackling the problems of the local areas.
2. Acts as individual units with statutory powers to fulfil the needs of the local community.

What is Municipal Corporation?

A municipal corporation is a body, created by the incorporation of the people of a specified area and invested with subordinate powers of legislation, for the purpose of assisting in the city government of the state, and of regulating and administering its local and internal affairs. Municipal Corporations are created by an Act of State Legislatures.

Civic Sense

The city is citizen—The city is the public character.

A nation is made up of its citizens, while the cities where the citizens live are schools of nationality. The city is not merely an aggregate of homes and families that comprise it. In fact, the city as a whole is a visible symbol of life.

It is the life of all its citizens and creators, past as well as present. The city treats citizens of all castes, religions and languages alike—as its sons and daughters.

JUSTIFICATION FOR PR IN CITY GOVERNMENT

Sustained education and public relations are required not only to tell and identify municipal problems, but also to create civic consciousness to seek people's cooperation in civic programmes. Attitudes of public towards corporations have to be ascertained. Public relations acts as a two-way traffic between the city corporation on the one hand and its internal public (employees) and citizens on the other hand.

Public relations has been described by Edward L. Bernays as "an attempt by information, persuasion and adjustment to engineer public support for an activity, cause, movement or institution".

What is municipal public relations? Public relations as practiced in municipal corporations to educate citizens on the functioning of a corporation and enable the citizens to participate in city government is called **municipal public relations**. Principles, techniques of public relations are applied by the municipal public relations to reach the goals of city government with citizen participation. Municipal public relations is concerned with what citizens think, know and do about city government, and at the same time, what city corporation thinks, knows and does about citizen. In fact, municipal public relations is a bridge between the municipal corporation and the citizens.

Judged by this definition, public relations can play a pivotal role in civic administration by creating the right environment and understanding between the civic government and their public. The functioning of a municipal government is essentially democratic. Popular involvement in civic affairs is the essence of its success. Without such cooperation and involvement of the public, civic programmes would lose all their meaning and the provision of civic amenities would be in total chaos. Street cleaning would be useless if people continue to litter the roads with garbage. Public roads would be dark if unsocial elements stone street lights. Pedestrian and vehicular traffic would be inconvenienced if petty traders operate on footpaths and road. True, such offenders could be dealt with by law. But law has its own limitations, and can deal with the problem only at the physical level. What is required for an enduring long-term result is the willing cooperation from the people, which can be achieved by appealing to their hearts and minds. It is towards this achieving of willing cooperation that public relations can contribute in great measure.

PR Effort

No doubt, maintaining public relations through the elected councillors is important. The councillors can be spokespersons for both the administration and the citizens. They do help in building up the image of the civic government through their meetings with the public. But all this is not enough to reach the goals of public relations. *First*, the role of a municipal government is more complex today. *Second*, the means of communication with the public have become too sophisticated in the modern world. Ours is the age of instant communication. Organisations vie with each other to draw people's attention through slick transmission of messages via variety of communication media, with each one trying to persuade the public to accept its ideas, products or services. In this melee, only an organised, concerted public relations effort can get civic messages across to the public and win their cooperation and confidence. Such communication with the people, informing them of the government's activities, policies and programmes, expressing its views on matters of vital civic importance and getting to know public opinions and reactions is one of the crucial ingredients for the successful functioning of a civic government.

PR Expert

To deal with the different aspects of municipal administration, officials are appointed with specific functions; engineers, tax officers, town planning experts, health officers, etc. These are the people specialised in their respective fields. In the same manner, the job of dealing with the communication of internal and external publics of the municipal government is to be left to a specialist in public relations. This task cannot be entrusted to an Engineer or a Tax Officer. Only a professional public relations person, specialised in the skills of mass communication, can perform this function with a degree of effectiveness. For these reasons, the appointment of public relations expert will augur well not only for the administration itself, but also for the administration's public.

Even small municipalities can have a public relations cell, with one man to deal with public information.

PR Organisation

Every major Municipal Corporation should have a full-fledged public relations department headed by a suitably qualified officer, trained in the skills of mass communication. The Municipal Corporation of Hyderabad has a full-fledged public relations department, headed by a Chief Public Relations Officer, who is under the direct control of the Chief Executive, Commissioner, Municipal Corporation. He is assisted by an Assistant Public Relations Officer and an Assistant Publicity Officer. Similarly, the Municipal Corporation of Greater Mumbai has a Public Relations Department with a Public Relations Officer assisted by two Deputy Public Relations Officers and three Assistant Public Relations Officers.

It is always advisable to create public relations department with professional staff as a separate operating unit rather than assigning it to other department in the corporation. Public relations in municipal governments is neutral to party politics. It should be the endeavour of the Public Relations Officer to publicise the policies of the civic government, as approved by a majority vote. It should not indulge in party politics of the party in power in the corporation.

MUNICIPAL PR GOALS

Municipal public relations attempts to provide information and inspiration to citizens so they may intelligently participate in municipal government. Administrative process on the city depends on elementary citizen response; selecting officials, expressing preferences in city plans, paying fees and taxes and utility charges, obeying regulations and supporting law enforcement. Apathetic people respond blindly or not at all. In either case, administration suffers.

Municipal public relations is basically bilateral. It should apply these following elements:

1. Adequate public understanding of how city government functions.
2. Current public information about city operations.
3. Channels through which the citizen can affect city government policy and action.
4. Channels through which the citizen can be reached by the city government, its officials, and other representatives.
5. To maintain better media relations with press, radio and television.
6. To make use of new media such as Internet. E-mail for quick transmission of messages.
7. To help municipal officials understand the role of the media in city corporation and citizen relations.
8. When the corporation is involved in a crisis, public relations must tell the facts to the media at the earliest possible moment.
9. To instil better civic consciousness among the citizens for proper utilisation of civic amenities.
10. To advise the municipal government on policy matters, gauge public reaction and suggest the administration on the means of gaining public acceptance and cooperation.
11. To conduct educative campaigns to seek public support for new taxation proposals and other schemes.
12. To inform the civic administration about public reactions and attitudes on civic policies as reflected in media.

In order to implement the objectives of the public relations department, the Public Relations Officer utilises various communication channels, such as the press, radio, television, house magazine, film, outdoor-publicity, advertising, and interpersonal media, etc.

(For case study on municipal PR, see 'Dogs Are Man's Best Friends' under the chapter 'Actions speak—case studies.)

POINTS TO REMEMBER

1. Public sector may be defined as a corporate body created by public authority with defined powers and functions and financially independent. It is administered by a Board of Management, appointed by the public authority to which public sector undertaking is accountable. However, with the disinvestments policy, shares have been offered to private individuals and institutions in some public sector organisations.

2. In the wake of economic liberalisation, privatisation and globalisation, the monopoly enjoyed by public sector has been removed. As a result, public sector is facing challenges which include: competition with national and multinationals, global market, technological upgradation, efficiency, communication strategy, competitive marketing. Change management is the essence of emerging challenges.

3. Functions of public sector's public relations like any other public relations include: employees' relations, shareholders' relations, media relations, community relations, consumers' relations, communications in crisis situations and reputation management.

4. Since the Government is committed to the public sector companies which are profit making in the competitive environment, public relations will have to play its role as a catalyst for change and development.

5. The need for public relations in municipal government arises as to create civic consciousness and to seek people's participation in maintaining civic programmes. Public relations acts as a two-way traffic between the city corporation and its internal and external public.

6. Public relations as practised in municipal corporation to educate its employees on the one hand, and citizens on the other hand to project as a better city to live in is called municipal public relations. Municipal public relations is concerned with what citizens feel, and know about city government. In fact, public relations acts as a bridge between the two—corporation and its publics.

7. As in the case of other departments, such as town planning, health and sanitation, taxation, there should be a separate public relations department headed by a professional public relations expert to handle the internal and external communication of a corporation as to build good relations with both the employees and the citizens. Many municipal corporations in India like the Municipal Corporation of Hyderabad, Kolkata, Mumbai, Delhi, etc. have public relations departments.

8. What are the goals of municipal public relations ? It is intended to provide full information from womb to tomb as to create better civic sense among the people of the corporation. Other goals include: adequate understanding of the functioning of city government, better media relations, to instil better civic consciousness, to gauge public reactions and keep the corporation informed of such reactions.

9. The modes of transport for the movement of people and goods include: the roadways, the railways, the waterways and the airways. Each transport system has its own role to play in the transport map of a country.

10. The need for public relations in a public transport organisation arises as it deals with millions of passengers whose goodwill is a prerequisite to the successful operation of its fleet. Education of employees, maintaining good relations with passengers by providing safe and comfortable travel, managing crisis situations or accidents by providing timely information and reaching the target audience through media are some of the factors that determine the scope of public relations in transport companies.

11. Functions of public relations in public transport corporation include: promotion of corporate objectives, plans, passenger amenities through various media; to instil better traffic consciousness among commuters to follow rules; to identify adverse criticism on operation of fleet, behaviour of crew as appeared in the media, to maintain better employees' relations, to bring out corporate publications including house-journal, to arrange for in-house training in public relations for the employees, etc.

REVIEW QUESTIONS

1. What is public sector? Explain its distinct characteristics as compared to a government department.

2. Define public sector public relations. Describe its functions in the changed public sector scenario of global competition.

3. The city is a citizen. What are the factors that justify for public relations in municipal government?

4. What is municipal public relations? Describe its role and goals in creating civic sense towards a clean and green city.

5. Transport is the lifeline of a nation. Discuss the role of transport management in providing safe and comfortable travel.

6. What is transport public relations? Explain its role and functions in creating better understanding between the transport corporation and its internal and external publics.

Public Relations in Police, Banks and Tourism

Chapter 17

Organisations either live or die on public perception.

C O N T E N T S

POLICE PR

A royal commission on the Police was appointed in the United Kingdom because of concern of lack of understanding and sympathy between the police services and the public. Even in our own country a police commission appointed by Andhra Pradesh Government among others sought suggestions and views of the public on questions such as:

1. What measures can be devised to bring about a better understanding of police by the public in day-to-day life and secure public cooperation in police work?
2. What role can be played by the mass media—press, television, radio, film in promoting healthy Police-Public relations?

Police is part of the community. It is the community that maintains the police force which, in turn, serves the community. The police exists for the welfare of the community. We find community participation in policing even in ancient India. If we study Kautilya's *Arthasastra*, we find an account of police in ancient India. Prevention of crime then was not the sole responsibility of the police administration. Reporting of strangers and suspicious individuals was incumbent on the average citizen, owners of rest houses, entertainers and physicians. This is a wholesome requirement which, while not given up entirely, has now become a mere ritual. This is to say that the community is not involved in policing and we are suffering from lack of community policing.

Distrust

Unfortunately, there is a growing distrust between the community and the police today. Unfavourable or bad police image is robbing the police of the community's support. Therefore, police-public relations programmes professionally organised by the police organisations may help to serve as an instrument through which mutual respect and understanding instead of fear and avoidance might be developed.

The role of police before independence was to preserve the rule of the British Government in India. After independence, the role of police has changed and it has to now function to promote the welfare State. We now belong to a sovereign, secular, socialist and democratic republic. The police force also has to function in promoting these ideals as enshrined in the Preamble of our Constitution. Thus, the need for effective police public relations.

FIVE DIMENSIONS OF POLICE PR

The police public relations can be discussed from six different dimensions which aim at bridging the communication gap between the police administration and the public.

1. The Constitution of India guarantees among others the right to protection of life and personal Liberty. It also envisages the right to protection against arrest and detention in certain cases.
2. Role of the police in democratic polity, public accountability and answerability. (People are masters.) Relationships between the police and the public are not merely administrative but more of human relations.
3. Projection of police services to the cause of the community.
4. Seeking people's cooperation, trust, in discharging the functions of community policing.
5. Relationship of the police with the media, the fourth estate of democratic government to seek their cooperation in building up healthy police-media relations.
6. Measures to ascertain the perception of the public about police services and its image. Feedback information.

A *Times of India*/Aditya Birla Group Opinion Poll was published in 1999 which commented that politicians, policemen and lawyers scramble for the bottom slot in terms of respectable profession. Police came 14th in order of preference as the most respected profession with only 10 per cent opting for it. The Armed forces were on the top of the list with 36 per cent thinking that they are the most respected profession. In terms of honesty and contribution to the society, police came again 14th in the list (S.A. Huda, Inside Police, 2004). In a voter survey 2007, conducted by national news magazine the *Week* to a question on "How much you trust among 16 institutions", such as army, media, universities, parliament, trade unions, private hospitals, etc. the respondents gave the sixteenth and last rank to the police while the army got the first rank. All these surveys are indicative of the bad image of the Indian police.

Twin Objectives

The above factors determine the need for the practice of public relations in the Police Department to motivate the police force to serve the public. A public relations department can also educate the public to make use of the police services for their security with better understanding, and extend all cooperation to the police for its successful functioning. In a democratic country like ours, the police has an obligation to attempt, achieve and sustain a positive image and maintain good public relations. What is the image of the police? What is the public perception of a police person? Many citizens tend to come in direct contact with the police only under unhappy circumstances and, most of the time, a citizen approaches the police in a distress situation. Naturally, in such a situation, citizens expect a patient hearing and a sympathetic attitude of possible police response and relief. If during this phase of important citizen contact, the police personnel exhibit lack of sympathy and understanding, and project a hostile, rude, negative and unhelpful attitude, it contributes a lot to tarnishing the police image.

The National Police Commission has rightly identified that the police because of their constant interaction with criminals, perhaps develop a style of functioning which may be suited and relevant to only hardened criminals, but is definitely unsuitable if the same disposition is exhibited towards respectable law-abiding, cooperative citizens.

Police Behaviour

The National Police Commission further analyses this phenomenon when it says, "The manner in which the Police Officers at the lower level behave is conditioned by the manner in which the police officers themselves are treated by their own higher-ups in the force". Therefore, the community's attitude and image towards police is influenced by the actions and behaviour of individual police officers and police constables on the streets, and how they generally conduct themselves.

We may have an efficient police officer but one survey shows that sometimes the attitude, behaviour of such efficient police officer is very poor. Efficiency is marred by bad behaviour. There are many negative factors which affect the image of the police in our country. The negative factors include: bureaucratic and unhelpful attitude of the police force towards law-abiding citizens, unjustified arrests; false criminal cases, encounter deaths; non-registration of criminal cases; use of third degree methods, corruption, etc. Police misconduct, whether defined as brutality, harassment, verbal abuse or gross discourtesy, contributes directly and in no small measure in lowering its respect as a profession. A basic growing distrust between the police and the community deprives the police of the cooperation and support from the citizens. Today, both the police and the community misunderstand and mistrust each other, and a growing antagonism between the two is leading to a point of total distrust and dissatisfaction.

Police Image

The Andhra Pradesh State Police Commission in 1983 assessed the **image** of the police force in the state. A questionnaire was sent to 3500 individuals of whom only 288 responded. Their views on the police image are as follows:

(a) 24 individuals said Police personnels are honest.
(b) 97 individuals said Police personnels are corrupt.
(c) 92 individuals said Police personnels are discourteous.
(d) 25 individuals said Police personnels are courteous in their behaviour.
(e) 66 individuals said Police personnels are efficient.
(f) 53 individuals said Police personnels are inefficient.
(g) 72 individuals said Police personnels are insensitive to people's problems.
(h) 52 individuals said Police personnels are responsive to people's problems.

From the survey, we may draw a conclusion that on the whole, the image is not totally unsatisfactory as there are some sections in the society though small who appreciate the police work and their disposition. In sum, we can say that the police is efficient but discourteous, insensitive to people's problems and, above all, corrupt. Therefore, there is every need to have a good public relations department in police force to improve its image by keeping the people informed of what they are doing for the public.

It is necessary for every police officer to understand the meaning and principles of public relations.

The Chartered Institute of Public Relations, U.K. defines public relations as: "public relations is about reputation, the result of what you do, what you say and what others say about you". It is the discipline which looks after reputation, with the aim of earning understanding and support and influencing opinion and behaviour. The understanding is between an organisation and its various publics – employees, customers, investors, local community and all of the stakeholder groups

Police PR

Every organisation, be it government, private or non-profit organisation, has a public relations department to deal with its public. It has public to serve the public who patronise them and others who generally constitute potential customers. Moreover, the police department has its own public and the need to maintain appropriate relations with such public constitutes police–public relations, which may be described as the management of a two-way communication between a police department and its internal force and external community—to earn public understanding for its services.

One needs to build a strong and enduring relationship between the police department and its internal as well as external publics in reaching the goals of the police department. In the process, the 1 lakh police force in Andhra Pradesh has formed a human bridge with its services to build up good community relations. How do we develop police-public relations? It is through effective police service and better communication.

PR PRACTICE IN THE POLICE DEPARTMENT

Professional public relations takes different dimensions depending on the nature of public such as:

1. **Employees relations:** Educating and motivating the police force.
2. **Community relations:** Educating the public in neighbourhood on police services (segmentation of target publics) and its problems, limitations and difficult situations.
3. **Media relations:** To seek the cooperation of the media in building up healthy police-media relations.
4. **Relations in crisis:** Relations both with the public and with the media in crisis situations, such as police firings, strikes of the police force, natural calamities.
5. **Feedback information:** Based on people's reactions including its employees about functioning of the police.

Each area of public relations demands a distinct approach with strategy and tactics. Police-public relations in any police organisation encompasses relationship with various publics such as employees, general community, opinion leaders, government, and other regulatory authorities and the media.

Two Watchdogs

Two watchdogs, namely police and press serve the cause of the society. Police provides security and safety to the community. The press acts as a sentinel of democracy and also watches the functioning of the police. These two watchdogs sometimes are found snarling at each other. It is unfortunate that occasions arise when the two take opposite sides of the fence, while working for a common cause of serving the people. Public relations in the police department must bring these two watchdogs together as and when they serve a common cause for the benefit of the society. There could be better cooperation between the two. It is for public relations to bridge the communication gap between the police and the media.

The Andhra Pradesh Police publishes *Suraksha*, a house journal which is serving a very useful purpose in educating the police force. The media for internal communication include house journal, public relations training, handbook for police constables, posters, video cassettes, audio-visuals, suggestion scheme, group meetings, computer messages, etc. The police department as a measure to motivate constables can produce a multi-colour posters highlighting their duties and accountability to the public.

Professional PR

It is against this background the police needs a trained professional public relations person to head the public relations department at the Director General of Police (DGP) office which can organise police-public relations at the state level. This PR head must give professional advice to the police at all levels. Similarly, there should be public relations cells from the police station level, DSP, SP to DIG level headed by regular police officers or professional PROs, and guided by the professional public relations department from the DGP's office. The police force must be trained in public relations and media relations.

Every year a week may be earmarked as 'Know Your Police Week'. Open house session may be organised at each police station for closer interaction between the community and the police. Various sports and games may also be organised to enable the public to come to police stations for better understanding as part of the police-community relations.

Administrative Set up

Efficient structure and set up are prerequisites for the effective implementation of police–public relations. Keeping in view the above-mentioned facts, a full-fledged public relations set-up has been created in the police department in Andhra Pradesh.

A DGPs conference held in New Delhi on 22 September 2000 had strongly recommended appointing Media Relations Officer not only at the State headquarters but also at each district headquarters to have a smooth coordination between the police and the media. This conference also recommended allocating a portion of police budget for implementing media policy. In July 1999, the Andhra Pradesh government accorded sanctioning of 25 posts of Public Relations Officers for all the district headquarters and at the Headquarters of Commissionerates in Police Department on a consolidated pay. The set up functioned for a few years. But this scheme was disbanded later, better known to the police department.

Impact of Police PR

What is the impact of professional public relations set-up in Andhra Pradesh Police? P. Ramulu, Director-General of Police, in 2002 in an interview to *Public Relations Voice* had said:

> *Before we had set up professional public relations in our State, we encountered much adverse criticism in the media. Due to many pre-occupations of the police with their normal work, the officials ignored such adverse criticism published in the newspapers. Now that we have a well-defined public relations setup, we issue rejoinders and clarifications as and when necessary giving the correct picture of events and this approach creates a dispassionate view among the newspapers and the media persons. As a result, the volume of criticism in the newspapers has considerably come down. From the DGP to a police constable, the police must be media savvy. It is in this context, we have a component of media relations in all our training courses.*

It must be made clear that the creation of a public relations department in the police force cannot be deemed an ad-hoc step but an integral part of the entire police management in a welfare State. Public relations should be organised on a sustained basis to create enduring relationships between the police and the community.

PR PRACTICE IN BANKS

'Banks live or die on public perception' said one Chairman of a major bank. Failure of Global Trust Bank in 2004 had turned depositors into a bundle of nerves. They rushed to the Bank to withdraw their money on a single day. A rumour that Mumbai-based South Indian Cooperative Bank made a loss witnessed mass withdrawals. The Punjab and Maharashtra Cooperative Bank, Mumbai also experienced withdrawals of Rs. 5 crore in one day in August 2004, only because its branch was situated next to that of South Indian Cooperative Bank.

Public Perception

Public perception is the key to the success of any bank. In the liberalized market economy and a more competitive environment with more players, and innovative products in banking industry, a question arises how do we build public perception on banks. It is through customer-friendly approach based on a two-pronged strategy: (i) customer friendly products and honest services, (ii) a public relations communication strategy.

Four Stages

The banking industry in India has passed through four key stages: (i) the money lenders table; (ii) the much elite owners banking; (iii) public sector banks and (iv) competitive banking in the liberalised economy. Indian banking entered its first stage with money lenders' table, purely a private affair and individual oriented, when the money lender attitude was "why should I care for a customer?"

In the second stage, banking was dominated by the rich elite owners, their aim being to earn profit out of their investments. However, in 1969 and 1980 witnessed a turning point in the history of Indian banking when 20 banks were nationalised and the commercial banks were brought into mainstream economic development with social objectives. That was the third stage. The new economic policy of 1991 resulted in the fourth stage towards a more competitive environment with more players, broader markets, wider and innovative products range, etc.

BANKING SECTOR REFORMS

The Indian banking system consists of commercial banks both in public and in private sector, Regional Rural Banks and Cooperative Banks. The Government of India appointed a high-level committee in 1997 on Banking sector Reforms headed by M. Narasimham. Based on the recommendations of this committee, certain guidelines were issued which among other include: setting up of new private banks to introduce greater competition, fair practices code for lenders, corporate governance; know your customer norms; merger and amalgamation of private banks for consolidation, operation of Indian banks abroad, liberalisation of bank branch licensing, setting up off-shore banking units in special economic zones; introduction of Banking Ombudsman scheme to settle customers' disputes, deposit mobilisation, etc. As a result, there has been a greater competition not only between nationalised banks and private banks, but also between nationalised banks. The interest rate war began among the banks.

JUSTIFICATION FOR PR IN BANKS

Sound public relations practices are the determining factors in improving the reputation of individual bank or financial institution to build up enduring relationships with the people inside and outside the bank. Banks deal with the public money, are the repositories of people's savings, serve people with financial services, have to maintain good relations with stakeholders, have to liaise with other financial institutions and government and non-governmental bodies, have to deal with media for effective communication, have to provide information under the Right to Information Act, etc. are a few to quote functions that justify the need for public relations in the banking industry. According to the German Associates, which is an association of the bankers of Germany, "every person in a bank from the President to the Record Keeper in the base and the Guard at the door are involved in public relations activity". From this statement, it is evident that directly or indirectly every person in any bank is involved in the public relations activity. Banking sector reforms pose a big challenge to the banks in dealing with the competitive marketing environment and to draw the attention of customers and potential customer.

Professional PR

Like human resource management, financial management or marketing management, banks also need a separate public relations management to handle relationships between the banks and their internal and external publics. Such relationships can be maintained only through a professional communicator equipped with skills in public relations techniques. The structure of a public relations department on par with marketing department is also a prerequisite for successful implementation of public relations activities in a bank. The public relations department in a bank forms the human bridge between the bank and its internal and external publics.

Public relations is a top management function. If this function is entrusted either to personnel or marketing department, it tends to promote the specific interests of only those departments. In fact, public relations is intended to promote the overall corporate image and such image can be built only when the subject of public relations is directly under the Chief Executive of the organisation. It is for this reason that public relations, by and large, is well established in banks.

Unique PR Structure in Bank

The State Bank of India has engaged the services of McKinsey and Co., a leading international consultant to review the bank's strategies, systems and structures, which among others deals with the subject of public relations. The consultants have made far-reaching recommendations relevant to the entire banking industry in India. Two important recommendations relate to public relations structure. One is about the merger of Community Services Banking (CSB) with the public relations department, while the second was placing public relations under the direct control of Chief Executive Officer. The State Bank of India has a unique public relations set-up worth emulating by all banks in the country.

In fact, a full-fledged public relations department was established in its head office Mumbai way back in 1963.

Corporate Office

The General Manager (Public Relations) who is the Head of Public Relations Department reports to the Chairman and Managing Director at the Corporate Office, Mumbai. The General Manager (PR) is assisted by one Assistant General Manager (PR). The public relations department in the corporate office is divided into four major sections, each section headed by an officer. These sections are: (i) corporate image, advertisements and crisis management, (ii) press releases and press conferences, (iii) media, liaison, and (iv) house magazine, *colleague*.

Local Head Office

The State Bank of India has 13 local head offices in the country. Each local head office is headed by a Chief General Manager. The Assistant General Manager or PR and CSB who is in-charge of public relations and community services at the local head office reports to the Chief General Manager.

He is assisted by four officers: (i) Officer—Community Services Banking, (ii) Officer—House Magazine, *Circle News*, (iii) Officer — liaison with media, (iv) Officer—press releases and press conferences, etc. The public relations set-up at local head office is a nerve centre for organising public relations programmes at the field level.

Zonal Office

The local head office is divided into various zones. Hyderabad Local Head office has four zonal offices at Hyderabad, Vijayawada, Visakhapatnam and Tirupathi. Each zone is headed by Deputy General Manager who is the head of office of the zone.

The Deputy Manager (PR) is placed in charge of public relations programmes at the zonal level who reports to the Deputy General Manager of zonal office.

STRATEGY

With a defined public relations policy and job profile, the public relations department in a bank forms a human bridge between the management on the one hand and its internal and external publics on the other hand. However, the public relations department based on the corporate mission and the banks services has to evolve a long drawn public relations strategy to reach the target audience.

Such a strategy has nine major components, viz.

1. Situation analysis or research
2. Identification of problems
3. Setting objectives
4. Segmentation of target audience
5. Service-oriented action plans
6. Designing media-wise public relations programme with multi-media approach
7. Budgeting
8. Communication or implementing public relations programme
9. Evaluation or the impact of the campaign

All these points have to be taken into consideration to evolve a programme both for internal and for external public relations. The media used in disseminating public information of a bank cover newspapers, corporate publications; radio; television; audio-visuals, photographs, exhibitions; hoardings; banners; wall paintings; posters; oral communication, management of customer meets, traditional folk arts, etc. Annual Reports, Annual General Meeting are the media through which relations are maintained with the shareholders.

In other words, a public relations manager in a bank must use the inter-personal media, traditional folk arts media, mass media and IT new media which alone will cover both urban and rural audience in creating awareness about the banks' services.

Corporate Relations

Public relations in banks takes different dimensions such as: employee relations; financial and investor relations; customer relations; government relations; community relations; media relations and relations in crisis situations. In other words, it is called **corporate public relations** or **corporate communications** embracing all types of relationships in a bank as to create better reputation for the banks.

Employees Relations

Employees are one of the publics that have to be cared for by public relations as they provide services to the customers. Banking transactions across the country came to a virtual standstill causing great hardship to crores of customers when 10 lakh officers and other employees of public, private cooperative and rural banks abstained from work to protest against the merger of public sector banks and an increase in foreign direct investment. Though employees of a bank are the key constituencies for public relations department, the management expects that public relations programmes must be directed towards external publics. A research in the area of customer services shows that customers can be satisfied if and only if employees are themselves satisfied. The main business of the bank is to satisfy customers and only a satisfied employee is capable of delivering the quality service expected by customers. It is against this background, employees' public relations comes to the fore.

House journals are the key tools of employees relations. *Colleague* —a quarterly house magazine of State Bank of India, *Sahavikas*— a quarterly house magazine of State Bank of Hyderabad, *Magicart*— a monthly house journal of Andhra Bank are examples which motivate employees towards higher productivity and better service to customers.

Relations with Customer

A bank customer is broadly defined as a potential user of bank's service. Ensuring his satisfaction is of paramount importance to a banker. The concept of customer satisfaction, therefore, has gained renewed emphasis in the present-day context. Definitely one must say that banks have profited from the ignorance of the customers. By saying it one does not mean to say that the banks have behaved unethically. But most banks take advantage of customers ignorance or lower bargaining power. Today, customer awareness has grown and, therefore, they are more demanding, vocal and consumer right oriented. The mass media, the consumerism and media exposure have raised the levels of expectations and this trend will continue. In the current scenario when banks have very little difference in interest rates, the only differentiation and most powerful weapon they have is customer service. The quality of customer service differentiates one bank from its competitor.

A customer evaluates the bank on the basis of his past experience, awareness and, above all, his perception of the banks service quality. Honestly, it is a product of cumulative memory of his experience during the service contact at various counters at the bank branch a customer had that results in the evaluation of its service quality.

Types of Customer

All customers can be classified as nine types, based on various combination of their moods:

1. Provider
2. Provider Transactor
3. Provider Seeker
4. Borrower
5. Borrower Transactor
6. Borrower Seeker
7. Transactor Seeker
8. Transactor
9. Seeker

These days there are growing expressions of dissatisfaction among the customers. It could be a realisation of the deterioration standards of service in the banks or the growing expectations of the customer. Whatever be the reason, it is the customer's participation that matters. What he thinks about the bank is more important than what the bank thinks about him.

It is, therefore, essential to manage customers experience in reality. We have to be alive to his requirements. Unless the bank provides what the customer wants in the manner he wants, the bank cannot survive in the long run.

Service Survey

Even customers' needs cannot be taken for granted. Attempts must be made to find out the true needs. First this would require a little amount of research to find out the true needs keeping in touch with the customer on a day-to-day personalized basis in one of the sure short emphasis. Foreign banks in India have affected the relationship approach to bank. They are successful in this area because the customers are few and of a high quality but when it comes to public sector banks, the customers are large and, therefore, the quality gets affected in terms of the volume of transactions.

Customer service is an important arm in the public relations exercise of any bank. Public relations in terms of customer service is performance, followed by recognition. If the bank staff and authorities do not perform, then its negative image will be built rather than a positive image. A satisfied customer is the best advertisement for any bank or for that matter any enterprise, and a dissatisfied vocal customer can cause damage to the reputation which cannot be repaired by a multi-media public relations campaign.

Most banks have customer service departments to ensure speedy redressal on grievances. Fornightly 'Customers' Day' is observed in each branch while 'Customers' Meets' are organised quarterly for an interface and pro-active participation of the management in redressing customers grievances.

Citizens' Charter

The Andhra Bank has published a citizen's charter as part of its accountability to the customers which has two sections. Section A envisages 'Service to the Citizens', while Section B offers remedies available to the customers in the case of any complaints. Customer complaints redressal cell in the customer service department deals with complaints. In case the customer is not satisfied with the grievance redressal mechanism, one can make appeal to the Banking Ombudsman located in the State capital, Hyderabad.

Banking Ombudsman

The banking ombudsman scheme, which is in operation since 1995, works under the control and supervision of Reserve Bank of India (RBI). Banking ombudsman is an independent body with legal powers to settle disputes quickly and inexpensively. RBI has appointed 15 Banking Ombudsman all over the country. If the customer's grievance has not been resolved by banks to his/her satisfaction can approach Banking Ombudsman. Grounds of complaints cover: Credit card complaints, pension complaints, failure to provide the promised facilities, delay in the payment or collection of cheques, drafts, etc. Banking Ombudsman scheme is a good exercise in customers' public relations.

Media Relations

Since media is the conduit of reaching publics of the bank, public relations is expected to create and maintain good media relations for getting fair coverage in both print and electronic media. Tactics, such as press kit, press release, press conference, advertorial, rejoinder, backgrounder, factsheet, news photograph, press interview, press clipping service, video films, video releases, talks, panel discussions are utilised for getting good coverage of banks activities, and also reaching the target audience.

A Case Study

Mobilisation of deposits in rural areas is a ticklish problem for banks. In India banks have been assigned a major role in promoting rural development by advancing loans particularly for agricultural development. As a result, banks are expected to build up their internal financial resources by mobilisation of deposits in both urban and rural areas. It is quite necessary for the banks not only to identify savings potentialities in villages but also evolve public relations communication strategies to inform and create awareness of the importance of savings.

For example, small farmers earn money by sale of milk which could be converted into savings.

It is in this context, in the 1990s the Karimanagar District Cooperative Bank in Andhra Pradesh launched a multimedia public relations deposit mobilisation campaign in villages for a period of one month. Press releases, advertisements, display of cinema slides in theatres, distribution of leaflets, cloth banners across major roads, use of cable television network, person to person communication were utilised to mobilise deposits with the support of District Collector. A mobile publicity van duly decorated with slogans and publicity material fitted with audio-visual equipment moved from village to village. The campaign resulted in reaching the targets. A sum of ₹1.97 crore was collected in the shape of deposits as against a target of ₹1 crore. As many as 3500 new accounts were opened from rural areas, thanks to the one month campaign.

COMMUNICATION STRATEGY FOR TOURISM

I heartily welcome the union of East and West provided it is not based on brute force.

—**Mahatma Gandhi**

Tourism has been a major social phenomenon of societies all over the world. It is driven by the natural urge of every human being for new experiences and the desire to be both educated and entertained by visiting new places of interest. The motivations for tourism also include religious and business interests. Progress in air transport and development of tourist facilities have encouraged people to travel beyond the boundaries.

The importance of tourism as an instrument of economic development and employment generation has been well recognized the world over. It is a large service industry globally in terms of gross revenue as well as foreign exchange earnings. India's performance in tourism has been quite impressive. If 60 lakh foreign tourists visited India, the number of domestic tourists who travelled within the country accounted for 65 crore in 2009. The Taj Mahal, one of the wonders of the world, is the star attraction for both foreign and domestic tourists.

While describing the glory of India, Mark Twain, the American Writer, over 100 years ago said, "India is the cradle of the human race, the birthplace of human speech, the mother of history, the grandmother of legend and the great grandmother of tradition. Our most valuable and most instructive materials in the history of man are treasured up in India only". That is the potential of tourism industry in India.

Tourism is a sunrise industry in India which provides employment and triggers economic activity, attracting both domestic and foreign tourists. Tourism means organising ways that facilitate travel, transport and accommodation for tourists who visit places of interest. It also means devising ways of stimulating the desire to travel in a particular direction, hence the provision of amenities, building of resorts and organising of leisure. India has moved from its 36th position in 2003 to 5th in 2004 among the top 10 global destinations.

The dictionary meaning of tourism is "commercial organisation and operation of holidays and visits to places of interest". The business of providing services for tourists includes organising their travel, hotels, entertainment, etc.

What is Tourism Public Relations?

Tourism public relations may be defined as "the application of principles and techniques of public relations to promote tourism industry so as to attract both domestic and foreign tourists to places of interest".

A key function of public relations is to create mutual understanding between tourism industry and its internal and external publics by providing both satisfactory services and need-based information.

Tourist places are full of life and attraction. In these places, there are monuments of architectural splendour and beauty, temples, churches, mosques and gurudwaras. There are also cultural treasures such as museums, centres of learning, along with places of scenic beauty such as waterfalls, beaches and lakes, etc. What is required today is to help bring the awareness of these places among the people through various PR communication strategies.

The tourism organisations, both at the Centre and at the States level, the Departments of Tourism, Indian Institute of Tourism and Travel Management and India Tourism Development Corporation Ltd. implement the policies for the development of tourism within the country and for attracting foreign tourists to India by way of developing tourism infrastructure, publicity and promotion and dissemination of tourist information.

These organisations at the Centre and State levels have public relations divisions to promote tourism. It is here the public relations plays a vital role.

Why PR in Tourism?

In the tourism, travel and leisure sectors, where the product is a service, promotion is even more vital than in other industries. Despite arguments over the essential differences between the marketing of goods and services, it is well established that where it is a service, the tourism and leisure product is a complex bundle of values—intangible, inseparable, variable and perishable. Promotion of service is rather different from the promotion of a product. Clearly, you cannot test drive a holiday beforehand, and thus promotion becomes critical, having a greater role in establishing the nature of the product than in most other markets.

The customer buys a holiday, a theatre ticket or attends a concert purely on the basis of symbolic expectations established promotionally through words, pictures, sounds and so forth. In this way, leisure and tourism experiences are literally constructed in our imagination through public relations and advertising. Indeed, it has often been said that tourism public relations is about selling of dreams and that tourism itself is about illusion, or about the creation of 'atmosphere' or awareness of tourist potentialities.

Need For PR

The need for public relations in tourism industry arises from the following propositions:

- To compile data and promote places of tourist interest among the prospective tourists.
- To bring out tourist literature including travel magazines for the benefit of both domestic and foreign tourists.
- To identify and encourage travel writers by providing tourist information for writing articles in travel magazines and other media.
- To organise travel and tourism exhibitions.
- To maintain media relations for fair coverage of tourist places and hotel industry in both print and electronic media.
- To launch multimedia public relations campaigns like the Incredible India Tourism Campaign implemented by the India Tourism Development Corporation in 2006–2007 to project India as a global tourist destination with a variety of places of interest and culture.
- To provide feedback information about the reaction of tourists to the facilities and services, so as to evolve policies to serve the customers with satisfaction.

Strategy

Travel agencies, tourism corporations, hotels and transport organisations have changed their concept of public relations by integrating marketing and communications as a single entity. Earlier, a guest relations officer was expected to entertain important customers, purchase travel tickets, handle customers complaints and go shopping with the wives of important customers. They never understood the real value of public relations. But things have changed. Aspirations of tourists have increased and the importance of media has grown manifold, which has forced the tourism industry to create a specialised professional public relations division in hotels, tourism corporations and travel agencies. Public relations, be it in a tourism department or in a hotel, has two primary goals: internal and external communication including media relations. If proper internal communication does not take place, an effective external public relations campaign can never be implemented. The entire tourism industry survives on its marketing and communication strategy. It is, therefore, said' "All marketing is communication, all communication is marketing". Integrated marketing communication includes public relations component. Data-based communication is the key to success in marketing communication.

Tactics

Public relations, in the modern context, has immense potentialities to promote the Indian tourism industry. Public relations can help tourism in several ways, such as the following:

- Identifying problems confronting the tourism industry, problems of tourist organisations and problems of tourists
- Advising tourist organisations to evolve a plan of action to provide the necessary infrastructure facilities at tourist places for attraction.
- Communicating tourism plans to create awareness on tourist places through the various media of communication
- Creating mutual understanding between tourist organisations and tourists
- Evaluating tourist campaign plans to assess their impact in terms of the influx of tourist traffic and improvement in economy

MULTIMEDIA PR CAMPAIGN

A multimedia public relations campaign must be evolved to promote tourism plan, based on public relations actions aimed directly at the target audience. Such a plan includes various media and methods. Media includes print communication, electronic media, travel writers, travel agents and tourism advertising. Stimulate the desire to travel and thereby promote tourists. Posters with good illustrations are effective media for communication in tourism. For example, a poster may be brought out on the importance of hotel customer with the quotation of Mahatma Gandhi "A Customer is most important visitor on our premises".

Similarly, phrases such as "how is our guest service—ask a guest", "it takes months to get a new guest and only seconds to lose a loyal one. You are the most important brand contact—you are our ambassador" and "clean data is as important as a clean kitchen" will tell the public relations culture of a hotel. Public relations with its informative, educative and persuasive skills can contribute considerably to stimulate the desire to travel and, thereby, promote tourism.

Case Study

The Ministry of Tourism, Government of India, launched overseas tourism promotion campaign to position India in the tourism generating markets as a tourism destination as to increase India's share in the global tourism market. The objectives were met through an integrated marketing and communication strategy and a synergised campaign in association with the Travel Trade and Indian Missions.

Promotional activities and media used include:

- Advertising in the print and electronic media
- Participation in Fairs, Exhibitions
- Organising seminars, workshops, road shows, India evening, publication of brochures
- Joint Advertising with Travel Agents/Tour Operators
- Inviting the Travel writers, media, and travel trade to visit India under hospitality
- India tourism offices overseas participated in the major International Travel Fairs and Exhibitions to showcase and promote the Indian tourism products. Such as Taj Mahal
- Arabian Travel Market in Dubai, World Expo 2010 in Shanghai, World Travel Market in London, etc.
- Advertising and outdoor publicity campaign during the Vancouver Winter Games 2010 in Vancouver
- Organised "Know India" seminar for the foreign tourists travelling to South India giving information about shopping, hotels, ayurveda and spas and safe travelling for women
- Outdoor advertising campaign including on taxis/buses/trains/hoardings and billboards have been undertaken in Beijing, Shanghai, Tokyo, Seoul, Sydney, Singapore, Dubai, Johannesburg, London, Paris, New York, etc.
- Road shows focussing on promotion of tourism to India as part of the Queen's Baton Rally were organised in Sri Lanka, Singapore, Malaysia, London, Melbourne and Auckland including holding run or walk relay through the tours

What is the result of this campaign?

Awareness has been created abroad about India as the destination of tourists. In the process, the influence of foreign tourists increased with foreign exchange earnings.

POINTS TO REMEMBER

1. There is a growing distrust between the community and the police due to which unfavourable or bad image is robbing the police the public's support. The National Police Commission as

well as the Police Commission of Andhra Pradesh felt the need for effective public relations in Police department towards better community relations.

2. There are five dimensions that justify the need for public relations in the Police department. (i) the police is accountable and answerable to the public in democratic government; (ii) projection of police services in the cause of society; (iii) to seek people's cooperation in community policing; (iv) maintaining media relations as part of healthy police media linkage; (v) collection of feedback information about police services and image.

3. Police–public relations may be defined as the management of "a two-way communication between a police department and its internal force and external community to earn public understanding for its services".

4. Public relations in the police department has five facets such as: (i) employees relations; (ii) community relations; (iii) media relations; (iv) relations in crisis situations; (v) feedback information mechanism.

5. The banking industry in India had passed through four stages, namely, the moneylender's table, the rich elite owners banking, public sector banks and competitive banking in the liberalised economy and globalisation.

6. As part of banking sector reforms, new private banks have been started for greater competition and bank branch licensing has been liberalised. As a result, competition between private and public sector banks has considerably increased.

7. Public relations structure is a prerequisite for effective implementation of public relations programme. The State Bank of India has a well-established public relations set-up with General Manager (PR) as the head in corporate office, Assistant General Manager (PR) at each of the local head offices and the Deputy Manager (PR) at zonal offices. They handle public relations in their respective areas.

8. Banks have published citizens charter as part of their accountability to the customers which envisages service to the customers and complaints redressal machinery.

9. Ombudsman in banking settles the complaints of customers.

10. Tourism public relations is defined as the application of principles and techniques of public relations to promote tourism industry as to attract both domestic and foreign tourists to places of interest. Management of mutually beneficial relationships between tourism organisations and their internal and external public is also called "tourism public relations". An important function

of public relations is to create mutual understanding between tourism industry, its related organisation and their internal and external public by providing better services and full information.

11. Justification of public relations in tourism arises from the following propositions: (i) compilation of tourist information and promotion of tourist places, (ii) bring out tourist publications for the benefit of tourists, (iii) identification and encouraging travel writers to write articles on tourist places and facilities, (iv) maintaining media relations for fair coverage in the print and electronic media, (v) provision of feedback information mechanism for ascertaining the reactions of tourists.

12. Public relations can promote tourism industry with activities, such as (i) identifying problems confronting tourist places and related organisation; (ii) advising tourist organisations to evolve a plan of action to provide necessary infrastructure facilities at tourist places; (iii) communicating tourism plans and creating awareness of tourist places; (iv) evaluating tourist campaigns as to study their impact.

13. Multimedia public relations strategy is adopted to promote tourist campaigns. For example, 'the incredible India' campaign launched by India Tourism Development Corporation was based on different media including advertising in both electronic and print media. Media used in tourism public relations campaigns include: print communication, hoardings, travel writers, electronic media, films, interpersonal media, etc.

REVIEW QUESTIONS

1. What is police public relations? Describe the justifications for public relations in the police department.

2. How does public relations help the police? Explain the broad areas of public relations in the police department.

3. 'Banks live or die on public perception'. Discuss the role of public relations in banks. Elaborate your answer with a public relations structure of any bank known to you.

4. What are the dimensions of corporate public relations in a major bank? Cite examples.

5. What is tourism?

6. Define tourism public relations. Explain the role of public relations in promoting tourist places.

7. Discuss a case study of Tourism publicity campaign.

Public Relations for NGOs and Political Parties

Chapter

18

C O N T E N T S

NGO—THE THIRD SECTOR

In modern society we find three distinct organisations or sectors that are involved in the service of the society. The first sector organisation is government whose objective is to protect, secure and regulate the lives and actions of citizens. The second sector is known as business sector that makes a livelihood and creates and accumulates wealth and the third sector is non-government organisation (Voluntary Sector) which is intended to pursue social concerns which are separate from gaining a livelihood but to serve the cause of community welfare. The functions and purposes of these three sectors sometimes overlap in reaching the target audience. It is because these three sectors are concerned with the issues and problems of the community.

What is a non-governmental organisation (NGO)? A non-profit or non-governmental organisation is a group of people interested in serving the community at large on an honorary basis in some area of community development. It seeks to raise its own funds through voluntary contributions or donations from both the individuals and the institutions for undertaking service-oriented schemes. An NGO is also assisted by the Government with financial grants.

Non-governmental organisations pursue various activities to relieve the suffering of the poor, protect the environment, provide health services and other development activities. Not-for-profit organisations are classified broadly as: socio-economic development organisations, rural development societies, cultural organisations, environmental groups, trade associations, professional bodies, foundations, service-oriented clubs, etc. An NGO can be any non-profit organisation independent from the government.

NGO Sector in India

Non-governmental or not-for-profit-organisations emerged in India to supplement the efforts of the government in the field of socio-economic development on the one hand and undertake philanthropic activities as part of community development on the other hand. In 1951, when the first Five Year Plan was launched, it was felt the need for people's participation and involvement in the successful implementation of the plan. As a result, NGOs like the Bharat Sevak Samaj came into being to involve the people as partners in progress and also supplement the efforts of the Community Development Department.

Notwithstanding the government effort, many industrial houses, business organisations in private sector, as part of their corporate social responsibility or corporate philanthropy have launched community welfare programmes for the upliftment of the poorer sections. They either undertake programmes themselves or create NGOs for implementing such welfare measures. The TATA Group of Companies have established a separate body called the Tata Council for Community Initiatives, while the Reddy Labs, Hyderabad have launched an NGO known as Centre for Social Initiative and Management (*Manavaseva Dharma Samavardhani*). The Tata Steel Rural Development Society, developed 500 villages in Bihar, Orissa and Madhya Pradesh by providing education, drinking water, transport, agricultural extension and the Reddy Labs' NGO has trained a number of workers of various NGOs in the cause of the society.

Business Partnership

An interesting development in the field of non-profit organisations is that some of the major corporations have entered into partnership with the NGOs to undertake philanthropic activities. It is because some of the Indian companies are ill-equipped to steer and administer community welfare programmes independently. Therefore, they tend to join NGOs which have specialised in implementing such programmes. This is a new trend in business–NGOs partnership.

International Perspective

Non-governmental organisations also developed international links as to participate in some of the global conferences organised by the United Nations Organisation on issues of public interest, such as environment, empowerment of women. For example, many NGOs from India attended the UN conference on the family, held in Cairo.

NEED FOR PR

A special feature of all NGOs is that they heavily depend on fund-raising activities to build their financial resources. Such fund-raising campaigns need public relations communication support. Of course, they are given tax exemption because their main objective is to enhance the well-being of the society. Fund-raising is a major public relations exercise for the NGOs.

Every organisation, be it an NGO or a business corporation survives only on public perception and their support. In ensuring the people's cooperation, communication plays a major role. The need for public relations communication in an NGO is more for four specific reasons. *First*, NGOs entirely depend for their finances on fund-raising campaigns. *Second*, an NGO has to project itself as a service-oriented or philanthropic organisation as to attract the attention of charitable trusts, and donors for financial help. *Third*, relates to the dissemination of information about its services, plans as to enable the people to make use of them for their betterment. *Fourth*, an NGO has to maintain good media relations so that the media carries their messages both to the donors and to the beneficiaries besides building image of the organisation. It is for these reasons that non-profit organisations must have public relations set up with adequate trained personnel to carry the goals and in the process gain the goodwill of their stakeholders.

Public relations is seen as an essential responsibility of NGOs in seeking donations on the one hand and projecting the organisation as service oriented for the cause of the public on the other hand. Of course, the basic approach to public relations in not-for-profit organisations may not be very different from that of public relations being practiced in business enterprises.

Public relations communication is the best way of promoting NGOs. It is not as costly as advertising and when properly handled public relations can produce far more positive results in fund-raising, media coverage and projection of the organisation.

AUDIENCES FOR NGOs

Before designing an organisational public relations strategy, one should first identify each of the key audience important for the message. For a non-profit organisation, the list of the audiences comprise two large categories: (i) those critical to fund-raising efforts such as charities, foundations, government agencies, individual donors, and (ii) those who are the beneficiaries of the NGOs programmes.

However, the typical audience for a non-profit or non-governmental organisation include:

1. The employees of the organisation.
2. The members of the Board of Management.
3. The beneficiaries or the people served by the organisation.
4. The leaders, workers whose attitudes or behaviour would influence the functioning of the organisation.
5. The individual donors, corporations, charities, government who give donations.
6. Similar NGOs involved in voluntary work.
7. Opinion leaders—local politicians, elected representatives of local bodies and Panchayat Raj Institutions.
8. Educational institutions and the student community who can assist in their voluntary work.
9. The media and their representatives.

PR GOALS

Every non-profit organisation should evolve a set of public relations goals based on which public relations plan could be implemented to reach the target audience. Goals vary depending on the purpose and nature of the organisation.

However, a non-profit organisation may set the following public relations goals:

1. Promote public awareness of the organisation's vision, mission, goals and programmes.
2. Design and implement public relations programme for fund-raising campaigns.
3. Induce individuals and institutions to make use of the services of the organisation for community development.
4. Produce publicity material on the services for distribution to the internal and external public.
5. Enrol and train volunteers for the community welfare programme.
6. Maintain good relations with media for fair coverage of the activities of the NGO.
7. Create feedback mechanism to monitor the reactions of the media and public on the functioning of the organisation.
8. Promotion of reputation of the organisation based on its performance.

MEDIA STRATEGY

The public relations division of NGOs must adopt a multimedia approach to convey its messages to the varied target audience. Since an NGO is a service-oriented organisation, it might get free editorial space or time in media which should be utilised appropriately. A combination of four media: interpersonal media, folk art media, conventional mass media and IT new media is an ideal media approach to carry out public programmes of NGOs.

The media include: oral communication, meetings, newspapers, magazines, corporate publications, electronic media—radio, television, films and video, traditional media such as puppetry, ballads, street plays, personalised letters or direct mail, e-mail, website, social media – blogs, facebook, etc. A small video is also an ideal medium to project the image of an NGO.

India is a democratic and developing country where the Government alone cannot provide all services. Therefore, the Government will extend financial support to NGOs for supplementing its efforts to eradicate poverty and strengthen democracy. As such a bright future beckons, the Indian NGOs and their public relations communication efforts.

MV Foundation: A Case Study

The MV Foundation (*Mamidipudi Venkata Rangaiah Foundation*), Hyderabad, a non-governmental organisation had mobilised the community in such a way that about 2.4 lakh child labourers in Ranga Reddy District of Andhra Pradesh were sent to schools. This work was done in a period of 12 years (1991–2003). The NGO did the work in alliance with the Government as to eliminate child labour in the country.

Shanta Sinha, a Professor of Political Science in the University of Hyderabad, and the founder Secretary of the Foundation worked with missionary zeal in the field of putting victims of child labour in school, was honoured with the *Ramon Magasaysay Award* in 2003 for Community Leadership. She was instrumental in guiding the people of Andhra Pradesh to end the surge of child labour and send their children to school.

Such voluntary organisations need public relations support and communication to mobilise people for the tasks and gain community recognition for the good work done.

The MV Foundation has adopted its own communication strategy in reaching its target audience in rural areas. It is because of its service and communication plan that the foundation could enrol over 2.4 lakh child labourers as students in different schools for studies. Effective public relations communication strategy, therefore, is central to the success of NGOs.

POLITICAL PUBLIC RELATIONS

Politics without principles is a sin. —**Mahatma Gandhi**

A unique feature of Indian political system is that apart from the recognised political parties by the Election Commission of India, there are about 700 registered political parties. All these political parties not only vie in General Elections at the National level and Assembly elections at the State level, but also fight among themselves in local body, Panchayati Raj elections and elections for cooperatives. It constitutes a major effort on the part of these political parties to mobilise public opinion in their favour at the grass-roots level. The Election Commission of India permits the recognised political parties to telecast political speeches containing election manifesto through the State owned electronic media—All India Radio and Doordarshan.

GENERAL ELECTIONS

Beginning in 1952, the country went to the polls in 2009 to elect the 15th Lok Sabha. A number of both national and regional political parties took part in the General Elections and no single party attained absolute majority to form the government in the Centre. The Indian National Congress Party emerged as the single largest party and formed a coalition Government in collaboration with other political parties in 2009. The regional parties had emerged as a strong force. Thus, the era of coalition parties in Indian democracy came to stay.

Communication within political parties and between political parties and the people is of vital importance in a democratic polity. Media also have an equal role to play in reaching the electorate. Intra-party communication is also important.

Since 1952 when the first general elections were held in India, public relations techniques have been used within the political context to promote candidates and key election campaign issues, to stage political events, to provide media contacts, to produce elections publicity material, to release political advertisements, to spin political information to candidates advantage and to offer advice on packaging political policies. Educating 75 crore voters on how to vote is itself a big exercise in political communication.

What is political public relations? Public relations takes different dimensions based on the nature of the organisation it represents and the audiences it serves such as the government public relations, public sector public relations, financial public relations. To this effect, public relations in the political context is termed as political public relations mostly used by political parties. Political public relations can be defined as a public relations process to create voting behaviour in favour of a political party and its ideology to win elections, to govern or retain power. Such a process is carried out through effective communication and multi-media strategy, by a political party in India.

Political Advertising

Advertising with party messages just before elections has been used as a means of reaching voters. Many national and regional parties have released full page advertisements. But this kind of advertising, we have noted, has one fundamental weakness of political communication. The voter as a receiver, always receives such messages with jaundiced eyes believing them to be propaganda material—biased and partial. The people think that such advertisements are politically loaded messages, reflecting the interests, ideas and values of the sponsor political party and are one sided. As a result, the effectiveness of political advertising as a means of persuasion became weak and limited. Therefore such limited use of political advertising has encouraged other forms of political communication that have proved to be more effective, which include household communication, public meetings, etc.

FREE MEDIA COVERAGE

Political leaders and political parties believe in 'free media editorial space and time', both in newspapers and in electronic media, to achieve their goals as opposed to the paid-for-advertising format. Through free media, political parties and their leaders gain exposure and coverage without having to pay any media organisations. Free media outlets include: press releases, press conference, press interview, press enquiries, press clarifications and rejoinders, individual face-to-face meetings. These tactics are not only applicable to the print media but also to the electronic media. They are also called tactics or methods of political public relations to reach the target audience. In order to handle the media and methods, political parties need professional public relations setup headed by a qualified public relations manager or a politician well-versed in public relations techniques. Therefore, political parties must employ professionals skilled in the working of the media. In the West, we have political public relations consultancy firms which deal with political issues. The ultimate objective of political public relations is not only intended to build up the image of political leaders, but also the corporate image of the party by creating the desired political awakening in the people.

Political Media Meet

Political parties almost everyday meet media to express their viewpoints on current issues. Each political party both at national and at regional level designates spokesperson to be in touch with the media. Heads of political parties also meet the media. Such media meets promote political media relations and also the views of political parties reach the target audience. Political media meets also enable the political parties to get feedback on their policies from the media representatives. Handling of political media meets demand public relations support. Since such media meets are instruments of public relations to influence the people, political parties need to engage professional public relations practitioners to handle the media meets.

How can public relations help to shape politics? Public relations strategy is used by political parties in six ways: (1) message formulation, (2) research, (3) media relations, (4) political advertising, (5) relations with voters and (6) feedback information containing the peoples' reactions and media reflections.

It is a well-established tenet that public relations is not a substitute for false propaganda. Nevertheless, narrow-minded political leaders all over the globe "turn life upside down for the right to rule the world, yet there may soon be no world for them to rule" (Prasad 2004). The "out" party fears the power of an army of "propagandists" to keep the 'ins' in and the 'outs' out.

INDIA SHINING

The National Democratic Alliance Government headed by Atal Bihari Vajpayee (of Bharatiya Janata Party) launched an election campaign 'India Shining' (2004) built around select buoyant economic indicators portraying a resurgent economy which ran into a considerable amount of money. The India Shining public relations campaign and 'feel good factor' slogan had not only proved "too exclusionist but also aggravated a feeling of being deprived of the goodies of the economic feel-good the urban and rural poor alike. The campaign strategy also reflected the misplaced feel good.... The campaign by a host of film stars to rub in the feel-good factor failed, as voters, reeling under drought or deprivation leading to farmer suicides, just felt excluded" (Prasannan 2004). The India shining campaign did not succeed because rural India was suffering (Prasad 2004). L.K. Advani, BJP leader, admitted the campaign title should have been "India Rising instead India Shining".

Aam Aadmi

The Congress party, the then main opposition party to the BJP, based its election campaign in 2004 on the perception of the party being one for the common man (*aam aadmi*). The Congress Party's slogan for the 2004 election was "Congress *ka haath, aam aadmi ke sath*" (the hand of the Congress is with the common man). Jairam Ramesh, the notable figure in the Congress Strategy Committee, said: "Sonia's *Jan Sampark* programme brought about the perception among the voters that the party was concerned about the plight of those who were left out of the Shining India orb" (Prasad 2004).

POLITICAL STARS—CINEMA GLAMOUR

If personal charisma of great political leaders such as Pandit Jawaharlal Nehru, Indira Gandhi won many votes for them, famous cine artistes such as M.G. Ramachandran, N.T. Rama Rao, Jayalalitha also won elections with their cinema glamour. Personal charisma and cinema glamour have acted as media to reach the voters with their past performance and promises of future. N.T. Rama Rao was elected as Chief Minister by getting full majority for his Telugu Desam Party in 1983, 1985 and 1994. Heroes on the screen became political leaders off the screen because masses identified them with the roles they played. Of course cinema glamour will not sustain if performance of the ruling party is not up to the expectations of the public.

NEW DIRECTIONS FOR POLITICAL PR

Political public relations cannot be a substitute for good governance. Political parties must realise that voters are capable of rejecting false claims. The downfall of the BJP-led government due to its jargon ridden 'India Shining' campaign and 'feel good' slogan is the proof that people are not easily taken in by nebulous ideas disconnected from reality. A political public relations cannot survive on false, distorted or irrelevant information.

PR Consultancy

The Indian political establishment which had earlier depended on internal sources to come out with popular slogans is now overtly dependent on public relations agencies and advertising companies to suggest the most appropriate way forward. It was evident from 2004 Lok Sabha elections that national political parties such as the Bharatiya Janata Party and the Indian National Congress Party engaged advertising and public relations agencies to design their election campaigns. Sam Balsara, Chairman and Managing Director, Madison said "Politicians are getting more and more savvy; we live in an over communicated world, and they think that the best way is to get professional help. The stakes are getting bigger and most of them are using professional agencies". The Congress too had started its campaign with the '*Aam aadmi ko kya mila*' theme. Its account had gone to Orchid Advertising Agency and was estimated at ₹50 crore. Its public relations account was handled by Dilip Cherian of Perfect Relations.

Bharatiya Janta Party's 'India Shining' and *'Bharat Uday Yatra'* campaign was handled by Grey Worldwide Multinational Agency. A political public relations consultancy is thus developing in India.

The role of public relations in politics is becoming more important with the increase in media competition. Exposure to media is creating an enlightened and well-informed voter. It is clear that press coverage is increasingly central to political campaign strategies and increasingly critical to its success. Public relations is, therefore, central to a political campaign in view of the fact that India has over 75 crore voters. Public relations in politics has a bright future in India, provided political parties develop public relations structure with professional outlook. And political public relations will emerge as a specialised area of public relations practice as being done in the United States.

The political public relations must refrain from ill-conceived propaganda or hard sell messages that may be well-received initially but backfire in the long run. The 2009 elections had indeed led all political parties to rethink their public relations and advertising strategies in the light of the people's verdict. Coalition politics in India will undoubtedly strengthen the political public relations.

US POLITICAL PR

In the USA, both the Members of the House of the Representatives and the Senate as part of their political relations have appointed individual press secretaries who perform the duties of political public relations officers and act as a 'bridge' between the Members and the Media and their constituencies. They monitor the home constituency or home state media, they write speeches, issue press releases, letters to the editor, they send out newsletters to their voters and arrange media conferences and interviews. The press secretaries not only do media monitoring, but also provide felt needs of the constituency.

An interesting feature of Political Public Relations in the USA is that the two major political parties, namely Republican Party and Democratic Party have their own television studios in Capital Hill (Washington), which are at the disposal of Press Secretaries of their respective political parties. Political Press Secretaries produce video news releases for the individual members and political parties, and transmit them to the local TV stations. Such a communication set-up testifies the fact that the political parties and the Members of House of Representatives and the Senate promote political public relations.

As in the United States, each Member of Parliament and Member of State Legislature, all Political Parties in India will have to promote professional political communications/public relations division manned by a professional public relations manager. Of course, party spokespersons, president of political party would oversee such political public relations set-up.

TV Channels

If All India Anna DMK headed by Ms. Jayalalitha has Jaya Television, DMK Party Chief M. Karunanidhi has established *Kalaignar* channel to promote their respective party ideologies.

Political Parties' Newspapers

A few political parties such as the Indian National Congress, Bharatiya Janata Party, Communist Party of India, Communist Party of India (Marxist) have established their own magazines and daily newspapers. Telugu dailies such as *Vishalandhra* and *Praja Shakti* published from Hyderabad represent CPI and CPI (Marxist) respectively. Political parties in India have their own weekly magazines like *Organiser* (BJP) *'Peoples' Democracy* (CPI (M)), *New Age* (CPI). These newspapers promote their respective party ideologies and are committed to them. They also act as a bridge between the party and its party workers.

> ## POINTS TO REMEMBER

1. A non-governmental organisation (NGO) is a group of people interested in serving the community on an honorary basis in some area of socio-economic development. It also supplements the governmental development programmes.

2. Industrial houses, business organisations as part of their corporate social responsibility take up community welfare programmes. They also establish their own NGOs to undertake such social welfare programmes. For example, the Tata Council for Community Initiatives (TCCI), an NGO of Tata Group of Companies provides services such as drinking water, education, health care to the needy poorer sections of the society.

3. Public relations support is required for NGOs because of four reasons.
   (a) Public relations communication is an essential task of NGO to launch fund-raising campaigns.
   (b) NGO has to project itself as a service-oriented organisation to attract the attention of donors.
   (c) Information on services of NGOs has to be disseminated to the target public a d beneficiaries.

(d) An NGO has to maintain good media relations with various representatives of media for better coverage.

4. Every NGO must determine public relations goals to achieve. They include:

(a) Designing and implementing public relations programme for fund-raising.

(b) Inducing individuals and institutions towards their services.

(c) Producing publicity material for distribution to the target audience, maintaining good relations with media for better coverage of the activities of the NGO.

5. In order to implement public relations plan of the NGO, the public relations department must adopt multi-media approach to reach the target audience. The media strategy includes four types of media such as: interpersonal media, folk-art media, mass media and IT new media.

6. Communication within political parties, between political parties and the people is of vital importance in a democratic party. The media also act as a bridge between political parties and the people in conveying political messages.

7. Political public relations is defined as a process to create voting behaviour in favour of a political party and its ideology to win elections, to govern or retain power. Public agitation movements of various political parties election campaigns need the support of political public relations.

8. 'India Shining' campaign of the 'National Democratic Alliance' government and the "Congress *Aam Aadmi Ke Sath*" by the Indian National Congress Party in 2004 General Elections are the two examples of political campaigns through advertising and free media publicity.

9. The Indian political parties which depended much on their internal sources for publicity have now adopted a new direction by engaging public relations firms/agencies for designing their political campaigns. Agencies like Madison, Orchid Ad, Grey Worldwide have handled some of political campaigns in 2004 elections.

10. The role of public relations in politics is becoming more important with the media explosion and the emergence of enlightened and well-informed voter. It is not only a challenge to Indian politics but also a great opportunity for political public relations to inform, educate and motivate the Indian voter. This political public relations has a bright future.

REVIEW QUESTIONS

1. Define a non-governmental organisation. Explain their major functions in the service of the society.
2. Discuss the need of public relations for NGOs.
3. What is the role of public relations in NGO? How does it help in fund-raising campaign.
4. What is political public relations? Explain its role in the Indian political system to reach the electorate as well as the general public.
5. Write short notes on:
   (a) Free media coverage for political parties
   (b) 'India Shining' campaign and *'Aam Aadmi Ke Sath'* campaign.

Celebrity Public Relations

Chapter

19

C O N T E N T S

Public relations is now a growing industry all over the world with a number of corporations, governments, and NGOs utilizing the services of professional public relations communicators to build good relations with their respective publics on the one side and improve their image on the other. Among others, there emerged celebrity public relations as a specialized form of communication to improve the reputation of celebrities, as well as making use of celebrities to promote a commercial product, service, a social cause or a brand.

DEFINITION OF PUBLIC RELATIONS

The Charted Institute of Public Relations, a PR professional body of UK, defines "public relations is about reputation the result of what you do, what you say and what others say about you. Public relations practice is the discipline which looks after reputation, with the aim of earning understanding and support and influencing opinion and behaviour. It is the planned and sustained effort to establish and maintain goodwill and mutual understanding between an organization and its publics".

This definition brings out an element of reputation management as one of the tasks of public relations practice. It could be reputation of an individual or reputation of an institution. Public relations as a discipline can promote the reputation of an individual celebrity, as a person in the service of society and also the reputation of an institution by using the services of a celebrity.

THIRD PARTY ENDORSEMENT

An important feature of public relations practice is the use of third parties, that is, VIPs and celebrities who endorse or promote organization's vision, mission, products or services. Such endorsements are more influential as they are seen as independent and not part of the corporation. An example of this is when a celebrity like Amitabh Bachchan endorses a brand and is associated with its launch or promotion through personal appearances and his statement relating to its performance is the focus of the campaign, that brand's stature and credibility are enhanced.

Public relations professionals engage celebrities to act as spokespersons for an organization to project an idea, cause or a service. This celebrity endorsement is a successful method of attracting media support and attention and can add substance to a public relations activity. Celebrity endorsement is most often used as part of organization's corporate social responsibility programme. In case of public service, celebrities offer their services free without a fee to support a cause in which they have faith.

Brand Creation

In their book *The Fall of Advertising and the Rise of PR*, Al Ries and Laura Ries made it clear that creating a brand and defending a brand are the two major functions of a marketing strategy. Public relations creates the brand, while advertising defends the brand. Therefore, they say that publicity/public relations must first create awareness of a brand, and then advertising comes as a next step to maintain the brand that has been created by public relations. One of the methods of creating the brand is to use a celebrity as a means of reaching out to the target audience.

What is a Brand?

Key Concepts in Public Relations by Sandra Cain describes a brand as 'a name, term, design or symbol which identifies and differentiates products'. It embraces everything which surrounds a company's offerings from external communication to staff behaviour and attitudes and environmental and physical surroundings. A brand may be a product but it can also represent an organization which has a unique identity.

BRAND EQUITY

The concept of brand equity and branding are intertwined and they are related to both advertising and public relations. Lisa Wood (2000) indicated that there are several different meanings of brand equity. First, it may be construed as the total value of a brand as a distinct asset, when it is actually sold in the marketplace. Second, brand equity may be interpreted as a measure of the strength of consumer loyalty to a brand. Finally, it may be considered a description of the associations and beliefs that the consumer has about a particular brand. It is also regarded as brand value. Advertising and public relations professionals build on the brand equity concept with ideas such as brand identity or brand image. The role of a PR professional is that of a corporate brand manager rather than merely as a communicator.

Five Ps

Brand image is built up with the needs and desires of a target market and target consumers by utilizing the five "P's"—Product, Price, Place, Promotion and Public relations. Fifth 'P' as public relations has also been added to four "Ps" by eminent marketing Guru Philip Kotler. The combined efforts of these five factors determine the brand strength.

Before a product or service can be bought by any consumer, it has to find a place in the market with name and fame. Famous brands have greater value to their consumers than obscure brands. Just as a famous actor like Amitabh Bachchan is popular, famous brands also have greater market value and better sales and higher margin of profits. However, the quality of product or service has to be ensured if brand value has to be sustained or improved.

WHO IS A CELEBRITY?

The Oxford Dictionary Thesaurus and Wordpower Guide defines a celebrity as a famous person. The attributes of a celebrity identified by the dictionary include: prominence, eminence, stardom, popularity, distinction, reputation, a sporting celebrity, a very important person. A celebrity is one who is not only famous but also familiar enough to the people based on his/her performance or service. Celebrity's popularity can be used to promote a brand like the Tata's Nano Car or a social cause like family planning. The origin of celebrity is from the Latin word 'Celeber' (frequented), which is also the origin of the verb, 'celebrate'.

Kinds of Celebrities

Celebrities are of varied kinds who influence the people. They are from the fields of politics, films, sports, music, social service and so on.

Mention may be made of celebrities such as Pandit Jawaharlal Nehru (politics), Mother Teresa (social service), Amitabh Bachchan (films), Saina Nehwal, Sachin Tendulkar (sports), Ravi Shankar (music), and Michael Jackson, the king of pop music, was a renowned celebrity in the USA.

Impact of Celebrities

Why should advertising and PR professionals use celebrities for creating a brand value or promoting a social cause? It is because they do impact on our daily life. Memorability and easy recall are important requirements for a brand to become popular. Associating a brand with a celebrity helps here. Famous actors and actresses as the leading icons of film industry and also with their heroic roles in a variety of films create an indelible impact on the minds of audience. For example, N.T. Rama Rao, from Telugu film industry, with his roles as Gods in mythological —films was adored by moviegoers and his cine glamour and popularity helped his Telugu Desam party and he became the Chief Minister of Andhra Pradesh in 1983. Similarly, when people keep watching films and get attracted to an actor repeatedly and start adoring that actor, they become his fans.

The impact of celebrity can also be seen in TV documentaries and chat shows where social, economic and commercial issues are discussed. The Mahabharat and Ramayana serials on Doordarshan and other channels created great impact on the Indian viewers.

Attracting the attention of customers is a problem for the marketer. The celebrities who by definition have considerable popularity and get attraction of the audience, than brands *per se*, can create the necessary environment to reach the target consumers/audience. Here, celebrities are very useful for public relations.

PR and feature films

About 1000 feature films are produced in India every year. To promote the film and its star cast, every film makes use of publicity public relations process. A few films even designate PROs for publicity purpose. Mahabharat, produced by Ramanand Sagar, had Ruben as PRO. Of course, the media is an essential means for generating publicity. PROs of celebrities are regarded as bang at the top of their profession in the West.

WHAT IS CELEBRITY PR?

Celebrity public relations is defined as 'a form of specialized communication process to promote the corporate brand/product/service/ reputation through the services of a celebrity'. The celebrity becomes the brand ambassador. Celebrity public relations has emerged as a distinct area of public relations practice with celebrity as a tool.

Compared to marketing, public relations has double advantage in making use of celebrities. Public relations can promote the image of celebrity or can market the celebrity and also it can use celebrity for promoting a brand or a social cause.

Celebrities are associated with publicity/public relations from its earliest days. Grunig and Hunt (1984) described the practice of celebrity publicities as the basis for one of the models of public relations—as Press Agentry/Publicity Model. Many celebrities approach PR agencies to market themselves with the help of professional publicists.

ADVANTAGES OF CELEBRITY PR

What are the advantages of celebrity public relations? Brand personality is basically based on the quality, ethics and the corporate social responsibility of the organization. A good product cannot be made out of rotten wood. Similarly, public relations cannot promote a cause which has no value of public interest. However famous the celebrity may be, the brand's quality is more important.

The following are the ways through which a celebrity can help public relations practice:

- Celebrity's messages of endorsements or testimonials with the help of interactive technology can be sent in the form of voicemail, audio messages direct to the mobile phones of the target group
- Launching a new brand and product in the market
- Creating a brand
- Maintaining a brand
- Reinforcing the brand in the global competitive marketing environment
- Acting as a brand ambassador
- Promoting sponsorships

Celebrity public relations with all its advantages has a bright future in India. As the Indian economy is growing and the Government is implementing several socio-economic development projects, the need for communication through celebrities increases in order to make people as partners in progress.

NEGATIVE ASPECTS

Use of Celebrity endorsement can also boomerang in some cases when celebrity's popularity slides. This is true of some of sports personalities. When a sportsperson is in his/her peak days, a brand can get quick recall and value with his endorsement. The brand can also suffer when the sportsperson's performance rate and popularity takes a beating. This does not, however, happen vice versa generally.

CASE STUDY: PULSE POLIO IMMUNIZATION

The Ministry of Health and Family welfare, Government of India launched the Pulse Polio Immunization Programme in 1995 to cover all children below the age of 5 years with polio drops. About 17 crores children were administered with polio drops in some of the camps conducted on a single day. Among others, celebrity public relations was also practiced to create awareness of the polio disease. Actor Amitabh Bachchan was appointed as the Goodwill Ambassador for UNICEF polio campaign in 2005, and thus he made an outstanding contribution in creating awareness with his personal messages on different media including the TV. In February 2012, the World Health Organization declared India as a polio free country. The 70-year-old actor Amitabh Bachchan who has fronted the polio eradication programme, was honoured for his key role.

Amitabh Bachchan is also the brand ambassador for Gujarat tourism. He has been the brand ambassador of several products/brands across the industry, such as Pepsi, ICICI Bank, Reid & Taylor, Maruti Versa and Cadbury.

Leading Cricketer Sachin Tendulkar popularizes Pepsi with the slogan 'Yeh Dil Mange More'. His major endorsements cover brands such as Toshiba, ITC, Boost and Reynolds. Tendulkar has also been named the Regional Brand Ambassador by the UNICEF to promote its total sanitation campaign in India, Pakistan, Sri Lanka, Bangladesh and Nepal. It may be mentioned here that 36 per cent of the world population do not have access to clean toilets (2013). Bollywood star Amir Khan through his talk show 'Satyameva Jayathe' has created greater awareness on subjects of social concern such as 'Honour Killings' and 'Doctors Atrocities', based on which State Governments took remedial actions. The Philips Company has appointed cine actress Karina Kapoor as the brand ambassador for its new product 'Intelligent Hair Care'.

Brand New Face for Michael Jackson

When the image of Michael Jackson (MJ), the king of pop (USA), was marred due to certain alleged accusations such as child molestation, financial troubles and more importantly his strange behaviour, the media commented "Changing the tainted public opinion of MJ would be the most challenging part of public relations". However, a public relations team launched a campaign to get MJ a Brand New Face so as to restore his image as a celebrity and icon of music.

POINTS TO REMEMBER

1. Celebrity public relations emerged as a specialized area of communication to improve the image of celebrities, as well as making use of celebrities to promote a brand or a social cause.

2. Public relations practice is the discipline that looks after reputation with the aim of earning understanding and influencing public opinion.

3. As part of public relations practice, celebrities issue endorsements and testimonials about a brand of products or services.

4. According to Al Ries and Laura Ries, public relations creates a brand while advertising defends or maintains the brand.

5. Brand is described as "a name, term, design, symbol or trade mark which indentifies and differentiates products". A brand may be a product or an organization. TATA Motors Nano car is a brand.

6. Brand equity is the total value of a brand as a distinct asset which is sold in the market. It may also be interpreted as a measure of the strength of consumer loyalty to a particular brand.

7. Celebrity is defined as 'a famous person'. The attributes of a celebrity include: prominence, eminence, stardom, popularity, and distinction.

8. Celebrities are of various kinds, such as Pandit Jawaharlal Nehru (politics), Mother Teresa (social service), Amitabh Bachchan (film), Sachin Tendulkar (sports) and Ravi Shankar (music).

9. Public relations professionals use celebrities because they impact on the daily life of the people.

10. Celebrity public relations is described as a form of specialized communication process to promote corporate brand/product/ service or a social cause by using the services of celebrity like Amitabh Bachchan. It also promotes the image of celebrity as an icon in one's own field—films/sports.

11. Compared to marketing, celebrity public relations has double advantage—on one side it can promote celebrity as an icon and celebrities are used in public relations to promote a corporate brand on the other.

12. Advantages of celebrities in public relations include: launching of a new brand, maintaining a brand, celebrity acting as a brand ambassador.

13. The image of a brand which is closely associated with a celebrity who endorses it can take a beating when that celebrity's popularity goes down.

REVIEW QUESTIONS

1. 'Public relations practice is the discipline which looks after reputation'. Discuss.

2. How does third party endorsement help public relations?

3. What is a brand? Explain the role of public relations in branding or creation of a brand.

4. Define celebrity public relations. Describe the way in which a celebrity promotes a brand as part of public relations practice.

5. Briefly discuss the advantages of celebrity in the practice of public relations. Cite a case study.

Global Public Relations

C O N T E N T S

UNO

The establishment of the United Nations Organisation in 1945 as an association of States to maintain international peace and security, and cooperate in solving international problems relating to political, economic, social, cultural and humanitarian paved the way for international communication and public relations. It is in this context that the United Nations has an exclusive communication and public information division to handle international communication. However, several other factors such as globalisation, information revolution have further strengthened the concept of international public relations.

WHAT IS GLOBALISATION?

The concept of globalisation and global village had great influence in globalising the public relations. What is globalisation? Thomas L. Friedman defined globalisation as "the integration of trade, finance and information that is creating a single market and culture". Globalisation can also be described as a process by which the people of the world are unified into a single society through a combination of economic, technological, socio-cultural and political forces. Added to this, the information revolution and proliferation of mass media has converted the globe into a 'Global Village', killing space and shrinking time and distance.

World is Flat

Christopher Columbus discovered America instead of India in 1492 and reported to his King Ferdinand that the world was round. After 500 years of this historical discovery, Thomas L. Friedman visited Bangalore, India's Silicon Valley, in 1994 on his Columbus-like journey of exploration and had said that 'the world is flat and not round'. His assessment of the world being flat was based on his experience of the IT industry in Bangalore. The explosion of information technology and the consequent knowledge pools and resources have connected the world, levelling the playing field as never before, so that everyone is not only equal but also a competitor. The world is wired so that Indian software engineers can now share an idea, team their skills or compete head-on for work with their US or European counterparts. Professionals everywhere, from China to Australia to Costa Rica, can work from home as if they were in offices. The rules of the game have changed forever but does this 'death of distance' which requires us all to run faster in order to stay in the same place mean the world has got too small and too flat, too fast for us to adjust. In fact, we are in a flat global village.

Two other important forces—outsourcing and offshoring—have not only flattened the world but also created greater impact on the global economy. Outsourcing is done by arranging for somebody outside a company to do work or provide goods for that company and then reintegrate that work into the overall operation of the parent company. Offshoring by contrast is that when a company takes its business to another country that has more generous tax laws than other places. There it produces the very same product in the very same way but with cheaper labour, lower taxes, subsidised energy and lower healthcare costs. India has been a beneficiary of both outsourcing and offshoring. All these changes are due to globalisation and information revolution.

Global Media

The concept of 'Global Village' which emerged based on revolution in information technology has changed the face of communication itself. Multinational companies and global information organisations enabled free flow of information at the international sphere. As a result, there emerged a demand for New World Information and Communication Order. This has been possible because of satellite communication. The Associated Press, United Press International (US), Agence France (France), the Information Telegraph Agency of Russia (ITAR), and international broadcasting agencies such as BBC, CNN are a few media organisations to name which have facilitated global communication. The most important outcome of international communication is the UNESCO sponsored Macbride Report published as 'Many Voices: One World' (1981). The Report suggested that the imbalance in the flow of information between the developed and the developing countries must be removed.

INTERNATIONAL COMMUNICATION AGENCIES

There are a number of international communication organisations, international broadcasting corporations and the global news agencies which act as tools of public relations in promoting international understanding. The impact of these agencies in the flow of global information is quite significant. They include the following:

1. United Nations Educational Scientific and Cultural Organisation (UNESCO) Unesco House, 7, Place de Fonteny, 75352, SP07, Paris, France (Media Development).
2. International Communication Union (ITU), Place Des Nations Ch 121, Geneva-20 Switzerland (allocation of frequencies and foster creation of telecommunications in developing countries).
3. International Programme for Development Communication (responsible to UNESCO).
4. Asian Media Information and Communication Centre (AMIC), Jurong Point, PO Box 36, Singapore - 916412.
5. British Broadcasting Corporation (U.K.)
6. The Cable News Network (CNN) (U.S.)
7. The Reuter Ltd., News Agencies (U.K.)
8. The Associated Press, U.S.
9. The United Press International U.S.
10. Agence France Presse AFP (France)
11. TelegrafnoI Agentsvo Souetsk vo Soyusa (TASS)
12. Information Telegraph Agency of Russia (Itar–TASS).

INTERNATIONAL PR ORGANISATIONS

In order to promote public relations with better standards, at the global level **International Public Relations Association (IPRA)**, **International Association of Business Communicators (IABC)** came into being in 1955 and 1970, respectively. They serve as a catalyst in the development of highest possible standards of public relations ethics, practice and performance. In addition, an organisation called **Global Alliance for Public Relations and Communication Management (2000)** with headquarters in South Africa was established to promote and coordinate public relations movements in various countries. Another organisation **Global Forum for Public Relations (GFPR)** with headquarters in Hyderabad, India was established in 2006 to promote professionalism, ethics and spirituality in public relations. It has the support of Media Wing, Rajayoga Education and Research Foundation of Prajapita Brahmakumaris. All these public relations professional organisations are involved in international public relations.

IMPLICATION OF GLOBALISATION ON PR/CORPORATE COMMUNICATION

The United Nations Development Programme (UNDP) defines globalisation as "the growing interdependence of the world's people through shrinking space, shrinking time and killing the distance". Marshall McLuhan's concept of 'Global Village', information revolution, emergence of single society through a combination of economic, technological, socio-cultural and political forces, creation of single market through globalisation all have far-reaching implications for global communicators and global public relations. The major challenge today is whether a global organisation can meet a myriad of voices and cultures without losing its local identity by trying to be everything to all markets and to all publics. There are many similarities between what public relations personnel do domestically and what they would do globally, yet some differences between local and global practices can make or break the efforts of the organisation. The differences include behaviour and interpersonal communication systems.

International PR Communication

From the concept of international communication, there developed the international public relations communication with international public. It has become a reality for both small and big organisations. The concept of 'think and act globally and locally' gave much leeway to the growth of international public relations. Its contribution in globalisation is of great importance.

What about public relations' contribution internationally? Public relations has global reach and is well-advanced throughout the developed world. Organisations that operate internationally often engage public relations consultancies in individual countries in order to benefit from local cultural understanding and contacts, recognising that it is preferable to handle public relations from the centre. Global and multinational companies may have presence in sufficient depth to enable them to establish public relations functions in each of their operating territories or markets, supervised and supported from the centre, or may fund regional distributors' public relations effort on their behalf.

Interest in public relations is fast becoming universal. For example, public relations in India is about ₹10,000 crore industry and about 1 lakh personnel are involved in this profession for dissemination of public information reaching around 80 crore people. With the entry of multinationals into India, Indian public relations has become global with international standards to project global voice of national and multinational companies.

WHAT IS INTERNATIONAL PR?

What is international public relations? "International public relations may be defined as the planned and organised effort of a company, institution or government to establish mutually beneficial relations with the publics of other nations". These international publics are those who either are affected by the decisions of organisation/government or who can affect the operations of a particular firm or government (Wilcox, Len and Cameron 2005).

A country's diplomacy is also based on international public relations. Any nation as a measure to maintain good relations with its neighbours and other countries has to practice and adopt the techniques of international public relations. The planning and implementation of concerted multinational public relations strategies and tactics constitute international public relations. At the corporate level, we see public relations in action communicating corporate messages to worldwide financial markets shaping corporate images, telling 'the stories of corporation' in times of crises and playing a key role in developing new identities and positioning for companies formed in the wake of mergers, acquisitions, and takeovers. As such public relations supports corporations/governments in their endeavour to promote international understanding.

Globalisation and India

In 1991, the Government of India introduced the New Industrial Policy, which envisaged economic liberalisation, privatisation and globalisation. As a result, foreign capital and foreign companies came to India and created competitive marketing environment. The Indian industry became internationally competitive. We are now producing world class goods and services and also exporting. Outsourcing has shifted to India. Now our country is not only number one in outsourcing, but also a recognised power in software development.

Vasudhaiva Kutumbakam

For India globalisation is not a new concept. India had enunciated the principle of *Vasudhaiva Kutumbakam*—the world is one family, Marshall McLuhan's concept of global village came only in the 20th century. In fact, the concept of globalisation had taken place in India with the birth of Buddhism in the 6th century BC. If Lord Buddha is regarded as the *Light of Asia* by spreading Buddhism in the East, Swami Vivekananda is considered as the *Voice of Indian Culture and Spirituality* when he delivered his lecture at the Parliament of World Religions at Chicago in 1893. Both of them became pioneers of globalisation.

What are the implications of globalisation? The Foreign Direct Investment (FDI) as a means to support domestic investment for achieving a higher level of economic development has been fully encouraged by the Government of India. Foreign investors are now finding India an attractive investment option. Major multinational companies have already entered the field of telecommunication, transport, automobile, finance, power, insurance, business and even the media. More can be expected in this direction.

TRADE WARS

As a result, a competitive environment has emerged in India between national and foreign companies on the one hand, and between the national corporations themselves on the other hand. In fact, we are witnessing *trade wars* in the form of car war, cell-phone war, insurance war, banks war, media war, television channel war, newspaper price war and so on. When TATA launched Indica in the market all other automobile companies including foreign companies slashed the prices of their cars. The insurance sector is yet another important area where there is severe competition. As against one Life Insurance Corporation of India, we have today about 25 insurance companies doing business with a variety of policies and aggressive communication methods for attracting customers. The customer has a 'tough time' in deciding who has the best product to offer. There is a war going on in every field be it automobiles or insurance. Aggressive and competitive messages of various companies attract the customers day and night. Here is a message of Life Insurance Corporation of India.

LIC has One Policy,
To Serve the People of India Better;
Yesterday, Today, Tomorrow
"We know India Better"
If the LIC says. We know India Better,
The Air India says "We know India the Best".

The New Colgate describes its product.

"I Shade Whiter Teeth in 1 week"

While the New Pepsodent advertises about it product

"4 Hours after Brushing, 130 per cent
Germ ATTAACK Power.
Brush Twice Daily"

GLOBAL COMPETITION: CHALLENGES FOR CORPORATIONS

The tables have turned in this competitive marketing environment. Change or be damned has become the order of the day. The fittest and fastest to change alone will survive in this competitive marketing. What are the challenges that the Indian industry is confronting to meet global competition?

- Reduction of cost of production and distribution
- High productivity with greater efficiency
- Quality of products and service of international standards
- Customer care and customer satisfaction
- Employees commitment to economic reforms
- Global perspective—faster and better adaptation of new technology
- Effective financial, human resource, marketing communication management to meet the competitive environment
- Effective public relations/corporate communications management

Three-Pronged Strategy

A big question arises as to who manages these challenges to achieve the national goals. The answer lies in a three-pronged strategy.

1. It is the corporate plan and performance of the organisation that manages these challenges
2. It is the mindset of the workforce of a corporation, stakeholders and the corporate culture of the organisation that manages these challenges
3. It is the public relations communication as a strategic management function and also as a catalyst of change that manages the challenges

ERA OF GLOBAL PR

If the Indian industry is facing several challenges, globalisation and information revolution have had far-reaching implications on public relations discipline/corporate communications. What are they?

Globalisation has facilitated many challenges as well as opportunities for public relations in reaching out to global markets and global stakeholders. If the challenge is professionalism of international standards, the opportunity has been that it has facilitated the process of globalisation by spreading values and promoting culture through public relations techniques and various media of communication.

However, globalisation affects public relations practice in the following areas:

- Offers opportunities for the amalgamation of ideas, products and services for different countries

- Increases opportunities and challenges for change in the profession towards greater professionalism
- More organisations, multinationals have international workforces and markets
- Public relations becomes part of global power such as UNO, International Communication agencies, National Governments, international PR associations like Global Alliance for PR and Communication Management
- The last but most important for public relations is that anti-globalisation requires the support of public relations discipline

Male Airport in Maldives: A Case Study

An Indian multinational company GMR under an agreement with Government of Maldives spent about $230 million on the construction of Male International Airport and that it was operating and maintaining the airport. GMR had signed a legally valid and binding contract. Unfortunately, another Government with different political dispensation came to power in Maldives. The new government cancelled the earlier agreement with GMR and took over the running and maintaining of the airport in December 2012. Even the appropriate court upheld the decision of the Maldives Government. Of course, the Maldives Government will pay the compensation.

It is a lesson worth pondering both by Indian corporates and Indian public relations in the context of globalisation. While investing in foreign countries, the Indian companies must also pay close attention to factors like the political dispensation and political stability. As part of its fact-finding stage, public relations must make an assessment of political environment and bring it to the notice of the company.

Communication Needs

- The need for communication increased to meet the competitive market economy and also the need for more public relations professionals.
- Global scope for public relations programmes increased and an upswing in public relations activity.
- Public relations agencies emerged. Indian agencies tie up with foreign public relations agencies is also on the rise.
- Advertising agencies opened public relations branches and also tied-up with foreign advertising agencies.
- Convergence of public relations, advertising and marketing communications.
- Media convergence as multimedia in computer. Public relations has become a 24 hour job.

- Number of in-house communication departments increased.
- Emergence of e-public relations, e-marketing.
- Privatisation and disinvestment, public issues increased the need for financial public relations.
- Globalisation, global markets, "Think and act globally and locally" concept emerged.
- Information revolution and proliferation of media, demassification of media and audience, distance killed, mass audiences reduced, segmented audience, segmented communication increased.
- Good governance, transparency, freedom of information, enactment of Right to Information Act.
- Learning public relations practice and partnering of public relations in other countries for global view.
- Global brands—global reputation.

INTEGRATED PR COMMUNICATIONS

As a result of globalisation and proliferation of media, public relations has been liberalised from the local or national public relations to global or international public relations. The importance of communication has grown manifold in the age of competitive marketing environment. In order to project their products and services, all companies both Indian and foreign have intensified public communication programmes to attract customers and educate the workforce. *Think and act globally and locally* has been the order of the day. This is not only a challenge for public relations, but also great opportunity to prove its worthiness. A paradigm shift is needed in public relations towards professional excellence with specialisation in international public relations.

Tata Communication Pvt. Ltd

Under the policy of privatization of the Govt. of India, the Tata Group of Companies has acquired the Videsh Sanchar Nigam Limited (VSNL), a public sector undertaking. The Tata Group has renamed Videsh Sanchar Nigam as Tata Communication Pvt. Ltd. Its corporate communications department is now known as Tata Communication's Global Public Relations, with its headquarter in Singapore, which handles companies' public relations in about 35 countries. The 'Rediffusion', a global PR firm, acts as PR Consultant to the Tata communication.

POINTS TO REMEMBER

1. Establishment of the United Nations Organisation in 1945, the concept of global village based on information technology, globalisation, proliferation of media on the one hand and the emergence of global information and communication agencies such

as BBC, CNN, Reuters, the computer and Internet technology on the other hand not only enabled the free flow of information across the world, but also paved the way for global communication.

2. From global communication agencies and global communication, there emerged international public relations to reach global community with corporate and government information towards international understanding.

3. International public relations may be defined as the planned and organised effort of a corporation or government to establish mutually beneficial relations with the publics of other nations. "Think and Act Globally and Locally" is the basic principle of international public relations.

4. Due to competitive marketing environment and global marketing, the Indian industry is confronting certain challenges which include: reduction of cost of production and distribution, high productivity, quality of products and services of international standards, employees' commitment to change management better adaptation of new technology, effective public relations/corporate communications strategy.

5. Global competitive marketing environment has had far reaching implications on Indian public relations. They include: the need for corporate communications has increased manifold to meet the competitive marketing; global scope for public relations has increased, new PR firms emerged and a number of multinational PR agencies have tied up with Indian PR agencies. PR has now become 24-hour business, the number of in-house PR departments has multiplied.

6. Public relations has to adopt an integrated communication approach to support all management functions, such as HRD, finance, production besides promoting corporate reputation. Such a new strategy with international standards will meet the global challenges for public relations.

REVIEW QUESTIONS

1. What are the factors that created the concept of global communication?

2. What is international public relations? Describe its role in building international relations with the public of other nations.

3. Enumerate the international information and communication organisations that support global public relations.

4. Define globalisation. Identify its implications on corporate India.

5. What should be the public relations/corporate communications strategy to meet global challenges?

Media Strategy and Tactics

✓ Public Relations and the Media
✓ Interpersonal Media
✓ Traditional Folk Media
✓ Newspapers in Public Relations
✓ Electronic Media—Radio and Television
✓ E-PR: IT New Mass Media
✓ Audio-Visual Media; Films
✓ Visual Media—Photographs and Exhibitions
✓ Event Management; Open House
✓ Multimedia PR Campaigns
✓ Media Relations

PART FOUR

MEDIUM

Public Relations and the Media

Chapter 21

> *Medium is the message.*   —**Marshall Mcluhan**

C O N T E N T S

- Medium Defined
- Medium is the Message
- Classification of Media
- Media Networking
- Functions of Media
- Media and PR
- Media Scene in India

MEDIUM DEFINED

What is a medium? *Reader's Digest Great Dictionary of English Language* defines medium as a "means by which something is expressed, communicated or achieved". The *Dictionary of Communication and Media Studies* defines a medium as "the physical or technical means of converting a communication message into a signal capable of being transmitted along a given channel." Television, for example, is a medium which employs the channels of vision and sound.

A communication channel for reaching the public with a particular message can be described as a medium. Moreover, any communication vehicle which transmits programme or messages to people is also a medium. Media is the established vehicle for providing the public with information or entertainment, especially one which sells the opportunity to advertise or promote a cause or service.

Media include: the means, instruments, avenues, vehicles, channels, forms of communication through which messages (news, entertainment, information, advertisement, etc.) are transmitted. The media serve as the vital 'link' between the communicator and the audience. An advertiser of a product and its potential consumers—a public relations professional and the organisational public or a political party and its followers are the examples to quote. The plural of medium is media. Mass media are designed to reach out a mass or very large audiences through the instruments of mass media such as radio, TV and newspapers.

MEDIUM IS THE MESSAGE

Marshal McLuhan (1911–1980), a Canadian Professor of University of Toronto and communication theorist, in his book *Understanding the Media—The Extensions of Man* had said, "The medium is the message". But the question arises how can medium in the form of an instrument be the message? Many people would be disposed to say that it was not the machine but what one did with the machine that was the meaning or message. To justify his theory, McLuhan gave an instance of the electric light. Electric light is pure information. It is a medium without a message unless it is used to show an advertisement or person's name in the dark. Whether the light is used for brain surgery or for night baseball, is a matter of indifference. It could be argued that these activities are in some way the 'content' of the electric light, since they could not exist without electric light. This fact merely underlines the point that the medium is the message because it is the medium that shapes and controls the scale and form of human association and action. The message of the electric light used is like the message of electric power in industry, totally radical, pervasive and decentralised. McLuhan suggested that the content of any medium was always another medium, the content of the press is literary statement, and the content of the movie is the story.

Extensions of Human Faculty

In his book *Understanding the Media—The Extensions of Man*, McLuhan further describes that "what is said is deeply conditioned by the medium through which it is said". The particular attributes of any medium help to determine the meaning of the communication and no medium is neutral. He believed that all media are extensions of some human faculty, psychic or physical. They are extensions of one or more five senses. For example, face-to-face communication covers all the five senses, *seeing, hearing, touching, smelling, tasting*. However, the print media extends only the eye, while radio the ear. Television is an extension of both the eye and the ear. Music, for example, is both the medium and the message.

CLASSIFICATION OF MEDIA

Media is classified in several ways on different parameters. John Fiske in *Introduction to Communication Studies* (UK 1982) divides media into three categories:

1. **The presentation media:** The voice, face-to-face communication, body language, the spoken word, where the communication

of the person actually is a medium. The presentational media are direct acts of communication.

2. **The representational media:** Communication methods, such as books, paintings, photographs, that use cultural and aesthetic conventions to create a text of some sort; they become independent of the communicator and are called representational media. The reader who reads the book or views a painting or photograph gets the message without the presence of a communicator as in the case of presentational media. Here, the book or photograph not only represents the communicator, but also communicates the message directly to the receiver.

3. **The mechanical media:** The media which act as technical vehicles or devices of transmitting messages are called mechanical media. Telephone, radio, television, film are examples of mechanical media. The advantage of mechanical media is that they can transmit messages of both presentation and representational media.

Sensory Media

The ultimate aim of public relations is to persuade and influence the mind of the people towards organisational goals, products, services. Therefore, the media are also classified on the basis of their appeal to the human sensory organs. They are put into three categories as:

1. The media which appeal *to the eye* are called **visual media** (sense of seeing).
2. The media which appeal *to the ear* are called **audio media** (sense of hearing).
3. The media which appeal *to both the eye and the ear* are called audio-visual media (sense of both seeing and hearing).

Visual media

Media which are attracted by the sense of sight and the messages that influence the mind through the eyes are called visual media. Newspapers, magazines, photographs, cartoons, pictures, books, etc. represent the visual media. Vision is the key instigator of thought in all these media.

Audio media

The media that influence the human mind and behaviour through the sense of hearing and ear are described as audio media. The deaf will have no effect of this media. Radio, spoken word, are called audio media as they persuade the audience through the sense of hearing and the ear.

Audio-visual media

The media that appeal to the sense of hearing and seeing belong to the category of audio-visual media. Television, cinema, dance, drama are examples of audio-visual media.

Another classification of media is based on the types of media that we use in communicating message. Media-wise classification is as follows:

Intrapersonal media

Communication that takes place within the self (with in the brain) is called intrapersonal media. It is convergence of both inner and outer stimuli. Lord Buddha attained enlightenment through meditation and intrapersonal communication. It is also called self-discovery and self-insight. Interpersonal communication is a prerequisite to all other types of communications.

Interpersonal media

Any mode of communication, verbal or non-verbal, between two individuals is called interpersonal media. Two persons in this process take the role of both the speaker and listener. These media include: face-to-face interaction, meetings; conferences; interviews; telephone; press conference; annual general meeting; etc.

Traditional folk art media

Traditional medium is defined as an art form through which message is communicated in the shape of spoken word, song, dance or drama. Theatre, music, and dance are the three age-old art forms which have been part of human culture and heritage. Traditional media such as drama, ballads, puppetry, folk dances are found everywhere in India. *Harikatha*, storytelling (Andhra Pradesh), *Villupattu* (Tamil Nadu), *Tamasha* (Maharashtra), *Yekshaganam* (Karnataka), *Jaatra* (West Bengal), *Garba* (Gujarat) are a few traditional forms to mention that are being used to communicate messages on political, economic and social themes.

Mass media

Various forms, means, avenues of communication through which an identical message is transmitted to a large number of people at different places at a time are called mass media. It is the mass medium that transmits the message. Newspapers, radio, television, film, photographs and videos are described as mass media. With the emergence of the computer, the mass media became the old media and the new media emerged in the form of e-mail, Internet.

IT new mass media

The computer brought information revolution with instant communication. The world-wide web emerged as the eighth wonder of the world which facilitated newspapers to deliver their colourful editions electronically to people on computer screens. The web is more flexible than other media. Users can navigate paths among millions of onscreen messages. The Internet is the wired infrastructure on which the web messages move. Today, the Internet is a user system tying institutions of different sorts together into an information highway. The modern information communication technology has created new media in the form of world wide web, Internet, e-mail, video conference, blogs, twitter, facebook, facsimile transmission, video news release, CD, etc. They are now known as new mass media and social media.

Other media

There are other media also that help in transmitting the target-oriented messages. They include: exhibitions, outdoor media (hoardings, bus panels), open house, bulletin boards, and public address system.

MEDIA NETWORKING

What is networking? Networking is the process of developing mutually beneficial and supportive relationships with like-minded individuals. Such relationships and social contacts are helpful in the practice of corporate public relations.

What is then media networking? Media networking is the linkage of a group of radio or TV stations that broadcast the same programme.

Public relations without media is like winking at a young pretty girl in the dark. All communication activities, both with internal and external publics of an organisation, are through the media network. Media in public relations practice are of two types. One is mass media, which consists of complex networks of news gathering and dissemination, as well as entertainment programming and editorial commentary. Daily newspapers, news magazines, television and radio are the conventional venues through which views, commentary and entertainment reach the audiences. If the mass media owned by other people is one type of media, the second type of media used by public relations practitioners is 'their own media', a media produced, controlled and distributed by themselves. They are their house journals, annual reports, pamphlets which act as tools of public relations to disseminate information. In this sense, media are print and electronic media networks that can be used to reach mass audiences. Media networks provide the public relations practitioner with a unique opportunity. Narrowcasting allows for a fairly high-level customisation and refinement of the message.

Public relations practitioners must be aware of media networking for making use of such networking in the practice of corporate public relations.

The term networking is used in broadcasting to describe the pattern of connection of broadcasting stations. For example, the Prasar Bharati (Broadcasting Corporation of India) is a public service broadcaster with All India Radio and Doordarshan as its two constituents. If All India Radio has a network of over 250 radio stations, the Doordarshan operates 35 satellite channels and has a vast network of 66 studio centres and 1415 transmitters. Such networking allows simultaneous broadcast of the same programme. To network programme means to broadcast it to the widest number of TV/Radio stations but within one network and in their network. The Republic Day message of the President of India is broadcast by all the channels of Doordarshan and all the stations of All India Radio simultaneously across the country. That is the good example of network programme.

FUNCTIONS OF MEDIA

Each medium has its own importance and utility in disseminating information. It will be futile to separate the media into watertight compartments. They are closely interrelated in their functions. All the media, verbal, print, electronic and photographic technologies have certain following basic functions:

1. **Information source:** Dissemination of news, messages.
2. **Interpretation forum:** Giving opinion on news, views, editorial comments, views articles.
3. **Education and persuasion forum:** Educating the people by giving due guidance and agenda setting.
4. **Entertainment source:** Short stories, comic strips, music, dance and drama.
5. **Economic, political and social source:** The media serves the economic, political and social systems.

In other words, media inform, interpret, educate and entertain the people. With the above-mentioned inherent functions, the media can play a vital role in transforming the society for the better. Media and society are intertwined. Each medium provides opportunities for public relations to reach the organisational publics. Media has a greater role to play in a country like ours, which is both democratic and developing, to inform, educate, motivate, and entertain people as active partners in the process of democracy and development.

MEDIA AND PR

Media is the lifeblood of public relations. In fact, media comes first in the scheme of public relations programme because a message cannot reach the target audience without it. The idea here is that no matter how well planned or creative a public relations programme/campaign is, it will fail if no one in the audience sees it, hears about it, reads about it, speaks about it, writes about it, experiences it. It is in this backdrop and to assure audience reach and to influence them, the first order of any organisation is to cultivate appropriate media relations, to inform, educate and motivate them towards one's goals.

Corporate public relations and media relations are intertwined. While media is hungry for information, public relations is the source of information. Any communication gap between the organisation and its publics can be filled with the information provided by the media. It can help in every area of corporate public relations, such as employees relations, shareholders relations, customers relations, community relations and also in crisis situations.

Unlike advertising media, the public relations media are as varied as its segmented internal and external public. It is so because that a public relations message has to cover all types of stakeholders who have interest in the organisation. Therefore, every available media from interpersonal media to Internet is used in the practice of public relations.

As media gets priority in the public relations plan, every public relations practitioner must know about the various types of media used in the practice of public relations. Understanding the media is the primary task of PR professionals.

MEDIA SCENE IN INDIA

The media from interpersonal media, old mass media to IT new mass media have great potentialities in creating awareness about corporate mission, products and services of any organisation. According to one estimate, the mass media—newspapers, radio, television and film reach about two thirds of India's total adult population. However, there is a gap between media reach and the people's access to media. Poverty, illiteracy are the main reasons for this communication gap which could be filled through traditional media. In fact, press which enabled to reach mass audience has graduated into mass media with the advent of radio and television. In the second stage, media turned into multimedia domain with the invention of computer and Internet. Public relations also in tune with the changing media scene has adopted multimedia approach for educating a variety of stakeholders.

A brief description of both mass media and IT new media is discussed hereunder.

Newspapers

Indian press is 234 years old (2014). James Augustus Hicky on 29, January 1780, started the first newspaper, a weekly *Bengal Gazette* or the Calcutta General Advertiser. He is, therefore, regarded as the father of the Indian Press. Raja Rammohan Roy (1772–1833) who started Sambad Kaumudi, the Bengali Weekly in 1821 as part of his social reforms and to create public opinion against the 'Sati' the burning of a wife along with dead husband is regarded as the Father of Indian Language Journalism.

When India became independent in 1947, there were 3000 newspapers and periodicals of which 300 were dailies. Over the years, the number of newspapers has considerably increased because of increase in literacy and development of the economy. According to the Annual Report for the year 2011 of the Registrar of Newspapers for India, the total number of registered newspapers/periodicals was 82,222. There were 10,205 dailies, 394 triweeklies and biweeklies, 27,321 weeklies, 10,422 fortnightly, 25,072 monthlies and 5208 quarterlies. Newspapers are published in English and 21 principal languages listed in the Eighth Schedule of the Constitution. Newspapers/periodicals were also published in 127 languages including dialects and a few foreign languages.

Circulation

The total circulation of newspapers was 33 crore copies per publishing day in 2011. The largest number of newspapers and periodicals registered in any Indian language is in Hindi (29,094). The second largest number of newspapers and periodicals registered in any language is in English (10,530).

Top Ten Daily Newspapers

Rank	Publication	Language	Circulation
1	The Times of India	English	3,314,493
2	Dainik Jagaran	Hindi	2,674,304
3	Malayala Manorama	Malayalam	2,129,934
4	Hindustan	Hindi	1,843,608
5	Eenadu	Telugu	1,737,086
6	Dainik Bhaskar	Hindi	1,674,790
7	Amar Ujala	Hindi	1,643,828
8	Daily Thanthi	Tamil	1,614,471
9	Rajasthan Patrika	Hindi	1,590,409
10	The Hindu	English	1,558,379

Top Five Weekly Newspapers

1	The Sunday Times of India	English	1,071,963
2	Ravivasriya Hindustan	Hindi	1,006,912
3	Ravivar Loksatta	Marathi	363,006
4	Karmasasgsthaan	Bengali	333,447
5	Mathrubhumi–Thozhilvartha	Malayalam	333,022

Source: ABC 2012

Radio

All India Radio is 87 years old (1927–2014). The beginnings of radio go back to 1923 when some enthusiastic amateurs tried hand at setting up low power transmitters in Bombay. However, the first radio station floated by the Indian Broadcasting Company (IBC) was inaugurated in Bombay by the then Viceroy Lord Irvin on 23 July 1927. This marked the beginning of organised and regular broadcasting in India. After liquidation of private Broadcasting Company in India, the radio came under the control of Government from 1 April, 1930 with the formation of the Indian State Broadcasting Service (ISBS). The ISBS was given the present name of All India Radio on 8 June 1936 and the name 'Akashvani' from 1957. Prasar Bharati (Broadcasting Corporation of India), the autonomous body for All India Radio and Doordarshan, came into existence on 23 November, 1997.

At the time of independence, AIR had nine radio stations of which three went to Pakistan. As such independent India began its radio service only with 6 radio stations and 18 transmitters which covered 11 per cent population and 2.5 per cent area of the country. The network in 2012 comprises 277 radio stations and 381 transmitters which provide coverage to 99.16 per cent of the population and reaches 91.82 per cent area of the country. All India Radio broadcasts over 647 news bulletins daily in 90 languages (Indian, foreign and dialects).

FM Radio (Frequency Modulation Broadcast)

The Supreme Court pronounced in 1995 that "the airwaves are public property" and that they cannot be the monopoly of government or private business. As a result, the government decided to privatise the airwaves. The monopoly of All India Radio ended in 1999 when the radio waves were opened up to private commercial FM Radio through auctions.

Major media organisations such as the Times of India (Radio Mirchi), The Hindustan Times (Radio Fever), Anand Bazar Patrika (Friends FM), Jagran Prakashan (Radio Mantra), Malayala Manorama (Manorama Radio) gained from the auctions and started operating FM Radio stations in different cities. However, Radio City and AIR's FM stations (Rainbow FM and FI [Gold) have been the main operators in the country. FM Gold Channel of AIR which was on air in September 2001 at Delhi earned as a niche infotainment channel with 30 per cent news and current affairs component and 70 per cent of entertainment programme.

The FM Gold channel is available in four metros i.e., Delhi, Mumbai, Kolkata, and Chennai. Radio industry has shown notable growth with the emergence of FM radio.

Vividh Bharati

The popular Vividh Bharati service provides entertainment for 15 hours a day from 37 CBS–VB centres and four Short wave transmitters in Mumbai, Delhi, Chennai and Guwahati on a synchronised metre which can be heard on the same wavelengths in any part of the country. Regional stations like Hyderabad originate a few programmes at some special timings in their respective languages.

Television

Television in India is 55 years old (2014). It began as a modest experiment as late as 15 September 1959, with one station in New Delhi radiating 25 miles, transmitting an hour's programme two evenings a week. The regular service with a news bulletin became operational in 1965. '*Krishi Darshan*', as a measure to educate the farming community, was launched on 26 January 1967. The national television called '*Doordarshan*' conducted a unique year-long project, the first venture of its kind in the developing world, to inform, educate and motivate the rural community. The project called Satellite Instructional Television Experiment (SITE) from 1975 had beamed special educational broadcasts and farming programmes to clusters of 2400 villages in six states: Andhra Pradesh, Bihar, Karnataka, Madhya Pradesh, Orissa and Rajasthan. A major landmark was the introduction of colour television in 1982 coinciding with the 9th Asian Games held in New Delhi that ushered a major revolution in broadcasting in the country. *Doordarshan,* earlier a part of All India Radio, was separated and made into a distinct department in April 1976. *Doordarshan* is now part of *Prasar Bharati*, the autonomous Broadcasting Corporation of India.

Doordarshan operates 31 channels, besides free-to-air DTH service—4 national channels; 11 regional satellite channels; 8 state networks; 2 Rajya Sabha/Lok Sabha channels; 1 international channel. *Doordarshan's* DD–1 is the largest terrestrial network in the world. It covers 90 per cent population in the country.

Free-to-air DTH Service

Doordarshan is providing free-to-air DTH service (Kuband), 'DD Direct+' in the country. This was started primarily for providing TV coverage to the areas uncovered by terrestrial transmission. Presently, there are 56 TV channels on DTH platform. DTH signals can be received anywhere in the country (except Andaman and Nicobar islands) with the help of a small sized dish. For Andaman & Nicobar islands, DTH service in C-band with a bouquet of channels is in operation.

There are more than 800 private TV channels in India, including transnational channels. The transnational channels entered the field in a significant measure in 1991 when CNN gave us the live coverage of the Gulf War (Iraq).

Major Television Services

The major television networks in India, among others, include 'NDTV, ZEE TV, STAR TV, SUN TV, JAYA TV, SONY TV, Eanadu (ETV), TV Today, Times Now, CNN–IBN, etc. TV network is very wide in India with a variety of services such as news, cinema, business, music, sports, etc. As per the TAM Annual universe update-2010, India has over 134 million households (out of 223 million) with television sets, of which over 103 million have access to cable TV or satellite TV, including 20 million householders which and DTH subscribers.

Information Technology, Communication and Internet

Awareness of information technology is highly essential for every PR professional to make use of the media such as internet, mobile phones, post offices to disseminate corporate information to the stakeholders. The subject of the 'Internet' and its uses has been covered in detail in Chapter 26. However, certain other media such as postal network, telecommunications and mobile phones are discussed here.

Postal Network

The postal network in India, which is the largest communication network in the world, acts as an important tool of public relations to reach out especially rural India. The postal system established by Lord Clive in the year 1766 was further developed by Warren Hastings by establishing the Calcutta GPO in the year 1774. As such postal network in India is 240-year-old (2014).

At the time of independence there were 23,344 post offices throughout the country. India has the largest postal network in the world with 154,979 post offices (March 2011), of which 139,182 (89.81%) are in rural areas and 15, 979 (10.19%) are in urban areas.

Postal Services for PR

The Department of Posts offers certain services which are very useful to public relations profession:

(i) *Media post:* It is a unique publicity/advertising medium to help the corporate and government organisations reach the target audiences through media post. Under this service public relations practitioners can use:

- Advertisements and publicity slogans on postcards, inland letters cards, Aerogram and other postal stationery.
- Space sponsorship options on letter boxes throughout country which are spread in different streets and locations.

(ii) *Business post:* It was launched in 1997 to meet the specific needs of bulk customers for pre-mailing activities. It provides value addition to all traditional services offered by the post office in the form of collection insertion, addressing, sealing, franking, etc.

(iii) *National address database management:* The Department has the National Address Database System under which the update address database of public/customers online help the customers in locating addresses with pin code. The application shall be hosted on India Post Website which will provide address and pin code search option to the public.

Telephones

Telephone is yet another tool of public relations, which facilitates direct communication between the sender and the receiver. The liberalisation of the Government enabled the private sector to enter the telephone industry which was the monopoly of the government. In March 2011, there were 282.29 million phones in rural areas. The number of mobiles, which is an effective medium for public relations, in India account for about 95 crores. There are 14 crore internet connections in India.

Cinema

Indian feature film is now 100 years old (2013). The first Indian feature film Raja Harishchandra was released for public exhibition on 3 May 1913 in Bombay. It was produced by Dada Saheb Phalke who has been rightly acclaimed as the Father of Indian Cinema.

India produces the largest number of feature films (1274 in 2010) every year in the world. The Films Division (established in 1948) of Ministry of Information and Broadcasting, Government of India also produces documentaries, short films animation films, and news magazines, which are shown in regular cinema theatres along with feature films. As many as 8500 cinema houses in the country screen both feature and short films. It is estimated that about 10 crore people view these films every week. The NRS indicates that cinema viewership is declining in India. However, the emergence of multiplexes is increasing the viewership.

Multiplexes with several screens in one premises offer a different experience to cine-goers for in most cases they are part of a shopping malls and restaurants complex. Major multiplex chains include: PVR Cinemas Ltd, Inox Leisure Ltd., Sathyam Cinemas, Cinemax India Ltd., etc. Cinema provides ample opportunity for public relations to educate and entertain stakeholders towards organisation's goals, products and services. Public relations professionals can organise film shows for both theatrical and not theatrical audiences. The Films Division organised special screening of 39 films on music and musical geniuses titled "Moments with the Maestros" in collaboration with Directorate of Film Festival and Entertainment Society of Goa in November 2009 at Black Box Kala Academy, Panaji, Goa during International Festival of India.

Each medium has its special attributes and imposes its own constraints. Newspapers have to be read, radio has to be heard and television has to be seen and heard.

POINTS TO REMEMBER

1. Medium is a means by which something is expressed or communicated. A medium is the physical or technical means of converting a communication message into a signal capable of being transmitted along with a given channel. Television, for example, is a medium which employs the channels of vision and sound.

2. "Medium is the Message" said Marshal McLuhan. To justify his theory, McLuhan gave an instance of electric light. The electric light is pure information. Whether light is being used for brain surgery or night baseball, the content of the electric light matters. The message of the electric light is used like the message of electric power in industry. Similarly, music is both a medium and a message.

3. Medium is classified in several ways than one. John Fiske classified media as presentation media (the voice or body language), the representational media (books, photographs, paintings) and the mechanical media (telephone, radio, television).

4. Media is also classified on the basis of their appeal to the human sensory organs. They are put into three categories as: (i) visual media (newspaper); (ii) audio media (radio); and (iii) audio-visual media (television).

5. Another classification of media is as follows:
    (i) Intrapersonal media (talking to oneself),
    (ii) Interpersonal media (telephone),
    (iii) Traditional folk media (street plays),
    (iv) Mass media (radio, television),
    (v) New mass media (computer, Internet, website).

6. Media networking is the linkage of a group of radio or TV stations that broadcast the same programme. All India Radio has a network of over 277 radio stations which broadcast network programme.

7. Functions of media are fourfold: to inform, to interpret, to educate and to entertain people.

8. Media is the lifeblood of public relations practice. Media comes first in the scheme of public relations plan because messages cannot reach the target audience without media. Public relations and media are intertwined to build up good relations between an organisation and its internal and external publics.

9. Media can help in every area of corporate public relations, such as employees relations, customers relations, shareholders relations, community relations and media relations.

10. Media scene in India includes: 82,222 newspapers with a circulation of 33 crore copies, 277 radio stations, 31 Doordarshan television channels, 800 private television channels, 12 crore Internet users, 90 crore mobile phones and 8500 cinema houses.

11. Postal network in India has about 1.55 lakh post offices, of which 1.39 lakh post offices are in rural India. PR can use postcards, inland letter cards and aerograms for publicity purpose.

REVIEW QUESTIONS

1. Define a medium. Explain the basis on which media is classified.

2. Medium is the Message. Discuss.

3. Give an example of your own to demonstrate each of the following types of communication media:
   (a) Intrapersonal communication
   (b) Interpersonal communication
   (c) Mass communication

4. What are the key functions of mass media? How do they help the society?

5. Media is the lifeblood of public relations practice. Describe the linkage between the media and public relations in disseminating public information.

6. What are the various types of media used in public relations practice? Explain the relative advantages, limitations and impact of media. Such as newspapers and TV.

7. Give an estimate of mass media scene in India.

8. Distinguish Multiplexes from normal cinema houses.

Interpersonal Media

I will pay more for the ability to deal with the people than any other ability under the sun.

—Rockefeller

CONTENTS

TYPES OF COMMUNICATION

Public relations as a communication process makes use of different forms of communications which may be intrapersonal, interpersonal, group and mass communications. Each type depends on the kind of message and the audience to be reached. Earlier public relations turned to mass communication for its operations. It was because, most of public relations professionals in the beginning came from journalism field and were trained in mass communication. As the profession developed, public relations professionals realised the importance of interpersonal communication and using it in various areas of corporate public relations to motivate employees, customers, etc. Each type of communication offers its own media for use.

Intrapersonal Communication

Communication that takes place within the individual mind is called **intrapersonal communication**. What goes on inside our minds is controlled and conditioned by our self-view that emerges from a vast complex of past and present influences. It is a convergence of both inner and outer stimuli. Through intrapersonal communication (self-view), we can create bridges or battlements; we can make connections or sever them; we can open ourselves up or establish self-defence. In fact, intrapersonal communication is a prerequisite to interpersonal and also mass communication.

Interpersonal Communication

Interpersonal communication may be defined as "a relationship in which two persons alternating in the roles of speaker or listener; engage in face to face interaction; because of their shared desire for social facilitation or fulfilment of a need or because they feel to exchange ideas or information about a topic of mutual interest". It may also be described as the means by which a person may reach a more satisfying relationship with other human beings. Interpersonal communication is a mode of communication—verbal or non-verbal between two individuals or more people. It is also called oral or verbal communication which is considered to be the most earliest common medium of communication. Interpersonal media of communication are superior even to the written media; because they normally are 'quick' and 'better understanding', and also save time. A good example of interpersonal media is telephone.

Characteristics

What is the basic characteristic of interpersonal communication ? It is an audio medium which appeals to the sensory organ of the ear. The most common form of communication is verbal communication and is based on face-to-face conversations. According to one survey most of the time in daily life, as much as 75 per cent is taken in talking and listening (30 per cent talking and 45 per cent listening). Writing takes 9 per cent and reading 16 per cent.

It is evident that we spend a major portion of time in talking and listening as part of interpersonal communication. Each person assumes the dual role of both sender and receiver of messages. A distinct advantage of face-to-face communication is the fact that feedback is immediate. The sender of the message can ascertain the reactions of the receiver of the message, if not in words but through the body language of how he is reacting to the message. Facial expression, gesture, and stance will communicate the receiver's feelings. The disadvantage in face-to-face communication is that messages intended for long distances cannot be communicated to a large section of the society. The instrument used in interpersonal communication is voice in the form of speech and talk to convey a message. While conveying oral messages various methods such as face-to-face meeting, conference, seminar, talks, etc. are used.

All these media are used not only to transform ideas from one person to another, but also is aimed at bringing about change in the behaviour/attitudes of persons and establish goodwill.

Uses of verbal media

As mass media has limited reach in India, the verbal media play an important role in educating the people particularly in rural areas. But many forms of mass media such as newspapers, radio, and television are not accessible to many people in villages. As such messages on development reach only that particular class of people who have access to newspapers or television. And they became opinion leaders. Such opinion leaders, under the two-step flow of communication interact with other people who are not exposed to mass media. Here interpersonal communication or verbal media play a significant role in carrying development messages from opinion leaders to others. A good example of such communication is creating awareness on increased agricultural production through green revolution. In the first instance the mass media educated rich farmers and, in turn, rich farmers through interpersonal communication educated other small farmers who were not exposed to mass media. It is in this context interpersonal media can play a major role in socio-economic development of our country.

White Revolution (milk production), Pulse Polio Immunisation Programme, health education, etc. were successful in our country because of contribution of both mass media and interpersonal media. Interpersonal media are most effective in employee communication, customer relations, rural development.

Directorate of field publicity

The Directorate of Field Publicity, Ministry of Information and Broadcasting, Government of India with its headquarters in New Delhi is the largest rural-oriented interpersonal communication medium in the country established to inform, educate, entertain and motivate people in the nation building activities.

As a two-way channel for dissemination of public information among masses and gathering feedback for the Government, the Field Publicity units in districts use a variety of interpersonal media including public meetings, group discussions, seminars, symposia to convey messages. Films and live song and drama performances are also utilised to communicate messages. About 80,000 oral communications were organised in the year 2012 to explain the schemes, such as national rural health mission, pulse polio immunisation, AIDS awareness, family welfare, public distribution system, national development programme.

Group Communication

Group communication is an interaction process that occurs among a group of people in an attempt to achieve commonly recognised goals either face-to-face or through mediated forms. This is sometimes included in the interpersonal level. The most obvious difference is the number of persons involved. Decisions made in a group will be very effective for implementation.

Mass Communication

If interpersonal communication is a mode of communication between two individuals, there exists another form of communication which reaches mass audience. Any mechanical device that multiplies messages and takes it to a large number of people simultaneously is called mass communication. The media through which such kind of communication takes place is called mass media, such as newspapers, radio, television, films. Mass communication can be defined as the process of using a mass medium to send messages to large audiences for the purpose of informing, entertaining or persuading. In mass communication, we find 'five Ms'—mass communicators, mass messages, mass media, mass communication and mass audience.

If interpersonal communication is between two individuals, mass communication involves one to many—mass audience. The technology of the mass media gives the mass communicator a 'mega phone' which is not available to other communicators. In interpersonal communication, for example, the sender aims a message at one other person or a few people. A journalist in contrast has the printing press or radio to reach lakhs of people. The printing press is a mega phone. Broadcasters have their transmission equipment which enable the mass communicators to amplify messages in ways that are not possible with interpersonal or even group communication. In interpersonal communication, feedback is immediate while in mass communication it is delayed. It might be a week after an article is published before a reader's letter to the editor arrives. The greatest advantage of mass communication over other forms is that it multiplies messages. In interpersonal communication, you can reach another person with what you have to say. With mass communication, however, a message can be amplified so that lakhs of people pick it up. Thus, mass communication has the potential to reach vast audiences and motivate them to action.

If mass communication creates awareness of a programme, the interpersonal communication impresses the people towards action. Therefore, combination of mass media and interpersonal media is an ideal process of communication in the Indian environment.

Non-verbal Communication

Non-verbal communication is the transmission of a message or meaning from one person to another, using non-word symbols or body language. In non-verbal communication, people send messages to each other without talking. Non-verbal communication takes place through facial expression, eye contact, head positions, arm and hand movements, body posture and positioning of legs and feet. These are collectively called **non-verbal media**. The face itself is an autobiography of a man and a major source of non-verbal messages.

FIVE MAJOR CHANNELS OF BODY LANGUAGE

The body angle, the face, the arms, the hands and the legs are the five major channels of non-verbal communication/body language. People ignore the non-verbal communication. But it assumes great importance in relationships management as an angry face creates negative effect, while a smiling face indicates positiveness. The open and relaxed hands with palms facing a customer are a positive signal, while twisted palms indicate tension. Talking to someone with two legs on a table is nothing but arrogance.

Organisational Communication

Communication in any organisation flows mainly in three directions:

1. **The downward communication:** This type of communication originates from top officials and flows to lower level functionaries.
2. **The upward communication:** It carries information from subordinates to top officials or immediate bosses, 'The Downward' and 'Upward' Communication is also known as two-way communication.
3. **The horizontal or side-way communication:** Communication between two or three subordinates or managers of the same rank or equals in the hierarchy is known as horizontal communication.

LISTENING PROCESS

A Chinese proverb says, "If I hear, I forget". There is a close linkage between speaking and hearing in the process of effective communication. If you forget what you hear, the message results in failed communication. Therefore, proper listening is an important element in interpersonal communication.

Poor Listening

Oral communication generally suffers due to poor listening on the part of the receiver. Studies show that only about a fourth of what has been heard is retained after two days. So, listening is a poor link in the chain of oral messages. Developing and improving the ability to listen is imperative in oral communication. It is important to train oneself to listen, attentively. Listening well is a matter of correct attitude. Since listening efficiency is poor, considerable oral information is lost even in the process of transmission.

Some of the reasons for faulty listening are as follows:

1. **External distraction:** Some of the distractions are caused by the speaker. For example, loud sound, stammering, excessive gestures, awkward postures, etc. The other source of distraction comes from the physical environment such as noisy fans, glaring lights, stuffy and musty rooms, heat, cold, draft, annoying background noise. All these disturb and distract the listener's attention.

2. **Prejudice against the speaker:** If one is not favourably disposed to the speaker, then one's listening is often 'turned off' or one could be easily distracted. This is because the listener is negatively oriented to the speaker.

3. **Time lag between thinking speed and speaking speed:** About 80–160 words per minute is the average speaking speed. The capacity to think is put at about 800 words per minute. This leaves the listener way ahead of the speaker in terms of time available for processing information. During the 'spare time', listener's mind can wander, lack attention, etc. This could lead to serious lapses in listening.

4. **Interrupting speakers:** Listeners interrupt speakers before they complete their sentences, interpret what they have said, draw conclusions, etc. In short, we behave as if we know their thoughts.

   So anticipation, concluding of details even before they have been said, takes place. This is indeed a serious problem for effective listening.

5. **Listening blocks:** There are certain words, sentences or phrases that create a block in the mind of the listener because of stereotypes, negative meanings, cultural barriers, etc. So one tends to block listening to such expressions. This could result in considerable listening impairments.

6. **Poor speaking and delivery styles:** Persons who speak poorly (hesitant, unclear, inaudible, in a drone, etc.) lose their audiences quickly. The listener gets bored and disinterested in what is being said. Good listening requires effort. It has to be cultivated, consciously.

LISTENING SKILLS

1. Get prepared to listen to the speaker patiently. Recognise that one could gain something by listening. This could hold attention better.
2. Develop a positive attitude. This would enable one to look for and find something useful or valuable in the speaker's presentation.
3. Listen with an open mind. This involves respecting the other person's point of view. Do not deny or discredit a counter position. This would totally cut off listening.
4. Be focused, attend to the speaker with good rapport. This would help in eliminating listening problems to a great extent.
5. Concentrate on the messages being given by the speaker. Mentally look for and absorb the main ideas and thoughts of the speaker. Follow the speaker closely, for grasping the full theme of the presentation.
6. Keep interruptions/questions to a minimum. One needs to interrupt the speaker only if one has to. Otherwise this could detract from the focus on listening.
7. Use the non-verbal cues to clarify/support what has been heard. This would help in the consolidation of what has been heard.
8. Stop talking. To listen, one should stop talking. This is a useful guideline for better listening.
9. Listen with the 'mind' not only the 'ears'.
10. Basic knowledge in the subject will facilitate effective listening. If you are listening a lecture on spiritual empowerment for the first time on the concept of spirituality, one needs a minimum understanding of the subject for better listening.

Since the speaker and the listener are two equal partners in the process of interpersonal communication and sometimes they alternate their roles, listening plays an important role in interpersonal communication. If there is no effective listening, there is no communication. A good communicator is one who listens the most.

Case Study: The Last Teaching of Confucius

During his last moments of life, the great Chinese Philosopher Confucius said to his disciple, "Son, look into my mouth and check if there is tongue inside".

The disciple said, "Master, yes, the tongue is there inside the mouth".

Then the Master asked, "Look again and see whether there are teeth inside".

The disciple said, "Master, there is none".

The Master said, "The tongue was born first and it is still there intact, but the teeth which were born later are missing. Why have they gone earlier"? Hearing this, the disciples were all silent and surprised and looked towards the Master, who said: "Look, the tongue, is soft, therefore it is still there. The teeth were hard, hence they broke away."

This was the last teaching of the great Master.

(The inference of the story is that softness in our communication makes a big difference in relationships management.)

POINTS TO REMEMBER

1. Communication process is classified as intrapersonal communication, interpersonal communication, group communication, mass communication, non-verbal communication. Each type has its own medium to transmit messages.

2. Interpersonal communication is defined as a relationship in which two persons alternate the roles of speaker and listener, because of their shared desire for fulfilment of a need. It is also called the means by which one may achieve a more satisfying relationship with other human beings.

3. Interpersonal media include: face-to-face communication, oral interview, conference, verbal reports, telephonic conversation, quality circles, press conference, meetings.

4. Mass communication is defined as the process of using mass medium to send messages to large audiences. In mass communication, there are five 'Ms' such as mass communicators, mass messages, mass media, mass audience and mass communications.

5. Non-verbal communication or body language is a process of communication through body angle, face, arms, hands and legs. No words are used in non-verbal communication.

6. Organisational communication has three types: upward, downward and horizontal communication.

7. About 45 per cent of time is spent everyday in listening as against 30 per cent in speaking. Listening well is a matter of correct attitude.

8. Listening skills are: listen to the speaker patiently, develop positive attitude, listen with an open mind, concentrate on the messages, listen with the mind, not merely ears.

REVIEW QUESTIONS

1. What are the various types of communication? Identify the advantages of each type of communication.

2. What is verbal or interpersonal communication? Discuss the role of interpersonal media in the practice of public relations.

3. Distinguish between interpersonal communication and mass communication. How is mass communication useful in public relations?

4. Compare and contrast upward and downward types of communication in an organisation to promote employee relations.

5. Examine listening process and explain the skills that improve listening.

Chapter

23

Traditional mind can be changed with traditional media.

C O N T E N T S

- Value of Traditional Art Media
- Historical Perspective
- Mahatma Gandhi and Traditional Media
- Song and Drama Division

VALUE OF TRADITIONAL ART MEDIA

What is a traditional art medium? Theatre, music and dance are the three traditional art forms which have been part of human culture. The language of the theatre is primarily spoken words, that of music is vocal while dance is based on movement of the body. They are performing arts which create great impact on the human mind.

Tradition is a custom handed down from one generation to another. When tradition is applied to an art, it is an artistic style established by an artiste and subsequently followed by others. Traditional art media by nature are those indigenous forms of communication which have their roots in the cultural tradition of the country.

Human Style

Traditional medium is defined as a folk art form by which a message is communicated in the form of spoken words, song and body language, facial expression. Folk media are personal, appear in the form of human style and the message is direct from the artistes to the audience. Traditional media were the only means of entertainment for the people in rural India. These media are still alive in villages and continue to provide both information and entertainment to the people in remote areas who are not exposed to the modern media of communication.

Traditional media are very useful in a country like ours to inform, educate and entertain the poorer and illiterate sections of the society. Every region in India has its own folk art form that is immensely popular in that area. *Jaatra* (West Bengal), *Burrakatha* (Andhra Pradesh), *Villupattu* (Tamil Nadu), *Tamasha* (Maharashtra), *Yakshagana* (Karnataka) are a few traditional forms to mention.

Tamasha

The tamasha, meaning fun is an extremely lively and robust form of folk theatre of Maharashtra, which dates back to over 400 years. It is pure entertainment specific, with the star performer being the female artist who has to sing the favourite songs of the patrons as they shout out 'Daulat Ziada' (may the wealth of the patrons increase). It takes its name from the Dholki, a cylindrical two-sided drum, and its leading player is the Sahir, the peoples' poet. A chorus of six to eight male singers cum performers and two or more female dancers/singers make up the rest of the troupe.

Yakshagana

'Yakshagana' is the song of the 'Yaksha', the most popular folk drama of Karnataka.

HISTORICAL PERSPECTIVE

The folk or traditional arts of India from ancient period have been used for moral, religious, socio-political and entertainment purposes. Some of folk art forms are community, caste, culture and language/dialect specific and bear value associations often unique to them. Mahabharat, the epic, as a moral value was popularised through folk arts only.

Earliest means of entertainment and education in India was only through traditional media. As such the folk art forms are our rich cultural heritage and hoary past. Folk song is defined as "neither new nor old, it is like a forest tree with its roots deeply buried in the past, but which continually puts forth new branches, new leaves and new fruits". From time immemorial when human beings started social pattern of living, poetry originated with it as a means of expression. At the same time, perhaps, folk art forms such as folk songs, folk dances, storytelling took shape to express the love for labour, social bondages, the joy of harvest festivals, and religious rituals. We find folk art forms in Indian mythology and ancient scriptures. And they are still popular in our villages. Historically, traditional or folk media have often played a role in the communication and promotion of new ideas and adjustment to a new social or political order, apart from its traditional role of pursuing Indian culture and our age old values. For example, the *puranas* like *Ramayana* and *Mahabharatha* in ancient India were popularised only through folk art media. During colonial rule in India when the mass media were under the control of British Government, the social reformers, the freedom fighters used only traditional media to mobilise public opinion against the oppressors, present strategies and rally public support for freedom movement.

Kabir

Saint Singer Kabir who lived in the medieval India propagated his philosophy among others through the medium of song composed by himself in simple language and local dialect that not only attracted the attention of the people but also impressed them with the philosophy of communal amity. *"Kabira Khada Bazaar mein; Mange Sab ki Khair"* (Kabir stands in the market, wishing everyone well).

MAHATMA GANDHI AND TRADITIONAL MEDIA

To me art in order to be truly great must, like the beauty of nature, be universal in its appeal. It must be simple in its presentation and direct in its expression like the language of nature.
—Mahatma Gandhi

Mahatma Gandhi had immense faith in the folk arts as media of communication. In modern India, Mahatma Gandhi used the traditional folk art media to communicate his message of freedom movement. His prayer meetings held in the evenings started with bhajans, *ram dhun*, *kirtans* and songs. Announcements of three major movements such as Non-cooperation Movement (1920), Civil Disobedience Movement (1930) and Quit India Movement (1942) were made known only at prayer meetings. In his entourage of 200 mile long salt satyagraha, Dandi March, of 24 days in April 1930 included musicians who recited *kirtans* and other songs that attracted huge gatherings.

Importance

"A nail is used to drive out a nail". Similarly, traditional art media are the most appropriate channels for changing the traditional Indian mind towards modernisation. Being the ancient form, it is very close to the hearts of people and became part of life. They influence the rural mind regardless of their education, social and financial background. Traditional art media has special significance in the Indian communication system. Three factors make it more important in the contemporary society. First is that traditional media are part of our culture and Indian life. Second, traditional media were used even during the freedom struggle to create public opinion against the British Raj. Burrakatha (story telling) was extensively used by the Communist party of India (CPI) to fight against the Nizam Rule in the erstwhile Hyderabad state. *Alha*, the popular ballad of Uttar Pradesh, *Laavani* of Maharashtra, *Gee-Gee* of Karnataka, *Villu Pattu* of Tamil Nadu, *Kaabigaan* of West Bengal were used by freedom fighters to arouse national consciousness among the people against the British rule. Third, the traditional media are being used along modern media in popularising the Five Year Plans, family planning and making people participate in the development schemes.

These media continued to play a meaningful role in rural areas in educating the masses on social evils such as drinking, illiteracy, untouchability, superstition, communal conflict, population explosion, malnutrition and insanitation. Against this background it can be inferred that the traditional art media assume great importance in contemporary Indian society.

Supplement the Mass Media

A question arises why should we use traditional media when the modern media of mass communication are good in quickly transmitting development information? While mass media like radio and television can be used in disseminating information on development activities particularly on agriculture, the traditional media can undoubtedly supplement the mass media. They have comparatively better impact on the motivational, behavioural or attitudinal aspect of the rural illiterate people.

Characteristics

Like other media of communication, the traditional media have the following characteristics:

1. Traditional media is classified as audio-visual media because one can see and hear the artistes and their messages. It has double impact on both seeing and listening.
2. Traditional media bring close relationship between the medium and audience, and engage them face-to-face. It allows, typically, an extremely high degree of physical closeness with costumes and often psychological closeness and intimacy.
3. There is more possibility of getting quick and instant feedback in the traditional media.
4. Being local and live, they are most intimate with the masses and command immense credibility and impact.
5. Traditional media like modern media inform, educate and entertain the masses.
6. Folk arts forms have a mix of dialogue, dance, drama, song, prayer, clowning and moralising.

Limitations

The greatest limitation of traditional media is that they cannot reach the mass audience. They cannot create greater awareness. However, this can be overcome by binding traditional media with modern media such as radio, television and film. The reach of traditional media compared to mass media is limited.

Advantages

Traditional art forms have certain following advantages over other mass media:

1. **Personal contact:** The audience comes into direct contact with the communicator and has a face-to-face interaction in the traditional media. As a result this medium establishes a direct link between the communicator and the receiver. In the case of electronic media, the message reaches the audience out of an impersonal box.

2. **Feedback:** An added advantage of traditional media is that the communicator gets immediate feedback vis-a-vis other media where the communicator cannot talk to the audience directly. Doubts, if any, are cleared on the spot when a message is communicated through traditional media. In other words this is the best form of a two-way communication.

3. **Language:** The language and dialogues used in traditional media are the spoken language of the local people and colloquial dialects. This enables the audience to understand the theme very easily and makes it acceptable to the rural folk.

4. **Audience participation:** Audience also participates in some of the folk media. The entire group assembled joins in the folk song. The audience participation creates greater attentiveness among them and leads to better understanding of the message. It is also called 'Sadharanikaran', a scene in drama where the audience developed traditional attachment with the artiste's role.

5. **Face-to-face:** Since audience in this form comes face-to-face contact with artistes, the expectation of the former can be assessed to tune the message.

6. **Flexibility:** The folk media have greater flexibility in utilisation than the electronic media. The theme and form can be adapted depending on the audience and the subject items on current events can be introduced into the traditional forms.

7. **Cost:** Compared to other media, the traditional media is less expensive and it is possible to repeat the performance any number of times depending on the need.

8. **Support medium:** Traditional media are employed in support of other media such as film, exhibition, radio, television, and oral communication. *Burrakatha* or *Harikatha*, street play, are now being used in almost all the media for the purpose of communication.

9. **Effective reach:** Though the electronic media has wider physical coverage of area, its impact on the people is not as effective as that of traditional media. Being limited to a local area and to the local audience, the traditional media create greater impact on the rural audience, and so it is very effective.

Forms of Traditional Media

India is known for its various art forms. Every state, and every region has its own folk art form born out of their own culture, and life style. Traditional media varies from simple story telling and puppetry to more complex, multimedia events as the *Veedhi Bhagavatham*, *Yakshagana* or wandering minstrels singing and enacting stories. The number is vast and include as many as 300 folk music styles varying from *Bauls* and *Bhatialis* of Bengal, to *Chaiti* and *Kajare* of Uttar Pradesh, to *Bihu* of Assam and *Duha* and *Garba* of Gujarat. There are the varied theatrical styles from the *Jaatra* theatre of West Bengal to the *Tamasha* of Maharashtra and *Yakshagana* of Karnataka.

Blend of Traditional with Electronic Media

Notwithstanding the expansion of electronic media, the traditional media have their own role and scope in our country. Since traditional art media is presented in the human form, there is a greater scope for a better impact. These forms can be utilised in rural areas and slums of urban areas where the poorer sections of the society are not exposed to the electronic media of mass communication. The poorer sections (below the poverty line) that constitute about 30 per cent of the population in our country will be too receptive to witness the performance of traditional media not only for entertainment purpose, but also for education purpose. Thus, the traditional media can be utilised by incorporating development themes or themes based on marketing, etc. This medium is now being utilised mostly by the Central and State Government information services. It can also be utilised by the private sector and public sector undertaking in influencing the customers towards their products and services in rural India.

There is every need to protect and patronise the traditional media as part of our culture. An ideal situation will be the co-existence of modern mass media and traditional media. A blend of these media can be of immense use. Electronic and traditional media can be blended for effective communication. Radio and television in India gave story telling a new lease of life. In rural situation, a story telling through electronic media would not only entertain but also function as a message carrier in human style. The performer uses the story as a tool of his profession and later provides information to motivate the audience. In fact, the dying traditional media are being revived by the electronic media which use them extensively in entertainment communications. Media experts also suggest the blend of modern media with traditional media.

Change Agent

In the post-independent era, the traditional media are being extensively used for information, education and motivation of people towards reaching national goals. They are being used as change agents among the rural communities for adult education, rural development, family planning, pulse polio immunisation. The experiences of Field Publicity Officers of the Central Government and the District Public Relations Officers of the State Governments have shown that street-plays, storytelling, puppet shows, folk songs, folk proverbs, sayings, *kavisammelanams, mushairs,* etc. have been useful to meet the communication needs of village folk. It has been proved by studies that comparatively traditional media can more effectively stir the feelings and affect attitudes of illiterate masses.

The First Five Year Plan Document on public cooperation in national development on reaching the people said: "A widespread understanding of the plan has, therefore, to be carried into every home in the language of the people with the assistance of creative writers and artistes which has to be specially enlisted. "All available methods of communication have to be developed and the people approached through the written and spoken words no less than through radio, film, song and drama". This statement is still valid even during the 12th Five Year Plan (2012–2017) period.

Case Study

Here is an example of how the art form *mimicry* brought deposits for a bank. A nationalised bank utilised the services of mimic to promote its deposit scheme among the rural people. Whenever bank officials visited villages, people generally tried to avoid them, fearing that they might have come for recovery of loans. The villagers hardly lended a ear to these officials who came to explain the deposit scheme. When the bank announced a mimicry programme in the village, the people flocked to it. The artiste mimicked politicians and cinema actors and when the audience was absorbed in the programme, he subtly put across a bank deposit scheme and explained how small savings would grow and come to the villagers' rescue in future. After listening to the mimicry programme, one villager expressed wonder and said he never knew that the banks had savings scheme. Thus, the artiste was able to deliver the message on deposits in the rural people's own language. The mimicry artiste gave about 30 performances in Guntur District of Andhra Pradesh and many people in rural areas came forward to open new accounts with the bank. If a bank is able to mobilise deposits through the medium of mimicry, every organisation, be it public or private sector, can make use of traditional art form in rural areas in communicating their messages. Similarly, a puppet show with a mix of song and dance was organised by a voluntary agency, the South India AIDS Action Programme, in the slums at Adayar, Chennai to educate the slum dwellers on the HIV infection and AIDS.

Bengaluru Municipal Corporation Applies Traditional Media to Collect Property Tax

The Bengaluru civic authority, the Bruhat Bengaluru Mahanagara Palike (BBMP), has adopted a unique method of collecting property tax dues by applying traditional folk art media with age-old drums. The country's third largest software company Wipro Ltd. earned a net profit of ₹1716 crores, but it owed property tax dues of five years to the Municipal Corporation. The Corporation officials engaged a team of traditional drumbeaters who did drumbeating outside Wipro's head office at Doddakannelli village, Sarjapur, Bengaluru in January 2013. The effect of drumbeating on the Wipro Company was indeed magical. Embarrassed company officials hastily handed over a cheque for ₹5 crore to the Deputy Commissioner Mahadevapura Zone with a promise to clear the remaining dues in a week. This is the effect of folk art media in changing the attitude of the people.

SONG AND DRAMA DIVISION

The Song and Drama Division of the Ministry of Information and Broadcasting is a unique organisation with a specific mandate of socio-cultural and development communication. It was set up in 1954 for tapping the resourceful and live media, particularly the traditional folk art forms for plan publicity. It is also known as "Live Media Wing". It utilises a wide range of stage forms, such as drama, folk and traditional plays, dance-drama, folk recitals and puppet shows besides the sound and light medium to focus the attention of the audience on important aspects of country's life and development in different fields. On an average, the Division puts up about 40,000 programmes all over the country every year involving 10,000 artistes. It has 700 registered cultural troupes of various categories, such as drama, folk and traditional recitals, mythological recitals, puppetry, magic.

Tribal Publicity

Ranchi Tribal Centre involves more tribal artistes in the development process. Programmes are presented in the tribal areas of Bihar, Chhattisgarh, Jharkhand, Madhya Pradesh and Orissa to educate the people about various development schemes designed for tribals. The Division also presents shows of plays on various themes such as Family Welfare, AIDS, Drug Abuse, National Integration, Communal Harmony, Environmental issues, etc. Such programmes are organised at local fairs and festivals where large number of people congregate.

POINTS TO REMEMBER

1. Traditional art medium is described as a medium of communication which has roots in the cultural tradition of the country, such as *Jaatra, Yakshagana*, puppetry. Theatre, music and dance are the three performing art forms that have been part of human culture. Traditional medium is also known as a folk art form by which a message is communicated in the form of spoken words, song and body language—facial expression.

2. A folk song, which was developed by our cultural tradition, is described as neither modern nor old, it is like a forest tree with its roots deeply buried in the past, but which continually puts forth new branches, new leaves and new fruits.

3. Traditional media has special significance in the Indian communication system. Since these media are very close to the heart of rural Indians, traditional media are used both for entertainment and for information.

4. The advantages of traditional media include: direct and personal contact with the audience, immediate feedback, audience participation and limited effective reach.

5. Traditional media were used in the freedom struggle to create public opinion against the British rule. Traditional media are now being used to publicise the Five Year Plans, family planning, Pulse Polio Immunisation Programmes.

6. Mahatma Gandhi compared an art with the beauty of nature. It must be simple in its presentation and direct in its expression like the language of nature.

7. The *bhajans, kirtans*, songs, parables, *ramdhun* were some of the folk art forms that were used by Mahatma Gandhi in his daily prayer meetings while communicating messages on the freedom

movement. His entourage of 200 mile long salt *satyagraha*—Dandi March in 1930 had included musicans, musical instruments to recite songs and bhajans.

8. Notwithstanding the modern mass media, traditional media are used in the Indian communication strategy because over 50 per cent of the Indian population have no access to mass media. Traditional media when blended with the electronic media, such as radio and television, supplement the mass media and reach a large section of the society.

9. The Song and Drama Division, a media unit of the Ministry of Information and Broadcasting Government of India exploits the traditional media in urban and rural India to motivate people towards national integration and development. It is also known as 'Live media wing'. Its special tribal troupes reach tribal areas for education purpose.

REVIEW QUESTIONS

1. What is traditional art medium? Explain its significance as a medium of communication.

2. Why should we use traditional media when we have modern mass media of communication? Describe the functions and scope of traditional media in rural development.

3. How did Mahatma Gandhi use traditional media in the freedom struggle?

4. How does Song and Drama Division promote development by using folk media?

5. Why are folk media important in the Indian communication system to reach out rural folk?

Newspapers in Public Relations | Chapter 24

C O N T E N T S

PR AND NEWSPAPERS

Press, which includes daily newspapers and periodicals, is the most potent, versatile and resilient of all communication media. It is so powerful that sophisticated electronic media could not kill it in the industrialised countries. As literacy grew in the developing countries, so did the press also to meet the communication needs of the literate population. Press is a medium that communicates the message in the form of printed word.

Press is an effective medium of public relations, particularly in reaching the most influential and educated section of the society. In fact, newspapers carry both news and views which are of great significance to the reader. Every reader of a newspaper is considered as an opinion leader whose views are much valued by others in the Indian context where illiteracy is on the higher side.

JOURNALISM

Since press is one of the formats of journalism, a student of public relations must also study about journalism which tells the ABC of newspapers and their application. Roland E. Wolseley, a famous American Journalism Professor described journalism as the "systematic and reliable dissemination of public information, public opinion and public entertainment by modern media of mass communication". The term 'journalism' embraces all the forms and through which news and the comments reach the public. Journalism by its writing style takes different forms such as print journalism, radio journalism, TV journalism, film journalism, photo journalism and online journalism.

Guardian Angel

What is the significance of press in relation to public relations? The press as a purveyor of information and source of public opinion assumes great importance in the modern world. Press has been described as *the guardian angel of democracy*. A free press is the sentinel of a free society. The Emperor of France Napoleon Bonaparte once said "four hostile newspapers are more to be feared than a thousand bayonets". Press is also called the *Fourth Estate of the Realm* next only to Executive, Legislature and Judiciary.

Thomas Jefferson, third American President, commented that "were it left to me to decide whether we should have Government without newspapers or newspapers without Government, I should not hesitate a moment to prefer the latter". He opined that newspapers are must for a society.

Pandit Jawaharlal Nehru, First Prime Minister of India, speaking on the significance of the press, had said "I would rather have a completely free press with all the dangers involved in the wrong use of that freedom than suppressed or regulated press".

As newspapers act as prime source of news, views and current affairs and they inform, educate and entertain the people, public relations makes use of the press as its media of communication to reach its target audience, particularly educated sections. Press acts as a *bridge* between an organisation and its internal and external publics. Each medium has its own characteristics. Press as a channel of communication belongs to the visual medium which appeals to the eye and sense of seeing.

Contents

The contents of a newspaper bear an eloquent proof to the importance of press as a medium of public relations. Newspapers' contents include: news and current affairs; editorial page which is known as opinion page with editorials, signed features, letters to the editor, business column (news about trade, markets, shares), entertainment (music, dance, drama, cartoons, comics, sports news). All these contents undoubtedly influence the mind of the readers in creating public opinion towards an organisation, product, service or an idea.

Mahatma Gandhi described the functions of a newspaper as "one of the objects of a newspaper is to understand popular feelings and give expression to it, another is to arouse among the people certain desirable sentiments and the third is fearlessly to expose popular defects".

Two Tasks

Press relations in any organisation has two tasks—*first* to maintain appropriate media relations with press representatives and *second* to provide corporate information to the media for coverage. In public relations campaigns, newspapers create awareness and build a healthy public opinion. If an idea, service or a product has to be promoted at national or international level, the press can be the best medium. The editorial page and other news columns create public opinion on several issues confronting the nation. The credit of exposing Bofors Gun deal, or 2G spectrum scam goes to the Indian press. The newspapers in India today play a significant role in bringing about the socio-economic change.

Indian public relations is remarkably fortunate in having 82,222 newspapers including 10,205 dailies (2011). The total circulation of newspapers was 33 crore copies. The newspapers in India offer good opportunities for public relations in reaching the urban and rural audiences with messages. Press can be utilised in several ways. They include (i) promoting institutional performance; (ii) product publicity; (iii) services promotion; (iv) advertorials; (v) reputation of the organisation, (vi) media monitoring (feedback).

PRESS TACTICS

The tactics that are used in the medium of press include: news release or press release, press conference, press tour, feature article, letter to the editor, rejoinder, press interview, press photographs, newsletter, media advisories, curtain raiser, fact sheets, press kit, pitch letters (short letter to the editors about news item), electronic news services, corporate press advertising, advertorials, press inquiries, press reception, press open day, press clippings service. Through these tactics a public relations manager ensures media coverage in newspapers for the organisation.

It should be the endeavour of a public relations manager to get fair coverage in the newspapers about the activities of an organisation. This is possible only when a public relations manager maintains a close rapport with the press by providing a good media service or readers-oriented information. In fact, a public relations practitioner acts as "a person in the middle" between the management of an organisation and the newspapers. The objectives of the management and the newspapers are quite different. It is here that the public relations manager has to *bridge* their viewpoints and bring each side around to understand the problems and perceptions of the other. This can be achieved only through planned press relations.

Case Study

The Andhra Pradesh State Road Transport Corporation (APSRTC) in order to develop good media relations and fair coverage for the organisation made use of all tactics. The public relations department first designed a press release format and got a blue colour letterhead printed for easy identification as 'Media Release' with APSRTC logo as masthead.

Press release

Press notes were released covering the Board Meetings and other important events and achievements of the Corporation. Another type of press release included 'curtain raiser'. As and when inaugurations of bus stations or major functions were held, the curtain raiser containing factual information and photographs of the proposed bus station, bus depot were released two days in advance of the event for coverage.

Press conference

A press conference was organised for Vice-Chairman and Managing Director who spoke on the new budget proposals and future plans of APSRTC. It got good coverage in all the newspapers.

Rejoinders

Rejoinders and clarifications were another tactics used by the corporation for providing factual information when newspapers publish adverse reports without any basis. *The Hindu* once under its column "Between You and Me" published a clarification of APSRTC about the difference of bus fare on its inter-state services. The clarification said "under the inter-state reciprocal agreement the fare structure of respective States has to be followed. As such the fare in Andhra Pradesh was at 13 paise

per km while in Maharashtra for the same bus it was ₹17.50 per km".
While appreciating the public relations department's clarification, the
column ended "Thank you for the prompt reply".

Bus timings

A unique tactic used by the Corporation was publication of inter-state
long distance services, and bus service timings to famous pilgrim
centres. It was the practice of newspapers in Hyderabad to publish only
the railway and airways timings. When bus timings were published,
the Vice-Chairman and Managing Director of APSRTC complimented
the public relations department.

Feature

Another tactic is feature article. Feature articles on "A Bus to Every
Village", "A Bus Ride to Progress" were published in many newspapers.
These features highlighted as to how the life of Komi, a tribal woman
at Chautapally bus stand in Krishna District changed from a casual
labourer to vegetable vendor after a bus was introduced to this village.
In all 19 newspapers carried this article providing a free editorial space.
When the clippings of this coverage were put up, the Managing Director
praised the department for its good work. A poster meant for drivers
to provide comfortable and safe travel to commuters was published in
all major newspapers to assure the passengers of APSRTC that the
management was taking all steps for safe driving. These are only a few
press tactics used by APSRTC to gain coverage in newspapers.

Three Masters to Serve

Whenever you think of media relations management, you are reminded
of three masters you serve as a public relations practitioner. *First* is
your own organisation and your Chief Executive. *Second* is the print
and electronic media, their representatives. And *third* is the various
publics, your target audience, who receive your information from the
media. You are responsible and accountable to all the three bosses—yet
you as a public relations manager have little or no authority or power
to influence or make final decisions. Is this not a challenge? Even then
your job is to get a fair or even better and favourable coverage. Well it
calls for many skills and experience.

Editor's Comment

One Chief Editor of a newspaper commented on the professionalism of
public relations professionals in the following words: "The Editors are
appalled to see the sloppy copy that comes in the form of press notes.

Though the author of such press notes is a qualified public relations manager, there is no professional touch in many of the press notes; every copy needs a re-write man. It does not mean that the editors look for such press notes that can go straight to composing. What is required is a good copy and up to the point. In a day, an editor receives 300 to 400 press notes and if every press note runs into a number of pages, he may not have time to go through all. As a result, important ones will go unnoticed". So the public relations manager's aim should be to vigorously crave for editor's attention with professionally drafted press release. It is in this context the public relations manager must overcome the shortcomings highlighted by the journalists.

Complaints from Press Against PR

Complaints are very often heard from the press about public relations press releases. Here are a few such complaints.

1. Public relations manager always tries to colour and or suppress free flow of legitimate news under the influence or pressure of the management
2. Public relations manager is not free to select news kindling readers' interest
3. Public relations press releases are boss oriented and not readers oriented. They use many adjectives to please their management
4. Public relations managers are ignorant of journalistic writing
5. Public relations managers give only positive news, suppressing news of negative nature
6. Public relations people are inept
7. Public relations managers indulge in over communication
8. Public relations managers have no news sense
9. Public relations managers deliberately withhold facts
10. Public relations people, of course, know better

The shortcomings mentioned above and the comments of the editor quoted earlier clearly highlight the defects in public relations press releases. One has to overcome such complaints with professionalism.

HOW TO WRITE A GOOD PRESS RELEASE?

Many attempts to communicate are nullified by saying too much

What is a Press Release?

A press release is one of the communication tactics of sending news of public interest to journalists for use in the media. It aims at conveying the essence of a story in a journalistic style for coverage in the medium being approached. Newspaper, radio and television are the media useful to public relations professionals, which accept press releases. The press release ensures effective media coverage than pay for advertisements because readers prefer news rather than its advertisements.

Good Press Release

A good press release is one which attracts the attention of the editor and communicates the message efficiently and effectively. But what goes into the making of a good press release? In the beginning, you must know the anatomy of a news release before identifying the golden rules for writing a press release. The anatomy gives you the basic structure of a press release as indicated here.

1. **Source**. It should be clear from where the press release has emanated, say Municipal Corporation of Hyderabad.
2. **Date of release or dateline**. It should be clearly stated in the press release.
3. **Headline**. It serves to attract the reader's attention.
4. **The first paragraph or the Lead**. "Five Ws and One H". It should contain the basic information: who, what, where, when, why and how.
5. **Additional paragraphs** or point-wise information. One paragraph for each additional point of information in the descending order. It is also called body copy.
6. **Statistics**, if any.
7. **Conclusion or the final paragraph**.

Three Parts

A public relations manager must think and act like a journalist when writing a press release. Construction of the 'story' is an important aspect in the writing of a press release. A news release should be divided into three main parts for the purpose of writing. They are as follows:

1. The heading
2. The lead or the opening paragraph
3. The body or the remainder story

Catchy Headline

Every news story in a newspaper requires a headline which is a signpost to the reader. Its primary function is to attract the attention of readers and tell them instantly what the story is about. It should be simple, crisp, news worthy and straight to the point. The headline should stand out in bold type that makes us stop and read the story. For example, **"Government Will Survive; No Trust Vote: PM"**. What does it mean? The Prime Minister said his Government would survive the no-confidence motion proposed to be introduced by the opposition in Parliament.

'India, Russia Ink, Military Deals' was the heading of a news story when Prime Minister Manmohan Singh and Russian President Vladimir Putin finalised two military contracts worth about ₹20,000 crores on 25 December 2012. Though headline writing is the job of newspaper editorial staff (sub-editors), the public relations practitioners also can give a headline to the news story, which enables the editors to assess its news value.

LEAD—FIVE 'Ws' AND ONE 'H'

The basic principle for news writing and for packaging the opening para is what is known as the Five Ws and one H. It is also called the 'lead'. The whole content is summarised in the first paragraph so that one does not need to read a word further in order to understand what the news is all about. The lead—the first paragraph or perhaps the first three or four sentences is the most important part of the release. You cannot write a good release without a good lead, and you cannot write a good lead until you have answered the question about what is important.

Deciding what is important sometimes needs a little judgement. Important areas must be construed broadly. What you really want to isolate is the most significant and most interesting aspect of your subject. And you have to keep in mind that the news is what is happening now. For example, if the release is about the opening of a new fertiliser plant, the most important thing is the fact that the plant is opening. The action is the news. But is there something especially interesting about the plant itself? Is it the largest plant of its kind in the world? Or the first? Will it provide lot of jobs for the local economy? Once you have decided what is important and also what is interesting, you can write a lead. The most important is the lead.

The Lead not only should sum up all the main points but also should indicate to the reader "Who has done, What, Where, Why, When and How it happened". This is known as 'Five Ws and one H'.

- Who is involved in the story?
- What happened?
- When did it happen?
- Where did it happen?
- Why did it happen?
- How did it happen?

For example, the Madras High Court appointed Justice R. Mohan, a retired Judge of the Supreme Court of India, to conduct the BCCI elections to be held in Kolkata on 29 and 30 September 2004. Another Lead says, "Amid Growing Demand for Stringent Rape Laws, Union Home Minister Sushil Kumar Shinde has asked all political parties to send their suggestions to the three-member committee headed by former Chief Justice J.S. Verma, constituted on December 23, 2012, to suggest amendments to criminal laws to sternly deal with sexual assault cases". This was the lead of a story after the death of a 23-year-old physiotherapy student (Delhi), the gang rape victim.

The body or remainder story

The third and the most important part of the news release is the body or the remainder story. This item is taken up after the headline and the lead. Having read the headline and the lead, the reader goes to the remainder of the story—the body. While quintessence of the story is covered in the lead, the body explains other details depending on their importance. The remaining paragraphs expand on each of the components and are arranged in descending order of importance and/or interest, because journalists and sub-editors cut from the bottom up.

The body is divided into several paragraphs. Each paragraph tells one aspect of the story. The reporter selects the most important fact of the story for the lead. Then the next most important incident or detail is mentioned and so on in the **descending order of importance**. The public relations practitioner will need plenty of practice in selecting paragraphs and arranging them in the order of the reader's interest. Sub-headings can be given to important paragraphs to lead the reader.

The points that are to be borne in mind when framing a news story are: (i) have the facts been presented properly and accurately so that the reader can actually picture the occurrence; (ii) if the story includes disputed points, have both the sides been fairly presented; (iii) does it answer the five Ws and the H; (iv) does it indicate the source of the information; and (v) is it covering all aspects to be comprehensive.

INVERTED PYRAMID

The inverted pyramid (or Triangle) puts pressure on journalists as well as PR professionals to present the entire story "up front". The first summery sentence of the inverted pyramid style is to provide the essence of the whole event. This is followed by background information of the story in importance. Further, it is followed by other details which are increasingly marginal in importance. Readers will gradually get less and less important news as they read the story further. The inverted pyramid is intended to ensure that only less essential details can be removed if the journalist is to cut short by the sub-editor because of lack of space on the page.

Graphically, the entire news story takes the shape of an 'inverted pyramid'. Information is arranged in the descending order of importance. Most important elements of the story come first with the next important aspect of the story getting less prominence and space.

The main objective of using the Inverted Pyramid pattern is that the reader gets all the essential news at a glance based on its importance. As a result, the reader gets the essence of the report or the most important facts in the very beginning and does not have to read it through till the end for being posted with the news. If the reader is not much interested, he can stop reading after first three or four paragraphs.

The advantages of using the Inverted Pyramid form are as follows:

1. It catches the reader's interest.
2. It tells the reader what the story is about, depending on its importance.
3. It facilitates the editor to get the gist of the story in a hurry.
4. It helps the editor to leave out less important paragraphs, if pressure on space demands it.

The Inverted pyramid is the newspaper writing style which should be practised by PR professionals to get the press release published without much editing and cut.

Length

Knowing how to write a release is important. But knowing when to end the release is equally important. If a release is too long, the editor may decide there is no time to read it, and to the file the release will go. The essential points can usually be covered in one page. Sometimes an important event will call for two or three pages, however, so if you need that much space to cover the subject, use it. But even then, write the release in such a way that the editor can chop a few paragraphs off the bottom without damaging the story.

Keep the release brief, at least in most cases. If you really think more information might be needed—statistics or background of the organisation for example—attach a factsheet to the release. A factsheet lists the basic elements of the institution and the event. The dateline is also important.

The checklist for an effective news release is as follows:

1. Is the lead direct and to the point? Does it contain the most important and most interesting aspects of the story?
2. Have who, what, when, where and why been answered in the first few paragraphs?
3. Are sentences and paragraphs short, concise? Words common and concrete? Avoid jargon and complicated language

4. Has the editorial comment been placed in quotation marks and attributed to the appropriate person?
5. Has newspaper style (AP or other) been followed faithfully throughout the release? Make it clear and complete
6. Are spelling and punctuation correct?
7. Have all statements of fact been double-checked for accuracy?
8. Has the release been properly prepared, typed and double-spaced on the one side of the paper? Keep the press release short, with a picture.
9. Is the release dated? Is the release time indicated?
10. Are names, phone numbers, fax numbers, and e-mail addresses for further information included?

A SUCCESSFUL PRESS CONFERENCE

Press conference is one of the tactics or opportunities available in the medium of press, which makes possible quick and widespread dissemination of corporate information through the news media. What is a press conference? A press conference is a media event at which corporations or CEOs announce an important news of public interest. The news is typically announced by the head of an organisation or in the case of a product launch, the Vice-President (Marketing) who can best explain the product and also answer questions raised by the media persons. A press conference is a staged forum in which journalists are invited to listen and witness a news announcement being made first hand. The media persons' questions are answered and doubts if any cleared on the spot at such conferences. A press conference is a bit like a game of Chinese whispers. The speakers present information to the press who in return deliver the content to their readers. In other words a press conference is all about presenting to the presenters (Journalists). And communication in this process is a two-way.

News can be disseminated through a press release also. A press conference is not necessary if the news can be conveyed by a press note. Press conference is necessary when a big news needs elaboration. Many of the big news stories in the business pages of daily newspapers come from announcements made at press conferences. If you are considering the press conference option, public relations manager need to know when and why to organise a press conference, and how to do. When you consider arranging a press conference, ask yourself three following questions:

1. What kind of announcement will generate the maximum attendance of journalists? It needs to be a big event.
2. Is the subject or product of major news value?
3. Is the subject of such a controversial nature that it demands to explain the issue fully?
4. Is the conference intended to divulge multiple decisions that need clarifications by the media?

Types

It is the practice to hold two types of press conferences. One is spontaneous news conferences arising out of a crisis situation. When a tidal wave hit the coastal Krishna district in Andhra Pradesh and 10,000 people died, the Chief Minister held an emergency press conference to explain the devastation caused to human beings and property. The second type of press conference is the planned and scheduled conference held by a CEO of an organisation at a prescribed time with advanced notice. The key element of a press conference is news of public interest wherein there is some big news to announce. A press conference can be planned when the budget is approved or a new product is being launched to explain the programmes of the organisation and the new product. Press conferences are held after the State or Central Government cabinet meetings to brief the media on the cabinet decisions which have far-reaching impact on the people.

Press conferences are organised in connection with product/services or portfolio announcement, financial results of the company, major mergers and acquisitions, new company strategy announcement, opening of new branches, announcement of new budget plans, announcement of annual performance report, important corporate achievements.

The following extracts from a news item titled "A Peculiar Press Conference" that appeared in *The Hindu* shows an example of a bad press conference.

> Pressmen bustling into the officer's room found him busy, excited and also nervous. He was telephoning to somebody saying. "The pressmen are here and I don't know what to say because I am only-dealing with such-and-such-subject. Why don't you also come around and help". He then turned to us and said "I know all of you are very much excited just as I am" and a reporter said the officer was obviously more excited but he ignored the remark.
>
> "Now Gentlemen", said the officer "what you want to know tell me." A reporter asked him how much a particular project was going to cost. "I know you will ask such a question, but wait a minute" he said, dialling somebody. "I say here are a group of pressmen in my room regarding that project you know and they are asking me how much it will cost. It is in that book on my table? You know I did not have time to read that book because it was rather suddenly arranged and in which part of the book is it? On the first page? Well you are right, it is, indeed, here. Thanks". He hung up and told us the cost, and the pressmen were afraid to ask him more questions lest he started dialing again. And so, a reporter asked him "please tell us about that portion of the project you are directly concerned with", and here again the officer was not sure of his ground, and as a 'supplementary' he produced a 10-foot long blueprint and asked somebody to count the figures there. And so went the press conference.

This, indeed, is a peculiar and a bad example of press conference which speaks of an amateurish way of handling it and reflects badly on the efficiency of the public relations department which did not prepare its spokesperson for the press conference.

Tips for a Successful Press Conference

Organising a press conference is an art. A few tips for holding a well-attended and successful press conference are presented here.

1. **Purpose.** The purpose of the conference should be clearly spelled out, understood and defined. The purpose of a press conference can be the announcement of the inauguration of the ₹1000 crore fertiliser plant. Press conference should be called only when a big news story is to be divulged.

2. **Venue.** The press conference should be organised at an easily accessible and decent conference hall of the organisation or a hotel. The convenience of the press persons must be the first consideration rather than the glamour of the place. Rather than taking the press conference to an interesting destination requiring transport, the easier is reaching the destination, the more likely you are to get a good turnout. The venue must have good conference facilities ranging from catering, telephone, internet, to audio-visual equipment.

3. **The date, day and time.** Assuming you have a newsworthy event to announce, the success of the press conference depends on your timing and date. Choose a date which does not clash with other major events. Check with the media about the important events in the city. The most convenient time for the media usually is mid-morning. It is advisable to arrange a press conference at about 11 a.m. followed by lunch. Never plan your press conference for late afternoon. The day of the week is also important. Select a day that gives you the best chance of good media attendance. Generally, the best days for a well-attended conference are Tuesday to Friday. Sunday being a lean day is also good for press conference.

4. **Invitation.** All press correspondents, radio and TV reporters concerned with the subject should be invited. Under no circumstances should a press correspondent be excluded. A list of accredited correspondents can be obtained either from the State Information and Public Relations Department or Press Information Bureau, Ministry of Information and Broadcasting. The invitation, about one page, must be addressed to the editor giving the details of the subject, day, date, time and place. It is usually a good idea to call all those you have been invited

to the press conference two or three days after you sent out your invitation, just to make sure they received it and to get an estimate of who plans to attend. The day before of the conference, check again by telephone to remind each invited guest of the day and time of press conference.

5. **Backgrounder.** A written statement giving all the details of the subject of the press conference for the spokesperson must be prepared by public relations manager for distribution at the conference. The spokesperson must understand the subject and rehearse before the conference. It will serve as an unofficial press release based on which questions can be raised by the media persons. A backgrounder must be prepared keeping the needs of the target audience who are going to be benefited. Such background material may be given along with a press kit with all relevant printed material and photographs. Make sure a professional photographer is available to take photographs of the conference and products if any. Backgrounder should serve as a form of press release.

6. **Spokesperson or speaker.** The success of the press conference depends on the way in which the chief spokesperson handles the event. The press conference speaker must be someone who has speaking skills and is best able to answer questions. Some of the qualities that a spokesperson should have are presented here:

   (a) The pressmen should be free to raise any point and ask any relevant question. The chief spokesperson, while sticking to the theme of the press conference should be prepared to answer the questions with confidence. A bit of humour will come in handy as it covers up inadequacies, if any, in the answers. Home work for the chief spokesperson is essential.

   (b) The chief spokesperson should always have his top executives at hand to help him in answering questions. The speaker must focus on the news and always must stay with the message.

   (c) The public relations manager should also brief the chief spokesperson on the likely questions to be asked and help him in preparing for the press conference.

   (d) Listening patiently will help the chief spokesperson to understand the questions in their proper perspective.

   (e) If television and radio correspondents want separate interviews, necessary facilities should be made available to them. The requirements will be different from those of newspaper correspondents. The spokesperson should tailor his/her presentation to the needs of the journalists.

   (f) The success of a press conference depends on good attendance, intelligent questions and lively proceedings. Efforts should be made to ensure all reporters attend the conference.

(g) When a public relations manager once suggested to the General Manager of a fertiliser company that a press conference should be organised, the General Manager advised him to cultivate the pressmen first. Personal rapport of public relations manager with the reporters will go a long way in the successful conduct of press conference.

(h) The speaker should never attempt to talk "off-the-record" at a news conference. Many editors forbid their reporters to honour off the record statements. Such off the record statements will be published in one form or the other.

(i) The speaker always must speak the truth—with a complete story.

7. **Signage.** It is particularly important when you expect television coverage, because it provides important on-camera identification for your brand or company. Project your logo on a screen behind the speaker, or hang a banner with the logo behind the speaker. Also put your logo on the front of the podium too for better coverage.

8. **Question and Answer Session.** The spokesperson usually makes a statement about the conference. Reporters are recognised for the types of questions they ask and the spokesperson may have one or two experts nearby to assist him with highly technical queries.

Professional standards demand that reporters confine their questions to the subject. The duration of the press conference should normally be 30 to 45 minutes, unless the subject and the personality of the spokesperson warrant more time. But in no case should it exceed an hour.

9. **Hospitality.** One of the Directors of State Information and Public Relations Department always used to advise his public relations officers to treat journalists as their 'sons-in-law'. You must treat attending journalists as important official guests or as appropriate to the occasion. If the event is to run over lunch time, a buffet is normally preferable to a formal sit down lunch. Such hospitality will enable the journalists come closer to the spokesperson for informal discussion. The hospitality should be good though not lavish. There is an editor's old saying that still holds true, "what counts is news, not booze".

10. **Follow-up.** A public relations manager's job does not end with the departure of media persons who came to attend the press conference. On the day of the event send the information pack or press kit containing the spokesperson's statement to those journalists who were interested but did not attend the conference. Issue appropriate thanks letters. Press conferences can achieve dramatic results for the management.

Therefore, when the subject of the press conference is published, the public relations manager must collect press clippings from all newspapers and audio and video coverage from radio and TV channels and make an analysis of the coverage. A set of clippings along with a brief note must be submitted to the CEO and other officials who matter in the organisation. That will not only enable the analysis of public relations work, but also public relations gains recognition.

PRESS TOUR

Press release, press conference and press tour are three important tactics through which a public relations manager can get wider coverage for the organisational activities. Both in the case of press release and press conference, the purpose is to disseminate information and opinion from the organisation to the news media in a business-like manner. The journalists have to depend entirely on what the management has to say.

It is the human instinct to believe what they see rather what they hear. And it is for this reason organisations have evolved another method called press tour to show to journalists their production centres, or programmes such as commissioning new projects, new plants, etc. *Seeing is believing*, a saying goes. Personal observation and personal experience of media persons are of great significance in press tour coverage.

Press Tour Defined

Press tour is a conducted tour of media persons to a project for personal observation and coverage. It is defined as an organised visit of selected media persons to a project, factory or a new installation of development project, for an on the spot study and reporting. It also includes trips on launching new plane services to destinations either within the country or outside the country. Press or media tours also are organised to places where natural disasters, such as cyclones, tsunami, earthquakes take place.

Types of Tour

There are three types of media tours. The most common is a press tour to cover a function or an important event. It is called **function-oriented press tour** when a press party is conducted to cover an event such as inauguration of a project or a scheme. The host company usually provides transport to journalists.

The second type of press tour is called **familiarisation or project of study tour** sponsored by the organisation enabling the journalists to see for themselves and report based on their experiences. Government organisations sponsor such familiarisation tours to irrigation, hydro-electric projects, tribal welfare development schemes. As many as 10–15 journalists can be taken in each tour by providing transport, lodging and boarding facilities.

The third kind of press tour called **individual journalist tour** is conducted by organisations to sponsor journalists on individual basis of one newspaper exclusively. Sometimes journalists take initiative to visit project while sometimes organisations take initiative to sponsor journalists. If a journalist from a major paper is sponsored to visit a project, the cost will be much less than an advertisement released. However, the editorial impact will be greater than an advertisement. While organising press tour, the public relations manager must follow the tips given in the case of a press conference.

EMBARGO

An 'embargo' is a deliberate request at the top of the press release, asking the editor that the content of a press release should not be published before a stated date and time. This practice is adopted when advance information is being provided, say a speech to be delivered by the Prime Minister of India at the meeting of the Planning Commission or Chief Ministers' Conference in order to overcome differences in advance notice period created by various deadlines, time zones or production schedules. The objective of embargo is to assist the journalist in providing time to assimilate the editorial matter, decide what use is to be made of it and plan accordingly, probably by trying to obtain some extra dimensions such as ancillary comment or reaction.

However, the speech with embargo has to be published only after the Prime Minister has delivered his speech. From public relations perspective, the embargo can be very useful to avoid the kind of embarrassment that may happen when, for example, a speech is published before it is delivered and the speaker then makes changes taking unexpected events into account, since it was written. Newspapers and the electronic media are expected to adhere to the embargo.

PRESS KIT

A 'Press Kit' is a set of press material for use by journalists. It is also a package of news and background information presented in a format that press persons need and relate to the event. The press kit containing all material is generally distributed at press conferences, opening ceremonies, exhibitions, press tours, and other occasions where the media are interested in a great deal of background information and statistics. It comprises agenda, a press release, factsheet, as a background briefing, copies of speeches, captioned photographs on the related subject, other relevant matter such as a CD, CD-ROM or diskette, biographies, press clippings, corporate profile, brochure, product sample and a writing pad and pen. It is usually contained within a folder or a bag for convenience of easy handling. A folder is acceptable to the media provided it is attractive and it is the contents in the kit that count. The press kit should be made available to the journalists neither too early nor too late. Basically, there are three different options available today to deliver the press kit. Hard copy on the spot; electronic format on a CD or a DVD and online through a website.

Any overdoing, or over communication is counterproductive. A public relations manager must know the **'don'ts'** in preparing the press kit. They are: Don't over doit, Don't spend too much money; Don't forget to highlight the story in all its perspectives.

ADVERTORIAL

Advertorial is a paid form of editorial matter. It is an advertisement presented in an editorial format. Instead of having independent features or news items written by journalists as usual, advertorials are separate features where editorial content is controlled or actually produced by public relations department or marketing department. Used as inserts in magazines, advertorials commonly focus on a single theme such as health, travel, etc.

The idea is to borrow the credibility of a genuine editorial and thereby, increase the readers' interest. Advertorial can take different formats. However, to make it different from normal advertising, the advertorial at the end is labelled as "ADVT".

Advertorial features, which contain even photographs and illustrations, are effective in providing additional information about products, services and also in encouraging product sampling. Readers gain added value from such features that the products or services are relevant to their tastes and interests. But this is a way of confusing the reader and concerns arise about editorial integrity. Yet advertorials can work very well in specialised magazines like women's interest magazines. The *Reader's Digest* very often carries advertorials, making a brief mention as advertising feature.

Example

Maruti Suzuki sponsored an advertorial published on the front page of *The Hindu* on 30 July 2006 with six column banner headline "Traffic Expected to Come to a Halt all Across India" along with a picture of WAGON R brand car. This advertorial continued even on the back page with pictures of the new Wagon R. The advertorial was presented in such a manner that it appeared as if the piece was written by the newspaper correspondent.

The advertorial began with "It has been repeatedly noted that when people see Monalisa for the first time in the Louvre in Paris, they literally freeze. It is just that beautiful objects and people catch our attention and for some moments keep us completely engrossed". It compares the new Wagon R. The advertorial ends "With its sleek looks and aerodynamic body shape, the changed Wagon R is bound to make people stop on their tracks. It has the potential to be a traffic stopper wherever it is seen. With the new Wagon R being launched all over the country, traffic might-just-come to a halt today ! ADVT". This is a shining example of an advertorial that gives the impression of a normal editorial matter.

One should be clear about the difference between an advertorial and an advertisement or an advertising feature. A copy refers to the text matter within an advertisement and also all the material needed for print reproduction of an advertisement. Editorial refers to non-advertising text that appears in the form of news report, editorial comment, and so on in the media.

How does an advertorial differ from an advertising feature? In the advertorial, the editorial matter supports the advertising that surrounds it. The editorial matter is used, for example, when the management of an organisation wants coverage for the inauguration of a new factory; the editorial flatteringly reports on the organisation, its products, its new factory, prospects, employment ambitions and so on. All around the article, advertisements from the suppliers of the new factory, such as the builders, professional advertisers, suppliers of raw material, etc. are printed. This indicates the clear difference between an editorial and an advertorial.

The editorial is written by a journalist from the newspaper and the advertisements are sold separately by advertisement sales people. If editorial matter is handled by a journalist, the advertising manager deals with advertisement. Both have different approaches in the newspaper world.

LETTER TO THE EDITOR

Every newspaper reserves one page called the editorial page or opinion page to voice not only its own views and opinions, but also the opinions of readers in the shape of Letters to the Editor, byline articles, etc. Letters to the editor touch a variety of subjects and offer an opportunity to ordinary citizens to give their views freely. Public relations managers can also introduce such a column in the house magazines enabling the employees to express their views, besides writing to the newspapers in the form of 'Letter to Editor' if any problem of the organisation is raised.

Feedback

Letters to the various newspapers are read with interest, provided they are crisp and written interestingly. They express the views of the readers and help the government and institutions know the defects in their policies or implementation, and correct them. These letters, therefore, are useful not only in formulating and modifying the policies of organisations but also in their implementation. Reaction of the readers, as published in the newspapers, is one of the sources of public opinion. The Letters to the Editor may conveniently be termed as *feedback* for the managements and to read the pulse of the public. The column is also seen as a safety valve for those who are agitated due to injustice done to them and to ventilate their grievances.

The humble letter may seem a quaint channel of communication but there are a plenty of reasons for writing such letters to editors. A covering letter that attaches a news item can serve several purposes:

- It reminds the editor of who the sender is, and his or her reputation as a source of 'good stories' well researched and written. This can be an aid to the digestion of what follows. Newspapers can carry investigative stories based on a single letter.
- It can be the means of developing the contact further, by sketching possible future contact, availability of more or different material, forthcoming events, and so on.

Letters can also be used to raise editorial ideas suited to the editor's particular publication. These 'query letters' have to provide something new, which in practice usually means a creative use of available resources, provide interest, be highly specific to the readers' interests, offer a choice of alternative treatments and establish both credentials and credibility. They are used to 'sell' ideas, in particular, for articles and reader competitions.

The letters are an outstanding means of putting across an opinion, comment, fact or rebuttal in a part of the newspaper or magazine that has proven high readership. Most editors encourage letters and such letters generate awareness and understanding. The only problem is that they can be subjected to substantial editing, to fit the available space, so what needs to be said has to be expressed economically to ensure that the message appears unaltered.

Grievances

Public relations can make use of this column in two ways: by understanding the grievances of the customers as ventilated through the letter and the public relations manager can also write a letter to the editor after the grievance is redressed. For example, most of the grievances relating to problems such as drinking water supply, drainage, garbage, stray dog nuisance, street lighting, etc. are highlighted in the form of Letters to the Editor. It offers a good opportunity to public relations of any Municipal Corporation not only to redress such problems, but also report back again through the same column. Such a process enhances the image and credibility of the organisation.

In Andhra Pradesh State Road Transport Corporation (APSRTC), passengers highlight their grievances through Letters to the Editor. Public relations department, with the assistance of Depot Managers, takes early action on such complaints. Such early action on the complaints and the prompt replies given to the passengers through the letters to the Editor column has resulted in gaining the confidence of media and passengers that APSRTC cares for passengers' grievances. As a result, the quantum of adverse remarks in the press on bus operations in Andhra Pradesh came down.

MEASUREMENT OF MEDIA COVERAGE

Publicity placement through media release is one of public relations tactics, where size does not matter. What you are actually looking for in placement results are quality (publications hit), content (important messages retained in the printed stories) and feedback (media follow-up calls or customer orders). You need this information to make your internal and external public happy.

There was a time when a stack of clips resulting from a news release, press conference or other event was sufficient evidence for the management to think that public relations managers were doing their job. And, even today, quantity is sometimes confused with quality. What about your intended message? With publicity being an uncontrolled form of communication, it is crucial for public relations manager to analyse not only the content of each press release placement, but also feedback.

With persuasion the usual goal of public relations writing, you must research your results in that light: who reads your material? Were attitudes changed? Did you convince people to come to your event? Did your publicity help swing attitude change towards your service? Is there a better understanding of your organisation's goals? You get the picture through measurement.

Now, what about putting "rupee values on placement results". One argument goes something like this: "Since everyone knows public relations is akin to a third-party endorsement because it appears as news, you should be able to devise a formula that takes into consideration what space would cost were you to buy it, and then multiply that cost by a factor that would give you a nice, tidy rupee figure to show your management. Space won't permit an in-depth discussion of the rupee value debate, but suffice it to say a number of very successful, ethical and well meaning firms have conjured up such formulas. Perhaps the best analysis of placement value was summarised in *Public Relations Voice* article. "The effectiveness (of public relations) cannot be measured at the end if you don't determine the objective in the beginning". Objective is a prerequisite for measuring results.

POINTS TO REMEMBER

1. Newspapers as the most potent, versatile and resilient of all communication media are highly useful in public relations to reach the literate public. Messages communicated through newspapers can change the attitudes of the people.

2. While discussing the significance of the press, the Emperor of France Napoleon Bonaparte once said "Four hostile newspapers are more to be feared than a thousand bayonets". Press is also called the Fourth Estate of the realm, next to executive, legislature and judiciary. As such the newspapers assume the same importance that of other estates have.

3. As the newspapers are the prime source of news, views and current affairs and they inform, educate and entertain people, public relations makes use of the press as its media for communication. Press acts as a 'bridge' between an organisation and its internal and external publics.

4. The press tactics through which messages are communicated cover press release, press interview, press conference, press tour, feature article, letter to the editor, rejoinder, press photographs, fact-sheet, backgrounder, press kit, advertorial, press advertising, etc.

5. Complaints from journalist against public relations managers include: Public relations manager tries to colour the news, suppress free flow of legitimate news, public relations manager is not free to select news of readers interest, public relations press releases are boss oriented, public relations managers give only positive news, suppressing news of negative nature.

6. A good press release has three parts: (i) the heading; (ii) the lead; and (iii) the body of the story in an inverted pyramid style. The lead must reflect five Ws and one H.

7. A press conference is a media event at which the CEOs announce important news of public interest to the journalists. It is a staged forum in which journalists listen to the presentations made by organisations. In other words, a press conference is all about

presenting news to the presenters (media) who will then present to the readers.

8. A successful press conference is based on certain key factors; such as the purpose of the conference; venue, the date, day and time; invitation; statement of spokesperson; question and answers session and follow-up to measure the press conference.

9. A press tour is defined as an organised visit of selected media persons to a project for an on the spot study and reporting.

10. An embargo is a deliberate request at the top of the press release, requesting the editor that the content of the press release should not be published before a stated date and time.

11. A press kit is a set of package—press material for use by the journalists. Its contents include an agenda, a press release, fact-sheet, a copy of the photograph, CD, corporate profile, a writing pad and pen.

12. An advertorial is a paid form of editorial matter. It is an advertisement presented in an editorial format.

13. Letters to editor offer an opportunity to citizens to ventilate their views freely and reflect public opinion in general. Public relations must identify the customers grievances as pointed out in the letter to the editor column.

14. Media coverage of the organisation published in the shape of news, features can be measured in terms of column centimetres and positioning of the news in the newspaper.

REVIEW QUESTIONS

1. Press as the 'Fourth Estate' of the realm is the most potent versatile and resilient medium of public relations. Discuss?

2. Explain the various written tactics used in the practice of public relations as part of media relations.

3. What are the complaints of journalists about public relations professionals' press releases?

4. How would you write a good press release?

5. Prepare a checklist for an effective news release.

6. What are the logistics of organising a successful press conference? Explain the benefits of press conference for a public relations manager?

7. What is a press tour? How does it differ from a press conference?

8. What is an embargo?

9. Why should we have press kit? Describe its contents.

10. Define advertorial? How does it differ from advertisement?

11. What is the significance of a Letters to the Editor? Why should public relations manager write letters to the editor ?

12. Some organisations want to measure their media coverage. How can we best give our managements some kind of rupee value analysis of media placement success?

Electronic Media—Radio and Television

CONTENTS

- Radio
- Future of Radio
- Writing for Radio
- Television
- Infotainment
- Writing for Television

RADIO

Radio, in the Indian context, as a means of mass communication is the most popular medium for it has wider reach in rural India. Perhaps a unique feature that makes radio different from all other media of mass communication and particularly of special interest to public relations professionals is that it is not only the cheapest, but also an instantaneous medium. The radio is described as an 'Electronic Magic Carpet' that carries messages around the world with lightning speed. It is also called the music box.

Immediate announcements can be made on the radio. For example, in 1969 a rumour was spread that Osmansagar Lake, 20 km west of Hyderabad had breached. People panicked and ran helter skelter. At that point of time, All India Radio, Hyderabad announcement that it was only a rumour and that Osmansagar was intact, saved the people. Similarly, the end of Second World War in 1945 was announced by BBC which was a great relief to humanity all over the world. Local radio stations have further increased the value of this medium and messages are intended for specific local area audience. The commercial radio programmes also give fillip to public relations in sponsorships.

FUTURE OF RADIO

History

Lee De Forest an American became the Father of radio communication when he succeeded in communicating the human voice through the wireless. However, it was only in 1920 that the first radio programme was broadcasted in England by the Marconi Company. Radio broadcasting started in India in the early 1920s. In 1923 the first programme was broadcasted by the Radio Club of Bombay. This was followed by setting up a broadcasting service in 1927 with two privately owned transmitters at Bombay and Calcutta. The then Viceroy, Lord Irwin inaugurated the first radio station in Bombay on 23 July, 1927 which marked the beginning of regular broadcasting service in India. The Indian broadcasting service which started two radio stations went into liquidation in March 1930. After liquidation, broadcasting in India came under direct control of Government of India from 1 April, 1930 with the formation of the Indian State Broadcasting Service (ISBS). In 1936, the ISBS was given its present name All India Radio, when Delhi station went on air. In 1947, when India became independent All India Radio inherited only six radio stations—Delhi, Calcutta, Bombay, Madras, Lucknow and Tiruchy. When the princely states were merged with the Indian union, the radio stations at Hyderabad, Aurangabad, Mysore, Trivandrum and Baroda were taken over by All India Radio. In 1957, All India Radio adopted its present Hindi name *Aakashwani*. By 2012, All India Radio's network comprised 277 stations and 431 transmitters which provide radio coverage to 99.16 per cent of the population and reach 92 per cent area of the country.

Characteristics

An authority on broadcast media who has written much on this subject gave radio's universality, contemporaneous and direct and individual appeal as its unusual characteristics. Radio is basically an audio medium which influences the human mind with the aid of ear. Radio has the intimacy of human voice which attracts listeners to hear voices with emotional impact. It has also become an interactive medium with phone-in-programme which enables to get immediate feedback. Being portable, a radio can be listened anywhere—home, office or factory.

All India Radio Services

The services of All India Radio can be classified into five categories as:

1. The National Service (Programmes emanating from Delhi)
2. The Regional Service (Catering to major linguistic groups from States and Union Territories)

3. The Local Service (Local FM radio stations/community radio to cater to the interests of local population)
4. The Vividh Bharati Service (Light entertainment, film music)
5. The External Service (like BBC, Radio Moscow); the External Services Division broadcasts to over 100 countries, projecting India's culture, in 27 languages
6. DTH Service (it is a satellite channel service with digital quality covering the entire country and neighbouring countries. DTH is a 24-hour service broadcast digitally)

Programme Pattern

The programme pattern of All India Radio (AIR) is based on three major components: (i) Entertainment, (ii) Information, (iii) Education. In fact, radio plays an important role in creating people's awareness about national policies and programmes by providing information, education and entertainment. The programme pattern can be classified as follows:

1. Music—folk music, classical, devotional, film music, Light music, Western music.
2. Spoken word programme: talks, symposium of poets, farm and home, interviews, specialised audience programmes on youth, children, women, industrial workers, family welfare, health, tribal, religious.
3. News and current affairs.
4. Commercials, FM channels of private companies, carry mostly entertainment and commercial programmes without much relevance to economic development.

PR Opportunities

The radio understandably provides ample opportunities and wide scope for public relations coverage. Various types of programmes broadcasted by All India Radio can be advantageously utilised by public relations managers in projecting the services of various organisations as related to specific audience. Public relations managers particularly government and public sector undertakings can send news releases direct to News Services Division of All India Radio for broadcast purpose. There are two types of new bulletins: *national ones,* which report major national and international news; and regional ones, mostly from States' Capitals which report regional and national news.

Opportunities for public relations include: (i) news bulletins; (ii) field taped interviews; (iii) studio interviews, discussions, talks; (iv) interactive phone-in-programmes; (v) sponsored serials; (vi) specialised audience programme on women, children; (vii) *Yuva vani*—youth programmes; (viii) educational broadcast; (ix) development broadcast; (x) radio news-reels; (xi) commercial advertisements; (xii) public service announcements promoting public causes, such as health and civic programme; (xiii) radio newsreels; (xiv) current affairs; (xv) audio news release.

In order to make use of opportunities available in radio, public relations managers are expected to know the variety of programmes being broadcast by All India Radio, private FM channels and AIR FM Rainbow Channel.

Public relations managers depending on the nature of the organisation they work in and the target audience, must fit in their messages into the specific radio programmes for influencing the people. Those working in Government and development departments can make use of farm and home, and also specialised audience programmes to convey development information. The News Services Division of All India Radio broadcasts a series of special programmes under the title "*Kahiye Mantriji*" in Hindi and "Tell us Minister" in English which are based on interviews with various Central Ministers.

With the advent of television, the popularity of radio lessened mostly in urban India. But it will not lose its premier position as a source of information nor will it ever be out of advertiser's media plans. It will continue to be the most relied medium. With the expansion of FM radio network, and the concept of local radio, it will be more popular as an area specific infotainment medium.

FM Service

In view of the superior quality of FM broadcasts, radio programmes are gaining popularity in the country. All India Radios' FM channel is named 'FM Rainbow' and other private stations are Radio Mirchi, Radio City. FM Gold channel of AIR, as a niche infotainment medium with 30 per cent news and current affairs and 70 per cent entertainment, has become popular.

Impact

Public relations should use radio to inform, educate, entertain and motivate people towards organisational goals and programmes. Such programmes must not only influence people's mind, but also be able to create an impact for action.

Green Revolution

Here is an interesting example of the impact of radio. A new variety of paddy popularised through the radio station is called 'Radio Rice' in

Thanjavur District of Tamil Nadu and it is not known by its genetic or marketing name. In Jalandhar district, a survey indicated that farmer families listen carefully to the price bulletins, weather forecasts, new agricultural practices and eagerly await the latest information from radio on high yielding varieties of seed, pesticides, etc. In fact, the credit for bringing 'Green Revolution', making India self-sufficient in food grains goes to All India Radio.

The author made a survey of three villages in Nalgonda district of Andhra Pradesh in 1992 to know the various sources of public information in rural India on government policies and programmes. Among the formal sources of information, All India Radio stood first in disseminating official information to 23 per cent of beneficiaries. About 45 per cent of the households in the cluster villages—Shali Gowraram, Shali Lingotam and Gurijala in Nalgonda district had radio sets.

In the 1970s, the Municipal Corporation of Hyderabad had launched a campaign "We have a beautiful city: Let's keep it clean" under which slum improvement scheme was taken up. Every sixth person in Hyderabad was a slum dweller. As part of multi-media public relations campaign, All India Radio, Hyderabad organised a unique programme "Radio Visits Slums". A team of AIR officials visited slums and recorded the views of Municipal Councillors and slum dwellers on the problems in slum areas. Municipal Officials were interviewed to project the corporation's efforts to solve the problems and grievances. AIR broadcast four different types of programmes, such as straight talks, panel discussions, face-to-face interview with slum dwellers. This had tremendous effect on both the Municipal officials and the slum dwellers as through this programme, a single platform was created to understand both parties problems. These studies indicate that the radio in our country has a bright future.

Audience Research

Audience Research Unit, AIR, provides research inputs for producing effective and listener friendly programmes by studying the target audience, their needs, tastes, preferences, etc. In order to gauge the popularity of the programmes, AIR carries out countrywide listenership surveys, which help the Marketing Division in selling airtime. The Audience Research Unit of DG, AIR has also launched impact studies sponsored by State Governments' departments. Some of the major studies taken by Audience Research Unit include: radio programme listenership study at 63 places across the country, radio programme listenership study on commercial broadcasting service; survey on Mass Media support to agriculture extension broadcast; survey on FM channels of AIR and analysis of listeners.

Community Radio Stations

The Government of India has decided to permit the establishment of community radio stations in our country. This is a major step in the expansion of radio broadcasting for the benefit of any community. It also creates a bright future for broadcasting in India.

Though community radio gained momentum in the West as an alternative to public and commercial radio in the late 1970s, it is a new concept in India. Tabing (2002) defines a community radio station as "one that is operated in the community, for the community, about the community and by the community". The community can be territorial or geographical—a township, a village or island and can also be a group of people with common interests who are not necessarily living in one defined territory. The community radio, as such, may be owned and managed by one group or by combined groups. It could also be controlled and run by people, such as women's organisation, children, farmers, fisher folk, educational institution, ethnic groups.

Community radio is thus characterised by public participation in production and decision-making management by listeners, and its operations rely mainly on the community owned resources. This involvement of community members distinguishes community radio from the dominant State controlled or commercial stations that are operated for profit or public service. Community radio is one of the best ways to reach excluded or marginalised communities and in giving them a voice that matters most in communication for social change.

India

Community radio stations are working in many countries such as USA, Australia, Latin America, Canada, Europe, Sri Lanka, etc. In India, non-profit development organisations campaigned for more than 10 years for the right to set up low-cost local radio broadcasting facilities to support their community development work. Similarly, educational institutions demanded that they may be permitted to launch community radio stations for educating the student community. In 2005, the Union Cabinet finally cleared the community radio policy for educational purposes. As a result, in 2005, the Anna University in Tamil Nadu established the first community radio station in India. In 2007, Sri Venkateswara Oriental College, Tirupathi in Andhra Pradesh established another community FM Radio Station.

The community radio centres started in India, among others, include: Kutch Mahila Vikas Sangathan (KMVS); Community radio project Ujas at Bhuj (Gujarat); the Deccan Development Society's Community Radio Project at Pastapur (Medak district, Andhra Pradesh); the Namma Dhwani, the Community Radio Project at Budikote village (Karnataka); and Radio Alkal in Trivandrum. Community Radio centres were also set up at five places in the North Eastern India to serve the local tribal population. As per the policy guidelines for setting up Community Radio Stations in India, framed by Ministry of Information and Broadcasting, Government of India, the community radio stations should serve a specific well-defined local community.

The key objectives of the community radio programme are:

- To enable the local people to produce locally the need-based programmes
- To build expertise among the rural people to speak about their issues affecting their lives
- To rejuvenate local art forms and culture

The area of operation is 5 km, and this facility is likely to be extended to NGOs also. Community radio brightens the prospects of radio listening in India with specific areas and audiences.

Reminder Medium

When radio came into being, people thought it would kill the print medium. Similarly, it was felt that television would kill radio. However, television did not kill radio. No medium can kill the other medium. Each medium has its own merits and demerits. Former Director-General, Doordarshan, Shashikant Kapoor once said "Television is a girl friend and Radio is the wife". Radio may never acquire its pre-television eminence in the Indian media scene as the most popular mass medium, nor will it acquire the kind of glamour and glitter of the visual electronic medium. But radio will never lose its premier position as a source of information or be out of public relations' and advertisers' media plans. In fact, it will continue to be the most relied 'Reminder Medium', and also marketing and public relations medium. The concept of local radio stations with FM facility became area specific, and *infotainment medium* with widespread network in urban and rural India. As a result, the importance of radio has gone high with local and area specific programmes very akin to the local people. Radio will survive in India as it survived elsewhere. Like area specific editions of newspapers, each district in India may soon have a local radio station. As a result of keen competition between FM radio operators and expansion of local radio stations, the radio in India is being rediscovered.

Digital

Digital radio further gives fillip to a very promising future for a medium that still commands vast audience throughout the country. It promises a surge of new interest for it eliminates, truthfully, the irritating interference that can hinder reception and provides automatic tuning and a leap in sound quality. As of today, about 7 per cent of time is devoted to rural programmes, hence there is a demand for launching a separate rural channel by All India Radio.

WRITING FOR RADIO

Writing for radio requires a distinct style as compared to writing for newspapers. The basic difference between the two is that if writing for radio appeals to the ear, newspaper writing is for the eye. A broadcast copy must attract the attention of the listener through both sound and word symbolism. A public relations manager is required to write for radio talks, radio news, panel discussions, radio interviews, etc. He or she must be conversant with the broad principles of writing for the radio.

Conversational Style

The radio is an audio medium where the message is heard rather than read as in the case of print medium. It is a conversation between two individuals, the presenter and the listener. Therefore, the writing style for radio is conversational as if one were conversing with another individual.

Spoken Language

In our real life, we communicate with each other either orally or by writing letters. When we speak or talk our speech is direct, short, crisp and to the point. We do not use long, and complicated sentences. Contrarily, when we write for the print medium long and ornate sentences are used. We also take full care of grammar. So when writing for radio one must use spoken language.

Easy to Listen Formula

According to Dr. I.F. Fang, any sentence that has more than 30 syllables is not easy to comprehend when you hear it. For this count of syllables, he categorised words based on the number of syllables they contained. Words with three syllables are acceptable and those with four and above are relatively harder to understand. As such one has to write in easy to listen formula. Sentences, therefore, should be short and simple.

Testing Copy

Broadcast copy is written to be read and the only way to test how it will sound is to read it aloud. A sentence that looks fine on paper may turn out to be too long to read smoothly, perhaps may be a tongue-twister, or may even mislead the listener. After writing one should always read the copy.

Figures

Numbers are difficult to follow and remember more so when they are heard and not seen. In writing for radio, one must use round figures. For example, the statement that the Government has allotted ten crore rupees is the correct format for easy listening. One should not write ten crore, fifty lakhs and five thousand rupees. Percentages should be converted into fractions, e.g. 25 per cent becomes one fourth, 50 per cent a half. Dates should be written as they are read.

It is better to spell out numbers from one to eleven as these can get lost in the copy, while numerals from 12 to 99 will do as these are easy to read. One should always spell out words such as thousands, lakhs, crores.

Honorifics

We use the honorific Mr., Mrs. in English and Shri and Shrimati in Hindi and other Indian languages. It is correct to say President Bush or President Pratibha Patil instead of the more formal President Mrs. Pratibha Patil. The designation always precedes the name and in case the designation is used as an attribute or adjective, the definite article is omitted. Dead persons are mentioned without any honorific—Jawaharlal Nehru and not Mr. Jawaharlal Nehru.

Abbreviations

Abbreviations are best avoided in writing for radio and a word should be written the way one wants it to be read. Lieutenant Governor helps the news reader and not Lt. Governor. However, acronyms such as UNICEF, SAARC, UNO, which are familiar to listeners and pronounced as a word can be used. If one has to use an abbreviation, the best way is to spell out the full name. The World Trade Organisation and then WTO, so that the listener gets the hang of it.

Dateline

In newspapers, the dateline of a story is given at the beginning and there is a frame of reference. In radio, however, there is neither a dateline nor a frame of reference. The dateline or the place and date of the occurrence of an event have to be included in the story. The US President, now on a visit to India arrived in New Delhi today. Instead of using a.m. or p.m. say this afternoon or last evening.

Language

The language has to be conversational and of a kind which the average listener understands. It should be easy on the ear, intelligible and yet elegant enough to hold the listener's interest. The choice of words should be precise and shorn of verbiage. Unwieldy words and phrases should give way to a vocabulary that corresponds to the one used in conversation. For example, male, female are used in formal language but man, woman are mentioned in conversational style.

Pronouns

Repeated use of pronoun for a particular noun also confuses the listener. Mohammad Hamid Ansari, the common candidate of the United Progressive Alliance and the Left Parties was on Friday declared elected as the country's new Vice President (2007). Instead of using, the pronoun 'he' in further statement, a better way of doing the story will be to alternate the name, the designation.

Tense

A certain amount of grammatical liberty is allowed in writing for radio. Instead of the correct language "India was committed", one can say, "The Prime Minister said 'India is committed to a peaceful nuclear policy'". In broadcasting, the present tense is the most engaging tense, since it shows an immediacy. For example, police are searching for clues is acceptable. But mixing of tenses is not advisable.

Mispronunciation

A mispronunciation or the use of wrong word can cause utmost and irreparable damage. The impact is instantaneous. Therefore, care should be taken to use appropriate words and correct pronunciation to avoid bad impression on the listener.

Typing

All broadcast stories are typed in triple space and written on the one side of the page. Such typing is not only clearer but also leaves room for corrections. Wide margins are best because they make the copy stand out. The golden rule is not to split words at the end of a line and never to split a sentence at the end of the page.

TELEVISION

The word 'television' is a combination of Greek and Latin expressions. The Greek word 'tele' means at a distance, while the word 'vision' comes from the Latin 'video', which means 'I see'. In other words, television is distance seeing.

Television is described as an electronic system of transmitting transient images or moving objects together with sound over a wire or through space by apparatus that converts them into visible light rays and audible sound.

Evolution

Television belongs to electronic medium which has the characteristics of vision, sound, movement and colour. Television (Doordarshan) made its beginning in India on 15 September 1959 when an experimental pilot television centre was established in New Delhi to transmit educational and development programmes. A major landmark was the introduction of colour television in 1982 with Indian Satellite coinciding with the 9th Asian Games held in New Delhi that ushered in a major revolution in broadcasting in the country. Private TV channels also entered the Indian scene in the 1990s. Over 800 channels are present in India having great impact on the Indian mind. Television has become the primary source of information. Though television in India is mostly an urban phenomenon, it has been brought within reach of those who cannot afford sets, by means of community television viewing.

Characteristics

As the message of television influences the human mind through eyes and ears, it is categorised as an audio-visual medium. It has the double impact of both sight and sound.Television has the strongest emotional impact of all the media. Its sound and sight power makes programmes more close to the viewers and influence better than radio or press.

Television always presents reality as things cannot be hidden from the television camera. A lion on TV screen is shown as a real lion with its majesty and colour. The strengths of television among others, include; high impact on the audience, audience selectivity; fast awareness; sponsorship availability.

Mixed Media

The greatest characteristic of television is that it combines in itself the media of sound, sight and colour. In fact, television may be called as a mixed medium for it blends and synthesis the advantages of many creative media, such as the printed word, the spoken word, the motion picture, slides, music, dance, drama, colour, animation and sound—'all in one'. Phone-in-programme technique made television as an interactive medium. Educational programmes of various Universities broadcasted are also now interactive.

Receptive Audience

While not as captive as a cinema audience, the television audience is always found in relaxed and receptive mood for a specific programme. The audience being ready to watch a programme becomes unconscious participants in the television communication process.

PR Medium

Television, the most modern mass medium offers some of the effective channels for public relations. Its enormous reach and speed have revolutionised the powers of transmitting and interpreting information 24 hours a day. As a public relations medium, television is fast becoming one of the most important outlets. It provides public relations departments with excellent opportunities for channelling information to people in specific areas and sometimes to the national audience where the general people interest is involved. Television offers opportunities for both advertising and non-advertising communication messages, and, therefore, has become a vehicle of public relations communication. Most of public relations firms maintain a list of television specialists for their clients. Television has played an important role in many public relations or corporate advertising programmes. For example, Pulse Polio Immunisation Programme had big support from Doordarshan. Osmania University celebrated the 75th anniversary in 1995, when TV gave its full support by telecasting its progress. Kheda District in Gujarat which is the birth place of white revolution, the farmers there were educated only through television.

Doordarshan: Programme Pattern

Doordarshan which is a part of Prasar Bharati (Broadcasting Corporation of India), an autonomous body, is a public service broadcaster regarded as one of the largest television networks in the world. It operates 31 TV channels besides free-to-air DTH service. DD-National is the largest terrestrial network in the world covering about 92 per cent population and 82% land area of the country.

Free-to-Air

Doordarshan provides the free-to-air DTH service (KU-brand), "DD Direct +" in the country. This was launched primarily for providing TV coverage to the areas uncovered by terrestrial transmission. DD News, DD Sports, DD Bharati (Art and Culture), DD India (International Channel), DD Commercial are a few important channels to quote.

As many as 11 regional language satellite service and regional state networks function to meet the needs of various linguistic groups, such as Telugu, Malayalam, Bengali, Gujarati, Tamil, etc. DD Bharati, for example, telecasts programmes on children, health, music, dance, and heritage. DD India acts as a chief window to the world especially for the Indian diaspora to witness the Indian social, cultural, political and economic scene.

Development Communication Division (DCD)

The Development Communication Division was established in Doordarshan to cater to the communication needs of government departments. It serves as a single window facility for programme production, generation of creative media planning and implementation for public sector. It has undertaken several media campaigns in accordance with the requirements of government departments and ministries. The campaign *'Kalyani'* on behalf of the Health and Family Welfare Ministry was a popular series to educate people on health care. DCD launched and completed 95 campaigns across the country in 2010.

Both private television channels and Doordarshan channels reach a large section of society with a variety of programmes. In fact, if one wants to know about any country and its people, then that country's television programmes must be watched because they reflect the people and culture of that particular country. Such is the importance of television as a medium of communication. In view of its importance and reach, public relations managers make use of television to *inform, educate* and *entertain* people.

Six Ways to Use TV

To a public relations manager, television provides the tactics for reaching the target audience with various public relations messages. A public relations manager must see the 'Programme Guide to Television' published in a newspaper to understand the types of subjects telecasted. A public relations manager must fit the organisational views into the television programme pattern so as to reach the target audience. However, there are five ways in which a public relations manager can fit an organisation's news, views and programmes on television.

1. **News:** The first approach is to make use of news channel both at national and regional level. A copy of the media release being sent to the print media can be released to the television channels, if necessary with a photograph. Another method of using news channel is to produce a video news release for immediate use by

television. Transnational channels like BBC can also be used for international or global news.

2. **Events coverage:** The second approach is a media advisory announcing the event that is to take place in the organisation, e.g. anniversary celebrations. Such an advice will enable television to cover the event and telecast the same programme. This would also cover field visits by television stations.

3. **Documentary films:** The third approach is to provide documentary films produced on an organisation to television studios for telecast on behalf of government departments, public sector undertakings, community organisations and charitable institutions. For example, documentaries such as "Dreams of Rabindranath" or a biographical film on R.K. Narayanan, produced by the Films Division were shown on television channels also.

4. **Products and Services:** A public relations manager can disseminate information on corporate mission, programmes, products, public causes, services of an organisation in the shape of talks, panel discussions, interviews or sponsored programmes and public service announcements.

5. **Commercial service:** Advertisements are telecasted in the form of television commercial. Public relations can supplement public relations programmes with commercial ads.

6. **TV monitoring:** PR manager can analyse TV programmes which reflect the pulse of the peoples' reactions, needs and aspirations. Such feedback will be useful to the organisations to adjust their policies.

Impact

Television in India, Doordarshan in particular, has created great impact on the Indian mind towards socio-economic development of the country. It had played a vital role in Green Revolution (self sufficiency in food grains), White Revolution (milk production), health care, etc. The Satellite Instructional Television Experiment (SITE) in 1975–1976 aimed to broadcast directly to satellite receiving dishes in 2400 villages to improve rural primary school education, teaching, training, agriculture, health and nutritional practices and contribute to family planning and national integrity. Another pioneering experiment in using television for educational purposes in India was Kheda Communication Project (1975–1985). It promoted rural development and social change at the grassroots level. *Hum Log* was India's first long running soap opera which utilised the entertainment-cum-education strategy to promote social themes as gender equality, small family size and national integration. Similarly, *Ramayana* and *Mahabharat*—the two great epics telecasted in the 1980s by Doordarshan had a great impact on the Indian society.

Tata Nano ₹ one lakh car was popularised among others through TV channels as a small car within the reach of ordinary people. It secured significant national media coverage, demonstrating its key feature as a cheap and small car.

Audience Research

The Audience Research wing of Doordarshan conducted an evaluative study on the narrowcast agriculture programme. It also assesses the performance of different programmes of Doordarshan channel to know their impact on the society. The unit manned by professional researchers has 19 field units all over the country for research studies.

INFOTAINMENT

Media basically has four-fold functions; to inform, to interpret, to educate and to entertain. Of late, a new term **infotainment** has been coined which is a blend of information plus entertainment for sustaining the attention of the audience. Both the content and presentation of the infotainment today pervades electronic media news and current affairs and much of the printed media. This trend seems to be that people not only sustain serious matter for long but also assimilate the message when information is mixed with entertainment. Public relations must adopt this theory in conveying messages mixed with entertainment for better understanding, both in urban and rural areas.

WRITING FOR TELEVISION

Two Approaches

There are two approaches to get PR news stories broadcast in local TV or Radio Stations:

- First, you can send to the TV station the same press release that you send to the local print media. The news unit of TV station will edit the release and broadcast.
- The second approach is to write and produce a video news release (VNR) as an audio news release and send it to TV station for immediate use. For example, the best way to launch a new product is to produce a VNR and promote the product through TV network.

Another important thing that PR manager has to consider is while writing for broadcast media, one has to keep the two target audience in view—One who reads your copy (announcer) and the second is listener or viewer.

Broadcast style of writing applies to both radio and television. But the television is an audio-visual medium. Over the television, you not only listen but also see the visuals. A distinguishing feature of television writing is that the message is both heard and seen. If the listener is the 'kingpin' in radio, the viewer is the master for television writing. Like radio, television writing also adopts the conversational style of communication. Therefore, short sentences in active voice, without complex words and expression are the ideal way to follow in television writing. Easy to listen formula and conversational style are best suited for this medium. The visuals which are commonly called graphics are shown on the screen along with the narration by the presenter.

Here are certain tips:

- If it is necessary to use a person's designation in a story, let the title precede the name. The Union Minister for Home Sushil Kumar Shinde.
- Time is the essence in TV. A newspaper can add more space, if there is more news. In broadcast style, the newscast has 30, 15, 10 or 5 minutes. Writing should be in tune with the time constraint.
- Use numbers infrequently and write them out in words.
- Instead of using a.m. or p.m. write this afternoon or last evening.
- In typing, don't split words between lines and don't split sentences between pages. Either way, it may cause embarrassing mistakes when being read on the air.
- Don't begin with prepositional phrases or with clauses. By the time your listener gets to the end, he/she may have forgotten the beginning.
- Subjects and verbs should be close together. The best sentence structure is subject-verb-object
- Don't use abbreviations unless you want your copy to be read on the air as an abbreviation, e.g., UNO.
- Avoid making value judgements in your writing. Avoid such words as "beautifully cleverer, etc".

POINTS TO REMEMBER

Radio

1. Radio is basically an audio medium which influences the human mind through the sensory organ—the ear.

2. The programme pattern of All India Radio has three major components: (i) entertainment, (ii) information, (iii) education.

3. Radio offers several opportunities or tactics to public relations manager for conveying messages to the target audience. Such

public relations opportunities include: news bulletins, current affairs, talks, panel discussions, audio news releases, sponsored serials, studio interviews, newsreels, public service announcements.

4. Radio as a mass medium has a great impact on the Indian mind. All India Radio must be proud of its role played in ushering Green Revolution in India by which we attained self-sufficiency in food production.

5. Radio may never acquire its pre-eminence on the Indian media scene as a most popular mass medium. But radio also will never lose its premier position as a source of information or be out of public relations and advertiser's media plan. The concept of local radio stations with FM facility and community radio scheme, the medium of radio has been rediscovered and it became area specific infotainment medium with widespread network in both urban and rural India.

6. Digital radio gave further fillip to a very promising future for radio that still commands vast audience throughout India.

7. There is a demand for launching a separate rural channel of All India Radio to meet the growing communication needs of rural folk. As such a bright future beckons for radio in India.

8. Radio writing demands a distinct style as compared to writing for newspapers. Writing for radio must be on the principle 'easy to listen formula' and in conversational style. Unwieldy words and phrases should give way to vocabulary that corresponds to the one used everyday in conversation.

Television

9. Programme pattern of television covers subjects such as news, current affairs, education, science, women and child welfare, youth programmes, health and family welfare, agriculture, public service broadcasting.

10. Opportunities for public relations in the medium of television include: news, talks, panel discussions, studio interviews, documentary films, specialised audience programmes (business, farming, women), public service announcements, phone-in-programme, etc.

11. Television, Doordarshan in particular, has created great impact on the Indian mind towards socio-economic development of the country. It had played significant role in green revolution, white revolution, health education, social development, etc. For example, *Hum Log* India's first long running soap opera with entertainment-cum-education strategy promoted social justice

such as gender equality, small family norm, and national integration.

12. Infotainment is a term coined to denote information as well as entertainment for sustaining the attention of the audience.

13. A distinguishing feature of television writing is that message is 'heard and seen'. Like radio, television writing also adopts conversational style of communication and easy-to-listen formula. The visuals get priority in television writing.

REVIEW QUESTIONS

1. Discuss the characteristics, advantages and limitations of radio as a medium of mass communication. Explain its uses in public relations.

2. Why is radio called ubiquitous and influential medium in the context of rural India?

3. Describe the historical perspective of radio in India.

4. How do you visualise the future of radio in the wake of television in India?

5. What makes a distinguishing style of writing for radio? Cite examples.

6. What are the characteristics of television as an audio-visual medium?

7. How is television influential in the practice of public relations? List out the various tactics that are used to reach out to the target audience with messages.

8. Define infotainment.

9. Write short notes on the following:
   (a) Satellite Instructional Television Experiment
   (b) Kheda Communication Project

E-PR: IT New Mass Media

An information bomb is exploding in our midst, showering us with a shrapnel of images and drastically changing the way each of us perceives and acts upon our private world.

—Alvin Toffler

C O N T E N T S

ELECTRONIC PR

Alvin Toffler, an American futurologist and the author of *Powershift* and *Future Shock*, in his yet another book *The Third Wave* refers to three waves and the three revolutions that the world has witnessed. In the first wave, we experienced *agricultural revolution* with human and animal muscle power as living batteries for energy and interpersonal and folk media for communication, while the second wave symbolised *industrial revolution* with the steam engine for power and mass media for global communication. The third wave paved the way for *information revolution* with computer and the Internet at the centre stage.

Information Revolution

Today, information is power; we are now in the information society. Information and communication technology is the most effective instrument of public relations, influencing all segments of public, namely, shareholders, employees, customers, suppliers, general community, media public, etc. IT as new mass media offers ample opportunities for public relations to reach out the target audience which has led to E-public relations. In fact, IT new mass media Internet, website, e-mail ushered in electronic public relations. As a result of IT technology, the conventional media such as newspapers, radio, film and television turned to be the old media. IT media such as the computer, Internet, e-mail, website and social networks have became the new mass media. However, a combination of old mass media and new mass media is an ideal media strategy for effective public relations.

MICRO-COMMUNICATION

With the emergence of internet and social media, the information system has been divided into two specific areas, mass communications and micro-communications. In fact, there is a significant difference between the two, one which is made available to mass audience without two-way communication process or asymmetrical relationship between the communicator and the receiver on a mass scale and the other one which is fundamentally an interaction between two individuals, where we may have a greater degree of symmetry. Mass communications cover newspapers, television, radio, whereas the micro-communications, which are more flexible in terms of timescale, reach and influence based on one-to-one or small group conversations, belong to new media such as e-mail, blog, chat, twitter, facebook and telephone. Micro-communications is assuming great importance in public relations practice.

Social Networking

After the emergence of Internet, first generation websites came into being. The websites slowly gave birth to personal websites. Later, these personal websites became blogs. Simultaneously discussion groups started gaining importance. Blogs and discussion groups were the major social media till the middle of 2000. From 2004, social networking sites started growing. Facebook and twitter became popular among the youth because of their brevity in communication. Audio and video podcasts also grew at that time. All these became tools of micro-communication as against mass communication media—radio, television, newspapers— and established a well-knit social networking.

What is E-PR?

Practice of public relations using the new mass media—the Internet, e-mail, blog, web in the centre stage may be called e-public relations. But what exactly does that mean:

'E' is for Electronic: The 'e' in e-public relations is the same 'e' that comes before 'mail and commerce' to mean the electronic medium of the Internet. E-public relations concerns every aspect of the Internet, including e-mail systems as well as the World Wide Web (WWW).

'P' is for Public: Both internal and external publics.

'R' is for Relations: Building relations between an organisation and its audience on the Internet. Thousands of one-to-one relations can be built up simultaneously on the Internet due to its instantaneous and interactive nature.

The Internet lends e-public relations the following advantages:

- **Constant communication:** The Internet enables one to communicate with people 24 hours a day, 7 days a week and 365 days a year (24 × 7).
- **Instant response:** One can respond instantly to emerging issues via Internet.
- **Global audience:** One can communicate all over the world at no extra expense.
- **Audience feedback:** As the Internet is interactive, one can get immediate feedback from one's public on one's policies and programmes.
- **Two-way communication:** If public relations is a two-way communication process, e-public relations helps build mutual relationship with to and fro communication.
- **Cost-effective:** E-public relations is more cost-effective as there is no stationery or printing costs involved.
- **Speed:** Speed is the essence of Internet which has not only reduced distance but also converted the world into a small global village.

NEW MASS MEDIA

Internet

What is Internet? The term 'Internet' is described as the interconnection of millions of computers that are linked usually by cable, satellite, or wireless telemetry in order to receive, re-route and transmit data. Internet and World Wide Web are terms that are frequently used interchangeably, although strictly speaking the WWW is the graphical, user-friendly end of the Internet that came to the fore in the mid-1990s. However, it has mushroomed into a new and personalised media, enabling individual access via a modem to uncensored pictures, sound and text from around the world. It is a relatively inexpensive way to accumulate or distribute data to and fro around the globe. There are a number of different Internet tools and tactics that are available to the public relations manager. We have 14 crores internet connections in India (2013).

Content uncontrolled

A public relations professional should keep in mind certain facts about the Internet. A message intended for local or regional use may draw reactions as good or bad from unexpected places. Content of the Internet is virtually uncontrolled. Anyone can say or show anything without passing it through 'gatekeepers', the editors and producers who approve the material that reaches the public. Lack of editorial control not only permits unfettered freedom of speech but also leads to distribution of unconfirmed, slanted or erroneous information. Internet, which is described as one of the wonders of the world, is like AK-47 riffle in shooting information. Another negative aspect of the Internet is hostile sites set up to imitate or mimic an organisation. For example, U-Haul in the US is a company that rents transports so that people can move their home furnishing to another location or move an office. An alternative site is called U-Hell and it carries equipment and services of companies.

E-mail

E-mail is sent automatically to a large number of users or individuals through a computer (Internet) network. Electronic mail (or e-mail) was the first commercial use of the Internet and has remained its most popular function. It has two significant advantages over snail mail. The first is its speed. An e-mail can arrive within seconds of transmission. The other its cost, where it is estimated that 10,000 individuals can be contacted for the price of one postal cover. The electronic mail includes messages to individuals, newsletters to staff members, transmission of news release and pitch letters to media offices, and despatch and receipt of copy between public relations firms and clients.

Internet is being used for live chat sessions. The then Union Minister for Finance, P. Chidambaram, held a chat session for a world audience on the Internet soon after he presented his budget. That was an inexpensive and personalised way of responding to his public, the taxpaying citizens.

Intranet

Intranet is a private Internet network intended for internal communication of a company that uses the same kinds of software that one would find on the public Internet. The importance of internal communication has increased manifold with globalisation. The Intranet offers the corporation a means of communication with employees around the globe. If internal communications are normally through a site with protected access, as is currently normally the case, then it is an internal Internet site as opposed to the externally available Internet site. It is a convenient way not only to shorten the communication cycle by providing information, but also to get feedback and store and retrieve information. Intranet and internal communication go hand-in-hand.

Intranets for all intents and purposes function as Internets, but operate within the confines of a private local network. Intranets allow an organisation to have its own private 'web' of sites used only by its users. Security, target audience, e-mail, traffic, cost and a variety of mail systems are some of the added advantages of intranet.

WEBSITE

It is an area on the web (computer) where information about a particular subject or organisation can be found. The retrieval of such information is possible via a web browser. The website has become a major communication point between organisations and their publics and as such is of considerable importance to public relations practice. The website as your electronic identity has two functions: it must provide information to the visitor and the site should encourage interrelations with the visitor to promote the mutual understanding, the end product of public relations. However, the information on your site needs to be relevant, current and interesting and all about your company, products and services. The Internet being interactive must enable the people to express their opinions and reactions, which they cannot do with newspapers. You can even promote discussion groups on the Internet which will involve people on important issues. To do the job on the website effectively, you need to make sure that your site is user-friendly and trusted.

Tirumala website

Websites can be created by individuals or organisations. The example of the Tirumala Tirupathi Devasthanam (TTD) that manages the Sri Venkateswara Temple in Tirumala, Tirupathi (Andhra Pradesh) is very instructive. It has got its own website *www.tirumala.org*. The website has about 300 pages of information regarding accommodation on the hills and in the city, the various *sevas* there, services of marriages and of barbers, publications, transport, places of scenic beauty and history of every temple. Pictures of entire Tirumala Tirupathi and places of interest are available on the web. Anybody from anywhere in the world can log on to the website and view page after page of information. Therefore, a website is an important tool of public relations.

News on web

Web-based news sites are yet another category of IT new media. Many websites are extensions of a particular newspaper, magazine, radio or television station or even television network. Internet users make use of this medium as a source of news and information. News, views and articles from *The Hindu*, the national newspaper, for example, can be found on *www.thehindu.com* Public relations professionals should not neglect such sites as both media of communication and media monitoring.

Blog

What is a blog? A blog is similar to a website. A weblog, shortened to blog, is a kind of website. It permits the blogger to write web-pages (posts) and make them available for surfing. Most blogs are public, but many companies have internal blogs for employees to read, create and write. Most blogs enable readers to make comments about the blogger as part of interactive communication. A weblog also allows to embed photographs, video, voicemail and diagrams into blog posts.

Weblogs or blogs have become an integral part of the Internet. The term describes a regularly updated website that points to links on other sites and has commentaries about the links. You can create a weblog that relates to your field, say, public relations, and can attract potential audiences for your write-up. Bloggers may be amateurs or professional journalists who like to express their opinions, observations and criticism about any subject of public interest. Public relations professionals can become bloggers on behalf of their employers and clients. In the process, they (blogs) take their business message right to the public without television news network or the local newspaper.

Twitter

Twitter is a form of micro-blogging with very limited space of 140 characters for text (http://www.twitter.com). The name is derived from chirping sound of birds-twitter. The small bird creates a series of short high sounds. In the same way, twitter, as social networking, allows sending out short regular messages about what you want to say and the people can access on the internet or on their mobile phones. It has become very popular as an interactive social network.

Shashi Tharoor, former Minister of State External Affairs, landed in trouble when he used the words "he would travel cattle class in solidarity with all our holy cows" in his twitter in response to a question about the Congress austerity drive to travel by economy class. The words 'cattle class' evoked adverse response. Twitter is like a weapon that hits the target once you use the words.

WHAT IS A PODCAST?

What is a podcast? Like a radio, a podcast is an audio format embedded into a web page (typically a blog) with show notes and the means by which listeners can comment on or respond to content in the show. These radio-like audio programmes can be listened on a PC or laptop, iPod or mobile phone. The term podcast is a fusion of pod and broadcast and one can download the podcast. Podcast is a recording of a radio broadcast or a video that can be taken from the Internet.

According to a podcaster, public relations practitioner will have the following advantages:

- They allow listeners to time-shift and place-shift media consumption.
- They are easily accessible to a global audience that is not defined by geographic boundaries.
- They provide an easy access to an educated, influential audience with a high income group.
- Electronic programming can be leveraged without an outside news media filter.
- They offer a cheap medium of transmitting message through voice to the target audience.
- They form the most cost-effective electronic media distribution channel available. An advantage of podcast is that it is a useful medium for both internal and external communication.

Podcasts are offered by organisations from giants such as the BBC to Srinivasan of PR Point.com Chennai, which offer podcasting under the name 'Poduniversal', a popular medium in India.

WHAT IS A WIKI?

What is a wiki? A wiki is a website that allows any user to change or add to the information it contains. There is a wiki page hosted by the conference where you can share ideas and information. Wikis are used inside organisations to allow a group of people to create reference and edit pages to form all evolving body of knowledge for the group. Wikis have become popular for PR professionals in the West because if you want to know more about any channel for online communication, it will almost certainly be described in detail by a number of experts in 'Wikipedia.com'.

TELECONFERENCE

An important advantage of satellite communication for public relations purpose is teleconferencing, which is also called video conferencing. A teleconference is a way through which information is exchanged among people and machines remote from one another through a telecommunication system. Whether you are exchanging information, reviewing performance, checking on the progress of a project, making a presentation or discussing strategy, there is often no substitute for a face-to-face conference. Teleconference allows people in different locations within India and abroad to meet face-to-face. It is almost like being in the same room even though the participants might be in different locations hundred or even thousands of miles away.

Public relations practitioners converse with clients, suppliers and media persons. Hill and Knowlton, a PR agency in the US, arranged a two-hour conference between Cairo (Egypt) and five US investors to talk directly with high ranking Egyptian officials about private investment in Egypt. A Chief Minister in India can interact with District Collectors and District administration very frequently through video conferences, instead of asking them to come to State's capital for a conference. It is an effective tool for public relations.

A public relations practitioner can arrange a teleconference by employing the use of Doordarshan that specializes in this format. Dr. B.R. Ambedkar Open University, Hyderabad organises teleconferences for the benefit of students and general public on every Sunday between 2 p.m. and 3 p.m. from 'Saptagiri Channel', Doordarshan Kendra, Hyderabad, on different subjects such as economics, political science and public relations. "The State-of-the-Art Public Relations: Problems and Prospects" was one of the topics discussed in one of the teleconferences, in which questions were asked in an interactive session not only from India but also from other countries. Dr. B.R. Ambedkar Open University, Hyderabad, pays a sum of ₹50,000 to Doordarshan for one hour slot, which is cost-effective in reaching out students spread across the country.

In teleconferencing, groups of students or people separated as listeners by thousands of miles across the globe can interact instantaneously with strong visual impact saving time and transportation costs. Many multinational companies organise teleconferences as to interact with their employees, customers, spread across the world. Public relations firms do undertake teleconferences on behalf of their clients between one country and another. A major limitation of teleconference is that it lacks personal touch that comes from face-to-face conversation.

Web Conferencing

Another method of conferencing is through the medium of website which is otherwise called 'web conferencing'. The web is less expensive compared to teleconferencing. In web conferencing, 'See-You—See-Me' format is available. Users with web camera and microphones mounted on their computer can engage in an Internet version of videcphone.

Public relations professionals can use the web for interactive webcasts that serve for the transmission of public information. For example, a press conference might be webcast to any and all who log into the event online. The participants can ask questions from the news source during the conference by e-mail. Similarly, web seminars can be organised.

SATELLITE MEDIA TOUR

Media tour is a format of media conference in which a CEO from one location can interact with journalists stationed at different destinations. In media tours, it has been the practice that the CEO or the celebrity visits different places for press conferences. Instead of making CEO or VIP tour the country on an expensive, time-consuming promotional tour, public relations professionals can advise the managements to use the format of Satellite media tour. Such tours are very useful in times of natural calamities or in crisis situations for interacting with local media representatives.

In a satellite media tour, the CEO or VIP is stationed in a television studio and media persons interview him or her through satellite from their home studios. Two-way satellite television is used, permitting a visual dialogue. Corporations can make use of satellite media tours to promote their products or services.

Mobile Phones

Mobile phones have become very popular in India. One estimate indicates that there were over 95 crores cell phones in India in early 2013 and that this number might cross 100 crores. Mobile phone can easily be used as a tool of public relations to reach out to the target public with small messages as SMS. Cell phones enable the PR professionals to be available anytime and at any place for the purpose of communication. Professional body such as Public Relations Society of India makes use of this device to be in touch with its members for meetings or any interaction on professional matters.

Facsimile Transmission

An invaluable tool in public relations practice is facsimile transmission, commonly called Fax. Facsimile transmission moves an exact copy of printed matter and graphics by telephone circuit from a machine or computer in one office to another across town or to the other side of the world. It allows exact reproduction of the original. A press release can also be sent to media through fax. Multinational companies deliver news release electronically to a large number of newspapers and other major news media offices. Fax transmission is a tremendous time saver. Delivery is almost immediate.

VIDEO NEWS RELEASES

Audio and video news releases can be converted into an Internet format. The video news release (VNR) is produced in a format that television studios can easily use or edit based on their needs. Such tailor-made VNRs sent by public relations managers will not only be useful to television stations but also organisations get good coverage in television. Of course, they are relatively expensive to produce but they have great potential for reaching large audiences.

Mizoram

The Department of Information and Public Relations, Government of Mizoram in the North-Eastern India provides Video News releases everyday to three TV channels: (i) LPS Vision, (ii) Skylines and (iii) Zonet, which are based in the capital city Aizawl. In turn, these channels transmit these tailor-made video news releases not only to their subscribers, but also to all the local cable TV networks that spread over about 500 villages in the state. It is through these VNRs and cable TV networks that the State Information Department reaches villages 24 hours a day with government messages. Indeed, it is an effective medium of reaching the grassroots. Transmission by satellite also makes possible fast distribution of video news releases. The 'picture and voice releases' are sent primarily to cable television networks, local cable systems and local television stations for coverage.

E-JOURNALS

Online journals which are similar to e-magazines can be produced. Electronic house journals are the order of the day. Many corporations have adopted this method for reaching employees quickly.

CD-ROM

The CD-ROM (Compact Disc Read Only Memory) is the multimedia version of the familiar compact disc that plays music and contains video, audio and text on the same surface. With an enormous capacity, the CD-ROM can display up to three lakh pages of text, colour pictures and graphics. Movies can also be seen through CDs. CD-ROMs are used for retrieval of text or data to a video screen and are normally used in association with personal computers (PCs). They can also be used interactively with the Internet. CD-ROMs are used extensively because they are relatively inexpensive to hold considerable data. From CD-ROM emerged high density Digital versatile Disc (DVD) as a tool of communication.

The Internet age has brought a revolution in the practice of public relations. This revolution not only involves the way we communicate, but also the nature of communication itself. In fact, the computer and the Internet in the centre stage have affected all areas of corporate public relations, be it employees communication, media relations or crisis public relations.

Driven by what we know of global transparency and organisations' accountability, the public relations practitioner has to elevate the profession of public relations not only into the board room but also into the very heart of management. Practitioners now need to think of high quality in the practice with latest information and communication technology as in the case of e-marketing and e-governance, which resulted in e-public relations. It is through e-public relations that public relations professionals could reinvent public relations profession to meet the emerging trends in the corporate world.

Writing for Website

Diane F. Witmer in her textbook *Spinning the Web: A Handbook for Public Relations on the Internet* says, "Writing for the Web is much like any other writing project. You need to follow many of the same basic guidelines, but also be aware that the text will be read on a computer screen". Witmer gives the following 10 basic tips:

1. As with all effective public relations writing, your text must be mechanically excellent and free of any grammar, punctuation, spelling, or syntax errors.
2. Avoid 'puff' words, cliches, and exaggerations.
3. Keep the sentences short, crisp, and to the point.
4. Use active verbs and avoid passive voice.
5. Support main ideas with proper evidence.
6. Keep individual paragraphs focused on one central idea.
7. Make sure each paragraph logically follows the one before it.
8. Set the reading level appropriate to the readership; use short words and sentences for young and inexperienced readers.
9. Avoid a patronising tone by talking 'with' rather than 'at' the reader.
10. Avoid jargon, acronyms, and other specialised language that may confuse the reader.

Impact of Social Media

With the introduction of Internet, the mass media has been demassified and mass audience and mass mind also have been demassified with segmented audience. This is clearly indicated by Alvin Toffler in his book

Third Wave. It is a great challenge for public relations to move away from 'mass' and begin to think of niche audiences for effective reach and better influence. The concept of mass media has become old media. As a result, PR practitioners have now adopted fresh communication management skills in the new social media. How can social media help public relations? The Guardian's media business correspondent Katie Allen wrote a straightforward business story about world's second largest advertising group WPP. Headlined "PR industry profits boosted by MySpace phenomenon", her piece credited the popularity of social networking sites such as Facebook and MySpace with driving unusually strong growth in public relations business. Allen also quoted WPP's Sir Martin Sorrell: "Social networking seems to underline the importance of editorial publicity.... Social networking is really recommendation between people about the things that they are interested in and they like... this has stimulated people's attention in terms of the importance of PR" (David Philips, 2009). In the process, the theory of advertising, a paid form of communication, will also fall as narrated in *The Fall of Advertising and the Rise of PR* by Al Ries and Laura Ries (2002).

However, social media in India will have greater impact when the educated section makes full use of the Internet. As of (2013), 14 crores internet connections exist in India. It may take more time for social media in India to impact the entire country as Western countries, where the Internet reach is 80 per cent.

ANNA HAZARE'S CASE

When Anna Hazare launched 'Anti-corruption Movement' for introduction of Lokpal bill in the Parliament during 2011, among others, social media not only made him popular but also gave greater fillip to the movement. Not many would have thought that a frail 73-year-old social worker would give such a jolt to the Government of India on corruption in the country. With more than one crore likes on the India Against Corruption Facebook page and thousands of others lending online support through twitter and their website www.indiaagainstcorruption.org, Anna Hazare had taken the Internet by storm. Social media played a pivotal role in spreading the message of Anna Hazare. The synergy between the Internet and the electronic media has acted as a bridge to connect more people on the movement. The social media compensated for the Leader who could not be present everywhere and decentralized the campaign. In the process, Anna became a global phenomenon only because of the social media.

Anna Hazare also candidly admitted that it was media which was responsible for his rise from regional figure in Maharashtra to a national icon in the field of anti-corruption movement. "If TV cameras and social media had not followed me everywhere who would know me" was the activist's honest response. Prime-time press conferences, made-for-TV spectacles, social networking campaigns, did benefit Anna Hazare with saturation media coverage.

In the last Presidential Elections in 2008 and in the elections of 2012, U.S. President Barack Obama used social media extensively. He used blogs, Facebook, Twitter, YouTube, etc. In fact, Obama launched his 2012 election campaign only through 'YouTube' by placing video. Since Internet use is more than 80 per cent in the United States, the social media had great impact in the elections.

POINTS TO REMEMBER

1. According to Alvin Toffler, the Third Wave paved the way for information revolution with Computer and Internet in the centre stage. Thus born IT New Mass Media—Internet, Website, E-mail.

2. Public relations practice with the help of IT New Mass Media such as the Internet, Website, Web logs, E-mail is called Electronic Public Relations. Here 'E' stands for Electronic, 'P' for Public and 'R' for Relations.

3. The Internet lends E-PR several advantages, such as the constant communication, instant response, global audiences, two-way communication and cost-effectiveness.

4. The IT New Mass Media include: Internet, E-mail, Intranet, Website, News on Web, Podcast, Wiki, Weblog, Teleconference, Video News Release, E-journal, CD-ROM, DVD, Facsimile.

5. Writing for website demands a distinct style of attracting the attention of Internet users. The guidelines for website writing cover: free of any grammar, punctuation, spelling or syntax errors, avoid puff words, clichés, keep sentences short, crisp and to the point; use active verbs; keep individual paragraphs focused on one central idea; use short words for young and inexperienced readers; and avoid jargon; acronyms and other specialised language that may confuse the readers.

6. Social media not only made Anna Hazare a popular leader in India but also gave greater fillip to his anti-corruption movement. Blogs, Facebook, Twitter, MySpace were extensively used in spreading the message of Anna Hazare, particularly to the youth.

REVIEW QUESTIONS

1. Define information revolution. Explain the three revolutions that created different types of media.

2. What is E-PR? Describe the use of IT new mass media in public relations for reaching out to the different types of audiences.

3. What is Internet? Explain its advantages in the practice of public relations.

4. How is the website used in public relations? Describe the basic guidelines for website writing.

5. What was the impact of social media on the anti-corruption movement of Anna Hazare?

Audio-Visual Media: Films

Chapter

27

C O N T E N T S

- Significance of Film
- Films Division
- Exhibition of Films
- PR Opportunities in Films
- Impact of Films

SIGNIFICANCE OF FILM

The word 'cinema' is derived from the Greek word *'Kinema'*, meaning movement or motion. The word 'movie' comes from the Latin word *'Movere'* which also means to move. The movement of images is called movie or film. Film is a transparent strip of plastic or celluloid with a silver emulsion, high sensitive coating used to produce motion pictures, photographs or television video with the aid of a camera. Cinema has been defined as an appearance of continuous motion created in the minds of the viewers by presentation of series of motionless images in rapid sequence.

Film or motion picture is the most exciting art form and is called the 'Art of All Arts'. Other art forms such as dance, drama, photography, song, music, painting, colour, creative writing form part of a movie. The viewers, therefore, have the perception of film as a 'mixed medium of entertainment'.

Audio-visual communication is the most effective method of disseminating public information. It has been scientifically established that we remember only 10 per cent of what we hear, 20 per cent of what we see, and 60 per cent of what see and hear simultaneously. The visual content of a film draws the attention of the viewer and creates an environment or mood for witnessing the film, while the voice or sound (audio) portion of the film provides emotional link which imparts realism and conviction. Film with its double impact of both sight and sound is the effective audio-visual medium of communication.

Darkened Auditorium

Another important feature of the movie is that the viewer in a darkened auditorium only concentrates on a giant screen with nothing to interrupt the experience. While watching a film, the rest of the world is excluded for the viewer and the mind is fully absorbed on the theme of the film. Therefore, the experience of the viewer is strongest in the darkened cocoon of a cinema theatre. Watching movies remains a thrill—an experience unmatched by other media. It is an all encompassing experience of the viewer that gives films a rather special power in shaping people's mind towards organisational goals, social and ethical values.

Blending of Film with TV

When television emerged, the people thought that film or movie will be killed. Film industry's initial response to television was to fight the medium. But it had mixed response. The film industry, therefore, adopted the idea that if you cannot beat television, join it. Today most of the entertainment fare on television comes from the film industry. We watch three to four movies everyday in a few TV channels.

Public relations must understand the change in the film industry, that blending of film with television is of great advantage for the film medium to communicate messages to a larger audience through television. Film gains double advantage of showing or conveying message to the theatrical audience through cinema halls and non-theatrical audience through television and mobile publicity vans. As such film becomes an important tool of public relations to reach both internal and external public.

PR and Films

Film is one of the media for public relations practice. Public relations messages are communicated effectively through the medium of film. Films are more useful in the Indian context because of high percentage of illiteracy in rural India. It can be used for educating the employees, customers. The entertainment component of the film medium creates greater impact on the people with any message. Therefore, film is not only used in public relations discipline, but also in advertising, marketing and educational fields.

Characteristics

1. It is basically an audio-visual medium which appeals to both the senses of seeing and hearing.

2. Cinema serves the journalistic trinity purposes—to inform, to educate and to entertain.
3. As the film combines, colour, sound and motion, it lends realism and authenticity to the messages.

Advantages

1. Ideas or messages received through the film are retained longer than those received by other media.
2. The film has no literacy barrier. Both literates and illiterates can understand the language of the film.

However, the limitations of film include: cost of production is high; film is urban oriented in India, it does not give immediate feedback, film is more an entertainment medium, information and education being subsidiary.

Types of Films

There are different types of films useful to different audiences. Films are categorised as feature films, short films or documentary films, news magazines, children films, advertising films, video films, animation films, cartoon films. Based on the theme, films are classified as social, crime, fantasy, historical, biographical, mythological, devotional, children, educational, advertising, public relations, etc.

Documentary Films

Documentary film is not only a short film but also non-fiction film based on educational or informative content meant for public exhibition. Documentary films which are educative and based on facts belong to public relations. A documentary is like a written document based on facts. Such short films are straightforward in nature present the reality and are termed as instructional and educative films. The Films Division, Ministry of Information and Broadcasting, for example, produced a documentary film on 'Fodder Grass for More Milk' to convey the message that in dairying better fodder yields more milk. The film intended to educate farmers. The Municipal Corporations produced short film on *"Kachra Mat Phenko"* to create civic sense. Some of the famous documentaries include: biographical film on late K.R. Narayanan, former President of India, "New Deal for Rural India," and "Population Stabilisation".

100 Years of Indian Cinema

Cinema came to India when the first screening was arranged at Bombay Watson Hotel with a bang on 7 July 1896. That was a red-letter day in the history of Indian cinema. Its growth has been incredible.

Cinema, which is very dear to the hearts of both urban and rural India, made its beginning on 18 May 1912 at Coronation Cinema in Bombay when the film 'Pundalik', the story of a saint in Maharashtra, produced by R.G. Torney and N.G. Chitre with the assistance of English technicians was released. However, the real pioneer of Indian Cinema was Dhundiraj Govind Phalke, affectionately, called "Dada Saheb Phalke", who made India's first indigenous feature film (silent) 'Raja Harischandra', which was released on 3 May 1913 in Bombay. Therefore, 'Dada Saheb' is regarded as the Father of Indian Cinema and the Government of India accords Dada Saheb Phalke Award to an eminent film personality every year.

FILMS DIVISION

The Films Division, constituted in January 1948 by rechristening of the erstwhile Information Films of India and the Indian News Parade set up in 1943 for war propaganda, is the key tool of Government of India to inform, educate and entertain the people through the medium of film. In fact, the Films Division acts as a tool of public relations of Government of India. The aims and objectives of the Division focused on national integration and to project the image of the land and the heritage of the country to Indian and foreign audiences. It has been motivating the broadcast spectrum of the Indian public with a view to enlisting their active participation in national building activities. With its headquarters in Mumbai, Films Division produces documentaries, short films, animation films and news magazines. It caters to about 8500 cinema theatres all over the country and to the non-theatrical circuits like units of the Directorate of Field Publicity, mobile publicity Vans of the State Governments, Doordarshan, field units of the Directorate of Family Welfare, educational institutions, film societies and voluntary organisations. The documentaries and newsreel of State Governments are also featured in the Films Division's release on the theatrical circuit.

Newsreel Wing of Films Division encompasses a network spread over main cities, towns, including State and Union Territory capitals, and is engaged in covering of major events. The coverage is used for making the news magazines and in compilation of archival material.

Distribution Wing

The Distribution Wing of the Films Division controls 10 Distribution Branch Offices located in different parts of the country for the supply of approved films to all cinema theatres for exhibition. It also distributes prints of selected films of Films Division to the Indian missions abroad through the External Publicity Division of Ministry of External Affairs.

The Central Board of Film Certification certifies film for public exhibition in India. The Board has its Headquarters in Mumbai and nine regional offices located in Bengaluru, Kolkata, Chennai, Cuttack, Guwahati, Hyderabad, Mumbai, New Delhi and Thiruvananthapuram. As many as 814 Indian feature films were certified in 2011.

EXHIBITION OF FILMS

Production of documentary/public relations film is one aspect and exhibition of such films before the target audience is another aspect. Both are equally important for a public relations manager. However, special care has to be taken in the exhibition of public relations films before both the theatrical and non-theatrical audiences. Film prints/VHS cassettes, VCDs, DVDs, Betacam cassettes, animation films, cartoon films, short feature films based on the theme of public communication and public education can be exhibited through cinema theatres, multiplexes and non-theatrical outlets such as Field Publicity Units of Ministry of Information and Broadcasting, District Public Relations units of State Information and Public Relations Departments, Public Relations units of Central and State public sector undertakings, educational institutions, NGOs, television channels, cable TV networks, Indian Missions abroad, etc. Certain guidelines have to be kept in mind while showing public relations films. The nature of the film/theme, composition of the audience, topicality of the film, place and time suited to the audience are some of the points for guidance. There is a close linkage between the theme of the film and the audience being exposed to such a film.

With the expansion of TV and Cable TV network, the number of cinegoers to the cinema theatres has to some extent dwindled. But the number is now growing because of multiplexes—multi-screen cinema houses which is a new trend even for public relations films.

Multiplex Theatres

Film exhibition in India, with a history of over 100 years (starting from the 1896 show by Marius Sistier, Assistant to Lumiere Brothers at Watson Hotel, Bombay) is in a sense older than the Indian film industry which started in 1913 with the release of Raja Harischandra. In the past, film industry has witnessed significant changes and improvements in technology, content and focus.

Historically, cinema in India was set up as a single screen theatre with a large seating capacity with inadequate infrastructure, slack maintenance, outdated technology, poor audio-visual quality, paltry-ticket prices, pathetic occupancy rates, high taxation and dwindling profits.

As the technology changed, the film exhibition scenario also changed for the benefit of cinegoers. As the single screen theatre was outdated, the state of affairs was ideal for the entry of multiplexes and India's first multiplex, PVR Anupam was established in New Delhi in 1997. Since then multiplexes, multiscreen theatres have grown phenomenally. Multiplexes differ from conventional theatres in many ways. With more than one screen in a single building, a multiplex controls costs by maintaining facilities on a shared basis as compared to single screen theatres. The costs incurred towards facilities such as ticket counters, food and beverages services, common utilities, manpower, electricity and maintenance can be distributed among all the screens. Movie shows for different screens are scheduled with a reasonable time-gap, so that the crowd is evenly distributed over a longer time period, instead of clustering it at one point of time. Multiplexes attract the maximum crowd during the first week by showing the movie on more than one screen.

Drive in Movies

In a bid to cater to the good life, leading hotels around the world offer drive in movies positioning a 3-by-5 metre projection screen at the end of a 20-metre-in-door pool so that swimmers can watch continuous screening of black-and-white classics. They can also see their favourite movies or satellite-television programmes. Of course, drive-in-theatres are also there on major highways. A bright future beckons the exhibition of films with the new technology of multiplexes.

PR OPPORTUNITIES IN FILMS

The film as a medium of communication is exploited by all public relations units in Government of India, State Governments, public sector, private sector undertakings and not-for-profit organisations. The Directorate of Field Publicity, Government of India, alone organises about 30,000 film shows every year in the country. Similarly, the 28 State Information and Public Relations departments organise film shows for educating the public. Film when produced is used in the form of prints, VHS cassettes, VCDs, DVDs, betacam cassettes. As such a film is not only screened through projectors but also through television in a video format.

With the objectives to focus on national perspectives and to educate and motivate people in the implementation of national programmes and to project the image of the land and the heritage of the country to Indian and foreign audiences, the Films Division arranges special screenings and film shows at various parts of the country. One such film show was on "moments with the Maestros"covering music and musical geniuses in Goa as part of the International Festival.

Tools of PR

How can a public relations manager use film in the practice of public relations. There are various types of documentary films depending on the theme and topic, ranging from agriculture to industry, food to festivals, health care to housing, science to technology, trade and commerce to transport, tribal welfare to community development. However, a public relations manager can make use of different types of films, such as feature films (family planning), documentaries, short feature films, news magazines, children films, animation films, cartoon films, corporate films, product films, film strips, advertising films, public relations films, cinema slides. Special films can be produced for motivating employees. Public transport organisations produced films on driver, conductor who are the link between the management and the passengers. Films are the best tools of corporate public relations which can be used in the areas of employees' relations, investor relations, customers' relations, dealers' relations, community relations, crisis situations and reputation management. Films are used for different purposes—from public relations to general education.

IMPACT OF FILMS

A film has immense potentialities to reach millions of people both in urban and in rural India. About 100 million people watch movies in India every week in about 9,000 cinema houses. However, the number of cinegoers is depleting because of television. A film has the potentiality to reach non-theatrical audiences in rural India through mobile film units of Government of India and State Governments' Publicity Units. Exposure of people to the documentary public relations films brings a change in the outlook of the people towards development. The impact of the medium of cinema in other spheres including development is equally impressive. In his book *Communication and Development*, Dr. Y.V. Lakshmana Rao described how mass media particularly films helped in the trade of a tailor in a village in Visakhapatnam district of Andhra Pradesh. It was based on the study of two Indian villages. A tailor in the village, Ayyanna, was asked by the study team, if he watched movies often. The answer was 'yes'. In fact he said, "I see every movie show in nearby town". His experience was very instructive. His business had picked up because of movies. The women of the village fancied the blouse styles worn by the actress of the movies. One woman reportedly asked the tailor "Can you make me a blouse like the one the heroine was wearing in the scene in which she eloped with the landlord's son in the film 'Modern Girl'". He complied with the request. That was a breakthrough. Other women in the village soon followed her and Ayyanna's business flourished. The reaction of the village men too was similar. More and more of them wanted to emulate the styles of city folks so much so that the traditional collarless shirt virtually went out of vogue. This is a clear case to show how the dress styles in the movies promoted urbanisation in the villages and how a source of entertainment like the film was also a means of change and economic betterment.

Political Stars

Film actors such as M.G. Ramachandran, Jayalalitha (Tamil Nadu) and N.T. Rama Rao (Andhra Pradesh) entered politics and became Chief Ministers in their respective States is an eloquent proof of the impact of films on the masses and society. Heroes on the screen became leaders off-the screen because the masses identified them with the roles they played.

Less tangible aspects of films such as rejection of untouchability, acceptance of widow remarriage, etc. were also propagated. V. Shantaram, under his Rajkamal production made a purposeful film like '*Dehej*' against dowry system. The films have become an important medium of social reform and economic development. A few films created impact on family welfare and small family norm.

POINTS TO REMEMBER

1. Cinema is the appearance of continuous motion created in the minds of the viewers by presentation of a series of motionless images in rapid sequence. Cinema is called 'the art of all arts' and the mixed medium of entertainment.

2. Film with its double impact of sight and sound acts as an effective medium of public relations in reaching out to the target audience.

3. The viewer, when sits in a darkened movie theatre concentrates only on a giant screen with nothing to interrupt and gains the strongest experience unmatched by other media.

4. Film gains an added advantage when it is blended with television, as its reach will be very wide.

5. Films are more useful in the Indian context because of high illiteracy and lack of adequate people's access to mass media.

6. Film by its characteristic is an audio-visual medium, which combines all arts—colour, sound, motion, etc. It lends realism and authenticity.

7. Messages received through the film are retained longer than those received by other media.

8. It is more an entertainment medium, information and education being subsidiary.

9. Films are classified based on the theme. They are: feature film, documentary short film, news magazine, children films, ad film, public relations films, animation films, cartoon films, historical films, mythological films, etc.

10. Public relations can use films in corporate public relations to inform, educate, entertain and motivate both the internal and the external publics of an organisation.

11. There are about 9,000 cinema houses in India in which about 10 crore people watch movies every week.

12. A new trend has set in the exhibition of films, with multiplex theatres in one building. Such multiplexes are a step in increasing the number of cinegoers in India. Movie shows for different screens are scheduled with a reasonable time gap as to distribute the crowd instead of clustering it at one point of time. Multiplex also is an opportunity for public relations to exhibit public relations films.

13. Films are not only useful for entertainment but also for economic development. Film artistes such as N.T. Rama Rao, M.G. Ramachandran, Ms. Jayalalitha could become Chief Ministers because of their influence on the audience. They used their influence for politics.

REVIEW QUESTIONS

1. What is the significance of film as a medium of public relations?

2. Describe the characteristics, advantages and limitations of films.

3. What are the public relations opportunities in the medium of film?

4. Film is a mixed medium of information and entertainment. Discuss the impact of films on the Indian mind. Cite examples.

5. Write short note on multiplex multi-screen theatre.

Visual Media—Photographs and Exhibitions

Chapter

28

C O N T E N T S

PR PHOTOGRAPHY

"One picture is worth a thousand words" is an old Chinese proverb. Many a person, who may not even care to read a news item, will undoubtedly look at a good picture in a newspaper. This is because photographs have immense eye appeal, and attractive photographs are described as inner poems of permanence. A photograph has validity and for most of us is synonymous with truth. "A camera cannot lie" is a well-known maxim. A photograph can tell a story, convey a message, provide an insight so effectively that to do the same as an alternative in text it would take many words.

Photography is the process of forming and fixing an image by the chemical action of light on a surface of film which is sensitive to light. A photo print is a photographic print or positive, while photomontage is an assemblage of photos or parts of photos. Photo call is a request to photographers to cover an event.

Photographers often specialise in one kind of photography. For example, commercial photographers take pictures of products, fashions, food or machinery. Scientific photographers take pictures for scientific magazines and books. Photojournalists take pictures of events, people, places or things for newspapers, while portrait photographers take pictures of people in their own studios or at schools, homes, weddings and parties. Aerial photographers take pictures from airplanes, for newspapers, business, research organisations or the military. Fine arts photographers take pictures for artistic expression.

Characteristics

Photography has certain distinct characteristics that make this medium more advantageous in the practice of public relations.

- Photography is basically a visual medium that appeals to the eye.
- Photography is described as the most 'universal of all languages' in the sense that photographs are not foreign to anyone, to whatever country on language one may belong.
- Photos know no barrier of illiteracy—both literate and illiterate understand the picture.
- Photographs 'spell out' a message more quickly and powerfully than other means of communication.

Photo Journalism

Newspapers carry both written words and photographs to present a news story. They have equal importance in presenting news. A picture in a newspaper requires all the qualities of a good news item. Therefore, there is as much journalism as there is in the printed word. The reporter is replaced by the photo journalist and notebook is replaced by a camera. As such, one who reports to the newspapers with the help of a camera and photographs is called a photo journalist. As such there developed photo journalism.

In concise *History of photography*, Gernsheim writes: "No other medium can bring life and reality so close as does photography and it is in the fields of reportage and documentation that photographs' most important contribution lies in modern times. Not least of its achievements, photographs and photo journalism have proved powerful agents in the awakening of social conscience".

PR Photographer

There is a category called **public relations photographers** employed either by in-house public relations department or a public relations agency who specialise in taking photographs for house journals, corporate publications, exhibitions, posters, newspaper, corporate advertisements. In fact, a public relations photographer provides support in terms of photographs and visuals to promote and undertake public relations programmes. Photos supplied by public relations department to the media are the work of public relations photography. The use of photos by public relations manager in corporate public relations is also termed as public relations photography. Paralleled with photo journalism is the term public relations photography which helps in communicating via the medium of photographs. A good public relations photographer is first of all a good public relations professional with complete knowledge of public relations requirements.

Aid to PR

It is against this background, photographs act as an 'aid' to public relations practice to convey messages with visual tactics. However, a distinction has to be made between photo journalism and public relations photography. If the photos published in newspapers constitute photo journalism, then the photographs used by public relations professionals in conveying messages to the target audience are described as public relations photography.

WHY SHOUD PR USE PHOTOGRAPHS?

Photos are used in public relations because the audience likes pictures, easily understands, remembers them and believes in them. These factors enhance the value of pictures in public relations profession. Photographs are used in public relations in several following ways:

1. Action shots of technical operations of machines
2. Product and services photos in newspapers and catalogues
3. Illustrate news stories and features or events of organisation
4. Illustrate reports, booklets, house journals, folders, posters
5. Illustrate press advertising and posters
6. Illustrate manuals, handbooks, annual reports
7. Illustrate record albums, photo features in house journals
8. Illustrate newscast in television
9. Illustrate exhibition and other outdoor publicity material
10. Human interest stories in photographs
11. To impart training with the help of pictures
12. Photographs in press kit

Editors of newspaper frequently complain about the poor quality of public relations photographs. All photographs should be supplied in the format specified by newspapers. It is usual to provide well-contrasted black and white gloss or semi-gloss prints in 15 × 10 cm or sometimes 25 × 20 cm. Captions should accompany all prints, so that when viewing the photographs, the related text may be read. Transparencies should be dispatched in protective packaging, and prints are placed in broad backed envelopes. Such precautions should also be taken when photos are used for all public relations purposes.

The success of public relations photography depends on the efficient briefing of professional photographer by the public relations practitioner. If a building is to be constructed, the architect is consulted about its design, elevation, etc. Then the engineer constructs the house. Similarly, the public relations practitioner has to tell the photographer what is required to communicate a message through a photo. Then the photographer takes appropriate photographs.

DIGITAL PHOTOGRAPHY

Digital photography is a relatively new development. With this new technology, film is being replaced by microchips that record pictures in digital format. Pictures then are downloaded on to a computer hard drive. Photographers use special software to manipulate the images on screen. Digital photography is used primarily for electronic publishing, advertising and e-public relations.

Digital photography has the advantage of getting material processed in reduced time. If e-mail is used, then public relations photographs can be sent to hundreds of recipients including newspapers via Internet within minutes at minimal cost. Digital photos must be sent to newspapers in compact disks with caption on the cover of the disk for use by newspapers.

Case Study

The Andhra Pradesh State Road Transport Corporation (APSRTC) had taken photographs of its poster on 'Safe Driving' and published them in newspapers, house journals used in exhibitions and television. A poster converted into photograph was used for several purposes in public relations. The cover page of *Prasthanam* house journal of APSRTC carried a photograph with the caption *"Driver Garu, Meeru Jagrathaga Duty Cheste"* ("Dear Driver, if you drive carefully..."). This photograph highlighted the role of the driver in providing a comfortable and safe travel to passengers and the same was displayed in all training schools, bus depots where drivers report for duty. The poster spelt out the benefits of careful driving and it also tried to sensitise the driver that if he drives carefully, the passengers, pedestrians and he too (the driver) would reach home safely. The poster also depicted the driver's wife and his children welcoming him with a smiling face along with his pet dog.

The big size poster displayed at all bus depots and the illustration in house journal educated the drivers on safe driving. The same poster-photo was released to all daily newspapers which was published prominently for education of the general public on safe driving and to make the passengers aware of the safety measures taken by APSRTC. In this case, the drivers and the trade unions appreciated the effort of public relations department for educating employees through house journal, multi-colour poster and newspapers.

When John Pope Paul II landed at the Palam Airport, New Delhi in 1980s, the first thing he did was that he kissed the Indian soil. The photo published in newspapers evoked the feelings of Indians irrespective of religion. Everyone appreciated the gesture of the Pope —the religious Leader of Roman Catholics.

EXHIBITIONS—SEEING IS BELIEVING

Exhibition, be it local, regional, national or international, is based on the principle "seeing is believing" and assumes great importance in the promotion of sales, services and socio-economic development schemes of a country. It has been established that about 87 per cent of impressions that we receive are through the medium of sight and the ideas received by this sense organ are retained longer. People are accustomed to accept most of the ideas in second-hand sources, such as books, newspapers, radio, television, film. How many of us have really seen the moon rock? Yet we formed some idea of the moon rock by seeing it in pictures and by reading in newspapers. This is otherwise known as knowledge by indirect methods. But the moon rock which was displayed at some places in India, however, enabled the people to see it in real shape. This makes all the more difference in framing an idea than by reading in newspapers and directly seeing things in three dimensions. 'Seeing' sense, therefore, gives the viewer greater scope for translating abstract concept into realities. It also creates a lasting impression on the human mind. In fact, it is the means whereby a message, whether it refers to a product or an idea, is brought to perception of a person by actual visual presentation. This is the concept of exhibitions.

Exhibition Defined

What is an exhibition? The term exhibition as generally used refers to a collection of display exhibits as arranged in a trade show or convention. Exhibiting is a communication medium such as public relations, advertising or marketing which involves conveying a message at a display stand. A public showing of art works or products of a manufacturer is called exhibition. Exhibition may be described as an attractively organised public show of certain objects. It also includes an eye-catching display of products, paintings, photographs, models or services. Exhibition is an event where companies or individuals (exhibitors) display products, services, or works (exhibits) on show for an appropriate audience for the purpose of either selling those products or enabling the audience to witness and appreciate them for their aesthetic value. It has both merchandising and public relations value.

The main function of an exhibition is to attract the attention of the visitor or potential users of the products and services, and see for themselves and judge their merit for use. Apart from the selling impact, exhibitions have an informative and educative function also. Therefore, exhibition is used as one of the media of public relations.

Is Exhibition a PR or Marketing Medium?

Exhibition has close 'linkage' to public relations, for it is a medium of promoting a product, an idea or a service which not only creates awareness, but also brings about human understanding between the promoter and the audience. There is some confusion about its use as a public relations medium. The question is asked whether the exhibition is a marketing medium or public relations effort. The answer lies in the purpose of the exhibition. If it is to inform and educate the public on an idea, say family planning or a service like life insurance, then it becomes a public relations medium. If the exhibition is intended to influence the consumer to purchase products on display, it becomes the marketing medium. Majority of trade exhibitions fall into the marketing category. Whatever be the technical classification, an exhibition benefits the organisation for public relations and marketing purposes. They are inter-linked and intended to promote the organisation. Sometimes conferences and seminars are organised in conjunction with exhibitions.

CATEGORIES OF EXHIBITION

Exhibitions are of different categories. They are classified depending on the nature of exhibitions; some exhibitions are categorised based on the geographical area they cover such as local, regional, national and international, while other exhibitions are classified based on the products, or the subjects they promote as agricultural exhibition, industrial exhibition, etc. Other types include: art exhibitions, commercial or trade fairs, informative exhibitions, rural exhibitions, mobile or travelling exhibitions. Specialised exhibitions such as Shoe-Tech (footwear), Home Fair (household appliances), Food Fair (food products), Book Fair, etc. are also organised.

Exhibitions as a medium have several following advantages:

1. It is a direct and face-to-face medium.
2. It has an enormous publicity potential for individual exhibitor.
3. It provides the use of multi-media at the same place. Public relations manager can arrange talks, film shows, song and drama performances, distribution of publications, display of photographs, relay of TV, radio programmes, etc.
4. It explains the product in three-dimensional effect (length, depth and height).

5. It informs, educates, entertains and motivates people for action.
6. It acts as a catalyst for socio-economic development.
7. It eliminates the middlemen and brings the seller and the buyer/consumer face-to-face.
8. It provides a market to introduce new products at regional, state, national and international levels.
9. It is a meeting point for comparing technological and economic progress.
10. It supports a well-established conference.
11. Unlike other media, it provides immediate feedback to the exhibitor.
12. Exhibition is a relaxed event where visitors see products and services in holiday mood.
13. Public relations and exhibitions are intertwined in promoting corporate image, products and services.

Norms for Participation

Before making a decision in regard to setting up of either an independent pavilion or participating in the exhibition, the public relations manager has to consider certain vital factors of the exhibition like its marketing and public relations purposes, besides trade values. They are as follows:

1. What is the purpose of the exhibition?
2. Whether it is necessary to use the medium of exhibition for sales promotion and public relations purposes at that time.
3. Whether the exhibition coincides with some local, seasonal gathering or events? Events may include: public events, trade events, conferences, or seminars.
4. What official support does it enjoy?
5. What is the reputation of the organiser?
6. What is the theme of the exhibition? Is it relevant? What are the messages to be conveyed?
7. Who are the public that are going to visit the exhibition and the size of the attendance? What have been the recent attendance figures?
8. What are the exhibits that have to be displayed in the exhibition?
9. Whether the location of exhibition is suitable both to the organisation and to the visitors.
10. What is the budget?
11. What will be the returns in terms of sales promotion, image building, promotion of ideas, etc.?

Having considered the above points, public relations manager should advise the management whether it should take part in the exhibition or not.

Four Components

In organising an exhibition, one has to follow four basic components for its success:

1. Booking the venue.
2. Theme, design, construction, displays of stands, products, photographs, lighting, decoration, human interest live models.
3. Management and running the exhibition—build-up to break down, (from state to conclusion) well-informed guides, visitors book, feedback from visitors.
4. Publicity and public relations support before, during and after the exhibition. Providing information services.

The Exhibition Division of the Directorate of Advertising and Visual Publicity, Ministry of Information and Broadcasting, Government of India organises exhibitions throughout the country every year. It organised exhibitions on the life of the Father of the Nation—Mahatma Gandhi, and on 'Sukhi Parivar' at the Family Welfare Pavilion at Pragati Maidan, New Delhi. The India International Trade Fair is organised every year in November at Pragati Maidan, New Delhi—a shining example of international exhibition.

Any failure of exhibition should be analysed carefully. It can be due to any or all of the following reasons:

(i) Bad choice of exhibition as a medium
(ii) Wrong choice of site unsuitable to the visitors
(iii) Unattractive or badly located stand
(iv) Lack of planning and preparation
(v) Unsuitable trade literature, or wrong language
(vi) Unskilled or ineffective staff on duty
(vii) Failure to follow-up inquiries
(viii) Failure to make advance use of information services for creating awareness
(ix) Lack of publicity

POINTS TO REMEMBER

1. "One picture is worth a thousand words" is an old Chinese proverb. Many people do not even care to read a news item, but look at good news picture. Photography is the process of forming and fixing an image by the chemical action of light on a surface (films), which is sensitive to light.

2. Paralleled with photo journalism, there emerged public relations photography to meet the needs of photographic communication

of public relations discipline. Photographs used for the purpose of communicating public relations messages as part of corporate public relations come under the category of public relations photography.

3. Photographs of public interest are used in the practice of public relations because people easily understand them. People enjoy photos, People remember good photographs and they believe them.

4. Public relations photographs are used in several ways to reach the audience:

   - Product and services photographs in promotional literature
   - News photos, photo features
   - Photos of audience interests in house journals, and annual eports
   - News photos for telecast purpose in television
   - Photos for exhibitions and other outdoor publicity
   - Photos in media kits
   - Record albums photographs

5. Digital photography is a relatively new development in the technology in which film is replaced by microchips that record pictures in the digital format. Photos then are downloaded on to a computer's hard drive. Such photos can be transmitted to newspapers and others via Internet.

6. "Seeing is believing", the theme on which exhibitions are organised to attract visitors towards ideas, products and services.

7. Exhibition is defined as a 'public showing' of art, works, ideas or products and services of an individual or an organisation. Exhibition, therefore, became as one of the tools of public relations to persuade the audience towards organisational goals and goods.

8. Exhibition is used both as public relations and as marketing outlet. However, if the purpose is to create awareness and build the image of an organisation, it comes under public relations, while the exhibition meant for selling products is termed as marketing exhibition. In both cases, public relations has a role to play.

9. Exhibitions are classified based on their nature of display. They are: agricultural exhibition; industrial exhibition; trade fair; informative exhibition; travelling exhibition; rural exhibition; shoe-tech (footwear); home fair (household appliances); food fair (food products); book fair, etc.

10. The advantages of exhibitions are many. Some of them include: it is a direct and face-to-face medium where seller and buyer meet. It acts as a catalyst for socio-economic development and provides a market to launch new products.

11. Four components are involved in the success of exhibition. They are: (i) Booking the venue; (ii) Theme design, construction and display of stands; (iii) Management and running the exhibition; (iv) Publicity 'before', 'during' and 'after' the exhibition.

12. An exhibition may be a failure due to certain factors such as bad choice of location, lack of planning, ineffective staff on duty, lack of publicity, etc.

REVIEW QUESTIONS

1. "One picture is worth a thousand words". Discuss.

2. Why is public relations photography a medium? Explain its advantages in the practice of public relations.

3. Discuss the ways in which photographs can be used in corporate public relations for conveying messages. Cite examples.

4. "Seeing is Believing". Describe the scope and role of exhibitions in public relations.

5. Is exhibition a public relations or marketing medium? Give reasons with examples.

6. What are the factors that result in the failure of an exhibition?

If public relations is the discipline of creating and maintaining mutual understanding between an organisation and its publics, events with the objective of communication are a powerful media to reach out to the target audience with messages to build good relations and also promote reputation. This approach will be in the form of face-to-face interaction and it will be more effective. An event becomes a platform to inform, educate, motivate and entertain the gathered audience towards organisational goals, products, values, qualities, services on the one side and also assess their valued opinions and reactions on the other. In a way, event is a two-way traffic. Any event, be it local, regional, national or international, needs public relations support for its success. Therefore, event and public relations are intertwined and they must go together to accomplish the goals.

WHAT IS AN EVENT?

The Oxford Dictionary—Thesaurus and Word Power defines an event as "a thing that happens or takes place". It is also described as a public or social occasion. Marketing Guru Philip Kotler defined events as "occurrences designed to communicate particular messages to the target audiences". Suresh Pillai, Managing Director, Events Management regards the event as an additional media whereby two-way communication is possible between the event manager and its audiences.

The author explains the event as 'a face-to-face occurrence with a defined objective to promote an organisation, an idea, product, service or reputation and gain understanding of the gathered audience'. Kumbh Mela, periodically held on the river Ganga in Uttar Pradesh, is a shining example of a national event. Similarly, the Annual General Meeting of a corporation is a local event, confined to shareholders of an organisation.

TYPES OF EVENTS

Events are of varied types. They are classified as local, regional, national or international based on their reach. India International Trade Fair, held in November every year in New Delhi, is an example of international event, in which manufactures from all over the world converge to showcase their products for marketing. Events also are classified based on the theme such as sporting event, cultural event or fund-raising event.

The classification of events based on the theme is as follows:

1.	Corporate Events:	Annual General Meeting, Award Ceremonies, Anniversaries, Sponsorships, Major Project Launches
2.	Sporting Events:	Sport Events, Sports Competitions, Sponsoring
3.	Cultural/entertainment Events:	Music, Dance, Drama, Folklore, Art Shows
4.	Fundraising Events:	Charity Shows
5.	Personal Events:	Weddings, Birthdays, Lunches, Dinners
6.	PR Events	Press Conference, Press Tour, Press Interview, Radio and TV Talks, Exhibitions, Open Houses, Round Tables, Conferences, Lectures, Seminars, Film Festivals, Visits of VIPs

Though public relations events are shown as a separate category, a public relations professional is charged with the responsibility of handling all types of events to generate media attention. A public relations professional should not only understand the art of event management but also act as an event manager.

OBJECTIVES

Every event must have an objective to reach its goal and accomplish results. An event without any objective will be as a train without destination. However, the objective is basically based on the theme and purpose of the event. Objectives of events are summarized as follows:

- Raising funds for community purpose
- Sponsorships to build image of the organisation
- Promote fine arts and performing arts to gain mileage out of social responsibility
- Promote sports events
- Launch new products/services/projects
- Organise meetings, conferences, seminars, Annual General Meetings
- Hold Press conferences, open houses, exhibitions, etc.
- Promote scientific temper among students

PR Tool

Event is a tool of both marketing and public relations depending on the nature and purpose of the event. For example, an exhibition or trade fair could be used as a medium of marketing, if its intent is sales or a medium of public relations if the objective is to promote organisational image.

The XI Conference of Parties (CoP 11) Convention on Biological Diversity, Hyderabad, India, 2012 is a good example of a major global event held for 19 days from 1 October 2012. Over 8000 delegates from 200 countries attended this mega event. The focus of this conference was on global biodiversity, its concerns and solutions.

EVENT MANAGEMENT

Event management is defined as the management of an event with careful planning, action projects, execution, coordination and evaluation so as to reach out to the target audience and accomplish its objectives.

Four-stage Process

As the event management forms part of public relations practice, the public relations practitioner must make it as an inbuilt public relations programme. Communication is a predominant component of event management which professionally is the prerogative of public relations discipline. In making the event successful, one should follow the four-stage public relations process or RPCE model: R stands for Research or Fact finding, P for Planning, C for Communication and E for Evaluation. This topic is covered in Chapter 7. These tips are also applicable to event management.

FIVE C's OF EVENT MANAGEMENT

Gaur and Saggere (2003) identified five "C's" of events. The first is Conceptualisation of the event. Second, the Costing, i.e. calculation of cost of production on the event. Third is Canvassing for clients/sponsors, customers/audience and networking. The fourth one is Customisation of the concept based the customers/audience needs. The fifth one, the most important part of event management, is the conclusion, the execution of the event as planned.

Planning

Planning is the key to the success of an event. Events such as press conferences or open house, need a formal planning process including risk or crisis assessment. In fact, planning is the backbone of a good event. A well thought out plan of an event executed efficiently can give the organisation tremendous image building mileage.

Among others, the planning stage must include areas such as Objective (sponsoring sport event or AGM); Venue, Date and Time (date should not clash with local major events); Target Audiences (invitees list—customers); Printed material (invitations, corporate profile); Facilities at the venue (clean premises, reception area, parking lot), Security, Public Address System; Speakers, Celebrities, Lighting, Display Stands, Hospitality, Catering, Entertainment, Stage Decoration with branded backdrop; Staffing, Permissions and Licenses (from police, municipalities); Promotion, Publicity and Public Relations (media coverage)—Photo, audio-visual coverage, cable network, outdoor hoardings, direct mail; Crisis Plan (fire accidents, first aid, weather conditions); Budget, Rehearsal of the Event, Evaluation (brief summary of the event).

Preparing for the Event

The Event Manager needs to have knowledge and complete data on different vendors who are required to provide various services. Following services are generally needed for an event:

- Audio-visual needs such as projection equipment, TV monitors, speakers, microphones and so on
- Recording of the proceedings by video and audio
- Badge makers, Carry bags/Kit manufacturers
- Decoration supply houses, Florists
- Furniture rental companies (for stage, seating, etc.)
- Transport operators
- Memento makers, Gift marketers
- Media Relations Consultants

- Trade Show organisers, Exhibit Display firms
- Printers and Digital operators

The list will vary depending on the size and nature of the event. However, it is absolutely essential to gather information and keep data on such service providers to be able to contact them for deciding on the requirements well in time before the event.

PR COMMUNICATION FOR EVENT

Public relations communication is a prerequisite to the event management. Creating awareness about an event is the primary job of PR. In fact, PR support is required for the event in three stages—pre-event, during event and post-event. The PR manager has to design a multimedia public relations plan to give wider media coverage to the event in all the three stages. Unlike the paid media publicity, public relations aims at free publicity to get due coverage for the event based on its importance to the society.

The public relations plan among others must include networking process with multimedia approach, newspapers, radio, TV, the Internet, cable network, outdoor media, direct mail, press releases, press conferences, letters to the editor, advertorials, institutional ads, exhibitions, etc.

The Conference of Parties 11 (CoP 11) to the Convention on Biological Diversity 2012 got much coverage both in print and in electronic media free of cost. It was because it relates to lives of the people. A key theme of the conference in one of the sessions was the impact of biodiversity loss on the poor. "Dependent directly on nature for food, clean water, fuel, medicine and shelter, poor householders were hit hardest by ecosystem degradation" the conference felt. Major newspapers highlighted this aspect with headings "Include the Poor in Biodiversity Conservation".

Case Study

'Sharan Incorporation', a well-established Event Management Company in Chennai in South India, has the credit of organising mega events with top celebrities such as Amir Khan, A.R. Rahman, Rekha, S.P. Balasubramanyam and Gulam Ali. One of the most prestigious events organised by Sharan Incorporation in Chennai was 'JAI HO' show of the Oscar Winner A.R. Rahman. It was a significant event of music lovers, which could reach out to many—because of publicity and public relations support.

OPEN HOUSE: A PR EVENT

Open house is one of the key public relations events to expose the functioning of an organisation both internal and external publics, including the family members of the workforce and stakeholders, such as shareholders, customers, suppliers, dealers, opinion leaders, members of the board, employees, etc. who could be invited. It is also an effective tool of public relations to show the corporate vision, as well as mission statement, services and products on the one side and its friendly attitude and corporate culture on the other. In the process, the organisation gets due recognition from the public.

What is an Open House?

The Oxford Advanced Learner's Dictionary describes Open House as "a place and time at which visitors are welcome", "Open day, a day when people can visit a school, an organisation, etc. and see the work that is done there, a time when people who are interested in buying a particular house or apartment can look around it". It is also called the plant/factory tour by individual visitors.

Community Visitation

Open house may be described as keeping the company open for the visit of community, enabling them to know what the company is doing for the society. Open house is regarded as community visitation. The community around can be invited to visit the plant and get assured that the factory is not likely to disturb the local ecological balance and pollute the environment with poisonous gas. The community then understands realizes that it is a good place to work, makes good products, is a leader in the field and a good welcome to the locality.

The term 'Open House' is derived from the concept of new houses built by real estate dealers to show them to the prospective buyers. One company says "A new town takes shape. We'd love to have you over for a city tour. You will discover that it feels like home. And you probably find one too". This is how they attract people through advertisements to the new colonies.

Open House London

Taking a cue from a simple but powerful concept Open House, major cities in the world have launched a programme showcasing outstanding architecture of the city for all to experience, completely free of cost. Open house initiatives of cities invite everyone to explore and understand the value of a well-designed built environment. Open House London Weekend, the capital's greatest architectural showcase, takes place every year on 22 and 23 September. About 700 buildings of all kinds with amazing architecture are kept open for the public to see for themselves. As a result, visitors become more knowledgeable, engage in dialogue and make informed judgments on the buildings and places where they live, work and play.

Open house in the corporate culture represents a corporation or an organisation because employees live there as one family in their second home. Any organisation for employees becomes the second home where they work about 8–12 hours. Thus developed the concept for open house in the corporate sector with corporation as a home of employees.

Theme

Open house with a particular theme will be effective in reaching all the target audience with an appropriate message. For example, a possible theme for employees' open house and their families could be "Family Day". If it is for the general public, it could be "the Company in the Service of Society" or "Friendly Neighbour".

Limitations

Open house has its advantages and limitations. The limitations include: it cannot reach distant public, time is limited and confined to local area.

Open House at CCMB: A Case Study

The Centre for Cellular and Molecular Biology (CCMB), nation's premier institute, in Hyderabad organises its open house every year on its foundation day. Marking the foundation day of the Council of Scientific and Industrial Research (CSIR), CCMB organised open house for one day exclusively for the benefit of students of the twin cities of Hyderabad and Secunderabad in September 2012. Over 16,000 students from different schools in the city apart from Intermediate and Degree colleges entered the world of biological research.

Administrative Staff, Scientists and Ph.D. scholars acted as Guides for groups of students who embarked upon a guided tour through the Research Institutes Lab facilities. Over 50 posters were displayed which simplified science for the students. Other posters included on subjects such as biometrics, immunology and biochemistry, which were a big attraction for the students. There was an interaction between the scientists and student's community on key concepts such as DNA fingerprinting, Nanotechnology and Cancer Research on Zebrafish.

POINTS TO REMEMBER

1. Event is a platform to inform, educate, motivate and entertain the audience to gain their goodwill.
2. Event is defined as a public or social occasion. It is also an occurrence organised to communicate a particular message.
3. Events are categorised as corporate events, sporting events, entertainment events, fund raising events and public relations events.
4. Key objectives of events include: raise funds for community purpose, sponsorships for building corporate image, organise cultural and sports activities; launch new products, organise press conference, open house, exhibition, etc.
5. Event management is described as the management of an event with careful planning, action projects, execution, coordination and evaluation to reach out the target audience and accomplish its objectives.
6. Four-stage public relations process is also applied to event management, such as Research, Planning, Communication and Evaluation.
7. Five C's of events cover: Conceptualization, Costing, Canvassing, Customization, Conclusion.
8. Public relations communication plan is a prerequisite to the successful event management to draw media attention. Media plan includes: print media, electronic media, new media, word of mouth, exhibitions, etc.
9. Open house is a public relations event to expose the functioning of an organisation to both internal and external public, including the families of the workforce.
10. Open house is also called community visitation as it involves keeping the company open for the visit of community, enabling them to know what the company is doing for the society.

REVIEW QUESTIONS

1. Define an event and give examples of three different types of events. Explain how they benefit the organisation.
2. What do you mean by event management? Describe its process to accomplish its objectives.
3. Public relations communication plan as to gain media attention is a pre-requisite to the success of an event. Discuss.
4. How does 'open house' help an organisation to reach its goals?
5. Make an objective assessment of a case study on event management and explain its results.

Multimedia PR Campaigns

> Media mix is an ideal strategy to reach out diversified audience and to accomplish the goals of public relations.

CONTENTS

- What is a Campaign?
- Types of Campaign
- Ten Commandments of a PR Campaign

WHAT IS A CAMPAIGN?

The *Reader's Digest Great Dictionary of the English Language* defines a 'campaign' as an organised course of action to achieve a goal. The word 'campaign' derives from the French *'Campagne'*, meaning open country. The change in meaning occurred in the 17th century, from the military practice of moving out at the start of summer from a fortress or town into open country where the soldiers would be camped in the open for the summer season or for the duration of one continuous series of operations. In modern times, military activity is less dependent on the weather, and campaign denotes the operations themselves rather than their season. Campaign is described as a concerted effort in support of a cause, product or service to achieve a marketing or public relations objective.

A campaign is the strategic design of a series of messages sent to one or more targeted populations for a discrete period of time in response to a positive or negative situation affecting the organisation. The key to the definition of a campaign is that it is created by an organisation like a profit-oriented corporation, a political candidate or a social agency to communicate to a single small audience such as employees within one office or to millions of persons in multiple audiences across the nation (*Encyclopedia of Public Relations*, 2005).

The term 'campaign' is often used in the context of media studies which refer to an organised action, a series of operations in achieving a specific result or a particular corporate goal or interrelated goals through the media and methods. A company runs a successful advertising campaign to promote say its new brand of washing powder Nirma.

A good reputation or better public understanding is not something that is earned with a press-button approach. It has to be carefully planned and considerably cultivated. Good reputation is something that is earned over a period of time which promotes not only understanding, but also develops people's support for an organisation. Therefore, public relations has to adopt a campaign approach to achieve organisational goals in a scientific manner.

Conceptualisation Model of Campaign

Five factors identify and distinguish a campaign designed by a PR professional. This is also known as conceptualisation model of a campaign which is based on five key elements:

1. Campaign problem (issue affecting the organisation—a crisis, or a positive project)
2. Nature of organisation (NGO or profit, sale of products, services, social cause)
3. Campaign plan objectives and action plans (plans to reach objectives)
4. Nature of audience (Employees, Stakeholders, Media)
5. Media strategy (media mix to reach out the audience)

Any campaign has to be developed on these five basic elements.

PR Campaign Defined

What is a public relations campaign? When the principles, techniques and media of public relations are applied in a campaign approach to accomplish a particular goal or goals of an organisation, it is termed as **public relations campaign**. It is against this background, campaigns are designed around a corporate mission statement or an objective with bearing on the corporate mission or goals. All campaigns are planned well and coordinated with specific objectives and purposeful actions to solve problems confronting an organisation.

Multimedia PR Campaign

What is then multimedia public relations campaign? Indian audiences are varied and represent multilingual, multi-religious groups with different socio-economic background. They comprise both literates and illiterates. Such a diversified audience cannot be reached with a single medium either newspapers or radio. Therefore, a multimedia approach is the best way to reach the Indian public. **Multimedia public relations campaign** may be defined as a planned and action-oriented public relations programme based on a judicious media mix aimed at persuading the target audience in accomplishing set corporate objectives or a specific project. The use of more than one media constitutes a special characteristic of multimedia campaign. Media mix is an ideal strategy to reach out diversified audience.

TYPES OF CAMPAIGN

Campaigns are divided into different types depending on the nature of the problem or campaign situation. The most accepted conceptual campaigns are: commercial campaigns, advertising campaigns, marketing, poverty eradication campaigns, political campaigns, social issue campaigns, health education campaigns, family planning campaigns, small savings campaigns. And now we have public relations campaign.

PR Campaign

Public relations campaigns can be divided further into sub-campaigns based on the type of audience to be targeted. Public relations campaigns include: media relations, employees relations, shareholders or investor relations, customer relations, dealers and suppliers relations, stakeholders relations. For each of these campaigns, the traits of the audiences inherently label and identify the kind of campaign.

Public relations campaigns can also be divided into different types depending on the purpose of the campaign, viz. public awareness campaign, public information campaign, public education campaign, advocacy campaign. Each campaign has a specific set of objectives. If public awareness campaign is to create and promote awareness about a new scheme or a new product, public information campaign provides full information about the scheme or a product besides creating awareness. The literacy campaigns are intended to educate the people.

LIC Campaign

'*Bima Nivesh*', a single premium payment campaign launched by the Life Insurance Corporation of India, was intended both for creating awareness and for providing full information on the new product. One advertisement on this new scheme with a heading 'Single Solution for Multiple Needs' gives more details of the new product. *Bima Nivesh*, its features such as single premium, short term, tax benefits, safety, liquidity, life cover, and attractive returns are highlighted in the advertisement for the benefit of the prospective LIC customers. Public education campaign using the word education in the pedagogical way, equips a person with instructional material for being sufficiently educated. For example, the National Literacy Mission is a campaign intended to eradicate illiteracy in the country by providing non-formal education.

Advocacy Campaign

Advocacy is one of the functions of public relations. Advocacy public relations arises from public issues that confront an organisation. Such issues are subject of legislation or regulation. They may result from outside forces threatening the organisation. Advocacy campaign may range from influencing the Municipal Corporation to change zoning restriction to lobbying for tax incentives. For example, the Government of India has issued orders that the symbol of 'Skull and Bones" be used on *beedis* packet as a warning symbol to avoid smoking. Based on the campaign and pressure of political parties, the Government of India has postponed the decision of Skull Mark in December 2006.

In such cases, organisations launch advocacy campaigns with specific messages as a part of their public relations strategy. Advocacy campaigns are elaborate, expensive efforts to influence the opinion of key publics on a particular issue or towards a particular cause. Such campaigns make use of the press and often television and direct mail, and certainly the web. Other strategies include advertising, letters to the editor, legislators or other decision-makers.

It is against this background, several types of campaigns have been launched in India, such as Family Planning Campaign, National Savings Campaign, Pulse Polio Immunisation Campaign, AIDS Control Campaign, Election Campaigns, etc. All such campaigns from public relations angle have three distinct components, namely *Information*, *Education* and *Motivation*. These campaigns based on multimedia, utilise both public relations and advertising techniques.

The difference between a public relations campaign and an advertising campaign is that an advertising campaign promotes sales, while a public relations campaign aims at the services, products or ideas by creating a favourable environment. Indeed, most organisations have more than one campaign in action at a given point of time. A good example can be taken from the Health and Family Welfare Department which runs several campaigns simultaneously to reach the goal of 'HEALTH FOR ALL'. They include: separate campaigns on AIDS Control, Pulse Polio Immunisation, Family Welfare, Malaria Eradication.

Goals of PR Campaign

There are five main goals of public relations campaign:

1. To inform and create awareness on the implementation of campaign plan.
2. To persuade, educate and motivate.
3. To mobilise public opinion towards ideas and actions.
4. To utilise appropriate media and methods in reaching out the target audiences.
5. To give results by implementing the programmes and solve the problem.

In fact, effectiveness of a campaign lies on the 'outcome' rather than one 'process'. In other words, what is the impact of a campaign on the audience can be known only through the measurement of the plan.

TEN COMMANDMENTS OF A PR CAMPAIGN

Grounding a public relations campaign or programme can be an overwhelming task. A systematic and scientific approach is needed. But as with any project, the secret of success lies in advanced planning and effective implementation. Ten Commandments constitute a public relations campaign. See Figure 30.1.

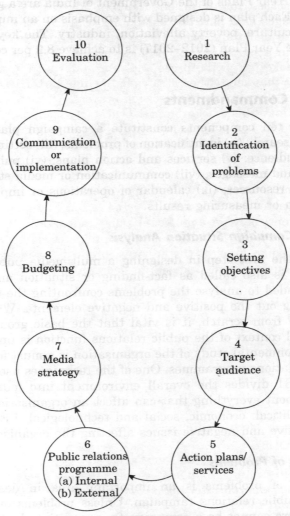

Figure 30.1 Ten Commandments of public relations campaign.

Planning

Planning is an important facet of campaign management. In fact, planning is the foundation for the success of any project. There are several good reasons for planning. Some of them are as follows:

- It determines priorities among many issues
- It enables to concentrate efficiently and work effectively
- It provides a vision for the organisation with long-term and short-term perspectives
- It minimises mishaps both at the micro and at the macro levels
- It promotes proactive activities and gives positive results

The Five Year Plans of the Government of India are a good example of planning. Each plan is designed with emphasis on an important area, such as agriculture, poverty alleviation, industry. The key objective of the 12th Five Year Plan (2012–2017) is to achieve 8.2 per cent economic growth.

Campaign Commandments

As many as ten components constitute a campaign planning. They include: (i) research; (ii) identification of problems; (iii) setting objectives; (iv) target audience; (v) services and action plans; (vi) public relations programme and messages; (vii) communication or media strategy; (viii) budgeting or resources; (ix) calendar of operations or implementation; (x) evaluation or measuring results.

Research or Campaign Situation Analysis

Research is the first step in designing a multimedia public relations campaign. It is also called as fact-finding or situation analysis. This stage is intended to analyse the problems confronting the organisation besides listing out the positive and negative elements. When starting a programme from scratch, it is vital that the basic ground research on the overall context of the public relations function is undertaken. A general environmental study of the organisation is a must for launching any public relations programmes. One of the techniques used is a PEST analysis. PEST divides the overall environment into four areas and covers just about everything that can affect an organisation. The four areas are: political, economic, social and technological. PEST analysis gives us positive and negative issues affecting the organisation.

Identification of Problems

Identification of problems is an important area in designing and planning a public relations campaign. Unless problems or issues are identified, there cannot be a campaign for any action. In the research or analysis of the functioning of Municipal Corporation of Hyderabad, among others, the stray dog menace in the city was one that came to light. There were over 10,000 stray dogs in Hyderabad city and about 200 persons became victims of dog bites every day. Such a problem had to be tackled through a public relations campaign.

Setting Objectives

Setting realistic objectives is absolutely necessary, if the campaign is to achieve something tangible. The kinds of objectives public relations campaigns can have are to inform, educate and motivate for creating awareness and understanding among the people.

Anne Gregory in her book *The Art and Science of Public Relations,* Volume 2, 2000 says that there are seven imperatives that must be borne in mind while setting objectives. They are detailed here.

1. **Set public relations objectives:** There is a tendency of public relations professionals to set objectives that public relations cannot deliver. It is not reasonable to say that public relations should increase sales by 20 per cent. That depends on the sales force. It is reasonable to say that presentations should be made to 50 per cent of key retailers to tell them of a new product and try it. It may well be that as a result, sales may increase by 20 per cent, but it is outside the scope of public relations to promise this.

2. **Ally to organisational objectives:** Public relations programmes and campaigns must support corporate objectives. If a corporate objective is a major repositioning of the company in its market, then the public relations effort must be directed to supporting that stance.

3. **Be precise and specific:** Objectives need to be sharp. To create awareness is not good enough. Creating awareness of what, to whom, when and how needs to be clearly spelt out. No element of ambiguity should be there.

4. **Do what is achievable:** It is better to set modest objectives and hit them than hitch your wagon to the stars. Wherever possible evaluate the likely benefits of ideas and pre-test the pilot schemes. If a major part of the programme is to contact all investors to inform them of a particular development, you must be sure you can do it within the framework of the stock market rules.

5. **Quantify as much as possible:** Not all objectives are precisely quantifiable, but most of them are. If the aim is to contact particular audience groups, say how many. Quantifying objectives makes evaluation much easier.

6. **Work within the budget:** This goes without saying. It is no good claiming to be creative, and, therefore, not interested in

money. A good planner and manager knows exactly how much the things will cost, and will run the budget tracking programme.

7. **Work to a priority list:** Public relations professionals always have too much to do and they could extend their list of activities without an end. Know what your priorities are and stick to them irrevocably. If you have to function on non-prioritised work, make sure you let your superiors know the consequence of their demands. Prioritising objectives enables you to see where the major effort is to be focused.

Some examples of workable objectives are as follows:

(a) **Trade:** Ensure 100 top dealers attend annual dealers' conference.
(b) **Media coverage:** Increase levered editorial coverage of service by 20 per cent.
(c) **Objectives:** Public relations campaign can be effective and produce tangible results only if objectives are developed in relation to identified problems.

Target audiences

Public are the lifeblood of an organisation. There are groupings of public that are fairly common to most organisations. Public relations' public could be divided into two broad segments: **internal public** (employees) and **external public** (customers and others). In fact, the general public in public relations is a myth. We have only specific target-oriented public, such as employees, shareholders, customers, media. The Hyderabad city population is about 50 lakhs. Though Hyderabad city is one, the people of the city are divided into two broad segments depending on their socio-economic background as urban and rural(slums), educated and illiterate. Different linguistic and religious groups live in the city. People who live in slums are those migrated from villages. Public relations campaign, therefore, is aimed at segmented public rather than general public. The best way to categorise public is to move from the general to the specific.

Services and action plans

If the campaign is intended to solve a problem, the management must design services and action plans for the benefit of the target audience. Programmes that aim to produce radical shifts in behaviour and attitude will be more useful. If there are no services or qualitative products, there is no campaign for the public. In fact, they are two prerequisites.

In a Pulse Polio Immunisation Programme, opening of centres with adequate provision for pulse polio drops acts as service plans. Such centres were opened at all hospitals, health clinics, bus stations, railway stations, community centres enabling the people to get their children administered with polio drops on a single day. As many as over eight lakh Aasha workers function in villages to inform and educate each household on pulse polio drops. The Municipal Corporation of Hyderabad has opened dog clinics and also increased dog catching squads to control stray dog menace as part of PR campaign.

PR programme

The next step in campaign planning after services and action plans relates to public relations programme. Organisations very often forget the communication component in many of the campaigns and development projects. In fact, eradication of information poverty is a prerequisite to the eradication of economic poverty. Unfortunately, removal of ignorance or information poverty is not given due importance. Therefore, public relations communication content assumes great importance in any public relations campaign.

Action projects/services of the organisation and messages of the public relations department act as two eyes of the campaign. Public relations programme based on the action projects encompasses all the communication activities which an organisation undertakes as part of campaign planning. The broad elements of a public relations programme include: corporate identity; corporate advertising; issues management; crisis management; employee communications; community relations; sponsorship; media relations; monitoring and reviewing. All these areas of public relations as applicable to a campaign must be grounded in the communication stage. Campaign plan should involve employees to provide service to the target audience.

Media strategy

How do we manage communication? It is only through an appropriate media strategy and tactics to keep the public informed of both services and action plans designed as part of the campaign besides grounding all plans. Communication programme of any campaign is meant to change the attitudes of both internal and external audience. Such a programme is based on persuasive messages which are important components of communication plan. TATA Indica car's message "More Car Per Car" is a good example of an advertising and public relations message. Another example can be taken from the India Post that has a main message on its commitment to the community which says that **India Post Delivers 4.3 crore Pieces of Mail Every Day linking Every Nook and Corner of the Country. No other media can match the sheer expanse of India Post in terms of volume and direct personal reach.**

A very clear example of media strategy and tactics can be derived from the multimedia approach adopted by the Ministry of Health, Government of India in the case of Pulse Polio Immunisation Programme to eradicate polio. Multimedia in Pulse Polio campaigns covers interpersonal media, traditional folk art media, mass media and IT new mass media to reach both urban and rural target groups. Media tactics include: press release, press conference, advertising, public meeting, radio, television talks, songs, street plays. A combination of four types of media: interpersonal media; traditional media, mass media and IT new media is an ideal communication model to suit the communication needs of the Indian public who belong to different religious, linguistic, rural and urban backgrounds. As a result of multimedia, the Pulse Polio Immunisation campaign, about 17 crore children were administered pulse polio drops on a single day in one of the campaigns. In the process WHO, declared India as a polio free country. That was the impact of the campaign.

Budget

Dr. Dough Newsom (US) compared a campaign to a building. The floor is the organisation's mission statement and acts as the foundation to support the entire campaign and the budget is the roof. Supporting pillars are the methods and research that give an insight into the correct approaches to the campaign. The roof of the building is equal to the budgeting of the campaign. Without a roof, a house is not habitable. So minus the budget, a public relations campaign is equal to a zero.

It will thus be seen that operating costs of the campaign are of vital importance. When costing out public relations activities, two vital aspects need to be borne in mind, effectiveness and efficiency. The budget may be divided into three parts—staff salaries, operating cost and equipment.

Communication or implementation

Two things are peculiar to a public relations practitioner's life. The first is that there will never be enough time to do everything that needs to be done because the tasks and possibilities for action are always far greater than the time available. The second is that because public relations tasks often involve other people and the coordination of several departments, the completion of the task always takes longer time than you think initially.

In addition, there are two interlinked facets that must be taken into account when considering calendar and timescales. The first is that deadlines must be fixed so that the tasks associated with a campaign can be completed on time. The second is that the right financial resources need to be allocated so that the tasks in hand can be completed satisfactorily.

There should be a well-thought out calendar of operations that have to be worked depending on the nature of the event. Topicality may be kept in mind. Any campaign in agriculture must be organised in the monsoon season so that the farmers could be fully involved. Services and messages must always go hand in hand in the implementation of a campaign plan.

Evaluation

The last and the most important step in campaign managing is evaluation or measuring the results. The principle *research before, research during,* and *research after* or pre-plan research, interim research and post-plan research are the guiding principles to strengthen the campaign planning and also evaluate the results. In fact, evaluation is an ongoing process. Research before represents fact-finding state, research during enables the public relations managers to adopt mid-course corrections in the communication stage and the research after deals with the last step evaluation, i.e. measuring results.

Evaluation is intended to:

- Demonstrate effectiveness
- Ensure cost efficiency
- Facilitate accountability
- Measure outcomes against objectives
- Measure exposure of audience to media and messages
- Measure impact of services and action plans
- Measure the image of your organisation in terms of the services and draw inferences to guide future campaign

There are three main ways to evaluate and measure public relations results:

1. Observation and self-experience
2. Feedback information and analysis
3. Research—primary and secondary research

Evaluation is always undertaken against the objectives set. If the dogs campaign of the Municipal Corporation of Hyderabad is to prevent dog bites, the number of dog bites per day whether increased or decreased could be ascertained only through evaluation. In this instant, the evaluation revealed that the number of dog bites in Hyderabad city decreased from 200 a day to 63 in a period of two years. You have succeeded in your campaign. For example, over 17 crore children between the age of 3–5 were administered pulse polio drops on a single day in the year 2000—thanks to the pulse polio immunisation campaign.

If professional excellence is our objective, the Indian public relations should adopt campaign planning approach either to achieve specific goals or to solve the organisational problems. But, very few public relations organisations in India go in for multimedia public relations campaigns. This approach will change for the better. See Figure 30.2. for media umbrella model.

Action Plan Messages

Media-Mix

Newspapers 1	Corporate Publications 2	Photographs 3	Television & Radio 4	Film 5	IT New Mass Media 6	Advertising Media 7	Exhibitions 8	Traditional Folk Media 9	Interpersonal Media 10
Press Releases	Books	News Photos	News	Documentaries	Computer	Press ads	Trade Fairs	Songs	Public - meetings
Features	Pamphlets	Photo features	Documentaries	PR Films	Internet	Radio ads	Agri-exhibition	Dances	Group discussion
Rejoinders	Folders	Product-photos	Features	Features	Intranet	TV ads	Art-exhibition	Drama	Round-table conference
Letters to the Editor	Handbooks	Photos for TV	Commercial spots	Ad-films	e-mail	Corporate-ads institutional ads	Leather Fair	Harikatha	Panel-discussions
Press Conference	Manuals	Photos in: Publications exhibitions	Interviews	News magazines	Website	Public Service ads	Mobile Exhibition	Burrakatha	Conferences
Press Tour	House-magazines	Ad. Photos	Panel discussion	Film stirrups	Weblog	Classified ads	Rural Exhibition	Street plays	Seminar
Press Kit	Annual Reports	Pictorial-albums	Talks	Tele-films	Video	Out-door Hoardings	Industrial Exhibition	Puppet-shows	Symposia
Specialised Newspapers	Calendars	Product Photos	Specialised audience programme	Cinema-slides	News Release	Electronic ads	Bulletin-boards	Folk forms	Annual General Meeting
	Diaries		Public Service announcements	Cinema-houses	Fax			Bhajans	Meet the - Customers
	Greeting-cards			Video cassettes	CD ROM			Keertans	Open house
	Pictorial Publications			Video magazines	DVD			Folk dances	
	Direct Mail			Video films				music	
	Posters							magic	

The Public and Messages

The Public Understanding of PR

Figure 30.2 The media umbrella model of PR campaign.

POINTS TO REMEMBER

1. What is a campaign? A campaign is the strategic design of a series of messages sent to one or more targeted population for a discrete period of time in response to a positive or negative situation affecting the organisation. A campaign is also defined as an organised course of action to achieve a goal by altering or changing the opinion of any group or groups. Advertising campaigns, for example, aim to change people's choice of product or to persuade them to buy new products. Election campaigns aim to reinforce or change people's voting behaviour.

2. What is public relations campaign? When the principles, techniques and media of public relations are applied in a campaign approach to accomplish a goal or goals of an organisation, it is termed as public relations campaign. All public relations campaigns are planned and well coordinated with specific objectives and purposeful actions to solve the problems confronting an organisation. Public relations campaigns always utilise multimedia to reach the diversified, multilingual and multireligious audiences.

3. What is multimedia public relations campaign? Since India's heterogeneous population cannot be reached with a single media, the concept of multimedia approach emerged. A multimedia public relations campaign is described as a planned and action-oriented public relations programme based on judicious media mix aimed at persuading the target audience in accomplishing set corporate objectives. The use of more than one medium in reaching the diversified audience is the distinct characteristic of multimedia.

4. There are five goals of campaign such as: to create awareness; to persuade and motivate; to mobilise public opinion to adopt multimedia approach in reaching the target audience; and to achieve designed objectives and give results to the management.

5. Campaigns are categorised as: commercial campaigns, advertising campaigns, marketing, political, social issues, public relations campaigns. In each type of campaign public relations has a role to play.

6. Ten commandments of a public relations campaign include: research, identification of problem, setting objectives, target audience, action plans, public relations programme, media strategy, implementation, budget and evaluation.

REVIEW QUESTIONS

1. Define a multimedia public relations campaign. Explain the key objectives of a campaign.

2. What are the various types of campaigns? Discuss their roles.

3. Design a multimedia public relations campaign to solve an identified problem of your organisation. Describe each component of the campaign with examples.

Media Relations

> *It is an immutable law in business that words are words, explanations are explanations, promises are promises—but only the performance is reality.*

CONTENTS

- What is Media Relations?
- Man in the Middle
- Principles of Good Media Relations
- Inter-media Publicity Coordination Committee

WHAT IS MEDIA RELATIONS?

In previous chapters we described two segments of public relations profession. The first part of this book described as to how public relations is practised. The second segment dealt with the media as a tool used in the practice of public relations to reach out the target audiences with messages. In this chapter, we deal with press relations which are applicable to electronic media—radio, television and, news magazines also. Public relations and press relations both have the initials 'PR'. Press relations is an integral part of public relations discipline. The success of media coverage depends on your relations with the news media. If PR manager has good relations with the media, the organisation's reporting in newspapers will be equally good. Of course, it depends on the readers' oriented service of the public relations manager. Dealing with the media in all its forms is one of the most important and most difficult aspects of public relations manager's role.

MAN IN THE MIDDLE

Public relations manager as a person in the middle has to understand the requirements of both the management and the needs of media to provide media-oriented press material for an effective coverage. Media coverage for an organisation depends on maintaining good media relations and serving the newspapers effectively. Therefore, media relations are based on certain principles and it is nothing more than serving the media. In fact, the public relations practitioner is a 'link' between the management and the media. Being a person in the middle, the public relations practitioner must gain confidence of the media and the management of the organisation. Gaining confidence is not an easy task because the interests of the management and the media often do not agree. Sometimes they become adversarial.

Managements want news to be published in a manner that will promote their policies and business interests. They do not relish any criticism whatsoever in the media. Whenever criticism or critical writings appear in the media they react. There are certain cases both in the private and in the government sector to stop advertisements to the newspapers, when critical writings were published. Some organisations tend to use advertisement support as a lever to control the press. But this is not the correct approach to deal with the press. The PR manager's first responsibility as an employee is to get maximum coverage for the organisation and its products and services. On the other hand the media particularly the newspapers like to publish only such news that interests a large number of readers. News of readers interest alone is useful to the newspaper. The journalist always tries to keep the master publisher—the reader, viewer or listener in view while publishing the news and not the management master of PR manager—CEO. It is not what the PR practitioner wants media to publish or broadcast. It may thus be seen that both sides—the managements of various organisations and media managements have legitimate ground about serving their respective masters, viz. chief executives and readers, respectively. Public relations manager who is a 'link' between the management and media has to 'bridge' their viewpoints and bring each side around to understand the problems and perceptions of the other. This can be achieved only through better media relations.

If public relations can be defined as managing relations and understanding between an organisation and its publics in getting company's products or services understood and acceptable, the media relations is termed as *the art of persuading the press that the same organisation is worth getting media coverage*. The most successful press campaigns are those which translate your company's marketing and corporate objectives into media objectives. Media relations is nothing more than serving the media, but there are some basic ground rules and guidelines that need to be followed.

Editor's Comment

"The editors are appalled to see the sloppy copy that comes in the form of press notes. Though the author of such press notes is a qualified public relations officer, there is no professional touch in many of the press notes. Every copy needs a 're-write man'. It doesn't mean that the editors look forward in such press notes any ready-made material that can go straight to composing. What is required is a good copy and up to the point. In a day, an editor receives 300 to 400 press notes and if every press note runs into a number of pages, not only he may not have time to go through all, but he will be terribly bored, with the result important ones will go un-noticed".

Propaganda Material

There is a tendency to stuff the press notes with propaganda material. Authors should first of all know the difference between publicity and propaganda and they should confine themselves to gain publicity for a particular event or activity, and not try to brain-wash the editors or propagate their viewpoint. If the press notes are losing credibility among the editors, it is because of this tendency of the public relations officers to load them with propaganda material. The public relations officers should make it a point to prepare the press notes in a crisp news form. On the contrary, if it is stuffed with propaganda, it is bound to reach its due place in a newspaper office, that is 'dustbin', or a waste paper basket.

Unlike other publics, media is both a constituency and a conduit to all other audiences—employees, shareholders, customers, general community who as stakeholders are concerned with your organisation. Media, therefore, gets priority in public relations plan. So, the Public Relations Officer's aim should be to fight for editor's attention with the limited time he has at his disposal by providing news of public interest.

What is media relations? Media relations may be defined as a process of public relations to achieve maximum media coverage of public relations information both in print and in electronic media as a measure to create knowledge among the publics and gain understanding towards organisational goals. Good media relations are created and maintained only through honest and newsworthy and public interest information provided in an atmosphere of mutual trust and understanding between public relations and media. News service is the watchword in media relations.

A means to an end

Once an Admiral asked a young midshipman what was the purpose of gunnery. "The reply came" "To fire the gun Sir". The Admiral's face purpled and he shouted "Boy" the purpose of gunnery is not just to fire the gun but it is to hit the target. So also the purpose of media relations is not just to issue press releases or handle press enquiries from journalists. The real purpose of media relations is to reach out the target audience with a specific message to influence them towards organisation's products, services and enhance its reputation. Therefore, media relations act as a means to an end—understanding of media as gate keepers and target the audience with a message.

Objectives

The objectives of media relations include:

- maintaining a media list with names/publications
- improving better relations with media persons and media organisations
- changing the attitudes and behaviour of target audience through media
- improving company or brand image
- increasing marketing share
- influencing government policy at local/national and international levels
- improving communications with shareholders, financial analysts and investors
- creating awareness, knowledge and gaining public understanding
- acting as a source of information to media
- providing press releases loaded with public interest information

Shortcomings of the Press

Media has both positive and negative areas. In fact, crowded and competitive media environment is a real challenge before any public relations outfit to carry the right information to the people. It is for public relations to understand these aspects of media before embarking on relations with the representatives of media. Here is a list of shortcomings of the press as pointed out by some experts.

Shortcomings of the Press

- Caters to the elitist, neglecting the issues of the less privileged
- Politicians and corporations try to win over journalists
- Crass communication: market-oriented but not mass-oriented
- Sensationalism
- Dishonest means of gathering information and tapping information sources
- The line between advertising and editorial matter is not kept clear-advertorials
- Proprietors of media dictate than working editors and devaluation of editor
- Paid news concept has emerged in the news coverage

It is against this background that Dr. A.S. Anand, former Chief Justice of India once said: "while commercialization has a legitimate place in the business office of a newspaper, it becomes a danger when it invades the editorial room".

Complaints Against PR

If there are some shortcomings in media, the media also point out the limitations of public relations. The complaints of the media against public relations are as follows:

- PR Press releases are not professionally written that can go straight for publishing in a newspaper
- PR Manager always tries to colour the press release with adjectives or suppress free flow of legitimate news under management pressure
- PR Manager is not free to select news kindling reader's interest
- Media relations are boss-oriented but not readers' oriented, who are the masters of newspaper
- PR Press releases project only positive news of an organisation, suppressing news of negative nature
- PR managers sometimes tell the stories off the record.
- Media releases are very long, difficult to use within limited space or time
- PR professionals make unsolicited phone calls to media, when they are busy in their work
- PR practitioners try to lure media for editorial coverage with advertisements
- As part of misinformation campaign, PR keeps the media in the dark to cover up the scams

An understanding of shortcomings of both media and public relations is an essential stage to launch media relations campaign by any public relations practitioner.

PRINCIPLES OF GOOD MEDIA RELATIONS

Better press relations are maintained by public relations managers by practicing certain principles as good service, honesty, frankness, impartiality, accuracy, truth, helping attitude, etc. The relationship between the public relations professional and the media largely depends on the news of public interest. The first challenge, therefore, that the news provided by public relations professional must be of public interest or it must answer the question; 'is it newsworthy?' It must answer the following—Ten Guidelines.

Good media relations are built and maintained only through honest and audiences'-oriented news service provided in an atmosphere of mutual trust and understanding between public relations and the media. Here are the guidelines:

Understanding the Media

You must have a thorough understanding of the functioning of newspapers, their deadlines, schedules, requirements of news, etc. Get an idea of the differences in style, contents of the national, regional and local newspapers. Then exploit them to the advantage of your organisation by feeding the press with readers'-oriented news. This can be acquired by examining the various items published in newspapers, news programmes broadcast by radio and television. In fact, every public relations manager must not only read Programme Guide to Radio and Television being published in newspapers but also see and listen programmes. Visits to publishers, printers and studios are also very helpful in understanding the media. However, public relations practitioner needs to know about the nature of the press-editorial policy, circulation area and readership profile.

Media list

Having understood, the functioning of media, public relations manager must compile and maintain a media list with personal contact names, telephone, e-mail, publication details etc for maintaining relations and sending press releases. It acts as an address book.

Good Service

Better service is the key to success of press relations. What the press expects is that the public relations should feed them with the news of public interest. The best way to gain confidence of media is, therefore, to provide them with press material in the form in which it is published. Newspapers publish news and views in various forms, such as news reports, features, letter to the editor, etc. A good copy will always deserve publication. Good photographs are important to illustrate appropriate news releases and other media services. Create a website with relevant corporate information. Keep it up-to-date with photographs and press releases. Public relations manager must think and act as journalists think. They must be a reliable source of information because media is hungry for information.

Remember, news is not just information it is about communicating value and benefit for the audience. Send short and concise press release. Long missives often go unread. Media loves stories with pictures, send press releases with picture for effective coverage. Media wants newsworthy items that are useful to the readers or benefit them.

Be proactive

Having understood the media expectations you can anticipate their needs and provide them with the appropriate news stories. Keeping in view market situations, you can create a news worthiness for your services and products. Press relations manager tends to be reactive with newspapers. That is not a correct approach. Be proactive and gain the goodwill of the media by providing newsworthy stories. Allowing journalists to see things for themselves is an added advantage.

Impartiality

Public relations should never develop partiality towards only a few media persons. A fundamental principle in public relations is that a public relations manager cannot favour only one news source, ignoring others or at the expense of other news outlets. When the pressmen come to know that a public relations manager has given a particular story only to a few favourite friends, the public relations manager then risks the confidence and goodwill of other newsmen. As part of good press relations, it is advisable that press releases should be sent to all and not to a few selected ones. One should be impartial. This will also establish your reputation and credibility. As most journalists view PR professionals as the source who can provide information, make media as friends. It will be a "win-win situation" for you.

Oral Request

It is the practice with some public relations managers to telephone and ask newspapers to publish their stories. It is interesting to know that once a public relations person representing the textile company went to a News Editor with a press note for publication. The public relations person after sometime asked the news editor to return the press note if there was any difficulty for its publication, so that it could be given to another newspaper. Nothing irritates the media persons more than a public relations manager who goes on requesting the newspapers to publish their stories. If the material is not newsworthy, any amount of personal effort in getting it published will be a waste. Never make any unsolicited phone calls to media.

No Suppression

Once a public relations manager working for a fertiliser manufacturing company was asked to suppress the news about the strike of the employees. But public relations manager told the management that it was not his job to suppress the facts. Public relations is based on truth.

The public relations manager then suggested that the news about the welfare measures taken by the company for the benefit of employees, the demands accepted and difficulties in not acceding to other demands of employees could be highlighted instead of prevailing upon the press to suppress the news about the strike. The management readily agreed to the suggestion and the views of the management and the news about the strike were published simultaneously.

A public relations manager, therefore, has no right to ask a newspaper, radio or television to kill a story or publish the way in which the management expects. To any media person such requests are nothing but an insult. It is asking media men, to betray the trust reposed in them by the readers. Such attempts will only bring ill-will and not goodwill from the press. Therefore, never try to slant the facts or tell only half the story. Never provide false information. Be a professional, when media will respect your professionalism as a source for journalists.

Over Communication

It is the practice with some of the public relations managers to send press notes regularly whether they are of news value or not. In fact we live in an era of information explosion and newspapers get endless messages from all over the world either from their own correspondents or from news agencies. Against this background, if public relations manager goes on flooding the newspapers with their material of no relevance to readers, it may result in negative relations. One should be very selective in sending press notes. Remember that any over communication is counterproductive. When there is any tie-up with celebrity or well-known personality, the PR event gets plenty of ink and airtime.

Helpful Attitude in Emergencies

Management confront with crises be it a strike, a natural calamity or an accident. In such situations, media persons would like to have full details of the incident which has great relevance to readers. An incident, if not handled properly can, at one stroke mar the reputation of the management built up over many years. Cyclones, rail, road, air and fire accidents are a few to quote. The public relations manager must be of great help to the media and extend all possible assistance to them. The presentation of unbiased facts and full information can prevent a bad situation from becoming worse.

Crisis guidelines

In all crises and emergencies, the following guidelines may be followed:

1. Give the media persons all the facts you have at your hand promptly and explain to them what the organisation is doing in meeting the crises.
2. Establish a control room or media centre which could feed the media round the clock.
3. Explain the measures taken by the organisation to provide relief and rehabilitation.
4. Explain the losses and the extent of damage.
5. Explain the preventive measures the organisation has proposed.
6. The best way to explain the situation would be to invite the media persons to the scene of accident and enable them to see for themselves and write stories.

Press Enquiries

Press persons often ask public relations managers certain information about the organisation. Since media work under tight deadlines, time is always important. The public relations manager must answer all such questions promptly and accurately. However, he or she should be careful in comments. Never tell the media anything 'off the record'.

Headless chickens-Off-the-record

India's Ambassador to the US, Ronen Sen in a telephonic interview with the Managing Director, *Rediff India Abroad* on political turmoil in India over the Indo-US Civil Nuclear Deal was reported to have said "It has been approved here (Washington) by the President and there New Delhi, it has been approved by the 'Indian Cabinet'. So why do you have all this running around like 'headless chickens' looking for a comment here or comment there, and these little storms in a tea cup".

The Ambassador's interview figured in the Indian Parliament during August 2007 and Members of Parliament in both the Houses felt the reference 'Headless Chickens' was about them and demanded that he be recalled. Some MPs even gave privilege motions objecting to such unwarranted remarks.

The Ambassador stated that he had an "Off-the Record" conversation with correspondent giving some assessment on the Nuclear Deal. Some of the comments were made in his personal capacity and did not reflect the views of the Government. His remarks Headless Chickens were about 'my media friends'. A number of the comments were, however, misunderstood, misquoted out of the context, the Ambassador said. Later the Indian Ambassador in Washington Ronen Sen offered "sincere and unqualified apology" to the members of parliament.

The Managing Editor, Rediff India Abroad who reported justified his coverage and said that the comments of the Ambassador were made over phone on 19 August, 2007 and at no point of time did Ronen Sen say the conversation was off-the-record (*The Hindu*). This off-the-record episode landed the Indian Ambassador in trouble.

If the public relations manager does not know the answer, instead of telling the press that he does not know, it would be more appropriate to tell the newsmen that he would check up from the Officer concerned and let him know. The public relation manager should follow it up and see that the answer is provided as early as possible. This type of helpfulness will help the public relations in building up long range media relations.

Rapport with All

One day when a public relations manager visited the news room for handling over a press note, a senior sub-editor indirectly commented 'How is that this public relation manager who only maintains contacts with the editor has come to the news room'. This indicates that public relations manager was only in touch with editor and not the news editor and sub-editors who actually handle the news desk and who really matter in selection of news.

Public relations managers generally keep contact only with the correspondents forgetting that there are a number of other news persons such as editors, news editors, sub-editors, leader writers, special correspondents, etc. who matter much in the publication of news. Public relation managers must establish direct contact and personal relationship with all levels of news persons—producers. Such contact should be regular and not only when you have work with them. Since public relations has become a 24 hours job, because of 24 hours news channels, public relations professionals must always be accessible to the media. Be polite and respectful to all media outlets. Courtesy keeps everybody happy.

No confrontation

Sometimes uncomfortable news and critical news are published in newspapers against the managements. To deal with such situations, highest skill is called for. If there is any criticism about the organisation in the press, it must be contradicted and corrected in prudent and restrained language. Rejoinders, contradictions of the management are bound to get coverage in the newspapers. Confrontation with the press will not augur well for public relations. We must remember that 'the press fires the last shot'.

Deserve and Desire

While dealing with the subject press and public relations, a very senior editor of a newspaper advised public relations managers to remember the dictum 'First Deserve and Then Desire'. This advice came in the context that the press should be approached only if there is something worthwhile for publication. In other words an item which has news value automatically deserves publication. This is the best principle of press relations. Deserve and Desire will go hand in hand.

Qualities

To be successful, the media relationship programme between public relations professionals and journalists should be based on mutual trust and confidence. The following qualities are essential if a public relations practitioner wants to gain confidence of media persons (*Public Relations Manual, Tymson & Lazar, Australia*).

Honesty	Courtesy
Frankness	Clarity
Fairness	Objectivity
Reliability	Commonsense
Helpfulness	Enthusiasm
Accuracy	Patience

Professionalism

Above all, PR manager must get recognition as a true professional with all qualifications and qualities of professional excellence. If he/she is an author, a writer, connected with a PR professional body, it is an added value. Your professional excellence is the watchword for your success in media relations.

INTER-MEDIA PUBLICITY COORDINATION COMMITTEE

The public relations manager is expected to maintain cordial relations with government media such as the All India Radio, Doordarshan, Films Division, Press Information Bureau, Directorate of Advertising and Visual Publicity, Directorate of Field Publicity, etc. which are charged with the responsibility of giving publicity to the various activities of the government departments and public sector undertakings. Public relations managers connected with government and public sector organisations can get fair coverage through these media units by adopting, the same principles of press relations.

The Government of India have constituted a State level Inter-Media Publicity Coordination Committee at each of the State capitals with heads of various Government of India media units, Director of Information and Public Relations of the State Government, Public Relations Managers of various Central and State Public Sector Undertaking as members. The senior most officer of the Ministry of Information and Broadcasting stationed in the State capital city will be the Chairman of this committee. The committee provides an excellent forum for various public relations managers of both the Central and the State Governments to design and launch publicity programmes in collaboration with the Government of India media units. The Committee meets once a month. All important publicity campaigns such as pulse polio immunisation, AIDS control, family welfare are discussed in the meeting and due publicity is given through various media units. As part of the nationwide intensified pulse polio immunisation programme, as many as 17 crore children aged below five years were administered with pulse polio drops in our country on a single day on 7 January 2007. The Inter-media Publicity Coordination Committees of 28 States in India have played a pivotal role in mobilising and sensitising parents all over the country through government media.

POINTS TO REMEMBER

1. Public Relations manager acts as a 'Man in the Middle' between the organisation he represents and the media which gives coverage for the organisation. But organisations and media differ in reaching the audiences. The management of an organisation does not relish any adverse criticism in the media. On the other hand, the media publish or broadcast only such news which is of public interest.

2. Public Relations manager must understand the requirements of both the organisation and the media, and bridge their viewpoints. He should bring each side around to understand the problems and perceptions of the other for the good of community.

3. Media relations may be described as a process of public relations to achieve maximum media coverage as a measure to create knowledge among the target audience and gain understanding towards organisational goals, products, services, etc.

4. However, good media relations are created and maintained only through honest and newsworthy and public interest information provided in an atmosphere of mutual trust and understanding between public relations and media. News service of public interest is the watchword in media relations.

5. The objectives of media relations include improving better relations with media organisations and media persons, conveying messages to the target-audience through media, creating better understanding between organisations and the public stakeholders.

6. The guidelines of good media relations are understanding the media, good news service of public interest, impartiality, no oral requests for publication of news, no suppression of news, over communication counter productive, helpful attitude in emergencies, answers to press enquiries promptly and accurately, maintain rapport with all media persons, and deserve and desire.

7. The Inter-media publicity coordination committee of the Ministry of Information and Broadcasting functions at each of the State capitals in India with local heads of media units of government of India, Public Relations Managers of State and Central Public Sector Undertakings and Director of the State Information and Public Relations Department. The Committee will design plans for giving good coverage of all government publicity campaigns through AIR, Doordarshan and other media units.

REVIEW QUESTIONS

1. What do you mean by media relations? Explain the factors that justify the need for good media relations.

2. 'Public Relations Manager is the Man in the Middle' between an organisation and the media. Discuss.

3. What are the objectives of media relations? How do they help an organisation?

4. List out a few shortcomings of the press? Cite examples.

5. What are the complaints of the media against public relations professionals?

6. Give some guidelines for building and maintaining good media relations.

7. How can the inter-media publicity coordination committee help better coverage of public relations campaigns in Government?

PART FIVE

Professional Excellence in Public Relations

✓ Effective Writing for Public Relations

✓ How to Be a Good PR Manager

✓ Public Relations into the Future

	Chapter
Effective Writing for Public Relations	32

> *Writing is man's greatest invention. It enables us to converse with the dead, the absent and the unborn, all at great distances of time and space. To it we owe everything which distinguishes us from savages. Take it from us and the Bible, all history, all sciences, all government, and nearly all social intercourse go with it.*
>
> **—Abraham Lincoln**

C O N T E N T S

10 GOLDEN GUIDELINES FOR EFFECTIVE WRITING

Public relations practitioners should have a command of the language they communicate in, and a mastery of basic writing principles. The ability to arrange words and express meanings clearly is a skill that has to be learnt and practised in a natural way. Here are the 10 golden guidelines for effective writing.

Writing Skill: Rock Foundation of PR

The emphasis on writing and expressing thoughts effectively matches closely with public relations functions. According to a survey conducted in the USA, news releases and media relations were ranked important by 99% of the practitioners. Public relations manager writes for corporate publications, speeches, talks, exhibitions, etc.

Thus, it will be clear that the foundation of all the above skills is writing of one kind or another in transmitting public relations messages.

Again, feedback from practitioners as well as the results of surveys indicate that writing is the most important skill that a public relations practitioner can have. How to cultivate this talent?

"... Many know and some will even admit they do not write well. Does this cut them out of the practice of ? No, not at all. Writing is first a skill, then a talent. Most people can learn to write well. The major traits of good public relations writing include: clear, concise and to the point use of words. Creativity is important, but after these points are mastered ..."

Becoming a good writer involves the desire to write better and practise. Most of us will agree that practice is needed, but we do not generally do it. This acts as a constraint in developing the skill.

Once a group of college students requested the novelist, Sinclair Lewis to give them a lecture on writing. Lewis asked them "How many of you really intend to write?" All of them raised their hands. "In that case" said Lewis "There is no point in my talking. My advice to you is go home and write, then rewrite and write".

We know that cricketer, dancer, musician, artist all develop their skills by long and sustained practice. So also practice is a long and sustained one spread over several years perhaps.

Writing is the rock foundation on which public relations is built. The art of writing is therefore a prerequisite for a successful public relations manager.

Outline of writing

The first thing that you must do before writing is you must prepare an outline of your press release, article or brochure, even for an editorial of your house journal. Define the key topics in the outline. It must contain various thoughts that will go into the writing, which can help you in dividing the matter into short sections.

The Message, the Audience, the Media

There are three important areas about which the public relations writer must have a clear idea before he writes to succeed in communicating. They are: The message; the audience; and the media. These three will help a person a long way in good writing for effective communication.

The message: A public relations writer or his writing has one goal—to convey a message. The first step is to decide what you want to say and to have a clear idea about it. If you do not have a clear idea of what you want to say, the understanding of your audience will also be negligible. In other words, you must make sure that you understand the message yourself before you begin to write.

The audience: It is not enough for you to understand the message. You must write it in such a way that your audience understands it. For this, you must know your audience—their educational background, values and beliefs. It is also important to know the interest of readers and their needs. This is called **audience profile**. Otherwise, you will not be able to communicate effectively. After having a clear audience profile, you must tailor your message. So, know your audience well before writing.

The Media: When you know your audience well, the next step is to choose the right medium to reach the audience. Different media are used for different audiences. Therefore, choosing the right medium is one of the important aspects in effective communication. It may be a single medium or a combination of media. This depends on the nature of the public relations campaign planned.

Writing for Clarity

"... Every successful piece of non-fiction should leave the reader with one provocative thought that he did not have before... not two thoughts or five... just one..." said a distinguished public relations author. Here the author emphasises the fact that the public relations writer should write in such a way that the audience understands what he means. This is the one provocative thought so well emphasised by the author.

Unfortunately, this lesson is not learnt by many who aspire to write well. Instead, they turn to grammar rules, tenses and cases and other language problems. All this obscures the purpose of writing, namely communication. In short, good writing is one that succeeds in communicating. Bad writing is nothing but failing to communicate. The objective of writing in public relations is to express, and not to impress the audience with literary writing.

Clarity is the number one aim of good writing. If the audience does not understand what the public relations writer has written, then his efforts go wasted. But if his writing is clear, a dull style will leave his audience uninterested and unenthusiastic. It follows that a public relations writer must cultivate the ability to write clear prose in an interesting style. This is achieved by paying good attention to two important aspects namely sentence length and word length.

Sentence Length

Lengthy sentences tire the reader and make your writing hard to read. The first principle is to keep most sentences short. When the sentences are short, the reader will grasp quickly what the public relations writer has to say. If they are long and tangled, they will obscure the meaning and confuse the reader, he may not understand what the public relations writer has said.

However, it does not mean that every sentence should be short. Some could be long. The prose written by the public relations writer must be a happy combination of short and long sentences. Research has shown that the readability of a piece is enhanced if the average sentence length is 16 words. Sometimes, sentences are too long simply because of extra words, not extra ideas. Writers frequently use three or four or even five words where one will do. Study the examples given here.

1. "Unless and until the employees at all levels both horizontally and vertically—are loyal, efficient and devoted to duty, the overall production of the company will not register an upward trend in the near future and lead it to our cherished goals of greater margins of profit".

The above sentence is long and tangled. One will also note the redundancies in it.

2. "The employees should be loyal, efficient and devoted to duty to increase the company's production and profits". The same sentence reads well as its length has been shortened and its redundancies eliminated.

Here a list of redundancies is provided. The word or words in brackets should be avoided.

- (absolutely) essential
- (already) existing
- (basics) fundamentals
- (current) trend
- (every) now and then
- (hard) facts
- my (personal) opinion

Word Length: Use Short and Simple Words

A public relations writer may have an exceptional command of vocabulary. But he must not show it off when it comes to good writing. He must prefer short words to long ones to achieve clarity, and long words to unfamiliar ones or difficult ones. If the word is unfamiliar, its meaning will also not be clear to the reader, with the result, the reader will not understand the sentence. If he/she does not understand the sentence, he cannot understand what the public relations writer wants to communicate. For example, "The Quinquennial statistical abstract of 2005 has many factual and typographical errors, in addition to registration deficiencies in the sophisticated offset printing of multiple bar diagrams".

The same sentence can be re-written using as follows short and simple words. "The 2005 Statistical Abstract has many factual errors and printing mistakes. Colour diagrams are not printed well". So, to achieve clarity, the public relations writer must write short sentences with short and familiar words.

Here is a list of a few big words with the substitute short words.

Big Word	Short Word
Terminate	End
Utilize	Use
Incombustible	Fireproof
Substantiate	Prove

Simple Language: Avoid Jargon

Scientists, economists, doctors, engineers, lawyers, space technologists, journalists and other professionals use certain terms restricted to their respective professions. They are called **jargon**. Members of the same profession will understand the jargons used. For example, only doctors will understand the medical jargon used by professional colleagues, whereas a common man will not. Nor professionals belonging to other professions.

For example "All solar thermal systems must accept diurnal transients and rapid transients from cloud passage during daily operation". This sentence was written by an engineer explaining some of the drawbacks of solar-electric power plants. When reword the sentence means: It gets dark at night; sometimes during daytime, clouds block out the Sun.

Avoid clichés, jargon and antiquated phrases. Use plain and simple language. Prefer active voice than passive voice. In the active voice, action is explained directly. 'Rama killed Ravana' in the passive voice, the action is indicated in indirect – "Ravana was killed by Rama". When you write in active voice, your writing will be more direct and vigorous. Your sentences, more concise.

So, one of the principles of good writing is: *Use plain language: Avoid jargon. This is most essential in public relations writing.*

One-step-At-a-time

The public relations writer can confuse readers by telling too many things at once. Readers can accept one new fact when written clearly. They must not be confused. So, one must introduce one new idea at a time and in a logical order. The first idea should explain the second, the second the third and so on.

Using this one-step-at-a-time approach, the public relations writer can eventually explain well the whole theme. The most important thing here is to make sure that the first step is in the right place. After you have identified the main points, put them in order. Readers will know what you are talking about.

Example

Asian workshop on sustainable agricultural research held in Thailand.

(A) ICRISAT, in conjunction with the International Rice Research Institute (IRRI), the International Irrigation Management Institute (IIMI), and the International Board of Soil Research and Management (IBSRAM), organised an Asian Regional Workshop on Sustainable Agricultural Research in Bangkok, Thailand, from 30 September to 2 October.

(B) About 45 Representatives from Bangladesh, Bhutan, China, India, Indonesia, Korea, Laos, Malaysia, Myanmar, Nepal, Pakistan, Philippines, Sri Lanka, Thailand, USA and Vietnam including ICRISAT, IRRI, IIMI, and IBSRAM participated in the workshop.

(C) The meeting aimed to determine jointly with the national agricultural research systems, the research being undertaken on sustainability by countries in Asia and the Pacific, and the gaps in sustainability research within each country.

In this example, published by the ICRISAT in *SAT News* each para contains one main point. The main points (first identified by the public relations writer) are stated in their logical order. The first point in the first para is explained by the second paragraph. The second by the third.

Make the central point clear

Whether the public relations writer writes a complex sentence or a simple sentence, his objective is still the same—*to convey a message.* Messages must be supported by facts and figures, descriptions and explanations; he cannot leave out important details. However, very often writers obscure the central point or the message with details and descriptions. The central point may be buried in a para full of, say, statistics or descriptions, or perhaps somewhere in the middle para. Make sure the main point stands out.

The public relations writer must do this by stating his main point clearly at the outset. Let the details come later. If the main point is not made clear, the audience not only will not get the message; they also will not attach much importance to what the public relations writer has to say.

Example: Study the following press release:

The Kenya Agricultural Research Institute has set up a task force for groundnut research and development in Kenya.

Dr. Lakshman Singh, ICRISAT's Principal Agronomist has been elected to the task force.

In the work programme that has been prepared, ICRISAT is called upon to provide support for multi-locational testing of improved groundnut seed production surveys of production systems, marking and utilisation potentials and identification of production constraints.

In the above example, the main point or the central point is made clear at the outset—in the first para itself. Good writing requires that the central point is made clear at the outset.

Figures and Abbreviation

The way in which you use the numbers is as important as you use the words in writing. The first rule is not to start a sentence with a figure. Spell it out instead with words. This style is followed universally in newspapers, and also in professionally produced publications. At the same time, it looks or reads odd to spell out a multi-digit number; either write out, the year 2014 or else recast the sentence completely.

However, there are occasions when it is difficult to avoid a figure at the beginning and when it happens say in a brochure or in giving statistical data, then there may be no alternative but to start with a figure.

The second rule and this is for numbers within a sentence is to spell out numbers up to and including ten and above that write in figures. If the numbers are higher than ten, the rule is to use figures throughout for the sake of consistency and clarity. Write out hundredth but after that put 101st and so on.

Abbreviations

If the initials are popular such as AIR, BBC, CBI, abbreviated form can be used in writing. If not, the name should be spelled out in full before using abbreviations, otherwise spelled out in full after the initials at first reference. AIR—All India Radio.

Vocabulary

There are two aspects to your vocabulary—passive and active. The passive vocabulary is made up of words which one hears, reads and understands but which one does not use in speech or writing. These are words which one understands rather vaguely, but they are not for normal use. They can, of course, become part of one's active vocabulary when they are used more regularly in speech and writing. In this way, words will move from passive vocabulary to active vocabulary.

When you want to become a good writer, you must pay greater attention to your active vocabulary. You must know their correct meaning. Therefore, conscious efforts must be made in this direction. Whenever you come across a new word in a newspaper or a magazine or a book, you make it a point to refer to the dictionary and learn its correct meaning and usage. Once you know its correct meaning, you will be able to use it with confidence in your speech or writing.

So, expand your passive vocabulary gradually. At the same time active vocabulary should also receive good attention. You must know the correct meaning of words, you use freely and frequently. In this area, the dictionary is your best friend.

Grammar

A mastery of good writing presupposes good knowledge of grammar that one has learnt during one's education. Therefore, this aspect need not be re-covered. However, it may be emphasised here that some areas such as infinitives, prepositions, sequence of tense, agreement of the verb in the sentence need special attention.

There are many standard language usage manuals that discuss points of grammar and usage. Such manuals help clarify doubts. *Reader's Digest Word Power Dictionary* is one such usage manuals. It will be a useful addition to one's library.

Spelling

Spelling is a skill that can be learnt. One can become an excellent speller, if one wants to. Spelling is largely a matter of convention. Sometimes a slight spelling error changes the meaning of a word. So, it is a good idea to refer a standard dictionary.

If an article is riddled with spelling mistakes, the readers might not believe in the facts presented. They might suspect the credibility of the writer also.

Spelling errors do crop up even in prestigious publications. But to avoid them one must be diligent. To avoid such overconfidence, good writers—especially public relations writers—should occasionally test themselves on commonly misspelt words.

Here a reference to word processing system may be relevant. A distinguished author said about the word processing system:

"... Most word-processing systems have spelling checks. The only problem with relying on spell check system entirely is that if, for example, you have used 'there' instead of 'their', the system will not find the error. The system will only find words that are misspelt as 'there' for 'their'...". So the word-processing system has its limitations.

Punctuation

A public relations writers while editing their articles must pay good attention to punctuation.

The aim of every punctuation mark is to make unmistakable the meaning of written words. Every mark of punctuation is a sign to help the reader catch what the writer intended to convey. Punctuation marks serve fourfold objectives: (i) to terminate, (ii) to introduce, (iii) to separate, and (iv) to endorse.

They help group related ideas. They set off words for emphasis, they indicate the model of what you write the words which are to be kept together or separate. The underlying purpose of punctuation is to make the meaning clear. Subtle changes in punctuation can change the meaning of sentence.

Punctuation marks include: capitalisation, period, exclamation point, comma, colon, semicolon, dash, quotation mark, an italics, parentheses, brackets, apostrophe and hyphen.

Here are a few punctuation marks:

Full stop (.)

A full stop is the mark of the end of a sentence. No stop is needed when ending a sentence with a question mark, exclamation mark and ending a quotation which ends with a full stop. They should not appear in heading for press releases. Do not put them after abbreviations like Mr, Mrs, unless they come at the end of a sentence.

Comma (,)

The comma is normally used to encase a job title or descriptive phrase after a name. A comma would only go before and in a list of items, if one of the items includes another and.

Colon (:)

The colon is used to amplify, explain or introduce a quote e.g., Abraham Lincoln said: "Democracy is of the people, by the people and for the people".

As part of grammar, PR professionals must practice all marks for better writing. Good public relations writing always strives for consistency in the use of numbers, hyphens, punctuation, grammar, symbols, capitalization and abbreviations. Therefore, one should be consistent in writing.

POINTS TO REMEMBER

1. The ten golden guidelines for effective writing include: (i) writing skill; (ii) the message, audience, the media; (iii) writing for clarity; (iv) Sentence Length; (v) Short and Simple Words; (vi) Simple language, avoid jargon; (vii) One step at a time; (viii) Figures and Abbreviation (ix) Vocabulary; (x) Grammar, spelling, punctuation.

2. Writing skill is the rock foundation of public relations.

3. The message, the audience and the media are the three segments which guide writing.

4. Clarity is the number one aim of good writing. The one major principle of good writing is that one must use simple, plain language by avoiding jargons.

5. One-step-at-a-time approach will avoid confusion in writing.

6. Don't start a sentence with a figure.

7. One must pay greater attention to active vocabulary.

8. A mastery of good writing presupposes good knowledge of grammar.

9. Spelling is a skill that one can learn by practice.

10. The aim of every mark of punctuation is a sign to help the reader catch what the writer intents to convey.

REVIEW QUESTIONS

1. Which are the 10 golden guidelines for effective writing? Explain with examples.

2. Writing skills are a prerequisite for successful public relations. Discuss.

3. Describe the linkage between the message, the audience and the media in public relations writing.

4. Explain the role of punctuation marks in writing.

How to Be a Good PR Manager | Chapter 33

> *Whatever you think that you will be. If you think yourself weak, weak you will be. If you think yourself strong, strong you will be.*
>
> **—Swami Vivekananda**

CONTENTS

FUNCTIONS OF A PR MANAGER

Good managers are not born, but made. They are fashioned by experience of business, education, training, and the realities of the workplace. The general principles of management are applicable to public relations discipline also.

One of the pitfalls in Indian public relations is the lack of a defined job profile of a public relations manager as approved by the CEO. However, there are some public relations departments which have clear cut functions. What do public relations people actually do? This is an often asked question. If in-house public relations staff does public relations activities of the company, those who work outside in public relations consultancies offer public relations services to the client on relationships management.

The 10 key tasks that public relations mangers will do are as follows:

1. **Planning:** Endlessly the public relations professionals plan, determining the objective, needs, priorities, desirable ends, targets for the public relations messages, time frame and, of course, costs! With their focus on the importance of ethics, public relations people have often taken the lead in the establishment of codes of conduct and even codes of ethics in many areas of national and

international business and industry. Therefore, planning is the first task of a public relations manager with clear objectives.

2. **Management:** Public relations is a strategic management function. Public relations managers need to be able to administer the overall public relations programme to ensure that it runs on time, within budget, and ends up with a successful record of achievement. It is true that until recently some public relations people did not rank well as managers: they were good as professionals at handling the public relations aspects of the task as technicians, but they did not give as much priority as they should to the management function itself. All that is changing now. However, for the person keen to be perfect at public relations, it is important to recognise the need to hone up management skills as much as to develop the operational public relations skills. PR manager has both managerial and technicians roles.

3. **Maintain relations:** Public relations manager maintain relations with journalists, technical experts, politicians, academics, opinion formers of one sort and another, and with the employees, customers of the organisations concerned, with charitable institutions, community leaders and so on. All public relations communications should be to some agreed and identified purpose which helps achieve their overall objectives in due course. Public relations people in many countries have been leading the development of networking—now widely recognised as a valuable communications tool—whereby people in complementary areas (and even in competitive ones) meet together to form a common cause on issues of importance. This job is otherwise known as stakeholders relations with employees, shareholders, customers, media etc. through IT new media networking. PR not only informs the public through various media, but also collects people's reactions on the organisational policies and keeps the management informed of such feedback information.

4. **Organise:** Public relations managers arrange special events from press briefings and conferences, from annual general meetings and press tours, to open houses (the day when the company welcomes visitors to see the factory) and anniversary celebrations, award functions and charity or sports sponsorship events. Organising events related to media and image building is the responsibility of public relations managers. Event management is a tool of PR.

5. **Writing:** PR professionals write news releases, newsletters, letters of all sorts, to groups which include opinion formers and journalists. They write reports, speeches, copy for booklets, posters, radio and television scripts, trade paper articles, magazine articles, letters to the editor, etc. They become sometimes as ghost writers for clients, CEOs.

6. **Editing:** They not only write but also edit house journals, newsletters, reports to shareholders, letters written by their peers, communications material prepared by technical and other experts for dissemination to external and internal publics. Editing of corporate publications is an important task of public relations managers.

7. **Production:** Writing and editing is one aspect while production is another area. Public relations professionals have the responsibility for welding together many aspects of communication involving the use of print, photography, design, art, audio and video materials, so that these are created into communications tools which are needed to transmit the messages relevant to the job. Production of folders, house journals, posters, films, audio-visuals is the job of public relations professionals.

8. **Speaking:** Public speaking is an essential quality for public relations managers. They speak at meetings, presentations, press conferences, in front of television cameras, on radio shows, at private and public functions of one sort or another. Public relations practitioners, therefore, adopt interpersonal media and spoken word for effective communication.

9. **Research:** One of the main areas of activity for public relations practitioners is gathering of intelligence information, and they have to be good at it. They need to know where to go for information, what to look for, how to analyse it, and monitor and update the information, evaluating it so that it can be 'mined' if needed to assist the campaign or project on hand. A public relations manager is the source of organisational information, which has to be gathered, stored and disseminated.

10. **Training:** As part of the training, public relations managers have to create public relations conscious in every employee of the company. Public relations for non-public relations people has to be organised to educate them. Organising in-house public relations training is the responsibility of public relations managers.

Multidisciplinary Function

Herbert M. Bans described public relations as "a combination of philosophy, sociology, economics, language, psychology, journalism, communication and other knowledge into a system of human understanding."

Since public relations is a multi-disciplinary function, it has to work in line with marketing, advertising, human resource development, finance, production and other wings of the organisation. It is against this background, that a public relations manager is expected to assume a variety of roles such as communicator, writer, speaker, photographer, journalist, psychologist, broadcaster, media specialist, marketing expert, financial analyst, protocol officer, event manager, exhibitor, speech maker, speech writer, publisher, image builder, researcher, editor and above all a strategic manager and a partner in operations.

MANAGEMENT EXPECTATIONS

Attributes of a public relations manager have to be in tune with the expectations of the management. Expectations of the management from a public relations manager as expressed by some of the CEOs include:

1. Sharpen communication skills and maintain good media relations by both receiving and transmitting information of public interest to the organisation.
2. Keep the eyes and ears of management open to people's reactions.
3. Act as an ambassador of the company.
4. Create an all-round understanding of management problems and actions.
5. Project the image to various publics and gain public understanding.
6. Serve as an antenna-cum-receiver by providing feedback, information and disseminating organisation's policies with all the employees, shareholders, customers and external public to improve relations.
7. Serve as lubricants of communication between management and publics.
8. Make the management and all employees public relations conscious.
9. Provide support to sales efforts by creating awareness of company's products, services and brand.

Management expects from public relations, business-like goal setting, campaign planning, sustained implementation through budget-control and realistic assessment of results as it does from any of its other departments such as production, marketing, finance, HR, etc.

Misconception

The effectiveness and success of a public relations programme of an organisation largely depends on the calibre and attributes of public relations professionals. Many aspirants for a career in public relations seem to entertain the notion that they can be successful public relations managers because they are extroverts and enjoy meeting and talking with people. Others seem to feel that, for success in the profession to come their way, all they need is to be courteous in their dealings and be good at the art of public speaking. A few candidates believe that they could be successful in public relations profession because they won prizes in debating and essay writing competitions. Some have the illusion that journalists can be good public relations managers. While these qualities are necessary concomitants for success in public relations practice, they are by no means sufficient by themselves. There are certain other essential qualities and qualifications fundamental to effective and better public relations manager.

Good and Bad

As in most other professions, there are two types of public relations professionals—good and bad, efficient and inefficient, ignorant and intelligent. Good public relations managers are those who possess the required qualities and professional qualifications, are efficient, experienced and conscientious and produce profitable results to the organisation in terms of communication and help build up its image. The other categories of public relations personalities—the inept, inefficient, inexperienced, non-professional and insincere ones who do not come up to the expectations of the management in giving positive results and building relationships with the stakeholders. Such public relations persons fail to bring credit to the organisation even though it performed well.

One criticism is that the Press Information Bureau and the State Information Departments tend to function as 'Trumpeters' and 'Drum Beaters' of the Government, and even of individual ministers, whereas the objective of the official information agencies should be to provide full and unbiased information to the public through the press. Correspondents posted at districts headquarters have complained that in many cases District Public Relations Officers become active only during the visits of ministers from the State Headquarters, and that they are of little help in the day-to-day collection and dissemination of development news (The Second Press Commission 1982). Such a scenario not only exists in government but also extends to private sector industries and business organisations.

Is PR a Profession?

A profession is a paid occupation involving formal qualifications and training. It is seen as both necessary and desirable for a decent society, provides a crucial link between the individual's struggle for a fulfilling existence and the needs of the larger society, and is a stabilising force in a society, protecting vulnerable people, social values, and providing quality of service. In fact, any profession be it marketing or public relations must act as a watchdog of public interest.

It is against this background that one should study whether public relations is a profession or not? Experience tells us that public relations is a profession. But a majority of public relations practitioners in India lack professionalism. A professional is one who engages in a pursuit or activity professionally. He or she is a person having impressive competence in a particular discipline.

J.E. Grunig and Todd Hunt in their book *Managing Public Relations* (1984) listed following five characteristics of a professional:

1. A set of professional values
2. A membership in a strong professional organisation
3. Adherence to professional norms
4. An intellectual tradition or established body of knowledge
5. Technical skills acquired through professional training

The above five characteristics identified are the best yardsticks to judge whether public relations is a profession or not? Public relations all over the world fulfils the above characteristics and prove, beyond doubt, that public relations is a profession.

However, when public relations did not give results to the management, became an odd person's job, lacks skills, and becomes a legitimiser of the company and a 'spin doctor', then the nomenclature of the profession changed from public relations to corporate communications. In the guise of a new name, corporations started doing the work of public relations.

Spin Doctor

The term 'spin doctor' emerged in the West, particularly in the USA during the 1980s. In the beginning, the meaning of spin was confined to what often were considered the unethical and misleading activities and tactics of political communication consultants. In the 1990s, the media widely used the term 'spin doctor' to describe any effort by public relations personnel to put a positive slant on an event or issue (Wilcox 2006). Spin is unethical to legitimise public relations which aims to enhance the image of corporations and individuals and to generate public understanding for the programmes.

The time has come for public relations professionals to condemn spin and the label 'spin doctors'. The original title 'Public Relations' should be restored by changing the term corporate communications as an art and science of relationships management through a two-way communication process.

The bad image acquired by public relations and the public relations professionals in the past is partly due to the fault of the practitioners themselves. It is because they entered the profession without any background in public relations education and training. Is it not our duty to create educational facilities and induction and in-service training for public relations professionals?

Professionalism

How do we ensure professionalism in public relations? We need a good public relations manager who is a true professional, has professional qualification and skills with positive personal qualities. We must look to the 21st century public relations manager who will handle public relations work professionally to gain recognition for the profession on the one hand and goodwill for the organisation on the other hand.

The basic characteristics of a manager apply to public relations managers too. However, managers including public relations managers need certain guidelines that will help them build their managerial knowledge and skills. Some of the guidelines include: achieving results, getting on with people, stress management, personality development, benchmarking, budgeting, change management, communicating, continuous learning, crisis management, creativity, managing one's boss, persuading, presentations, effective speaking and patient listening, productivity improvement, report writing, strategic public relations management, team building, time management, trouble shooting, etc.

Good Public Relations

What is good public relations? It goes beyond communications to business strategy and business issues and should, therefore, be an integral part of organisation's corporate strategy and decision-making. This is possible only when a seat for public relations is made available at the board table or in the role of a professional adviser it ranks alongside finance, HR professionals. Good public relations strategy making involves pulling things together, taking a holistic view and achieving alignment of public relations and other communications activities. Good public relations strategy making is based on high quality audience research and a thorough understanding of the attitudes and issues affecting different publics. Good public relations strategy making is objective driven, starting with organisational objectives and goals, and then reaching consensus on strategies for achieving the desired results. The senior management commitment to effective public relations communications is a key differentiator of good public relations performance. The CEO should act as the integrating force between different communication functions.

Act as an Adviser

Good public relations planning is essential to the success of public relations practice. It is highly dependent on the skills, knowledge and attitudes of individual public relations practitioners. The professionals, therefore, require well-developed public relations specific professional skills, interpersonal business and critical thinking competencies.

A broad understanding of business, marketing, management in order to understand the organisational public relations issues is required along with a global mindset. A good public relations professional accepts the reality of e-communications increasing the porosity of organisations to the outside world. Good public relations should integrate communications to reach the internal and external publics. The professionals should have a broader communication role acting as 'advisers' to other communication professionals concerning interactions between different communicators and between different stakeholders.

Does good public relations really add to society and organisations? Public relations can be seen as giving dignity and respect to the organisations and all its varied stakeholders and publics.

WHAT MAKES A GOOD PR MANAGER?

What are the attributes of a Good PR Manager? The doyen of American public relations, Edward L. Bernays, defines a PR counsel as "the practitioner, a professional equipped by education, training and experience to give counsel to a client or employer on relations with the publics. He sets about his task by analysing the relations of the subject and the public. He then interprets the subject to the public. PR counsel of an agency or PR manager of in-house department functions on a two-way street. He interprets public to client and client to public".

T.J. Ross, one of the early leaders of PR profession lent emphasis to the point when he said, "A public relations man is not worth his salt, if he succumbs to pie-in-the sky" (a pleasant prospect that is very unlikely to be realised) or (a plan with little chance) thinking divorced from the realities of his business. And he will not stay long on the management team if he does. In his zeal to place his corporation in the most favourable public light, he must not forget that a business is first and foremost, a profit making enterprise, not an eleemosynary institution. In the relationships, he seeks to create between the corporation and its publics, he may be 'Soft-hearted'. But he must not be 'Soft-headed'.

Skills Oriented

To be a good public relations professional one has to master two inter-related areas, the art of mass communication and the theory and practice of public relations. However, the most important quality, valued is above all 'Creativity'. Lastly, one should have the 'ability to write'. If these skills are strongly present in a person, there is scope for him to excel in public relations practice. Creativity involves not just thinking but also the ability to perceive and understand from outside the prevailing conventional thinking and to use often desperate bits and pieces in order to provide added value. Writing skill does not confine to production of press releases, but the ability to write, to a wide range of a styles for a variety of purposes and communication channels. In fact, writing makes a public relations manager perfect.

FOUR 'As' AND FOUR 'Ps'

The success of a public relations manager is entirely dependent on the following four 'As' and four 'Ps':

Analyst

It is the primary responsibility of a public relations manager to analyse the situation and the environment of an organisation which includes the attitudes, opinions of the people and their problems. In a way, it is a process of 'pulse reading' of the public, through which we identify problems.

Adviser

Based on the situation analysis and problems identified, the public relations manager has to formulate a policy of action and communication programme for solving the problems confronting the organisation and improving the relations with the people. The policy and programme as designed by the public relations manager as an adviser are placed before the management for approval.

However, the manager must be part of top management for being an effective adviser.

Advocate

The public relations manager is considered an advocate who not only speaks for the organisation but also implements the public relations policy through various media of public relations. This becomes the most important aspect of organisation's public relations activity. As an advocate, the public relations manager has to implement the programmes through the various communication channels. The public relations manager here acts as a communicator and his advocacy on organisational services will have a great impact on customers and other stakeholders.

Antenna

The public relations manager, who acts as an antenna, must evolve a system of collecting and conveying correct feedback information to the management periodically to enable it to fine tune its policies and programmes in accordance with the wishes of the people.

In the making of a good or successful public relations manager, a survey conducted by *Public Relations Voice* revealed that a good public relations manager and public relations needs four 'Ps' to undertake the four 'As'.

Personal characteristics

The efficient public relations practitioner, no matter what his or her background may be should have certain personal characteristics such as:

    (a) Self-realisation

    (b) Ability to get along with all kinds of people with integrity

    (c) Ability to use imagination in designing public relations programmes

    (d) Ability to advise management and interpret organisational environment

    (e) Genuine interest in people around and patience

    (f) Positive mindset and ability to face challenges unfazed

    (g) Inspiring leadership qualities and role model

    (h) Empathy and responsiveness to the problems of people

    (i) Life-long learning process

    (j) Ethical and spiritual values

Professional qualification

There is a close relationship between qualifications and quality of the profession. The minimum qualification of a public relations professional must be graduation in arts/science/commerce or any discipline. Professional qualifications such as Bachelor of Public Relations, Bachelor of Communication and Journalism, or Diploma in Journalism, Public Relations, Master Degree in Communication and Journalism, Public Relations, Advertising and Public Relations is also important. One should be computer literate with the capacity of handling IT new media such as computer, Internet, website, fax, E-mail, etc. M. Phil., or Ph.D. in Communication or Public Relations is considered as additional qualification.

These days possessing an MBA degree is also beneficial. Therefore, prospective public relations managers may acquire MBA degree besides professional degree in public relations. It is advisable for business schools to start MBA with specialisation in public relation/corporate communication.

Professional skills and experience

Those who plan careers in public relations should develop eight basic professional skills. They are as follows:

- Skills in tactics: Written tactics, Spoken tactics; Visual tactics and IT new media tactics.
- Skills in effective communication: Skills in speaking, listening, reading and writing. (A good communicator is one who listens

the most.) Skills in media relations, skills in presentation of body language as non-verbal communication. Being a writer one should be a wordsmith with skills in words.

- Research ability
- Planning strategies with multimedia
- Problems solving ability—Ability in reputation management
- Business management and marketing management background
- Source of information—Ability to collect information
- Integrated public relations communication approach with sound judgement and experience.

Public relations manager is primarily a communicator. Being a communicator for the organisation, the public relations professional is also the source of organisational information. In fact, he or she is considered to be the repository of information at the organisation. As the source of information and communicator, the public relations manager has to interpret the policies and programmes to both internal and external stakeholders. In performing the duties, a public relations practitioner acts as a person in the middle between the management and the media, public relations manager is both 'eyes and ears' of an organisation on the one side and the public on the other hand. As such, public relations profession is skill oriented. Working in public relations can be absolutely fabulous when you know what you want to do and then do it successfully with techniques and skills.

Psychologist's bent of mind

Public relations professional is primarily a psychologist, a master of human behaviour. A successful public relations manager must be in a position to study and understand the human mind and behaviour. It is because the quintessence of public relations is to influence and change the attitudes of publics towards one's organisational goals, products or services. Therefore, one must possess psychologist's bent of mind and one must study psychology. A good public relations manager is also a good psychologist.

PR MANUAL

Like financial code there should be a public relations manual for every public relations department within the organisation as a guide to public relations personnel for effective functioning without any confusion. The public relations manual must contain information such as:

- Public relations policy and structure within the organisation
- Functional chart of public relations manager and the public relations team
- Financial and administrative powers of public relations manager

- Media-wise and public-wise programme content
- Checklist for various events
- Media relations—do's and don'ts
- Public relations reporting
- The last but not the least a synopsis of Four 'As', and Four 'Ps' for ready reference.

PR REPORTING

"We should take pride in what we do, why we do it and how we do it, never hesitate to tell it like it is" said John E. Sattler, a veteran American public relations practitioner. The idea is that every public relations manager should never shirk responsibility of reporting to the top management about the contribution and results of public relations programme. This is all the more necessary when public relations profession is fighting for its recognition as a strategic management function on par with HR or finance. In other words, this process of keeping management informed about the role of public relations is called 'Public Relations Reporting' or 'Public Relations for Public Relations'.

Why public relations reporting?

You must understand that the management is not at all interested in the process of public relations communication. What the management interested is how communications can do actionable tactics to give better results in terms of creating good relations with the public, and building the image of the company. Public relations reporting is a sort of progress report document giving a picture as to what the public relations department is doing.

Achievements

There are several ways to keep the management informed about public relations activities through public relations reporting. Personal meeting reports, monthly, quarterly, annual status progress reports, submission of annual plan, interject achievements in conversation with CEO. When opportunity is prime, take advantage of the situation and interject an anecdote that highlights the achievement of public relations team. Public relations reporting should be very subtle. It should not appear as if one is blowing one's own trumpet. Some well-executed, self-promotion can be a matter of revealing in an informative and factual way what you in the public relations functions have been doing for some time. Just be sure to tailor your approach to the style of the CEO whom you are trying to educate or create awareness about the role of public relations.

In fine, most people who get 'to the top' be it in business, the academic or the public relations profession, get there because of the standards they have set themselves—not the standards others have set for them. Try to evolve your own good public relations standards for yourself based on what we have discussed here and aim at becoming a good public relations manager and role model.

Four 'Don'ts'

A careful study of attributes discussed earlier would give us a clear impression of 'Dos' of a public relations manager who is expected to follow. But there are also 'Don'ts' to be avoided by all those who wish to make a successful career in public relations. The four 'Don'ts' are as follows:

1. Do not speak public relations as a panacea for everything or every problem.
2. Do not indulge in panegyric on your boss achievements. Never act as a trumpeter and drum beater of an institution or an individual.
3. Do not seek personal publicity for yourself. It is counterproductive.
4. Do not have negative attitude.

In sum, if one follows the four 'As', four 'Ps', four 'Don'ts', and PR reporting he or she will be a better public relations manager, getting credit for the PR profession.

POINTS TO REMEMBER

1. According to one author, the Public Relations Manager performs 10 key tasks. They are: Plan; Manage; Maintain Relations; Organise; Write; Edit; Produce; Speak; Research and Public Relations People Train.
2. Expectations of Management from public relations include: maintaining good media relations for better coverage; act as an ambassador of the company, project the image of the corporation; serve as an antenna-cum-receiver to provide feedback information; act as lubricants of communication between management and public; creating public relations consciousness in every employee. Management also expects business techniques such as goal setting, campaign planning; assessment of results, etc.
3. Like in other professions, there are good or bad and efficient or inefficient public relations managers. Good public relations managers are those who possess the required professional qualifications, experienced and produce positive results, while bad public relations managers are those who are not professionals, inept, inefficient and not up to the expectations of the management.

4. The Second Indian Press Commission (1982) commented that the Press Information Bureau of the Government of India and the State Information and Public Relations Departments tend to function as 'trumpeters and drum beaters' of the Government and even of individual ministers where as the objective of official information agencies should be to provide full and rounded information to the public through the press.

5. Experience has proved that public relations which is based on a specialised knowledge and academic preparation is a profession. J.E. Grunig (1984) has listed five characteristics of a professional. They include: a set of professional values, a membership in a professional body, adherence to professional ethics, established body of knowledge and technical skills.

6. When public relations professional lacked skills and became legitimiser of a company, the media described such people as 'spin doctors'. Spin is unethical to legitimise public relations to build the image of corporations and even of individuals.

7. What makes a good public relations Manager? Edward L. Bernays describes a public relations counsel as the practitioner, a professional equipped by education, training and experience to give counsel to a client or employer on relations with the publics. Public relations manager of in-house department functions on a two-way street. T.J. Ross said that "A Public Relations Man is not worth his salt if he succumbs to pie-in-the sky".

8. Eight attributes make a good public relations manager. These characteristics include four 'As' based functions and four 'Ps' based qualities. The 'As' stand for 'Analysis', and Ps represent for 'Performance'.

9. The functions of a PR manager cover fourfold 'As'. They represent the four roles such as The Analyst; The Adviser; The Advocate; The Antenna. The entire edifice of PR manager is based on these four key tasks.

10. If public relations managers have to function efficiently and effectively as envisaged in four 'As', they need four 'Ps' based qualities and qualifications. They are: (i) personal characteristics (positive mindset); (ii) professional qualifications (Bachelor of Public Relations); (iii) professional skills and training (skills in writing, speaking) and (iv) psychological mind (to understand human behaviour).

11. Alongside four 'As' and four 'Ps' which are considered as 'Dos', the public relations manager in order to be a good professional must avoid four 'don'ts. These four Don'ts are: (i) Do not say public

relations is a Mumbo-Jumbo; (ii) Do not involve in panegyric; (iii) Do not seek personal publicity for yourself; (iv) Do not have negative attitude.

12. The process of keeping the management informed of what public relations has done in a set period is called 'public relations reporting or public relations for public relations'. This is a sort of progress report document giving a picture as to what public relations department is doing in the organisation.

REVIEW QUESTIONS

1. What are the key elements of public relations manager's job?
2. Describe the expectations of management from a public relations manager.
3. Is public relations a profession? Why or why not?
4. What makes a good public relations manager? Elucidate the key attributes of successful manager.
5. What are the 'Don'ts' that have to be avoided in the practice of public relations?
6. What do you mean by Public Relations Reporting?
7. Write short notes on:
   (a) Public relations manual
   (b) Public relations reporting

Public Relations into the Future

> You need to live your today with tomorrow's maturity. For such people alone future awaits.

C O N T E N T S

PR IN THE FOREFRONT

Who are the masters of a country or an organisation? It is the people and the people alone who are not only the masters but also the motive force in the making of a nation or an organisation. They make or mar the organisation.

If the people are the first in any organisation, the relations with them comes next in priority for its survival. Who handles relations with the internal and external public for the smooth functioning of a company? Public relations as a two-way communication process and as relationships management discipline promotes mutual understanding between an organisation and its publics, besides building its reputation. Therefore, public relations should be in the forefront among all the management disciplines, such as finance, human resources and marketing. But as of today, it is not.

Public relations has been defined as the art of presenting a company (or person) to the public, usually via the media, ideally in a positive manner that improves the reputation of that company (or person) and subsequently impacts positively on that company's sales/uptake of that company's services/the company or individual's overall reputation (Cathy Bussey 2011). In future, according to a few experts, public relations as a strategic management discipline to deal with relationships and communication with stakeholders on whose support the organisation depends will come to be regarded as a major force of top management. Peter Gummer, Chairman of Shandwick firm stated, "I believe that public relations will increasingly be seen for what it really is—an indispensable tool of management (1990). It is in this context that public relations professionals should take full advantage of this emerging trend and strive for professional excellence with high international standards by acquiring qualifications and skills, failing which their role will be usurped by others, preferably marketing, human resource, finance or management discipline. This is a wake-up call for today's PR professionals to enter into the future of public relations.

GROWTH AND CONTRIBUTION OF PR: FOUR MAJOR ACCOMPLISHMENTS

The independent India must be proud, among others, of four major accomplishments due to which public relations in India has not only grown but also contributed for such outstanding achievements. What are they?

1. **Democracy:** India, a sovereign, socialist, secular, democratic, republic with a parliamentary system of government, has emerged as the world's largest vibrant democracy with over 75 crore voters. Education of voters as partners in all democratic institutions has been the task of public relations communication. As a result, PR has grown and also contributed to the sustaining of Indian democracy.
2. **Globalisation:** India as a developing country which was known for its starvation deaths is now a global economic player and poised to become the third biggest economy in the world. The New Industrial Policy 1991, that envisages economic liberalisation, privatisation and globalisation has not only contributed to the growth of Indian economy and development but also intensified the Indian communication system to meet the global competitive marketing environment and trade wars such as car war, cell phones war and insurance war and media war. It is in this context that the public relations process took its global form and resulted in an era of global public relations. Think Globally and Act Locally has been the guiding force.

3. **Media explosion, including the Internet and 24/7 News:** The third biggest achievement of independent India has been the media explosion including the Internet and 24/7 news channels. There were only 3,000 newspapers, including 300 dailies, and six radio stations in India at the time of independence in 1947. What is the present scenario? According to the Annual Report for the year 2011 of the Registrar of Newspapers for India, the total number of registered newspapers/periodicals was 82,222. There were 10,205 dailies, 394 triweeklies and biweeklies, 27,321 weeklies, 10,422 fortnightly, 25,072 monthlies and 5,208 quarterlies. Newspapers are published in English and 21 principal languages listed in the Eighth Schedule of the Constitution. Newspapers/periodicals were also published in 127 languages including dialects and a few foreign languages. The total circulation of newspapers was 33 crore copies per publishing day in 2011. The largest number of newspapers and periodicals registered in any Indian language is in Hindi (29,094). The second largest number of newspapers and periodicals registered in any language is in English (10,530).

The Radio network in 2012 comprised of 277 radio stations and 381 transmitters which provided coverage to 99.16 per cent of the population and reached 91.82 per cent area of the country. All India Radio broadcasts over 647 news bulletins daily in 90 languages (Indian, foreign and dialects).

The growth of public relations profession is in direct proportion to the ascendance of the media explosion. As the media grew, the awareness and aspirations of the people also rose beyond expectations. Organisations have never been under so much scrutiny. In the past, customers could easily be isolated or ignored, but today they can join together quickly online and seek to change either in the product or in the service if they so desire. When there was a problem of battery discharge, Nokia replaced them at the doorsteps of the customers.

Therefore, the 24/7 rolling news and explosion in media channels including print and social media mean that there are greater opportunities for public relations, proactively to communicate either to project the point of view or to contradict the wrong notion appeared in the media. More media, demassification of media, demassification of audience mean more challenges for public relations, more work and the need for more PR professionals, if the organisations want to communicate their messages. Media is the lifeblood of public relations. Public relations Communication Mantra with the support of media could contribute to both the success of democracy and the development process of the country.

4. **Right to Information Act:** The fourth and key achievement of independent India has been the Right to Information Act, 2005 which provides easy access to the people to the

government held information. The Act which is regarded as the oxygen of Indian democracy has heralded a new era in public relations communication enlightening the people on policies and programmes of the Government. Under the Act, every public authority, in both Central and State Governments, has to appoint a public information officer in every administrative unit to provide information as demanded by the public. It shall be a constant endeavour of every public authority to provide as much information suo motu to the public at regular intervals through various means of communication, including internet, so that the public have minimum resort to the use of this Act to obtain information. As a result, the dissemination of public information got a fillip which directly reflected the growth of public relations communication in India.

WHITHER INDIAN PR?

What is the State-of the-Art Public Relations? According to one estimate, the Indian information and public relations network, representing the government, public sector, private industry, NGOs, with about one lakh professionals directly involved in public information and about 20 lakh public communicators working in the extension wings of agriculture, health and family welfare, rural development, women's welfare, etc., reaching out about 75–80 crore people with development messages, constitutes the biggest communication network in the world. About 9 lakh accredited social health activists (ASHA), trained women community health volunteers alone work in rural and urban areas to reinforce community action for universal immunisation, safe delivery, the care of new born, control of communicable diseases and promotion of household sanitary toilets. WHO has declared India as a Pulse Polio Free Country, thanks to the health communication network.

Mixed Bag

However, a million dollar question arises as to what is the State-of-the-Art Public Relations in India? It is a 'Mixed Bag' containing a few highly competent public relations professionals, second to none in the world, on the one side and many non-professionals without any professional qualification, education and training on the other. The distinguishing trait of Indian public relations is the 'Quantity of Public Relations Personnel' rather than 'Quality of the Public Relations Profession'. The need of the hour is professional excellence with international standards so as to promote India as a global economic player and also the world's largest democracy.

FIVE CHALLENGES

At a time when we discuss about the likely future, Indian public relations is confronting with five major challenges.

Identity Crisis

First challenge is the identity crisis of public relations. It is still a misunderstood profession with several nomenclatures, such as public relations, corporate communication, corporate relations, publicity, public affairs and public communication. The term public relations coined in the early 20th century cannot be disposed of so readily. All the alternative terms lack clarity. Communications is a vague term and also lacks the brand recognition that PR has. Public relations has staying power compared to other titles because it is thoroughly institutionalised. Professional bodies such as the Public Relations Society of India, the Public Relations Society of America, the Chartered Institute of Public Relations, London, the International Public Relations Association, the European Public Relations Confederation, Public Relations firms as distinct from advertising agencies, and the 28 State Information and Public Relations Departments in India are unlikely to change their nomenclatures overnight and the same goes for professional journals such as *Public Relations Voice* (India), *Public Relations Strategy*, *Public Relations Tactics*, USA. Many training courses and some University degree programmes also use the name of public relations.

A debate is on as to whether the poor reputation of PR as spin doctor could be partly solved by coming to an understanding for a common definition of public relations as corporate public relations.

Strategic Planning

The next challenge in public relations is performing the role of a technician instead of strategic management function. It has the roles of both strategic management and technician. The need to improve strategic planning and link it to communications is the need of the hour. Mere technician's role will not augur well for the profession. PR practitioners should act as strategic partners too.

Public Relations Education and Training

Lack of public relations education, induction and in-service training is the major third challenge which has to be overcome to enter into the future of public relations. There is a demand for qualified PR professionals, but the supply is not in tune with demand because Indian universities do not offer PR professional courses. One Survey says that only 40 per cent of PR professionals in India possess PR qualification. Investment in public relations education will improve the quality of the profession.

Lack of Research and Measurement

The fourth challenge of public relations is lack of research and measurement of its programmes to show results to the management. In fact, research is the weakest link in the practice of Indian public relations. The IBDO Report (1994) observed that 'evaluating the effectiveness of PR remains a hotly debated issue' and that 'the public relations industry may never be fully respected unless it can provide measurement of its value'.

'Evaluation is the rocky but sunlit pathway for public relations practitioners to climb, once and for all, out of the quacks and where our work is judged by instinct, gut-feel and intuition. It has also a warning that there is a pain factor in submitting work to the acid test of evaluation and it is one that both clients and consultancies are frequently inclined to dodge' (Alison Theaker 2011). Such measurement problem can be solved if Indian public relations follows the principle of the two-way symmetric model wherein both parties—the sender organisation and the receiver public—will have an equal say and importance in the feedforward and feedback information mechanism.

Grassroots Public Relations

The fifth and the last challenge is grassroots public relations. India lives in its 6 lakh villages where 72 per cent of the population resides, but the Indian public relations predominantly concentrates in urban India where 28 per cent population resides with about 4,000 towns and cities. Indian future looks to its villages. Similarly, the future of Indian public relations depends on its penetration into rural India. Fast changes are taking places in villages. PR executives not only function from their corporate or divisional offices but also move into the rural India to share customers' experience and stakeholders' reactions so as to capture rural market. For example, the Amul Brand has expanded its rural network to reach over 4000 villages.

A BRIGHT FUTURE BECKONS INDIAN PR: FIVE IMPORTANT FACTORS

A bright future beckons Indian public relations in the next decade because of the following five important factors. These factors not only provide greater opportunities to PR but also enable it to strengthen PR and enlighten the people with full information.

1. India continues to sustain as the world's largest democracy with over 75 crore voters. The success of democracy presupposes free flow of information between democratic institutions and their public or vice versa.
2. India which was known for its starvation deaths and poverty is now poised to become the third biggest economy in the world. Eradication of information poverty is a prerequisite to the eradication of economic poverty. This can be handled by PR.
3. The third factor is that Indian education in the backdrop of English media and English as one of the languages will make India the largest English speaking nation in the world. It will surpass USA in the near future. Consequently, Western publishing and broadcasting houses might shift to India for collaboration with the Indian media houses.

   It brightens the international communication—a challenge for Indian PR.
4. The fourth factor is that with the increase in literacy and per capita income, there will be an increase in the media and also in the media consumers in proportion to the rise of literacy and economy. It is estimated that the increase in the media will be about:

   - One lakh newspapers including over 15,000 dailies
   - Over 1000 TV channels with fragmentation of audiences
   - Over 100 crore mobile phones spread over both urban and rural India. About 90 crore cell phones will have internet connection with multipurpose usages like iPad
   - Over 30 crore computer-based internet connections with several options for social media

   The opportunities offered by development in new information and communication technology will help PR in the tactical area and direct communication with stakeholders through websites, social media and also in the strategic management area of advising the companies.

   In fact, social media has ended the age of one-way messaging and ushered in a new era of 'Dialogue' with stakeholders rather than 'Monologue'. Dialogue is yet another challenge for public relations.
5. The fifth and the last factor that will promote public relations set up in India is the emergence of new States. According to the predictions of media, the number of States in the Union of States will increase to 50 from the present number of 28. More States create more PR departments and more PR professionals to handle the public information of public authorities. The Union Cabinet in December 2013, has approved a Bill for the creation of Telengana State, which has to be cleared by the Parliament Telengana will be the 29th State.

MELBOURNE MANDATE FOR THE FUTURE OF PR

The 7th World Public Relations Forum organised by the Global Alliance for Public Relations and Communication Management (a representative body of over 1.6 lakh PR and Communication professionals across the world) in Melbourne, Australia in November 2012 came out with a Mandate for Public Relations in the Future to promote global PR more effectively, more professionally and more responsibly to the cause of organisational excellence and strong relationships with stakeholders. Among others, the Mandate casts heavy responsibility on public relations professional.

(i) To demonstrate social responsibility with open, honest and credible communication.
(ii) To demonstrate professional excellence responsibility through research and professional standards.
(iii) To demonstrate personal responsibility by ensuring one's personal communication consistent with truth and actions that create mutual benefit between an organisation and its publics.

PUBLIC RELATIONS VISION: FIVE GROWTH ENGINES

Against this background, what is needed today is a vision for public relations to shape the future of this profession. The public relations vision to be designed by PR professional bodies must be centred around the following five growth engines, which leads to a paradigm shift for public relations.

- Public relations education and training
- Adoption of the two-way symmetric public relations model with emphasis on feedback information mechanism
- Multimedia approach based on ITMN theory of Gandhian public communication
- Research and measurement of public relations programme to show outputs on investments to managements
- CEO who is accountable for total corporate vision, mission and policies should assume the role of Chief of Public Relations strategy at the board level

Public Relations Education and Training

Academicians and Chief Executives have suggested that the future of PR depends on the increased investments on public relations education and training. The University Grants Commission and the Universities in our country should be persuaded to launch public relations courses.

Dr. B.R. Ambedkar Open University Hyderabad which has been the pioneer in launching Bachelor of Public Relations course in 1984, has launched a new courses Mass Communication and Public Relations as one of the optional subjects at the undergraduate level in 2013 and that MA in Mass Communication and Public Relations will be started in 2014.

Two-way Symmetric PR Model

Though we call PR a two-way communication process, it has been one way without giving much importance to feedback information of the audiences. If the 20th century, by and large, had experimented the one way asymmetric PR model, the 21st century should adopt a two-way symmetric PR model with a balance flow of information from organisation to the target public and from the pubic to the organisation. Both the parties—the sender organisation and the receiver public—will have equal say in both feedforward and feedback information so as to promote mutual understanding between the organisation and the target audience.

Multimedia Approach Based on ITMN Theory of Gandhian Public Communication

Though the Internet age has brought revolution in communication with social media, India cannot afford to stay only on online public relations. Alongside, the internet public relations must adopt age-old Indian traditional media to reach the people below the poverty line who constitute about 30 crores and all those lower middle class who do not have access to modern mass media. The ITMN theory of Gandhian Public Communication involves four types of media in tune with the Indian environment. There was no new media Internet when Gandhiji promoted his own theory of non-violence to create public opinion against the British. In ITMN, I stands for intrapersonal and interpersonal media such as meditation, prayer meetings, word of mouth, public meetings; T represents traditional folk arts media—songs, bhajans, drama, dance, puppetry; M relates to the mass media such as newspapers, radio, TV, film; and N covers new media such as internet, e-mail, twitter, YouTube, blog, website.

Convergence of these four types of media is best suited to the Indian conditions. Such media strategy alone will bridge the communication gap between the information rich and the information poor, so to say, besides covering both urban and rural areas.

Budgetary Provision for Research and Measurement of PR Programmes

Public relations research is the weakest link in the chain of public relations practice. In fact, the entire public relations process is based on four cornerstones, which are Research, Planning, Communication and Evaluation. Unfortunately, research and evaluation which help to measure the success or failure of PR and also to design future strategy are generally ignored due to lack of money, time, understanding and personnel. In the process, PR is unable to show results, and as a result it is also not gaining management recognition. We must clearly understand that public relations will not be fully respected unless it can provide measurement of its value with necessary budgetary provision.

CEO as Chief of PR Strategy at the Board Level

If public relations is regarded as strategic top management function, the Chief of PR must find a place in the Board which formulates policies for all management disciplines. Unfortunately, the PR by and large is at the middle level under HR or Marketing. Therefore, public relations must be placed at the top management level with a Director or Vice-President (PR) who should be made responsible to the CEO and Board of Directors. And CEO, who is accountable to all disciplines, must assume the role of Chief of PR for designing PR strategy at the corporate level.

If challenges are converted into opportunities and if all such opportunities are tackled with a vision, a bright future beckons for Indian public relations.

POINTS TO REMEMBER

1. Who are the masters of an organisation? It is the people and the people alone are not only the masters but also the motive force in the making of a nation or an organisation.

2. If the people are the first, the relations with them comes next in priority for the survival of the organisation. Such relations are handled by public relations as a discipline of two-way communication process. In fact, PR should be in the forefront among other management disciplines such as HR or Marketing. But it is not.

3. According to a few experts, in future, public relations as a strategic management discipline to deal with the relationships management and communication with stakeholders on whose support the organisation depends will come to be regarded as a major force in top management.

4. Peter Gummer, Chairman, Shandwick firm, once stated, "I believe that public relations will increasingly be seen for what it really is an indispensable tool of management". Therefore, PR professionals must strive for professional excellence, failing which their role will be usurped by others, preferably marketing or HR.

5. The growth of Indian Public relations was due to four major achievements of independent India: (i) India emerged as the World's largest democracy with 75 crore voters; (ii) India today has become Global Economic Player and is poised to become the third biggest economy in the World; and (iii) Media explosion including Internet and 24/7 news; and (iv) Right to Information Act which provides free access to information held by government and all public authorities. Public relations as information management discipline must be proud of its role in accomplishing these four key achievements. In the process, publicity has graduated into public relations and today it has become global public relations.

6. The distinguishing trait of Indian public relations is "the quantity of public relations professionals" rather than the "quality of the PR profession". The need of the hour is professional excellence with international standards so as to promote India as a global economic player and also the world's largest democracy.

7. **Five major challenges:** Indian public relations is confronting five major challenges as to enter into its future. These challenges include (i) identify crisis of public relations (it has different nomenclatures such as corporate communication and public affairs); (ii) as a strategic management function, PR professionals must act as strategic planners, but as of now majority of them are working only as technicians as directed by the management; (iii) lack of public relations education and training; (iv) lack of research and measurement of PR programmes to show results to the management and (v) and lack of grassroots public relations at the village level where 72 per cent population lives.

8. **A bright future: five factors:** Notwithstanding its limitations, a bright future beckons public relations in India, among others, because of five important factors which provide opportunities for PR to communicate and educate people. These factors include (i) India continues to sustain world's largest democracy; (ii) India is poised to become the third biggest economy; (iii) India will become world's biggest English speaking nation; (iv) India will be the hub of world's largest media network with over one lakh newspapers, over 1000 TV channels, over 100 crore cell phones, including 90 crore cell phones with internet connectivity; and (v) India is likely to have 50 states instead of 28 as of now in 2013.

9. **Melbourne mandate for the future of PR:** The 7th World Public Relations Forum organised by the Global Alliance for Public Relations and Communication Management in Melbourne, Australia, in November 2012 came out with a Melbourne Mandate for Public Relations Future which among others casts heavy responsibility on PR practitioners to demonstrate professional excellence through research and professional standards.

10. **Public relations vision:** The future growth of Indian public relations is based on a vision for public relations to be designed by PR professional bodies like Public Relations Society of India. Such a vision will have five growth engines, which are (i) PR education and training; (ii) Adoption of the two-way symmetric PR model; (iii) multimedia approach with ITMN theory of Gandhian Public Communication; (iv) research and measurement of PR programmes with the required budget; and (v) CEO should assume the role of Chief of Public Relations Strategy at the board level.

REVIEW QUESTIONS

1. Why public relations should be in the forefront among the disciplines of management?

2. What are the four major achievements of independent India? Explain the contribution of public relations in these accomplishments.

3. What is the State-of-the-Art-Indian PR? Describe its distinguishing feature.

4. 'Five major challenges have to be overcome if Indian public relations has to grow'. Discuss.

5. A bright future beckons Indian PR. Elaborate your answer with five major factors.

6. Write short notes on:
   (a) Melbourne Mandate
   (b) Public Relations Vision with five growth engines

Actions Speak: PR Case Studies

Chapter

35

> *Achievement requires character, discipline, united action and readiness to sacrifice the individual self for the larger cause.*
> **—Pandit Jawaharlal Nehru**

C O N T E N T S

Public relations is basically an applied science. When the theory and principles are applied in public relations practice, the organisation not only solves the problem but also gets good results. For this reason, the case study method of learning about public relations is an essential part of a practitioner's career. Case histories are developed based on measurement and scientific research to show the results accomplished.

There is a dearth of PR case studies in India as public relations research is yet to develop. Certain case problems have been discussed in each chapter. A few case studies are listed below.

DOGS ARE MAN'S BEST FRIENDS: MULTIMEDIA APPROACH

Let us study a case as to how the Municipal Corporation of Hyderabad (MCH) tackled stray dogs menace through public relations campaign. Hyderabad is a beautiful city with over 400 years history with about 40 lakh population.

In the analysis, among other civic problems, the stray dog menace in the city was one that came to light. There were over 10,000 stray dogs in Hyderabad city in 1970s. Everyday over 200 persons became victims of dog bites. Every dog owner is expected to take dog license and get their dog vaccinated against rabies. But only about 200 people took dog licenses. About 25 people were dying of rabies every year. The public relations department of MCH made a research of the various problems confronting the Corporation. The dogs menace as one key problem was identified.

Setting Objectives

Public relations objectives were set to tackle the stray dog menace. The main objective was to create awareness among the people on the threat of dog bites to human beings and also to eliminate stray dogs which are not licenced.

Action Projects

Mere public relations programme will not yield the desired results. It should be accompanied by action projects and services. The Animal Husbandry Department of the Corporation had set its own service objectives to tackle the dog menace. They are as follows:

- Reduce the number of stray dogs
- Increase the number of licensed dogs
- Increase the number of dog clinics to provide anti-rabies vaccine
- Modernise dog catching methods by importing tranquiliser guns
- Provide immediate relief to dog bite victims
- Reduce the incidence of rabies deaths

Target Audience

The people of the city were divided into two segments—depending on their socio-economic background. The first category were urbanites, educated class, with better economic status and exposed to modern means of mass media such as newspapers, radio, television, films, etc. The second category was the population that lives in slums. Most of them had migrated from rural areas to slums for employment and are uneducated, poor and not exposed to mass media.

PR Programme

The public relations campaign was developed based on the theme "Dogs are Man's Best Friends: Let's Protect Them Against Rabies".

Services and action plans to solve the dogs menace included: public assistance cells, increase in the number of dog catching squads with modern tranquiliser guns, adequate supply of vaccine for anti-rabies, opening of more dog clinics to treat dog bite victims, etc.

The media mix was designed in such a way as to meet the needs of both the educated people who lived in sophisticated localities and those who lived in slums. Every fifth person in the city was a slum dweller. In fact, two types of campaigns were launched; one for the general public and educated ones, and the other for the benefit of slum dwellers.

Media Mix

The media strategy included: newspapers; radio; television; film and audio-visuals; cinema slides; photographs; exhibitions; printed literature, folders, leaflets; oral communication, public meetings, symposia; traditional media, songs, *burrakatha*, play; and outdoor advertising— hoardings, exhibitions.

Fifty huge and impressively illustrated hoardings with catchy slogan "Dogs are man's best friends. Let's Protect them against rabies" erected in all parts of the city not only attracted the audience but also created great awareness.

The action projects of the Animal Husbandry Department to catch stray dogs and the educative campaign of the Public Relations Department went on simultaneously for two years. The components of the Public Relations Department constituted as 'messages' while the action projects of the Animal Husbandry Department acted as 'services'. Messages and services created credibility for the campaign.

Negative

Any campaign when launched gives both positive and negative feedback. In this campaign, the organisation received negative feedback. People felt that the Corporation was passing the buck on to the people. They felt the Corporation's slogans tell that instead of practising, it is only preaching.

A newspaper editorial commented that propaganda and education were two different things and the objectives of the Corporation cannot be realised merely by what it thinks to be catchy slogans and hoardings.

In a letter to the editor, one reader pointed out that the slogans in the newspapers and the hoardings on the streets perhaps remind the Municipal Corporation **"Practice Before You Preach"**.

Even some of the Corporation's officials did not like the campaign, for, the increase of grievances about stray dogs and dog bites had correspondingly increased their responsibilities.

It was the view of the public relations practitioners that the negative feedback was due to the fact that the local citizens had never before been exposed to such a campaign in Hyderabad on dog menace with catchy slogans on huge hoardings, front page advertisements in newspapers supported by radio programmes—all appealing to the people to share responsibility in eliminating stray dogs. Their doubt was whether the Corporation would rise to the occasion and put into practice what it preached.

The public relations department was perplexed from the adverse reaction in the press and negative feedback from the public. How did it then tackle this problem?

Positive Perception

To arouse the enthusiasm of the citizens, the Corporation swung into action and launched a series of programmes to catch stray dogs and also provided anti-rabies vaccination by opening more dog clinics. Dog clinics were opened at several places in the twin cities of Hyderabad and Secunderabad to provide dog licences and anti-rabies vaccine besides increasing the dog catching squads.

The action projects of the corporation aroused public interest and developed confidence in the Corporation. People felt that the Corporation was interested in doing things for the citizens. There was a continuous flow of information through all the media on the campaign and duties of citizens to protect the dogs against rabies and elimination of stray dogs, which had bridged the communication gap between the Corporation and the public. As a result, negative perception changed to positive feedback and people extended their whole-hearted cooperation in the implementation of the campaign.

Impact

What was the effect of this multimedia public relations campaign on the dogs menace? Evaluation of the campaign was entrusted to an independent organisation like the Department of Communication and Journalism, Osmania University. The evaluation was undertaken by the department in about 300 localities of the city. The specific objectives of the evaluation were: (i) to study the level of media exposure; (ii) to find out the effectiveness of the public relations campaign.

Campaign Exposure

The per cent of respondents who were exposed to the media are as follows:

Hoardings	:	73
Newspapers	:	58
Radio	:	49
Cinema slides	:	52

Almost three-fourths of the respondents (72 per cent or 211) interviewed were educated on the campaign and knew the objectives of the campaign.

When asked if they had read about the campaign in any of the daily newspapers of the city, 58 per cent replied they had while 42 per cent (82) replied in negative. About half of the respondents (49 per cent or 102) heard about the campaign on radio, while the other half of the respondents (51 per cent) did not. A little more than 52 per cent of the sample recalled cinema slides on the campaign shown in cinema houses.

Results

The Number of dog licenses taken increased from 200 to 6,000 in two years. The cases of dog bites showed a steady decline from 200 a day to 63 and the number of rabies death came down from 24 to 14 a year. The number of stray dogs eliminated were 21,000 in a period of two years. About 71 per cent of the respondents said that they had been educated on protecting the dogs from rabies.

The public relations department of the Corporation helped in solving the 'Dog Menace' confronting the Corporation through public relations techniques. This was indeed a result-oriented public relations campaign. If the campaign had succeeded in educating the people it was because dog problem related to every individual and it was his/her duty to take care of one's dog.

Future

Public relations is a sustained effort. As long as there is Municipal Corporation of Hyderabad and that there are dogs in the city, the campaign as a continuous effort must be on. Unfortunately, the campaign was suspended. As a result communication gap was created between the stray dogs' problem of the Corporation and the people who keep dogs and the dog bite victims.

What happened for not continuing this campaign? The number of dog bites per day which was 200 a decade back has now increased to 500–600 per day. As many as 53,000 cases of dog bites were reported in 1995–96. A dog had eaten away a three-year old girl in Secunderabad. This could be tackled again through a multimedia public relations campaign. Wiser counsels will prevail on the Municipal Corporation of Hyderabad to restart such a campaign.

HIGHER PRODUCTIVITY REQUIRES EMPLOYEES SATIS-FACTION: THE SINGARENI COLLERIES SUCCESS STORY

Among others, one of the key roles of a public relations department in any organisation is to create loyalty and commitment among the employees towards organisational goals. Here is a case study to tell as to how camraderie among the workforce of Singareni Colleries Ltd was created to bring down the incidence of strikes from 350 to 11.

The Singareni Collieries Company Ltd. (SCCL), Hyderabad is the only coal mining company in South India with a workforce of about 93,000 spread over in four backward districts of Andhra Pradesh—Adilabad, Karimnagar, Warangal and Khammam. The corporate communication head who is designated as Executive Director (Marketing and Public Relations), reports only to Chairman and Managing Director. Because of the involvement of CMD who is also the CEO of the company, the Singareni Collieries could implement a well-planned employees communication programme to maintain better industrial relations and achieve higher productivity.

Cat Call Strikes

The industrial relations scenario in SCCL before 1997 was characterised by a number of illegal and cat call strikes. There was a spurt in activities of militant trade unions especially during the period 1989 to 1993. The average number of strikes during these four years was 446 with a coal production loss of 1.3 million tonnes per year. This had contributed to gross indiscipline and deterioration in work norms in the company.

Poor communication with the workmen and their lack of awareness of the financial situation of the company helped the trade unions to mislead the workforce and organise cat call strikes. The management failed to communicate the significance of change in the work culture and faced a strong opposition to the introduction of technological innovations.

The management grasped the potential risk of lack of strong internal communication and workforce reach out programmes. There was also a growing perception among the workmen that the management was isolated and insensitive to the employees. Therefore, the management realised that an effective two-way communication was necessary to achieve understanding and cooperation of the workforce at all levels.

Communication Objectives

The company as a measure to handle the employees' communication, a corporate communication policy was evolved in 2003 with the following objectives:

- To foster a sense of organisational pride among the workmen to bring out an attitudinal change in their outlook so as to make SCCL vibrant, dynamic and forward looking company.
- To create an understanding amongst executives about the importance of communication to reduce the communication gap between the workers and the management.
- To create an environment wherein the management effectively interacts with workers on a continuous basis and tries to resolve the genuine problems of the workmen and increase the productivity.

Communication Strategy

The innovative steps taken as a part of communication strategy were as follows:

- To promote spirit of Singarenism among Singarenians, celebrating 'Singareni Day' on 23 December, every year.
- Full-fledged communication cells were established in each area with separate budgetary allocation for communication and public relations activities.
- Production of two high-quality documentary films on SCCL—one for general viewers and the other for workers and their families.
- Coordinating with the media and advertising agencies on bringing out important innovations and best practices in the form of short write-ups in various media.
- Briefing the press on important developments of SCCL.
- Engaging/hiring a professional consultant/agency for specific purposes depending on the exigencies of requirement.
- Publication of multi-colour posters and Singareni Newsletter on various developments.
- Mobile van with audio-visual communication facilities for extensive communication campaign in all area mines and colonies.
- Production of short films for Singareni *Tharangaalu* and other communication techniques such as *Burrakatha* (story telling), short films, etc.

Macro-level Communication

Padayatra

The management adopted the communication strategy at the Area Level. *Padayatras* are conducted by a group of executives headed by the Area General Manager on 1st of every month. The *Padayatra* team consists of some identified executives drawn from all major disciplines, including medical and health, best workmen, members of Singareni Seva Samithi, Singareni Employees' Wives Association, Scouts and Guides, NSS volunteers numbering about 30. The *Padayatra* was conducted in all the colonies by rotation and it started at 9 in the morning and ended by 12 noon. Some of the members hold placards and banners containing good slogans relevant to the situation and also appeals such as "All employees, executives of SCCL as One Family" to the residents of the colony and ask them to cooperate with the management in its efforts to make the company vibrant and viable.

The *padayatra* team also makes note of the status of civic amenities prevailing in the colony and takes necessary steps for augmentation/amelioration of civic amenities. Every executive would interact at regular intervals with minimum 50 workers, particularly productive workers, and look after their requirements. The local media is also involved in the *padayatras* and this is hailed as one of the best transparent initiatives that has brought the administration to the doorsteps of the workforce.

Mine Manager

In the organisational set up, the unit is a mine at the micro level where large number of workmen function. For the workmen in the mine, the face of the management is represented by the manager and other executives working under him. It is but natural for the workmen of the mine to look forward to the manager and other officers of the mine for guidance to get certain issues concerning them clarified. The Mine Manager and his team of officers will educate the workmen on the company policies and philosophy non-communication or miscommunication of the policies and the philosophy of the company will result in misunderstanding and misapprehensions among the workmen. Hence, the managers of the mines have adopted the following micro communication strategy:

Mine Sadassu

Fortnightly 'Sadassu' (convention) was conducted between 4. p.m. and 5.30 on 15th of the month and on the last day of the month at a mine or department level, and if it falls on a holiday, then it is held on the immediately following working day involving the manager and all the executives in the mine at a convenient place in the premises of the mine wherein the workmen of the mine and their family members participate.

In the above 'Sadassu', the Mine manager / HOD and the executives address the workmen explaining the current issues concerning the coal industry, SCCL, policies communicated by corporate management, etc.

The views of the workmen/the family members on those issues are invited. This *Sadassu* is apolitical in nature, and it is ensured that non-workmen and political leaders are not permitted to participate.

Cultural programmes

The Communication cell conducts one cultural event in the form of a playlet, skits, *'khawwali'*, *'oggukatha'*, etc. in the colonies itself once in a month, i.e. 20th of every month at 6.30 p.m. lasting for about one to one and half hours. Staging of the cultural programmes is arranged in all the colonies in the area by rotation. Executives also witness these cultural programmes along with the workmen and residents of the colonies.

Dial your General Manager

'Dial your G.M.' programmes are conducted in each area every month to facilitate the workers and their families to contact the Area General Manager to ventilate their grievances, viz. civic amenities, water supply, power supply of their residential colonies, etc. The respective Heads of Department take up the matter raised by the workmen or his family and initiate appropriate follow up action.

Singareni Tharangaalu

Pre-recorded video programmes under the caption *'Singareni Tharangaalu'* are telecasted in the Siti Cable Channel in all the areas of the company without any let up including the following items:

- Weekly talks/interviews with children of workmen, best workers, etc. followed by playlets.
- Monthly debates/lectures by outside industrial relations experts.
- Directors/GMs' monthly messages on previous month's achievements by workers and congratulating the achievers.

House magazine

A house magazine *'Singareniyula Samacharam'* is being published and distributed among the employees covering the information about various activities throughout the company for the benefit of the employees. Further, colour posters (*Singareni Samachara Prabha*) publicising the current events are displayed for the knowledge of the employees.

Impact

The company's imaginative macro and micro communication policy touched the right chords and helped immensely in sensitizing the employees on various aspects such as higher education, thrift, antialcoholism, AIDS, etc. As a result, workmen are not resorting to illegal *cat call strikes*. The number of strikes has been reduced from 350 in 1998 to 11 in 2004. It had fostered a sense of belongingness and camaraderie by way of *'Singarenism'* and *'Singarenians'*. It worked as the elixir for the organisation in improving its organisational culture as 'One for All and All for One Singareni'. The productivity of the company also increased. The company is regarded as one of the best managed coal companies in the country.

MEDIA RELATIONS IN A CRISIS SITUATION: ONGC

Oil spill, blow-outs, uncontrollable flow of oil and gas, fire are disastrous incidents which no organisation wants to happen within their premises. However, companies in the oil industry are involved in highly risky jobs of exploration, production, refining and marketing of petroleum products. Despite utmost care and following safety procedures, history tells us that disasters do take place in every part of the world.

Opinion Leaders

In such an eventuality the organisation where this disaster happens will be under pressure and is subjected to public scrutiny. To come out of this situation, the organisation should take immediate steps to control the disaster and minimise the damage to the environment and loss of public property. In this task, the organisation should take along with it, the support of the parliamentarians, environmentalists, media personnel and other opinion leaders so that all these people are involved in combating the disaster rather than criticising the organisation. ONGC has a tradition of managing crisis situations effectively.

ONGC

The Oil and Natural Gas Commission (ONGC) was established in August 1956 as a statutory body under Oil and Natural Gas Commission Act for the development of petroleum resources and sale of petroleum products. This Commission was converted into a Public Limited Company and named as Oil and Natural Gas Corporation Ltd (ONGC) from February 1994. In 2004 its 10 per cent equity shares were disinvested. Indian Offshore Oil industry began in 1974. It had encountered three major crisis situations. A blow-out at well No. SJ-5 in Bombay High in July 1982. An oil pipeline leak which occurred at the main Bombay High-Urban trunk line in May 1994 and an uncontrolled flow of gas and fire at B-121 platform in March 1999. ONGC effectively maintained relations with the media and the public opinion in all these situations and had come out without any damage to the corporate image. As an uncontrolled flow of gas took place in 1999, this case study demonstrates how ONGC dealt with this crisis situation and in the process took the nation along.

Fire on B-121 Platform

A gas leak took place on one of the wells connected to B-121 platform in Bombay Offshore which is located about 140 km away from Mumbai shore on 11 March 1999, followed by fire on 12 March 1999 at 12.20 p.m. The Regional Management immediately took steps to control the situation. The members of the crisis management team located in different parts of the country were mobilised. International experts on Well Control were contacted. The United India Insurance Company, with whom ONGC has taken an insurance coverage, was informed. Well control experts from Houston arrived in less than 60 hours and the insurance surveyors arrived in about 48 hours time.

Strategy

On 12 March, 1999, the Regional Contingency Plan was activated and the Regional Contingency Committee comprising ONGC, Navy, Coast Guard, Mumbai Port Trust, Jawaharlal Nehru Port Trust, State Government Authorities and other organisations involved in Marine activity held a meeting and a strategy was planned to tackle the situation and all organisations were alerted for their role if the situation became worst. The Ministry of Environment, both at the State and at the Centre, were informed about the uncontrolled flow of gas and other details.

Day 1—report to the nation

Simultaneously, the media was taken into confidence and involved in dealing with the situation. The fire took place at 12.20 p.m. on 12 March 1999 and the first press release giving details of the incident was ready at 3.30 p.m. which was sent to all newspapers and news agencies and television channels both in India and abroad. This release emphasised on the safety of the employees working on the rig, steps taken for the protection of environment and details of the incident. After this release was given, the Corporate Communications Division received a series of calls from the media, ONGC family members, environmentalists and various State Government authorities. All the queries were replied, technical details were given wherever required. This immediate action and responsive attitude by ONGC produced fruitful results and the entire media reported the details given by ONGC, leaving no scope for rumours.

Day 2—interface with the media

As ONGC plays an important role in the national economy and its well-being is of vital importance to the Nation, so any incident, which takes place in ONGC concerns every citizen. Therefore, ONGC decided to report to the Nation all the details of the incident and organised a Media Conference on 13 March, 1999 in less than 36 hours after the incident took place. The conference was addressed by the Board of Directors, Executive Director and other senior executives of the Region. As media personnel could not be taken to offshore, video footage on high resolution Beta tape and photographs taken were made available to the media. The press conference, the question-answer session and availability of visuals and photographs to the media helped in getting a positive coverage by all the newspapers and television channels.

The pictures of action by ONGC personnel and the visuals on all television channels showing ONGC dealing with the situation, controlling the fire, mobilising men and material, and planning ahead has given an impression that ONGC has the capability to deal with such situations. Though this is a disaster to the organisation, a positive tone was already set in the minds of the media and the people. This was possible through the proactive role played by ONGC.

Day-to-day media releases

Further, a press release was given everyday giving an update on the incident to newspapers, news agencies, television channels, All India Radio and news agencies on the Internet. By reporting to the Nation every day a correct and factual situation was reported to the people.

Control of fire

On 20 March, 1999 the Rig Sagar Ratna which was close to the B-121 platform was lowered and towed 1 km away from the site. Later, on subsequent days the ONGC crew and the foreign experts moved closer to the fire and made alternate plans of controlling the fire. The plans included a shallow water survey, re-equipping the rig with fire fighting equipment, drilling of relief wells and killing the well.

Day 12—the media reassembles

As significant developments took place from the day the fire incident took place, ONGC felt that there was a need to share with the media about further developments and action plans. Therefore, a second press meet was organised on 23 March, 1999 which was attended by both national and international agencies, news channels and newspapers. This press conference was addressed by the Executive Director of MRBC and the international expert on Well Control was also present. The international expert explained to the media that such incidents occurred in other parts of the world, appreciated the action taken by ONGC in isolating the fire and mobilising emergency equipment.

Foreign expert

This interaction with the foreign expert on well control helped media in understanding that such events occur in other parts of the world and gave credibility to ONGC efforts. Again ONGC made available video footage of control operations and photographs to the media. Media appreciated this gesture and reported the actual details of the incident. As new developments unfolded everyday, the media was dutifully informed through press releases, phone calls, responding to the queries and facilitating technical data. On 22 May, 1999 the first relief well was successfully completed. As one of the sources of gas has been plugged, the intensity of fire has come down considerably. This was reported by print and electronic media.

Supply Vessels Controlling the Fire

Gas cut-off

Finally, on 6 June, 1999, 86 days after the incident took place, the source of the gas was cut-off and the fire was totally extinguished. The media was informed and the same was covered by major newspapers and television channels in India and abroad.

Thus ONGC proved its capabilities of managing crisis, managing environment and earning goodwill of the people.

Gains Achieved

The open policy of ONGC and sharing of all the information with the media led to a positive reporting of a fire incident, which could have been termed as a major disaster because of negligence. When the incident took place, the Parliament was in session and the Minister for Petroleum and Natural Gas gave the House the details about the uncontrollable flow of gas and fire. Similar reports appeared in the newspapers. The Members of Parliament appreciated the efforts of ONGC and showed confidence on the capabilities of ONGC in dealing with the crisis situation.

Morale of employees

Positive information and the statement that all the 85 members on Rig Sagar Ratna were shifted to safety enhanced the morale of all the employees offshore and their family members who are spread across the length and breadth of the country.

Openness

Quick response by top management as well as the Corporate Communications Division for all the media queries projected a factual position of the incident. Because of this openness and credibility of information, the media personnel did not go to any other source for information on this event. Video footage on high resolution cassettes which are internationally acceptable, photographs, negatives, transparencies, scanners for scanning photographs and Internet connectivity for transferring data and information to different parts of the world were made available to the media. This facility has helped in getting both visual and print media coverage, which indirectly depicted the high risks and dare devil action, involved in the oil industry.

Stake Down

On the first day of the incident the share price of ONGC plummeted in the stock market, but continuous positive reporting by the media made financial newspapers report that the incident was small when compared to the size and degree of operations of ONGC and this incident will not affect the profitability of the company. This restored the confidence of the shareholders and the ONGC share price rose to the pre-incident level.

The Corporate Communication Executives were in constant touch with the top management, the control room, and all information channels within the organisation. The Department interacted with different disciplines within the organisation, searched various books on such incidents, surfed the Internet and made available all relevant information to the media. The responsive attitude of ONGC paid rich dividends in the form of correct reports about the incident. And the Corporate Communications of ONGC department played its role not only in keeping the internal and external public informed of the situation but in sustaining the reputation of ONGC.

Multi support Vessels Spraying on the rig.

CORPORATE SOCIAL RESPONSIBILITY: TISCO

There is a broader recognition today that corporate self-interest is linked to the well-being of the society of which the business is an integral part. It is in the self-interest of the business to accept a fair measure of responsibility for improving society because "insensitivity to changing demands of society sooner or later results in public pressures for governmental intervention and regulation to require business to do what it was reluctant or unable to do voluntarily".

This case study takes a closer look at the Tata Iron and Steel Company (TISCO) and its corporate social responsibility (CSR) programmes.

The concept of social responsibility was defined by Tata Steel's founder Jamshedji Nusserwani Tata, "The wealth which comes from the people, as far as possible, go back to the people". JRD Tata and Ratan N. Tata have carried forward the vision of Jamshedji. In the Tata Iron and Steel Company (TISCO), CSR is not a peripheral activity that could be taken up if resources permit, but a key business process. Adhering to the concept, 'charity begins at home', Tata Steel established benchmarks in caring for its employees. Commitment to social responsibility and obligations to the community are in Tata's Articles of Association, which emphatically stated that the company would be mindful of its social responsibilities to its consumers, employees, shareholders, society and the local community.

Tata Main Hospital

Tatas focused on meeting the objective of improving quality of life within Jamshedpur, while the autonomous societies work towards building better communities in the hinterland. The 740 bedded Tata Main Hospital (TMH) at Jamshedpur acts as the apex health care service centre for people of Jamshedpur, handling on an average of

2,300 patients everyday. Complementing TMH are the nine dispensaries handling on an average of 2800 patients daily. The Centre for Family Initiative (CFI) deals with family planning norms. It operates 27 clinics in Jamshedpur and serves over six lakh people, both employees and non-employees. CFI has bettered the national average population growth and considerably reduced infant and maternal mortality. Some of these projects are being implemented in collaboration with Care International.

Mobile Clinics

The Tribal Cultural Society set up to meet the needs of the tribals continues to fulfil the medical needs through three mobile clinics each day to ensure 100 per cent coverage under immunisation, planned family norms and awareness campaigns. The company is fully aware of HIV/AIDS and over four years the entire workgroup was covered under the programme of AIDS awareness. Through the Education Department, the company supports 15 co-educational schools catering to 10,000 students, besides assisting four girls and four boys schools, to co-educational high schools and intermediate college. To empower tribals, the company runs need-based vocational training programmes. The aim is to make tribal people employable.

Ecology

TATA Steel is committed to preserve ecological balance. Years ago, before bio-diversity became a buzzword, TATA Steel was environmentally conscious. An average operating expenditure of ₹100 per tonne of crude steel is incurred on maintaining environmental control system.

Audit

In order to ensure the expected impact of the projects on the lives of the poor and less fortunate target community, TATA steel keeps on collecting feedback from the community and getting the projects audited by involving internal and external agencies.

The TATAs Corporate Communications / Public Relations Department played its own role in carrying the message of social responsibility to the target people who could make use of the services to better their health.

MIRACLE OF MINI POSTER IN MOTIVATING EMPLOYEES IN A CRISIS: APSRTC

The employees of the A.P. State Road Transport Corporation (APSRTC) gave a strike notice for wage revision in 1980. Negotiations were held with the recognised trade union and other unions of employees on their demands. Conciliation meetings with labour department officials were held. While negotiations were on, the Public Relations Department brought out a 'Mini Poster' 20" × 15" size explaining the Corporation's stand on employee demands. The title of the poster was "Employees Are the Life-blood of Corporation". The contents of the poster were that the wage revision was done earlier involving an additional burden of ₹16.5 crore and the Corporation is ready to appoint a committee for revising the pay scales. Detailing the welfare measures, the poster mentioned about temporary relief, additional dearness allowance, payment of ex-gratia, incentive bonus, housing loans, medical aid, new dispensaries, child welfare centres, concessional bus passes to the children of employees and loans through cooperative credit society.

Financial Crisis

The poster also presented the other side of the financial burden on the Corporation due to increase in the cost of inputs such as fuel, spare parts, tyres, etc. "In view of the positive approach of the Corporation to demands of the employees the strike is not advisable", the poster read. The employees were advised to keep the financial crisis of the Corporation in view and await the decision of the Pay Revision Committee.

This poster was displayed in all the bus depots, bus stations, work-shops and at all work-places where the employees of the Corporation met including canteens. It was the practice earlier that the management negotiations be confined only to the trade union leaders and that there was no direct communication with individual employees. This 'Mini Poster' exposed all the employees to the positive attitude of the management to their demands and created positive impact on the minds of the employees that they could wait till a decision is given by the Pay Revision Committee. Passengers were also exposed to this poster. Sensing the favourable mood of the employees and the passengers, the trade unions also realised the difficulty of the Corporation and called off the strike. This was the miracle of the Mini Poster, which helped maintaining direct contact with individual employees of the Andhra Pradesh State Road Transport Corporation. In the process, the communication work of the Public Relations department was also recognised by the management.

MEET THE COMMUTERS: A CASE STUDY IN CUSTOMER RELATIONS

Every organisation, be it airways, railways or roadways, is basically linked with the interest of four types of publics: (i) the top management,

(ii) the employees, (iii) the customers, and (iv) the community at large and the opinion leaders. In fact, these groups constitute four strong pillars on which the organisation rests firmly. A successful organisation is one which provides a common forum for regular interaction of these four types of people to understand the problems of each other which in turn help in the smooth running of the organisation. But managements tend to implement communication programmes for each group of these publics independently either through internal communication for employees or under external communication for customers. No integrated approach is made in the Indian setting to bring these four groups on a single platform for the purpose of exchanging views. The Andhra Pradesh State Road Transport Corporation (APSRTC) has attempted on such integrated approach in its communications with the publics inside and outside the Corporation.

A unique programme *"Meet the Commuters"* was organised for the first time in its history on 4 May, 1980 at the Mehdipatnam Depot in Hyderabad city. The General Manager and his top managers representing the management, select traffic inspectors, mechanics, cleaners, drivers, conductors representing the employees, a cross section of commuters such as government employees, petty traders, lawyers, doctors, industrial workers, students, women, physically handicapped, etc. representing the customers and fourth segment opinion leaders represented by the media, people's representatives, consumer associations participated in the meet. Due publicity was given through all the media about this programme, besides extending personal invitations to select commuters and their associations, media representatives to take part in this face-to-face dialogue.

Management Views

"Meet the Commuters" session started with the views of the management as presented by the Vice-Chairman and the General Manager. In his opening remarks, the General Manager highlighted the basic corporate philosophy as comfortable travel of passengers—the passenger being the master of the Corporation and that the employees who serve the passenger are the public servants. In his view, three persons assume great importance, the garage worker who keeps the bus fit and clean for operation; the conductor who conducts the bus and comes into direct contact with the passengers and the third most important person is the passenger. It is the basic responsibility of both the employees and the passengers to safeguard the interests of the Corporation so that the buses can run smoothly.

The views of the management include:

1. Passenger is the master, the passenger is always right.
2. Employees should work with devotion as public servants—they are accountable to passengers.

3. The crew must answer the questions and doubts raised by the passengers with all courtesy.
4. Bus timings should be displayed at important bus stages.
5. Passengers should tender exact fare and demand the correct ticket.
6. APSRTC is a public corporation. The people should protect the buses without burning or damaging them in crisis situations.
7. Passenger amenities such as bus shelters, bus stations be provided.
8. Welfare measures for employees.

Passengers' Grievances

Next to management, passengers ventilated their problems in the Meet. Chinta Subba Rao, an advocate initiating the discussion complimented the management by stating "this is the first time that a forum like 'Meet the Commuters' has been organised by the Corporation as a step in furthering good relations between the APSRTC and the passengers". His complaint was that if the general pass was not renewed on time, the passengers would forfeit the deposit. Buses run without any destination boards, leading to confusion to the passengers. When the Corporation had spent about ₹3 lakh on a bus, there was no reason why a destination board which costs about ₹30 should not be fixed. Another complaint was non-availability of bus time tables.

Dr. Tilak, who represented the passengers' association was very balanced in his views and said even a family had its own problems. Similarly, the Corporation dealing with lakhs of passengers would have problems and that the meet organised would mitigate such problems.

The President of Vijayanagar Colony Welfare Association, Swamy vehemently criticised the Corporation stating there was 'no service' to the passengers but only '*Peedana*' (curse). He compared the service as a curse because buses do not come to the colony as scheduled, sometimes the buses come in sequence, some of the buses are dirty. He suggested the renewal of bus passes could be arranged in different colonies of the city instead of in one or two places.

The views of passengers were summarised as follows:

- More buses should be run during peak hours
- Destination board should be fixed to every bus
- Buses should not be cancelled without advance notice to passengers
- Buses should be stopped at all designated stages
- Bus timings should be displayed at all important stages
- Conductors, drivers and controllers should always be in uniform for easy identification
- Rash driving which results in accidents to be avoided

- Such 'meet the commuters' programme should be organised at every depot level for solving the problems of passengers and the employees.

Media

Representing the media and opinion leaders, G. Satya Rao, correspondent, All India Radio observed that there was every need to give public relations training to the crew for developing a spirit of accountability to the passengers. He was of the view that a bus passengers' council should be established for every bus depot to interact on the problems of passengers and such meetings should be arranged at every bus depot level. He suggested that the bus time tables should be displayed at all important bus stages of the city, besides running more buses to slum areas.

Employees' Response

After listening to the views of the management and the grievances of the passengers, the employees of the Corporation got an opportunity to present their viewpoint. Narsaiah, a conductor initiating the discussion from the employees side narrated the difficulties of the bus crew. They come into contact with about thousand passengers every day in the city and face people with innumerable behaviours and different attitudes in every trip. It is here that the cooperation of the passengers also is required for the bus crew. Some of the problems were that passengers give ₹10,50,100 notes for a small denomination ticket; male passengers sit on the seats earmarked for women; ticketless travelling in heavy rush. This poses a biggest challenge to the conductor in operating the bus. As the conductor has to work for about eight hours a day dealing with the different types of passengers, Narsaiah urged the sympathy of passengers for their smooth working.

Referring to the complaint of passengers that sometimes buses are very unclean, Chinta Narsing Rao, a mechanic explained his difficulty that power cut comes in their way of cleaning the bus. As a result the bus sometimes leaves the depot on time without being cleaned. In this case, he stated, that RTC should not be blamed.

The driver L.A. Khan said "though I am a small worker in this mighty Corporation, this is the first time that I got an opportunity to share a platform in which the General Manager on the one side and the passengers on the other side are present". Pointing out to the complaint of passengers that the drivers waste most of their time at bus terminals drinking tea, Khan said if a driver goes on drinking tea several times is he not conscious of his health? Zaheeruddin, another driver explained that buses in the city are not stopped sometimes at the bus stages, because '*rikshaws*', autos and petty traders park their vehicles very near to the bus stop.

Views Summarised

1. Passengers should extend their full cooperation to the conductors and drivers.
2. Passengers should not stand on the footboard causing inconvenience to the co-passengers. The passengers should discourage such travelling.
3. Passengers should tender exact fare, while taking the ticket to avoid the problem of change.
4. Police should ensure that autos, *rikshaws* and *thelas* are not parked near the bus stops.
5. One conductor versus hundred passengers should be borne in mind whenever a passenger deals with the conductor.

Results

The programme organised at Mehdipatnam depot enabled each section of the public to understand others' problems. The employees could understand the grievances of passengers while the passengers could understand the difficulties of the employees. At the same time, management was able to grasp the views of both employees and passengers.

At the end of the meet, a spirit of brotherhood and mutual understanding was visible. They exchanged greetings and even hugged each other while departing. The major result of this meet was organising of such programmes at every bus depot in a year-long schedule and action plan for redressing the grievances of passengers and employees. The meet also resulted in bringing out handbooks for drivers and conductors besides launching a multimedia public relations campaign to educate both employees and passengers.

JANMABHOOMI: A UNIQUE EXERCISE IN RURAL COMMUNICATION

Jawaharlal Nehru, first Prime Minister of India, had said, "*Freedom from ignorance is as essential as freedom from hunger*". In other words, eradication of information poverty must precede the eradication of economic poverty. *Janmabhoomi* is a programme to inform, educate and enlighten people in rural areas.

Communication

Society, it may be said, is communication. Communication is used as a social process—the flow of information; the circulation of knowledge and the ideas in human society, and the propagation and internalisation of thoughts. Earlier communication projects such as Satellite Instructional Television Experiment (1975); The Kheda Communication Project (1975–1985); and Jhabua Development Communication Project (1996) —proved beyond doubt that media would undoubtedly transform the society from traditional to a modern status.

A great economic, social and political transformation is sweeping across India. Green Revolution, White Revolution, Blue Revolution, Health Extension, Pulse Polio Immunisation, Education of 750 million voters are some examples which contributed for socio-economic transformation. India today is the tenth largest economy in the world, tending to become the third largest economic global player. All these significant achievements have been possible, thanks to media and public communication. This case study examines the role of both private and government media in the eradication of information poverty on development schemes intended for rural folk, with special reference to the first round of '*Janmabhoomi*'.

Janmabhoomi (motherland)

A people-centred development process aimed at rebuilding the villages and towns modelled after a successful South Korean experience named "*Saemul-um-Dong*" (New Community Movement) was implemented by the Government of Andhra Pradesh for a period of over six years from January 1997 to July 2003. The main communication objective of *Janmabhoomi* was not only to sensitize the rural masses but also seek their participation in rural development programmes.

Media Strategy

In tune with Indian environment a multimedia strategy with a blend of four types of media—interpersonal media; folk art media; mass media and modern IT new media was used in reaching the target audience. Human Chain Communication with 10 million people, arranging 226 rounds of *Dial Your Chief Minister* through television and radio network as phone-in-programme; mass distribution of 50,000 audio cassettes containing songs on *Janmabhoomi*; chief minister's printed message of one million copies for oral presentation; conduct of 53,600 gram sabhas (village general assemblies) for micro planning; use of over 26,000 village drums as tool of rural communication and interaction of 400,000 college students with village folk; grassroots people's self-help groups for education and motivation; feedback information mechanism to identify people's felt-needs and grievances were some of the action programmes.

Impact

What was the impact of this rural communication exercise on development? Over 30 million people constituting 50 per cent of the State's population were exposed to the multimedia communication campaign and they were also enlightened on the new programme, *Janmabhoomi*. In terms of economic development, community works worth ₹182 million were completed under 100 per cent and 50 per cent people's contribution. As many as 47,500 school buildings, neglected for years for want of annual maintenance, were whitewashed. A number of irrigation canals were renovated. Over 300,000 public grievances were received as part of feedback information mechanism in the first round of the programme. Chandrababu Naidu as Chief Minister became very popular soon thanks to Human Chain Communication via All India Radio and Dial Your Chief Minister through Doordarshan. When he interacted face-to-face with about 10 million people in each round. Such Dial Your Chief Minister at the State level was indeed an innovative communication system. *Janmabhoomi,* according to experts, is a unique rural communication experiment in a developing nation worth emulation by other countries.

SATELLITE INSTRUCTIONAL TELEVISION EXPERIMENT (SITE)

The Satellite Instructional Television Experiment (SITE) started on 1 August 1975 was an important landmark in the history of television in India. It was the first experiment in the developing world to use a satellite for telecasting educational and entertainment programmes to far-flung rural areas. With this experiment, India entered into space age.

Four Linguistic Groups

UNESCO recommended that since the conditions were favourable in India, the satellite could be used for national development. In 1969, the Department of Atomic Energy entered into an agreement with the National Aeronautic and Space Administration (NASA) of the USA for the loan of ATS6 satellite, free of cost for one year from August 1975. It was meant to relay educational television programmes direct from satellite to receivers. As many as 2,400 villages spread over six States comprising Orissa, Madhya Pradesh, Bihar, Rajasthan, Andhra Pradesh and Karnataka–spanning four linguistic groups—were covered by SITE. Languages covered included Hindi, Oriya, Telugu and Kannada.

SITE was described as the biggest communication experiment of its kind in the developing world. The satellite had a powerful transmitter which enabled it to be used with inexpensive movable 'Chicken-mesh' ground antenna. No costly stationary and relay stations as commonly used in conventional communication network were required. The SITE beamed four-hour programmes everyday from earth stations at Delhi and Ahmedabad on education, agriculture, health and family planning. One hour and a half daily was devoted to programmes for pre-primary and primary school children in Telugu, Oriya, Kannada and Hindi languages so as to reduce the drop-out rate and improve children' skills.

Limitation

One of the shortcomings of SITE was its limited reach. There were only three base production centres at Delhi, Cuttack and Hyderabad to produce the bulk of the programmes for villagers with varied linguistic and cultural backgrounds and spread over six states. As a result, only a few area specified programmes in the relevant local dialect could be telecast. That was the limitation of SITE. However, India being the first country to try this experiment and do it successfully inspired other developing countries to draw on its experience in planning programmes for their socio-economic development including agricultural development.

When the NASA could not extend the contract for leasing satellite further, SITE came to an end on 31 July 1976, and a new SITE Continuity Project was initiated. This provided for the installation of six terrestrial transmitters in far-flung backward areas, such as Raipur (Chattisgarh), Jaipur (Rajasthan), Muzaffarpur (Bihar), Sambalpur (Orissa), Gulbarga (Karnataka) and Hyderabad (Andhra Pradesh). The new transmitters covered not only 954 of the earlier 2,400 villages, but also extended the coverage to some additional villages.

Impact

Several studies lauded SITE for having contributed substantially to gaining knowledge and creating a positive change in the attitude of the viewers. Through the studies useful lessons were learned. Its success can be illustrated by one example. A fire broke out in Kheda village in Rajasthan. When people started running for water, an illiterate farmer who was exposed to SITE telecast shouted "Throw some sand. Did you not see it on TV". This is only one example to quote. The people derived many benefits and there has been a sea change in the outlook of the villagers exposed to this programme towards development.

Tub and Lantern

Television is an effective tool for changing farmers' attitude. Doordarshan used to telecast a programme on "Tub and Lantern" methods of killing insects infesting the paddy fields. A ditch was dug and a brick elevated platform built at the centre. The ditch was filled with water below the level of brick platform. A lantern was kept on the brick platform throughout the night. Insects were attracted towards the light and got killed in the water. An illiterate farmer who watched this programme experimented the method in his farm and the ditch was full of insects. In the normal course, he would have used insecticides to tackle the menace. Thus, he saved money and as a 'knowledgeable person' shared his experiment with other farmers. That is how television had created an impact on the farming community. The key lesson learned was that broadcasting television programmes, produced in local languages, relevant to the needs and aspirations of rural people were needed.

KHEDA COMMUNICATION PROJECT (UNESCO AWARD WINNER)

Another pioneering experiment in using television for educational purposes was the Kheda Communication Project (KCP). Inspired by the lessons learned from SITE, KCP was designed which was a decentralised experiment in community-based television. The site chosen for the experiment was Kheda district, an area near the Space Application centre headquarter in Ahmedabad. One low-power transmitter was located at Pij village, about 50 kilometres south of Ahmedabad, which was connected to a local studio, to the local Doordarshan station and to a satellite earth station in Ahmedabad (Singhal and Rogers 2001). As many as 650 community television sets were installed in 400 villages at public places (Panchayats, schools), where village audience gathered in the evenings to view the broadcasts.

Kheda district comprises some 1000 villages with over three million inhabitants. The people of Kheda district, in particular the villagers where community television sets were provided, daily watched independent television programmes telecast by Space Application Centre from Pij transmitter for ten years (1975–1985). The KCP collaborated with extension agencies working in dairying, agriculture and health services, as well as with local banks, cooperatives and employment exchanges. As such, the KCP fully tapped the development infrastructure in Kheda district to facilitate the use of information transmitted by the television broadcasts. The project was independent of commercial interests as it relied mainly on government funds for financial support.

Need-based Programmes

The project produced television programmes based on audience research by conducting needs assessments of villagers and carrying out formative and summative evaluation. The focus was on rural development and social change at the village level. Audience participation was aggressively encouraged at all levels. Villagers were involved as actors, writers and visualisers in the production of television programmes dealing with local issues such as exploitation, caste discrimination, minimum wages, alcoholism, cooperatives, local and national elections. Television serials, puppet shows, folk dances, folk dramas and other local folk art forms were blended with television to highlight the issues, such as family planning, gender equality and village sanitation. Among the KCP programmes, *Ka Firyad*, a weekly feature, used to take up a specific problem confronting the villagers and discussed it in detail with interviews of both the affected villagers and the Government officers. *Chatur Mota* (Wise Elder) and *Nari Tu Narayani* (Women you are Powerful) were yet two other popular infotainment serials produced by KCP with the active participation of local people. The television producers went into villages of Kheda district and involved the local people to speak out about their problems and development. The Kheda project represented a model of community level, decentralised television broadcasting from the grassroots level in India. As a result, the Kheda experiment gained worldwide recognition and it received the prestigious UNESCO prize of US$20,000 in 1984 for rural communication effectiveness. The Kheda communication project continued till 25 July 1985, when a high-powered transmitter was commissioned in Ahmedabad with a range that covered Kheda district. The Government shifted Pij transmitter of Kheda district to Chennai in order to facilitate a second entertainment channel for its metro residents.

A study on the benefits of the project by Space Application Centre Research cell showed that the villages having community television sets had a greater level of awareness than villages which were not covered by the KCP. It was found that 96 per cent of those who watched Pij transmission knew of the advantages of immunisation as against 24 per cent of those who did not watch the transmission. The farming community greatly benefitted by the programmes and if they are well-to-do today, it is because of the project. Kheda district became a major centre for milk production in India as part of the White Revolution. India is now number one in milk production in the world. KCP played its role in ushering 'White Revolution' beginning from Kheda district.

Missed Opportunity

SITE (1975–1976) and KCP (1975–1985) were the two successful television experiments for education and socio-economic development of the country. But the Government of India and Doordarshan did not replicate these two television models in other parts of the country. The failure to replicate SITE and Kheda Communication Project demonstrates missed opportunities in utilising television for socio-economic progress of rural India.

JHABUA DEVELOPMENT COMMUNICATION PROJECT: A NEW MILESTONE IN THE EDUCATION OF TRIBALS

- Increase in Farm Production
- Decrease in the habit of drinking alcohol
- Tribal women came forward to watch TV for infotainment

Jhabua is a remote, hilly hinterland region in Madhya Pradesh noted for its large extension of tribal folks. About 85 per cent of population belongs to tribal communities, majority of them (85 per cent) are illiterates. Though the district is blessed with abundance of natural resources, the people here are the poorest ones in the STATE. Infant mortality rate is high. Transport and communication facilities are very limited. Agriculture is the main source of livelihood.

Objective

The Development Education Communication Units (DECUs) of the Indian Space Research Organisation (ISRO), Ahmedabad as a measure to cater to the development needs of this under developed sections of Jhabua region launched the Jhabua Development Communication Project (JDCP) with satellite communication and provided programme support to development efforts. The project is located in Jhabua, primarily a rural area, and was started on 1 November 1996.

The purpose of Jhabua Development Communication Project was to experiment with the utilization of an interactive satellite-based broadcasting network to support development and education in remote and pastoral area of Madhya Pradesh. As many as 150 direct reception centres such as satellite dish TV sets, VCRs and other equipment were installed in selected villages of Jhabua, which received television broadcasts for two hours every evening from DECUs Ahmedabad studio uplinked through satellite. In addition, 12 talkback terminals were also installed in each of the block headquarters of Jhabua district through which village functionaries such as teachers, anganwadi workers, hand pump mechanics and local panchayat members asked questions, provided feedback and report on the progress they accomplished. Talkback terminals were also used for training programme. The evening telecast provided communication support to field development activities so as to cover a wide range of issues such as health, education, watershed management, agriculture forestry, panchayati raj and cultural heritage. A variety of programme formats from specific factual information to dramatized stories were telecast to promote additional and behavioural change towards development. Active participation of local people in the programmes was an integral part of the project. The State Government, Jhabua district administration, local panchayats and NGOs joined hands to implement the project. The ISRO has beamed over 1500 TV programmes in a period of two years which were produced by ISRO and private entities. These programmes not only created greater awareness but also changed the mindset of the people towards development.

Impact

Since it was an effort by ISRO to enter the tribal area which belonged to the backward and poverty stricken people, evaluation studies were made on the impact of Jhubua Development Communication Project. The studies revealed that 75 per cent of the viewers who regularly watched the programmes that dealt with development issues were exposed not only to TV medium but also to development programmes such as watershed developments, health, education, panchayati raj and other local issues. With emphasis laid on participatory and local issue programmes, over 85 talkbacks training sessions were conducted, with over 8,000 participants given training in their respective fields such as anganwadi workers, teachers, employees of panchayati raj wing.

An interesting feature of the study was that the pre-transmission survey had indicated that the overall general knowledge of the tribals was very low. About 46 per cent of the Jhabua district population had never viewed television and majority of respondents never participated in Gram Sabhas organized by the panchayats. However, the mid-transmission survey indicated that people's awareness of development programmes had increased among respondents and average attendance was about 50 people per reception centre. The overall impact of Jhubua Development Communication Project was that there was a considerable increase in the awareness of programmes telecast by ISRO which resulted in an increase in farm production and a decrease in the act of drinking alcohol. The neglected half earlier women came forward to watch TV programmes for infotainment.

INDIA: A POLIO FREE COUNTRY—A CASE STUDY IN HEALTH COMMUNICATION

The Ministry of Health and Family Welfare, Government of India is not only instrumental but also responsible for implementation of various programmes on a national scale in the areas of Health and Family Welfare as well as prevention and control of major communicable diseases. Pulse Polio Immunization Programme is one of such schemes intended to eradicate the polio disease.

According to one estimate, about two to four lakh children, all under five years of age, were affected with polio paralysis annually in India in 1980s. There was a daily coverage of 500–1000 cases. In other words, one per cent of infants born were destined to develop polio.

In pursuance of the World Health Assembly Resolution of 1988, in addition to administration of routine OPV through the Universal Immunisation Programme, India not only joined the global movement for polio eradication but also launched the Pulse Polio Immunisation (PPI) programme in 1995–1996 to cover all children under the age of five years.

Amitabh Bachchan: A Goodwill Ambassador

Since the PPI initiative in 1995, significant success has been achieved in reducing the number of polio cases in the country. Of the three types of polio causing viruses, type two was eradicated in 1999 and we also succeeded in preventing the transmission of type three in 2010 and type one in 2011. The last child with wild virus polio was detected in Howrah, West Bengal on 13 January 2011. In February 2012, the World Health Organisation (WHO) declared India as a polio free country. Not only India was declared a polio free country, but also the celebrity actor Amitabh Bachchan who has been the Goodwill Ambassador for Polio UNICEF Campaign from 2005 was honoured for his outstanding contribution to the cause with his personal messages on different media. The 70-year-old actor had fronted the polio eradication programme successfully. People eagerly looked to him for his persuasive messages on polio disease.

However, the National Polio Eradication Certification Committee will wait for three years from the last virus detection before certification procedures, which is expected after January 2014. Polio eradication will then mean 'no infection without polio virus wild or vaccine'.

How did India eradicate Polio from four lakh cases to zero?

Eradication of polio disease is one of the major achievements of our independent India. The Ministry of Health and Family Welfare, must be proud of its role in implementing the pulse polio eradication programme with twin objectives. One was the service of administering pulse polio drops at the doorssteps of the people. The second one was its multimedia communication approach to reach every household in the country with the message "get administered polio drops 'Eradicate Polio'".

Social Mobilisation

A nationwide social mobilisation campaign was launched to sensitize people on polio problem. This involved better social mobilisation of frontline workers from the private health sector, members of Rotary International, volunteers, anganwadi workers, besides the massive public health workforce. In addition, the PPI created systems, such as cold chains for storage and transportation of the vaccines, ensuring vaccine vial monitors on each vial, follow up and mop up campaigns to track children left out during immunisation campaign.

'ASHA' Workers: Household Communication

As many as 8.50 lakh Accredited Social Health Activists (ASHAs) and link workers had been selected in the country at the rate of 1 ASHA per 1000 population. In tribal, hilly and desert areas, their norm could be relaxed to 1 'ASHA' per habitation depending on the workload. These ASHA workers visited every household in the village and provided them access to primary health care including polio eradication. The ASHA workers educated people on polio eradication and took children with parents to polio centres. This was otherwise known as micro-level household health communication, and house-to-house vaccination of missed children was also introduced to vaccinate children missed during the fixed booth based vaccination of children. This resulted in increasing coverage of two-to-three crore additional children. With covering of almost 100 per cent children in their homes, while travelling in brick kiln, sugarcane, farms where temporary migrant labour set up homes, wild polio viruses had no place to hide.

24 Lakh Vaccinators: 20 Crore Households

India spent more than ₹12,000 crores on PPI, according to Union Ministry of Health and Family Welfare. In each PPI, 24 lakh vaccinators visited over 20 crores households to ensure that nearly 17.2 crore children, less than five years, of age were immunised with the OPV. Mobile and Transit Vaccination Teams immunised children at railway stations, bus stands, market areas and construction sites. Special rounds were held to give OPV to children of migrants and refugees.

Rotary International

The Rotary International (India) as one of the major partners as an NGO made a significant contribution in the eradication of polio in India. It is the largest private sector donor for the cause. In India alone the Rotary spent about ₹825 crores for polio eradication activities. As many as 7,000 polio inflicted children have been operated upon and rehabilitated. In a major boost to the eradication campaign, the Gates Foundation (US) joined hands with Rotary International and through Bill & Melinda Gates Foundation contributed a sum of US $355 million for the final push. Rotarians are involved in myriad ways, before, during and after national immunization days, in providing funds for vaccine, promoting upcoming publicity campaigns in the community, distributing vaccine to local health centres, serving as monitors, working with local officials to reach every child and participating in surveillance efforts.

Multimedia

Multimedia approach was adopted to reach out to literate, illiterate, urban, rural, rich and poor in the nook and corner of the country. Media used included interpersonal meetings, traditional folk arts such as Tamasha, Street Plays, Puppets, Mass Media, newspaper, radio, TV, Film and new media Internet, e-mail, twitter, blogs, etc. Actor Amitabh Bachchan was the Ambassador of Pulse Polio Immunisation Programme, who became spokesman on all the media and had great impact on the people. India could eradicate polio disease because of its service-oriented action plans on the one side and the multimedia communication campaign to sensitize people on the other. Eradication of polio disease not only decreased the disability of the people but also increased the national gross productivity.

INDIA SHINING (2004)

Two innovative Government Publicity Campaigns 'India Shining' (2003–2004) and *Bharat Nirman* (2004–2012) were part of public relations effort of Government of India with a difference.

India Shining

The National Democratic Alliance government led by Bharatiya Janata Party launched ₹500 crores 'India Shining' multimedia publicity campaign in 2003–2004, to project its five-year achievements, before Parliamentary Elections in 2004. The campaign designed by a multinational advertising agency involved the release of pleasing advertisement series throughout the country. What made India Shining stand out and get noticed was the release of attractive advertisements with better visuals and easy-to-read copy. Each advertisement had a theme with particular emphasis on a given subject, such as 'Roads are Lengthening, Distances are Shortening'; 'Schools are Bustling, Children are Sparkling'. The theme for rural economy was 'Villages are Progressing, Eyes are Twinkling' to portray the changing face of rural India in which many villages resemble small towns with television, cell phones and Internet.

But many political leaders of all shades and communication experts admitted that the epithet 'India Shining' was not applicable to the rural sector, which was ridden by a crisis in agriculture, farmer suicides, drought, drinking water, shortage of power supply, unemployment, etc.

Even the then Chief Minister of West Bengal, Buddhadeb Bhattacharjee, at the valedictory session of 26th All India PR Conference in Kolkata on 19 December 2004 told the author that 'India Shining' was not in tune with the environment of rural India. BJP leaders also later admitted that 'India Rising' would have been much better than

'India Shining'. The campaign failed as it was only one way and that the pulse of the public towards the campaign was not ascertained. The ruling party tasted defeat.

BHARAT NIRMAN PUBLIC INFORMATION CAMPAIGNS 2004–2013

In May 2004, the United Progressive Alliance (UPA) supported by the left parties formed the government in New Delhi and Lauched a National Common Minimum Programme for the equitable social and economic development of the country. As 'India Shining' campaign of NDA Government was mostly urban and elite oriented, the UPA Government thought of yet another campaign aimed at reaching the grassroots of the country.

The Chennai Regional Office of the Press Information Bureau, Ministry of Information and Broadcasting organized a week-long innovative multimedia publicity campaign in Sivaganga Parliamentary Constituency in September 2004 in which all the media units of Government of India and development of departments both State and Central Governments including nationalised banks participated. Assets and loans worth ₹3.5 crores were distributed as part of the publicity campaign. Later the UPA Government published 'Report to the People 2004–2006', the message of which had to be carried to the common man in the villages.

Public Information Campaign

Encouraged by the great success of multimedia publicity campaign in Sivaganga Lok Sabha Constituency, the Ministry of Information and Broadcasting decided to organise 100 multimedia publicity campaigns at the rate of three each by the PIB Offices in the country during 2006–2007. However, the nomenclature of the campaign was changed to *Bharat Nirman* Public Information Campaign (BNPIC). The BNPIC was, indeed, an innovative method of disseminating development information at the village level by achieving synergy between the Government media and the development departments including the banks. The campaign was aimed at creating awareness among the common people about their legal entitlements, empowerment and the employment opportunities available to them through various developmental schemes. The focus was on the empowerment of Aam Aadmi and improve their quality of life.

Salient Features of BNPIC

- It is a three-day information mela organised at a rural venue or a backward area

- Communication strategy combines information dissemination with the delivery of services at the doorsteps of the beneficiaries
- Exhibition showcasing Government of India's flagship/welfare programmes. Stalls of various Central/State Government Departments, public sector undertakings, nationalised banks, NGOs and Self-help Groups
- Coordination with local banks for distribution of loans
- Participation of school children in creating awareness on Bharat Nirman Brand
- Feedback in the form of 'Logon ki Vani'

The campaign involved a two-tier mode of communication. In the first tier, the main BNPIC base camp organised an exhibition of various departments where symposia, public meetings, press conferences, group discussions, song and drama programmes were held. In the second tier, about eight mobile publicity units of the Directorate of Field Publicity and State Public Relations departments accompanied by department officials of agriculture, health, etc. not only arranged rural communication programme but also delivered public services at the doorsteps of the villagers in and around the base camp. The flagship programmes included: rural housing, drinking water supply, Rural Employment Guarantee Act, Tribal Welfare, National Rural Health Mission, etc.

Pre-campaign

An interesting feature of this campaign has been that the mobile publicity units also organised pre-campaign publicity for one week in at least 100 villages around the base camp so as to enable the people not only to participate in the publicity campaign but also to make use of the benefits extended. Handbills, banners, publicity through newspapers, announcements through loudspeakers, sms, press meets, press and releases were the media.

In Andhra Pradesh, the first BNPIC was organized at Nalgonda for five days in September 2006 in which banks distributed loans to the tune of ₹7.5 crores. Such campaigns are being organised by the PIB branches all over the country.

Evaluation

Though the two campaigns 'India Shining' (2003–2004) and 'Bharat Nirman (2004–2012) are important segments of government public relations, their effectiveness have not been measured through any independent research agency. As such the campaigns cannot show any tangible results.

The Press Information Bureau continues to organise these campaigns every year across the country to disseminate information on

Government's Flagship Programmes directly to the target beneficiaries. All the media units of the Ministry of Information and Broadcasting such as Films Division, Song and Drama Division and Field Publicity Division participate in these campaigns which make it a multimedia approach. During the period 2011–2012, as many as 140 public information campaign programmes were organised throughout the country, in which services like loans were delivered at the doorsteps of the beneficiaries, particularly in rural area. Ninety BNPICs were organied in 2012–2013. The Government of India should take steps to evaluate the impact of public information campaigns through independent research organisations to know the way in which people have been benefited.

Mahatma Gandhi: World's Greatest Communicator

(A Public Relations Exercise in the Freedom Struggle)

> *Our country gave birth to a mighty soul (Gandhi) and he shone like a beacon not only for India but also for the whole World.*
>
> **—Pandit Jawaharlal Nehru**

CONTENTS

In his autobiography, Gandhi mentioned about his journals—Public Opinion, Young India, Navajivan as a means of communication to accomplish his mission in life. He wrote, "Satyagraha would have been impossible without Indian opinion". Through these journals, I commended to the best of my ability the work of educating the reading public. The journals enabled me to ventilate my views and to put heart into the people.

Many biographies and articles have been written about Gandhi—all of them have focused either on political or social dimensions of his life. However very few have described how Gandhi conducted freedom struggle through mass communication and public relations strategy. The story of "Gandhi as the World's Greatest Communicator" is an excellent public relations exercise in the freedom struggle.

> *Gandhi was a man of the centuries. He was Buddha, the first of Jains, Francis of Assisi for love of fellow creatures, St. Paul and St. Augustine, Socrates with his catechism, Garibaldi marching with his followers, Rousseau, Abraham Lincoln. To present him as a teacher, as a moral*

genius, as a practitioner of truth and as a political leader only is to present the torso of a sculptured God. He cannot be compartmentalized. He was a complete man who did not turn his back on life (Chalapathi Rau 1972.)

Mohandas Karamchand Gandhi was born in a middle class orthodox family on 2nd October, 1869 in Porbandar, a small princely State in Kathiawar district of Gujarat. His father Karamchand Gandhi and mother Putlibai were devout Vaishanvites and his father and grandfather were Divans in the Porbandar princely State. Gandhi had his early education in his hometown and later he went to London to become a barrister. After his return to India in 1891, Gandhi set up legal practice in Bombay but was drawn into public life humiliated by the insults, injustices and racial discrimination on persons of Indian origin in South Africa which he had to visit in 1893 as part of his professional assignment in a lawsuit.

Mahatma Gandhi

GANDHI IN SOUTH AFRICA

Gandhi's life in South Africa dramatically changed him from being a barrister to a fighter for social justice as he faced the discrimination commonly directed at blacks and Indians. Gandhi was thrown off a train at Pietermaritzburg when he refused to move from the first class coach to a third class coach, while holding a valid first class ticket. Indians were not allowed to travel in first class coaches. Gandhi realized that an Indian in South Africa was held in scant respect.

At the end of his legal suit contract, Gandhi instead of returning to India, based on the request of Indians, stayed back in South Africa to fight against the injustices levied on the Indians. Gandhi founded the Natal Indian Congress in 1894 with himself as the Secretary to unite

Indians for a just cause. He moulded the Indian community of South Africa into a homogeneous political force by publishing pamphlets, leaflets detailing the grievances of Indians and the evidence of British discrimination in South Africa. He launched the weekly journal 'The Indian Opinion' in 1904 which became an official organ to disseminate information about the struggle of the Indians.

BIRTH OF SATYAGRAHA

'Satyagraha' means the pursuit of truth, passive resistance and non-violent protest. It is the use of 'soul force' or 'love force' against the British, against brute force to fight for justice. Satyagraha in the words of Gandhi is a '"Dharma Yuddha', one of the most powerful methods of direct action; it is a force that (though) works silently and apparently slowly (but) in reality, there is no force in the world that is so direct or so swift in working; it excludes every form of violence, veiled or open and whether in thought, word or deed. A Satyagrahi respects the law, but offers non-cooperation in regard to its evil elements only".

This new way of struggle 'Satyagraha' based on truth and non-violence for the first time in the political history of the world was born in South Africa to fight for the rights of Asians against the Asiatic Registration Act in Transwall in 1907. The Asiatic Act had stipulated that all men and women of Asian origin above the age of eight years should get their names registered. The Government recognized only Christian marriages as legal and the Hindu and Muslim couples who were married according to Hindu and Muslim religious rites were not considered legal. Tax was imposed on indentured labourers.

PEACE BRIGADE

Against this background, Gandhi launched his new weapon of protest 'Satyagraha', not to honour and obey the Registration of Asiatic Law and suffer punishment. This led to a fierce fight between Indians and South African Government. Gandhi called his band of workers as Peace Brigade. Satyagraha continued for six months. All the Satyagrahis including Gandhi were arrested and put into the prison. They were flogged, even shot for striking, for refusing to register, for themselves burning their registration cards or engaging in other forms of non-violent resistance.

What was the result of Satyagraha? It forced the Government of South Africa to come to an honourable settlement with Gandhi. Some of the major issues on which Satyagraha had been waged were conceded to the Indians. The citizenship rights of Indians were recognized. The tax on the ex-indentured labourers was abolished; marriages performed according to Indian rites were legalized.

INDIAN NATIONALISM

Having spent more than two decades in South Africa to combat racial discrimination, Gandhiji as advised by Gopala Krishna Gokhale returned to live in India in 1915. Gokhale, a veteran congress leader, became Gandhi's mentor. When Gandhi came on the Indian scene, the nationalist movement had already secured a foothold among the educated and professional classes in the country. Indian political life was however at low ebb. Great leaders such as Lokmanya Bal Gangadhar Tilak, Gokhale, Dadabhai Naoroji were at the helm of affairs to fight for the nationalist movement. Gandhi found that nationalist movement was confined to the upper middle class and the few elite. The poor peasants, artisans, workers and most of the village folk were out of the freedom movement. There was a yawning gap between the urban middle class and the rural poor, which was difficult to bridge through the conventional mechanism of politics. What was needed then was a mass movement with effective communication strategy to reach out to every village and every section of the society in the Indian environment to give a fitting fight to the British Empire.

EYES AND EARS OPEN BUT MOUTH SHUT

How did Gandhi accomplish this? Instead of entering into active politics, Gandhi as advised by his political guru Gokhale travelled the length and breadth of India to gain first-hand experience about the people and the country with his eyes and ears open, but his mouth shut. Like Aadi Shankara Gandhi started criss-crossing the country, mingling with the common man.

In the year of probation (1915), Gandhi eschewed politics severely. In his speeches and writings, he confined himself to the reform of the society and the individual and avoided issues which dominated Indian politics. His restraint was partly due to self-imposed restraint and partly due to the fact that he was still studying conditions in India and making up his mind. In today's public relations parlance, this stage of probation is called situation analysis or fact finding.

The tour of the country spurred him to identify himself with the common man and transformed him into "Daridranarayan", a half-naked true representative of his fellow impoverished Indian. Subsequently, his knowledge of the common folk and his straight, direct and heart-to-heart dialogue with them in simple language helped him create an immense impact on them.

SABARMATI ASHRAM: A HUMAN LABORATORY IN WALK THE TALK

At the end of his year's wandering the country, Gandhi settled at Sabarmati where he founded an ashram, which he called Satyagraha Ashram. Charles F. Andrews, a close friend of Mahatma Gandhi, commented "it is impossible to understand Mahatma Gandhi's principles in their entirety without studying their embodiment in his Ashram. Everyone felt the benediction of his presence as he sat facing the visitors and ashramites. Every inmate of the ashram cleaned one's own plates and washed clothes. There were no servants. There was a weaving wheel where people were involved in spinning and weaving as a constructive activity.

The environment in the Ashram was like a settlement house of a large family under a benevolent but exacting patriarch. Gandhi was Bapu, the father of the whole household; Kasturba was Ba, the mother. Indeed the ashram was a great human laboratory where Gandhi tested the cardinal principle of walk the talk or preach and practice. Winston Churchill, his British critic and Prime Minister, described Gandhi as a 'Half-naked Fakir' while the Noble Laureate Rabindra Nath Tagore called Gandhi in contrast 'Great Soul in Beggar's Garb'.

THREE MASS MOVEMENTS FOR INDEPENDENCE

Gandhi had launched three major mass movements of All India nature against the British rulers during his stewardship of the Indian National Congress from 1919 to 1947. These movements are popularly known as Non-cooperation Movement (1919–1922), Civil Disobedience Movement (1930–1932) and the Quit India Movement (1942). In fact, these mass movements were great exercises in the history of communication in India to mobilize public opinion against the British.

NON-COOPERATION MOVEMENT

The non-cooperation movement was the first ever series of nationwide mass struggle of non-violent resistance led by Mahatma Gandhi and the Indian National Congress. This movement had launched Gandhian Era in the Indian Independence struggle.

The Rowlatt Act promulgated by the British Parliament imposed authoritarian restrictions upon Indian people. The notion of Habeas Corpus was discarded and the police and army were empowered to search and seize property, detain and arrest any Indian without the need for evidence. In protest against the Rowlatt Act, Gandhiji called for observing Satyagraha Day on 6th April 1919 all over India—the beginning of non-violent, non-cooperation movement with a mass meeting at Chowpatty Beach, Bombay under the Presidentship of Gandhi.

JALLIANWALA BAGH MASSACRE

A major tragic incident took place at Jallianwala Bagh in Amristar when the British General Michael O'Dyer ordered shooting and massacre of about 15,000 unarmed and peaceful citizens assembled there to protest against Rowlatt Act. It was estimated that 1200 people were dead and 3600 wounded. In fact, 13th April 1919 was a Black Day in the annals of British India, marking a new turn towards freedom. In retaliation Gandhiji roused a storm of protest in the heart of our countrymen with a clarion call for non-cooperation with the ruthless British. In the Biblical style of speech after speech, and article after article in his two weeklies, 'Young India' and 'Navajivan', Gandhiji poured his passionate utterances which galvanized the people all over India. Bonfires of foreign cloth lit the sky everywhere and the hum of the spinning wheel was heard like a sacrificial chant. The nation rose as one man against the bloodshed of Jallianwala Bagh. The British Prime Minister David Cameron who visited India in February 2013 described Jallianwala massacare as a "shame to the British Nation" and it marked a new turn towards freedom for India.

The success of the non-cooperation movement was a total shock to British Government. However, on 4th February 1922, after a clash between the local police and the protestors in Chauri Chaura, three satyagrahis were killed in police firing. Gandhi felt that the movement should not degenerate into an orgy of violence where police and angry mobs attack each other back and forth victimizing civilians in between. Hence, non-cooperation movement was withdrawn because of the Chauri Chaura incident. Despite stopping the struggle on 10th February 1922, Gandhi was arrested on 10th March 1922 and was sentenced to two years imprisonment for seditious writings.

'PURNA SWARAJ'

In 1927, the Congress wanted Indian administration to function as Dominion Government and all political prisoners should be freed forthwith. But the Viceroy rejected the Congress demands outright. At the end of December 1929, the AICC met in Lahore amidst lot of tension and declared 'Purna Swaraj' as its goal. The first step Gandhi took was to call for the celebration of Independence Day on 26th January 1930. Hundreds of thousands of people in the towns and villages of India took a pledge that it was a crime against man and God to submit to British rule, and they undertook to join a campaign of Civil Disobedience and non-payment of taxes.

CIVIL DISOBEDIENCE MOVEMENT (1930–1932)

Gandhiji was greatly encouraged to see the response to the call for celebrating Independence Day. Four days later he published in the Young India his 11-point demand for consideration of Viceroy which, in his view, would mean the substance of independence. These points were: abolition of the liquor trade, reduction in the expenditure of the army and in the salaries of the bureaucrats, fifty per cent reduction in land revenue, imposition of protective tariff against foreign cloth, abolition of salt tax, abolition of the CID and release of the political prisoners But the Government did not take notice of these demands. Gandhi felt the country was ripe for a mass movement. Therefore, he suggested launching of Civil Disobedience Movement with breach of the Salt Laws. The Salt Tax, though relatively light in incidence, hit the poorest in the land. Gandhi announced that he would himself perform the first act of Civil Disobedience by leading a group of Satyagrahis to the seashore for the break of the Salt Laws.

240 MILES LONG DANDI MARCH

The long and great Dandi March took off from Sabarmati Ashram on 12th March 1930 at 6.30 a.m. After reciting his favourite prayer song 'Vaishnavajanaho', the frail and energetic 61-year old Gandhiji with staff in hand in the lead followed by his band of 78 dedicated satyagrahis started the march. The roads were decorated with flowers and arches through which the satyagrahis passed by, followed by a crowd of supporters and well-wishers. Gandhiji described his inner mind on the march, "My feeling is like that of the pilgrim to Amarnath or Badri-Kedar. For me this is nothing less than holy pilgrimage." Jawaharlal Nehru burst into eloquence, "Today, the pilgrim marches onward on his long trek. Staff in hand, he goes along the dusty roads of Gujarat, clear-eyed and firm in step, with his faithful band trudging along behind him.... It is a long journey, for the goal is the independence of India and the ending of the exploitation of her millions."

The march was like a mighty river starting as a small pool at its place of birth Sabarmati Ashram and picking up momentum with the joining of various rivulets and canals in its course towards the sea. Bapu's Dandi March witnessed unprecedented scenes of enthusiasm with people attending his meetings in large numbers en route. Gandhiji stopped at several villages and made numerous speeches, exhorted people to join in the march, boycott foreign goods, wear khadi dress and give up the evil of drinking and advised women to picket liquor shops and foreign goods outlets. His entourage included musicians who recited bhajans, kirthans, Ram Dhun and other songs.

A view of Dandi March

GLOBAL MEDIA

Gandhi enlisted support of worldwide media for the March by issuing regular statements from Sabarmati at his daily prayer meetings and through direct contact with the press. Gandhi said, "we are entering upon a life and death, struggle, a holy war; we are performing an all embracing sacrifice in which we wish to offer ourselves as oblation'. Correspondents from dozens of Indian, European and American newspapers along with film companies responded to the Salt Satyagrah and began actively covering the event. As a result, the struggle drew worldwide attention.

LAW BREAKER

The Dandi March concluded on 5th April 1930 after 24 days of trekking during which Gandhiji with his band of Satyagrahis halted at 22 places and carried out the daily regime of prayers, charka spinning, replying to letters, granting interviews to media representatives, interacting with and addressing the villagers, etc. After his morning prayers on 6 April 1930, he took bath in the sea and picked up a lump of salt and defied the Salt Law as Sarojini Naidu hailed him "Law Breaker." Gandhiji in a statement announced, "Now that the technical breach of the Salt Law has been committed, it is now open to anyone who would take the risk of prosecution under the Salt Law to manufacture salt, wherever he wishes and wherever it is convenient." Millions defied the law in spite of police brutalities. Salt depots were attacked and illicit manufacture of salt went unchecked. In a single attack on the salt depot at Dharasana, 289 volunteers were wounded in the lathi charge.

With the 'Long March' of 240 miles, Gandhiji and his gallant band of satyagrahis united a nation of 350 million against the British Empire. It was an electrifying moment as the nation rose as one man against what Gandhiji called 'Goonda Raj.' Gandhi was released unconditionally on 26th January 1931 to pave the way for Gandhi–Irwin talks on 17th February 1931. The subsequent Gandhi–Irwin Pact envisaged Round Table Conference in London. On his return from London on 28 December 1931, Gandhi was again arrested and the Civil Disobedience Movement was resumed.

QUIT INDIA MOVEMENT 1942

The last but the most important mass movement launched by Gandhi was Quit India. The All India Congress Committee at its session in Bombay 'Passed Quit India' resolution on 8 August 1942. It was also the period of Second World War that broke out in 1939. Gandhi declared that India could not be a party to a War ostensibly being fought to democratize freedom. As the British were not able to ensure India's defence against the Japanese advance into the Indian soil, Gandhi intensified his demand for independence drafting a resolution calling for the British to Quit India which brought in a head-on-collision with the British administration.

GANDHI SUFFERED TWO TERRIBLE BLOWS

What was the result? Gandhi, Jawaharlal Nehru, Maulana Azad, and the entire Members of the Congress Working Committee were arrested in Bombay by the British on 9th August 1942. Gandhi was held for two years in the Aga Khan Palace in Pune. It was during his jail term Gandhi suffered two terrible blows in his life. His 50-year-old Secretary Mahadev Desai died of heart attack and his wife Kasturba died after 18 months imprisonment on 22nd February 1944. Six weeks later Gandhi suffered a severe malarial attack. The news of the arrest of Congress leaders produced violent reactions. In several provinces the fury of the people burst the dykes and turned on the instruments and symbols of British Rule. Post offices, police stations and courts were burnt, railway lines, buildings and rolling stocks were damaged and telephone and telegraph wires were cut. The Government hit back with all its might; mobs were dispersed with firing and even machine-gunned from the air. Gandhi's Quit India pamphlet was banned. As all the Indians fought unitedly, the bold Quit India movement shook the British Government. Meanwhile, Gandhi was released before the end of the War on 6th May 1944 because of his failing health. At the end of the War, the British gave clear indications that power would be transferred to Indian leaders. At this point Gandhi called off the struggle and around one lakh political prisoners were released. India attained independence on the midnight of 15th August 1947 with Pandit Jawaharlal Nehru sworn as Prime Minister and he announced "at the stroke of the midnight hour when the world sleeps India will awake to life and freedom".

TWO FACTORS FOR SUCCESS

What was the secret of success of Mahatma Gandhi as the Man of the 20th Century and also the World's Greatest communicator? Why is he called Mahatma? His success was due to two key factors: one is his ideology of Satyagraha based on 'Truth, Non-violence' and Constructive Action-oriented Programmes. The second reason is his Communication strategy with unique media and methods in tune with Indian environment. These two key elements symbolize Gandhiji's basic philosophy 'walk the talk or practice that you preach'.

VILLAGE AS THE BASE

Gandhiji always believed that 'India Lives in Her Villages'. True to his firm belief, Mahatma Gandhi involved villagers in the freedom movement. The flag of nationalism was planted in every village, and in every village of any size, a dozen or more peasants' households were actively drawn into the orbit of freedom struggle. Walking tour from village to village and one night in one village tour were Gandhiji's specialties of inspiring rural folk to freedom struggle. Gandhiji could literally mobilize 10 per cent of the nation's population which came to about four crore people in action against the imperial power, and he also bridged the gap between the town and the village in the nation's struggle for freedom.

PRAYER MEETINGS

One of the weapons of his communication was prayer meeting. His prayer meetings held in the evenings always had packed audience. Every prayer meeting ended with his appeal to the people. Bhajans, kirtans, devotional songs and music and Ram Dhun, Vaishnavajanaho, were the regular feature of his prayer meetings which attracted the attention of visitors. He discussed various issues of current interest at such meetings. Major announcements of large-scale mass movements were made known only at prayer meetings. Each prayer meeting had a message and purpose.

On 30th January 1948, a congregation of about five hundred had assembled at Birla House in New Delhi for Gandhiji's regular prayer meeting. He was just a few yards away from the wooden platform from where he was to address when he was shot dead with automatic pistol. Gandhiji fell, his lips uttering the name of God 'Hey Ram'. True to his media (prayer meetings), Mahatma Gandhi laid down his life just at one such prayer meeting. What a coincidence!

SLOGANS

Gandhian catchy slogans caught the imagination of common people. Gandhiji's grasp of the perception level of the Indian people was so vast that he always concretized most difficult and abstruse concepts into simple language for better understanding. Gandhiji coined slogans that conveyed exact meaning and images which he wanted the masses to perceive.

If Bal Gangadhar Tilak coined the slogan 'Swaraj is my birthright, and I will have it', Gandhiji translated Tilak's Swarajya into 'Ramarajya', an expression with which the Indian mind was very much familiar. Quit India, Purna Swaraj, Harijan, Satyagraha, Swadeshi, Gram Swaraj and Dharma Yudh were some of the expressions of the native tongue that became instantly popular with the people the moment they were announced by the Mahatma as programmes of mass action.

SYMBOLS

Use of symbols, flags and images is the best way to educate the illiterate and ignorant people. Symbols form an important part in Gandhiji's thought and scheme of communication. He adopted the spinning wheel as a symbol of economic emancipation. The charkha was another visual item he made famous as a symbol of peaceful productive labour. This charkha had been incorporated into the Indian National Congress flag as a powerful symbol. People identified the freedom movement with this flag. The tricolor flag itself was an effective medium of communication.

Neville Chamberlain's Umbrella, Winston Churchill's 'V' for victory sign, Joseph Stalin's Military Uniform, Swami Vivekananda's Saffron Robes were famous images of the last century that equally matched powerfully by Gandhiji's appearance with half-naked fakir's loincloth attire, shaven head, bespectacled face and a familiar walking stick. His dress and appearance itself as a medium of mass communication not only acted as an embodiment of his personality but also identified Gandhiji as a man of the masses. Through the use of symbols, he was able to achieve and maintain close contact and rapport with millions of masses. He adopted this technique at a time when the means of communication were primitive by today's standard.

REPLIES TO LETTERS

After finishing his personal tasks and prayers, Gandhiji meticulously used to answer the letters he received. Everyday about 1000 to 2000 words, sometimes even more, poured out of his heart in his letters loaded with persuasive messages. They always had a personal touch of sincerity and tender human concern as one-to-one communication.

SILENCE AS COMMUNICATION

Ramana Maharishi, who was an Indian spiritual icon, taught devotees by communication in silence rather than word of mouth. Visitors flocked to him with bundles of questions, but as they got into his presence, they found that their question needed no answer.

Among his many measures devised voluntarily to maintain tight and regular discipline over himself, Gandhiji practiced complete silence on Mondays. But so great was the demand on him by others that even on Mondays that he could not seclude and cut himself off entirely for communicating with others. He still received visitors and heard them in silent observance. His answers and comments to them were, however, written in his own hand as notes on pieces of paper. He was an attentive listener who seldom interrupted those conversing with him so that his views and replies could be framed thoroughly and delivered neatly to the point. Gandhiji did not speak at prayer meetings on days of silence. Instead, his written replies to questions were read out to the audience. A good communicator is one who listens the most.

PRECEPT AND PRACTICE

Gandhiji believed in the dictum 'an ounce of action is worth a ton of preaching'. A great quality of Gandhiji was that what he preached, he also practiced it. His thoughts and actions always went together.

Once a mother came to Gandhi with her son who was fond of eating more sugar. She wanted Mahatma to advise her son on the ill effects of consuming a surfeit of sugar. Gandhiji asked her to bring her son after 15 days. Accordingly, the mother and son again came to Gandhiji who tutored the boy not to eat more sugar as it would adversely affect his body and health and that would ruin his life too. Later, the mother asked Gandhiji, why he took 15 days to give such a simple advice. He replied that he was also in the habit of eating more sugar and it took him 15 days to reduce the quantum of sugar consumption and become eligible to advise the boy. How many of our leaders, even public relations personnel, do this action-oriented practice?

CONSTRUCTIVE PROGRAMME

Gandhiji knew that mere propaganda communication without action does not yield any results. Therefore, for better impact he carried out constructive programmes alongside the freedom movement. His constructive programmes included: abolition of untouchability, promotion of communal amity through the removal of all discriminations among the communities, introduction of prohibition, popularizing khadi production, wearing of khadi and handwoven cloth, development of rural industries such as hand grinding, hand pounding, soap making, match making, tanning, oil processing, introduction of basic education in every village, adult education, empowerment of women, organisation of the peasantry, improvement of village sanitation, upliftment of adivasis, improvement of cattle, etc.

HARIJAN SEVAK SANGH

To implement his scheme of removing untouchability, Gandhi started an organisation called the All India Harijan Sevak Sangh. The programme of Harijan Sevak Sangh consisted of two sections: one was the constructive work and the other was propaganda. The aim of Sangh was to educate and canvas opinion among caste Hindus in favour of removal of untouchability in all its forms. If the constructive work was based on education of Harijan children, vocational training, welfare work, housing, temple entry, common drinking water supply facility, the propaganda work included holding of meetings for bringing together caste Hindus and Harijans on one platform, organising Harijan Days, processions, demonstrations, publication of books and periodicals and house to house visits to secure the objectives of removal of untouchability.

Gandhiji also undertook an All India Harijan Tour from 7th November 1933 to 12th April 1934 commencing from Wardha and ending in Benaras (now Varanasi). This yatra created an infinite urge among the people that untouchability must go. 'Harijan', his popular journal, was also devoted to the cause of abolition of untouchability.

FASTING

One of the tools of his communication was 'fasting'. The spectacle of voluntary suffering in his fasting embraced for a noble cause could not but win sympathy and admiration of all who care for human good and moral values. Pandit Jawaharlal Nehru said the fast does two things: it introduces a sense of urgency to the problem and forces people to think out of the rut to think afresh'.

Gandhi undertook a 'Fast-unto-Death' on three notable occasions:

- When he wanted to stop all revolutionary activities after the Chauri Chaura incident of 1922
- When he feared that the 1934 communal award giving separate electorates to untouchable Hindus would politically divide the Hindu people
- In 1947 when he wanted to stop the bloodshed between Hindus and Muslims in Bengal and Delhi

In all the three cases, Gandhi was able to communicate message for peace and communal amity.

NEWSPAPERS

Alongside the interpersonal media and traditional folk art media, Gandhiji made full use of modern mass media—newspapers. In fact, his ascendancy in Indian politics gave much needed fillip to Indian journalism. Gandhiji was not new to journalism. 'Indian Opinion' which he edited in South Africa was an effective tool for his movement against apartheid.

When he launched the Non-cooperation Movement, he felt the need for print media to educate the people. Therefore, Gandhi took over 'Young India' in 1919 from Jamnadas Dwarakadas of Bombay and also started a Gujarati Weekly Navajivan. Later he changed the title of 'Young India' and then to Harijan to promote the cause of the downtrodden and propagate against untouchability.

He described the objects of a newspaper as: "one of the objects of a newspaper is to understand the popular feelings and give expression to it. Another is to arouse among the people certain desirable sentiments; the third is to fearlessly expose popular defects'. While explaining why he had taken up journalism, Gandhi said, "I have taken up journalism as a means to communicate my mission in life—independence for the country".

Gandhiji was accepted as a noted writer. He never aimed at a style or flowery words which suit the ears. His style of writing was simple, precise, clear and devoid of artificialities and passive voice as the life of the author himself. In fact, Gandhiji became a good copy for journalists. Millions of people all over the country waited every week to read in their newspapers what Gandhiji had written and what his message was for them.

SEVEN SOCIAL SINS

As a measure to reform the society, Gandhi had identified seven social sins in the form of messages which he expected everybody to avoid. They are: Politics without principle is a sin, Wealth without Work, Pleasure without Conscience, Business without Morals, Education without Character; Science without Humanity and Worship without Sacrifice is a sin.

At the time when the modern means of mass communication were not available, the question arises as to how Gandhiji could communicate with millions of diversified and illiterate masses. This perspective is of great relevance to the present-day public relations professionals.

ITM THEORY OF GANDHIAN PUBLIC COMMUNICATION

If I am asked to answer to the secret behind Gandhiji's success, I would say it was "Gandhian Technique of Public Communication" which was in tune with the Indian environment, an environment inherited by the country with its 5000-year-old civilisation. In fact, Gandhiji had laid the strong foundation for the Indian public relations techniques with his double-edged weapon 'Preach and Practice'. Therefore, Public Relations Voice, the only journal for Indian public relations professionals, in its inaugural issue in 1997 aptly described Mahatma Gandhi not only as the World's Greatest Communicator but also the Father of Indian Public Relations.

The Gandhian Communication edifice is based on a new theory called the ITM Theory of Gandhian Public Communication, wherein he synthesized the age-old traditional media and modern mass media.

'I' stands for interpersonal media and identification with people (prayer meetings, public meetings, wayside meetings, interviews, Gandhiji's dress and way of living).

'T' represents traditional folk art media (bhajans, keertans, devotional songs and music, etc.).

'M' represents mass media; Gandhiji's own in-house newspapers such as 'Young India', Navajivan' and the 'Harijan' and other Indian and Foreign newspapers.

Gandhiji's communication style baffled the western communication experts who believed that mass communication was effective only in transmitting information and not in influencing the attitude and behaviour of the people (Malhn, 1985)

What inference do we draw from the communication life of Mahatma Gandhi?

- Public Be Understood
- Public Be Informed
- Public Be Sensitized
- Public Be Empowered towards Peace and Prosperity

That is the quintessence of his public communication/public relations strategy in the freedom struggle.

POINTS TO REMEMBER

1. Mohandas Karamchand Gandhi was born on 2nd October 1869 in Porbander, a small princely State of Gujarat. He studied law in London and became a barrister, had setup legal practice in Bombay.

2. He went to South Africa in 1891 as part of law suit to fight against the insults, injustices and racial discrimination on persons of Indian origin.

3. Gandhi was thrown off from the first class coach of a train to a third class as the Indians were not allowed to travel in first class coaches. Gandhi realized that an Indian in South Africa was held in scant respect.

4. Gandhi founded the Natal Indian Congress in 1894 to unite Indians to fight against discrimination in South Africa.

5. 'Satyagraha' means 'the pursuit of truth', passive resistance and non-violent protest. It is the use of 'Social Force' or 'Love Force' against the British. Satyagraha in the words of Gandhi is a 'Dharma Yuddha' which excludes every form of violence. A satyagrahi respects the law, but offers non-cooperation in regard to its evil elements. This word was born in South Africa to fight for the rights of Asians against the Asiatic Registration Act 1907.

6. As a result of 'Satyagraha Protest', the Government of South Africa came to an honourable settlement with Gandhi and the citizenship rights of Indians were recognized. The tax on the ex-indentured labourers was abolished, marriages performed according to Indian rites were legalized.

7. Having spent more than two decades in South Africa to combat racial discrimination, Gandhiji has advised by Gopala Krishna Gokhale returned to India in 1915 for participation in the Indian freedom struggle.

8. Gandhi in the first instance travelled the length and breadth of India to understand the people and the Indian environment with his eyes and ears open but his mouth shut. After the tour, to identify himself with the common man, Gandhi transformed into 'Daridranarayana', a half-naked true representative of Indians.

9. Gandhi founded an Ashram at Sabarmati, which he called Satyagraha Ashram, where he tested his cardinal principle of 'Walk the Talk' or Preach and Practice. If, Winston Churchill his British critic called Gandhi as a 'Half-naked Fakir', the Nobel Laureate Rabindranath Tagore described Gandhi in contrast as 'Great-Soul in Beggar's Garb'.

10. A major tragic incident took on 13 April 1919 at Jallianwala Bagh in Amritsar when the British General Michael O'Dyer ordered shooting and massacre of about 15,000 unarmed and peaceful citizens assembled there to protest against Rowlatt Act. As many as 1200 people were dead and 3600 wounded. It was a Black Day in the annals of British India. The Prime Minister David Cameron who visited India in February 2013 described Jallianwala massacre as a "shame to the British Nation"

11. In retaliation of massacre Gandhi roused a storm of protest among Indians with a clarion call for non-cooperation with the British. However, non-cooperation movement was withdrawn because of a clash between the local police and the protesters at Chauri Chaura where three Satyagrahis were killed in police firing.

12. The great 240 miles Long Dandi March in 1930 as part of civil disobedience movement was a great success and it is also regarded as an exercise in communication to mobilize public opinion against the British Rule.

13. Two factors, according to few experts, were responsible for the success of Gandhi: one was his philosophy of Satyagraha based on truth and non-violence and the second reason was his communication strategy in tune with the Indian environment.

14. Prayer meetings, slogans, symbols, his journals, Young India, Navajivan, Harijan, were the key media of communication to reach out with his messages.

15. ITM Theory of Gandhian Public Communication was his media strategy of communication accessible both to urban and rural Indians.

REVIEW QUESTIONS

1. What makes Gandhi as the World's greatest communicator? Elaborate your answer from his life and message.

2. Briefly discuss about the three mass movements (Non-cooperation movement, Civil disobedience movement and Quit India movement) and explain the media used in these movements to mobilize public opinion.

3. Mahatma Gandhi is regarded as the Worlds' Greatest communicator and the Father of Indian Public Relations. Discuss

References

1. Gandhi, M.K., *An Autobiography or the Story of My Experiments with Truth*, Navajivan Publishing House.
2. Sarvepalli Radhakrishnan, *Mahatma Gandhi: Essays and Reflections*, Jaico Publishing House.
3. Nanda, B.R., *Mahatma Gandhi: A Biography*, Oxford University Press.
4. *Mahatma: A Golden Treasury of Wisdom Thoughts & Glimpses of Life*, Mani Bhavan, Gandhi Sangrahalaya, Mumbai.

Glossary

*(Terms in the Glossary reflect the key
terms used in each chapter)*

ABC: Audit Bureau of Circulations. This Bureau audits the number of copies sold for newspapers/magazines. It takes into consideration only the net paid circulation in a particular period. ABC certificate boosts the advertising rate of a newspaper.

Above the Line and Below the Line Advertising: Payments/or the cost of the service made for media—television, radio, newspapers is known as above the line. It is because commission is paid to the advertising agency for the services of media. Public relations, promotional activities such as free publicity for a press release is regarded as the below the line activity. Direct mails, point of sale displays are examples of below the line where no commission is paid.

Account Executive: An executive in an advertising agency or public relations firm acts as a link between PR firm and a client. An expert in public relations/advertising. The AE is responsible to look after public relations programmes of a client such as media planning, developing PR strategy, designing PR campaigns and client relations.

Accredited Public Relations (APR): A title given to a PR professional by Public Relations Society of America based on an examination that meets the professional standards. It is a recognition to a qualified PR practitioner who is given preference in recruitment.

Active Publics: Active publics are those who are concerned about the activities of an organization in which they are affected These are the group of people or a subset of overall publics of an organization who react to the public relations problem/message. If a company acquires land for a small car project, a section of the local people may actively oppose the proposal of acquiring their land for a car project. They may even involve the media to highlight their grievance. Active publics can be further divided into two categories as 'all issue publics' and 'single issue publics'.

Advertorial: Advertorial is a paid form of editorial matter marked as a feature article. It is an advertisement presented in an editorial format. Advertorial is also considered as a mix of an advertisement and a newsworthy media release. The idea is to derive the credibility of a genuine news item as to increase readers interest. Advertorial writing is controlled by PR manager and at the end of the matter, it is labeled as 'Advt' or 'Advertiser's announcement'.

Advertising Agency: An agency of advertising business or a firm specialized in preparing and placing advertisements in media on commission basis. The agency is fully equipped with professionals and material to handle the clients with expertise services by purchasing space and time in media. The Indian Newspapers Society gives accreditation to ad agencies for getting media commission from newspapers.

Agenda Setting Theory: This is a mass media theory in which mass media influence the mind of the people towards an issue set by the media as an agenda. Media decide the subjects as agenda for people to think. Before elections, media highlight issues based on which people can vote. PR practitioners could suggest issues to the media. Mc. Combs, M.E and Shaw D.L (1972) are the authors of this theory.

AIDA Model: A—Awareness; I—Interest; D—Desire; A—Action—public relations practitioners use this model in promoting an idea, product or service as to enable the audience to adopt them for action.

Animation: The technique of photographing successive drawings or positions of puppets or models to create an illusion of movement when the film is shown as a sequence.

Annual General Meeting: Once–a–year meeting held by a company to discuss the annual report and future programmes. It is a shareholders meeting held under Companies Act.

Annual Report: Once in a year communication document of a company published under the Companies Act for the benefit of shareholders with audited reports including balance sheet, profit and loss account.

ASCI: The Advertising Standards Council of India. This is a self regulated body in advertising to promote professional standards and gain credibility for advertising. The ASCI was formed with the support of four sectors connected with advertising: advertisers, ad. agencies, media, PR agencies.

Audience: A group of people/viewers, listeners, readers who receive a message through a medium of communication such as TV or newspapers. Audience is the key in the practice of PR.

Audience Measurement: It is an opinion research to quantify or qualify the audience feelings or experiences gained through media—radio, TV or newspaper. It is also known as feedback mechanism.

Audience Profile: Socio-economic background of a readership, viewership or listenership. The profile gives an indication of spending habits, age, education, social status etc. It is useful to know the audience profile for determining the message and type of medium to reach out to the audience.

Backgrounder: A document or a note that gives full information on a given subject to supplement a public relations press release. Backgrounders are included in media kits. It is also called factsheet.

Bandwidth: Range of frequencies available for carrying data and expressed in hertz. (cycles per second). The amount of information a communication channel can carry is in tune with its bandwidth. TV channel requires around 8 megahertz.

Bar Coding: A technique of coding goods by printing bar code on packages which are read by scanning machines.

BBC: British Broadcasting Corporation.

Benchmark: A measurement used as a standard to compare other things or set objectives for communication plan.

Bernays Edward L.: The father of modern American Public Relations who in his famous book (1923) Crystallizing Public Opinion 'coined' the phrase 'Public Relations Counsel'.

Bibliography: A list of references/books/sources given at the end of the book.

Billboard: A hoarding that carries cinema poster or advertising message as an outdoor media.

Blog: Also web log. A website where a person writes regularly about events or topics that interests. It is linked to other websites. Blogs are used both for internal and external public relations.

Body Type: Text or printed matter as differentiated from the headlines. It is also body copy or body matter.

Bottomline: The ultimate result of an action such as the net profit or loss—the essential point in an issue.

Booklet: A small book similar to leaflet but with more contents and pages.

Boundary Spanning: Boundary spanning is intelligence gathering by public relations about the internal and external environment of an organization. Analysis of organizational environment and attitudes of stakeholders.

Brainstorming: A session of people gathered to generate new ideas.

Brand: A brand is a name, term, design or symbol that distinguishes and differentiates from other products or companies. Public relations creates a brand while advertising maintains brand.

Brand Equity: The total value of a brand as distinct asset in the market. It can be described as a measure of the strength of consumer attachment to a brand.

Brochure: A small booklet with about 10 to 20 pages. They are also called pamphlets which are part of corporate publications. Brochures are distributed as direct mail.

Bulletin Board: A board on which corporate information is displayed as a tool of internal communication for the benefit of employees. It is fixed in office at a prominent place.

Business to Business Advertising: Advertising of a business product or service by a business to a business audience called industrial advertising in contrast to consumer advertising.

Business to Business Communication: Communication between two business organizations for the purpose of selling or buying goods or services.

Buzz-Words: Word or phrase connected with particular subject that provoke response or emotive cliches. For example: the word 'unique'. This word has become popular and used very often.

Byliner: A story in a newspaper with the name of the author or writer is called byliner.

Cable Television: A television distribution network through which TV signals are sent to the TV audience through cable (insulated wire rather than air waves).

Campaign: The planning, implementation, communication and evaluation a of public relations programme of action, aimed at solving a corporate problem or achieving goals. e.g. Family Planning Campaign. It is a planned programme to contain population.

Case Study: A study based on research to know the results, impact of a campaign. Achievements of a campaign are indicated in a case study.

Catchword: A word used on the right hand side of the last line of a book page (bottom of the page) that is repeated as the first word on the following page—guide word.

CD-ROM: The abbreviation for 'Compact Disk–Read–Only Memory; a medium for storage of digital data, music, software etc.

Celebrity: A famous person is known as celebrity. Mother Teresa was a celebrity.

Celebrity Public Relations: It is a form of public relations practice to promote corporate brand, product/service by using the services of a celebrity as a brand ambassador.

Chequebook Journalism: The use of payment in procuring information needed for media from a source. Price can be very high when the story of the source is regarded as of high news value.

Circulation: Number of copies of a newspaper/journal as per the sales. The figure is as opposed to a number of copies read or readership.

Classified Advertisement: A small advertisement set in a single column and published in a newspaper under classified column, such as matrimonial, rentals, sales.

Client: An organization which has engaged the services of an advertising agency or PR firm, by payment for the services.

Code of Professional Ethics: Professional standards, conduct, values set by a professional organization to follow by its members. Public Relations Society of India has adopted Global Protocol on PR Ethics evolved by Global Alliance for PR & Communication Management.

Communication: Communication is sharing of information, or transmission of ideas from one person to another for better and common understanding between the sender and receiver.

Communication Audit: The analysis research or audit of communication programmes of an organization to know its results and impact on the audience. The audit identifies messages, public, media, methods and impact on the audience.

Communication Model: An illustration or a diagram that depicts the key elements of the process of communication.

Communication Strategy: A set of plans, communication objectives, communication plan, media strategy to reach out to the target audience in realizing corporate goals or corporate strategy.

Community Relations: Relations between an organization and the community based on community development programmes. As part of corporate social responsibility, corporation undertakes community welfare schemes like provision of drinking water, construction of community centre for the benefit of local community.

Competitive Advantage: The advantage of a product, idea that puts an organization over its competitors in this global competitive marketing environment.

Consumer Public Relations: Public relations process aimed at maintaining better consumer relations and to meet their needs with products of quality and better service.

Content Analysis: A research methodology by which the written, spoken and broadcast messages are measured into quantifiable form through a systematic approach to defining message categories through specified units of analysis. Content of mass media, press coverage, publications produced by PR department is analysed.

Controlled Media: Controlled media are such type of media where the sponsor can control the presentation of message. In contrast to interactive media, public relations professionals assume full responsibility in controlled media for the content, design, production, and distribution of messages. Brochures, direct mail are the examples of controlled media.

Convergence of Media: A blending of media made possible through internet and digitalization. Convergence means many things, convergence of telecommunications, information media and entertainment.

Cool Media and Hot Media: It is the innovation of Marshall McLuhan who distinguishes between a hot medium like radio from a cool medium like the telephone or hot medium like movie from a cool one like television. A hot medium is one that extends one single sense in high definition. High definition is the state of being well filled with data. A photograph is visually high definition; a cartoon is low definition, simply because very little visual information is provided. Telephone is a cool medium or one of low definition, because the ear is given a meagre amount of information. And speech is a cool medium of low definition, because so little is given and so much has to be filled in by the listener. On the other hand hot media do not leave so much to be filled in by the audience. Hot media are therefore, low in participation and cool media are high in participation. Naturally a hot medium like radio has very different effects on the user from a cool medium like TV.

Copy Editing: Copy editing is the process of going through the written material to check in detail the actual words written, spelling, grammar, syntax, readability etc. It should adhere to the house style.

Copyright: The exclusive right of a writer/author on the script, creative work which others cannot copy. Copyright Act regulates the copy rights. Copy writing includes body copy, slogans, press release, advertisement, TV/radio script.

Corporate Advertising: Advertising of a corporate enterprise to build the total image of an organization based on its unique achievements rather than advertising of its products or services.

Corporate Culture: Corporate culture is the culture of an organization developed over a period based on its values, attitudes, beliefs. Behavior of employees towards customers constitutes corporate culture.

Corporate Citizen: A corporation is regarded as a citizen that is socially conscious. Laws applicable to individuals also are applied to corporations as corporate citizens.

Corporate Identity: It is the distinctive insignia or logo of a corporation easily recognized and remembered by the public. A corporate identity is the overall image of a corporation or firm or business in the minds of diverse publics, such as customers and investors and employees. Burning lamp protected by two hands is the corporate identity of the Life Insurance Corporation of India. It is a visual symbol that improves the identity and image.

Corporate Communication: Corporate communication is a management function that offers a framework for the effective coordination of all internal and external communication with the overall purpose of establishing and monitoring favourable reputations with stakeholder groups upon which the organization is dependent. It is a total communication activity of a corporation to reach out both to internal and external publics.

Corporate Public Relations: A total public relations activity of a corporation to create and maintain mutual understanding between the corporation and its internal and external public. It embraces all types of relationships with corporate stakeholders and prospects through various media of communication. It includes relations with shareholders, employees, customers, media etc.

Corporate Reputation: The image of a corporation in the eyes of the public. Corporate reputation is the sum total of the corporation's daily actions, the quality of the brand, behavior of employees, values which impact on the perception of its internal and external public.

Corporate Social Responsibility: It is a commitment of a corporation to the welfare and improvement of quality of life of internal and external public including their families as well as the society at large. This is to the advantage of both the organization and the community concerned. The Tata Steel Rural Development Society as part of the Tatas social responsibility developed 32 villages around Jamshedpur.

Crisis: A situation or an event when normalcy is disturbed. A time of great danger, difficulty, when problem must be solved with determination. In economic recession, business crisis arises. Product defect, sabotage, fire, fraud cause crises.

Crisis Management: A plan of action to solve the crisis through the principles of management. Provision of timely information to the media is part of crisis public relations.

Crystallizing Public Opinion: Edward L. Bernays the father of American Public Relations authored Crystallizing Public Opinion in 1923 in which he defined 'public relations counsel'.

Cost Effectiveness: An outcome of the message that is measured in public relations research which evaluates the relation between overall expenditure (costs), results produced, usually the ratio of changes in costs to change in effects. It is an outcome on the expenditure incurred as input to produce an effect.

Cyber Public Relations (e-PR): It is a process of public relations through internet and new and social media. Internet is used in gathering, collecting and disseminating public information on various subjects to the target audience. Research, surveys and interviews are also conducted.

DAGMAR: D-Defining, A-Advertising, G-Goals, M-Marketing, A-Advertising, R-Results. This thesis was coined by R.H. Colley in USA during 1961.

Dateline: It is the first line of a news story or press release that indicates dates and the place from which the news has emanated.

Deadline: A deadline is a line with day and time fixed by media in which a story/press release has to be sent for publication. PR professionals must adhere to deadlines for getting stories published or broadcast.

Dealer Magazine: House journal brought out by an organization to educate dealers, distributors about a company and its products. It is an external house journal.

Declaration of Principles: It is historic principles in the practice of public relations when Ivy Ledbetter Lee the father of American PR issued a declaration in 1906, in which Lee committed his publicity agency would adhere to a professional standards of openness, truth and accuracy in dissemination of information to media.

Decoding: Process of converting messages into symbolic forms by the receiver.

Demassification: Coined by Alvin Toffler in his book "Third Wave" to describe move away from network TV to narrowcasting with special programmes for certain specialised viewers. With information revolution both media and audience have been demassified into several units and groups.

Demassified Media: Channels of communication- radio/TV, newspaper, divided or classified to reach out to small or selective audience as opposed to mass media. A newspaper has 30 editions–demassified into various units to reach the readers of that particular edition area.

Demographic: Relating to the study of population in terms of age, income, type of occupation, education levels.

Desktop Publishing: It is a system of publishing wherein the use of a computer and a particular software will combine text and graphics to create a document that can be printed on either a laser printer or a typesetting machine. The original text and illustrations are produced with software such as word processor and with photograph scanning equipment and digitizers.

DESTEP: The short form of D—Demographic, E—Economic, S—Social, T—Technological, E—Ecological and P—Political analysis. It is an analysis of organizational environment from different angles.

Development PR: Development public relations is the process of development information by public relations departments to create awareness among the public about the planning and development through a two-way communication street to seek people's participation in the socio-economic development. It may also be described as social marketing for the removal of illiteracy, ill-health and poverty.

Dialogic Communication: A two-way symmetrical attempt in communication process that promotes relationship building through dialogue.

Dialogic Public Relations Model: From dialogues between two persons their developed Relationship Management, a process of public relations. Such relationship management has resulted in the Dialogic Model of Public Relations. The World Wide Web, for example, became an important tool of dialogic public relations model where in public relations professionals can communicate directly with internal and external publics for feedforward and feedback information. Direct dialogue with the public through media is dialogic public relations.

Digital: It is a system of receiving and sending information as a series of the numbers, one and a zero showing whether an electronic signal is there or is not there. Presenting data in the form of numerical methods by discrete units as compared to analog method. Digital, now is commonly used as a synonym for computer. Digital satellite broadcasting, digital clock watch, digital camera, digital TV have become popular.

Digital Camera: A type of camera that stores photographed images electronically on magnetic disk instead of an traditional film. The disk can be played on computer or on a TV screen. Once stored in the computer the image can be manipulated and processed.

Digital Communication: A communication system, used with electronic and light based methods, that transmits audio, video and data as bits of information.

Digital Photography: Photography wherein film is replaced by microchip that records pictures in digital format. Pictures then are downloaded from the chip on to a computer hard drive. Digital photography is used for electronic publishing, e-public relations and advertising.

Direct Mail: Mail/letters sent direct to individual consumers by post/ courier service about a product or a service for direct response. Direct mail formats include: catalogues, commercial post cards, envelope mailers.

Direct Marketing: A process of marketing by which goods or services are sent direct to purchasers by post, or other direct means.

Disinformation: Manipulated or misleading information given to the media during war as propaganda material.

Display Advertising: Advertising in print medium that displays illustrations as well as type to attract the attention of a reader towards advertisement and its content message.

Documentary: A film, television or radio presentation of actual events rather than a fiction. It is also a short film or short presentation of facts, as a story, based on real life, but produced with creativity.

Dummy: Booklet of blank pages and pasting of proofs before going for printing.

DVDs: A DVD is a Digital Video Disc for storage of data which can be used as promotional media in public relations.

Dyadic Communication: Dyadic Communication is a communication on interpersonal level between two persons. Face-to-face communication within the process of public relations.

Editorial: It is a write up giving opinion of the editor/policy of the paper published in a newspaper on the editorial page. Editorial presents views by interpreting the news. It is also called leader.

Edit: To prepare/correct or alter the manuscript, film or any media work. Editing a house journal is the job of PR.

Edition: A particular issue of a newspaper published for a specific area. Daily newspapers publish city editions for a particular city like New Delhi or a particular district—Nalgonda.

Electronic Communications: Transmission of symbols, signals, writings, images, sounds or data through wire, radio, electromagnetic, photo electronic or photo optical system and internet.

Electronic Newspaper: Screening of a newspaper on computer or television.

E-Mail (electronic mail): Messages/mails transmitted by electronic impulses through a computer to be read from a video display screen or printed on printer.

Embargo: A deliberate request for the media not to publish or broadcast press release or a speech of a VIP before a stated date and time.

Employee Communication: Public relations communication with employees as to create belongingness towards organizational goals. House journal is the medium of employees' communication.

Employee Participation: Suggestion scheme evolved by the management wherein employees can participate by giving suggestions which will be useful to the organization in saving money or improving the productivity.

Environmental Monitoring: Monitoring of internal and external environment of an organization through research in the backdrop of socio-economic and political climate. A feedback of public opinion about the organization,

e-PR (electronic public relations): Practice of public relations using the new media—internet, e-mail, blogs, web in the center stage, is called e-PR.

Ethics in Public Relations: Ethics is the moral principles governing the conduct. Public relations ethics is defined as "the code of professional conduct and standards evolved by a PR professional body as a useful guide for its members on their ethical responsibilities in disseminating public information". PRSI has adopted Global Protocol on Ethics in Public relations.

Evaluation: It is an ongoing process of review or research of public relations programmes to determine their impact or results. For example, press clippings indicate the media coverage in the newspapers. It is a critical analysis of the results derived through PR programmes. Measurement of PR programme.

Evaluation Research: A form of research that decides the relative effectiveness of a public relations campaign or programme by measuring programme outcomes(changes in the levels of awareness, understanding, attitudes, opinions and or behaviours) are ascertained.

Event Management: Management of an event with careful planning, action projects, coordination as to reach out the target audience and accomplish its objectives. Organizing Annual General Meeting is an event for public relations. Public relations has the key role to draw media attention for the event. Conducting an "open house" is a PR event.

Exhibition: Seeing is believing. Exhibition is an attractively organized public show of products, services, paintings, photographs to project accomplishments of an organization and its products.. India International Trade Fair held every year in Delhi is an example of international exhibition when products from all over the world are displayed for sale. Success of exhibition depends on PR support. PR department is also entrusted with the task of organizing an exhibition.

External Publics: Groups of people with a common interest connected with an organization in relation to its products/services. Customers are the external public.

Extranet: The process of using internet-oriented technology and products between different companies for presenting documents. It increases the productivity and functions between partner companies.

Facebook: A small media networking site where one can project ideas, pictures for circulation. An interactive new medium on computer.

Face-to-face Communication: It is a process of direct communication between two individuals on a given topic of mutual interest. A good tool of PR to create better understanding.

Facility Visit: A visit or tour of journalists organized by the public relations department facilitating them to see for themselves and write story for media.

Factsheet: Key information/facts of an organization incorporated in a sheet for giving to media.

Faux Pas: Blunder; *especially* a social blunder.

Feature Article: An article that falls between the news story and wholly opiniated material with human interest. Interview-based feature. House journals carry feature articles.

Feedback Information: Information/response, reactions of public towards policies, programmes, products of an organization as collected by the PR professionals. It helps organization to correct their policies.

Financial Analysts: Experts in financial matters who advise people on investment of their money either in stocks or banks.

Financial Public Relations: A process of communication between a listed company and its financial audiences. It helps in public issues. Annual Report, financial media are the key tools of financial PR.

Five Ps: Marketing Strategy—1. Product, 2. Price, 3. Place, 4.Promotion and 5. Public Relations.

Five Ws: Press release or news story structure of a journalist/PR professional Who is involved, What is the news?, When did it happen?, Why did it happen? Where did it happen? Sometimes 'H' is also added. How did it happen?

Focus Group: A group of people invited for eliciting their opinion in a research project of public relations/marketing.

Folk Media: Media developed by tradition in villages for entertainment. Harikatha, Thamasha, Yakshagana are examples, which have access to rural people.

Forecasting: Presentation of future trends or events and performance.

Four Ps: Four Ps are: Picture, Promise, Prove and Push. A formula for motivation. PR professional writer can create a Picture of what the product or service can do for the consumer then promises that the picture will be useful if the consumer purchases the product, Later Proves that the product has been useful for other customers finally pushes for action.

Freelance Writer: A writer who writes on an ad hoc basis to cover short assignments for different newspapers/organizations. Available for anyone who wants to use freelance writing.

Games Theory: Behavioral theory based on study of individual preference in decision making.

Gandhian Public Communication: The communication system Mahatma Gandhi practiced in the freedom struggle to mobilize public opinion against the British rule is called Gandhian Public Communication. This was based on three-tier media, e.g. Interpersonal media (prayer meeting), traditional media (bhajanas, music), and mass media-newspapers (his own newspapers, The Young India, The Harijan & Navajivan).

Gatekeeper: The journalists who have the power to decide which news stories should be communicated to media consumers—newspaper readers, TV viewers, radio listeners or net surfers. Editors, producers, reporters, sub-editors belong to this category. Communication professionals also come under this category who decide as to which material should go to the public.

Ghostwriting: It is a process of writing wherein a professional writer, writes a speech for others to deliver lectures/speeches.

Globalization: "The integration of trade, finance and information that is creating a single market and culture is globalization". Growing interdependence of the world's people through shrinking space, time, and killing the distance is also called globalization. Globalization led to international public relations to meet the global competitive marketing. BBC is a global broadcasting corporation.

Global Brand: A product that has world-wide recognition (**e.g. Pepsi cola**).

Global Village: Marshal McLuhan (1911-80) evolved the concept of global village. The information revolution and modern information technology not only killed the distance but also brought people of the world together into a small global village in thoughts and actions (linking people all over the world through telecommunications). He advocated this theory in his book—Understanding the Media-1964.

Goebbels Joseph (1897–1945): He was the Propaganda Minister of Adolf Hitler during the Second World War. He poisoned his six children and wife Magada and shot himself, when Berlin was occupied by Russians.

Going Public: The initial public offer for sale of shares to the general public also called IPO.

Goodwill: Socially responsible behavior/helpful feelings of people towards an organization or an individual. The companies act in a responsible and ethical way to gain the goodwill of customers. PR is to create goodwill for the organization.

Government Relations: Public Relations practice in organization to maintain relations with the Government by publicizing policies and programmes of the organization. Government is one of the key publics for any organization. Maintaining good relations with government is process of government relations. Public relations has to create better relations through communication techniques with the government. It is also a relationship with government departments by an organization but not the relations of Government with its publics.

Graphics: Any illustrative material or visual presentations used in page design to inform, illustrate or entertain audiences. TV art work, lettering, diagrams, electronically generated symbols and all pictures, maps, charts and graphs belong to graphics.

Grapevine: The rumour mill communication through unofficial or informal sources within an organization. It is also known as informal communication, moves very fast.

Grassroots: The basic level of society or of an organization. Village in India is called the grassroots level unit of the society.

Green Public Relations: A process of public relations activity intended to promote environment in an organization. Commitment to preserve environment in an organization referred to as 'Going Green'. Green PR is a sub-field of public relations that communicates an organization's corporate social responsibility or environmentally friendly practices to the public. The goal is to produce increased brand awareness and improve the organization's reputation. Tactics include placing news articles, winning awards, communicating with environmental groups and distributing publications.

Griswold Denny: Denny Griswold (1908–2001) co-founder and editor of PR News (USA).

Gross Domestic Product: Total value of net domestic output of national products.

Group Dynamics: The study of the interpersonal relationships between the members of a work group.

Grunig James E: Prof. Emeritus, a PR theorist Grunig is the co-author of Managing Public Relations – Public Relations Techniques, Managers Guide to Excellence in Public Relations (USA) Grunig evolved four models of public relations. Press Agentry; Publicity, Public Information; two-way Asymmetrical communication and two-way Symmetrical communication.

Gutenberg Johannes: A German Printer (1400–1468) who developed one of the first printing presses with movable type which was used to print books. Bible was printed by him in 1452.

Handbill: A single sheet of publicity based paper usually 81/2" × 11" in any colour with a public relations/advertising message. Handbills are also called throwaway material.

Handbook: A book that gives information to the employees about job profile, duties, responsibilities as a guide. It could be for customers also. It is also called a manual with reference material.

Hard Copy: A printed version on paper of data held in a computer.

Hardware: The electrical and mechanical equipment used in telecommunications and computer systems as against software which consists of programes and files that are in the equipment.

Harlow-REX: He is one of the pioneers and prime promoter of professionalism in public relations of USA. Professor Harlow founded the American Council on Public Relations in 1939 as an association of West-Coast-Counsellors and in that organization started, the Public Relations Journal which is now published by the Public Relations Society of America (PRSA). The PRSA was formed in 1948 by merging the National Association of Accredited Publicity Directors and the American Council on Public Relations. He is regarded as the Father of Public Relations Research.

Headline: Headline is the sign post of a news story or of good writing. Short headline attracts the attention of the reader. It is also known as short summary of a news story or a title as to give a complete message of the story.

Hegemony: It is a concept which highlights the power or control of one social group over another. In public relations practice, the hegemonic group may be inculcated in the populace through education, influence and persuasion.

Hicky James Augustus: He is the Father of Indian Journalism who started the first newspaper in India—a Weekly Bengal Gazette in January 1780.

Hidden Persuasion: It is an attempt to influence public opinion by unidentified sources such as advertising or PR sources. A term coined by US, author Vance Packard, on motivation research.

Hierarchy Needs: It is a model of hierarchy needs evolved by American Psychologist Abraham Maslow which is based on the fundamental needs or desires of human beings and that they will seek to satisfy such needs. The needs are: 1. Self actualization needs, 2. Economic needs, 3. Social needs, 4. Safety needs and 5. Physiological needs. Public relations must take these needs into consideration while reaching out to the target audiences with persuasive messages.

Hitler Adolf: Adolf Hitler (1989–1945) the German dictator tried to impose his ideal of One Empire, One People and on Leader on his country at the expense of millions of lives. He achieved absolute power in Germany provoked the Second World War by invading Poland in 1939 and conquered much Europe, before committing suicide in April 1945 when Soviet troops entered Berlin.

Holistic: The whole thing but not in parts. Holistic approach in public relations is the total communication strategy to reach out to the stakeholders.

Hot Media: Marshall Mcluhan described radio, cinema as hot media as they provide plenty of data to be absorbed. Because, the medium is so full of information, it is aggressive and hot.

House Journal: A periodical brought out by an organization to inform, educate and motivate either employees or customers. It is basically a tool of internal public relations to promote the loyalty of employees towards a company or a sense of belongingness.

Human Interest Story: A news story which is of great interest to the audience in which it focuses on the success/failures, tragedies of the persons involved. It makes the story more appealing because real people are involved. For example, a child is kidnapped and killed for ransom.

Hyper Media: It is the combination of text, video, graphic images, sound hyperlinks and other elements in the form of typical of web documents.

Hyper-text: The text in one document that is linked electronically to text in another document or another part of the same document.

Hypodermic Needle Model: It highlights the power of media over audiences by injecting information into the minds of the masses. It is also known as magic bull perspective, emerged from the Marxist Frankford School of Intellectuals in the 1960s to explain the rise of Nazism in Germany. The model claims that the message is wholly and passively accepted by the receiver and that mass media has a direct and powerful effect on its audiences.

Information Society: It is a term coined by Alvin Toffler in his book 'The Third Wave (1980). He described that the world passed through the Agricultural Revolution (agricultural society), Industrial Revolution (industrial society) and that we are now passing through Information Revolution (Information Society). These three revolutions have impacted on the society. The Third Wave or the third revolution based on information and knowledge created information society like industrial society in the industrial revolution.

International PR Association (IPRA): The International Public Relations Association is a PR professional body of individual members. It holds world PR Congress for every three years. IPRA received recognition by the UNO in 1964 as an international non-governmental organization and has been granted consultative status by the Economic and Social Council.

International Association of Business Communicators (IABC): The International Association of Business Communicators (IABC) is a professional body of business communicators, headquartered in San Francisco, California, to support members in their work to create strategic, interactive, integrated and international organizational communication. Besides accreditation programme of its members, IABC gives awards in an annual international competition.

Investor Relations: It is a process by which we inform and persuade investors about the values in the securities that we offer as a means to raise capital for business. Investor relations is a strategic management function that integrates finance, communication, marketing and securities laws compliance to enable the most effective two-way communication between a company, the financial community and other constituencies, which ultimately contribute to company's securities and capital.

Issue Management: Issue management is a strategic function used to solve a problem or reduce friction and increase harmony between organizations and their publics in the public policy area. Issue management involves four core functions. (a) engaging in smallest business and public policy planning that is sensitive to public policy trends; (b) playing tough defence and smart offense through issue communication; (c) getting the house in order by meeting or exceeding stakeholders' expectations; (d) scouting the terrain to gain early warning about trouble issues. Applied properly, it gives organizations the opportunity to reduce the harm of threats and to take advantage of opportunities created as and when public policy changes occur. It is the process of identifying or anticipating problems issues relevant to an organization and then executing a programme to solve the problem.

IBM: The world's largest computer company formed in 1911. IBM also is known as IBM International. The actual name being is IBM Corporation, which previously was International Business Machines Corporation.

Image: Mental impressions/feelings or opinions regarding a company held by its public.

Information: Knowledge acquired in any manner, ideas and facts that have been communicated in any format are known as information.

Information Highway: The inter-linking of telecommunications for speedy access by the general public.

Initial Public Offering: The first shares of a company to be offered for sale to the public as mentioned in a prospectus approved by the Securities and Exchange Board.

Integrated Marketing Communication (IMC): Marketing mix in which public relations, advertising and other activities are integrated to reach out to the target audience. It covers the strategy, theme, messages and media including the audience.

Inverted Pyramid: It is a journalistic style of writing in which most important news elements are presented first and less important later. The most important news is presented in the lead or the first paragraph.

Infotainment: When information and entertainment are blended in media is called Infotainment. It attracts the attention of the audience and adds value to the message.

Integrated Public Relations: It is a process of public relations in which the communication activities of all disciplines such as Marketing, HR, Finance are integrated in public relations process to project the image of a company with one voice.

ITMN Theory of Gandhian Public Communication: A blend of (I) Interpersonal, (T) Traditional folk arts, (M) Mass media and (N) New media is known as ITMN Theory of Gandhian Public Communication. This theory is developed based on the techniques of Gandhian communication minus new media.

IIMC: The Indian Institute of Mass Communication, New Delhi, known for offering journalism, public relations and advertising courses, besides imparting in-service training.

Intranet: A private network inside a company for internal use, of employees.

Institutional Advertising: Advertising covering corporate image of an organization. It is intended to create goodwill for an organization rather than to advertise goods or services. It is also called image advertising.

Intellectual Property: Content of the human intellect deemed to be unique and original and to have market value and thus to warrant protection under the law. It includes ideas, inventions, literary works, products etc. Intellectual property protections cover: copy right, trademarks, patents and trade secrets.

Internet: The worldwide amalgamation of individual computer networks that are interconnected by a routing language for the exchange messages and sharing of data. It is the backbone of high speed data communication lines between host computers across the world. Designed for educational institutions in '70s', it is now used by millions of individuals for multi purposes. The present type of internet took shape in January 1983.

Industrial Relations: The relations between the management of a company and its employees and employees union is regarded as industrial relations.

Interpersonal Media: Media such as a telephone, word of mouth, meetings, used in person-to-person communication are known as interpersonal media.

Imprint: The name of the printer published at the foot of last page as a legal proof in case of any dispute.

In-house Public Relations: Public relations practiced through in-house PR department rather than PR consultancy is called in-house public relations. It is a full time PR service within the organization managed by a PR professional.

Indian Newspapers Society: It is an association of the owners and publishers of newspapers in India. It gives accreditation to advertising agencies which get commission from newspapers on ads given to them.

Information Overload: The people who have access to different media get a lot of information beyond their capacity to use it in a meaningful way, is termed as information overload.

Intrapersonal Communication: Communication taking place within one's own brain or talking to oneself. It gives self-view generated by experience and external stimuli. It is a prerequisite to other forms of communication.

Interactive Media: Interactive media allow people to communicate with people and people in turn could interact with sender of messages. Computers, mobile phones, TV, Radio now allow people to interact with each other on any subject. Interactive media facilitate two-way communication process between sender and the receiver.

Internal Communication: Communication within the internal public such as employees through house journals or other media is known as internal communication or internal public relations. A strategic management of interactions and relationships between internal stakeholders of an organization.

Jefferson Thomas: The third American President who is believed to have been the first person to use the phrase Public Relations in his address to the Congress in 1807. In his Seventh Address to the congress, Jefferson in one passage wrote: 'State of Thought' and then crossed it out and substituted it with 'public relations'.

Jargon: It is a technical language or terms of a subject or a profession.

Jingle: It is a catchy slogan with melody and tunes for broadcast on radio and television.

Journal: A newspaper or magazine published regularly with news and views. For example, house journal.

Journalist: A person involved in the profession of journalism for disseminating information through various media—newspaper, radio, TV.

Keywords and Phrases: The important words used in messages of a communication to attract the attention of the readers and also influence them.

Kickback: An illegal payment to an individual for favouring in a contract or a purchase. It amounts to bribe.

Kudos: Recognition or praise for a good job done by an individual.

Laminate: It is a process of sticking a transparent plastic film on a printed surface to create a glossy surface. Plastic film is stuck on book jackets, picture post cards, for a better look.

Layout: It is a page makeup with spatial arrangement of graphic elements such as photographs, illustrations, display, type, body-copy, headline, etc. for a printed publication. Layout displays size and position elements.

Lee Ivy Ledbetter (1877–1934): Lee is regarded as the father of American Public Relations who along with George F. Parker established America's third Publicity Bureau in 1904. Later on his own represented private companies like Coal Mines, Pennsylvania Rail Road where he proved his transparency in dissemination of corporate information. He is known for his Declaration of Principles (1906) which stated 'we aim to supply news' this is not an advertising agency. Our matter is accurate.

Lead: The first paragraph of a news story which is based on Five 'Ws' and one 'H' is known as the Lead. The essence of news is presented in the lead. Who, Where, What, Why, When and How.

Leaflet: A printed sheet of two or four pages with information for free distribution as part of publicity.

Libel: A written statement which is not true and also damages the reputation of an affected person is called libel. One can sue for the libel.

Line Function: The function of line executives who have authority and responsibility to implement plans and oversee that the work is done. They are the field staff who look to guidance from the staff executives who design strategies and plans at the corporate office. For example, a lineman in power distribution company.

Lobbying: It is a process of communication to influence those in power —decision makers, bureaucrats, legislators, regulators, etc. Lobbying is regulated in USA under an Act. There is no such Act in India.

Logo: It is a graphic design of a company to symbolize its products or services. Logo is created by using type, illustration or any graphic device. The logo of LIC with burning lamp being protected with two hands is a popular one in the field of life insurance.

Marketing: It is a social and managerial process by which individuals and groups obtain what they need and want through creating, offering and exchanging products of value with others. Marketing is based on Five Ps—Product, Price, Place, Promotion and the fifth 'P' is Public Relations. PR promotes marketing.

Marketing Communication: It is a process of communication of marketing department to create awareness of the products and services among the prospective buyers through various media of communication. Public relations also contributes to the promotional element of marketing mix.

Marketing Mix: A combination of marketing activities in the sale of products and services such as sales, advertising, promotion, public relations, distribution, pricing and product.

Marketing Public Relations: When public relations is integrated with marketing mix, it is called Marketing Public Relations. PR helps marketing with press releases, community relations and corporate social responsibility.

Mass Communication: Dissemination of information through mass media (radio, TV, newspapers) to large audiences as distinct from inter-personal or group communication is mass communication.

Mass Media: Media such as newspapers, radio, TV aimed at reaching very large audiences is called mass media.

Masthead: The top portion of a publication that indicates its name and other information such as year founded, motto. For example: The Hindu—India's national newspaper since 1878.

Measurement: Evaluation of public relations programme through research methods so as to give a precise dimension of the impact of the programme on the audiences. Exposure of audiences to the media also is measurement.

Media Advisory: A factsheet or a brief communication sent to news media to alert them of an event they may wish to cover.

Media Coverage: Media exposure to an organization's activity/ products or services. Coverage of news of an impending organization in the media.

Media Monitoring: Media coverage of an organization is monitored to the management by analyzing the press clippings. Monitoring or reporting (positive and negative); the quality of coverage, positioning of the news in the media.

Media Planning: Selection and planning of media to reach out to the target audience. Media is selected based on the socio-economic background of the audience.

Media Relations: Relations of public relations professionals with the media representatives to get fair coverage of the activities of an organization. Better media relations are created by providing newsworthy material to the media as useful to the readers. Press releases, press conference, articles, media tour, photo calls are the media tactics through which media relations are built.

Media Strategy: A media plan of public relations practice to use various media depending on the nature of audience to accomplish the objectives of PR programme. It is the key process in the implementation of PR campaign.

Message: Content of communication or statement is known as message to persuade the audience.

Mexican Statement: One of the best definitions of PR came from an International PR Conference held in Mexico City in 1978. It says, PR serves both the organization's and public interest.

McLuhan Marshall: Marshall McLuhan the Canadian author of "Understanding the Media (1964) in which he stated 'The Medium is the Message" and also visualized the concept of Global Village.

Mission Statement: It is a short statement of an organization that highlights the main objective of the organization. It provides a direction to the management in regard to its standards, values stakeholders relations, etc.

Mutual Understanding: Understanding between organization and its publics through public relations process based on performance and service.

Narrowcasting: Producing and distributing information for specialized audiences by narrowing the public—women, youth, farmers, health, sports. If broadcasting is for general public, narrowcasting is only for specialized group of people.

NASA: National Aeronautics and Space Administration (NASA–USA).

New Media: Media developed over computers, telecommunication to interact with each other as interactive media such as You Tube, Twitter, Facebook.

News: Fresh Information about a recent event that is of interest to reader, listener and viewers.

News Agency: A media organization which gathers information through its correspondents and disseminates such information through its network to various newspapers, magazines, radio, television etc. Press Trust of India is a news agency.

Newscast: Straight news broadcast on radio or TV.

Newsletter: A regular periodical of small size issued by an organization with useful information to the employees or customers. Unlike house journal, the contents of a newsletter are very brief with few pages.

News Release: A press note containing news story of an organization released by a public relations manager to the media for publication or broadcast.

Networking: It is a pattern of communication through which persons share information and programmes on individual basis. It is a process of interactive communication through media network like computers, TV, radio etc.

NGO: Non-governmental organization which functions on voluntary basis without any profit motive.

Non-publics: These are one category of publics identified by James Grunig who are neither affected by nor affect an organization. This group of publics remains unidentified and is ignored in public relations.

Non-Verbal Communication: Conveying messages without the use of words, but through body language—head posture, face, arms, hands, legs.

Objectivity: Reporting of events as observed by the reporter without including one's own feelings. Objectivity is the key principle of journalism.

Off-the Record: Information given to a journalist not for publication is termed as off-the record.

One Way Communication: It is a process of communication from sender to receiver without getting any feedback information.

On-line Press: Newspapers available on internet for readers is on-line press. Internet facilitates on-line journalism.

Opinion Leaders: The leaders or influential persons who are respected in the community and whose opinions are trusted by the public.

Opinion Polls: Polls conducted to elicit opinions on elections/marketing research constitute opinion polls. Such polls are used to measure the attitudes and the state of mind of the people.

Oral Literacy: Verbal literacy which is not written. Communication through speaking and listening is called verbal literacy or oral literacy.

Organizational Communication: It is a process of communication between an organization and its internal and external publics to influence them towards organizational goals.

Organizational Culture: The values, beliefs, attitudes, behaviours used by members of an organization constitute organizational culture.

Osgood Schramm Model of Communication: It is a circular model of communication (1954) which tells that the receiver as well as sender are engaged in a continuous act of communication. No mass media is used in this model.

Outdoor Advertising: Process of advertising out of doors, displayed on hoardings, billboards on the main roads.

Page W. Arthur: Vice-President of American Telephone Company (1927) who established a new trend that PR is a top management function which should have an active voice in the overall management.

Paradigm Shift: Change in the policy, model or thought towards a new pattern of operation.

Personal Selling: It is a one-to-one communication between a seller and prospective buyer as distinct from mass communication.

PERT: Programme, Evaluation and Review Technique.

PEST Analysis: A technique of research that analyses the overall environment of an organization into four broad areas such as Political, Economic, Social and Technological. Some organizations are affected by one of the four PEST areas.

Photo Call: An important event that demands media or PR to photograph for release to the media. It is a PR opportunity to make use of photo as a medium.

Podcasting: Dissemination of information about events through social network sites such as blog, facebook. It is audio form of blogging.

Pitch: Presenting a programme to a prospective client or informing media about an event. Derived from sales pitch.

Plan Publicity: Dissemination of information on Five Year Plans to create awareness on plan schemes so as to enable the people to participate in such plans.

Political Public Relations: Public Relations practiced by political parties to influence the public towards party ideologies and voting behavior. It includes media relations, public speaking, speech writing.

PRCI: Public Relations Council of India.

Press Release: It is one of the tactics of media relations through which news is sent to media for publication. Press release has headline, the lead, the remainder story in the order of importance, written in a journalistic style.

Press Conference: It is a media event at which CEOs announce important corporate decisions to the journalists for publication. VIPs too address press conferences.

Press Kit: It is a set of press material for use by journalists. A package of background information, press release, factsheet, photographs, CDs, corporate profile, product sample, etc., are kept in the kit.

Primary Research: Original research through which information is collected by observing the people or doing a survey.

Product Recall: Companies recall the products from the market when they are found to be defective.

Propaganda: A deliberate manipulation by means of symbols, words, gestures, images, flags of other people's thoughts, behavior, attitudes and beliefs. The systematic widespread promotion of a certain set of ideas, doctrines etc. to further one's own cause. Religious propaganda is to influence the people on a particular religion.

PRSA: Public Relations Society of America.

PRSI: Public Relations Society of India.

Publics: A group of people. Publics are segmented as employees, share holders, customers, general community, financial community. They are also categorized as audiences, stakeholders or internal and external public of a particular organization.

Public Affairs: It is the professional maintenance of legislative, and government and community relations to influence legislators, bureaucrats, policy makers, towards organizational goals and issues. Planned management of public and political issues which may have an impact on the operations of any business organization. It is a specialized area of public relations which involves government relations, community relations and management of internal and external communication.

Publicity: The dissemination of information, making matters pubic from the point of view of one who wishes to inform others on products or services. Placing information in a news medium to attract the attention of the public towards products/services.

Public Information: Information of public interest communicated by a PR professional to the general public.

Public Opinion: Public behavior, attitudes towards a particular issue constitutes public opinion. It represents a consensus on problems of an organization or a nation.

Public Relations: The management of a two-way communication process between an organization and its public to promote the corporate vision, mission, products, services, reputation and gain public understanding. It is also a science of relationships management based on information, service and persuasion.

Public Relations Agency: It is a firm/consultancy specialized in the practice of public relations to counsel the client's organization on public relations.

Public Relations Effectiveness: The impact of PR campaign on the target audiences or the outcome of PR programme.

Public Relations Professional: PR professional is one who is equipped by education, training and experience to give counsel to a client or employer on public relations practice.

Public Relations Professional Organization: A body of PR professional body to promote public relations as a strategic management function, besides enriching the knowledge of its members. For example, Public Relations Society of India (PRSI).

Public Relations Reporting: It is a process of keeping management informed about the public relations activities and its accomplishments within the organization. PR manager has to undertake this task of reporting periodically.

Public Relations Return on Investment: The impact of public relations activity on investment made by the corporation. Impact should commensurate with the investment.

Public Relations Voice: A quarterly professional journal launched in 1997 in Hyderabad by its founder editor Dr. C.V. Narasimha Reddi as the only journal for Indian PR professionals, devoted to the cause of public relations discipline. Till 2013, it has brought out 52 issues.

Public Sector: It is a corporate body created by public authority with defined powers and functions and financially independent. Air India is a public sector undertaking in the field of air transport.

Quality Circles: A group of employees who gather together to discuss their productivity, cost effectiveness and performance under their supervisors. Problem solving techniques are used to offer suggestions and increase their productivity. This concept had originated from Japan.

Qualitative Research: A method of research that measures empirical evidence–information dealing with the feelings of the public rather than numerical.

Quantitative Research: A method of research to investigate the reasons for human behavior or opinions and to identify the numbers or percentage of people. It helps to observe a situation or the outcome of a PR programme.

Questionnaire: A list of questions designed for the purpose of research to gather information.

Quota Sample: A quota sample is where specific number of people of a particular sex, age and social group are found by interviewers in a survey research.

RACE: It is a public relations model evolved by Marston(1979) which stands for * Research * *Action*, *Communication* and *Evaluation*

Random Sample: Selection of respondents on random for interviewing on a given topic for research.

Rate Card: A card with details of advertising rates, discounts, special positions and mechanical and printing requirements issued by a newspaper to advertisers, PR and advertising agencies.

Reach: The range of audience who watched a programme in a particular period.

Readership: Readership of a newspaper is based on the number of readers who read a particular newspaper. They are distinct from those who receive or buy a newspaper.

Relationship Management: Managing good relations between an organization and its public through both management and public relations techniques. The bottomline of PR is to create and sustain relationships.

Reputation Management: Management of reputation of an organization in the eyes of its stakeholders through PR techniques based on its performance. Good reputations are developed over a period through effective services.

Research: Research is a systematic study of collecting data and interpreting such data on a given subject. Research is always conducted against corporate objectives to know what results are accomplished.

Resume: A brief biodata of a person, also called curriculum vitae.

Reuters Ltd.: World news agency located in London with fulltime correspondents all over the world. Reuters World Service provided international news.

RNI: Registrar of Newspapers for India, who certifies the launching of a newspaper with a registration number and maintains a register of newspapers and magazines in India.

ROPES: It is a model which stands for *Research. *Objectives *Programming *Evaluation and *Stewardship. This model highlights the process of public relations practice with research against specific objectives.

Roughcut Film: It is a work print of a film after shooting the various aspects of the film. A fine cut is the outcome of rough cut. Fine cut is prepared by editing the rough cut.

Sales Promotion: Marketing techniques, apart from personal selling which create demand from both the trade and the consumers. Displays, shows demonstrations, sales processions are part of sales promotion.

Satellite: An equipment circling the globe, satellites are based on channels or paths that receive signals from earth and then retransmit them back to the ground to reach various TV sets.

Satellite Media Tour: A series of interviews conducted through satellite channels called a media tour, because it replaces travel of journalists as well as spokesperson.

Satellite Transmission: It is a system of transmitting text, pictures and sound by beaming an electronic signal to a transponder on a satellite orbiting 22,300 miles above the earth, from where it bounces back to receiving dish antennas on the ground.

Scoop: An important and exclusive news story published, broadcast exclusively in a particular newspaper, radio or TV channel, which other channels missed.

Script: It is a written matter of a news story, radio, TV talk, a film etc., Script can be divided into various formats such as newspaper book, radio, TV film, speeches, online etc. PR practitioner must be good at script writing for a newspaper or corporate publications.

Selective Perception: A perceived notion of a particular person about a programme or subject. This suits to one's own attitude.

Set-top Box: An electronic machine that decodes and decrypts a TV signal so that it can be viewed by a viewer. Typically a pay TV device. It is a small 'box' that is placed on the 'top' of the TV set.

Seven Cs of Communication: *Credibility *Context *Content *Clarity *Consistency* *Channels *Capability* of the Audience.

Silk Screen Printing: A method of printing for printing small quantities of items such as invitations, posters, billboards. Works on the principle of blocking out specific areas on a silk screen, followed by drawing on ink or paint across the screen.

Situation Analysis: Public relations process starts from situation analysis, which means an analysis of the organizational situation/ environment. It is otherwise a type of communication audit to identify the strengths, weaknesses and problems of the organization from PR angle.

Slogan: A word or phrase used to express characteristic position or stand or a goal to be achieved. A brief attention getting word used in public relations campaigns ' Garibi Hatao' is a slogan adopted by Indira Gandhi as Prime Minister to eradicate poverty in the country. Slogan should be catchy. Slogans always should 'be memorable, be original, be competitive and be believable.

SMART: It is an acronym that sets/organizational objectives which should be *Specific *Measurable * Achievable * Realistic and *Timebound.

Soap Opera: A serial on TV channel of true-to-life around family affairs and its problems and tragedies. 'Humlog' was a good example of soap opera on Doordarshan.

Social Marketing: It is a marketing of social communication of social ideas beneficial to the society. An example of social marketing is family planning campaign to promote small family norms and contain population.

Software: It is a programme that controls the computer. Equipment is called 'Hardware' PR practitioner must have knowledge of both the systems.

Supplement: A separate section added to a newspaper, particularly the Sunday edition 'Education Plus' is a supplement as a Chief window to courses and careers added on every Monday to the daily The Hindu.

SPIN: It is a pejorative or negative term meaning a biased portrayal about a person or profession. Media describes PR practitioner as SPIN Doctor because he/she is alleged to be manipulating corporate information.

Spokesperson: A person who speaks to the media on behalf of an organization, a product or service. Authorised person of an organization to speak to the media.

Spot Announcement: A short announcement on radio or TV usually running less than a minute that either informs or sells such as a public service announcement or commercial.

Staff Function: Strategic function of staff (executives) who advice management on corporate strategies for implementation by line executives. Public relations is a staff function in an organization.

Stakeholder: Stake means 'interest' the interest of a stakeholder in an organization. 'A stakeholder is any group or individual who can affect or is affected by the decision/achievement of the organization's purpose and objectives. Stakeholders may be divided into three types based on their interest in the organization. Equity Stakes; Economic Stakes; and Influencer stakes. Equity stakes are held by those who have some direct ownership of the organization, such as shareholders, directors. Economic stakes are held by those who have an economic interest but not an ownership interest, in the organization such as employees, customers, suppliers and competitors. The last category of stakeholders belongs to the influencer stakes are held by those who do not have either an ownership or economic interest in the actions of the organization, but who have interests as opinion leaders such as consumer advocates, environmental groups, trade associations and government organizations.

Strategy: It is a public relations programme or plan designed at the corporate level for implementation. It describes the design how PR campaign will be implemented though various media tactics.

Stringer: A reporter who works in a newspaper on a retainer/word rate basis but not on a regular salary.

Stylebook: Every newspaper has its own stylebook for its own staff which outlines the rules for capitalization, spelling, figures in order that all editorial matter could form to a particular pattern.

SWOT Analysis: It is an acronym for *Strengths *Weaknesses *Opportunities and *Threats. This is a prerequisite for designing a PR programme.

Tableau: An important scene, a thing, a stationary group of performers, an elaborate stage presentation on a moving vehicle, a medium of PR. Tableaus depicting the progress of the country are presented at the Republic Day Parade in New Delhi.

Tabloid: Small size page newspaper like The Times. The London Times converted into Tabloid. Half the size of the normal big size paper is called tabloid.

Tactic: An activity or a tool used to achieve objectives. Strategy and Tactics are the twins of PR. If strategy is the PR plan, tactic is the tool to reach the objective of strategy. Press release, press conference, photo calls are the media tactics to gain media coverage. Exhibition is also a tactic of PR.

Talk Show: A TV show based on interviews, telephone conversations with viewers. It is also called a chat show.

Tangible PR: A PR programme which is planned to achieve specific results after evaluation. Planned press conference based on major policy decisions will get good media coverage and also gives results.

Target Audience: A very specific segmented audience as against general audience by some measurable characteristics such as employees, customers, shareholders, farmers, women. Specific messages are designed for specific target audience. Audience meant for PR messages is the target audience.

Teleconference: It is a type of electronic conference held at more than one place and that such places are linked simultaneously by audio and or video network. The students are linked with professors and others subject matter specialists in a teleconference.

Teleprompter: A device attached to the TV camera so that the anchors, newsreaders can look into the camera and follow the text. It is called teleprompter that enables newscasters to read the script while directly looking into the camera. However, newscasters do keep the typed script as a back-up material.

Terrestrial: Television signals broadcast from the ground based transmission in contrast to satellite transmission from the sky.

Themed Message: Messages that are identified as central to the organization's vision, mission, reputation and that are designed to change or reinforce perceptions in tune with the organizations needs and reputation.

Third Party: Credible opinion leaders who give independent opinions or views about organizations, products or services.

Three-D: A technique used in films, which provides images of three dimensions—length, breadth and depth.

Trade Fair: A national or international exhibition with national and global pavilions for selling products. India International Trade Fair is held in New Delhi every year as a commercial exhibition is a good example.

Trademark: Logo, sign, often with distinctive lettering that distinguishes a particular brand from other products.

Trade Press: Publications/newspapers that deal with trade and business such as the Business Week or the Business Standard.

Traditional Media: Media such as folk arts—Tamasha, street play, puppets developed out of lives of the people for information and entertainment.

Train Exhibition: Exhibition on board trains that tours from place to place to inform and educate people on a specific subject like Science and Technology.

Transport Advertising: It is system of advertising on transport vehicle, and vessels and property belonging to transport undertakings. Such vehicles include: trains, buses, ships, aircrafts and properties like bus stations, rail stations, sea ports, airports. Travelling public will have easy access to such advertising.

Trend Analysis: A system of analysis to predict future events and collect information to identify such predictions.

Two-way Communication: It is a process in which the sender not only sends the message as one way but also receives the feedback from the receiver which makes it two-way communication. The sender and the receiver alternates their roles as speaker and listener.

Two-step Flow of Communication: It is a communication model in which messages from mass media reach first to opinion leaders who have access to the newspapers or electronic media and who in turn in the second step communicate to others who are not exposed to media.

Two-way Asymmetric PR Model: This model was evolved by James Grunig (USA) as a two-way communication system from sender to the receiver, but the power rested with the sender whose primary aim is to persuade the receiver so as to accept and support the sender's organization, and its products, or services. It is in a way a scientific approach in communication based on two-way communication process with imbalanced effects more titled towards organization without much importance to the total perceptions and needs of the receivers. This model has a feedback loop, but the objective is to get the feedback only to the advantage of the organization and to help the sender of the message as to understand the audience and their attitudes and how to persuade them. This PR model relies only on persuasion and is used to influence the behavior of the audience for buying products or services and voting.

Two-way Symmetric PR Model: This model in contrast to asymmetric model was developed when USA was confronted with certain basic issues such as Vietnam War Protests, the Civil Rights Movements, the Environment Movement and also the Corporates wanted that their policies should be in tune with the pulse and needs of customers. Therefore, a two-way symmetric model was evolved by James Grunig wherein both the sender and receiver parties are capable of being persuaded to adjust and modify their attitudes and behaviours according to the needs of each party as a result of public relations effort. The element of two-way dialogue is prominent in this model with balanced views unlike titled in asymmetric model towards sender party. Such a dialogue between both the parties who adjust their attitudes to their respective needs will result in mutual understanding and that is called two-way symmetrical PR model.

Unmediated: It is a system in which the internet allows for information to go directly to the public without being mediated by a third party such as a journalist or a gatekeeper.

UNI: United News of India, a news agency.

UPI: United Press International a syndicated news service.

Uplink: Transmission path from an earth station up to a satellite in the sky.

UNESCO: United Nations Educational Scientific and Cultural Organization.

Upward Communication: Communication in an organization from bottom to the top management.

Unique Selling Proposition (USP): A special feature of a product or service that adds value to the thing which no other product offers This special feature becomes the focus of the selling message.

Unduplicated Audience: The total number of people or households that listen to or view a specific radio or TV commercial programme.

Verbatim: Exactly as spoken or written. The actual comments that participants make in a group or individuals. Oral presentation word for word using exactly the same word or words.

Vernacular Press: Newspapers/magazines which are published in national language such as Telugu, Urdu, Hindi. It is also called language press.

VHF: Very High Frequency. TV/Radio channels whose transmission is in the range of 30 to 300 MHZ.

Video: The visual portion of a broadcast or a film.

Video Conference: (See Teleconference).

Video Magazine: A house journal produced on video cassette for showing on TV sets to employees as part of internal communication. A medium of PR.

Video News Release(VNR): it is a pictorial news release recorded on a video tape with camera for broadcast by TV channels in contrast to printed news release.

Video Tape: Recording and playback tape for showing on Television.

Video Text: It is a two-way communication process in which information is communicated to the receiver home/office on a screen and in turn the receiver sends messages by keyboard.

Viewpoint: An opinion of a person on a given issue or a problem.

Vision: A long-term plan of an organization with its key objectives and aspirations to accomplish. Promotion of corporate vision is the job of PR amongst both internal and external publics.

Visual Aids: Aids in presentations such as films, slides, posters, charts and other devices involving symbol are known as visual aids.

Visual Communication: Communication based on the principle of human sensory organ—eye.

Visual Identity: It is the visual projection or symbol of an organization through its logo and other physical presentations such as colour scheme, typography, interior design etc. people identify or recognize a company through its visual identity like logo, visual identity is also known as organizational symbolism.

Voice Mail: It is a process of communication that answers calls and allows users to reply to save, delete or forward messages. Mobile phone is a medium of voice mail. Voices received on a mobile phones or computer.

Voice Over: Commentary or reading news by unseen anchor/speaker on film, video tape, or TV programme. Narrator's message without showing him or her on the screen of TV.

Vox Populi: (Latin) for, the voice of the people. Public opinion.

VTR: Video Tape Recording.

Wall Media: Media such as posters, wall newspapers that are affixed to walls of exterior and interior spaces of companies and public places for publicity.

Wall Newspaper: It is a big size one sheet printed paper with information of public interest for display on street walls. It is good PR medium for educating both literates and neo-literates with big size letters and attractive pictures in the wallpaper.

Web2.0: The process in the way that people use the internet that allows users free access and give them more control over the information.

Weblog: It is an updated website that links on other sites for information. Anyone can create weblog relating to his/her field.

Web-Offset-Litho: Offset-litho printing from a continuous web or reel of paper instead of from single flat sheets.

Webpage: Websites are collections of electronic pages. Each webpage is an HTML document that has text, images etc.

Whistle Blower: A person within an organization who divulges information which is corrupt, a scandal, unsafe etc. Since he cannot be a silent spectator for such corrupt/dishonest practices, whistle blower out of inner conscience leaks out information to the media or it is like going 'public'.

White Paper: A key document prepared either by government or by any organization as an argument on a given issue. A government paper that explains policies and programmes.

Window Display: Display of products/services of companies for drawing the attention of customers. The art of arranging goods in shop windows in an attractive way.

Win-Win: A process of negotiation whereby the interacting parties find a solution which benefits both of them. The success of negotiations in an issue.

Wire Photo: Telephonic photo transmission system operated by news agencies like PTI. Photo transmission is now done through satellite as Wire Photo.

Wire Service: News agencies like PTI, UNI which send news to newspapers and electronic media—radio and television studios by tele-printer, radio and satellite.

Wives Visitation Programme: It is a system of open house programme organized by a corporation when the wives of employees are invited to see the factory/company where their husbands are working. They spend a few minutes watching their husbands at work and examining the conditions, environment under which they work. An effective PR tool involving the wives in corporate communication. This system is yet to gain importance in India.

Word Processor: Smart typewriter which stores typed information using a daisy-wheel or matrix system so that the information can be retrieved in parts or in any order required for editing purposes.

Word-of-Mouth: It is a process of oral communication in which information is transmitted through the sensory organ—mouth. It is also called interpersonal communication—the most effective process in public relations.

World Wide Web: It is a process/system or internet service that uses color, printed word, pictures and sound to transmit information and entertainment. Easy for users to retrieve hypertext and graphics from various sites. The first on-line website came into being in 1990, while the world wide web became free for everyone on April 30, 1993.

Writeup: A written report, an article in a publication, written matter for a booklet or folder.

Xerography: A process of dry photographic or photocopying reproduction in which powdered ink is distributed electronically so that a negative image is formed on an electrically charged plate and then electronically transformed and thermally fixed as a positive on pages or other material. The Xerox corporation headquartered in Stanford CT makes trademarked xerographic copying and duplicating machines and other equipment. It is also known as electro photography technique that produces an image on paper, using electronically charged particles.

Xerox: An electronic process for producing copies of letters, documents using Xerox machine—xerography.

Yahoo(computer): An online directory of World Wide Website. The company **Yahoo** Corporation is based in Mountain View, CA, USA.

Yardstick PR Model: This is an evaluation process PR model known as Lindenman's Public Relations Yardstick Model (1993) aimed to make evaluation process more accessible. Lindenman claimed that public relations evaluation need be neither expensive nor laboriously time consuming. This model passes through a two-step process.

1. Setting public relations objectives
2. Determining at what level public relations effectiveness is to be measured

Three levels of evaluation show the extent of programme measurement.

1. The basic level which measures public relations outputs such as media relations, here the measurement is in-terms of media coverage, space given, position of news and the reach of the target audience. Press clippings are the source of measurement.
2. The second level which uses 'outgrowth' measures to show whether audiences actually receive the messages and evaluates retention understanding and awareness of the message. Interviews are the source of measurement level.
3. The last and the third level measures 'outcomes' which can include opinions attitudes and changes in behavior of the audience.

Yellow Journalism: A phrase used in the US to describe newspapers involved in the inter warfare of the popular metropolitan press empires of the late 19th century, a battle which has continued to the present-day with mass circulation tabloids competing for readership with all sorts of exploitative offers. Lurid revelations and block buster bingo. Exaggerative exploitatively sensational cheap articles designed to attract a mass audience comes under yellow journalism. The origin is the use of Yellow ink to print. The yellow kid a trouble maker in a comic strip created in 1895 by Richard Outcault in the New York world, a free wheeling sensationalist newspaper. Later William Randolph Hearst was called the yellow kid, and the term became derogatory, implying irresponsible journalism. The owner of the New York World Joseph Pulitzer who engaged in yellow journalism founded the prestigious Pulitzer Prize in 1917.

Yellow Pages: Telephone numbers of classified advertisements of different trades published on yellow pages of telephone directory. The pages are distinct in the directory with yellow colour.

Zero-Time-Communication Environment: Public relations operates in a zero-time communication environment in that the rapid and readily changing advances in technology are resulting in instant global communications. Space as well as time are shrinking. As such, not only is this communication space instantaneous it also allows for direct and rapid competition with other significant role players in the local and global economies.

Zoom: To bring picture into close up by using zoom lens on a camera. A lens which can be adjusted automatically to give the effect of movement away from or towards the stationary camera, on a still camera, the zoom brings an object much closer.

Zones Campaign: PR/advertising campaigns and marketing strategies limited to a particular region or zone. This is a measure to intensify in a particular area. The Bharat Nirman Public Information Campaign is organized by the Press Information Bureau only to cover a particular area in a district.

Zones of Influence: Stone (1995) quotes research which identifies six main zones of influence within families when making buying decisions. They are; 1. Man, 2. Woman, 3. Children 4. Man & Woman; 5. Man and Children 6. Woman and Children. The research in 1991 indicated that women were dominant in the purchase of household goods. Information on buying decision is useful to PR practitioners when planning campaigns and selecting appropriate messages and tactics to carry messages about products or services to the target audiences.

Zero-based Media Planning: A review of media during communications planning based on research analysis and insight, but not habit and preference.

References

Alison Theaker, *The Public Relations Handbook*, Routeledge, London, 2001.

Bahl, S., *Making PR Work*, Wheeler Publishing, New Delhi, 1994.

Banick, G.C., *Public Relations and Media Relations*, Jaico Publishing House, Mumbai, 2005.

Bhimani, R., *Face up Tenets, Techniques and Trends of Public Relations for the 21st Century,* Rupa, New Delhi, 2002.

Caywood, C.L., *The Handbook of Strategic Public Relations and Integrated Communications*, McGraw-Hill, New York, 1997.

Croft, A.C., *Managing a Public Relations Firm For Growth and Profit*, Routledge, New York, 1996.

Cutlip, S.M., *The Unseen Power: Public Relations, A History*, Lawrence Erlbaum Associates, New Jersey, 1994.

Daymon, C. and Hollway, I., *Qualitative Research Methods in Public Relations and Marketing Communications*, Routledge, London, 2003.

Dennis L., Wilcox, Glen, and T. Cameron, *Public Relations—Strategies and Tactics*, Pearson, New York, 2005.

Foster, J., *Effective Writing Skills for Public Relations*, Kogan Page, New Delhi, 2008.

Gordon, A.E., *Public Relations*, Oxford University Press, 2011.

Hart, N.A., *Strategic Public Relations*, Macmillan Press, London, 1995.

Hill, J.W., *The Making of a Public Relations Man*, David McKay, New York, 1963.

Illustrated History of India, Wilco Publishing House, Mumbai.

Johnston, J., *Media Relations: Issues and Strategies*, Allen and Unwin, Australia, 2008.

Larry Tye, The Father of Spin, Edward L. Bernays and the Birth of Public Relations, Crown Publishers, New York.

Marshall McLuhan, *Understanding Media—The Extension of Man*, The MIT Press, London, 1994.

Narasimha Reddi, C.V., *Public Information Management: Ancient India to Modern India*, Himalaya Publishing House, Mumbai, 2002.

Natrajan, J., *History of Indian Journalism*, Publications Division, Delhi, 1955.

Newsom, D.A., J.V. Turk, and D., Kruckeberge (Eds.), *This is PR—The Realities of Public Relations*, Wadsworth, Belmont, CA, 2000.

Perse, E.M., *Media Effects and Society*, Lawrence Erlbaum Associates, London, 2001.

Sahay, M., *A Text Book of Communication, Media and Society*, Wisdom Press, New Delhi, 2013.

Singhal, A. and E.M. Rogers, *India's Communication Revolution: From Bullock Carts to Cyber Marts*, Sage Publications, New Delhi, p. 94, 2001.

Venkateswaran, K.S., Mass Media Laws and Regulations in India, AMIC Singapore, 1993.

Weinstein, S., *The Multimedia Internet*, Springer, 2005.